Exile and Return

Beihefte zur Zeitschrift für die alttestamentliche Wissenschaft

Edited by
John Barton, Ronald Hendel,
Reinhard G. Kratz and Markus Witte

Volume 478

Exile and Return

The Babylonian Context

Edited by
Jonathan Stökl and Caroline Waerzeggers

DE GRUYTER

ISBN 978-3-11-057809-6
e-ISBN (PDF) 978-3-11-041928-3
e-ISBN (EPUB) 978-3-11-041952-8
ISSN 0934-2575

Library of Congress Cataloging-in-Publication Data
A CIP catalog record for this book has been applied for at the Library of Congress.

Bibliographic information published by the Deutsche Nationalbibliothek
The Deutsche Nationalbibliothek lists this publication in the Deutsche Nationalbibliografie; detailed bibliographic data are available on the Internet at http://dnb.dnb.de.

This volume is text- and page-identical with the hardback published in 2015.
Printing and binding: CPI books GmbH, Leck

♾ Printed on acid-free paper
Printed in Germany

www.degruyter.com

Table of Contents

Introduction —— 1

Laurie E. Pearce
Identifying Judeans and Judean Identity in the Babylonian Evidence —— 7

Kathleen Abraham
**Negotiating Marriage in Multicultural Babylonia:
An Example from the Judean Community in Āl-Yāhūdu —— 33**

Gauthier Tolini
From Syria to Babylon and Back: The Neirab Archive —— 58

Ran Zadok
**West Semitic Groups in the
Nippur Region between c. 750 and 330 B.C.E. —— 94**

Johannes Hackl and Michael Jursa
**Egyptians in Babylonia in the Neo-Babylonian
and Achaemenid Periods —— 157**

Caroline Waerzeggers
**Babylonian Kingship in the Persian Period:
Performance and Reception —— 181**

Jonathan Stökl
**"A Youth Without Blemish, Handsome,
Proficient in all Wisdom, Knowledgeable and Intelligent":
Ezekiel's Access to Babylonian Culture —— 223**

H. G. M. Williamson
The Setting of Deutero-Isaiah: Some Linguistic Considerations —— 253

Madhavi Nevader
**Picking Up the Pieces of the Little Prince:Refractions of
Neo-Babylonian Kingship Ideology in Ezekiel 40–48? —— 268**

Lester L. Grabbe
**The Reality of the Return:
The Biblical Picture Versus Historical Reconstruction — 292**

Jason M. Silverman
Sheshbazzar, a Judean or a Babylonian? A Note on his Identity — 308

Katherine Southwood
**The Impact of the Second and Third-Generation Returnees
as a Model for Understanding the Post-Exilic Context — 322**

Peter R. Bedford
Temple Funding and Priestly Authority in Achaemenid Judah — 336

Abbreviations — 352
Non-bibliographical abbreviations — 358
Index — 359

Introduction

Since the appearance of the first Āl-Yāhūdu tablets a few years ago, there has been growing awareness among biblical scholars that cuneiform texts from the Neo-Babylonian and Persian periods might offer useful information that will elucidate questions related to the historical reconstruction of the Babylonian Exile, its impact on ancient Judaism and its relevance for understanding certain biblical texts. The Āl-Yāhūdu tablets preserve a unique imprint of an actual Judean / Jewish community living in central Babylonia during the period conventionally identified as the era of the Babylonian Exile. It is certainly not the first time that we find evidence of Judean exiles in the cuneiform record – Weidner's identification of king Jehoiachin in tablets from Nebuchadnezzar's palace comes to mind – but the Āl-Yāhūdu texts offer the most vivid, most complex and most direct testimony of life in the Babylonian Exile so far. Indeed, they appear to be the archives of a Judean community itself. However, the relevance of the cuneiform text corpus for understanding the Exile is not restricted to its preserving the names and actions of concrete individuals affected by it – the corpus is so dense and diverse that it reveals the cultural and social context within which not only the individual experiences of the individuals in question need to be interpreted but also those of other deported communities and those of the host society at large. Here, then, is an opportunity to contextualize a formative era in the history of ancient Judaism.

Most biblical scholars would agree that the many books of the Hebrew Bible were either composed in some form or edited during the Exilic and post-Exilic periods among a community that was to identify itself as returning from Babylonian captivity. At the same time, a dearth of contemporary written evidence from Judah/Yehud and its environs renders any particular understanding of the process within its social, cultural and political context virtually impossible. This has led some to label the period a dark age or black box – as obscure as it is essential for understanding the history of Judaism. To be fair, such a defeatist view of the Babylonian and Persian periods in Judah/Yehud is not widely shared today, especially not since archaeologists have stepped up their effort to look for and study material remains from the period in recent years. Historians have also added to the momentum by drawing on the advances in the study of Achaemenid Persian history in order to integrate the local history of Yehud, the return from Exile, and the restoration of Jerusalem's temple more firmly within the regional, and indeed global, developments of the time. These efforts have increasingly led to a realization that the story of the Exile and return as narrated in the biblical text is a construct that replaces a much more complex and socially contested history. Despite its constructed nature, however, a majority of biblical scholars concedes

social norms in the various ethnic communities living together in Southern Babylonia in the Neo-Babylonian and Persian periods.

The case of the still relatively little known Neirabean community who, like their Judean counterparts, were exiled to Mesopotamia by the Babylonians and later returned to their ancestral homelands in Syria, is the topic of Gauthier Tolini's study ('From Syria to Babylon and Back'). He carefully traces their lines of communication and business between Mesopotamia and Syria as well as their (apparent) devotion to the moon-god. For scholars interested in the Biblical tradition, the Neirabeans provide a parallel case – albeit with rather scant data; for those interested in the study of ethnic minorities and the history of forced migration, the material illuminates a little more some of the impact of the historical *Großwetterlage* in the ancient Near East.

Ran Zadok's contribution to the volume ('West Semitic Groups in the Nippur Region between c. 750 and 330 B. C.E.') offers a large collection of data for groups of people of West Semitic origin in the Nippur region from 750–330 BCE, including, among others, the Āl-Yāhūdu texts. Zadok identifies people of Western Semitic background mostly on the basis of onomastic data; in the concluding remarks, Zadok offers a short interpretation of his data with regard to the integration of ethnic minorities in Babylonian society.

Following Zadok, Johannes Hackl and Michael Jursa look at 'Egyptians in Babylonia in the Neo-Babylonian and Achaemenid Periods'. Following the – Babylonian – data, they classify the attested Egyptians as temple slaves, slaves of Egyptian origin, free Egyptians and as Egyptians associated with the royal administration. They finish with an appendix on Egyptian material culture in Mesopotamia. Hackl and Jursa argue that the nature of their data is most easily explained if we assume that Egyptians at least occasionally assumed Babylonian names, thus becoming invisible to the modern scholar. This 'invisibility' has interesting ramifications also for the studies by Zadok and Pearce.

Caroline Waerzeggers' ('Babylonian Kingship in the Persian Period') interrogates the consequences of the loss of 'indigenous' kingship in Mesopotamia after the Persian conquest of Babylon. Whereas biblical scholars attribute great significance to the loss of indigenous kingship in Yehud, the issue is often thought not to be significant in Mesopotamia as the Persians were much more present and were at least in name, Kings of Babylon. Waerzeggers, however, shows that the situation is considerably more complex and that the increasing absence of the Persian rulers in the Mesopotamian heartland can be found refracted in Babylonian historiographical texts.

In his essay on Babylonian knowledge in Ezekiel ('Ezekiel's Access to Babylonian Culture'), Jonathan Stökl reflects on the social location of the author of the book as well as the channels of transmission of Mesopotamian knowledge to

Judean / Jewish literature. He tentatively identifies the author of the initial stages of the book of Ezekiel as an upper class Judean in the Babylonian heartland who had access to and attended a cuneiform school.

Hugh Williamson ('The Setting of Deutero-Isaiah') contributes to the question of the physical location of the author(s) of Deutero-Isaiah. To that end he looks at terms for trees in Isaiah 40–55, and identifies a number of them as Akkadian loanwords which would make very little sense in Persian Yehud. This goes counter to a trend in modern Isaiah scholarship which seeks to find the location of the book in Yehud rather than in Babylonia. While his argument is initially strictly philological Williamson reflects more widely on the methodologies used by scholars to identify the setting of ancient literature.

In her essay ('Picking Up the Pieces of the Little Prince'), Madhavi Nevader looks at the figure of the *nāśī'* ('Prince') as he is found in the book of Ezekiel 40–48 and compares him to the figure of the king in Neo-Babylonian kingship ideology. She describes the curiously ambiguous nature of the prince and sees his actions as stipulated in Ezekiel as reminiscent of the position of the Babylonian rulers in the rituals of the Neo-Babylonian temple: a ruler and a cult performer who is both central to the ritual performed but also subservient to other cult officials. She also notes the absence of two important aspects of the Neo-Babylonian kingship ideology: that of the king as judge and the king as temple builder.

The tenth contribution to the volume is written by Lester Grabbe ('The Reality of the Return') who presents the various forms in which the return from Exile narratives are presented in biblical texts showing that they are different and should be kept separate. Grabbe then offers his historical reconstruction in which he provides explanations for the diverging traditions as the literary echo of various groups whose experience of Exile and Return differed at times starkly from each other.

In 'Sheshbazzar, a Judean or a Babylonian?' Jason Silverman focuses on this figure by looking at potential parallels for Persians appointed governors. Based on such practices Silverman suggests that Sheshbazzar may be the last Neo-Babylonian governor who was reconfirmed by the new Persian overlords.

Katherine Southwood ('The Impact of the Second and Third-Generation Returnees as a Model for Understanding the Post-Exilic Context') looks at the impact of socio-anthropological data theory in particular regarding second generation return migrations on our understanding of the Judean / Jewish community in Persian period Yehud. Southwood emphasises the emotional attachment of the exiles to their homeland as it is expressed in many biblical texts, as well as the emerging understanding of itself from within Judaism as a religio-ethnic entity that defined itself in contrast to others. In this process, it appears, that the migration from Babylon on Yehud may have had more impact than the initial Exile to Babylon itself.

The final essay in the volume, 'Temple Funding the Priestly Authority in Achaemenid Judah', Peter Bedford assembles the available economic evidence for the rebuilding of the temple in order to assess who was responsible for its rebuilding and to elucidate some of the power structures in the society of Persian Yehud. Bedford's conclusion is that according to the available evidence it is most likely that the temple was financed through 'informal taxation', that is through 'voluntary' gifts enforced through social pressure rather than formal taxation. This indicates that the temple did not have the social power to insist on more formal forms of taxation, suggesting that the boundaries of the various communities in Persian Yehud continued to shift for a considerable amount of time and that the temple community achieved central power only at a later date.

The editors hope that Assyriologists, biblical scholars and ancient historians will continue to interact with each other. May this volume and the essays in it be an encouragement and an invitation that this dialogue between specialists on different sources is interesting, enriching and productive.

Caroline Waerzeggers & Jonathan Stökl
Leiden and London, September 2014

The Āl-Yāhūdu texts were published by Laurie Pearce and Cornelia Wunsch early in 2015 at a time when the manuscript for this volume was already in its final stages. We hope that the volume will stimulate further research into this fascinating archive; see Laurie E. Pearce and Cornelia Wunsch, *Documents of Judean Exiles and West Semites in Babylonia in the Collection of David Sofer* (CUSAS 28; Bethesda: CDL Press, 2014).

Laurie E. Pearce

Identifying Judeans and Judean Identity in the Babylonian Evidence

The terms 'exile' and 'return' suggest a number of dualities – of movement away from and back to a native land; of power hierarchies between captors and captives; of geographic location and dislocation of returnees and 'remainees'. The activities and legacies of those who returned to Judah and those who remained resident in Babylonia can be revealed only in so far as the people (both as individuals and as groups) can be identified. For this reason, any comprehensive understanding of 'exile and return' depends in the first place on determining those mechanisms by which Judeans may be identified and in the second on assessing what those identifications reveal.

Under ideal circumstances, the identification of Judeans and exploration of Judean identity should be possible equally from both Judean and Babylonian points of view. Identity, like 'ethnicity', the more value-laden term it often replaces, is a two-sided mirror – reflecting the perceptions, presumptions and constructs of the viewer as well as the viewed. The images received by modern viewers depend on the reception by one cultural community of the record produced by the collective pen of another. Writing conventions and media thus bear directly on the recovery and assessment of individual and community identification. In this study, the focus will be on the identification of Judeans and Judean identity in the Babylonian documentation of the long sixth century B.C.E.,[1] a historical construct that corresponds chronologically to the period of exile and return.

The present study will consider the following as presented in the native Babylonian sources: (1) What criteria may be used to identify Judeans in the cuneiform sources?, (2) What problems may inhere in that data?, (3) What do the markers of identity tell us about Judean self-identification and about Babylonian perceptions of Judean identity?, and (4) What generalizations do the Babylonian perception and presentation of Judean identity hold for a study of Babylonian society as well? Discussion of specific features preserved in the Babylonian documentation may bring us closer to answers to these and other questions.

1 Michael Jursa, *Aspects of the Economic History of Babylonia in the First Millennium BC: Economic Geography, Economic Mentalities, Agriculture, the Use of Money and the Problem of Economic Growth* (AOAT 377; Münster: Ugarit-Verlag, 2010), 5.

Laurie E. Pearce: University of California, Berkeley

1 Texts and Context

Excavated at Nippur in the late 19th century, the texts of the Murašû archive document the activities of a Babylonian extended family whose livelihood derived largely from leasing and subleasing crown lands.[2] Among the Murašû's clients were a number of individuals of Judean origin, readily identifiable on the basis of the Yahwistic component of their names. The Judeans drew immediate attention, as, in the introduction to BE 9, Clay acknowledged the presence and importance of the large number 'of Jewish names known from the Old Testament, especially from the books of Ezra and Nehemiah.'[3] These names stood out, even against 'the large foreign element living in the rich alluvial plain between the Euphrates and Tigris as during the centuries following the fall of Babylon, 538 B. C.'[4]

Although the Yahwistic names in the Murašû texts securely establish a Judean presence in Mesopotamia in the post-exilic period, they pose many additional questions and present a number of challenges when viewed against the biblical reports of the exile. The first concerns chronology: dated to 454 B.C.E., the earliest Murašû text leaves unaccounted approximately 135 years of Judean history from the time of the destruction of the Temple. The length of this gap grows if reckoned from the first wave of deportation in 597 B.C.E.[5]

2 The major groups of Murašû texts have appeared in the following, listed in chronological order of publication: Hermann Hilprecht and Albert T. Clay, *Business Documents of Murashû Sons of Nippur Dated in the Reign of Artaxerxes I (464–424 B. C.)* (BE 9; Philadelphia: University of Pennsylvania, Department of Archaeology and Palaeontology, 1898); Albert T. Clay, *Business Documents of Murashû Sons of Nippur Dated in the Reign of Darius II (424–404 B. C.)* (BE 10; Philadelphia: University of Pennsylvania, Department of Archaeology and Palaeontology, 1904); Albert T. Clay, *Business Documents of Murashû Sons of Nippur Dated in the Reign of Darius II* (PBS 2/1; Philadelphia: University Museum, 1912); Matthew W. Stolper, *Entrepreneurs and Empire: The Murašû Archive, the Murašû Firm, and Persian Rule in Babylonia* (Leiden: Nederlands Historisch-Archaeologisch Instituut te Istanbul, 1985); Veysel Donbaz and Matthew W. Stolper, *Istanbul Murašû Texts* (Istanbul: Nederlands Historisch-Archaeologisch Instituut te Istanbul, 1997). Small groups of texts or isolates appear in: Henry F. Lutz, 'An Agreement Between a Babylonian Feudal Lord and His Retainer in the Reign of Darius II', *UCP* 9/3 (1928): 269–277; Oluf Krückmann, *Neubabylonische Rechts- und Verwaltungstexte* (TuM 2/3; Leipzig: J. C. Hinrichs, 1933); Ira Spar and Eva von Dassow, *Cuneiform Texts in the Metropolitan Museum of Art: Private Archive Texts from the First Millennium B. C.* (CTMMA 3; New York: Metropolitan Museum of Art; Turnhout: Brepols, 2000); Matthew W. Stolper, 'Fifth Century Nippur: Texts of the Murašûs and from Their Surroundings', *JCS* 53 (2001): 83–132.

3 BE 9 27.

4 BE 9 26.

5 2 Kgs 24:15–16.

The second issue is geographic. In contrast to the impression the biblical record gives of the resettlement of the deportees who had once been residents of an urban environment, in the decidedly urban capital Babylon,[6] the cuneiform record confirms a wider distribution of the populace across the landscape. Murašû texts record exiled Judeans engaged in agricultural activities – some saddled with debt, all constrained by the economics of tenant farming, in the countryside around Nippur.[7] The dissonance between these accounts was striking enough to have caused some scholars to express surprise that the descendants of the 'Babylonian Exiles' were small-scale farmers and not the smiths and valiant men recorded in the description of the deportation in 2 Kings.[8]

To be sure, cuneiform texts did document the presence of Judeans in Babylon itself, but it is important to emphasize that this evidence appears in a limited number of texts belonging to highly stylized genres. The aforementioned Weidner Ration Lists record a straightforward administrative activity, the dispensing of rations to individuals of high social standing. In the secondary literature, the names of the Judean king Jehoiachin and his five sons are those most frequently cited as recipients of generous ration allowances. But prominent, if unnamed, Egyptians, Elamites, Ionians, Philistines and Tyrians are included as well. While strategic considerations may have prompted the settling of defeated royals in the capital as state dependents, it is clear that Babylonian policy considered all deported royals and their retinues, regardless of origin, to be of equal social

6 2 Kgs 25:7 and Jer 52:11 identify Babylon as Zedekiah's destination. The subsequent verses do not explicitly state that the Judeans were taken to Babylon, although the report on the delivery of the broken brass Temple implements to Babylon contributes to the impression that Babylon was these exiles' destination. The Weidner Ration Lists (Ernst Weidner, 'Jojachin, König von Juda, in babylonischen Keilschrifttexten', in *Mélanges syriens offerts à monsieur René Dussaud: secrétaire perpétuel de l'Académie des Inscriptions et Belles-Lettres, par ses amis et ses élèves. Tome II* [Paris: Geuthner, 1939], 923–935) identify Jehoiachin, the deported Judean king, by name, and reference his sons as recipients of ration portions. Support for the impression that, at the least, upper-class or royal deportees resided in or near Babylon comes from the tablets' excavated context, the Kasr Südburg 21s area of Babylon (Olof Pedersén, *Archive und Bibliotheken in Babylon: die Tontafeln der Grabung Robert Koldeweys 1899–1917* [ADOG 25; Berlin: SDV, 2005], 112).

7 Admittedly, in the course of the 135 years that separate the destruction of the Temple and the date of the earliest Murašû texts, any number of factors could have affected the demographics of the exiles. What is of concern here is the clarification of the various sources' reports on the distribution of the population across urban and rural environments.

8 Israel Eph'al, 'On the Political and Social Organization of the Jews in Babylonian Exile', in *XXI. Deutscher Orientalistentag: vom 24. bis 29. März 1980 in Berlin: Vorträge* (ZDMGSup 5; ed. Fritz Steppat; Wiesbaden: Franz Steiner, 1983), 106–112 (110).

standing. For the Babylonians, the identification of Judeans, Egyptians, and others was merely a regular detail in this type of documentation.

Another textual product of the royal (and therefore urban) circle that mentions Judah and Judeans is the 'Chronicle Concerning the Early Years of Nebuchadnezzar'. In general, the rhetorical style of Babylonian chronicles is terse, preserving only the most sparse details of royal campaigns, as in this, the entire report on Nebuchadnezzar II's march against Judah and Jerusalem:

> The seventh year: In the month Kislev the king of Akkad mustered his army and marched to Hattu. He encamped against the city of Judah and on the second day of the month Adar he captured the city (and) seized (its) king. A king of his own choice he appointed in the city (and) taking the vast tribute he brought it into Babylon.[9]

Similarly, the chronicle passages that report on military actions against the Egyptians[10] and Arabians[11] focus on benefits accrued to the Babylonian king. From Judah, Nebuchadnezzar gained 'vast tribute'; extensive plundering transferred the Arabians' possessions, animals and goods to the Babylonians. In the encounter with the Egyptians, 'both sides suffered severe losses' and no particular advantage accrued to Nebuchadnezzar.[12] The straightforward tone avoids privileging the defeat of any one enemy over another, and establishes that royal captives from diverse origins received comparable treatment. This equanimity permeates much of Babylonian historical rhetoric, insofar as all subject lands furnish the goods and personnel necessary to establish and maintain Babylon as the center of the world.[13]

Although the ration lists and chronicle confirm the presence of royal Judeans in the urban environment of sixth century B.C.E. Babylon, the Murašû texts focus on a rural locus of Judeans in the later fifth century B.C.E., even as they interacted with the imperial administration. This dichotomy might suggest that over the course of 135 years a dramatic demographic shift had occurred which forced

---

9 A. K. Grayson, *Assyrian and Babylonian Chronicles* (Winona Lake: Eisenbrauns, 2000), ABC 5: rev. 11–13.

10 ABC 5: rev. 5–7.

11 ABC 5: rev. 9–10.

12 ABC 5: rev. 7.

13 David Vanderhooft, *The Neo-Babylonian Empire and Babylon in the Latter Prophets* (HSM 59; Atlanta: Scholars Press, 1999), 34–49, esp. 40. Along with ABC 2, 3, 4, and 6, ABC 5 belongs to a group of texts referred to in the scholarly literature as 'Chronicles of the Neo-Babylonian Dynasty'. Caroline Waerzeggers ('The Babylonian Chronicles: Classification and Provenance', *JNES* 71 [2012]: 285–298 [295]) identifies ABC 5 as the final component in a three-text series consisting of ABC 3–4–5, which focus 'primarily on military history; religious concerns are secondary at best'.

urban dwellers into tenant-farming in the Nippur countryside. However, recent scholarship confirms that the cuneiform record depicts an upward trend in the social and economic conditions in Babylonia in the long sixth century.[14] Against that background, differences in the demographics, location and economic interactions of the various subsets of the Judean exilic population await explanation.

The first pieces of additional evidence bearing on this problem came from three tablets in the Moussaieff collection published by Francis Joannès and André Lemaire.[15] The texts mention individuals bearing Yahwistic or West Semitic names. Two of the texts were composed in small, previously attested, rural locales: Bīt-Našar[16] and Bīt-rē'i.[17] The third text's remarkable contribution to the study of Judeans in the Babylonian Exile is in the name of the town in which it was composed, the previously unattested settlement Āl-Yāhūdu, 'Judahtown'.[18] Written in 498 B.C.E., it reduces by almost half a century the temporal gap in documentation between the date of the earliest deportations and the first Murašû texts. This single, brief text offered positive proof that Judeans, identifiable on the basis of their characteristic Yahwistic names or patronymics,[19] inhabited a rural settlement named for their place of origin. This text is one of fifty-one tablets known to belong to an Āl-Yāhūdu 'archive',[20] the remainder of which appear (or

---

14 Michael Jursa, *Aspects of the Economic History of Babylonia.*

15 Francis Joannès and André Lemaire, 'Trois tablettes cunéiformes à l'onomastique ouest-sémitique', *Transeuphratène* 17 (1999): 17–34.

16 TuM 2/3 91:7; see also Ran Zadok, *Geographical Names According to New- and Late-Babylonian Texts* (RGTC 8; Wiesbaden: L. Reichert, 1985), 98.

17 BIN 2 118: 12, NBDM 89: 32. On the basis of a small orthographic difference, Zadok (RGTC 8: 102) lists these toponyms separately. He locates the Bīt-rē'i attested in NBDM 89 in the Uruk region and suggests it may be associated with the Bīt-rē'i in Bīt-Amukāni, attested in Neo-Assyria sources. Uruk, at the southern end of Bīt-Amukāni (Grant Frame, *Babylonia 689–627 B. C.: A Political History* [Istanbul: Nederlands Historisch-Archaeologisch Instituut te Istanbul, 1992], 39), is close to Karkara, one of the vertices of the triangular region in which Āl-Yāhūdu and Bīt-Našar are believed to be located. Cf. Laurie E. Pearce and Cornelia Wunsch, *Documents of Judean Exiles and West Semites in Babylonia in the Collection of David Sofer* (CUSAS 28; Bethesda: CDL, 2014), 6–7.

18 For the transliteration, translation and copy of this Āl-Yāhūdu tablet, see Joannès and Lemaire, 'Trois tablettes cunéiformes', 18, 33. An interpretation of this text is offered by Wilfred G. Lambert, 'A Document from a Community of Exiles in Babylonia', in *New Seals and Inscriptions, Hebrew, Idumean, and Cuneiform* (HBM 8; ed. Meir Lubetski; Sheffield: Sheffield Phoenix Press, 2007), 201–205.

19 Nīr-Yāma, son of Ahīqam (ll. 6–7, 15); Yāhu-azar, son of Abdi-Yāhu (ll. 11–12); Yāhu-azar, son of Ṭāb-šalam (ll. 16–17); Nadab-Yāma, son of Ṣadduqu (ll. 17–18); Nahhum, son of Yāhu-azar (ll.18–19); Abdi-Yāhu, son of Šama-Yāma (l. 21).

20 Preliminary reports on the Āl-Yāhūdu archive are found in: Laurie E. Pearce, 'New Evidence for Judeans in Babylonia', in *Judah and the Judeans in the Persian Period* (ed. O. Lipschits and

will appear) in two publications.[21] Entirely ordinary and regular in their administrative and legal details, the Āl-Yāhūdu texts, along with those from the neighboring settlements Bīt-Abīram and (Bīt) Našar, contribute data relevant to the exploration of Judean identity and identification.[22]

These rural locales positively correlate with Nebuchadnezzar II's well-known policy of deporting defeated populations and resettling them in the Mesopotamian countryside, especially around Nippur.[23] However, the place of composition

M. Oeming; Winona Lake: Eisenbrauns, 2006), 399–411; Laurie E. Pearce, '"Judean": A Special Status in Neo-Babylonian and Achaemenid Babylonia?', in *Judah and the Judeans in the Achaemenid Period: Negotiating Identity in an International Context* (ed. O. Lipschits, G. Knoppers and M. Oeming; Winona Lake: Eisenbrauns, 2011), 267–277; Michael Jursa, *Neo-Babylonian Legal and Administrative Documents: Typology, Contents, and Archives* (GMTR 1; Münster: Ugarit-Verlag, 2005), 151.

21 Pearce and Wunsch, *Documents of Judean Exiles*; Cornelia Wunsch, with contributions by Laurie Pearce, *Judeans by the Waters of Babylon. New Historical Evidence in Cuneiform Sources from Rural Babylonia: Texts from the Schøyen Collection* (Babylonische Archive 6; Dresden: ISLET, forthcoming). Texts in these volumes will be identified with the *sigla* CUSAS 28 and BaAr 6, respectively. The *siglum* CUSAS 28 + tablet number given here supersedes the designation TAYN + tablet number that appeared in Pearce, 'New Evidence'.

22 *Ālu ša Našar* (attested in several different orthographies) is the place of composition of the text published as no. 2 in Joannès and Lemaire, 'Trois tablettes cunéiformes', 27–30. Yahwistic names appear in that text, as well as in the other Našar texts in the new publications. Bīt-Abīram is the site of composition of seven texts published in Francis Joannès and André Lemaire, 'Contrats babyloniens d'époque achéménide du Bît-abî Râm avec une épigraphie araméenne', *RA* 90 (1996): 41–60 (52). Although the Bīt-Abīram texts do not contain Yahwistic names, they do link the local administrator, Zababa-šarra-uṣur, with a village at the edge of the Kabaru canal (previously known from BE 9 4: 9, 84: 2; YOS 3 111: 28; cf. RGTC 8: 373), biblical נהר־כבר, Nᵉhar Kᵉbar, (Ezek 1:3, 3:15). This location places him in geographic proximity to descendants of the Judean deportees (Joannès and Lemaire, 'Contrats babyloniens', 52). For preliminary comments on the Zababa-šarra-uṣur archive, see Jursa, *Neo-Babylonian Legal and Administrative Documents*, 151, and Caroline Waerzeggers, 'The Babylonian Revolts Against Xerxes and the "End of Archives"', *AfO* 50 (2003): 150–173 (157 n. 38) and Pearce and Wunsch, *Documents of Judean Exiles*, 7. The remaining forty-seven texts known to belong to the Zababa-šarra-uṣur archive will be published as BaAr 6 43–57, 59–65, 67–76, 78–84, 86, 87, 90–95. Several dozen new toponyms appear, most attested only once or twice throughout the corpus. Many of them assist in developing a more comprehensive understanding of the southern Mesopotamian landscape at this time, but few, if any, provide direct evidence for the Judeans and their activities.

23 See, for example, Israel Eph'al, 'The Western Minorities in Babylonia in the 6th and 5th Centuries B. C.: Maintenance and Cohesion', *Or* 47 (1978): 74–90 and Vanderhooft, *The Neo-Babylonian Empire*, 110–114; for the geographic information see Ran Zadok, 'The Nippur Region during the Late Assyrian, Chaldean and Achaemenian Periods Chiefly According to Written Sources', *IOS* 8 (1978): 266–332, and Ran Zadok, 'Phoenicians, Philistines, and Moabites in Mesopotamia', *BASOR* 230 (1978): 57–65.

that precedes the date formula at the end of Neo-Babylonian legal and administrative texts is rarely brought into discussions of identity. Yet, the geographic name Āl-Yāhūdu and its orthographies, especially those in the two earliest documents, prompt a consideration of toponyms (including those of other settlements named for deported or non-native populations) in attempts to detect means by which Babylonians identified Judeans (and others) now present on their landscape. Dated to the 33rd and 38th years of Nebuchadnezzar (20 Nisannu 572 B.C.E. and 7 Kislīmu 567 B.C.E., respectively), CUSAS 28 1 and BaAr 6 1 document Āl-Yāhūdu's existence on the Mesopotamian landscape fifteen and twenty years after the destruction of Jerusalem; they confirm a Judean presence in the Babylonian countryside from the earliest days of the exile. Thus, the urban/rural dichotomy thought to obtain between the descendants of deportees to Babylon and the tenant farmers in the Nippur region and to reflect the Judeans' apparently changed and constrained economic status is bridged. As the Āl-Yāhūdu texts range in date from 572 (33 Nbk) to 477 (9 Xerxes) B.C.E., there remain undocumented only fourteen years at the beginning and twenty-three years at the end of the 135-year documentary gap between the destruction of Jerusalem and the earliest Murašû texts.

In CUSAS 28 1 and BaAr 6 1, the place of composition is written with the standard Akkadian gentilic *-āya* and is preceded by lú, the determinative designating 'people'.[24] Thus the Akkadian toponym *ālu ša Yāhūdāya* must be translated as 'the town of the Judeans'. These texts suggest that Āl-Yāhūdu was one of the places in which Judean deportees were resettled. The gentilic disappears from the toponym by the first year of Amēl-Marduk's reign (561 B.C.E.);[25] from that point on, the settlement is known simply as Āl-Yāhūdu, 'Judahtown'. These are the earliest known instances of Babylonian identification of Judeans as a population on the Mesopotamian landscape. In order to assess whether the shift in orthographies of this new settlement's name offers any insight into Babylonian perceptions of Judean identity, the orthographies and contexts of other toponyms should be considered.

In the Nippur area, many of the settlement names which include the gentilic refer to members of an eponymous household or Aramean tribe.[26] Very few of the attestations of settlements named for Levantine cities include the gentilic,[27] and

---

24 CUSAS 28 1: URU ^{lú}*ia-a-hu-du-a-a*; BaAr 6 1: URU ^{lú}*ia*$^{!}$*-<<da>>-hu-du-a-a*.

25 CUSAS 28 6: 18: URU *ia-a-hu-du*, written 5.iii.1 Amēl-Marduk (561 B.C.E.).

26 E.g. Bīt-Tabalāya (Zadok, 'Nippur Region', 297; RGTC 8: 107); Gambulāya (Zadok, 'Nippur Region', 302; PBS 2/1 12: 11).

27 **Hazatu** (Gaza): BE 8 56: 5, 14 (URU *ha-za-tu*$_4$, Nbn [year broken]); BE 10 9: 2, 20, 24 (URU *ha-*

then never in the statement that indicates the place in which the text was composed. That is to say, while no tablet is known to have been written in the 'town of the Ashkelonites' or 'town of the Tyrians', or the like, the gentilics [lú]*Išqillūnāya*[28] and [lú]*Ṣurrāya*[29] (among others) appear as descriptors of the background of an individual or group of individuals, as in the Weidner Ration Lists. Yet the number of those documents is small and most of them were written in the Achaemenid period, well after the toponym *Ālu ša* [lú]*Yāhūdāya* had been transformed into Āl-Yāhūdu. Thus, these gentilics carry little weight as evidence for Babylonian markers of identity.

Another documented shift from the use of the gentilic in the construction of the name of a town to a more abbreviated form of the name occurs in the orthography of the 'town of the Arabians', *Ālu ša* [lú]*Arbāya*. It appears in the place of composition of two texts, BE 8 26:13 and 50:15,[30] dating to 42 Nbk (563 B.C.E.) and 9 Nbn (547 B.C.E.), respectively. Zadok equates the locale with the toponym Arbā ([uru]*ar-ba-a*),[31] the place where, in 4 Dar (518 B.C.E.), the text TuM 2/3 147:3 was composed. The loss of the gentilic in the toponym recalls the orthographic shift from *Ālu ša* [lú]*Yāhūdāya* to Āl-Yāhūdu. The (admittedly small corpus of) evidence suggests that the gentilic form of each toponym appears earlier than the form that

---

za-tú/-tu₄, 1 Dar); RGTC 8: 155; Zadok, 'Phoenicians, Philistines, and Moabites', 61. CUSAS 28 101, a promissory note for barley written in [uru]Hazatu in 5 Cyr (534 B.C.E.), records the debt of Nabû-uṣur, son of Dala-Yāma, and thus provides evidence of a Judean there; **Išqillūnu** (Ashkelon): BE 9 86a: 8 (URU *iš-qal-lu-nu*, Artaxerxes [place of composition and year destroyed]), BE 10 118: 4, 9; 7 (URU *iš-qal-lu-nu*; URU *šá iš-qal-lu-nu*), CBS 12895: 8' (published in Matthew W. Stolper, *Management and Politics in Later Achaemenid Babylonia: New Texts from the Murašû Archive* [PhD Thesis, University of Michigan, 1974], 432–435; RGTC 8: 183. Zadok notes that Išqillūnu 'was also inhabited by Jews' (Zadok, 'Phoenicians, Philistines, and Moabites', 61); **Qidiš** (Qadeš): Qidiš is the place of composition of ROMCT 2 2: 17 (URU *qí-⌜di⌝-iš*), written in 41 Nbk (564 B.C.E.); RGTC 8: 255 also cites an instance of the name Qidiš in Pinches, *JTVI* 49 129–130: 3–4; **Qidari** (Qedar): URU *qí-dar-ri* appears in BE 8 65: 7; the tablet's place of composition is destroyed. RGTC 8: 255 (other references for Qedarians: Qedarians are identified in two letters written during the reign of Esarhaddon: ABL 350:8 [SAA 18 143 {P237241}] and ABL 811:7 [SAA 18 145 {P237645}], see Postgate *apud* Eph'al, '"Arabs" in Babylonia in the 8th Century B. C.', *JAOS* 94 [1974]: 108–115 [112 n. 28]); **Ṣurru** (Tyre): for citations see Francis Joannès, 'La localisation de Ṣurru à l'époque néo-babylonienne', *Semitica* 32 (1982): 39–41 (35–43) and RGTC 8: 280–281.

28 Weidner, 'Jojachin', 928: VAT 16283 = Babylon 28178 (plate 3) line 6: [x+]2 *mārī ša* [m]*Agâ šarri ša* [kur]*Išqillūnu* plate 3 r. 8, plate 4 l. 22, plate 5 l. 25, 26; RGTC 8: 183. The recipients are identified as the 'supervisor of the people of Ashkelon' and 'chief of the singers of Ashkelon', *rēš Išqillūnāya* and *rēš nârê Išqillūnāya*, respectively.

29 Weidner, 'Jojachin', 924: text A, line 32.

30 In both, the toponym is written URU *šá* [lú]*ar-ba-a-a*.

31 RGTC 8: 23.

does not include it. The orthographic shift from *Ālu ša* [lú]*Yāhūdāya* to Āl-Yāhūdu occurs after such a brief period of time that it suggests an almost immediate transformation of the Babylonian perception of these deported people into a resident population. Although the orthographic shift from *Ālu ša* [lú]*Arbāya* to Arbā is documented over a greater span of time, the direction of the shift over time parallels that of the development of the change in the writing of the name of Āl-Yāhūdu. The parallel chronological development of these orthographies suggests a tendency to assign toponyms formed with the names of the regions in which their transplanted population originated rather than with the explicit names of cities located in that homeland.[32] More compelling evidence for Babylonian identification of subjugated peoples on the basis of their geographic origins appears in the designation of certain economic units.

2 Marks of Identity in Social and Economic Institutions

Bow(-fief) lands (*bīt-qašti*), known to exist in the reign of Nebuchadnezzar II,[33] and especially well-documented in the Murašû archives, were an important component of Babylonia's economy. People obligated to serve on these lands were organized into *haṭrus*, groups labeled with professional or geographic designations, e.g., the *haṭru* of the Urartians and Meliteans ([lú]*Uraštāya u Miliduāya*),[34] or the *haṭru* of the pastry cooks ([lú]*kaškadinnū*).[35] Of these appellations, Stolper says:

> ... because the Murašû texts deal with *haṭru* members chiefly as holders of land and attached obligations, the texts provide no real evidence that *haṭru* names actually characterize the members' professional or social statuses, that is, that the names have descriptive as well as

32 In the evidence presented in note 27 above, citations from Hazatu, Qidiš and Ṣurru all date to the reigns of Nebuchadnezzar or Nabonidus, placing them squarely in the Neo-Babylonian period and relatively close in time to the conquest of the Levant. None of the names of these cities appears with a gentilic, lending strength to the suggestion that the Babylonians named new settlements both for the regions from which deportees came and for cities. The reasons for two approaches to the nomenclature are not known.

33 Michael Jursa ('Bogenland schon unter Nebukadnezar II', NABU 1998/124) demonstrates that this economic institution was already functioning in Uruk by the 35th year of Nebuchadnezzar (570 B.C.E.). For evidence of bow-lands in the reign of Nebuchadnezzar in the Āl-Yāhūdu corpus, see the discussion of Bēl-šarra-uṣur on p. 32.

34 Stolper, *Entrepreneurs and Empire*, 78.

35 Stolper, *Entrepreneurs and Empire*, 74.

> identifying value. Nevertheless, there is some indirect evidence that the names are descriptive: administrative connections between *haṭrus* named for estates and the estates themselves; and the incidence of foreign personal names among members of *haṭrus* which have foreign ethnic names. Assuming that the *haṭrus* of fifth-century Nippur were comparatively recent creations, and that their names had not become mere proper nouns, those names give a general notion of the membership of *haṭrus*.[36]

haṭrus consisted of *šušānû*, individuals of dependent juridical status,[37] working under the supervision of the *šaknu*, manager, or other officers, who themselves bore the designations of their professions or named estates.[38] The Murašû texts do not document the existence of a Judean *haṭru*, which might have been termed *haṭru ša Yāhūdāya*, or the like. However, other terminology in the Āl-Yāhūdu texts points to the existence of a Judean *haṭru* or *haṭru*-like organization in Achaemenid Babylonia.[39]

The phrase *šušānê ša* [lú]*Yāhūdāya*, '*šušānû* of the Judeans', appears in three texts written in Āl-Yāhūdu[40] and identifies a group of Judean state dependents on the basis of their place of origin. This designation is consistent with Stolper's observation that identification of members of a *haṭru* was: 'a condition of economic and juridical dependence on the state or the state's concessionaires that is strongly marked by frequent use of the term *šušānû* in *haṭru*-names'.[41] Even without the explicit identification of a Judean *haṭru*, it is clear that by the Achaemenid period, Judeans were but one of the many groups organized into and labeled with respect to social organization and administrative units.[42] Babylonian (and Achaemenid) efforts at identifying populations were comprehensive, inclusive of all groups that came under their administrative and imperial jurisdiction.

The suggestion that the explicit designation *haṭru ša* [lú]*Yāhūdāya* is not necessary to establish the existence of a Judean *haṭru* is supported by the fact that the

---

36 Stolper, *Entrepreneurs and Empire*, 72.

37 For the etymology of the term, see CAD Š/3 379–380.

38 Stolper, *Entrepreneurs and Empire*, 72–79.

39 Pearce, 'A Special Status?', 271–274.

40 With minor orthographic variation, the fields are called A.ŠÀ [lú]*šušānê* [lú]*Yāhūdāya*, 'the fields of the Judean *šušānû*': CUSAS 28 19 (5.vi.11 Darius); CUSAS 28 20 (6.<vi>.11 Darius); CUSAS 28 21 ([x+]1.ii.11 Darius), all promissory notes for barely due to be paid at the harvest.

41 Stolper, *Entrepreneurs and Empire*, 79.

42 The Achaemenid empire's concern with workers' origins extends only so far as to organize the population into service units. See Wouter Henkelman and Matthew W. Stolper, 'Ethnic Identity and Ethnic Labelling at Persepolis: The Case of the Skudrians', in *Organisation des pouvoirs et contacts culturels dans les pays de l'empire achéménide* (Persika 14; ed. P. Briant and M. Chauveau; Paris: Editions de Boccard, 2009), 277 with note 69.

complete description of the lands further demonstrates the organization of the Judeans into groups located on lands under the jurisdiction of the royal administration. In CUSAS 28 19, 20 and 21, fields designated A.ŠÀ ^{lú}*šušānê* ^{lú}*Yāhudāia* are under the authority of Uštānu, governor of Across-the-River, and managed by Iddināya, son of Šinqā, deputy of (the one in charge of) the mares.[43] Previously published documentation dating to 521–516 B.C.E. assigns Uštānu the title 'Governor of Babylon and Across-the-River'.[44] The present texts all date to 11 Dar (512/11 B.C.E.) and confirm Stolper's speculation that Uštānu may have continued to serve as a governor beyond 516 B.C.E.[45] The exceptional use of the single geographic term 'Across-the-River' in Uštānu's title in the new attestations deserves attention. Variations in the title 'Governor of Babylon and Across-the-River' typically have been cited in attempts to refine the date of the separation of the enormous province into two discrete regions. Here, attention is called to the striking and heretofore unattested use of 'Across-the-River' to define the geographic parameters of Uštānu's authority in texts concerned with lands described with the gentilic 'Judean'. Thus it opens for consideration the potential of this title to contribute to the discussion of Babylonian expressions and perceptions of Judean identity.

Examination of Stolper's list of Achaemenid officials bearing the title 'Governor of Babylon and Across-the-River' or its abbreviated forms reveals that only two individuals, Tattannu and Bēlšunu, are called 'Governor of Across-the-River'.[46] Notably, they are the only documented Achaemenid governors who may be iden-

43 *šá* ŠU.2 ^{m}*uš-ta-nu šá e-bir* I_7 *šá* ^{m}SUM.NA-*a* A-*šú šá* ^{m}*ši-in-qa-ʾ* ^{lú}2-*ú šá* SAL.ANŠE.KUR.RA.
44 Matthew W. Stolper, 'The Governor of Babylon and Across-the-River in 486 B.C.', *JNES* 48 (1989): 283–305 (290). On p. 289 (with n. 5), Stolper references three texts which mention an untitled individual named Uštānu, possibly the satrap. Based on the documented dates for Uštānu then known (1–6 Dar), he suggested that the poorly preserved Babylon fragment VAT 15617, which refers to a slave of Uštānu and is dated to year 10, be attributed to the reign of Xerxes (see also Wilhelm Eilers, *Iranische Beamtennamen in der keilschriftlichen Überlieferung* [Abhandlungen für die Kunde des Morgenlandes 25/5; Leipzig: Brockhaus, 1940]). However, at least on chronological grounds, the CUSAS 28 evidence establishes that the mention of Uštānu in VAT 15617 could have occurred in the reign of Darius.
45 Stolper, 'Governor of Babylon and Across-the-River', 292.
46 Stolper, 'Governor of Babylon and Across-the-River', 290; Tattanu VS 4 152:25 (23.ii 20 Dar). Stolper's identification of Huta-x-x-' as a 'governor of Babylon and Across-the-River' in a text dated to 486 B.C.E. provided convincing proof that the province could not have been divided prior to that point. Thus, the 512/11 date of the texts identifying Uštānu as Governor of Across-the-River is unlikely to bring new evidence to bear on the determination of the date of the provincial division. However, it does push back the date for the earliest witness to the use of single geographic references in the governors' title.

tifiable in non-Babylonian sources: Tattannu with Tattenai (Ezr 5:3, 6; 6:6, 13), and Bēlšunu with Xenophon's Belysis.[47] The biblical narrative makes clear that Tattannu directly intervened with and traveled to Jerusalem, a journey facilitated by his residence in Damascus.[48] All previously known documentation of Uštānu in official capacity refers to him as 'Governor of Babylon and Across-the-River'. The attestation of the shorter title 'Governor of Across-the-River' occurs in the latest known documentation of his career, in connection with his administration of lands with which Judeans were associated. Regardless of whether Uštānu was in Babylon (or southern Mesopotamia, more generally) or the more distant reaches of Transeuphrates in Darius' eleventh year, it is striking that several generations following Nebuchadnezzar's reign, Uštānu's title highlights the origin of the people whose fields figure prominently in the relevant transactions. While it may be premature to declare this a focus marker for Babylonian recognition of Judean identity, the evidence is suggestive.

3 Personal Names as Identifiers and Markers of Identity

The rosters of personal names and associated prosopographical evidence are the most accessible points of entry into the study of individual identity. Recovery of Judean names in cuneiform texts is facilitated by the interaction of two factors, one theological, the other the formal conventions common in naming patterns throughout the ancient Semitic-speaking world. In Semitic onomastica, the subjects of personal names constructed as nominal or verbal sentences are most frequently theophoric elements, be they kinship terms or divine names and attributes.[49] In constructing their offspring's names, Babylonian families might privilege the name of their respective cities' divine patrons,[50] but names of other Babylonian deities could and did appear as well. Thus, while individuals named

47 Stolper, 'Governor of Babylon and Across-the-River', 289, 292. Michael Jursa and Matthew W. Stolper affirm the association of Tattannu with Tattenai in 'From the Tattannu Archive Fragment', *WZKM* 97 (2007): 243–281 (244).

48 Pierre Briant, *Histoire de l'empire perse* (Paris: Fayard, 1996), 503.

49 Ran Zadok, *On West Semites in Babylonia During the Chaldean and Achaemenian Periods: An Onomastic Study* (Jerusalem: H. J. & Z. Wanaarta, 1977), 51–57 (kinship terms), 67–68 (nouns that serve as theophoric elements).

50 Michael P. Streck, 'Das Onomastikon der Beamten am neubabylonischen Ebabbar-Tempel in Sippar', *ZA* 91 (2001): 110–119; Jursa, *Neo-Babylonian Legal and Administrative Documents*, 7.

Marduk-X, Nabû-X or Šamaš-X are likely to have origins in Babylon, Borsippa or Sippar, there is no guarantee that the people bearing them were Babylonians, Borsippeans or Sippareans, respectively.[51]

Similarly, many Judean personal names included a theophoric element. Those names which included the distinctive name of YHWH, which does not appear in the pantheon of any other population group, serve as a nearly fool-proof marker of its bearer's Judean origin.[52] While the presence of a Yahwistic element is a reliable marker for identifying Judeans in cuneiform documentation, it does not guarantee recovery of them all. Identification of the maximum number of Judeans in the Babylonian record is a desideratum for the reconstruction and analysis of the Judean exile and return.

It is a major challenge to identify Judeans who do not bear Yahwistic names. Individual Judeans may be recovered if their names: (1) reflect cultural or religious practices that could be Judean, but which are not exclusively so, (2) are associated through prosopographical data with children, parents, and perhaps grandparents who bear Yahwistic names, and (3) can be demonstrated to preserve orthographic or phonological curiosities that conceal a Yahwistic name.[53]

---

51 Characteristics that may be used productively to distinguish West Semitic from Babylonian names are discussed in Michael D. Coogan, *West Semitic Personal Names in the Murašû Documents* (HSM 7; Missoula: Scholars Press, 1976), 3–5. He identifies many of the features that distinguish these onomastica from each other as well as from the contemporaneous Persian and Egyptian onomastica. Heather D. Baker ('Approaches to Akkadian Name-Giving in First-Millennium BC Mesopotamia', in *Mining the Archives: Festschrift for Christopher Walker on the Occasion of His 60th Birthday, 4 October 2002* [ed. C. Wunsch; Dresden: ISLET, 2002], 10–11) discusses the hierarchy of deities utilized in the names of sons of a single family and points out that some families, notably landed families in Babylon, avoided the use of any theophoric element except that of their city's chief deity.

52 Ran Zadok (*The Jews in Babylonia During the Chaldean and Achaemenian Periods According to the Babylonian Sources* [Haifa: University of Haifa, 1979], 7) notes that the Yahwistic theophoric element is occasionally found in names outside the Israelite and Judean environment. While the focus in this essay is on Judean names, the reader is reminded that the combined Israelite and Judean onomasticon preserves features that set it apart from the West Semitic and Babylonian onomastica in general.

53 Hypocoristica (shortened forms of names) pose special problems for the identification of individuals who bear them. It is not always possible to ascertain whether a single individual known in a text corpus is referenced both by the full form of his name and a closely related hypocoristicon. For example, not every instance of Nādinu can or must be correlated with a fully expressed name (e.g. Nabû-nādin-šumi) or with a specific individual bearing that name, although it may be possible to confirm such an association. The limitations of the cuneiform writing system in rendering West Semitic phonology and morphology complicate the assessment of orthographies of the Yahwistic element and, as a result, recognition of Judeans who bear hypocoristica of Yahwis-

In practical terms, these ambiguities complicate efforts to assess the demographics of an ancient settlement or town. Yet, a rough computation of the percentage of individuals in Āl-Yāhūdu who can be identified confidently as Judeans may suggest that the scope of the problem is not insurmountable. The Āl-Yāhūdu texts preserve the names of just over 400 individuals, including those whose existence is known only from the patronym of a two-tier filiation statement.[54] Of these, approximately 140 persons, a significant subset, bear Yahwistic names. The Judean population of Āl-Yāhūdu can thus be calculated at a minimum of 35 %, a percentage that stands in marked contrast to the barely 3 % of the Nippur population that Zadok computed for the Judeans in the Murašû texts.[55] In contrast, the fourteen Yahwistic names in the Našar corpus of 293 individuals suggests that this nearby town had a Judean population of 5 %, a figure that more closely correlates with the Judean population of Achaemenid Nippur.[56] The Bīt-Abīram texts preserve the names of some 272 individuals of West Semitic background, but only one Yahwistic name appears among them. Outside of Āl-Yāhūdu, the limited inventory of Yahwistic names likely correlates with a smaller population of Judeans; thus it is likely that few Judeans outside of Āl-Yāhūdu who do not bear Yahwistic names wait to be identified. Nonetheless, it is important to discuss lexical and

---

tic names is problematic. When prosopographical data permit the correlation of an individual bearing a Yahwistic personal name (i.e., with subject and predicate) to a corresponding hypocoristicon (even if it resembles a fine Babylonian name or hypocoristicon), additional Judeans may be recovered. In the Āl-Yāhūdu corpus, this is demonstrated in the case of a certain Bania, son of Nubāya, discussed on p. 22.

The new corpus extends the evidence of Yahwistic names and orthographies beyond that presented in Coogan, *West Semitic Personal Names*, and in Zadok, *West Semites*. The contributions of the new data to the topic of the present study are presented in the introduction to Pearce and Wunsch, *Doucments of Judean Exiles*, 10–29.

54 A general discussion of the composition of a two- or three-tier genealogy (termed here a filiation statement) appears in John P. Nielsen, *Sons and Descendants: A Social History of Kin Groups and Family Names in the Early Neo-Babylonian Period, 747–626 B. C.* (CHANE 43; Leiden: Brill, 2011), 2. Nielsen also tabulates the orthographic variants attested for these filiation expressions by city: Babylon, p. 26; Borsippa, p. 69; Dilbat, p. 105; Sippar, p. 130; Kish, p. 143; Nippur, p. 163; Uruk, p. 189; Ur, p. 212.

55 Zadok, *Jews in Babylonia*, 78. These figures are computed on data that span the full chronological range of the documentation. It would be quite difficult to assess whether these statistics reflect a consistent percentage of Judeans in Nippur over the course of 150 years or whether the data conceal demographic shifts.

56 For a discussion of the implications of statistical analysis (size and percentage) of the non-Babylonian population in general and that of the Judeans in particular, see Ran Zadok, *The Earliest Diaspora: Israelites and Judeans in Pre-Hellenistic Mesopotamia* (Tel Aviv: Diaspora Research Institute, 2002), 61–63.

orthographic features, the presence or absence of which might conceal the identity of additional Judeans.

4 Names Reflecting Cultural Practices

Cultural practices inhere in names like Haggai and Šabbatāya, which are said to commemorate the birth of a child on a festival or the Sabbath, respectively. Although they constitute a very small group of names reflecting a family's perpetuation of religious practice, not all who bear these names can be identified securely as Judeans.[57] Etymologically, these names are West Semitic and do not include the Yahwistic element. Thus, the cultural background of individuals who bear them can be securely determined only from prosopographical evidence, i.e., the names of their fathers or sons.[58] Individuals who bear these ambiguous names can be confirmed as Judean only if one position in the ubiquitous two-tier filiation statement is occupied by an unequivocally Judean, i.e., Yahwistic, name. Of the nine individuals named Šabbatāya listed in Coogan's study, only two can be securely identified as Judean:[59] one is the son of a certain Gadalyaw, the other, the father of Abī-Yāma.[60] Unfortunately, the name and patronym of Šabbatāya, son of Haggai, heretofore offered no secure markers of Judean identity.[61]

However, the instances of the names Haggai and Šabbatāya appearing in CUSAS 28 37 and BaAr 6 10 can be securely identified as Judean on the basis of prosopographical data.[62] With one exception, all of the relevant texts which preserve place of composition derive from Āl-Yāhūdu, their dates of composition in the reign of Darius placing them squarely in the post-Exilic period. But even the exception, a single text from Babylon (CUSAS 28 45 || HBM 8), records the activity of individuals known to have been at Āl-Yāhūdu. The names Haggai (identifying three individuals) and Šabbatāya (identifying one) are borne by sons, three of whose fathers bear Yahwistic names,[63] and one who bears the West Semitic name

57 Bezalel Porten, *Archives from Elephantine. The Life of an Ancient Jewish Military Colony* (Berkeley: University of California Press, 1968), 127.

58 Coogan, *West Semitic Personal Names*, 73, 84; Zadok, *Jews in Babylonia*, 22–24.

59 Coogan, *West Semitic Personal Names*, 35.

60 Gadalyaw, BE 9 69: 21; BE 10 7: 17; Abī-Yāma (^{m}AD-ia-a-ma), PBS 2/1 185: 2; 218: 3.

61 BE 10 85: 16, left edge; PBS 2/1 12: 15.

62 Two individuals named Haggai bear Yahwistic patronyms: Matan-Yā and Natan-Yāma, respectively, thus confirming the Judean context of this name.

63 Haggai, son of: Matan-Yā, CUSAS 28 37: 4, 11; Natan-Yāma, BaAr 6 10: 21; Šabbatāya son of Bana-Yāma CUSAS 28 42: 5, 13.

Ahīqam.[64] As this Ahīqam had four other sons who bore Yahwistic names (Nīr-Yāma, Yāḫu-azza, Yāḫušu, and Yāḫu-izrī) and is himself son of a father named Rapa-Yāma,[65] there can be little doubt that Ahīqam was of Judean lineage. Thus, prosopographical notices confirm that the names Haggai and Šabbatāya can, in fact, identify Judeans.

5 Ambiguous Orthographies

In addition to the attested orthographies known to represent the Yahwistic element, a few surprising orthographies appear in names in the new corpus and can be demonstrated to refer to the Judean god. The ability to confirm the Yahwistic element in these exceptional writings is possible because they appear in contexts that provide additional, positive identification of the Judean background of the individuals so named. In a text from the town of Našar,[66] Abdâ-Yāhu, son of Barak-Yāma, the *dēkû*, is responsible for the collection of silver due for administrative financial obligations. This Abdâ-Yāhu received the payment from ᶠBunanītu, wife of Ahīqar, the governor (ˡᵘ́en.nam = *pīhātu*). The witnesses included individuals who bore Babylonian and West Semitic names. One of them was Bania, son of Nubāya, whose name (written ᵐ*ba-ni-ia*) would appear to be a well-attested Babylonian hypocoristicon, written syllabically ᵐ*ba-ni-(e-)a/-ia/-ía*, and logographically ᵐDU_3-*a/-ia/-ía*.[67] The text offers no particular reason to suggest that he should be identified as a member of a non-Babylonian population group. However, orthographic evidence from the new corpus demonstrates that this Bania is, in fact, a Judean named Bana-Yāma.

In Našar, four years after the composition of the aforementioned text, the same scribe wrote a promissory note for a certain Bana-Yāma (written ᵐ*ba-na-a-ma*), son of Nubāya, stipulating the repayment an amount of dates in Āl-Yāhūdu

64 CUSAS 28 27: 17, CUSAS 28 29: 19, CUSAS 28 30: 5, 8, 10, CUSAS 28 39: 4, CUSAS 28 45: 3, 8 || HBM 8: 3, 8 (written in Babylon); BaAr 6 10: 5, 8, 12, BaAr 6 13: 11.

65 All of these are attested together in CUSAS 28 45 || HBM 8. The duplicate to CUSAS 28 45 is published in Kathleen Abraham, 'An Inheritance Division among Judeans in Babylonia from the Early Persian Period', in *New Seals and Inscriptions, Hebrew, Idumean, and Cuneiform* (HBM 8; ed. M. Lubetski; Sheffield: Sheffield Phoenix Press, 2007), 206–207.

66 Joannès and Lemaire, 'Trois tablettes cunéiformes', 27–28.

67 Knut L. Tallqvist. *Neubabylonisches Namenbuch zu den Geschäftsurkunden aus der Zeit des Šamaššumukîn bis Xerxes* (Acta Societatis Scientiarum Fennicae 32/2; Leipzig: E. Pfeiffer, 1906), 21.

to Bēl-uṣuršu, son of Nūr-Šamaš.[68] These references to Bania/Nubāya and Bana-Yāma/Nubāya undoubtedly refer to the same individual. Alternation between the use of an explicit orthography of the Yahwistic element and the seemingly Babylonian hypocoristicon points to one of the difficulties attendant to perceptions of Judean identity, both by Babylonians and by Judeans. At this point, the limited corpus of evidence may serve to initiate the discussion and help to define its course. The contexts in which the variant orthographies of Bana-Yāma's name appear suggest that it may be productive to investigate agency on the part of the individuals in determining the contexts in which variant forms of their names are used.

As mentioned, the Moussaieff collection text records ᶠBunanītu's payment of her governor-husband's *ilku* obligation to the Judean *dēkû*, Abdâ-Yāhu, son of Barak-Yāma. Individual witnesses often had some connection to the principals of transactions to which they attest.[69] As the witnesses in this text would affirm ᶠBunanītu's fulfillment of her duty on behalf of her husband, the governor, it is understandable that they would be selected from her social milieu, which undoubtedly was populated by Babylonians or West Semites. On the other hand, CUSAS 28 84 records an indebtedness of the Judean, Bana-Yāma/Nubāya, to the Babylonian, Bēl-uṣuršu. Although the text was written in Našar, the delivery is to take place in Āl-Yāhūdu. The proximity of Našar and Āl-Yāhūdu facilitate Bania a.k.a. Bana-Yāma's presence at activities in both settlements. But it is in the context of the demographics of the population involved in each transaction that he may choose the form of his name by which he will be known. Thus, in Našar, where he serves the Babylonian administration, he uses a form of his name that could appear to be Babylonian; in Judahtown, he opts for the Judean name Bana-Yāma.

This new evidence expands the corpus of orthographies which betray deliberate attempts at ambiguity.[70] In the Murašû corpus, ambiguity appears not only

---

68 CUSAS 28 84: 2.

69 Eva von Dassow, 'Introducing the Witnesses in Neo-Babylonian Documents', in *Ki Baruch Hu: Ancient Near Eastern, Biblical, and Judaic Studies in Honor of Baruch A. Levine*. (ed. Robert Chazan, William W. Hallo and Lawrence Schiffman; Winona Lake: Eisenbrauns, 1999), 6–7. Simonetta Ponchia provides an overview of the social contexts in which witnessing occurs (in Nicoletta Bellotto and Simonetta Ponchia, eds. *Witnessing in the Ancient Near East: i testimoni nella documentazione del Vicino Oriente antico: Proceedings of the Round Table Held at the University of Verona, February 15, 2008*. [Acta Sileni 2; SARGON, 2009], 225–251). Regrettably, witnessing procedures in the Neo-Babylonian and Achaemenid periods are not specifically addressed in this volume.

70 Michael D. Coogan, 'Life in the Diaspora. Jews at Nippur in the Fifth Century B. C.', *BA* 37 (1974): 11.

in names which can be explained as scribal idiosyncrasies in rendering West Semitic names in cuneiform, but also in names that reflect intentional reshaping into forms with tenuous connection to the standard Babylonian onomasticon. For example, the individual named Mannu-danni-Yāma (written *man-nu-ta-ni-* and *man-nu-d/tan-nu/i-*) also bears the name Mattan-Yāma. The forms appear to have been considered interchangeable variants, with Mannu-danni-Yāma a reformulation of Mattan-Yāma into a quasi-Babylonian name form. Late Babylonian orthographic practices preclude etymologizing the element *mannu-* as an orthographic variant of *mattan*, and thus the initial element of the name must be the interrogative pronoun *mannu*, 'who', rather than West Semitic 'gift'. Stolper termed this 'simply another example of the widespread and venerable practice of reducing foreign names to a shape at least approaching local forms'.[71] In addition to these variants that reflect an individual scribe's perception of his identity or the contribution of the individual to the marking of his own identity in Babylonian contexts, there is another small group of orthographic changes that are particularly instructive with regard to the Babylonian perceptions of Judean identity.

6 Replacement Orthographies

The term 'replacement orthography' adopted here designates names in which the theophoric element (i.e. *not* its orthography) varies in different instances of a single individual's name. The distinctiveness and cultural specificity of some of the theophoric elements attested in replacement orthographies point to a degree of tolerance of or ambivalence toward the newcomers in the Babylonian cultural environment.

Three documents written at Āl-Yāhūdu reference a single individual whose name is remarkably written both as Bēl-šarra-uṣur and Yāhu-šarra-uṣur.[72] In each of the three texts in which he appears, he is the creditor for an amount of barley or barley and silver, owed to him by an individual named Ṣidqi-Yāma, son of Šillim(u). In the two earliest documents, he is referred to as Bēl-šarra-uṣur, in the third, Yāhu-šarra-uṣur. The name Bēl-šarra-uṣur, meaning 'Bēl, save the king!', is of course the Babylonian construction of the name rendered Belshazzar in the biblical book of Daniel.[73] The replacement of Bēl, whose name references

71 Matthew W. Stolper, 'A Note on Yahwistic Personal Names in the Murašû Texts', *BASOR* 222 (1976): 26–27.

72 ^{md}EN-LUGAL-URÙ, in CUSAS 28 2: 2, CUSAS 28 3: 2; ^{md}*ia-hu-ú*-LUGAL-URÙ in CUSAS 28 4: 2.

73 Dan 5:2.

Marduk, the head of the Babylonian pantheon, by the name of the Judean god Yāhu, is striking.

Coogan stated that '[t]he use of clearly Babylonian deities (such as Marduk or Ninurta) in a name is usually an indication of Babylonian origin, while the opposite holds true for West Semitic ('Attar, Yāhu, etc.).'[74] Against this assertion, the striking juxtaposition of these two names borne by a single individual – Bēl-šarra-uṣur/Yāhu-šarra-uṣur – can hardly be accidental. This replacement certainly underscores that the inclusion of the divine determinative in orthographies of Yahweh's name reflects the scribe's understanding not only of the theophoric nature of the element Yahweh (in multiple orthographies), but his primacy in Judean circles. Yet, why would such a shift appear in a single individual's name? If acculturation to Babylonian society were its intention, would the transformation not be expected to proceed from a Yahwistic name to a Babylonian name?[75] And would the original Yahwistic name not contain, at the very least, a West Semitic, if not Hebrew predicate?

When the two forms of this individual's name are considered in context, another solution appears plausible. CUSAS 28 2 records a debt of barley and silver owed to Bēl-šarra-uṣur by the Judean Ṣidqi-Yāma/Šillimu, whose bow-land serves as a pledge against the loan.[76] Apart from this relationship defined by Ṣidqi-Yāma's indebtedness to Bēl-/Yāhu-šarra-uṣur,[77] it is impossible to determine Bēl-/Yāhu-šarra-uṣur's professional status. Yet the meaning and form of the predicate of his

---

74 Coogan, *West Semitic Personal Names*, 4.

75 This question calls to mind the naming practice of the so-called 'double names', in which an individual bears two names, typically expressed in the formula PN *ša šumšu šanû* PN_2, 'PN, whose other name is PN_2'. The individuals who bear double names may be difficult to identify in contexts where only one of their equally valid names is recorded. The concentration of double names in the corpus of legal texts from Hellenistic Uruk is catalogued and discussed in Tom Boiy, 'Akkadian-Greek Double Names in Hellenistic Babylonia', in *Ethnicity in Ancient Mesopotamia: Papers Read at the 48th Rencontre Assyriologique Internationale Leiden, 1–4 July 2002* (PIHANS 102; ed. W. van Soldt, D. Kalvelagen and D. Katz; Leiden: Nederlands Instituut voor het Nabije Oosten, 2005), 47–60. The long-standing allegation that the Akkadian-Greek double names serve to identify individuals with Hellenizing tendencies is revisited in Stephanie Langin-Hooper and Laurie E. Pearce, 'Mammonymy, Maternal-Line Names and Cultural Identification: Clues from the Onomasticon of Hellenistic Uruk', *JAOS* 134 (2014), 185–202.

76 Although the year number in CUSAS 28 2 was omitted by the scribe, it likely dates to 42 Nbk (563 B.C.E.; see Pearce and Wunsch, *Documents of Judean Exiles*). In the Murašû texts, ten of the 250 known bow-fiefs were in Judean hands (Zadok, *Jews in Babylonia*, 88).

77 Further documented in CUSAS 28 3 and 4, the latter dating to 5 Nbn (551 B.C.E.). In addition to these three promissory notes, Ṣidqi-Yāma appears as a slave-owner (CUSAS 28 5), a witness (CUSAS 28 6), and as a guarantor for the repayment of a quantity of silver (CUSAS 28 9), but Bēl-/Yāhu-šarra-uṣur is not mentioned in any of those texts.

name, *-šarra-uṣur*, is striking for an individual who, on the basis of the Yahwistic element in one of his name instances, should be securely identified as Judean. It is improbable that Judean parents would bestow on their offspring a name that invokes Yahweh's protection of the king reigning over the Judean exiles. Another motivation for this curious onomastic construction should be considered.

In the three texts, Bēl-šarra-uṣur/Nubāya is the creditor to Ṣidqi-Yāma, holder of bow-land that he pledged as security for the debt. It is not difficult to imagine that Bēl-šarra-uṣur may have occupied an administrative position that involved his collecting payments of silver and grain from Ṣidqi-Yāma. On the basis of analogy to the onomasticon at Neo-Babylonian Sippar, the composition of Bēl-šarra-uṣur's name may support this interpretation of his status. There, names including the element *šarru*, 'king', are well-attested in the roster of *ša rēši* officials.[78] There is no reason to assign Bēl-šarra-uṣur to such a lofty position, but in Judahtown, he may well have served in a low-level administrative capacity. From the Murašû documentation, it is apparent that administrative units were frequently led by individuals from the unit's constituency.[79] Might such a practice not be in place in towns populated by deportees? If so, then the appearance of Bēl-šarra-uṣur in the transformed name Yāhu-šarra-uṣur is hardly surprising. This onomastic transformation is contemporaneous with and parallels that of another important change in Babylonian naming practices.

By late summer or early fall of his fourth year, Nabonidus had established the double kingship and Belshazzar was serving as regent, a position he held until the beginning of the thirteenth year, when Nabonidus resumed his rule.[80] Just as the use of the name Nabû-na'id drops from the list of acceptable names for non-royals once Nabonidus assumed the throne, so too, the use of the programmatic name Bēl-šarra-uṣur ended with the crown prince's regency.[81] This shift appears to have been implemented even in the onomasticon of the small

---

78 A. C. V. M. Bongenaar, *The Neo-Babylonian Ebabbar Temple at Sippar: Its Administration and Its Prosopography* (PIHANS 80; Istanbul: Nederlands Historisch-Archeologisch Instituut te Istanbul, 1997), 100, 108–112. See also Baker, 'Approaches to Akkadian Name-Giving', 4–5 for a reassessment of the interpretation of Neo-Assyrian names containing the word *šarru* as markers of an individual's status as a eunuch; Michael Jursa addresses the linguistic and ethnic diversity of the royal establishment and the difficulty of identifying members of the administrative hierarchy on the basis of onomastic practices ('Families, Officialdom and Families of Royal Officials in Chaldean and Achaemenid Babylonia. Version 01.' (IOWP July 2012. http://iowp.univie.ac.at/?q=node/254, accessed 10/19/2012, see esp. p. 3); Streck, 'Das Onomastikon der Beamten'.

79 Stolper, *Entrepreneurs and Empire*, 79.

80 Paul-Alain Beaulieu, *The Reign of Nabonidus King of Babylon 556–539 B. C.* (New Haven: Yale University Press, 1989), 159–160.

81 Baker, 'Approaches to Akkadian Name-Giving', 7.

settlement Āl-Yāhūdu, where the latest attestation of the name Bēl-šarra-uṣur appears in CUSAS 28 3, dated to 9.ix.4 Nabonidus (6 January 552 B.C.E.). This delay of several months in abandoning the use of the royal name for non-royals is easily tolerated, as changes in naming practices in the wake of the crown prince's elevation to coregent may not have immediately been implemented in small rural settlements. The use of the Yahwistic iteration of the name appears in 6 Nbn (550 B.C.E.), well within the time-frame of Belshazzar's coregency. Additional evidence that changes in Babylonian naming protocols were implemented in the countryside comes from the name of the scribe of several early Āl-Yāhūdu texts. Nabû-na'id/Nabû-zēra-iqīša wrote CUSAS 28 1 (33 Nbk), while Nabû-nāṣir/Nabû-zēra-iqīša wrote CUSAS 28 3, 4, and 10 (in 4, 6, and 6 Nbn, respectively); this is likely to be the same individual scribe, known by two personal names. The parallel transformations of two names that circulated in the royal onomasticon can hardly be coincidental. In view of these changes and the contexts in which the names appear, it is reasonable to suggest that a Judean adopted the Babylonian name Bēl-šarra-uṣur upon assuming administrative duties and changed it (or the Babylonian scribe did it for him) to Yāhu-šarra-uṣur in conformity with local tradition.

Additional instances of names containing the predicate *-šarra-uṣur* confirm that: (1) there were a number of Judeans who adopted Babylonian names and whose Judean identity would remain undetected were it not for collateral evidence, and (2) *-šarra-uṣur* had currency among individuals with administrative or social connections. A case in point is the prosopographical evidence preserved on the seal of Yehoyišmaʿ, daughter of Šawaš-šarra-uṣur.[82] Avigad suggests that

82 The seal impression is discussed, inter alia, in: Nahman Avigad, 'Seals of Exiles', *IEJ* 15 (1965): 228–230; Michael Heltzer, 'Again on Seals of Exiles (from Israel to Judah and Mesopotamia)', in *Ethnicity in Ancient Mesopotamia: Papers Read at the 48th Rencontre Assyriologique Internationale Leiden, 1–4 July 2002* (PIHANS 102; ed. Wilfred van Soldt, R. Kalvelagen, and Dina Katz; Leiden: NINO, 2005), 176; Nahman Avigad and Benjamin Sass, *Corpus of West Semitic Stamp Seals* (Jerusalem: Israel Academy of Sciences and Humanities, 1997), 403. I am unaware of any discussion that disputes the authenticity of this seal, but it should be noted that the seal is unprovenanced and belongs to the Collection de Clercq (see Avigad, 'Seals of Exiles', note 20 for its initial publication information). All assessments of the dating of the seal thus depend exclusively on epigraphic evidence. For the problems associated with reliance on such criteria see André Lemaire, 'Les critères non-iconographiques de la classification des sceaux nord-ouest sémitiques inscrits,' in *Studies in the Iconography of Northwest Semitic Inscribed Seals* (OBO 125; ed. Benjamin Sass and Christoph Uehlinger; Göttingen: Vandenhoeck und Ruprecht; Fribourg: Academic Press Fribourg, 1993), 1–26. These matters notwithstanding, it is certain that the epigraphy and the linguistic background of the names preserved on this seal bear on the present discussion in additional ways. Among the features of note is the fact that Hebrew script was utilized

the father received his Babylonian name in exile and bestowed a Yahwistic name on his daughter in 'a revival of religious and national feelings among the Jews in Babylonia ...' and that Yehoyišmaʿ subsequently achieved some prominence and acquired a seal in connection with her engagement in business activities.[83] In view of the fact that a woman would transcend her native social class in only the most exceptional of circumstances, her presumed social standing reflects that of her father as well. Thus, while Šawaš-šar-uṣur's parents may have bestowed a Babylonian name on their child, it is equally plausible that he originally bore a West Semitic (Hebrew, Aramaic, or even Yahwistic) name and adopted the Babylonian one as he achieved standing among the ranks of businessmen or administrators. Regardless of which scenario better accounts for the origin of his name, the fact that the names appear on a seal suggests a family of relatively high social position. The formation of the patronym suggests Šawaš-šar-uṣur was an individual who interacted at some level with the administrative apparatus of the empire.

7 Self-Identification in Genealogical Evidence

This investigation has, to this point, focused on naming practices that distinguish Judean names from those of members of other population groups and thereby facilitate their recognition in Babylonian texts. This final area of investigation considers evidence that suggests that some Judeans consciously employed means to self-identify as Judeans, a conclusion that can be drawn from the names adopted over the course of several generations of a single family. Nearly every name instance in administrative and legal texts of the period is formulated as a filiation statement, in the form 'PN, son of FN'.[84] Even the limited prosopographical data in two-tier filiations contribute to the reconstruction of multiple generations of a single family which, in turn, may uncover a tendency of a family to self-identify with a particular cultural community. One of the texts in the new corpus, an inheritance division, fills in some of the lacunae in the previously published

to write the first line and Aramaic for the second (Lemaire, 'Les critères non-iconographiques', 20). It is of interest that Yehoyišmaʿ and Yehošamaʿ were popular names among the women at Elephantine in the fifth century (Avigad, 'Seals of Exiles', 228). Too few women's names appear in the cuneiform evidence to determine the popularity of this name among the Judean women exiles in Mesopotamia.

83 Avigad, 'Seals of Exiles', 229–230.

84 Nielsen, *Sons and Descendants*, 2.

duplicate.[85] Combining this with evidence from a number of other new documents, the focus can turn to the family genealogy and its nearly uninterrupted line of Judean names (see Figure 1: The Ahīqam Family Tree).

The duplicate texts were written in 16 Dar (507 B.C.E.), just over eighty years after the destruction of Jerusalem. At an average of twenty to twenty-five years per generation, the family history can be reconstructed back to pre-exilic days. Some of the family members whose names are documented in patronyms may well have themselves been deportees. The transmission of Judean names across multiple generations suggests an established mechanism for preserving a strong Judean identification within this family. Unfortunately, at this time, no other five-generation genealogy can be reconstructed for Judeans in Babylonian texts.[86]

Even in the absence of multi-generation family trees, it is clear that there was a tendency for individuals across generations of a Judean family to bear Yahwistic names. Of the 140 individuals with Yahwistic names documented in the Āl-Yāhūdu texts, seventy-six have either a father or son who also bears a Yahwistic name. Some forty individuals who bear Yahwistic names have fathers or sons who are not so named. The naming patterns in the family relationships of twenty-four individuals can not be determined: some filiation statements are irreparably damaged; some have relatives who bear West Semitic names or the names Haggai or Šabbatāya, and one or two bear titles (such as *dēkû*), which replace the filiation statement, in accordance with Babylonian naming practice. Taken together, the appearance of multiple generations of individuals bearing Yahwistic names and the high percentage of families at Āl-Yāhūdu that perpetuate the use of Yahwistic names across generations point to a pattern of Judean self-identification. Surely, if this were not a goal, fewer Judean names would have been recovered within the contemporaneous West Semitic and Babylonian onomastica.

8 Conclusion

The biblical narrative is undoubtedly responsible for the prominence of Judah and the Judeans in the historical memory of the lands which Nebuchadnezzar II destroyed and peoples he deported; the native record makes no such assertions. The ease with which many Judeans may be recognized in the native Babylonian

---

85 Abraham, 'An Inheritance Division', 206–221; the duplicate is published as CUSAS 28 45.

86 Coogan ('Life in the Diaspora', 8) reconstructed three generations of the Ṭob-ya family.

cuneiform documentation invites investigation of their social standing and associated questions of identity marking and perception. While the sources ranging from the books of Kings and Jeremiah, the Murašû texts and the Babylonian ration lists touch on different aspects of the exile and return, they leave many questions open for investigation. New evidence, texts from the town of Āl-Yāhūdu, corroborates much of the picture of Judean status presented in the Murašû texts and contributes new historical, onomastic, and social-economic information to the study of Judeans and Judean identity in the Babylonian exile.

Research in the early 20th century established that Yahwistic names are diagnostic, but not exclusive markers of Judean identity. Singly or in combination, orthographic, linguistic, and social factors leave many Judeans unidentified in the documentation, hidden by a veil of onomastic camouflage. The onomasticon preserved in the Āl-Yāhūdu texts expands the repertoire of Yahwistic names and provides additional evidence for the way the writing of Akkadian cuneiform may conceal Judean names. Some of these instances raise questions of Judean self-identification or acculturation. Prosopographical evidence is crucial if the Babylonian guise of a name such as Bania can be proven to represent a clearly Yahwistic name such as Bana-Yāma. Such secure identifications support the identification of additional orthographic variants for the Yahwistic element.

A more sophisticated level of onomastic confusion appears in names termed intentionally ambiguous: names that resemble known monikers but which, in reshaping through linguistic and orthographic manipulation, evolve into unique forms that enable their bearers to identify with multiple social environments. Names that would appear to be, but need not have been Judean complicate the disentangling of things that are not always as they seem: although most instances of the names Haggai and Šabbatāya demonstrably label Judeans, not all can be confirmed. The presumption that the adoption of personal names that reflect cultural practices assumed to belong exclusively to a particular community may lead to errors in discovering identity.

Although linguistically ambiguous names are readily identified in the documentation, and the reason for their creation may be assumed to have been for the (broadly stated) purposes of 'acculturation', it is possible only to guess at the point of motivation and process through which the name came to exist. Did parents bestow ambiguous names on their children with the expectation that they would facilitate integration into a host society? Did individuals change their names in the hopes of the same? In their interaction with Judeans at various administrative levels, did Babylonian scribes intentionally or unintentionally transform names into ones resembling the native onomasticon? At the heart of these speculative questions, lies the fundamental activity of self- and external identity marking, which, in turn, impinges on understanding the social, cultural,

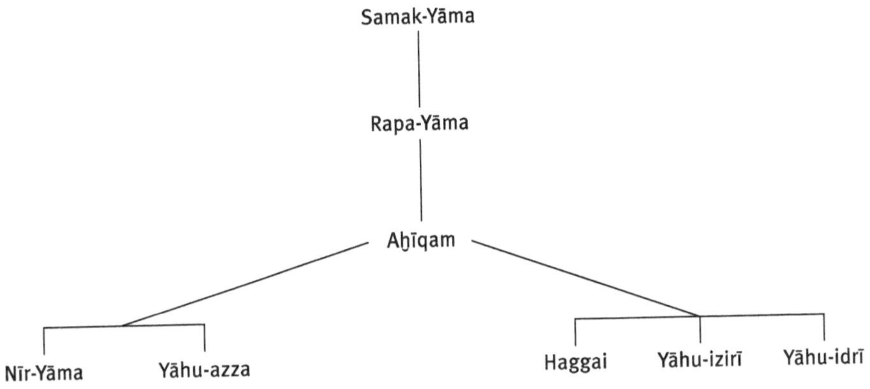

Figure 1: The Ahīqam Family Tree

and economic integration of the Judean deportees and their descendants into Babylonian society.

The interchange of Babylonian and Yahwistic theophoric elements in the otherwise Babylonian names of individuals whose filiation securely establishes their Judean background may offer some secure ground on which to explore such questions. The exchange between the elements Bēl- and Yāhu- in the name Bēl-/Yāhu-šarra-uṣur may well have evolved from an attempt to conceal or reveal Judean identity or stem from a Babylonian scribe's recognition of the primacy of Yahweh in Judean belief. This interchange can hardly have been unintentional and provokes consideration of the agency that resulted in its implementation. While exceptional in its instance, Yāhu-šarra-uṣur belongs to a well-known type in the Neo- and Late-Babylonian onomasticon, the so-called 'Beamtennamen', or professional designations, which include the element *šarru*, 'king', to indicate the bearer's membership in the Babylonian administrative hierarchy. Appearing in a context with such secure grounding in known social practice, this new evidence will undoubtedly contribute to a greater understanding of the mechanics and processes of identification of deportee or alien populations in Babylonian society.

The value in recovering Judean names and creating a comprehensive roster of Judeans lies not in a 'more is better' approach to data, but rather in the potential of such data to contribute to a more nuanced and more in-depth exploration of matters of identity marking. Such foundational research may then serve as the basis for the study of networks of interactions, among Judeans, and between Judeans and Babylonians. Recovering the repertoire of identity markers, both those utilized by self and those imposed by social practice, should provide further means with which to reconstruct the nexus between Babylonians and Judeans and to more fully understand Judean participation in the social and economic life of the region, and recognize developments that contributed to the transformation, over time, of the exilic Judeans into the enduring Jewish community of Babylonia.

Acknowledgment

This study had its first reception in the workshop 'Exile and Return: the Babylonian Context' at University College London, 10–12 November 2011. Presenting preliminary observations on matters of Judean identity and identification in the collegial environment of archaeologists, Assyriologists, and biblical scholars resulted in feedback and encouragement necessary to bring the work to this stage of its development; I thank all the participants for their contributions and assure them that any weaknesses are my responsibility alone. It is a special pleasure to thank Caroline Waerzeggers and Jonathan Stökl for their invitation to participate in the community of scholarship and friendship they created and nurtured during this workshop.

Kathleen Abraham

Negotiating Marriage in Multicultural Babylonia: An Example from the Judean Community in Āl-Yāhūdu

1 Introduction

Clay tablets written in Akkadian in cuneiform script are a major source of information concerning Judaism in the exilic and post-exilic periods. They allow us to get some idea of what happened to the Judean exiles and their descendants upon their arrival in Babylon, during the 70 years of their captivity in Babylonia, and after Cyrus the Great granted them permission to return to Jerusalem and rebuild their temple.

The latest addition to the documentary evidence on this crucial period in Jewish history is a cache of around 200 tablets that were found in modern-day Iraq but are currently in privately owned collections.[1] They are better known as the Āl-Yāhūdu tablets because of one of the places mentioned in them, namely Ālu-ša-Yahudāya 'Town of the Judeans', also known as Āl-Yāhūdu, which is best translated in English as The city of Judah or Jerusalem.[2] It seems to have been located in the Nippur-Keš-Karkara triangle.[3]

The Āl-Yāhūdu tablets depict the daily life of a rural community of Judean exiles and their descendants in ancient Babylonia beginning soon after their captivity (Nbk 33 = 572 B.C.E.). They lived away from the great cultural centra of Babylonia, often in places that had previously not been inhabited. Occasionally they travelled to the capital for their businesses. Otherwise they stayed in the

1 The David Sofer Collection (London-Jerusalem), the Schøyen Collection (Oslo), and the Shlomo and Aliza Moussaieff Collection (London-Herzeliya).
2 Francis Joannès and André Lemaire, 'Trois tablettes cunéiformes à onomastique ouest-sémitique', *Transeuphratène* 17 (1999), 17–27 (26); Laurie Pearce, 'New Evidence for Judeans in Babylonia', in *Judah and Judeans in the Persian Period* (ed. M. Oeming and O. Lipschits; Winona Lake: Eisenbrauns, 2006), 399–411 (401–402).
3 F. Rachel Magdalene and Cornelia Wunsch, 'Slavery Between Judah and Babylon: The Exilic Experience', in *Slaves and Households in the Near East* (ed. L. Culbertson; OIS 7; Chicago: The Oriental Institute of the University of Chicago, 2011), 113–34 (116).

Kathleen Abraham: KU Leuven

countryside, in and around Āl-Yāhūdu where they lived from the land that the King had given to them in return for service in the army and corvée work. Some of the Judeans held low-level administrative functions, such as *dēkû* or 'summoner (for taxes and corvée)'.[4]

The community of Judeans in rural Āl-Yāhūdu maintained some degree of social cohesion and adherence to tradition. The full extent of these phenomena cannot be assessed as long as most of the textual material from Āl-Yāhūdu remains unpublished. From what we know so far, it is clear that the Judeans in Āl-Yāhūdu were perceived by the Babylonians as an identifiable group of people, namely 'the people from Judah' ([lú]*ia-a-ḫu-du-a-a*).[5] The town in which a large concentration of them lived was officially named after them or after the major city in the geographical area from where they 'originated'. Part of the land that they worked was categorized as '*šušānu*-fields of the Judeans' by the local Babylonian administration which collected rent from it.[6] It is not unlikely that there also existed a '*ḫaṭru* (administrative unit) of the Judeans'. Yahwistic, Hebrew and Aramaic names persisted among them even after decades of exile. This adherence to names from the homeland should most likely be interpreted as a sign of attachment to tradition.[7] The fact that they were settled as a collective on crown land in Āl-Yāhūdu may have made it easier for them than for their colleagues who lived in an urban context to maintain their identity.

The community of Judeans in rural Āl-Yāhūdu gradually integrated into Babylonian society. A decade or two after their arrival they record their economic, administrative and some of their private legal activities on clay tablets in Akkadian conform to the well-attested cuneiform text types. They did not use Aramaic for these purposes although some of them knew how to write it,[8] and for most of

4 For details, see Pearce, 'New Evidence,' 403, 405–407; cf. Paul-Alain Beaulieu, 'Yahwistic Names in the Light of Late Babylonian Onomastics', in *The Judeans in the Achaemenid Age: Negotiating Identity in an International Context* (ed. M. Oeming and O. Lipschits; Winona Lake: Eisenbrauns, 2010), 245–66 (249).

5 Cf. Laurie Pearce, '"Judean"': A Special Status in Neo-Babylonian and Achemenid Babylonia?', in *The Judeans in the Achaemenid Age: Negotiating Identity in an International Context* (ed. M. Oeming and O. Lipschits; Winona Lake: Eisenbrauns, 2010), 267–77 (275): 'Judean ... was a presence but not a special status in Neo-Babylonian and Achaemenid Babylonia'.

6 Pearce, 'New Evidence', 405–406 and '"Judean"', 272.

7 Beaulieu, 'Yahwistic Names', 253: 'Judah was the main referent of their identity (not Jahweh) and one could express that identity with a Yahwistic or Hebrew name.'

8 The existence of Aramaic epigraphs in alphabetic script on some of the Āl-Yāhūdu tablets proves that at least some of the Judeans in Āl-Yāhūdu knew how to write and read Aramaic (or Hebrew), see Pearce, 'New Evidence'. In fact, it is not excluded that the community also pro-

them it must have been their mother tongue[9] or at least the language they spoke in Babylonia[10] in their daily contacts with the native population, the royal administration and other foreigners who lived in their vicinity. Moreover, we know that Aramaic was used for various purposes in Babylonia and that it owned a well-developed legal vocabulary and formulary in the Achaemenid period.[11] There was, no doubt, a pragmatic reason for the choice of Akkadian by the Judeans in Āl-Yāhūdu. It may be that scribes who sufficiently mastered the Aramaic legal language were not ready available in Āl-Yāhūdu. More importantly, the use of Akkadian facilitated recourse to Babylonian jurisdiction in the future,[12] and was the only option open in those cases in which local Akkadian speaking Babylonians entered into a legal transaction with a member of Āl-Yāhūdu's Judean community or acted as witness on their behalf.

---

duced legal documents in Aramaic written on parchment or leather but these have not survived in the Mesopotamian climate.

9 It is not excluded that Hebrew rather than Aramaic was their mother tongue, see Angel Sáenz-Badillos, 'Hebrew as the Language of Judaism', in *The Semitic Languages: An International Handbook* (ed. S. Weninger; Berlin: de Gruyter Mouton, 2011), 537–45 (538–39; on the use of Hebrew by Judeans and Israelites in their homeland before and after the exile).

10 On Aramaic as the vernacular language in Babylonia from the second half of the first millennium B.C.E. onwards, see Paul-Alain Beaulieu, 'Official and Vernacular Languages: The Shifting Sands of Imperial and Cultural Identities in First-Millenium B. C. Mesopotamia', in *Margins of Writing, Origins of Cultures* (ed. Seth L. Sanders; OIS 2; Chicago: The Oriental Institute of the University of Chicago, 2006), 187–216; Michael P. Streck, 'Akkadian and Aramaic Language Contact', in *The Semitic Languages: An International Handbook* (ed. S. Weninger; Berlin: de Gruyter Mouton, 2011), 416–24.

11 On the usage of Aramaic in legal contexts in Babylonia, see for instance the legal document that was written in 571/570 B.C.E. (Jean Starcky, 'Une tablette araméenne de l'an 34 de Nabuchodonosor (A) 21.063', *Syria* 37 [1960], 99–115 = André Lemaire, *Nouvelles tablettes araméennes* [Geneva: Droz, 2001], 64–68), the Aramaic epigraphs on Babylonian legal and administrative tablets (Joachim Oelsner, 'Aramäische Beischriften auf neu- und spätbabylonischen Tontafeln', *WO* 36 [2006], 27–71), and the Aramaic legal terms that infiltrated the Babylonian language in the late period (Kathleen Abraham and Michael Sokoloff, 'Aramaic Loanwords in Akkadian – A Reassessment of the Proposals', *AfO* 52 [2011], 1–92, s.v. *ḫarara* 'objection', *te'īqtu* 'injury', *qubbulu* 'received'); see also Streck, 'Akkadian and Aramaic', 420. In general, Aramaic legal formularies were well developed by the Achaemenid period, as is clear from the documents that were found in Egypt (esp. Elephantine, *TAD* B).

12 Cf. Francis Joannès, 'Diversité ethnique et culturelle en Babylonie récente', in *Organisation des pouvoirs et contacts culturels dans les pays de l'empire achéménide* (ed. P. Briant and M. Chauveau; Persika 14; Paris: de Boccard, 2009), 217–36 (228): 'On trouve des exemples où pour des procès on a fait appel à des experts lisant l'araméen ou l'égyptien (…), à l'intention d'akkadophones, mais le cas inverse a dû aussi se produire avec des traducteurs officiels mettant le contenu des tablettes à disposition d'administrateurs non-akkadophones.'

Even if we take the view that the Judean exiles and their descendants had largely assimilated to the local Babylonian environment as is often done, that does not entail the conclusion that they should not adhere to certain non-Babylonian customs, for instance in the area of family law. In fact, family values are often considered as at the very core of a community's cultural identity and accordingly particularly resistant to change. Their preservation and enforcement are envisaged by a set of laws that are transmitted from generation to generation. Thus, it is not excluded that specifically Judean customs are reflected in the Judean community's legal documents, in particular those pertaining to family law, even if the latter were formulated in Akkadian and cast in standard Babylonian formats.

It is the aim of this study to investigate the level of acculturation of Āl-Yāhūdu's Judean community from the vantage point of the legal documents that have come to us from this community. Unfortunately, most of this evidence remains unpublished and unaccessible. The few tablets from Āl-Yāhūdu that are in the Shlomo and Aliza Moussaieff private collection are the exception to that rule. Most of them are in a deplorable state of preservation and hardly legible, except for five documents, among them one recording the division of an inheritance, the other a marriage agreement.[13] The latter two provide the kind of evidence that could be used to conduct the study that I proposed above, namely an investigation into the Judean character of the Āl-Yāhūdu community, because they specifically pertain to family law, which is, as explained, the area of law that tends to preserve a group's cultural identity more than for instance business or property law. In the present study I will focus on the marriage contract from Āl-Yāhūdu with its Judean bride and Judean witnesses (henceforth abbreviated AYMC), and ask 'how Judean is the Judean marriage contract from Āl-Yāhūdu'?

---

13 Kathleen Abraham, 'West Semitic and Judean Brides in Cuneiform Sources from the Sixth Century B.C.E. New Evidence from a Marriage Contract from Āl-Yahudu', *AfO* 51 (2005–2006), 198–219; Kathleen Abraham, 'An Inheritance Division Among Judeans in Babylonia from the Early Persian Period', in *New Seals and Inscriptions: Hebrew, Idumean and Cuneiform* (ed. M. Lubetski; Hebrew Bible Monographs 8; Sheffield: Phoenix Press, 2007), 206–11.

2 The Neo-Babylonian[14] Marriage Contract with Judean Parties[15] from Āl-Yāhūdu: Standard Babylonian Practice?

In an earlier article I discussed in detail the ways in which the Neo-Babylonian marriage contract from Āl-Yāhūdu is similar to and differs from other marriage contracts from Babylonia that are dated to around the same period.[16] The problem with which I was confronted at the time and which arose again during the workshop in London (November 2011) is how to relate to the apparent combination of standard[17] and non-standard Neo-Babylonian features in one and the same document. Should we focus on the standard ones, deconstruct the so-called 'dissimilarities', disregard the Aramaic parallels as insignificant, and declare the document genuine Babylonian? Or should we focus on the non-standard features, stress the similarities with documents from outside Babylonia (such as the Aramaic material from Achaemenid Elephantine) and declare the document basically non-Babylonian in an Akkadian garb?

---

14 The AYMC is dated in Cyrus' 5th year which places it, in political-historical terms in the Persian rather than the Neo-Babylonian period. The term 'Neo-Babylonian' is used here in a broad sense, the way it is often done by legal historians, and includes documents that are dated in the Persian period because there are no significant differences between both periods from the point of view of legal history.

15 The AYMC is a document in which the bride, her brother and probably also her mother have Aramaic names, and several of the witnesses and/or their fathers bear Yahwistic or Aramaic names. On identifying Judeans in cuneiform tablets on the basis of onomastic data, and the problems it raises, see Beaulieu, 'Yahwistic Names' and Pearce in the present volume.

16 For details, see Abraham, 'West Semitic and Judean Brides', 202–206.

17 I consider a Neo-Babylonian marriage contract 'standard' if it follows the general outline, formularies and legal practice that is commonly found in Neo-Babylonian marriage contracts. See Martha T. Roth, *Babylonian Marriage Agreements 7th – 3rd Centuries B. C.* (AOAT 222; Neukirchen-Vluyn: Neukirchener Verlag, 1989), Introduction. This includes clauses about the formation (*binâmma, šemû, ana aššūti nadānu*) and dissolution of the marriage through divorce by the husband (*muššuru*) or remarriage (*aššata šanīta aḫāzu/rašû*), the giving of direct dowry (*nudunnû*), sanctions against the adulterous wife (Martha T. Roth, '"She Will Die by the Iron Dagger": Adultery and Marriage in the Neo-Babylonian Period', *JESHO* 31 [1988], 186–206), and stipulations regarding the paternal inheritance rights of offspring and the status of children born prior to the marriage. These standard elements are found in marriage contracts that belong to families from different social backgrounds. Thus they occur in the marriage contracts of oblates (e.g. BaAr 2 no. 3), manumitted slaves (e.g. BMA nos. 4, 5 and 14), priests (e.g. BMA nos. 21–22) and princesses (BMA no. 7). Anything that significantly deviates from these features in either form or content, could be categorized as non-standard, non-normative or special.

Let us first reiterate the features that I consider as 'special' in my previous study and which will dominate the discussion below. The AYMC stands out within the Neo-Babylonian corpus of more than fifty marriage contracts[18] because it (1) (a) refers to a gift from the groom to the bride's agent, (b) with which the former covers (*katāmu*) the latter, and (c) which is apparently labeled 'a provision? for the bride' (*z/ṣindu ša* ᶠPN).[19] Hence this gift functioned as an endowment upon the bride (i.e. an indirect dowry) rather than as a price paid for her (i.e. a bride price).[20] The AYMC also (2) (a) disconnects the case of divorce by the husband from that of his desire to take another wife in marriage (the latter option is left out of consideration all together), and instead speaks of divorce by the husband in terms of him 'releasing' (*muššuru*) the wife and (b) declaring 'She is not a wife'. Finally, it (3) stipulates that the husband is to tie the divorce settlement in his wife's hem (instead of simply giving it to her) when she leaves the house.

It may be argued that parallels for most of these features exist in Babylonian legal sources from the Neo-Babylonian period. A gift from the groom's side (1a) is attested in five, perhaps six other Neo-Babylonian marriage contracts,[21] although, it took different forms and its function significantly varies from one attestation to the other, as will be explained in more detail below. It was a widespread custom in Babylonia in earlier periods (*terḫatum*). The same is true for formulaic expressions such as 'to cover ⁽ᶠ⁾PN with a garment' (1b) which is attested in one other Neo-Babylonian marriage contract[22] and in several Neo-Babylonian

18 There are more than fifty published Neo-Babylonian marriage contracts: forty-five are edited in BMA, seven in BaAr 2 (nos. 1–7), and one in Francis Joannès, 'Textes babyloniens de Suse d'époque achéménide', in *Contribution à l'histoire de l'Iran: Mélanges offerts à Jean Perrot* (ed. F. Vallat; Paris: Éditions Recherche sur les Civilizations, 1990), 173–80 (no. 1).

19 The interpretation of the signs *z/ṣi-in-di* in line 21 remains enigmatic. A noun *zindu* is attested nowhere else in Akkadian. A noun *ṣindû* exists in Akkadian but means '(measure) of three seahs (capacity)' or 'bandage, arrangement' (from the verb *ṣamādu* 'to make ready, tie, harness', *CAD* Ṣ 196–97 and 200), which does not fit the current context. In my article 'West Semitic and Judean Brides' (p. 204–205) I offered possible Akkadian and Aramaic etymologies for the noun which all place it in the semantic field of 'provisions, support'. None of them are entirely convincing, but I still think that it is the most promising direction in which to look for a solution.

20 This point is picked up again and elaborated upon below (p. 50–52).

21 BMA no. 4, BMA nos. 34–35, BM 64195⁺ (Caroline Waerzeggers, 'A Note on the Marriage Gift *Biblu* in the Neo-Babylonian Period', *Akkadica* 122 [2001], 65–70), BaAr 2 no. 1, and perhaps BaAr 2 no. 5.

22 BaAr 2 no. 1 (left edge). The passage is fragmentary but seems to imply that the groom covered his mother-in-law with a garment.

house sales, adoptions and antichretic pledges,[23] and 'She is not a wife' (2b) which is attested twice more in the corpus of Neo-Babylonian marriage contracts[24] but belonged to the standard Babylonian divorce terminology in the Old-Babylonian period.[25] The legal idiom 'binding (silver) in the hem (of the beneficiary)' (3) is rarely used in the Neo-Babylonian period but was known in earlier periods (Old-Babylonian and Nuzi).[26] In other words, it seems that most characteristic features of the Āl-Yāhūdu marriage contract have sound Babylonian roots. They may not have been commonly practiced in Neo-Babylonian marriages, but still they were not foreign to Babylonian legal practice. Consequently, so it may be argued, there is no compelling reason to link them to the non-Babylonian origin of the bride (and perhaps also the groom) or their supposed deviant marriage and divorce customs.

One would agree with the above deconstruction of the so-called 'special' features of the Āl-Yāhūdu marriage contract or its 'deviations' from the normal Neo-Babylonian pattern were it not, first, that other ethnically marked Neo-Babylonian marriage contracts display similar features, and secondly, that for some of the more substantial features interesting parallels can be found in the Aramaic marriage contracts from 5th century B.C.E. Elephantine which are difficult to simply sweep under the carpet.

3 The Ethnically Marked Marriage Contracts within the Corpus of Neo-Babylonian Marriage Contracts

The existing corpus of fifty-three Neo-Babylonian marriage contracts includes eight ethnically marked contracts (the AYMC excluded). It concerns contracts in

23 See Abraham, 'West Semitic and Judean Brides', 203–204. In the house sales and adoption contracts it was a symbolic act that accompanied the transfer of property rights or rights over a person. It helped to compensate for the loss of the house or child. In antichretic pledges it fulfilled the obligation of providing the basic needs of a dependent person.

24 BMA no. 5 and BaAr 2 no. 3.

25 Ray Westbrook, *Old Babylonian Marriage Law* (AfOB 23; Horn: Ferdinand Berger & Söhne, 1988), 69 and 80.

26 Meir Malul, *Studies in Mesopotamian Legal Symbolism* (AOAT 221; Neukirchen-Vluyn: Neukirchener Verlag, 1986), 179–85. For the garment's hem in the late period, see CAD Q 84: *ardat lilî* incantations refer to the custom of binding silver in a garment's hem as part of marriage rites, and silver is placed in a garment's hem for safekeeping according to UET 4 130: 11.

which at least one of the parties to the marriage, usually the bride's one, and often also several of the witnesses, were of foreign descent, judging by their names and patronymics. Below follow the onomastic details for each of these contracts, and the ethno-linguistic affiliation that can be derived from them.[27]

BMA no. 11 (Neirab, 17/i/[...])

		Ethno-linguistic affiliation
Bride:	^{f}Bazīti	WS$^{?}$
Bride's family:	Nabû-ēṭir/Ea-zēra-iddina (Bro)	Bab.
Groom:	Bar-aḫḫaya	WS
Groom's family:	Kukizza (Fa)	Unkn.
Scribe:	Bēl$^{?}$-aḫa$^{?}$-iddina/Marduk-erība	Bab.
Witnesses:		Mixed Bab. – WS

BMA no. 17 (Ālu-ša-banê, 27/ix/14 Nbn)

		Ethno-linguistic affiliation
Bride:	^{f}Tallaya-Uruk	WS
Bride's family:	El-natan/Bara-el (Bro)	WS
	^{f}Bānītu (Mo)	Bab.
Groom:	Nabû-aḫa-uṣur	Bab.
Groom's family:	Ḫatāma (Fa)	WS
Scribe:	Šamaš-iddin/Nabû-aḫḫē-ēreš	Bab.[28]
Witnesses:		Mixed Bab. – WS

BMA no. 23 (Babylon, 2/v/11 Dar)

		Ethno-linguistic affiliation
Bride:	^{f}Taḫê-[...]	Eg.
Bride's family:	Samannapir/[...] (Fa)	Eg.
Groom:	Paṭmiustû	Eg.
Groom's family:	Pir (Fa)	Eg.
Scribe:	Marduk-iqīšanni/[...]	Bab.
Witnesses:		Pers., Edom, Eg., Bab.

27 Abbreviations used: Bab. = Babylonian, Bro = brother, Eg. = Egyptian, Fa = Father, Jud. = Judean, Mo = mother, Pers. = Persian, Si = sister , Unkn. = unknown, WS = West Semitic.
28 Note that his brother is among the witnesses and had a West Semitic name, Natan-El.

BMA no. 26 (Sippar, 11/ii/5 [Cyr])[29]

		Ethno-linguistic affiliation
Bride:	ᶠKaššāya	Bab.
Bride's family:	Bēl-uballiṭ/Hawše' (Bro)	Bab./Jud.
	ᶠGudadītu (Mo)	Unkn.
Groom:	Gūzānu	Bab.
Groom's family:	Kiribtu from Ararru family (Fa)	Bab. with family name
Scribe:	Nabû-mukīn-[...]/Bēl-iddina//[...]	Bab. with family name
Witnesses:		Mixed Bab. (a. o. with family names) – WS, Judean

BaAr 2 no. 5 (Ālu-ša-rab(-ša)-rēši, date broken)

		Ethno-linguistic affiliation
Bride:	ᶠNabê-ḫ̮innī	WS
Bride's family:	[PN]/Sîn-zēra-iddina (Bro)	Mixed Bab. – WS
	Aḫ̮-immê/Sîn-zēra-iddina (Bro)	
	ᶠMamītu/Sîn-zēra-iddina (Si)	
Groom:	Aqrāya	Bab.
Groom's family:	Arad-Eš(š)u(Fa)	Bab.
Scribe:	[...]/Šellibi//[...-B]ēl	Bab. with family name
Witnesses:		Mixed Bab. – WS[30]

Joannès, 'Textes babyloniens' no. 1 (Susa, [...] Art)

Ethno-linguistic affiliation

Bride:	ᶠŠammandu'	Pers.
Bride's "family":	Kīnunāya/Peṭi'u (Master)[31]	Eg. (or Bab./Eg.)
Groom:	Mannu-kī-Nanāya	Bab.
Groom's family:	Ḫ̮ūru	Eg.
Scribe:	Bēl-tattannu-uṣur/Bēlšunu	Bab.
Witnesses:		mainly Eg., Pers., Unkn.

29 For this document and BM 68921, which was written a month later and concerned the same marriage, see now Michael Jursa, 'Kollationen', *NABU* 2001/102. Yigal Bloch,'Judeans in Sippar and Susa during the First Century of the Babylonian Exile: Assimilation and Perseverance under Neo-Babylonian and Achaemenid Rule', *Journal of Ancient Near Eastern History* 1(2) (2014), 119–172
30 Attâ-panā/Dāgil?-el; [...]-el/[...]-eššu; [...]-idrī/[...]-ḫ̮u.
31 Servant of Šamu, see Michael Jursa, '"Höflinge" (*ša rēši*, *ša rēš šarri*, *uštarbaru*) in babylonischen Quellen des ersten Jahrtausends,' in *Ktesias' Welt / Ctesias' World* (ed. J. Wiesehöfer, R. Rollinger, and G. Lanfranchi; CleO 1; Wiesbaden: Harrassowitz, 2011), 159–73 (170).

BMA no. 34 ([Susa], date broken)

		Ethno-linguistic affiliation
Bride:	[...]-ṣunu	Eg.$^{?}$
Bride's family:	^{f}Ari-Esi (Mo); Ku'pi (Fa)	Eg.
Groom:	[broken]	
Groom's family:	^{f}Tadia (Mo)	Unkn.
Scribe:	[...]-šu-uṣur	Bab.$^{?}$
Witnesses:		Mixed Eg. – Bab.

BMA no. 35 ([Susa], date broken)

Ethno-linguistic affiliation

Bride:	^{f}Nahdi-Esu	Eg.
Bride's family:	Pisisamaska/[...] (Fa)	Eg.
Groom:	Harrimenna/[...]	Eg.
Groom's family:		
Scribe:	[broken]	
Witnesses:		Mixed Bab. – Eg.

The list above contains four marriage contracts from Egyptian communities that lived in the capitals Babylon and Susa, and four from communities of West Semitic origin that lived at Sippar or in the Babylonian countryside.

3.1 Neo-Babylonian Marriage Contracts with Egyptian Parties from Babylon and Susa

We know of four marriages between Egyptians recorded in Akkadian. Three originate from the Egyptian community in Susa,[32] one is from Babylon.[33] The parties involved and the men who witnessed the transaction often worked for the royal administration or were associated with the court in another way. The lists of witnesses had an outspoken international character containing men of Babylonian, Persian and Egyptian background, showing the high level of economic and cul-

32 On Egyptians at Susa (and other places in southwestern Iran) in the Achaemenid period, see Wouter F. M. Henkelman, *The Other Gods Who Are: Studies in Elamite-Iranian Acculturation Based on the Persepolis Fortification Texts* (Achaemenid History 14; Leiden: Nederlands Instituut voor het Nabije Oosten, 2008); Joannès, 'Contrats de mariage'; Joannès, 'Diversité ethnique'.
33 On Egyptians in Babylonia, see most recently Hackl and Jursa in the present volume.

tural exchange between the communities. The brides were married off with a dowry, except, so it seems, ᶠŠammandu' but she was a bondwoman.[34] The individuals we meet in the legal documents from Susa's Egyptian community[35] preserved their identity by keeping their Egyptian names and giving their children Egyptian names, and by marrying within their own community. Yet, when it came to writing down the agreements they reached at marriage concerning marital property, divorce and adultery, they turned to scribes with Babylonian names.[36] The marriage contracts which these scribes wrote on behalf of their Egyptian clients were definitively (Neo-)Babylonian in language, general outline and formulary. However, as far as their content is concerned, they significantly differ from their Babylonian contemporaries in matters regarding the dissolution of marriage and marriage gifts (whenever this information is preserved in the document). This is clear from BMA nos. 34 and 35.[37] BMA no. 34, for instance, considers the possibility that divorce be initiated by the wife (and not only by the husband), a condition unheard of in the Babylonian marriage contracts of the first millennium B.C.E.[38] It also includes a payment of indirect dowry by the groom (called *biblu*) in addition to a dowry by the bride's family, a custom that is found in BMA no. 35 as well, but only rarely practiced among the proprieted Babylonians in Neo-Bab-

34 The document that mentions her upcoming marriage (Joannès, 'Textes babyloniens', no. 1) is more concerned about arranging her transfer from Ecbatana to Susa (where the groom lived) and her master's relinquishment over her (and by implication also her future children) than with marital property, divorce or adultery. This is probably why these matters are not discussed in her marriage contract.

35 There are five such documents: a sale, an apprenticeship and the three marriages under consideration (Joannès, 'Textes babyloniens').

36 Why the Egyptians in Susa turned to these scribes and asked them to write in Akkadian whereas 'scribes of the Egyptians' were available in Susa (Henkelman, *Other Gods*, 341 + n. 800) remains to be seen. On the scribes who wrote in Akkadian on behalf of businessmen and refugees from Babylonia permanently living in Iran in the Achaemenid period or on an occasional visit, see Henkelman, *Other Gods*, 337–40. Further note that in the Elamite texts from the Persepolis Fortification Archive a 'Babylonian scribe' was one who wrote on leather in Aramaic (Henkelman, *Other Gods*, 93), and often had a Babylonian or West Semitic name (Henkelman, *Other Gods*, 149 and 340 + n. 798).

37 It cannot be proven for the other two Egyptian marriage contracts because of their fragmentary state of preservation: BMA no. 23 breaks off after the dowry clause and Joannès, 'Textes babyloniens', no. 1 is relatively well preserved but had other concerns than property or divorce (see n. 34 above).

38 See Roth, *Babylonian Marriage*, 14: 'No 34 is the only Neo-Babylonian marriage agreement – in fact, the only evidence from the Neo-Babylonian period – to consider the wife's right to divorce.'

ylonian or Persian times.[39] Therefore, it seems that the Egyptian parties to the recorded marriages had negotiated their own terms. The content of these terms, most scholars agree, does not reflect Babylonian custom, but derives from the parties' non-Babylonian background. Thus Joannès concluded his discussion of one of these marriage agreements (BMA no. 34) with the observation that 'le texte présente non seulement une onomastique particulière, mais aussi des dispositions juridiques spécifiques qui montrent que le droit utilisé ici n'est pas du pur droit babylonien: ...' (Joannès, 'Textes babyloniens', 227).[40]

3.2 Neo-Babylonian Marriages with West Semitic Parties from Sippar and Rural Babylonia

West Semitic communities in Babylonia[41] have left us four marriage contracts: BMA no. 26 from Sippar, which follows the known Neo-Babylonian practices in every respect, BMA no. 11 from Neirab, which breaks off after the marriage formation clauses so that not much can be learnt from it and is therefore further left out of consideration, and finally BaAr 2 no. 5 and BMA no. 17 from small villages in Babylonia. The latter two are at the center of the discussion below because they display interesting features that are reminiscent of the AYMC and therefore require further attention.

---

39 The only instance of the practice in a fully Babylonian milieu is found in the document published by Waerzeggers, 'Note on the Marriage Gift'.

40 Cf. Roth, *Babylonian Marriage*, 14: 'Given the foreign influences evident in this document, we must be cautious about extrapolating any general legal principles from this one document.' See also Francis Joannès' ('Contrats de mariage d'époque récente', *RA* 78 [1984], 71–81 [81]) conclusion that the Egyptian community at Susa followed 'un droit matrimonial coutumier qui lui est particulier.'

41 On people of West Semititic origin in Babylonia in first millennium B.C.E., see Ran Zadok, *On West Semites in Babylonia during the Chaldean and Achaemenian Periods: An Onomastic Study* (Jerusalem: Wanaarta, 1977); Ran Zadok, 'West Semitic Names in N/LB Unpublished Documents', *NABU* 1995/6; Ran Zadok, 'West Semitic Names in Neo-Assyrian Sources', *NABU* 1998/20; Ran Zadok, 'More Assyrians in Babylonian Sources', *NABU* 1998/55; R. Zadok, 'West Semitic Material in Neo/Late-Babylonian and Neo-Assyrian Sources', *NABU* 1998/56; Ran Zadok, 'The Representation of Foreigners in Neo- and Late-Babylonian Legal Documents (Eighth through Second Centuries B.C.E.)', in *Judah and the Judeans in the Neo-Babylonian Period* (ed. O. Lipschits and J. Blenkinsopp; Winona Lake: Eisenbrauns, 2003), 471–589; Ran Zadok, 'West Semites in Administrative and Epistolary Documents from Northern and Central Babylonia', in *Shlomo: Studies in Epigraphy, Iconography, History and Archaeology in Honor of Shlomo Moussaieff* (ed. R. Deutsch; Tel Aviv: Archaeological Center Publications, 2003), 255–71, and his contribution to the present volume.

BMA no. 26 records a case of intermarriage in Sippar, in which a Judean bride[42] was married to a Babylonian man. The latter belonged to one of Sippar's traditional families, and accordingly possessed a family name, Miller (Bab. *Ararru*). It does not display any peculiar feature. In other words, it is a standard Neo-Babylonian marriage contract in structure, content and technical language, regardless of the bride's Judean background. The key factor in this case is that of social status and prestige. When a bride from the West married a Babylonian man from Babylonia's urban middle class, or in other words, when such a bride married up, her family fully adapted itself to the established Babylonian law. It was certainly of a less prestigious status than the groom's family due to its immigrant background, and accordingly did not possess a family name. Nevertheless, its employment in the royal administration as merchant must have enabled it to build up some wealth,[43] and it was this wealth that was used to compensate for its lack of status. Its daughter was provided with a dowry and thus the family bought its way into the world of Babylonian matchmaking. By endowing ᶠKaššāya at the occasion of her marriage to Gūzānu from the Miller family this immigrant family moved up one more step on the social ladder. The head of the family, Hawše' had already adapted the names of his children to Babylonian standards: the bride and her brother had Babylonian names, whereas he himself kept his Judean name (Hawše', wr. ᵐ*a-mu-še-e* = *Hōšēăʿ*).

BaAr 2 no. 5 records another instance of intermarriage, but this time among families of comparable socio-economic status in rural Babylonia. It is in many respects unusual, as was already pointed out by Wunsch who published it.[44] She lists the following peculiarities: 'Mehrere Geschwister gemeinsam (wohl drei, darunter eine Frau) verheiraten ihre Schwester. Ihre Namen klingen nicht babylonisch, sondern überwiegend westsemitisch. ... Wenn ferner das letzte Zeichen ...]*ru* auf dem Rand eine Verbform im Plural anzeigen sollte, dann

42 For the Judean origin of the bride and her family see Jursa, 'Kollationen'; Michael Jursa, 'Eine Familie von Königskaufleuten judäischer Herkunft', *NABU* 2007/22.

43 On the merchants' commercial activities and their financial resources, see M. A. Dandamaev, 'The Neo-Babylonian *tamkāru*', in *Solving Riddles and Untying Knots: Biblical, Epigraphic, and Semitic Studies in Honor of Jonas C. Greenfield* (ed. Z. Zevit, S. Gitin and M. Sokoloff; Winona Lake: Eisenbrauns, 1995), 523–30; Michael Jursa, *Aspects of the Economic History of Babylonia in the First Millennium BC: Economic Geography, Economic Mentalities, Agriculture, the Use of Money and the Problem of Economic Growth.* With contributions by J. Hackl, B. Janković, K. Kleber, E. E. Payne, C. Waerzeggers and M. Weszeli (AOAT 377; Münster: Ugarit-Verlag, 2010), 580–84. On families of Judean merchants in Babylonia, see Jursa, 'Familie von Königskaufleuten'.

44 Cornelia Wunsch, *Urkunden zum Ehe-, Vermögens- und Erbrecht aus verschiedenen neubabylonischen Archiven* (BaAr 2; Dresden: ISLET, 2003).

könnte sich dahinter eine Quittungsklausel (*maḫrū, eṭrū*) verbergen, die auf den Erhalt von Silber durch die Geschwister der Braut deutet. Zahlungen in dieser Richtung sind bei Eheabsprachen zwischen Familien der städtischen Mittel-und Oberschicht nicht üblich, aber das Personal unserer Urkunde ist diesen Kreisen auch nicht zuzurechnen. ... Interessanterweise wird ... der Status ihrer Nachkommen explizit ... geregelt: Die männlichen sollen mit ihrem Vater in dessen ‚Haus' gehen. Was diese Bestimmung eigentlich bedeutet, ist völlig unklar; Parallelen sind m.W. nicht bekannt. ... Die Bestimmung Rs 2'f. gestattet dem Ehemann ausdrücklich, eine zweite Frau zu nehmen, sie stellt aber zugleich sicher, dass Nabê-ḫinnī nicht zur Nebenfrau degradiert werden darf. Eine solche Regelung ist höchst ungewöhnlich und singulär.'[45] As can be seen, peculiarities occur in matters that concern breach of contract by the husband (*in casu* demotion of the first wife to second in ranking), the status or affiliation of future children, and possibly also marital prestations.

BMA no. 17 concerns a marriage among members of the same community of immigrants from the West, rather than one of intermarriage. It stands out in the corpus of Neo-Babylonian marriage contracts in the way it deals with the dissolution of the marriage by the husband. Normally, two possibilities are considered, divorce by the husband, on the one hand, expressed by the verb *muššuru*, and demotion of the first wife to second in ranking, on the other hand, expressed by the idiom *aššata šanīta aḫāzu* or *rašû*. The same penalty is attributed to both possibilities so that they are combined in one clause and this constitutes the standard Neo-Babylonian 'divorce clause'.[46] However, in BMA no. 17 the two actions are expressed in two distinct clauses although the same penalty applies, separated by a clause dealing with adultery.[47]

45 Wunsch, *Urkunden*, 23–24. It seems that this unusual arrangement caused the scribe considerable headache judging from the frequent writing errors: *ina ūmi a[ššatu šan]ītu* {x} *ītaḫ*{x}*zu* {xxx} ᶠPN <*aššа*>*tu*! *rabītu* 'when he takes a second woman in marriage, ᶠPN is to remain first-ranking wife'.

46 Roth, *Babylonian Marriage*, 12–15.

47 Further note that the case of demotion is expressed by the verb *šūrubu* (not the usual *aḫāzu* or *rašû*). Interestingly, the latter recurs in another of the ethnically marked marriage contracts, namely BMA no. 34 (marriage between Egyptians) and is hitherto not found in any of the Babylonian marriages.

4 Evaluation: Negotiating Marriage in Multicultural Babylonia

The examples of ethnically marked marriages in the Neo-Babylonian language that were assembled above can be organized in three groups depending on ethnic and socio-economic parameters. A first group contains those Neo-Babylonian marriage contracts that record marriages among members of the same ethnic minority. To it belong the marriages within the Egyptian communities of Susa (BMA nos. 34–35) and Babylon (BMA no. 23), on the one hand, and those within the West Semitic communities in rural Babylonia (BMA no. 17), on the other hand. A second group consists of marriages among members of different ethnic communities who have a similar socio-economic status. These are the marriages of West Semitic brides with Babylonian grooms from rural Babylonia (BaAr 2 no. 5, cf. the AYMC). Nothing in the documents suggests that the grooms were descendants of any of the prestigious families that usually resided in Babylonia's urban centres or that they were much wealthier than the brides. In other words, the general impression one gets is that bride and groom (in BaAr 2 no. 5 and the AYMC) were of the same socio-economic class but had a different ethnic background. A third group consists of marriages among members of different ethnic communities and different socio-economic status, as in the case that is recorded in BMA no. 26.

As we saw above, the marriage of the third type was in no way different from the standard Neo-Babylonian marriages. It proves that when a West Semitic bride married up, her family accepted all Babylonian marriage customs. In contrast, the ethnically marked marriage contracts of the first and second groups abound with special features. They contain proportionally more peculiarities than those marriages in which both parties were of Babylonian descent. Moreover, one can discern a pattern in the assemblage of special features. They all occur in either the divorce clause or the one on marital property, or in both. In other words, Egyptians in Susa and West Semites in rural Babylonia made changes to the standard Neo-Babylonian divorce clause, and several also contain payments or gifts that were no longer customary in the Neo-Babylonian period. For instance, BMA no. 34 attests to indirect dowry and mentions the possibility of divorce by the wife in addition to that of divorce by the husband and demotion of the first wife. BaAr 2 no. 5 may contain a reference to a payment by the groom at marriage, does not consider divorce by the husband and explicitly forbids demotion of the first wife to second in ranking. BMA no. 17 considers both divorce by the husband and demotion of the first wife but treats them in two separate clauses. BMA nos. 17 and 34 describe the case of demotion by using the verb *šūrubu* rather than the standard *aḫāzu* or *rašû*.[48]

The same pattern of special features is also found in the AYMC. It attests to indirect dowry, penalizes the husband who divorces his wife and denies her the status of married woman, but is silent on the possibility of his demotion of the first wife to secondary in ranking.

In short, the Āl-Yāhūdu marriage contract with its special characteristics is not an isolated case. It follows the pattern of marriage contracts that were written in a multicultural environment among members of the same socio-economic class in rural Babylonia, and is comparable to the marriages that the Egyptians concluded among themselves in Babylon and Susa.

In view of this evidence, an approach that is more nuanced than the previously adopted ones of Babylonian vs. non-Babylonian or standard vs. non-standard is called for. It should start from the following observation, namely that Babylonia (and Susa) in the first millennium B.C.E. was a multicultural society, in the countryside as well as in the cities. Populations of various 'nationalities' lived side by side, and must have interacted on various levels (economically, legally, socially, culturally) and in various degrees of intensity. There may have been differences from place to place in the way in which Babylonia's different ethnic groups interacted. For instance, in the cities we must reckon with the presence of a traditional elite class that owned prebends in the temples and favored endogamous marriages.[49] Intercultural exchange is to be expected less frequently in such a segregative environment. As a matter of fact, Babylonian prebendary families never seem to have given their daughters in marriage to foreigners.[50] When they accepted a foreign bride into their midst (as in BMA no. 26), they probably had good reasons. Perhaps the bride was extremely beautiful, or they hoped to expand their commercial relations by marrying into a family of royal merchants. When they married down, as for instance in the case that is recorded in BMA no. 4, where the Babūtu family of Babylon gave a foster-daughter in marriage to a man of lower social ranking (but not necessarily of foreign descent), they demanded a financial compensation from him.

---

48 The contrast with BMA no. 26 from Sippar is clear: it follows standard Babylonian customs in that the bride is endowed by her family (not the groom's) and the case of divorce (*muššuru*) and demotion (*aššata šanīta aḫāzu/rašû*) are dealt with in juxtaposition.

49 Caroline Waerzeggers, *The Ezida Temple of Borsippa: Priesthood, Cult, Archives* (Achaemenid History 15; Leiden: Nederlands Instituut voor het Nabije Oosten, 2010), 97.

50 Zadok, 'West Semites'.

Intercultural exchange was probably most pronounced in the environment of the army and the king. Indeed, in military circles, at the court and in the royal administration contact between various population groups was intense. We know that soldiers, merchants, craftsmen, and clerks from foreign extraction worked for the king alongside Babylonians throughout Babylonia (and southwestern Iran), in the cities as well as in the countryside.[51] Some lived from rations that they received either directly from the palace or from Babylonian citizens via an officially controlled ration system.[52] Others were settled in the countryside and lived from the land that they had received from the king. Their daily contacts at work created a fertile ground for interculturalism, was no doubt one of the driving forces behind the widespread use of Aramaic as vernacular language, and must have accelerated their absorption in Babylonian society.

Daily contacts between different ethnic populations in an open and inclusive society inevitably lead to intermarriage. Conflicts of personal laws may have arisen, as often would be the case in intercultural encounters of this sort. To diffuse tension the parties would have to sit down together and negotiate the conditions of the marriage. The result in the specific cases under consideration was that the parties to the marriage choose to marry conform the local Babylonian law and notary tradition, and even under invocation of the local gods (the AYMC), provided that certain changes be allowed to the agreement's content and formulary. Changes were necessary in order to accommodate non-Babylonian traditions and other special circumstances. In other words, the shape and content of these marriages were determined by the circumstances in which they took place. Some must have been of a cultural and multi-cultural nature, others of more economic nature.

The Neo-Babylonian marriage contracts from the Egyptian communities at Susa and Babylon, and from the rural communities of West Semitic origin within Babylonia show that at times the established Babylonian law regarding marriage, with its great emphasis on direct dowry, its constraints upon female behavior (e.g. adultery), its restrictive attitude to polygyny and divorce must have ran counter to the multicultural nature of Babylonian society. The problem could be met should it present itself by making minor changes to the structure and formu-

51 Olof Pedersén, 'Foreign Professionals in Babylon: Evidence from the Archive in the Palace of Nebuchadnezzar II', in *Ethnicity in Ancient Mesopotamia: Papers Read at the 48th Rencontre Assyriologique Internationale Leiden, 1–4 July 2002* (ed. W. van Soldt; PIHANS 102; Leiden: Nederlands Instituut voor het Nabije Oosten, 2005), 267–71.

52 Caroline Waerzeggers, 'The Carians of Borsippa', *Iraq* 68 (2006), 1–22, on Egyptian-Carian soldiers and Judean workers (or soldiers, VS 6 128) receiving rations from Borsippean citizens.

lary of the existing format of the marriage contract. Non-Babylonian phraseology or explicitly foreign legal concepts were generally avoided (except perhaps in BMA no. 34). The parties remained within the borders of the acceptable Babylonian practice and legal jargon.

5 The AYMC Reconsidered

ᶠNanāya-kānat's marriage contract (the AYMC) looks like a normal Neo-Babylonian marriage contract because, first, every legal concept in it is attested in other Neo-Babylonian marriage contracts, and secondly, its formulaic peculiarities still basically reflect Babylonian traditions even if for some of them no exact parallel can be found in the legal jargon of the Neo-Babylonian period as we know it today. However, her marriage contract also contains at least two practices that are decidedly non-normative from a Neo-Babylonian point of view: indirect dowry and divorce by declaration.

What prompted their insertion in the AYMC? Were they included out of socio-economic or legal considerations? Or did they result from the specific cultural and multicultural circumstances in which the marriage took place?

Gifts from the groom's side at marriage in general, and indirect dowry in particular, were known but not normative in the Neo-Babylonian period. There are no more than six (perhaps seven) attested cases – the AYMC included – in the corpus of over fifty marriage contracts from this period. They were given under diverging conditions and accordingly had more than one function. In the Old-Babylonian period, gifts from the groom (known as *terḫatum*) functioned as a legal instrument to establish the legitimacy of the marital union and to transfer rights over the bride and future progeny to the husband. This function seems to have been lost in the Neo-Babylonian period. In that period gifts from the groom were given as an indemnity for the loss of access over the bride's productivity and reproductivity (esp. in those cases in which female productive labor was highly valued). An example at stake may be found in the Neo-Babylonian marriage contract of Lā-tubāšinni (BMA no. 4). Her marriage to the manumitted slave Dāgil-ili must have been a financial set-back for her single mother and may also have endangered the free status of her future children.[53] For Dāgil-ili it was an opportunity to improve his social status and for that he was

53 Cornelia Wunsch, 'Findelkinder und Adoption nach neubabylonischen Quellen', *AfO* 50 (2003–2004), 174–244.

willing to pay in hard cash, especially since he had the financial resources to do so.

In most cases, the groom's gift in the Neo-Babylonian period was intended as an endowment upon the bride and went by the name *biblu*.[54] It was originally transferred from the groom's side to the bride's one at marriage, and subsequently turned over to the bride by her family as part of her endowment. Anthropologists call this type of endowment 'indirect dowry' in order to distinguish it from the 'direct dowry' or dowry that came directly from the bride's side.[55] In at least three of the attested Neo-Babylonian cases of a gift from the groom's side the gift functioned as indirect dowry (BMA nos. 34–35 and BM 64195⁺), because it did not stay with the bride's family but was added to her dowry and thus left the family.

In my opinion, the groom's gift in the AYMC was also a type of indirect dowry, because it is qualified as a 'provision?' for the bride (*z/ṣindu ša* ᶠPN). In other words, its ultimate purpose was to provide for the bride. This could only be achieved if we assume that her mother transferred the garment with which the groom had covered her, or its equivalent in silver or part of it, to her daughter at some later stage. A similar scenario may be surmised for the destiny of the garment that was given in BaAr 2 no. 1, although the passage is fragmentary and does not seem to have qualified the gift as *biblu* or gift for the bride in any other way.[56]

In short, four to five of the attested Neo-Babylonian cases of a gift from the groom's side (including the AYMC) refer to endowments upon the bride (indirect dowry). Accordingly, indirect dowry was practiced among the Egyptians in Susa (BMA nos. 34–35), and occasionally also among the Judeans in rural Babylonian (the AYMC) and the Babylonian urban population of Sippar (BM 64195⁺; perhaps also BaAr 2 no. 1).

Why did these brides receive a dowry from their husbands or his family, either in addition to a dowry from their own family (BMA nos. 34–35 and BM 64195⁺), or in absence of one from their family (the AYMC, and perhaps also BaAr 2 no. 1)? The Egyptians probably followed a custom that they had brought with

54 BMA nos. 34–35: 'gift for the bride' *bibil* ᶠPN; and BM 64195⁺ (Waerzeggers, 'Note on the Marriage Gift'): 'gift that was placed upon the bride' *biblu ša ana* ᶠPN *taškunu*.

55 Jack Goody and S. J. Tambiah, *Bridewealth and Dowry* (Cambridge Papers in Social Anthropology 7; Cambridge: Cambridge University Press, 1973), 1–58.

56 The text in BaAr 2 no. 5 is too fragmentary to reach any conclusions regarding the money that is received in lines 18'-19' (left edge). A possible interpretation is: 'three shekels of silver [the bride's agents (i.e. her sisters)] have received (*maḫrū*).' If it indeed did entail the receipt of a payment from the groom by the bride's agents, it is noteworthy that the groom, bride and her agents bore Aramaic names.

them from Egypt (cf. indirect dowry in the Demotic marriage contracts).[57] One of the Babylonian families from Sippar used the practice of indirect dowry as a legal device to allow the groom's mother to transfer some of her personal belongings to her daughter-in-law. The latter case also shows that indirect dowry was not necessarily considered the lot of poor brides in Babylonia,[58] because the bride in BM 64195⁺ came from a relatively well-to-do Babylonian family judging from her family name and the content of her dowry.

An economically motivated explanation for the groom's gift in the AYMC can easily be perceived. Considering the rather obvious fact that ᶠNanāya-kānat was a relatively poor bride from a family where there was no father or any other adult male to provide for the family, her mother could use an incentive from the groom's side to 'give up' her daughter and make up for the economic loss of a helping hand. Moreover she could use the garment or rather its equivalent in silver (5 shekels) to endow her daughter. It must have been particularly embarrassing not to be able to provide a dowry in a society in which the endowment of the bride at marriage was widespread custom, culturally (even oblates married off their daughters with a dowry, see BaAr 2 no. 3) and economically important. The groom's support in this respect came in handy. When interpreted this way, his gift was the result of the economic circumstances in which the marriage took place. It was a poor bride's endowment and a compensation payment for her mother. Cultural or multicultural circumstances do not seem to have played a role.

The dissolution of a marriage in the Neo-Babylonian period was either the consequence of divorce (*muššuru*) or remarriage (*aššata šanīta aḫāzu/rašû/šūrubu*). The penalty for divorce was five or six minas. The one for demotion of the first wife to second in ranking in a polygamous marriage was the same. Consequently, both cases were usually dealt with in one clause rather than in two separate clauses: 'Should Husband divorce (lit. 'release') W (his wife), or take another wife (in preference to her), ...'[59] The less aggravating case, in which the husband only takes a second wife in addition to the first wife but does not reduce

57 J. G. Manning, '"Demotic Law"', in *A History of Ancient Near Eastern Law* (ed. R. Westbrook; HO 72; Leiden / Boston: Brill, 2003), 819–62, here 835–36.

58 Different from North India, for instance, where one finds more dowry and less indirect dowry among the upper castes, and less dowry and more indirect dowry among the lower castes (T. M. Lemos, *Marriage Gifts and Social Change in Ancient Palestine: 1200 BCE to 200 CE* [Cambridge: University Press, 2010], 15).

59 BMA nos. 2, 6, 17, 19, 20, 26 and BaAr 2 no. 2 (all six minas). BMA no. 8 (five minas payable to bride's mother). BMA no. 34 (five minas and return of dowry). It is not entirely clear whether the cases in which only five minas was paid also involved the actual dissolution of the marriage, because the contracts do not grant the wife to 'go wherever she please' or 'go (back) to her father'.

her in ranking nor desires to divorce her (the verb *muššuru* is left out), is met by a penalty of only one mina of silver.[60]

Deviations from this pattern occur whenever specific legal circumstances or other sensibilities needed to be addressed. This happened frequently at the marriage of foreigners (BMA nos. 34–35, no. 17, BaAr 2 no. 5 and the AYMC), but not exclusively (BaAr 2 no. 3 and BMA no. 5). It appears from these marriages that the standard Babylonian practice to combine divorce and remarriage in the same clause was considered problematic in particular. Therefore, its components were reshuffled or one component was left out and the other one formulated differently from the norm. For instance, BMA no. 17 'expresses these two actions in two distinct clauses, separated by a clause dealing with adultery'.[61] BaAr 2 no. 5 does not talk about divorce and explicitly forbids demotion of the first wife to second in ranking. BaAr 2 no. 3 and BMA no. 5 talk about divorce but 'without reference to another marriage and without using the verb *muššuru*'. They refer to divorce by recording 'an oral declaration that the husband would utter to dissolve his marriage: "ᶠPN will not be a wife (to me)"'. By uttering these words, the husband denied his wife the status of married wife, and thus effected the abolishment of the marital bond (*verba solemnia* of divorce). It is not immediately clear why remarriage was not considered by the parties[62] or why the type of divorce they envisaged could not be formulated in the 'normal' way, namely by the verb *muššuru*.

The AYMC is another instance in which the parties' decision to consider divorce but not remarriage obliged the scribe to reformulate the divorce clause.[63] This time the verb *muššuru* is kept (unlike in the previous two cases in which it was substituted by the *verba solemnia* of divorce). It is followed by a declaration by the husband that recalls the very same *verba solemnia* of divorce. The result is a clause in which divorce is expressed twice (so it seems): once by the verb

60 BMA nos. 4 and 25; or no penalty at all, solely the guarantee that the wife gets her dowry back (BMA no. 15).

61 This and the next two quotes are from Roth, *Babylonian Marriage*, 13.

62 Had it anything to do with the groom's status of legal dependency? In BaAr 2 no. 3 the groom was an oblate and dependent upon the temple. In BMA no. 5 he was a manumitted slave but still dependent upon his adoptive father in matters pertaining to marriage and personal status. Did he depend on the temple, respectively his adoptive father in order to arrange marriage to another woman, and is it unlikely that this would be granted to him, hence the entire case is dropped to begin with?

63 I do not see any specifically legal or socio-economic reason for leaving polygyny out of consideration in the AYMC. Perhaps it was not discussed because it was in conflict with certain cultural sensibilities? This is no more than speculation.

muššuru ('Should H divorce W'), and once by the *verba solemnia* of divorce ('and say "She will not be a wife"'). This is rather peculiar. Therefore it is more likely that the husband's statement in this case did not function as the *verba solemnia* of divorce but as a declaration of intent.[64] The husband's statement 'She is not a wife' was added in order to reveal something about his aims and intentions. A husband who is willing to declare 'She is not a wife' makes clear that he has no other cause for divorcing his wife than his own desire to be released from her. His declaration brings out the one-sided and unmotivated character of the divorce. He is not divorcing her because she remained childless, or he found any other wrong in her, or he wants to remarry. He is divorcing because of a simple change of heart with regard to his desire to be married to his wife. It was this legal concept of divorce, namely divorce without cause, that the parties wanted to be reflected in an unambiguous way in their marriage contract. The verb *muššuru* or the formula 'She is not a wife', when used alone, were considered insufficient or ambiguous.[65] It was by adding the latter to the former that the verb's true content was brought out explicitly and unambiguously.

Remarkably, precisely this practice, namely the presentation of divorce as an act of repudiation in the third person followed by a declaration of intent by the divorcing party finds its closest parallel in the Aramaic legal tradition. In the Aramaic marriage contract TAD B 3.8 from Elephantine (dated 410 B.C.E.),[66] lines 24–28 we read: 'If ᶠPN hates PN her husband and says to him: "I hate you; I will not be a wife to you"'.[67] The Aramaic 'if X hates Y' parallels the Akkadian 'if X

64 Cf. the use of direct speech in Neo-Babylonian legal disputes, see Cornelia Wunsch, 'Legal Narrative in Neo-Babylonian Trial Documents: Text Reconstruction, Interpretation, and Assyriological Method', in *Law and Narrative in the Bible and in Neighbouring Ancient Cultures* (ed. K.-P. Adam, F. Avemarie and N. Wazana FAT 54; Tübingen: Mohr Siebeck, 2012), 3–34 (31).

65 Could it be that the Neo-Babylonian term for divorce *par* excellence, *muššuru*, had secondarily acquired the added meaning of divorce with a cause due to its frequent juxtaposition to the case of remarriage? Thus it came to refer not just to any divorce but to specific types of divorce, for instance, to divorce that was motivated by the husband's desire to take another woman in marriage?

66 There are in total eight Aramaic marriage documents from Elephantine, but only three are basically complete (TAD B 2.6; TAD B 3.3; and TAD B 3.8). The remaining marriage documents are more fragmentary in nature (TAD B 2.5; TAD B 6.1–4).

67 The protasis of the other preserved divorce clauses have only the declaration of intent, namely 'I hate W. She will not be a wife to me' (TAD B 3.8: 21–24), which is shortened to 'I hate PN my husband (/ᶠPN my wife)' in TAD B 2.6: 22–29; TAD B 3.3: 7–10. On the technical meaning of the verb 'to hate' in this context, see Henri Zvi Szubin and Bezalel Porten, 'The Status of a Repudiated Spouse: A New Interpretation of Kraeling 7 (TAD B3.8)', *Israel Law Review* 35 (2001), 46–78 (55–68); Hélène Nutkowicz, 'Concerning the Verb śnʾ in Judaeo-Aramaic Contracts from Elephan-

releases (Y)' in the AYMC, and the Aramaic 'I hate you. I will not be a wife to you' parallels the Akkadian declaration 'She will not be a wife' in the AYMC.

The Elephantine marriage documents also attest to the practice of indirect dowry among Judeans in the exilic period. At times, the bridegroom gave a certain amount of shekels to the bride's agent, who then added it to the goods with which he endowed his daughter.[68] The bridegroom's gift is called *mhr* in the texts (= Biblical *mohar*). There are at least two if not three attested cases of *mhr* in Elephantine (TAD B2.6, B3.8, and perhaps B6.1) and in both dowry is paid as well. Esḫor, the bridegroom in TAD B2.6, for instance, points out (in the first person) 'I gave (as) *mohar* for your daughter Miptahiah: [silver], 5 shekels by the stone(-weights)s of [the] king' (lines 4–5), and from the total worth of dowry goods stated in lines 13–15 it is clear that the five shekels had been added. The inclusion of the *mohar* into the bride's dowry is also clear from TAD B3.8 where at the end of the dowry list it is said: 'All the garments and br]onz[e vessels] and mo[n]ey and the *mohar*: (in) silver seven kars, that is [7], eight [she]ke[l]s, that is 8, 5 hallurs by the stone(-weight)s of the king, silver zuz to the ten' (lines 15–17). Thus, Lemos concluded that 'there exist two texts in which both a dowry and a *mhr* were paid, but in both cases the amount of the *mhr* is insignificant (...) and is far outstripped by the value of the dowry. And in one,[69] if not both of these texts, the *mhr* which in the preexilic period always designated bridewealth, goes from the bridegroom to the bride herself, in effect becoming dowry, and more specifically, indirect dowry'.[70]

In my opinion, it would be a mistake to rely solely on socio-economic or legal explanations and deny the Aramaic parallels. I tend to believe that they are not mere coincidence. First, they are significant in the sense that they reflect the bride's side's desire to emulate some of its homeland marriage customs.[71] In the

---

tine', *JSS* 52 (2007), 211–25; Alejandro F. Botta, *Aramaic and Egyptian Legal Traditions at Elephantine: An Egyptological Approach* (London: Continuum, 2009), 60. On similar declarations, made in the context of divorce, from the West Semitic world, see the book of Hosea (Markham J. Geller, 'The Elephantine Papyri and Hosea 2.3', *JSJ* 8 [1977], 139–48) and a 13th century B.C.E. marriage contract from Emar (references at Abraham, 'West Semitic and Judean Brides', 203).

68 This is clear from a combined reading of the Elephantine material. For details, see Lemos, *Marriage Gifts*, 62–69.

69 TAD B3.8.

70 Lemos, *Marriage Gifts*, 69.

71 Note in this respect that from a practical point of view it was easy to integrate marriage customs of foreigners into the Babylonian format when these customs were not completely unknown in Babylonia, such as indirect dowry and divorce by declaration, because the Babylonian scribes could rely on formularies that were ready available in their language and did not have to translate the foreigner's customs into Akkadian.

culture from which at least the bride originated a gift from the groom had been a central part of marriage. Judeans in pre-exilic Israel considered it necessarily for a legal marriage.[72] By exilic times it may have morphed into indirect dowry and lost much of its juridical function, but it retained high cultural value. For instance in the marriage contracts from the Judean community in Elephantine it was still singled out and listed separately among the items of the conjugal fund, and called by its old name *mohar* although it had evolved from bride price to indirect dowry. Furthermore, in the culture from which the bride originated a declaration of intent by the divorcing party was considered essential in the divorce procedure.

Secondly, as we saw above, tempering with the content and formula of divorce and endowment clauses is found not only in the example from Āl-Yāhūdu but in all other instances of ethnically marked marriages from rural Babylonia (as well as in those from multicultural Susa). It is as much a sign of negotiating marriage in a multicultural environment as one of lining up the established law with conflicting socio-economic or legal realities.

Hence, I would not go so far to claim that the provisions in ᶠNanāya-kānat's marriage contract systematically represent another legal system, but I would not claim either that they perfectly fit the usual Babylonian standards.

6 Summary and Conclusions

Notwithstanding the economic integration and linguistic acculturation of Āl-Yāhūdu's Judean community, some of its members adhered to certain practices from their homeland as a means of self-identification, not only in the area of name-giving, but also, as I hope to have shown, in that of family law.[73] The only marriage contract that has survived from this community is predominantly

72 Lemos, *Marriage Gifts*, 230–31.

73 Perhaps also in their choice of the day on which they concluded legal transactions. Caroline Waerzeggers, 'Happy Days: The Babylonian Almanac in Daily Life', in *The Ancient Near East, a Life!: Festschrift Karel Van Lerberghe* (ed. T. Boiy et al.; OLA 220; Leuven: Peeters, 2012), 653–64, here 658, showed that the other ethnically marked marriage contracts were written on days on which Babylonians would rather not write their contracts. Unfortunately, the date of the AYMC is broken. It would be interesting to further investigate this issue once all legal documents from Āl-Yāhūdu are published. The inheritance division from Āl-Yāhūdu was written on Tašrīt 7th. In modern Judaism the first ten days of the year (Tishre 1–10) are days in which business should be avoided, but it is hard to say whether this habit was already practiced by Jews in early post-exilic times. In any case, for the Babylonians, Tašrīt 7th was a favorable day and a good day in court (Waerzeggers, 'Happy Days', 654 and 660).

Babylonian, in language and in concept, but it is not exclusively Babylonian. It was argued above that adaptations were made to its formulary by its Babylonian scribe in order to accommodate his Judean clients' requests and to diffuse tension between the Judean side and the Babylonian one. Both sides had negotiated the terms of the marriage in accordance with their socio-economic status and cultural background, and the results of these negotiations are reflected in the adaptations that were made to the standard format.

The example from Āl-Yāhūdu is not an isolated case. The corpus of more than fifty Neo-Babylonian marriage agreements, albeit its apparent conformity and stereotypical formulary, attests to knowledge of foreign marital practices. These are reflected in the special features that were noted above in several of the ethnically marked Neo-Babylonian marriage contracts, both the Egyptian and West Semitic ones, and then in particular those from rural Babylonia.

It cannot be ascertained which percentage of the non-Babylonian population in Babylonia stuck to their own traditions in family related matters, but by no means should the family of ᶠNanāya-kānat be considered as representative for the entire Judean community in Babylonia. Her neighbors, Nēriah and his brothers, who appear in an inheritance document from Āl-Yāhūdu, divided their deceased father's property according to Babylonian law, and the document recording the division of their inheritance shares does not deviate from the Babylonian notary norms.[74] Her compatriots in Sippar, the family of Hawše', married their daughter to a Babylonian man, gave her a dowry as was customarily done in Babylonia, and recorded the agreement conforming to Babylonian practices (BMA no. 26).

Babylonian family law (and in particular the exchange of gifts at marriage and the dissolution of marriage) in the first millennium B.C.E. should not exclusively be conceived in economic terms. Matters of ethnic origin also played a role in determining its shape and found their expression in the preserved marriage agreements. It would not surprise to find, once the study of the social history of Babylonian society in the first millennium B.C.E. is fully under way, that also matters of social structure, status and prestige helped shape Babylonia's family law.

Acknowledgment

The Research for this essay was supported by the Interuniversity Attraction Poles Programme initiated by the Belgian Science Policy Office.

74 Abraham, 'Inheritance Division'.

Gauthier Tolini

From Syria to Babylon and Back: The Neirab Archive

In 1926 and 1927, archaeological excavations in Neirab, a town ca. 10 km southeast of Aleppo in Syria, brought to light a small archive of twenty-seven Neo-Babylonian tablets.[1] The archive spans the reigns of Neriglissar (560–556 B.C.E.) to Darius I (521–486 B.C.E.).[2] The majority of these texts date to the reign of Nabonidus (556–539 B.C.E.) and mention descendants of one Nusku-gabbe. To understand the Neirab texts one must take into consideration several limitations and problems. First, the archaeological context of their discovery is extremely imprecise. The excavation reports are vague about the 1926 discoveries: 'C'est un peu avant d'atteindre le bord de la tranchée F que nous avons découvert, le 31 octobre et le 1er novembre, à un niveau variant entre 7 m. 23 et 7 mètres, un gisement de 27 tablettes cunéiformes ou fragments; parmi ceux-ci, plusieurs présentaient un texte continu et ont été à nouveau réunis, d'où le nombre total des tablettes ou fragments de tablettes doit être réduit à 25'.[3] The archaeological context of the texts discovered in 1927 is not specified at all: 'Deux fragments de contrats qui figurent au butin de cette année ne sont pas moins précieux à ce titre: l'un d'eux

1 About the digs in 1926, see Bertrand Carrière and Georges Augustin Barrois, 'Fouilles de l'École Archéologique Française de Jérusalem effectuées à Neirab du 24 septembre au 5 novembre 1926', *Syria* 8 (1927), 126–142, 201–212; G. A. Barrois, 'Fouilles à Neirab: Septembre-novembre 1926', *RB* 36 (1927), 256–265, pl. IV–IX. About the digs in 1927, see Félix-Marie Abel and Georges Augustin Barrois, 'Fouilles de l'École Archéologique Française de Jérusalem effectuées à Neirab du 12 septembre au 6 novembre 1927', *Syria* 9 (1928), 187–206, 303–319.

2 Texts no. 1 and no. 2 mention Nebuchadnezzar's reign. Goetze showed in a convincing manner that the first text concerned in fact Nebuchadnezzar IV. Cf. Albrecht Goetze, 'Additions to Parker and Dubberstein's Babylonian Chronology', *JNES* 3 (1944), 43–46 (45 n. 22). In return, the identification of the king cited in text no. 2 stays open. For Goetze, it is Nebuchadnezzar IV (*loc. cit.*). Oelsner prefers to date this text back to the reign of Nebuchadnezzar II (605–562 B.C.E.). Cf. Joachim Oelsner, 'Weitere Bemerkungen zu den Neirab-Urkunden', *AoF* 16 (1989), 68–77 (69). But dating to Nebuchadnezzar IV seems preferable to us (see footnote 54).

3 Carrière and Barrois, 'Fouilles à Neirab 1926', 138. The archaeologists are very imprecise on the relations between the tablets and a skeleton found nearby: 'Immédiatement au nord du gisement, et peut-être en rapport avec celui-ci, un scarabée de pâte bleue a été retrouvé parmi les débris d'un squelette'. See also Barrois' testimony: 'Avoisinant le corps, nous avons découvert un gisement de tablettes d'argile crue couvertes d'écriture cunéiforme', Barrois, 'Fouilles à Neirab', 263.

Gauthier Tolini: UMR 7041, 'Archéologies et Sciences de l'Antiquité', Nanterre

porte la date du règne de Darius et l'autre, très mutilé, authentique la découverte par la triple répétition du nom ancien de Neirab: *Ni-ri-bi*'.[4] Second, given its size, the chronological scope of the archive is quite long. Twenty-seven texts document a period of several decades. As a consequence, we are only informed about a small proportion of the activities of Nusku-gabbe's descendants. Indeed, the composition of this archive, which consists mainly of promissory notes, shows that it is a 'dead' archive. This means that the texts we have at our disposal were discarded by their owner(s) because they had lost their immediate utility.[5] Third, several texts fail to mention any member of this family and this poses the problem of the general coherence of the 'archive'. Fourth, I should add that the fragmentary state of many texts makes them difficult to read and interpret. Thus, despite their publication by E. Dhorme in *Revue d'Assyriologie* in 1928,[6] it was necessary to collate the tablets. After their discovery, the Neirab tablets were divided in two lots, between the École Biblique et Archéologique Française de Jérusalem, and the National Museum of Aleppo.[7] The first lot has been photographed by Denis Bouder during a research trip carried out in 2008 and funded by the UMR 7041 ('Archéologies et Sciences de l'Antiquité', Nanterre). These photographs are the basis of the new readings which I propose in this article.[8] After Dhorme's first study, the scholarship on this archive has focused on four issues: the dating of the texts, their onomastics, the localisation of the town 'Neirab' mentioned in the texts, and the economic aspects of the family's activities.[9] The most contro-

---

4 Abel and Barrois, 'Fouilles à Neirab 1927', 318.
5 About this question, see below § 4.2.
6 The first 25 texts discovered in 1926 were presented in Édouard Dhorme, 'Note sur les tablettes de Neirab', *Syria* 8 (1927), 213–215. For the full publication of all 27 texts, see Dhorme, 'Les tablettes babyloniennes de Neirab', *RA* 25 (1928), 53–82.
7 Texts preserved in Jerusalem: no. 2 (=SÉ 77), no. 4 (=SÉ 78), no. 7 (=SÉ 79), no. 9 (=SÉ 80), no. 10 (=SÉ 81), no. 12 (=SÉ 82), no. 14 (=SÉ 83), no. 17 (=SÉ 84), no. 18 (=SÉ 85), no. 19 (=SÉ 86), no. 21 (=SÉ 87) et no. 23 (=SÉ 88). Cf. Marcel Sigrist and Allan Millard, 'Catalogue des tablettes cunéiformes du Couvent Saint-Étienne', *RB* 92 (1985), 570–576 (574). Texts preserved in the Aleppo Museum: no. 1 (= M 3468), no. 3 (= M 3466), no. 5 (= M 3467), no. 6 (= M 3461), no. 8 (= M 3471), no. 11 (= M 3472), no. 13 (= M 246), no. 15 (= M 3470), no. 16 (= M 244), no. 22 (= M 3473), no. 24 (= M 247), no. 26 (= M 3495), no. 27 (= M 3494). About these last references, cf. Luigi Cagni, 'Considérations sur les textes babyloniens de Neirab près d'Alep', *Transeuphratène* 2 (1990), 169–185 (174). Texts no. 20 and 25 were not identified in the Syrian collection. However, a text is registered as coming from Neirab: 'no. 39 (= 252, M 3474)'. Cf. Cagni, 'Textes babyloniens de Neirab', 174.
8 The new readings are followed by an asterisk (*). A new edition of the archive is scheduled for publication on the website www.achemenet.com.
9 F. M. Fales, 'Remarks on the Neirab Texts', *Oriens Antiquus* 12 (1973), 131–142; Israel Eph'al, 'The Western Minorities in Babylonia in the 6th-5th Centuries B. C.: Maintenance and Cohesion',

versial debate is the one regardig the place where they were written. For Israel Eph'al the texts were written in Babylonia by Syrian deportees, who were settled in a village named Neirab according to their native land. At the end of exile, the deportees would have brought back a part of their documents drafted in Babylonia.[10] This hypothesis has generally been accepted,[11] but it continues to arouse scepticism.[12] In my present article I will focus on the following topics: the geographical and historical context of the Neirab texts (§ 1), the onomastics and other cultural aspects of the Neirabean community (§ 2), a study of the role of Nusku-gabbe's sons inside their community (§ 3) and a comparison between the living conditions of the Neirabeans in the Neo-Babylonian and Persian periods (§ 4).

1 The Geographical and Historical Context

1.1. Where Were the Neirab Texts Written ?

The archive of the sons of Nusku-gabbe was discovered in Neirab, Syria, and it mentions this town on several occasions. One contract was drafted in the 'town of Neirab' (*āl-Nēreb*; no. 23: 19) and another one in the 'town of the Neirabeans'

Or 47 (1978), 74–90; Oelsner, 'Neirab-Urkunden'; Cagni, 'Textes babyloniens de Neirab'; Stefan Timm, 'Die Bedeutung der spätbabylonischen Texte aus *Nērab* für die Rückkehr der Judäer aus dem Exil', in *Meilenstein: Festgabe für Herbert Donner zum 16. Februar 1995* (ed. M. Weippert and S. Timm; Ägypten und Altes Testament 30; Wiesbaden: Harrassowitz, 1995), 276–288. The Aramaic epigraphs were studied by Eleonora Cussini, 'Palaeography of the Aramaic Epigraphs from Tell Neirab', in *Studi sul Vicino Oriente Antico Dedicati alla Memoria di Luigi Cagni* (ed. S. Graziani; Naples: Istituto universitario orientale, 2000), 1459–79. Some comments can be found in Olof Pedersén, *Archives and Libraries in the Ancient Near East 1500–300 B.* C. (Bethesda: CDL Press, 1998), 192–193 and Michael Jursa, *Neo-Babylonian Legal and Administrative Documents: Typology, Contents and Archives* (GMTR 1; Münster: Ugarit-Verlag, 2005), 152.

10 Eph'al, 'Western Minorities', 84–87. This assumption has been reiterated in Israel Eph'al, 'On the Political and Social Organization of the Jews in Babylonian Exile', in *XXI. Deutscher Orientalistentag vom 24. bis 29. März 1980 in Berlin, Ausgewählte Vorträge* (ed. F. Steppat; ZDMGSup 5; Wiesbaden: Harrassowitz, 1983), 106–112 (108).

11 See for example Francis Joannès, 'La localisation de Ṣurru à l'époque néo-babylonienne', *Semitica* 32 (1982), 35; Oelsner, 'Neirab-Urkunden', 70; Timm, 'Texte aus Nērab', 282–283; Cussini, 'Aramaic Epigraphs', 1472–1473.

12 Stephanie Dalley, 'The Cuneiform Tablet from Tell Tawilan', *Levant* 16 (1984), 19–22 (20–21) and Cagni, 'Textes babyloniens de Neirab'.

(*ālu-ša-*^{lú}*Nērebāya*; no. 17: 14). Two other texts, drafted elsewhere, mention the town of Neirab in passing (no. 19 and no. 26). On this basis, it seems natural to conclude, with E. Dhorme, that the texts were all written in Syria, except for no. 19 and no. 1, which were drafted in Ḫīt and Babylon respectively. Dhorme also related other toponyms of the Nusku-gabbe archive to Syrian geography. For instance, he identifies the town of Ammat with Ḫamath and locates the town of Bīt-dayyān-Adad in the vicinity of Aleppo due to the importance of Adad's cult in this region.[13] But the identification between Ḫamath and Ammat has been rejected on philological and contextual grounds by L. Lewy, and I. Eph'al questioned the Syrian setting of the archive, arguing that the texts were drafted in Babylonia, and more precisely in the region of Nippur.[14] Three decisive arguments prove that the Neirab texts were indeed drafted in Babylonia:

1) In the Neo-Babylonian period, and particularly during Nabonidus' reign, the activities of Nusku-gabbe's sons concentrated around four agricultural villages:[15] Bīt-dayyān-Adad (no. 3, 5, 7, 10, 11, 13, 15), Ammat (no. 8, 9, 12, 14, 16), the Town of the Neirabeans on the Bēl-aba-uṣur canal (no. 17) and Ālu-ša-kutimmī$^{?}$* (the Town of gold- or silversmiths) (no. 4).[16] Based on information provided by the archive, the towns of Bīt-dayyān-Adad and Ammat were located at a distance of only two days travel from each other. Nuḫsāya, son of Nusku-gabbe,

13 Dhorme, 'Neirab', 54.

14 Julius Lewy, 'The Old West Semitic Sun God Hammu', *HUCA* 18 (1943–44), 429–488 (431–433); Julius Lewy, 'Tabor, Tibar, Atabyros', *HUCA* 23 (1950–51), 357–386 (373–374), and Eph'al, 'Western Minorities', 85.

15 We have excluded toponyms from texts with uncertain datings, only to retain texts with a secure Neo-Babylonian date. Text no. 23 was written in Neirab city (line 9'), but the date is partly broken: (10') ^{iti}bár u_4 17-kam mu x-kam (11') [PN lugal] e^{ki}. Dhorme restores the name of Nabonidus in the broken part without reason (Dhorme, 'Neirab', 66). Fales hesitates between Nabonidus and Nebuchadnezzar IV (Fales, 'Neirab Texts', 138). Actually, the sole title of 'king of Babylon' seems to exclude the Persian kings, whose full title used to be 'king of Babylon, king of the lands', or more simply 'king of the lands'. It is with this title that Cambyses is mentioned in text no. 22 (line 13'). Dating prior to Nabonidus seems to be possible too. Text no. 26, mentioning the town of Neirab (lines 3, 6, 10), cannot be dated due to its fragmentary state.

16 Reading of the toponym is unclear. Dhorme read the town's name: (*âlu*) *Ša ... ḫa-tim* ('Neirab', 57). Oelsner proposed *Šala*$^{?}$*-ḫati* ('Neirab-Urkunden', 77 n. 41). Tablet no. 4 is broken in two parts and the crack is all over the town's name on line 14. Furthermore, it seems that the tablet condition worsened since Dhorme's study, and many signs having been drawn perfectly by Dhorme (see the copy of the tablet in 'Neirab', 77) have become illegible. We are proposing the following reconstructions, based upon Dhorme's copy and the photographs: (l. 14) uru *šá* $^{[lú]}$kù*.dim / *Ālu-ša-kutimmī* (the Town of gold- or silversmiths). The sign *šá* is no longer visible on the tablet, but is clear on Dhorme's copy. The signs kù.dim are visible on the tablet. The toponym *Ālu-ša-kutimmī* is not attested in other texts from the Neo-Babylonian period.

and Nargiya, son of Ḫananāya, are both present in Bīt-dayyān-Adad on the second day of *tašrītu* (vii) (no. 11) and in Ammat on the fourth day of *tašrītu* of the tenth year of Nabonidus (no. 12; 546 B.C.E.). We also notice that the same people appear in all four villages. Thus, Nuḫsāya, son of Nusku-gabbe, is attested in all of four places:

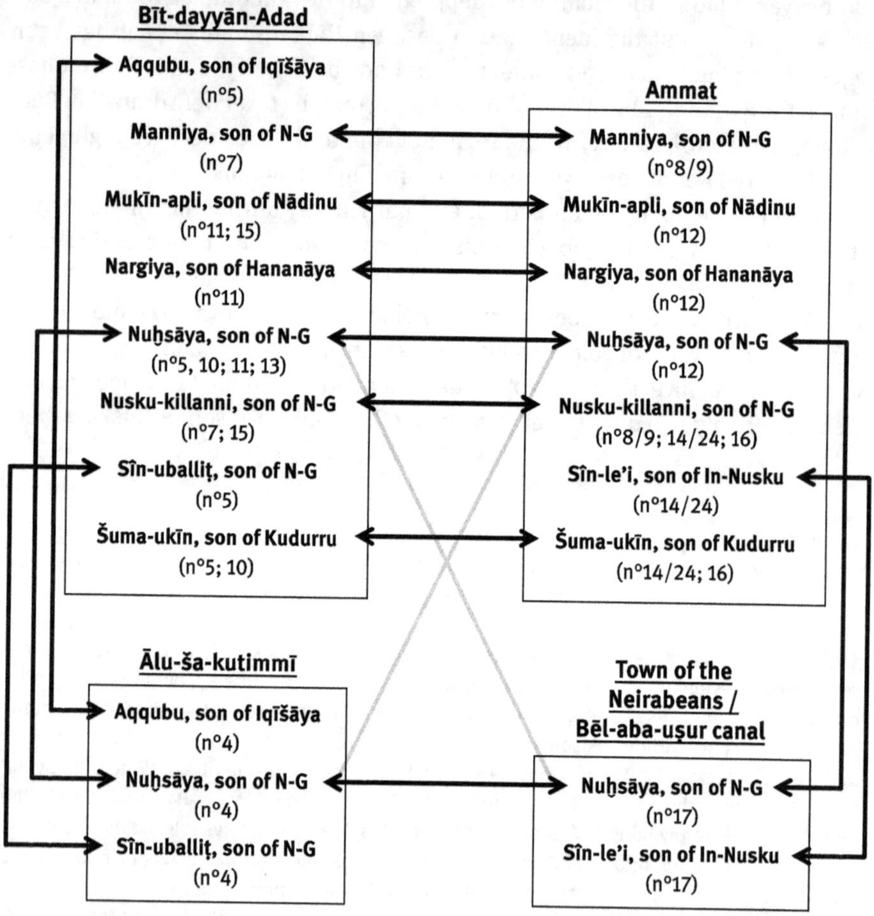

Fig. 1: The Neirabeans and the surrounding area during the Neo-Babylonian period

This ability of people to move around these four villages shows that they were relatively close to each other. As noticed by Eph'al, two of these toponyms are located in Babylonia, and more precisely in the region of Nippur. The village of Ammat is mentioned in several cuneiform texts from Nippur dated to the Neo-

Babylonian and early Persian periods,[17] and the Bēl-aba-uṣur canal is attested in the Murašû archive from fifth century B.C.E. Nippur.[18] Given that the four villages mentioned in the Neirab archive were close to each other and that two of them were located in the Nippur region, we should locate all four of them in that area.

2) Text no. 18, written in Bīt-dayyān-Adad or in Ammat, records a transaction of dates that were produced locally.[19] Date cultivation, typical in Babylonia, did not exist in northern Syria. In fact, the western limit of date palm cultivation lies in the Sūḫu region.[20] Text no. 18 therefore fits the Mesopotamian agricultural environment, but not that of Syria.[21]

3) Finally, the paleographic study of Cussini shows that the alphabetic letters of the Aramaic epigraphs on five of the Neirab tablets display characteristics very different from those found on texts from northern Syria at the time. She concluded that their shape and subject matter rather resemble those known from cuneiform tablets written in Babylonia during the Neo-Babylonian and Persian periods.[22]

1.2 Exile and Return: Historical Context of the Neirab Archive

As argued by I. Eph'al, deportation is the most likely hypothesis to explain the presence of a community of Syrian natives from Neirab in Babylonia.[23] Their deportation could have taken place some time towards the end of Nabopolassar's (626–605 B.C.E.) or the beginning of Nebuchadnezzar II's reign (605–562 B.C.E.).[24]

---

17 Ammat is attested in BE 8 40 dated 7/vii/0 Nbn (line 15: ^{uru}*am-mat*). It is also attested in several unpublished texts in the Istanbul Museum from the Nippur excavations: Ni 2673 from 19/viii/19 Nbk II (line 14: $^{\text{[uru]}}$*am-ma-tu*$_4$) and Ni 709 dated 25/vi/1 Camb (line 6: ^{uru}*a-mat*; line 11: ^{uru}*a-mat-tú*). I thank Francis Joannès for these references. For a short presentation of these unpublished tablets, see F. Joannès, 'Les tablettes cunéiformes d'époque néo-babylonienne de Nippur conservées au Musée de l'Ancien Orient d'Istanbul', *Travaux et Recherches en Turquie II* (1985), 187–194.

18 The Bēl-aba-uṣur canal is attested in the following: BE 9 65: 2, 14; PBS 2/1 104: 3, 6 and PBS 2/1 14: lower edge.

19 Cf. translation below § 3.2.1.

20 Paul-Eugène Dion, *Les Araméens à l'Âge du Fer: Histoire politique et structures sociales* (Études Bibliques Nouvelle Série 34; Paris: Gabalda, 1997), 334.

21 I thank Mustapha El Djabellaoui who suggested this argument to me.

22 Cussini, 'Aramaic Epigraphs', 1472–1473.

23 Eph'al, 'Western Minorities', 86–87.

24 Oelsner, 'Neirab-Urkunden', 76 and Timm, 'Texte aus Nērab', 285–286.

The Neo-Babylonian chronicles tell us that both kings carried out regular military campaigns against Ḫatti, the name traditionally given to northern Syria in these texts.[25] The following passage, for example, refers to an expedition in 604 B.C.E.:

> In (his) accession year Nebuchadnezzar (II) returned to Ḫatti. Until the month of *šabāṭu* (xi), he marched about victoriously in Ḫatti. In the month of *šabāṭu* (xi) he took the vast tribute of Hatti to Babylon (ABC 5: obv. 12–13).

Unlike Neo-Assyrian royal inscriptions, the Neo-Babylonian chronicles never explicitly mention deportations.[26] Instead, they use the general term of 'tribute' (*biltu*) without itemizing the different elements it consisted of, like in the following passage about Nebuchadnezzar II's first siege of Jerusalem in 597 B.C.E.:

> He encamped against the city of Judah (*Āl-Yāḫūdu*) and on the second day of the month *addaru* he captured the city (and) seized (its) king. A king of his own choice he appointed in the city (and) taking the vast tribute (*biltu*) he brought it into Babylon (ABC 5: rev. 12–13).

The Biblical account of these events leads us to think that deportees were included in the general term of 'tribute'.[27] In the same way, the mention of this term in connection with Ḫatti could also refer to deportees. The influx of Syrians in the region around Nippur is reflected in so-called 'toponymie en mirror', the practice of naming villages in Babylonia after the place of origin of their re-settled inhabitants:[28]

---

25 ABC 4 and 5. About the Babylonian military expeditions in the West and against Hatti specifically, see Oded Lipschits, 'Nebuchadrezzar's Policy in 'Ḫattu-Land' and the Fate of the Kingdom of Judah', *UF* 30 (1998), 467–487, and David Vanderhooft, 'Babylonian Strategies of Imperial Control in the West: Royal Practice and Rhetoric', in *Judah and the Judeans in the Neo-Babylonian Period* (ed. O. Lipschits and J. Blenkinsopp; Winona Lake: Eisenbrauns, 2003), 235–262.

26 For attestations of deportations in Neo-Assyrian sources, see Bustenay Oded, *Mass Deportations and Deportees in the Neo-Assyrian Empire* (Wiesbaden: Harrassowitz, 1979), 1–8.

27 The Hebrew Bible mentions several distinct waves of exiles. The first wave included king Jehoiachin (2 Kgs 24:8–17); a second wave of exiles is mentioned in 2 Kgs 25:8–12 (see also Jer 39:1–10 and 52:1–16). Jeremiah, controversially, also knows about a third wave following the murder of the governor of Judah (Jer 52:28–30).

28 For a detailed study of this phenomenon, we refer to Charpin's work on the Old Babylonian period, see Dominique Charpin, 'La "toponymie en miroir" à l'époque amorrite', *RA* 97 (2003), 3–34.

Syrian toponyms	Names in Babylonia	References	Dates
Neirab	*Town of the Neirabeans*	no. 17: 14	1/x/15 Nbn
	Neirab	no. 19: 7; 23: 9'; 26: 3, 6, 10	17/i/[-]; 13/[-]/1 Camb; [-]
Quramat	*Town of the Quramateans*	BE 8 25	8/viii/40 Nbk II
	Quramat	Ni 3149: 12[29]	21/iii/1 Ner
Qadeš	*Qadeš*	BM 81-4-28, 88[30]; ROMCT 2 2: 17	22/iv/40 Nbk II; 24/iv/41 Nbk II

Fig. 2: 'Toponymes miroirs' from northern Syria in the Nippur region

These Syrian towns are part of a greater set of 'toponymes miroirs' known from 6th century B.C.E. Babylonia, such as Sidon, Tyre, Judah and Gaza.[31] They were

29 I thank Francis Joannès for the reference of this unpublished text in the Istanbul Museum. This village named Quramat, or Town of the Quramateans, has probably been established after deportations concerning Quramati in northern Syria where a military campaign led by Nabopolassar in 606 B.C.E. took place and where the king settled his military camp, see ABC 4: 20–25, in Albert Kirk Grayson, *Assyrian and Babylonian Chronicles* (TCS 5; Locust Valley: Augustin, 1975), 98. This strategy, which consists in deporting a population and in settling on this place a garrison, is attested too during the Neo-Assyrian Period, see Oded, *Deportations*, 45.

30 T. G. Pinches, 'Babylonian Contract-Tablets with Historical References', in *Records of the Past, 2nd Series, Vol. IV* (ed. A. H. Sayce; London: S. Bagster & Sons, 1890), 96–108. See also: F. Joannès, 'La localisation de Ṣurru', 37 (text no. 4).

31 About toponyms of exiles from Asia Minor, Phoenicia, Syria and Palestine, see Eph'al, 'Western Minorities', 80–83. Since then, Francis Joannès published several articles about the case of Tyre in Babylonia, the place where deportees from Tyre settled. Its location between Sippar and Uruk remains relatively imprecise, cf. Joannès, 'La localisation de Ṣurru' and 'Trois textes de Ṣurru à l'époque néo-babylonienne', *RA* 81 (1987), 147–166. We can also add the town of Sidon (YOS 19 32: 8, 14 and Paul-Alain Beaulieu, *Legal and Administrative Texts from the Reign of Nabonidus* [YOS 19; New Haven: Yale University Press, 2000], 7 n. 18) and the town of Judah (see the article by Laurie Pearce in this volume). This last toponym *Āl-Yāhūdu* refers to Jerusalem. Indeed, this expression is used by the Babylonian scribes in the *Chronicle* which reports the siege of the city in 597 B.C.E. (ABC 5: rev. 12'), see Francis Joannès and André Lemaire, 'Trois tablettes cunéiformes à onomastique ouest-sémitique', *Transeuphratène* 17 (1999), 24–25. S. Dalley contested the reality of these 'toponymes miroirs' in Babylonia while publishing a cuneiform tablet from Harran found at Tell Tawilan in Jordan. According to Dalley the document proves the use of cuneiform in these regions, see Dalley, 'Tell Tawilan'. Joannès proposed a new reading and interpretation of the text to explain the 'journey' of this tablet suggesting that it moved by military movements at the beginning of the reign of Darius I or II, see Francis Joan-

created by the Neo-Babylonian kings for two reasons: to gain control of northern Syria, Phoenicia and Palestine, and to re-invigorate the region around Nippur by settling deportees on abandoned farmlands. This last point was made by Eph'al: 'All these data give the impression of masses of people brought to the Nippur region (and perhaps also to other areas in Babylonia) as part of an intensive effort by Nebuchadnezzar and his successors to rehabilitate that region, which had suffered severely during the Assyro-Babylonian wars in the seventh century B. C.'.[32]

To conclude, a town with the name of Neirab was situated in the region of Nippur, in the midst of a number of 'toponymes miroirs' connected to the deportations of the first Neo-Babylonian kings. Soon after their settlement in Babylonia, some deportees from Neirab started to use the clay tablet and cuneiform script to record their business affairs. Then, during the reign of Darius I, after a period of exile of more or less forty years,[33] they returned home to their original Neirab in Syria, bringing with them some of the documents they had drafted in Babylonia. The Neirab texts thus allow us to follow the activities of a community of Syrian deportees during their exile in Babylonia.

2 Cultural Aspects within the Community of Neirabeans in Babylonia

Onomastics and the study of the language and script of the texts of Neirab allow us to obtain some information about the cultural identity of the community settled in the Nippur region and to measure the influence exerted by their new Babylonian environment.

nès, 'À propos de la tablette cunéiforme de Tell Tawilan', *RA* 81 (1987), 165–166. Cagni critically assessed Eph'al's work regarding Neirab and Joannès' work regarding Tyre by asserting that the cuneiform tablets mentioning the towns of Milid, Ashkelon, Gaza, Tyre and Qadeš have been 'trouvées en Syrie' (Cagni, 'Textes babyloniens de Neirab', 179). But those tablets come from Babylonia, chiefly the region of Nippur (Eph'al, 'Western Minorities', 80).

32 Eph'al, 'Western Minorities', 81–82. The same policy of repopulating abandoned or desolate regions was in place during the Neo-Assyrian period, see Oded, 'Deportation', 67–74.

33 The regnal year of Darius I is broken in text no. 27. However, Eph'al considers this text as being from the beginning of his reign, arguing that there should only be a small gap between text no. 27 and the second last text (no. 21 from the reign of Cambyses) because both mention Nusku-na'id, son of Sîn-le'i among the witnesses (Eph'al, 'Western Minorities', 87 n. 39).

2.1 Onomastics and Cultural Aspects

The Neirab texts contain numerous names from the western part of the Ancient Near East. Édouard Dhorme noticed that twenty-two names, out of one hundred, were West Semitic.[34] New studies later added to this list. Mario Fales estimated that 29 % of the Neirab names were Aramaic, 52 % Babylonian, and the remaining ones of uncertain origin.[35] However, onomastics alone are insufficient to identify the members of the Neirab community in Babylonia. Many Syrian deportees appear with Babylonian names in the contracts, such as the descendants of Nusku-gabbe.

2.1.1 Onomastic Aspects of the Nusku-gabbe Family

According to the Neirab texts, Nusku-gabbe had at least five children – Nuḫsāya (or Nuḫšāya),[36] Sîn-uballiṭ, Manniya, Nusku-killanni, and Sîn-aba-uṣur – and one grand-child, Nusku-iddina. Only Nusku-gabbe bears an Aramaic name, meaning 'Nusku is exalted'.[37] In the Aramaic epigraph of text no. 12, he is perhaps mentioned with the nickname *Aba*, 'Father'.[38] His six descendants all have Babylonian names.

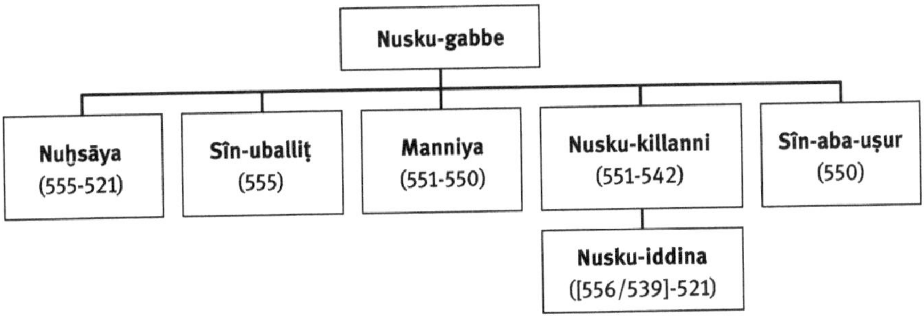

Fig. 3: The sons of Nusku-gabbe[39]

34 Dhorme, 'Neirab', 54.
35 Fales, 'Neirab Texts', 141 n. 32.
36 This name is written Nuḫsāya: no. 6: 4; 10: 3; 11: 4; 12: 3; 13: 8; 17: 4; 18: 6, Nuḫšāya: no. 2: 4; 5: 3 and Našuḫāya: no. 4: 4. In the remainder of the article, we will generally use the form Nuḫsāya which is the most frequent spelling in the Babylonian texts. It is also the only spelling (*nhsy*) used in the Aramaic epigraph (no. 12: left edge). For a discussion of these various spellings, see below.
37 The term *gabbe* (written *gab-e* or *gab-bi-i/e*), comes from the Aramaic root *gbh* ('to be high'), see F. Mario Fales, 'West Semitic names in the Šēḫ-Ḫamad Texts', *SAAB* 7 (1993), 139–150 (145).
38 Cf. below § 2.2.
39 For the chronological data of the Nusku-gabbe family, see Fales, 'Neirab Texts', 132–137.

Studying these names reveals two essential points. We notice that some Babylonian names are in fact adaptations of West Semitic names and we observe a strong affection for the lunar cult.

1. ***Babylonian names adapted from Aramaic names.*** One may wonder whether this constitutes a deliberate choice of the parents, for instance to ease their children's integration in the new Babylonian environment by giving them Babylonian names, or whether this results from an 'Akkadianization' of West Semitic names by the Babylonian scribes responsible for drafting the contracts. Text no. 4 sheds some light on this issue. In this text, Nuḫsāya and Sîn-uballiṭ, two sons of Nusku-gabbe, appear with slightly different spellings:

No. 4

(1–5)2.700 litres of barley, capital belonging to Šar-gabbi-le'i, son of Ilqataru*, is the debt of Našuḫāya and Šena-uballiṭ, sons of Nusku-gabbe. (6–7)In *ayyāru* (ii) they will deliver barley with 48 *qû* per *kurru* (as interest), at the door of the silo.

(8–9)They shall each bear responsibility for one another for payment of barley.

(10–12)Witnesses: Aqqubu, son of Iqišaya; Nusku-rimnu, son of Rimiya.

(13)And the scribe: Rēmūt, son of [...]-zakir.

(14–16)*Ālu-ša-kutimmī*?*, 24th *ulūlu* (vi), accession year of Nabonidus, king of Babylon (556 B.C.E.).

M. Fales noticed that the name Nuḫš/sāya was written here as Našuḫāya (Id*na-šuḫ-a-a*), a West Semitic pronunciation of the name of the god Nusku.[40] In most contracts, however, the Aramaic name Našuḫāya (NŠḪ) was transformed by a metathesis in Nuḫš/sāya, a proper Babylonian name derived from the root NḪŠ ('abundance, plenty').[41] In the same way, we notice that in text no. 4 the divine name in the name Sîn-uballiṭ is written following a West Semitic pronun-

40 Fales, 'Neirab Texts', 134–135. For different Aramaic pronunciations of the god Nusku (Našuḫ, Nušuḫ, Nušḫu), see Edward Lipiński, *The Aramaeans: Their Ancient History, Culture, Religion* (OLA 100; Leuven: Peeters, 2000), 621.

41 Fales, 'Neirab Texts', 134. The origin of the phonetic alternation between the name Nuḫšāya and Nuḫsāya is difficult to determine. For Dhorme the sounds *šin* and *śin* were not very relevant in Aramaic (Dhorme, 'Neirab', 55). Two explanations seem to be possible. First, the Babylonians themselves made this alternation: the same scribe, Šuma-ukīn, son of Kudurru, wrote the name Nuḫsāya (no. 6: 4 and 10: 3) or Nuḫšāya (no. 5: 3). Let us add that a few names are written with the sound *śin* instead of *šin* (Ištar-nuḫsi, Ili-nuḫsi, cf. *CAD* N/2, 320b). Secondly, it is possible that the Aramaic pronunciation of the two sounds was not realized to the extent that Akkadian scribes might not have been able to distinguish the two sounds as allophones. In both cases, the resemblance of sound between the roots *naḫāšu* ('abundance, plenty') and *naḫāsu* ('to go back, to return') facilitated the alternation of the name Nuḫš/sāya.

ciation by adding a phonetic complement: Šena-uballiṭ (^{Id}30na-din).[42] Besides the spelling of these two names, text no. 4 shows two more peculiarities: it is the only text drafted in the city of *Ālu-ša-kutimmī*$^{?}$* and it is the only one written by the scribe Rēmūt son of [...]-zakir. In fact, we notice that only a small number of scribes appear in the Neirab contracts. Thus, of ten contracts mentioning Nuḫš/saia[43], six were written by Šuma-ukīn, son of Kudurru, and by Mukīn-apli, son of Nādinu in the villages of Bīt-dayyān-Adad and Ammat.[44] They usually wrote a Babylonian version of his name: Nuḫš/sāya. It is difficult to know who is responsible for the 'Akkadianization' of this name: Nuḫš/sāya or the scribes? What does become clear, however, is that some of Nusku-gabbe's sons still bore West Semitic names, and that their Babylonian names were simply adapted from their original Aramaic ones. Whatever the case may be, the scribe of no. 4 took care of writing the names of Nusku-gabbe's sons following their Western pronunciation. There is one other clue that shows the Aramaic origin of the family members despite their Babylonian names. In the Aramaic endorsements of texts no. 7 and 15, the divine name included in Nusku-killanni is written Nušku (*nwšk*); this spelling is closer to the Aramaic form Nušḫu.

In most cases, the divine names Sîn and Nusku are written with ideograms (^{d}30 and ^{d}enšada) but we do not know how they were pronounced. The three examples from the names of Nusku-gabbe's sons which we presented show that these divine names could be pronounced with West Semitic versions: Šena and Našuḫ/Nušḫu.[45]

2. *Names related to the lunar cult.* The study of the names of Nusku-gabbe's sons reveals a particular affection for the lunar cult. Most names – whether their pronunciations are Babylonian or West Semitic – are related to the moon-god Sîn and his son Nusku: Našuḫāya, Sîn-uballiṭ, Nusku-killanni, Sîn-aba-uṣur and Nusku-iddina. The cults of the moon-god, his consort Nikkal, and his son Nusku occupied a special place among people coming from Northern Syria.[46] The city of Neirab was a religious centre dedicated to the moon-god, as testified by two

42 Fales, 'Neirab Texts', 135 and n. 15.

43 Texts no. 4: 4–5; 5: 3–4; 6: 4; 10: 3–4; 11: 4; 12: 3–4; 13: 8–9; 17: 3–4 and 18: 6.

44 Texts written by Šuma-ukīn, son of Kudurru, are no. 5 (Bīt-dayyān-Adad), 6 ([GN]) and 10 (Bīt-dayyān-Adad); by Mukīn-apli, son of Nādinu, are no. 11 (Bīt-dayyān-Adad), 12 (Ammat) and 18 ([GN]). One text has been written by another scribe, Iddin-Marduk, son of Nab-ēṭir, in the town of the Neirabeans (no. 17). Additionally, the scribe's name is broken in two texts mentioning Nuḫsāya: no. 2 ([GN]) and 13 (Bīt-dayyān-Adad).

45 See also the remarkable case of Bēl/Yāhu-šarra-uṣur discussed by Laurie Pearce in this volume.

46 Lipiński, *The Aramaeans*, 620–623.

funeral stelas discovered *in situ* dated from the seventh century B.C.E.[47] The cult of the moon-god in Neirab can be traced back at least to the first half of the second millennium, as shown by a votive statuette dedicated to 'the god of Neirab'.[48] If the affection for the cult of Sîn and his family is obvious in the onomastics of Nusku-gabbe's family names, it is also in text no. 26 which mentions several times in a very fragmentary context the god 'Sîn of Neirab'.[49]

2.1.2 General Onomastic Aspects of the Neirabean Community

The example of the Nusku-gabbe family shows that it is impossible to determine an individual's ethnic origin solely through a philological analysis of their names. Thus, in the case of the Neirabeans, two criteria are relevant: a full name (PN, son of PN) comprising a West Semitic element and a name related to the lunar cult. We must specify that the coming examples do not constitute an exhaustive study of the onomastics of the Neirab texts. There are still many problematic readings that await collation in the Aleppo Museum.[50]

---

47 The Neirab stelas were the subject of a first publication by Charles Clermont-Ganneau, *Études d'Archéologie Orientale* II (Paris: Librairie Émile Bouillon, 1897), 182–223. G. Conteneau dated them to the Neo-Babylonian period (Georges Conteneau, *Manuel d'archéologie orientale depuis les origins jusqu'à l'époque d'Alexandre: vol. III: Histoire de l'art (fin); Premier millénaire jusqu'à Alexandre; Appendices* [Paris: Picard, 1931], 1365–1366), while Rosenthal asserted that they are from the seventh century (Franz Rosenthal, *Die aramäistische Forschung seit Th. Nöldeke's Veröffentlichungen* [Leiden: Brill, 1939], 27). For an edition of the inscriptions on the stela of Neirab, see John C. L. Gibson, *Textbook of Syrian Semitic Inscriptions: Volume II: Aramaic Inscriptions, Including Inscriptions in the Dialect of Zenjirli* (Oxford: Clarendon, 1975), 93–98. See also the edition and recent bibliography in Dirk Schwiderski, *Die Alt- und Reichsaramäischen Inschriften: Band 2: Texte und Bibliographie* (Berlin: de Gruyter, 2004), 306.

48 Georges Dossin, 'Une inscription cunéiforme de Haute Syrie, ext. de Revue d'Assyriologie, 1930, 85', *Syria* 11 (1930), 387–388.

49 For Dhorme this text records the transfer of a sanctuary (*atmanu*) of Sîn (Dhorme, 'Neirab', 67). However, his reading of line 10 ([*ina muḫḫi a*]*t-man* (*ilu*) *Sin šá* (*âlu*) *Ni-ri-bi*) seems to us difficult to accept. Indeed, the term *atmanu* is mostly used in a literary context and is unexpected in a simple contract from daily life (*CAD* A/2, 495b–497a). Collations are desirable on this tablet which is preserved in the Aleppo Museum with the museum number 3495 (Cagni, 'Textes babyloniens de Neirab', 174).

50 For general comments on names mentioned in the Neirab texts, see Ran Zadok, 'The Representation of Foreigners in Neo- and Late- Babylonian Legal Documents (Eighth through Second Centuries B.C.E.)', in *Judah and the Judeans in the Neo-Babylonian Period* (ed. O. Lipschits and J. Blenkinsopp; Winona Lake: Eisenbrauns, 2003), 471–589 (556–558).

1. ***West Semitic names.*** In the Neirab texts, people bearing West Semitic names can be split up into two groups: the first with full West Semitic names and the second with mixed Babylonian and West Semitic names. A third group consists of family groups including people whose name is broken.

In spite of the fragmented state of the Neirab texts we can identify some people with a full West Semitic name among the hundred or so names registered: Abī-râm, son of Idrāya (no. 17: 10); Adad-râm, son of Iddiya (no. 14: 13 / no. 24: 11); Amsuri*, son of Iqqubā (no. 7: 10); Bar-aḫḫāya, son of Kukizza (no. 23: 1, 9); Bīt-il-ḫadir, son of Iliya-šimmu (no. 14: 14 / no. 24: 11); Ilteri-nūru, son of Nusku-rape (no. 19: 11); Našuḫ-râm, son of Aḫi-nūri (no. 2: 16); Samsa-igmur, son of Giḫilā (no. 20: 10);[51] Zabidāya, son of Ḫariya (no. 8: 16 / no. 9: 17); Zabini, son of Ruqqā (no. 8: 14 / no. 9: 15).

Individuals with a Babylonian name, but whose fathers bear a West Semitic name, are also present: Allānu, son of Abdā (no. 23: 14); Nargiya, son of Ḫananāya (no. 6: 11 / no. 11: 2 / no. 12: 2 / no. 19: 10); Šar-gabbi-le'i, son of Ilqataru* (no. 4: 2); Ušēzib, son of Qatirā (no. 10: 8). To these names, we can add those of Nusku-gabbe's sons and grandson: Manniya, Sîn-aba-uṣur, Nusku-killanni, Sîn-uballiṭ and Nusku-iddina. The Neirab texts also register people bearing a West Semitic name, while their fathers had a Babylonian name: Aqqubu, son of Iqīšāya (no. 4: 10 / no. 5: 10); Barīkiya and Gur-[...], sons of Nabû-bani (no. 20: 6);[52] Barīki, son of Nusku-šarra-uṣur (no. 23: 3'); Dalanī, son of Isinnāya (no. 8: 15 / no. 9: 16); Ḫidirāya, son of Nargiya (no. 2: 14); Iltammeš-ili, son of Šar-gabbi-le'i (no. 10: 2); Šer-idri, son of Sîn-kāṣir (no. 15: 11); Za<ba>du, son of Edu-ana-ummīšu (no. 16: 1). In some families, there was a succession of Aramaic and Babylonian names.[53] This fact is particulary visible within the family of Ḫananāya, whose name is of West Semitic origin. As for his son Nargiya, he bears a Babylonian name. This man was active between the third year of Nabonidus (no. 6) and the first year of Cambyses (no. 19), i.e. between 553 and 528 B.C.E. A witness mentioned in a sale contract concerning Nuḫsāya could be his son (no. 2). He appears with a West Semitic name: Ḫidirāya, son of Nargiya (lines 14–15). This last text can be dated to Nebu-

51 The reading of the name Samsa-igmur is proposed by Dalley, 'Tell Tawilan', 21 n. 2. A collation of the tablet in the Aleppo Museum is necessary to confirm this reading.

52 Though lacunal, the name Gur-[...] can be put together with the many West Semitic names beginning with this syllable. See Ran Zadok, *On West Semites in Babylonia during the Chaldean and Achaemenian Periods: An Onomastic Study* (Jerusalem: H. J. & Z. Wanaarta, 1977), 369b.

53 In spite of mixed onomastics, some individuals are clearly of Babylonian origin. This is the case of the scribe Nabu-šuma-uṣur whose father Zabini bears a West Semitic name, but whose ancestor's name, Dābibī, shows that his family was Babylonian (no. 19: 15). The choice Zabini as a name may then relate to a personal choice of the family.

chadnezzar IV.[54] To conclude, it seems that the Babylonian names which appear in these family groups with mixed names are mostly Akkadianized names.[55]

Some people bear West Semitic names, but due to damages their ancestors' or descendants' names cannot be identified: [PN], son of Amše (no. 13: 4); Adad-[...], son of Ḫarimmā (no. 17: 1); Addiya, son of [PN] (no. 3: 11); Barīkiya, son of [PN] (no. 22: 1); Iltammeš-dalā, son of [...]-riya (no. 20: 3); Ninurta-[...], son of Kuššiya (no. 12: 7); Šamaš-tallamā (no. 26: 2); Šamašiya (no. 26: 5, 12); Šena-il*, son of [PN] (no. 10: 6). Finally, we notice that Šer-idri, a slave of the Nusku-gabbe family, appears without patronym, as was the Babylonian custom (no. 8: 2, 5, 13 / no. 9: 3, 5, 10).

2. *Names related to the lunar cult.* A large number of names mentioned in the Neirab archive contain the divine name Nusku: Nusku-šarra-uṣur (no. 5: 2 / no. 23: 3), Tabni-Nusku (no. 27: 2), Pāni-Nusku-lūmur (no. 7: 3 / no. 15: 2), Nusku-iddina (no. 1: 3 / no. 18: 7 / no. 19: 4), Nusku-irakkas (no. 27: 3), Nusku-KUR-AL-šu (no. 3: 8), Nusku-na'id (no. 21: 1 / no. 27: 2), Nusku-rimnu (no. 4: 4), Nusku-šešir? (no. 26: 7), In-Nusku (no. 7: 4 / no. 14: 4 / no. 17: 3 / no. 18: 5), Nusku-mat-tukkin (no. 1: 2) and Nusku-rape (no. 19: 3). In the majority of cases, the divine name Nusku is written logographically, i.e. ^{d}enšada. On rare occasions, the god's name is spelled following a typically Aramaic pronunciation such as Našuḫ-râm (^{d}*na-šuḫ*; no. 2: 16). The moon-god is also well-represented in the archive. Although Sîn was a popular deity in Babylonia as well, it is often possible to distinguish between persons of West Semitic and Babylonian origin bearing names referring to this deity. Some people have West Semitic ancestors such as Sîn-uballiṭ and Sîn-aba-uṣur, Nusku-gabbe's sons.[56] In other cases the moon-god's name is written phonetically (^{d}*še-e-ri*; no. 8: 2, 5, 11 and 13) or with a phonetic complement added

54 Oelsner prefers to date this text to Nebuchadnezzar II (605–562 B.C.E.). For him, it seems rather impossible that Nuḫsāya, son of Nusku-gabbe, mentioned up to the 15th year of Nabonidus, i.e. 541 B.C.E. (no. 17), reappears under Nebuchadnezzar IV, in 521, after 20 years of inactivity (Oelsner, 'Neirab-Urkunden', 69). But several difficulties remain for dating this text securely to Nebuchadnezzar II's rule: 1) The archive of the Nusku-gabbe family is not fully preserved and it is therefore uncertain whether archival lacunae reflect periods of inactivity. 2) Our proposition to identify Ḫidirāya, son of Nargiya, mentioned in text no. 2, with the son of Nargiya, son of Ḫananāya, mentioned under Nabonidus' and Cambyses' reigns, would date this text under Nebuchadnezzar IV reign, at the moment when the second generation of the Ḫananāya family becomes active.

55 See Zadok, 'Foreigners', 556–558.

56 On the contrary, some people with an ancestor's name containing the name Sîn, are clearly of Babylonian origin, like Kalbāya, son of Iqīša-Marduk, descendant of Sîn-tabni, who appears among witnesses in no. 7: 7–8).

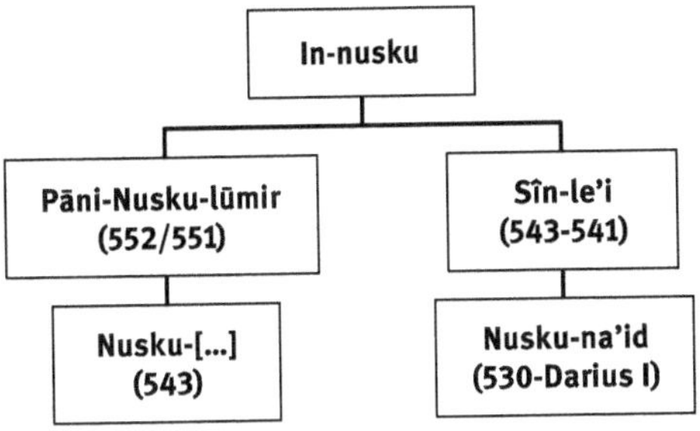

Fig. 4: The descendants of In-Nusku[57]

to the ideogram to indicate an Aramaic pronunciation ($^{d}30^{er}$; no. 9: 3, 5, 10 and 12 / no. 15: 11). Names composed of Nusku and Sîn often circulated in the same family, like in the case of Nusku-gabbe (see Fig. 3) and one Nusku-irakkas, son of Gabbe-[...]-Sin (no. 27: 3). This phenomenon is also illustrated by the In-Nusku family (see Fig. 4). The data from Neirab allow us to mark out the genealogy of this family, whose members appear in relationship with Nusku-gabbe's sons over two generations.[58] The names in this family show the same characteristics as those in Nusku-gabbe's family: they are Babylonian in origin but their theophorous element is composed only of Sîn and Nusku.

In the context of the Neirab archive, we can therefore conclude that a majority of the families whose members bear names containing the divine names Nusku and Sîn originate in the Western provinces and more precisely in the Northern Syria. Their Babylonian names are an adaptation of West Semitic names.[59]

2.1.3 A Large Community of Exiles?

We can consider as Neirabeans the majority of people who are mentioned with a complete West Semtic name, people who belong to a family group with mixed Babylonian / West Semitic names and people whose names contain the divine names Nusku and Sîn. Following these criteria, it seems that more than 3/5th of the people mentioned in the Neirab texts must be of West Semitic origin. We also notice that the Babylonians in the Neirab texts are mostly cited among the wit-

57 On members of this family, see Fales, 'Neirab Texts', 139–141.
58 On links between the two families, see Fales, 'Neirab Texts', 139.
59 About this question, see Zadok's remark about text no. 1: 'Both parties bear Akkadian anthroponyms and father's names (as far as they are fully preserved), but containing Nusku (therefore it is likely that they are Akkadianized North-Syrians)', Zadok, 'Foreigners', 557.

nesses; the scribes are always of Babylonian origin.[60] In several contracts, only the scribe is of Babylonian origin, such as in text no. 10:

Text no. 10

(1–4)2.790 litres of barley, capital belonging to Iltammeš-ili, son of Šar-gabbi-le'i, is the debt of Nuḫsāya, son of Nusku-gabbe. (4–5) In *ayyāru* (ii), he will deliver the barley in its capital amount.

(6–9)The witnesses: Šena-il*, son of [PN]; Nusku-killanni, son of Nusku-gabbe; Ušēzib, son of Qatira'.

(9–10)The scribe: Mukīn-apli, son of Kudurru.

(10–12) Bīt-dayyān-Adad, 20th of *šabāṭu* (xi), ninth [year] of Nabonidus, king of Babylon (= 546 B.C.E.).

Due to the presence in the Neirab texts of individuals with a West Semitic background it is necessary to discuss the nature of the mixture of languages attested in the archive.

2.2 Babylonian and Aramaic: Linguistic Aspects of the Neirab Archive

Text no. 7 illustrates the complexity of the linguistic questions that arise from the Neirab archive. It registers a loan of 8½ shekels of silver by Manniya, son of Nusku-gabbe, to his brother Nusku-killanni:

Text no. 7

(1–4)8 shekels ½ of one eighth alloy belonging to Manniya, son of Nusku-gabbe, is the debt of Nusku-killanni, son of Nusku-gabbe. (5–6)At the end of *dūzu* (iv), he will pay the silver according to the current tariff of* the land*.

(7–11)Witnesses: Kalbāya, son of Iqīša-Marduk, descendant of Sîn-tabni; Pāni-Nusku-lūmur, son of In-Nusku; Amsur[i]*, son of Iqqubā.

(11–12)Scribe: Kidin-Marduk, son of [PN].

(13–15)Bīt-dayyān-Adad, seventh [day of MN], fourth year of Nabonidus, king of Babylon (= 552–551 B.C.E.).

Aramaic epigraph: (Edges)*Document of Nusku-killanni, silver.*

60 See Oelsner, 'Neirab-Urkunden', 77 and n. 41.

Two witnesses probably belonged to the Neirabean community: Pāni-Nusku-lūmur, son of In-Nusku, and Amsuri, son of Iqqubā. A third witness, Kalbāya, son of Iqīša-Marduk, descendant of Sîn-tabni, and the scribe Kidin-Marduk, son of [PN], are Babylonians. The contract bears an Aramaic epigraph written on the tablet's edges: *šṭr nwšklny ksp'* ('Document of Nusku-killanni, silver'). This endorsement shows that Nusku-gabbe's sons were able to read and/or write in Aramaic. In that case, one wonders why they needed to record this transaction in Babylonian on a clay tablet instead of one single contract in Aramaic on parchment. Of the 27 texts in their archive, five have an Aramaic epigraph:

Text	Abstract	Aramaic epigraph
16/xi/[-] Ner **(no. 3)**	Promissory note of barley belonging to [PN], son of [PN], against [Nuḫš/sāya], son of Nusku-[gabbe][61]	(reverse)*[šṭr nḫs]* ⌜*y*⌝ (left edge)*y k[...]*[62] [Document of Nuḫsa]ya, ...
7/[-]/4 Nbn **(no. 7)**	Promissory note of silver belonging to Manniya, son of Nusku-gabbe, against Nusku-killanni, son of Nusku-gabbe	(obverse-lower edge)*šṭr nwšk* (left edge)*lny ks* (upper edge)*p'* Document of Nusku-killanni, silver
4/vii/10 Nbn **(no. 12)**	Sale contract of Nargiya, son of Ḫananāya, to Nuḫsāya, son of Nusku-gabbe	(left edge)*nḫsy* (obverse)*br 'b'*[63] Nuḫsāya, son of Father
27/xii/12 Nbn **(no. 15)**	Promissory note of barley belonging to Nusku-[...], son of Nabu-ri-[...], against Nusku-killanni, son of Nusku-gabbe	(obverse)*nwšklny* (left edge)*š 'r[n]* Nusku-killanni, barley
15/xii/[-] Nbn **(no. 18)**	Promissory note of barley belonging to [PN] against Sîn-le'i, son of In-Nusku, Nuḫsāya, son of Nusku-gabbe and Nusku-iddina, son of Nusku-killanni	(left edge)*lsn'l* To Sîn-le'i

Fig. 5: The Aramaic epigraphs on the Neirab texts

61 For the reconstruction of the name of Nuḫš/sāya, see Oelsner, 'Neirab-Urkunden', 75.
62 Reconstruction proposed by Oelsner, 'Neirab-Urkunden', 69. See also Cussini, 'Aramaic Epigraphs', 1462–1463, who points out that the interpretation of the two letters on the left edge remains difficult.
63 Oelsner suggested reading the last letters: *g'b'*, for (Nusku)-gabbe (Oelsner, 'Neirab-Urkunden', 75). Cussini disputes this suggestion and prefers: *'b'* ('Father'), Cussini, 'Aramaic Epigraphs', 1464. This reading had already been proposed by Dhorme, 'Neirab', 60.

In promissory notes, it is always the debtor's name which is written in Aramaic. Sometimes, the epigraph also adds information about the nature of the loan with the terms 'silver' or 'barley'. Perhaps the epigraphs were meant to be read by the creditor as 'aide memoire', to point out the debtor's name and the object of his loan. But it is also possible that these epigraphs were meant for someone else whose knowledge of Babylonian cuneiform was not enough to read the original contract. It is also conceivable that, in addition to these contracts in Babylonian cuneiform, a copy in Aramaic on parchment also existed. Compared with a hypothetical Aramaic copy, the cuneiform version had several advantages: the clay tablets were more easily handleable and available for consultation than papyrus or parchment documents generally closed by seals.[64] Furthermore, we may wonder if they were more admissible in a dispute in front of the Babylonian judicial authorities. In this case, the legal value of the clay tablets could be more important.

2.3 Conclusions from the Neirabean Onomasticon and the Linguistic Aspects of the Texts

The onomastic study of the Neirab texts reveals that some members of the Neirabean community deported to Babylonia adapted themselves to their new cultural environment by adopting Babylonian names and by getting involved in numerous activities (loans, purchases, marriage, witness statement, *etc.*), which required the drafting of documents in Babylonian cuneiform, on clay tablets with a legal value. At the same time, we notice that the Neirabean families preserved cultural traits of their own. The onomastic data show that during their exile in Babylonia they remained loyal to the lunar cult of their place of origin and some of them continue to use their mother tongue as we can see through a few letters inscribed in Aramaic, which helped those who did not master the Babylonian language to understand and to manage a part of the documents produced by their activities.

---

64 See Philippe Clancier, 'Les scribes sur parchemin du temple d'Anu', *RA* 99 (2005), 85–104 (92).

3 The Activities of the Sons of Nusku-Gabbe within the Community of Neirabeans

Among the twenty-seven contracts making up the Neirab archive, there are twenty promissory notes (*u'iltu*) of silver and barley.[65] Several historians have described the activities of Nusku-gabbe's sons as a 'firm', on a par with those of the Egibis and Murašûs.[66] When we have a closer look, however, it seems that Nusku-gabbe's sons played a particular role inside their own community, unlike the Egibis and Murašûs. In the following pages, I will argue that they were community leaders who provided loans and financial backing to their fellow Neirabeans in times of need.

3.1 A Particular Activity at the End and Beginning of the Babylonian Year

Most promissory notes in the Neirab date to the end and the beginning of the Babylonian year, i.e. before the new harvest of barley which took place in the month of *ayyāru* (April/May). The seasonality of the debt notes suggests that they may have sprung from periodic shortages in the barley supply.

---

65 Promissory notes of silver: no. 1, 7, 13, 14/24, 16, 19, 20, 21, 27. Promissory notes of barley: no. 3, 4, 5, 6, 10, 15, 17, 18. Others: no. 11, 12.

66 Fales, 'Neirab Texts', 137–142; Oelsner, 'Neirab-Urkunden', 72–74; Cagni, 'Textes babyloniens de Neirab', 172–173; Timm, 'Texte aus Nērab', 279.

3.1.1 General Characteristics of Promissory Notes of Silver

Eight promissory notes document silver loans (Fig. 6).[67]

Text	Amount	Creditor	Debtor	Term	Place
7/[-]/4 Nbn **(no. 7)**	8 shekels 1/2	Manniya, son of Nusku-gabbe (N-G)	Nusku-killanni, son of N-G	Month iv	Bīt-dayyān-Adad
29/xi/12 Nbn **(no. 14/24)**	4 shekels	Nusku-killanni, son of N-G	Sîn-le'i, son of In-Nusku	Month xii	Ammat
10/ii/13 Nbn **(no. 16)**	2 shekels 1/4	Za<ba>du, son of Edu-ana-ummīšu	Nusku-killanni, son of N-G	Month ii	Ammat
[-]/ii/3 Camb **(no. 20)**	[x] shekels	Iltammeš-dala', son of [...]-riya	Barīkiya et Gur-..., son of Nabû-bani	Month i	[...]-a'
1/xii/[-] Camb **(no. 21)**	4 shekels	[PN], son of Nusku-[...]	[PN], son of Nusku-[...]	Month xii	[...]
4/vi/Nbk IV **(no. 1)**	6 shekels 1/4	Šamaš-udammiq, son of Nusku-mat-tukkin	Nusku-iddina, son of Nusku-killanni	Month [-]	Babylon
[-]/[-]/[-] Dar **(no. 27)**	[x] mina	Nabû-iqbi, son of Tabni-Nusku	Nusku-irakkas, son of Gabbe-...-Sîn	Month i	[...]

Fig. 6: Promissory notes of silver

Their general characteristics are similar, even though they were drafted in the course of several decades:

1) The loans were contracted between the months of *šabāṭu* (January/February) and *ayyāru* (April/May) and usually concerned a modest quantity of silver (between 2 and 8 shekels, except for no. 27).
2) They were interest-free and short-term.

---

67 We do not consider here no. 13, which tells of the remainder of the sale of a donkey (see below § 3.2.1) and no. 19, the contract for the sale of the donkey, drafted as a promissory note (see below § 4.1.2). About the different transactions allowed by the promissory note formularies, see Cornelia Wunsch, 'Debt, Interest and Forfeiture in the Neo-Babylonian and Early Achaemenid Period: The Evidence from Private Archives', in *Debt and Economic Renewal in the Ancient Near East: Vol. III: A Colloquium Held at Columbia University, November 1998* (ed. M. Hudson and M. Van De Mieroop; Bethesda: CDL Press, 2002), 221–253 (224–229).

3) The loans were given among people who can be identified as members of the Neirabean community according to the criteria defined in the preceding pages. The following scenarios are documented:[68]

1. Sons of Nusku-gabbe exchange silver with other members of the Neirabean community. In this setting, sons of Nusku-gabbe borrow quantities of silver from or to people outside their own family. In no. 16 Nusku-killanni is debtor of 2.25 shekels of silver from Za<ba>du, son of Edu-ana-ummīšu. In no. 1 his son Nusku-iddina is debtor of 6.25 shekels of silver from Šamaš-udammiq, son of Nusku-mat-tukkin. The first creditor, Za<ba>du, bears a West Semitic name.[69] The name of Šamaš-udammiq's father, Nusku-mat-tukkin, betrays an affinity with the cult of Nusku popular in Neirab. Text no. 14/24, kept in two copies, refers to a quantity of 4 shekels of silver lent by Nusku-killanni, son of Nusku-gabbe, to Sîn-le'i, son of In-Nusku. This loan is without interest, but the debtor's cow is seized as a pledge. We saw that the onomastics of the In-Nusku family showed a strong attachment to the lunar cult which characterizes people of northern Syria and Neirab in particular.

2. Members of the family exchange silver to each other. Text no. 7 records an interest-free loan of 8.5 shekels of silver by Manniya to his brother Nusku-killanni.

3. Creditors and debtors not belonging to the Nusku-gabbe family. Two promissory notes mention no member of the Nusku-gabbe family, neither as debtor nor as creditor. In text no. 20, the creditor (Iltammeš-dalā) and debtors (Barīkiya and Gur$^{?}$-[...]) bear West Semitic names. In text no. 27, the divine name Nusku in the names of the creditor (Nabû-iqbi, son of Tabni-Nusku) and debtor (Nusku-irakkas, son of Gabbe-[...]-Sîn)[70] enables us to identify them as members of the Neirabean community.

68 No. 21 is too fragmentary to be included in any category. Note that the creditor's name ([PN] son of Nusku-[...]) and the debtor's ([PN] son of Nusku-[...]) both contain the divine name Nusku, which can be a criterion to identify members of the community of Neirabeans.

69 Zadok, *West Semites*, 119 and 335.

70 The reading of these names remains problematic. A collation of the tablets is desirable. No. 27 is kept in the Aleppo Museum with the museum number 3494 (Cagni, 'Textes babyloniens de Neirab', 174). No. 20 was never identified among the Neirab texts kept in Syria (Cagni, 'Textes babyloniens de Neirab', 174).

3.1.2 General Characteristics of the Promissory Notes of Barley

Text	Quantity	Creditor	Debtor	Term	Interest	Place
16/xi/[-] Ner **(no. 3)**	7,200 [+x] litres	[PN]	[Nuḫš/sāya], son of N-G[71]	[Month ii]		Bīt-dayyān-Adad
24/vi/0 Nbn **(no. 4)**	2,700 litres	Šar-gabbi-le'i, son of Ilqataru	Nuḫsāya, son of N-G	Month ii	27 %	*Ālu-ša-kutimmī*$^{?}$*
[-]/[-]/0 [Nbn] **(no. 5)**	[x] litres	Šar-bēlšunu, son of [...]-tarra	Nuḫsāya, son of N-G	Month ii	20 %	Bīt-dayyān-Adad
14$^{?}$-24$^{?}$/i/3 Nbn **(no. 6)**	3,600 litres	Barley from the royal treasury, belonging to [PN] son of Itti-Šamaš-[...], at the disposal of Ardiya	Nuḫsāya, son of N-G	Month ii	20 %	[...]
20/xi/ 9 Nbn **(no. 10)**	2,790 litres	Iltammeš-ili, son of Šar-gabbi-le'i	Nuḫsāya, son of N-G	Month ii		Bīt-dayyān-Adad
27/xii/12 Nbn **(no. 15)**	1,800 litres	Nusku-[...], son of Nabû-ri-[...]	Nusku-killanni, son of N-G	Month ii		Bīt-dayyān-Adad
1/x/16 Nbn **(no. 17)**[72]	4,620 litres	Adad-[...], son of Ḫarimma', the royal <mer>chant*	Nuḫsāya, son of N-G	Month ii		Town of the Neirabeans
15/xii/[-] Nbn **(no. 18)**	1,200 litres	The dates (must be paid off with barley) belong to [PN], from the farm rent due Nabu-ri-[...] under the control of Iqūpu	Sîn-le'i, son of In-Nusku, Nuḫsāya, son of N-G, and Nusku-iddina, son of Nusku-killanni	Month ii		[Bīt-dayyān-Adad / Ammat?][73]

Fig. 7: Eight Promissory notes of barley

71 This text is a contract drafted during Neriglissar's reign, at the end of the year (month xi), in which an individual, [PN] son of Nusku-[...], borrows barley (lines 4–5). This contract resembles the different promissory notes concluded at the end of the year by Nuḫsāya, son of Nusku-gabbe (no. 4, 5, 10, 17 and 18) and Nusku-killanni, son of Nusku-gabbe (no. 15). It is tempting to restore, like Oelsner, '[Nuḫš/saia] son of Nusku-[gabbe]' in lines 3–4 (Oelsner, 'Neirab-Urkunden', 69).

72 About this text see below § 3.2.2.

73 For the reconstruction of the city name, cf. below § 3.2.1.

We can make several observations about these promissory notes of barley:

1) Most of the barley loans were concluded at the end of the Babylonian year, between the months of *ṭebētu* (month x = December/January) and *nisannu* (month i = March/April), and they had to be reimbursed in the month of *ayyāru* (month ii = April/May), that is to say during the new crop (no. 3, 6, 10, 15, 17 and 18). These promissory notes therefore represent short-term loans. Only text no. 4 is a long-term barley loan, contracted in the month of *ulūlu* (month vi = August/September).
2) Why some barley loans were interest-bearing and others were not, is hard to explain. It is noteworthy that two out of three interest-bearing loans were drafted in the inaugural year of Nabonidus (555–554 B.C.E.). The first of these (no. 4) records an exceptionally high rate of 27 %. The second one (no. 5) evokes a previous promissory note due from Nuḫsāya and his brother Sîn-uballiṭ.[74] This means that the sons of Nusku-gabbe made at least three interest-bearing barley loans during the inaugural year of Nabonidus. The only other interest-bearing barley loan (no. 6) dates from shortly before the new crop, at a time of year when cereal reserves were running low. It is therefore possible that charging interest was a custom specifically related to times of shortage.
3) The loans of barley involve people of Western origin and particularly members of the Neirabean community. Nusku-gabbe's sons, including Nuḫsāya, Sîn-uballiṭ and Nusku-killanni, appear as debtors in these texts.[75] Some creditors were of West Semitic origin: Adad-[...], son of Ḫarimmā (no. 17), Iltammeš-ili, whose father Šar-gabbi-le'i bears a Babylonian name (no. 10), and Šar-gabbi-le'i, whose father Ilqataru bears an Aramaic name (no. 4).[76] Although originating in the Western provinces, it is not sure that all the creditors belong to the Neirab community, indeed, some belong to the crown administration.
4) Certain texts are connected with the royal administration. This is the case in no. 6, which records a more complex transaction than the other promissory notes in the archive, involving three persons: [PN] son of Itti-Šamaš-[...], a certain Ardiya, and Nuḫsāya son of Nusku-gabbe. The contract specifies that the barley originated in the royal treasury (*makkūr*

74 Text no. 5: '(7–9)Not including an earlier promissory note with which he (= Nuḫsāya) and Sîn-uballiṭ, his brothers, are debited.'

75 It is not sure that Nusku-gabbe's sons were not farmers or that they did not grow barley by themselves as Oelsner wrote ('Neirab-Urkunden', 74). The nature of the Neirab texts as a 'dead archive' leads us to be careful with arguments from silence (see below § 4.2).

76 The creditor's name is entirely destroyed in no. 3 and partially in no. 5 (Šar-bēlšunu, son of [...]-tarra) and no. 15 (Nusku-[...], son of Nabû-[...]).

šarri).[77] It is also the case in no. 17 where the creditor, Adad-[...], son of Ḫarimmā bears the title of 'royal <mer>chant*'.[78]

3.1.3 What Was the Purpose of These Exchanges of Silver and Barley?

In conclusion, we have seen that silver circulated inside the Neirabean community at the end of the Babylonian year. The sons of Nusku-gabbe were involved in silver exchanges, as creditors as well as debtors. The quantities of silver were modest and lent without interest. This kind of transaction can be qualified as loans of sociability, that is an exchange between two parties of which the purpose is not the enrichment of one of them but the strengthening of the personal links or the mutual aid within the community, especially in the harsh time before the new crop. At the same time, the sons of Nusku-gabbe borrowed barley from small farmers in agricultural villages close to Neirab and from the royal administration. The purpose of these loans of barley stays difficult to determine. All of them were too high for private use by the Nusku-gabbe family alone. For example, if we consider no. 10, we see that the quantity of barley (2,790 litres) exceeded the needs of the Nusku-gabbe family, as it could feed at least ten nuclear families during the three months until the new crop.[79] The loan may have been intended for redistribution within the community. As I will show in the following section, the particular status of Nusku-gabbe's descendants within the Neirab community explains their capacity to carry out interest-free exchanges.

3.2 A Leading Role within the Neirabean Community?

There are several signs that Nusku-gabbe's sons occupied a particular place within the Neirabean community in Babylonia. They enjoyed a rather comfort-

77 A collation of this text registered in Aleppo with the museum number M 3461 (Cagni, 'Textes babyloniens de Neirab', 174) is desirable.

78 About the reading of this title, see footnote no. 83 below.

79 On the nutritional value of barley, see most recently Michael Jursa, 'The Remuneration of Institutional Labourers in an Urban Context in Babylonia in the First Millennium B. C.', in *L'archive des Fortifications de Persépolis: État des questions et perspectives de recherches* (ed. P. Briant, W. Henkelman and M. Stolper; Persika 12; Paris: de Boccard, 2008), 387–427 (411) and Bojana Janković, 'Travel Provisions in Babylonia in the First Millennium B. C.', in *L'archive des Fortifications de Persépolis: État des questions et perspectives de recherches* (ed. P. Briant, W. Henkelman and M. Stolper; Persika 12; Paris: de Boccard, 2008), 429–464 (440–441).

able economic situation, as witnessed by the silver loans they granted and by their slave ownership.[80] Finally, several contracts show that the sons of Nusku-gabbe intervened in favour of a debtor to help him settle his debt. It seems that these texts illustrate the leading role played by the members of this family within the Neirabean community in Babylonia.

3.2.1 Guarantor for Purchases

Several texts show that Nusku-gabbe's sons played the role of guarantor for payments due by community members. In text no. 13 Nuḫsāya intervened to guarantee the purchase of a donkey:

Text no. 13
(1–4)[6 shekels of sil]ver, the remainder of the [price] of the donkey belonging to Balāṭu, [son of ...]-šame, is the debt of [PN], son of Amše. (5–6)[In month x], he will deliver the 6 shekels of silver in its capital amount. (7–8)[Nuḫ]saia, son of [Nusku]-gabbe, guarantees the payment of the silver.
(10–12)(Witnesses and scribe).
(13–15)[Bīt-dayyān]-Adad, the [-]th *ayyāru* (ii), 11th year of [Nabo]nidus, king of Babylon (= 545 B.C.E.).

In this text, Nuḫsāya assumes guarantee for the payment of 6 shekels of silver, due from the sale of a donkey by a person of West Semitic origin ([PN], son of Amše).[81] This sale had given occasion to the drafting of a first contract (not preserved) which was not paid by the buyer. Nuḫš/sāya resolved this conflict between the seller and the buyer by assuming the debt obligation of the latter (no. 13).

Text no. 18 may illustrate a similar role by the sons of Nusku-gabbe. This contract evokes a deal implying several participants:

Text no. 18
(1–7)1,200 litres of bar[ley in exchange*] for* dates belonging to [PN], which constitutes the rent due by Nabû-ri-[...], which (is) in the hands of Iqūpu, [son of PN, the debt of] Sîn-le'i, son of In-[Nusku], Nuḫsāya, son of [Nusku-gabbe], and Nusku-iddina, son of [Nusku-killanni]. (8–10)In *ayyāru* (ii), they will give the barley in its capital amount, at the door of the silo, in the *maši*[*hu*-measure of 1 PI] into the standard quality. (11–12)They shall each bear responsibility for one another for payment of barley.
(13–16)(Witnesses and scribe).

80 See no. 8/9 below § 4.1.1.
81 Zadok, *West Semites*, 112.

(16–18)[Ammat/Bīt-dayyān-Adad][82], 15th *addaru*, [-]th year of Nabonidus, king of [Babylon] (= 555–539 B.C.E.).
(19–10)This year, Nusku-iddina [gave] 234 litres [...].
Aramaic epigraph: (left edge)*To Sîn-le'i.*

The dates were grown in a palm grove of an owner whose name is broken (line 2), tended by a farmer named Nabû-ri-[...] (l. 3), and placed under the control of a rent farmer named Iqubu (l. 4). The text specifies that these dates are borrowed by Sîn-le'i son of In-Nusku, Nuḫsāya son of Nusku-gabbe, and his nephew Nusku-iddina son of Nusku-killanni. However, they have to reimburse the creditor with barley from the next crop. It is surprising to see the names of three debtors mentioned for a lower quantity than the amounts that Nuḫsāya and Nusku-killanni used to borrow on their own. This contract could illustrate, once again, the role of guarantor played by Nusku-gabbe's sons. The real debtor of these dates would in fact be Sîn-le'i, son of In-Nusku, already mentioned in first position among the debtors. He is also mentioned alone in the Aramaic epigraph of the contract ("*to Sîn-le'i*"). It is possible that Nusku-gabbe's sons are mentioned as co-debtors to guarantee the reimbursement of the claim. Besides, the contract stipulates that Nusku-iddina made a first installment of 234 litres.

3.2.2 Payment of Debts

Text no. 17 shows a concrete case in which Nuḫsāya had to exercise his obligation as guarantor:

Text no. 17
(1–4)4,620 litres of barley, belonging to Adad-[...], son of Harimmā, the royal <mer>chant*,[83] is the debt of Nuḫsāya, son of Nusku-gabbe. (5–6) In *ayyāru* (ii), he will deliver the barley. (6–9)

82 The scribe of the contract, Mukīn-apli, son of Nādinu (line 16) is the author of several texts drafted in Bīt-dayyān-Adad (no. 11 and 15) and in Ammat (no. 12).

83 Dhorme read the professional title as (*amēlu*) *qīp šarri* (Dhorme, 'Neirab', 63). The title *qīp šarri* ('royal agent') has been resumed by Oelsner, 'Neirab-Urkunden', 74 and Timm, 'Texte aus Nērab', 278. But the title *qīpu* is never written phonetically with just one sign *qip*, see the attestations in *CAD* Q, 264–268. On the copy we clearly see the sequence lúgàr lugal. A collation on the tablet itself confirms the reading. Therefore it can only be a mistake by the scribe for the title lú<dam>.gàr lugal = *tamkār šarri* ('royal merchant'). We notice that this royal merchant has a West Semitic name: Adad-[...], son of Harimma'. In fact, numerous royal merchants in the Neo-babylonian and Persian periods were foreigners from the Western provinces. Cf. Michael Heltzer, 'The "Royal Merchants" (*tamkārū (ša) šarri*) in Neo-Babylonian and Achaemenid Times and the West-Semites among them', *UF* 38 (2006), 347–351.

The barley is the remainder of 4,500 litres of barley and 4 [shekels] of silver from a previous promissory note for which he guaranteed[84]. [...].
(10–13)(Witnesses and scribe).
(14–17)Town of the Neirabeans which is on the Bēl-aba-uṣur canal, 1st *ṭebētu* (x), 16th year of Nabonidus, king of Babylon (= 539 B.C.E.).

Nuḫsāya took over a debt contracted by a person for whom he stood surety. The initial debt had consisted of silver and barley, but it was entirely converted into barley on this occasion.[85] Nuḫsāya agreed to settle this debt from the new crop. As we have seen, he and his family could rely on their contacts with small farmers in the agricultural villages around Neirab, in the Nippur region, for easy access to barley stocks.

3.2.3 Preservation of Litigious Contracts

The presence in the Nusku-gabbe archive of contracts without apparent relevance to their private concerns could be explained by their leading role in the community of Neirabeans. Persons who called upon their services as guarantors may have deposited their litigious contracts in their archive. This may be the background of texts no. 20 and no. 27:

Text no. 20	**Text no. 27**
(1–6)[x shekels of silver] of one-eighth alloy belonging to Iltammeš-dalā, son of [...]-riya, is the debt of Barīkiya and Gur-[...], [sons] of [...]-ni. (6–7)In *nisannu* (i), he will pay [the silver in its capital am]ount. (8–9)They shall each bear responsibility for one another for payment. (10–11)Witness: [Sam]sa-igm[ur?], son of Giḫila. (12)And the scribe: Iddin-Bēl, descendant of Šangû-Šamaš.	(1–4)[x] mina of refined silver belonging to Nabû-iqbi, son of Tabni-Nusku, is the debt of Nusku-irakkas son of Gabbe-[...]-Sîn. (5–6)... Sîn-kabtu and Balāṭu will give the silver to him. (7)In *nisannu* (i), he will pay the silver in its capital amount. (7–9)Anybody to Nabû-iqbi [...], he will give [x] mina of silver. (10–13)Witnesses: Nusku-na'id, son of Sîn-le'i; Nusku-..., son of Sîn-[...].

84 For the expression *šá ma-hi-iš* <*pu*>-*tu*-[*tu*] ('warranty'), cf. *CAD* M, 101b.
85 The prime debtor owed 4,500 litres of barley and 4 shekels of silver. If we convert the silver into barley, we get 5,220 litres (considering 1 shekel = 1 *kur*/1,800 litres of barley, which is the standard rate attested in Uruk, at this date, cf. Michael Jursa, *Aspects of the Economic History of Babylonia in the First Millennium BC: Economic Geography, Economic Mentalities, Agriculture, the Use of Money and the Problem of Economic Growth* [*AOAT* 377; Münster: Ugarit-Verlag, 2010], 445–448). The text specifies that Nuḫsāya should settle 4,620 litres of barley. The initial debtor had been able to fulfill only 600 litres of barley (about 3 shekels and a half of silver).

Text no. 20	Text no. 27
(13–15)[...]-uma', [-]th *ayyāru* (ii), 3rd year of Cambyses, [king of Babylon], king of the lands (= 527 B.C.E.).	(13–14)[The scribe]: Nabû[...], son of [...]ēṭir. (15–17)[NG], [xth of MN], [xth year] of Darius I, [king] of Babylon and the lands (= 521–486 B.C.E.).

3.3 Conclusion

The promissory notes in the Neirab archive provide information about activities that clustered especially at the end and beginning of the Babylonian year, just before the new barley crop. During this period, Nusku-gabbe's sons participated in exchanges of silver, as creditors or debtors. They also borrowed significant quantities of barley from farmers from surrounding villages. Part of these loans of silver and barley allowed Nusku-gabbe's sons to assist members of their community, paying debts or acting as guarantors. Thus, it seems that the sons of Nusku-gabbe occupied a leading role within the deportee community of Neirab in Babylonia.

4 From the Neo-Babylonian Period to the End of Exile

The study of the Neirab texts shows some evolution in the living conditions of Nusku-gabbe's sons in Babylonia between the Neo-Babylonian and the early Achaemenid Periods. Furthermore, the repatriation of part of their archive to Syria yields information about the end of their exile.

4.1 The Geographical, Social and Economic Changes

4.1.1 The Neirab Deportees' Status during the Neo-Babylonian Period

In the Neo-Babylonian period, Nusku-gabbe's sons were mainly active in four agricultural villages, located in close proximity to each other in the region of Nippur: Ammat, Bīt-dayyān-Adad, *Ālu-ša-kutimmī*?* and Neirab. The town of 'Neirab' was probably the main place of residence for deportees from the Syrian town of Neirab. Their status was determined by the status of the land they were settled on. Unfortunately, none of the texts clarifies the status of these lands, but indirect information can be gleaned from text no. 8/9 (preserved on two copies) which mentions an obligation to serve the king:

Text no. 9

(1–4)Manniya, Sîn-aba-uṣur and Nusku-killanni, sons of Nusku-gabbe, said to Šer-idri, their slave, as follows: (4–5)"Come and serve the king with us". (5–11)Šer-idri, Manniya, Sîn-aba-uṣur and Nusku-killanni made an agreement with each other: every year, Šer-idri will serve during 6 months for Kidināya, his brother, with Manniya, Sîn-aba-uṣur and Nusku-killanni, his brothers. (11–13)And every month, they will give to Šer-idri 24 litres of flour as travel provisions. (13–14)When he will serve the king with them, his status of slave will be lifted*.
(15–17)Witnesses: Zabini, son of Ruqqā; Dalanī, son of Isinnāya; Zabidāya, son of Ḫariya.
(17–18)The scribe: Rēmūt, son of Marduka, descendant of Purk[ullu][86].
(19–20)Ammat, 28th of *tašrītu* (vii), 5th year of Nabonidus, king of Babylon (= 551 B.C.E.).

In this text, Nusku-gabbe's sons entrust their slave Šer-idri with the task of performing the 'king's service' (*palāḫ šarri*) during six months of the year. The nature of this service is not specified, but the *palāḫ šarri* is more often attested in texts from Persian period Nippur and these reveal that it was a duty typically connected to bow-lands.[87] This suggests that Nusku-gabbe's sons and other members of the community of Neirabeans had been settled as dependent workers on crown land.

4.1.2 Greater Freedom in the Persian Period?

From the early Achaemenid period onwards, the geographic environment of some members of the community widens. At the same time, we notice a certain change in their economic activities.

1. *Evolution towards a new living horizon?* In the Persian period, the geographic horizon of the Nusku-gabbe family seems to have widened. Two documents situate them at a considerable distance from their area of settlement: in Babylon (no. 1) and in Hīt (no. 19). The latter text (no. 19) is particularly intriguing:

---

86 We follow the reading of the ancestor's name proposed by Oelsner, 'Neirab-Urkunden', 77 n. 41. The state of the tablet preserved in Jerusalem seems to have degraded compared to the copy of Dhorme, 'Neirab', 7.

87 Matthew W. Stolper, *Entrepreneurs and Empire: The Murašû Archive, the Murašû Firm, and Persian Rule in Babylonia* (PIHANS 54; Istanbul: Nederlands Historisch-Archaeologisch Instituut te Istanbul, 1985), 61–62.

Text no. 19
(1–5)9½ shekel of silver of one-eighth alloy, price of a donkey, belonging to Lu-aqriya, son of Ilu-enašu-šaḫ, is the debt of Nusku-iddina, son of Nusku-killanni. (6–7)In *nisannu* (i), he will pay the 9½ shekel of silver and its interest at Neirab. (8–9)Each month one shekel of silver per mina will accrue against him.
(10–12)Witnesses: Nargiya, son of Ḫananāya; Ilteri-nūru, son of Nusku-rape,
(13–14)And the scribe: Nabû-šuma-uṣur, son of Zabinu, descendant of Dābibī.
(14–16)Ḫīt, 13th of [MN], 1st year of Cambyses, king of Babylon, king of the lands (= 529–528 B.C.E.).

In the beginning of Cambyses' reign, Nusku-iddina, the grandson of Nusku-gabbe, bought a donkey in Ḫīt, a city located on the Middle Euphrates some 300 km away from Nippur. The contract stipulated that payment was to be made in Neirab. Oelsner wondered whether this referred to Neirab in Babylonia or in northern Syria.[88] If Syrian Neirab was meant, this could indicate that the family had already returned from its Babylonian exile in 528 B.C.E. But we notice that Nusku-iddina is still mentioned in a tablet drafted in Babylon about a decade later, during the reign of Nebuchadnezzar IV (= 521 B.C.E.) (no. 1). So, it seems more likely that no. 19 talks of the Babylonian town of Neirab and that, as a consequence, the family had not yet returned home.

The presence of Neirabeans in Ḫīt remains difficult to explain. Ḫīt was an important centre of the bitumen industry, and Nusku-iddina may have visited the city for trading purposes. We are unaware, however, whether Ḫīt was his final destination or a stopover in a longer journey. It is also possible that he visited Ḫīt to perform some kind of corvée duty, rather than to engage in entrepreneurial activities. Workers from the Eanna temple of Uruk and the Ebabbar temple of Sippar were regularly sent there to collect bitumen,[89] and it is not inconceivable that members of the Neirabean community were obligated to participate in similar expeditions on behalf of the state.

---

88 Oelsner, 'Neirab-Urkunden', 70–71.

89 The evidence comes from the reigns of Nabonidus and Cyrus. For Ebabbar, see *Nbn.* 976; BM 63926/Bertin 1231, published by A. C. V. M. Bongenaar, *The Neo-Babylonian Ebabbar Temple at Sippar: Its Administration and its Prosopography* (PIHANS 80; Istanbul: Nederlands Historisch-Archeologisch Instituut te Istanbul, 1997), 38–39; CT 55 346; BM 63003, published by John MacGinnis, *Letter Orders from Sippar and the Administration of the Ebabbara in the Late-Babylonian Period* (Poznań: Bonami, 1995), no. 4; and CT 56 755. For the Eanna, see YOS 3 119. Although this letter was not dated, the addressee, Muranu, is probably attested in the 12th year of Nabonidus and 5th year of Cyrus; cf. Hans Martin Kümmel, *Familie, Beruf und Amt im spätbabylonischen Uruk: Prosopographische Untersuchungen zu Berufsgruppen des 6. Jh. v. Chr. in Uruk* (ADOG 20; Berlin: Mann, 1979), 118. For the use of bitumen, see P. R. S. Moorey, *Ancient Mesopotamian Materials and Industries* (Oxford: Clarendon, 1994), 332–335.

2. ***Different economic activities?*** There are some indications in the archive that the activities of Nusku-gabbe's sons may have changed in the Persian period. First, barley loans date exclusively to the Neo-Babylonian period (see Fig. 7), which might suggest that the family became less involved in agricultural affairs in the Persian period. Secondly, whereas silver loans date from both the Neo-Babylonian and the early Achaemenid periods (see Fig. 6), the quantities of silver seem to increase, with the last contract (no. 27; dated to the reign of Darius the Great) referring to one or more minas of silver. It cannot be excluded that these patterns merely result from archival practices, but in this regard it should be noted that the disappearance of contracts concerning agricultural staples coincides with the moment when Nusku-gabbe's sons seem to have embraced a wider geographical field of action.

4.1.3 The End of the Exile: A Political Decision or a Natural Development?

The descendants of the Syrian deportees gained a certain freedom of movement in the Persian period. This freedom materialized, in the first instance, in their ability to travel more widely than before, and secondly in their ability to return home. One may wonder where this freedom comes from. Oelsner considers that the lack of texts from Cyrus' reign (539–530 B.C.E.) shows a break in the Babylonian activities of Nusku-gabbe's sons during this time, possibly caused by their return to northern Syria.[90] Timm maintains that the return to Syria must be dated to the reign of Darius, and sees in Oelsner's hypothesis an attempt to establish a connection with the Judeans, who, according to Ezra 6:2–12, were given permission by Cyrus to return to Jerusalem.[91] Although this does not seem to be Oelsner's point of view, it is worthwile to bear in mind that the historicity of Cyrus' decree is disputed,[92] and that there are no Babylonian or Persian records that confirm such an action by the Persians, neither of the Judeans, nor of any other deported group settled in Babylonia by the Neo-Babylonian kings.[93]

---

90 Oelsner, 'Neirab-Urkunden', 71–76.

91 Timm, 'Texte aus Nērab', 286–287.

92 On the subject, see Lisbeth S. Fried, 'The Land Lay Desolate: Conquest and Restoration in the Ancient Near East', in *Judah and the Judeans in the Neo-Babylonian Period* (ed. O. Lipschits and J. Blenkinsopp; Winona Lake: Eisenbrauns, 2003), 21–54 and Lester L. Grabbe, 'The Persian Documents in the Book of Ezra: Are They Authentic?', in *Judah and the Judeans in the Persian Period* (ed. O. Lipschits and M. Oeming; Winona Lake: Eisenbrauns, 2006), 531–570.

93 Unfortunatly it is still necessary to recall emphatically that the *Cyrus Cylinder* does not contain any information on the Babylonian deportees' fate, see on the subject, Amélie Kuhrt, 'The Cyrus Cylinder and Achaemenid Imperial Policy', *JSOT* 25 (1983), 83–97.

Since the beginning of the first millennium B.C.E. Babylonia, and in particular the region of Nippur, had been subject to several waves of settlement by West Semitic population groups. This phenomenon is visible in the deep changes of Babylonian toponymy.[94] The deportation policy of the Neo-Babylonian kings was, in effect, a continuation of this trend. One may actually wonder if the royal administration set up a system to control deportees settled in Babylonia. Or, asking the question in a different way: How did the royal administration distinguish between foreigners settled in Babylonia through voluntary migration and those settled in Babylonia through deportation? Did the former move around freely, whereas the latter depended on political decisions? In his work on the deportation policy of Neo-Assyrian kings, B. Oded studied the evolution of the social and economic conditions of deportees. He distinguished three steps in this evolution. 1) First, deportees arrived in their new environment as 'royal slaves' controlled by the administration. 2) In a second instance, they received land from the crown, in return for fees and duties. They lived a family life, and agricultural lands could be inherited. They were allowed to own property and to enjoy the remainder of the agricultural yield after fees and obligations had been deducted. 3) In the third and final phase, the land became private property.[95] Aspects of this model seems to fit the cursory evidence about the Neirab community in Babylonia. 1) The first stage is admittedly not documented because it falls before the start of the archive, but 2) Nabonidus' reign seems to correspond to the second phase. At this point, the Neirabeans appear as tenants of crown land for which they had to fulfil the 'king's service'. Meanwhile, the ownership of slaves and the promissory notes of barley and silver show that some of them succeeded in creating profits from their participation in the local system of exchange. 3) The texts from the early Achaemenid period correspond more or less to the third phase of Oded's model. The Neirabeans now appear less bound to the land. At this point, they chose to invest in economic activities in a new geographical landscape, quite distant from their place of residence. Whereas the royal administration could control the deportees during the two first steps, it seems more difficult for the authorities to check on their movements during the final phase, and to distinguish at that point between them and other foreigners living in Babylonia. So, rather than a political decision emanating from the Persian authorities, one may wonder if the return to Neirab could be connected with the upgraded socio-economic conditions of the sons of the deportees and their personal choice to go back to their homeland.

94 See Ran Zadok's contribution in this volume.
95 Oded, *Deportation*, 98–99.

4.2 The End of the Exile: Return to Neirab and the Babylonian Texts

The fact that the archive of Nusku-gabbe's family was discovered in Syria but redacted in Babylonia raises questions about its status. It would seem that there are two features which allow us to classify it as a 'dead' archive:

1) The archive is predominantly composed of promissory notes (20 of 27 documents) and contains only a few property (5 of 27) and family documents (2 of 27).[96] This composition is typical for a 'dead' archive, as it is devoid of texts with actual legal value for its owners.[97] We notice, for example, that amongst the promissory notes, there are eleven texts in which Nusku-gabbe's sons were debtors of silver (no. 1, 7 and 16) or barley (no. 3, 4, 5, 6, 10, 15, 17 and 18). The fact that they were in possession of these texts shows that they had settled their debts, since creditors held on to the debt notes until payment had been made, at which point they were handed to the debtors.[98]
2) The chronological spread of the Neirab documents is very uneven. Most texts relate to Nuḫsāya and Nusku-killanni, the sons of Nusku-gabbe (17 of 27).[99] The second generation, with Nusku-iddina, son of Nusku-killanni, is poorly documented (3 of 27).[100] This imbalance is a characteristic of 'dead' archives, as specified by Jursa: 'The final years of such a "dead" archive's life are usually not well documented because of the removal of current files before deposition'.[101]

---

96 Business documents: no. 1, 3, 4, 5, 6, 7, 10, 11, 12, 13, 14/24, 15, 16, 17, 18, 19, 20, 21 and 27. Property documents: no. 2, 8/9, 22 and 26. Family documents: no. 23 and 25. The presence in the Nusku-gabbe archive of no. 26 (concerning the transfer of a commodity) and no. 23 (a marriage contract) raises questions because they do not mention any members of the family. Two hypotheses are possible. 1) The commodity mentioned in no. 26 and one of the wedding partners of no. 23 joined the Nusku-gabbe family by acquisition or by another marriage at a later date. In this scenario, texts no. 26 and no. 23 would be retro-acta. 2) It is also possible, however, that the sons of Nusku-gabbe kept these contracts because they had acted as arbitrators or advisors in disputes among community members. This would befit their role of community leaders (3.2.3).
97 On this classification, see Michael Jursa, *Neo-Babylonian Legal and Administrative Documents: Typology, Contents, and Archives* (GMTR 1; Münster: Ugarit-Verlag, 2005), 57–58.
98 On this practice, see Wunsch, 'Debt, Interest, Pledge and Forfeiture', 222.
99 Nuḫsāya, son of Nusku-gabbe, appears in no. 4: 4; 5: 3; 10: 3; 11: 4; 12: 3; 13: 8; 17: 9 and 18: 6. He is mentioned without patronymic in no. 2: 5, and his name is possibly to be restored in no. 3: [4]. Nusku-killanni is active in no. 7: 3; 8: 1, 6, 10; 9: 1, 6, 9; 10: 7; 14: 1, 8; 15: 3; 16: 3 and 24: [1], 7.
100 Nusku-iddina is mentioned in no. 1: 13; 18: 7 and no. 19: 4. His name possibly appears among the witnesses of fragmentary text no. 27: 12.
101 Jursa, *Neo-Babylonian Legal and Administrative Documents*, 58, n. 358.

Nusku-iddina, grandson of Nusku-gabbe, inherited the family archives from his father Nusku-killanni, or from his uncle Nuḫsāya. It seems that Nusku-iddina is the one who organized the transfer of the archives to Neirab. This transfer raises several questions. What is the purpose of repatriating texts several decades old? Our understanding of this phenomenon is limited by the lack of archeological data surrounding their discovery. It should be recalled that they were discovered during two missions, in 1926 and 1927, and one may wonder, therefore, whether the archive has been fully excavated. But even if we have the complete archive as it was brought to Syria at our disposal, it is still difficult to assess which percentage of the original archive was brought back to Syria, but we may think of two scenarios. It is possible that Nusku-iddina repatriated the entire archive, and that he discarded some of it upon arrival in his ancestral hometown. It is also possible that he had already sorted out the archive in Babylonia, but that he nonetheless decided to take the obsolete pieces with him to Syria. Whatever the case may be, it is clear that Nusku-iddina took care not to leave behind the cuneiform records gathered by his family and by other members of the Syrian community during their exile in Babylonia. Why was this? It is possible that this was motivated by political considerations. We have seen that Nusku-gabbe's descendants played a leading role in the Neirab community deported to Babylonia. We can suppose that the members of this family already occupied a similarly high social rank in Syria before the deportation.[102] The documentation about northern Syria does not allow us to learn much about the history of Neirab in the sixth century B.C.E., but it is not inconceivable that newcomers took the place of the elites deported by the Neo-Babylonian kings. Anticipating clashes upon his return, Nusku-gabbe's descendants might have felt the need to justify their ambition to reoccupy their social rank from before their exile in Babylonia.[103] So, maybe, keeping the docu-

---

102 During their exile in Babylonia, the leadership of the Judean community belonged to the descendants of the House of David, to the descendants of the priestly class and to the 'Elders of Judah'; see Israel Eph'al, 'On the Political and Social Organization of the Jews in Babylonian Exile', in *XXI. Deutscher Orientalistentag vom 24. bis 29. März 1980 in Berlin, Ausgewählte Vorträge* (ed. F. Steppat; ZDMGSup 5; Wiesbaden: Harrassowitz, 1983), 106–112 (110–112). These people or their ancestors already played the leading role in the kingdom of Judah before the deportation.
103 About the opposition between the Judeans coming back from the exile and the inhabitants of Judah, see Mario Liverani, *Israel's History and the History of Israel* (London: Equinox, 2005), 270–291. To justify their return and their right to occupy the land and to claim the leadership, the exiles set up a strategy to dispute the legitimacy of the inhabitants of Jerusalem who did not experience the deportation and the exile. There are numerous studies about this subject, *e.g.* recently Dalit Rom-Shiloni, 'From Ezechiel to Ezra-Nehemiah: Shifts of Group Identities within Babylonian Exilic Ideology', in *Judah and the Judeans in the Achaemenid Period* (ed. O. Lipschits, G. Knoppers and M. Oeming; Winona Lake: Eisenbrauns, 2011), 127–151.

ments drafted in Babylonia might have enabled them to testify that they were still the leaders of the Neirab community.

5 Conclusions

Though consisting of a small number of texts, the Neirab archive contains valuable information about a group of Syrian deportees settled in Babylonia in the course of the sixth century B. C. The coherence and unity of this community clearly comes to the fore in our texts. The deportees were settled in villages close to each other in the Nippur region. This enabled them to preserve elements of their community organisation, such as the leading role of the Nusku-gabbe family. The community's geographic concentration and its intact social patterns allowed for the continuation of cultural traditions, as witnessed by the popularity of the lunar cult in onomastics. In spite of the community's unity and cohesion, some of the exiles became integrated in their new environment, taking Babylonian names, participating in the local economy, and using documents written in cuneiform. Nevertheless, the return to Neirab of at least some of their descendants reveals that in spite of their eventual integration, some deportees always felt the desire to end their exile, and go back to their hometown.

Acknowledgment

I am very grateful to Denis Bouder and Farnoush Mansourian for their help in the translation of this article into English. They should not be held accountable for the remaining shortcomings in this respect.

Ran Zadok

West Semitic Groups in the Nippur Region between c. 750 and 330 B.C.E.*

1 Introduction

This paper is about the presence of three West Semitic ethno-linguistic groups (Chaldeans, Arameans and Arabians) in the Nippur region during the early Neo-Babylonian (c. 750–627 B.C.E.), Chaldean (626–539 B.C.E.) and Achaemenid (538–330 B.C.E.) periods. The documentation from the early Neo-Babylonian period consists mainly of Neo-Assyrian royal inscriptions, Sargonid correspondence, and the so-called 'Governor's archive'.[1] The Chaldean and early Achaemenid periods mostly coincide with the peak of the cuneiform archival documentation predominantly belonging to the temples and the Babylonian urbanite elite, whereas that of the late Achaemenid period consists of the Murašû archive and the other, somewhat dwindling, cuneiform material (basically archives of temples and *homines novi* acting as businessmen).[2]

---

* All of the cuneiform material below is Neo/Late-Babylonian unless otherwise indicated. The months (in Roman numerals) are the Babylonian. All the documents in sections G-H were issued in Nippur and belong to the Murašû archive unless otherwise indicated. The West Semitic anthroponyms are generally italicized below. Individuals with non-West Semitic names occurring in these sections are put in brackets. Abbreviations of editions of cuneiform texts are as in the Chicago Assyrian Dictionary (CAD), unless otherwise indicated. Addu, Ahi, Bēl and Nabû in the West Semitic names below are invariably written with the Sumerograms ^{d}IŠKUR, ŠEŠ, ^{d}+EN and ^{d}+AG respectively in the cuneiform texts. On the other hand, the *pluralis maiestatis* DINGIR^{meš} renders *il* in such names. Therefore only DINGIR^{meš} but not the other four Sumerograms are indicated below in order to avoid ambiguity. A single (/) and a double (//) stroke in filiations denote 'son of' and 'descendants of' respectively. The formula +x AC stands for 'with anonymous coparceners whose number is not indicated'.

1 For early Neo-Babylonian Nippur see John P. Nielsen, *Sons and Descendants: A Social History of Kin Groups and Family Names in the Early Neo-Babylonian Period, 747–626 BC* (CHANE 43; Leiden: Brill, 2011), 157–180.

2 For an overview of cuneiform texts from first millennium B.C.E. Nippur, see Michael Jursa, *Neo-Babylonian Legal and Administrative Documents: Typology, Contents and Archives* (GMTR 1; Münster: Ugarit-Verlag, 2005), 110–116.

Ran Zadok: Tel Aviv University

Most of the West Semitic onomastic material from Nippur dates from the second quarter of the first millennium B.C.E. This concentration is due to the nature of the documentation. The Chaldean onomasticon is residual: only a handful of explicit Chaldeans bore non-Babylonian names. The main problem is to distinguish between the Aramaic and the other north West Semitic names on the one hand, and the Aramaic and Arabian names on the other. In most instances, especially where the geographical-historical context is clear, the referents are plausibly Arameans. The Arabians kept their separate identity basically in the borderland between the Babylonian alluvium and the Syro-Arabian desert, while in the alluvium they came under Babylonian and Aramean cultural influence and as a result were in various stages of assimilation to the Arameans. Unlike the infiltration of the Arameans into the alluvium (from the Jazira), which is recorded in historical sources, the process of the penetration of Chaldeans into Babylonia is not recorded. The form *Kaldu* in Neo-Assyrian is with the shift of the sibilant to *l* probably a Babylonianism in Assyrian.[3] Regarding the delineation of the Aramaic onomasticon from the Canaanite-Hebrew one, the Phoenician onomastic component can be isolated relatively easily. There were very few Transjordanian deportees in Mesopotamia.[4] The overwhelming majority of the Judeans in Babylonia, who bore compound names, had the theophorous element Yhw,

3 See Simo Parpola, *Letters from Assyrian Scholars to the Kings Esarhaddon and Assurbanipal: Commentary and Appendices* (Volume 2; AOAT 5/2; Kevelaer: Butzon & Bercker, 1983), 243; cf. Jaakko Hämeen-Anttila, *A Sketch of Neo-Assyrian Grammar* (SAAS 13; Helsinki: Neo-Assyrian Text Corpus Project University of Helsinki, 2000), 22 with n. 30 who points out that in most cases this shift did not occur in Neo-Assyrian; Mikko Luukko, *Grammatical Variation in Neo-Assyrian* (SAAS 16; Helsinki: Neo-Assyrian Text Corpus Project University of Helsinki, 2004), 80–81.

4 Only two individuals of Moabite extraction – viz. Itti-Nabû-balāṭu/^{d}*Ka-mu-šú-šarra-uṣur*, possibly with the alias Amurru-si-im-ki-' (Marten Stol, 'Un texte oublié', RA 71 [1977], 96) and Ha-an-ṭu-šú/*Ka-mu-šu-i-lu* (both with paternal names containing the Moabite theophorous element Kemosh, Ran Zadok, 'Phoenicians, Philistines and Moabites in Mesopotamia', BASOR 230 [1978], 57–65 [61–62]) – and possibly just one Ammonite, namely *Mil-ki-<<KU?>>-mu-šarra-uṣur* (end of the Chaldean period) are recorded in Babylonia and Susa (see Ran Zadok, *The Earliest Diaspora: Israelites and Judeans in Pre-Hellenistic Mesopotamia* [Publications of the Diaspora Research Institute 151; Tel Aviv: Diaspora Research Institute, 2002], 80, n. 7). Both individuals of Moabite extraction are from the early Achaemenid period. They may be descendants of people who were deported to Babylonia as a result of the campaigns of Nebuchadnezzar II and Nabonidus in southern Transjordan (cf. Erasmus Gass, *Die Moabiter – Geschichte und Kultur eines ostjordanischen Volkes im 1. Jahrtausend v. Chr.* [Abhandlungen des Deutschen Palästina-Vereins 38; Wiesbaden: Harrassowitz, 2009], 210–212 with literature). ^{d}*Ka-mu-šú-šarra-uṣur* and *Mil-ki-<<KU?>>-mu-šarra-uṣur* probably belonged to the palatial sector in view of the fact that the predicative element of their names contains *šarru*, "king". They might have belonged to the Transjordanian elite. For Edomites cf. below, Part II.c with n. 85.

which is not recorded in the original Aramaic onomasticon. It is very probable that all the West Semitic groups in Babylonia were thoroughly influenced by the local Aramaic language and culture. There is every reason to believe that what is overcautiously defined as the 'West Semitic' onomasticon from Babylonia is in fact mostly Aramaic.

Part I Historical Overview

1 The Early Neo-Babylonian Period

Chaldeans

Most of the recorded Chaldeans in Neo-Assyrian and Neo-Babylonian/Late Babylonian sources bore Akkadian (Babylonian) names.[5] Originally there were five Chaldean tribes whose territories stretched from the coast of the Persian Gulf as far north as the region of Cutha: Kār-Nergal (^{d}IGI.DU) of the northernmost territory within Bīt-Dakkūri in Sennacherib's list[6] is probably identical with Kār-^{d}U.GUR (once mentioned with Cutha at the time of Sargon II).[7] Bīt-Sa'alli was near Bīt-Dakkūri. Appak belonged – like Ma-li-la-tu – to Bīt-Dakkūri in Sennacherib's time, but Ma-li-la-tu (or Am-li-la-tu) had belonged to the Chaldean territory of Bīt-Sa'alli before it was conquered by Tiglath-pileser III. Ma-li-la-tu is not included in the list of the towns of Bīt-Sa'alli conquered by Sennacherib, and Bīt-Sa'alli itself is not mentioned at all after Sennacherib's time. Neo-Assyrian *A-pak*^{ki} (Late Babylonian ^{uru}*Ap-pa-ak*^{ki}, *Dar.* 533: 15) was west from Marad if it is identical with Ur III *A-pi*$_5$*-ak*^{ki}. If *A-pak*^{ki} and *Ma-li-la-tu* were near each other, then Bīt-Sa'alli is also

5 A comprehensive survey of the Chaldean onomasticon is presented in Ran Zadok, 'The Onomastics of the Chaldaean, Aramaean and Arabian Tribes in Babylonia during the First Millennium', in *Arameans, Chaldeans, and Arabs in Babylonia and Palestine in the First Millennium B. C.* (ed. A. Berlejung and M. P. Streck; LAOS 3; Wiesbaden: Harrassowitz, 2013), 261–336, section A, e.g., A-di-nu son of Merodach-baladan II's sister, who was captured by the Assyrians during Sennacherib's 1st campaign (703 B.C.E.). See Eckart Frahm, 'New Sources for Sennacherib's "First Campaign"', *Isimu* 6 (2003), 129–164 (138).

6 Frahm, 'New Sources', 138.

7 H. W. F. Saggs, 'The Nimrud Letters, 1952 – Part III; Miscellaneous Letters', *Iraq* 18 (1956), 40–56 (no. 35: 23); F. R. Kraus, 'Provinzen des neusumerischen Reiches von Ur', ZA 51 (1955), 45–75 (58); Dietz Otto Edzard und Gertrud Farber, *Die Orts- und Gewässernamen der Zeit der 3. Dynastie von Ur* (RGTC 2; Wiesbaden: Reichert, 1974), 12–13.

to be sought not far from Babylon. Dūr-Balīhāya, which belonged to Bīt-Sa'alli in Tiglath-pileser III's time, is mentioned between Dūr-La-di-ni (of Bīt-Dakkūri) and Larak in connection with Bīt-Awkāni[8] in a letter from Sargon II's time. Bīt-Šīlāni, which was near Larak and Nippur, is not mentioned after 691 B.C.E.[9] At least part of it was later annexed by Bīt-Awkāni, which was south of it. The southernmost Chaldean territory was Bīt-Yakīn in the Sealand.

'Explicitly' Aramean tribes

Arameans, whose tribal affiliation is not given, are recorded from 1111 B.C.E. onwards, but specific Aramean tribes are mentioned from the time of Tukulti-Ninurta II onwards (890–884 B.C.E.). Thereafter references to unspecified Aramean tribes in Assyrian sources become relatively rare. A very detailed history of the Arameans until the demise of the Assyrian empire is presented by Lipiński.[10] Tribal names can be plural forms, but in fact early Syro-Aramean, Transjordanian, Israelite, Arabian and Palmyrene tribal names are mostly singular, originally anthroponyms and gentilics or with a geographical allusion.[11]

Mesopotamia gradually became part of the vast Aramaic-speaking continuum of the Fertile Crescent. Apart from tribesmen, there probably was – possibly non-voluntary – migration of non-tribal people from the middle Euphrates. More than one settlement in the western section of the alluvium was named after Hindaneans, Hi-in-da-i-na of Bīt-Awkāni (to be preferred over the hapax Gi-in-da-i-na)[12] and Late Babylonian Hindāya in the Murašû archive; see also Neo-Babylonian Gab-li-ni on the middle Euphrates and the homonymous settlement near Nippur. An anonymous governor of Hindānu possessed a field in the Nippur region as late as 423/2 B.C.E. (BE 10 54).

Anonymous sheikhs of Arameans without tribal affiliation are recorded in a letter from the so-called Governor's archive from Nippur (c. 755–732 B.C.E.).

---

8 For the eponym cf. the Sabaic surname *'wkn* (P. Stein, *Die altsüdarabischen Minuskelinschriften auf Holzstäbchen aus der Bayerischen Staatsbibliothek in München. 1: Die Inschriften der mittel- und spätsabäischen Periode* [Epigraphische Forschungen auf der Arabischen Halbinsel 5; Tübingen: Wasmuth, 2010], X.BSB 83/2).

9 See Frahm, 'New Sources', 146.

10 Edward Lipiński, *The Arameans: Their Ancient History, Culture, Religion* (OLA 100; Leuven: Peeters, 2000), 422–489; cf. also Zadok, 'The Onomastics', 271–304, section B.

11 Cf., e.g., J.-B. Yon, *Les notables de Palmyre* (BAH 163; Beirut: Institut Français d'Archéologie du Proche-Orient, 2002).

12 Cf. Frahm, 'New Sources', 149–150.

Another letter from that archive refers to 'all the Arameans'. This notion of 'Aram' is an ascribed cover name of several tribal groups and their territory, which in the case of the early Sargonid province of Gambūlu formed a continuum. Cultivators coming from Aram (or rather from among the Arameans, *lúA-ram*) to Nippur turn up in OIP 114 no. 96: 24–25.[13]

There is evidence for the presence of 13 specific Aramean tribes dwelling in the Nippur region (out of 42 such tribes in Babylonia). Nos. 1–3, 10–13 below are first mentioned in the so-called Governor's archive from Nippur (mid-8th century B.C.E.):

1. **Puqūdu**'s lengthy and massive presence near Nippur left its mark on the local toponymy: the important canal named after them (Nār- or Harri-Piqūdu) flowed in the western section of the alluvium, near the Euphrates, Babylon and Nippur.
2. **Ubūlu** was dependent on the important tribe of Puqūdu. Its anonymous sheikh may have possessed land near Nippur, presumably a precursor of the settlement of 'Ibuleans' (*I-bu-le-e*) near Nippur in the late Achaemenid period (see below, III.i).
3. **Hinda/eru** and **4. Ru'a** were associated with Puqūdu and Gambūlu in south-eastern Babylonia. Nār-*Hi-in-da-ri* in the Nippur region was named after the former.
5. **Gambūlu** is recorded from the reign of Sargon II onwards. It retained its status as a tribal (Aramean) region at least as late as the early reign of Nebuchadnezzar II, when 'Marduk-šarra-uṣur of Gambūlu' (Akkadian) is mentioned in the so-called 'Hofkalender' (vi*: 26').[14] His name (with *šarru*) betrays his connection with the palatial sector: *šarru*- names among chieftains in the Hofkalender may be a hint that the central authorities strove to have the decisive role in their nomination. This trait is as old as Old-Babylonian Mari,[15] an aspect of the long durée phenomenon of a dimorphic state (interaction between urban and initially non-urban elements). The settlement of the 'Gambuleans' (*Ga-am-bu-la*-A+A) was located near Nippur in the late-Achaemenid period (see below, III.e).

---

13 Steven W. Cole, *The Early Neo-Babylonian Governor's Archive from Nippur: Nippur 4* (OIP 114; Chicago: The Oriental Institute, 1996), 200–201.

14 On the Hofkalender, see most recently Rocío Da Riva, 'Nebuchadnezzar II's Prism (EŞ 7834): A New Edition,' ZA 103 (2013): 196–229. For the formula "PN (sheikh) of (Aramean) tribe" in the Hofkalender see Zadok,'The Onomastics', 285.

15 Cf. Michael P. Streck, 'Zwischen Weide, Dorf und Stadt: Sozio-ökonomische Strukturen des amurritischen Nomadismus am Mittleren Euphrat', *BaghM* 33 (2002), 155–209 (181).

6. **Amlātu** is mentioned only by Tiglath-pileser III. *Am-la-te* is perhaps identical with the later Neo-Babylonian settlement of *Im-ma-lat* (possibly in the Nippur region).
7. **Amatu**. A homonymous settlement (Neo-Babylonian *Am-mat*) is mentioned in documents from 'Chaldean' Nippur. Neo-Babylonian uru*Am-mat* in the Neirab documentation is to be sought not far from Nippur. A connection between this tribe and the estate or household (*bītu*) of Hammatāyu near late-Achaemenid Nippur (cf. below, Part II.f) cannot be established.
8. **Haṭallu**. A homonymous settlement is Late-Babylonian Haṭallūa near Nippur (cf. below, Part III.e).
9. **Rabb-ilu**. The tribe might have existed as late as the 5th century B.C.E. (cf. lú*Rab-bil-lu*? in the Murašû archive).
10. **U/Itū'**. People of Sarrabānu (near Larak) were scattered in several Babylonian cities and among the *I-tú-'*.[16]
11. **Gulūsu, 12. Rupū', 13. Dunānu**.

'Implicitly' Aramean tribes

The following tribes are either associated with Aramean tribes or bear typical Aramaic names. All the seven tribes listed in this section, except for Yašumu, are first recorded in the so-called Governor's archive from Nippur (mid-8th century B.C.E.), and except for Tanê and Naqru, they occur only there.[17]

1. **Tanê** is first mentioned together with the Aramean tribes of Hindaru and Naqru.[18]
2. **Hamdānu** went together with the leaders of the Aramean tribe of Puqūdu to the Chaldean territory of Bīt-Awkāni.
3. **Gāmu** joined the Rupū' tribe.
4. **Halapu**. Like the tribes lú*B/Pu-û-sa-li*, lú⌜*xx*⌝*-ru* and lú*Ú-a-sa-ha-nu*, lú*Ha-la-pi* is mentioned together with the Aramean tribe Hindaru and the tribes Naqru and Tanê.
5. **Habi'**.
6. **Naqru** is the same tribe as the referent of the base of the gentilic lú*Na-qi-ra*-A+A, whose sheikh, *Ia-da-'-il* (8th century B.C.E.), bore an Aramaic name.

16 Cf. Frahm, 'New Sources', 146.
17 See Zadok, 'The Onomastics', 304–322, sections C-F.
18 See Lipiński, *Arameans*, 471.

7. **Yašumu.** His descendant was settled together with his clan and with his Aramean allies by Merodach-baladan II in 710 B.C.E., presumably in Larak.

Brinkman points out the different terminology employed by the Assyro-Babylonian scribes while describing the tribal organisation of the Chaldeans and Arameans.[19] A Chaldean chieftain is called **ra'š* (extant in pl. *ra'sāni, rēšāni*)[20] or simply *mār* + tribal name (i.e. of *bīt* + tribal name), whereas an Aramean sheikh is named *nasīku*. However, none of the three terms referring to Chaldeans is exclusive to them, but belong to the common West Semitic socio-political vocabulary.[21] Aramean entities are also preceded by *bīt*- (e.g. Bīt-Agusi). Thus, an Aramean tribe (Litamu) was related to a unit of *bīt*-PN (e.g. *bīt-Ikkari* = É [lú]ENGAR).[22] Likewise, *nasīku* refers to non-Aramean sheikhs in Neo-Assyrian texts and in the Hebrew Bible.[23] Last, but not least, the Chaldeans' non-Akkadian names are all Aramaic and – if to judge by the linguistic situation of later Babylonia – they spoke Aramaic and eventually merged with the Arameans.

Arabians and others

1–2. The names of the tribes ***[lú]B/Pu-ú-sa-li*** and ***[lú]Ú-a-sa-ha-nu*** look Arabian. They are mentioned together with the Aramean tribe Hindaru and the unspecified tribes Naqiru and Tanê in the Governor's archive.

3–4. **Ahenna** and **Birru**, both attested in the Governor's archive, refer to unspecified West Semitic tribes.

---

19 John A. Brinkman, *A Political History of Post-Kassite Babylonia, 1158–722 B. C.* (AnOr 43; Rome: Pontifical Biblical Institute, 1968), 265.

20 The latter title is based on an Akkadianised form *rēšu* or Aram. *ryš* (/*rēš*/), being a case of Akkadian-Aramaic linguistic interference.

21 Cf., e.g., Willem A. M. Beuken, 'ראשׁ *Rôʾš*', ThWAT 7, 278–279 (277a).

22 See John A. Brinkman, 'A Legal Text from the Reign of Erība-Marduk (c. 775 B. C.)', in *DU-MU-E$_2$-DUB-BA-A: Studies in Honor of Åke W. Sjöberg* (ed. H. Behrens, D. Loding and M. T. Roth; Occasional Publications of the Samuel Noah Kramer Fund 11; Philadelphia: The University Museum, 1989), 37–47 (42 ad 2).

23 Non-Israelites: *nsyky Syḥwn* (Jos 13:21); *nsykmw* || *ndybmw* of Midian (Ps 83:12); *nsyky ṣpwn* in a highly literary style (Ezek 32:30); and eight *nsyky* after seven shepherds (Mi 5:4). Cf. Christoph Dohmen, 'נָסַךְ *nāsak̲*', ThWAT 5, 487–493 (492). The word occurs only once in Aramaic (if at all, cf. Jacob Hoftijzer and Karel Jongeling, *Dictionary of the North-West Semitic Inscriptions* [Handbuch der Orientalistik I/25; Leiden: Brill, 1995], 735–736). The poor record of indigenous political vocabulary in early Aramaic may also be due to the relatively early demise of the Aramean polities.

A letter from Ashurbanipal's time states that speakers of many tongues *(lišānāti mādāti)* resided in Nippur then.[24] The author of the letter hardly had any interest in linguistics, but intended to point out the ethnic diversity of late-Sargonid Nippur. The city had commercial links with the Iranian plateau as early as the mid-8th century B.C.E. (cf. the occurrence of the Median regions of Sangibuti and Parnakku) and Nippurean exiles were found in Elam during the Sargonid period.[25] It is possible that some traders from the Iranian plateau settled in Nippur but this very thin non-Semitic layer assimilated within few generations.

'Suteans' is not a category of its own, but an archaic term for unspecified West Semitic tribes typical of a highly literary style. Thus Nergal-nāṣir, an ally of Merodach-baladan II is singled out as a 'Sutean' with a clear derogatory sense, after Merodach-baladan II's concrete allies: the Elamites, Arameans and Chaldeans in Sennacherib's first campaign (703 B.C.E.), who defeated Merodach-baladan II and his allies in the battle of Cutha.[26]

2 The Chaldean and Early Achaemenid Period

While in the preceding periods the evidence for Arameans is direct and explicit, in post-Sargonid Babylonia it is mostly implicit as the documentation of Aramean tribes is negligible. The latest direct evidence for the existence of Aramean territories within the Neo-Babylonian imperial framework is from the beginning of the 6th century B.C.E. (in the 'Hofkalender'). The pertinent sample presented here is almost entirely reconstructed on the basis of a linguistic-onomastic analysis of the abundant prosopographical material. Most of the private archives from Chaldean and early Achaemenid Nippur (626–484 B.C.E.) refer to transactions among urbanites with a very low percentage of West Semitic names (altogether 14 individuals).[27] An exception is the rural archive of Nergal-iddina and his descendants, where most documents bear Aramaic notations. West Semites, notably Arabians, are well-represented in this archive. At least two settlements where documents were issued are named after West Semitic entities (Ālu-ša-Arbāya and

24 ABL 238, see also Ran Zadok, *On West Semites in Babylonia during the Chaldean and Achaemenian Periods: An Onomastic Study* (Jerusalem: H. J. & Z. Wanaarta, 1978), 1.

25 See Ran Zadok, *The Ethno-Linguistic Character of Northwestern Iran and Kurdistan in the Neo-Assyrian Period* (Tel Aviv-Jaffa: Archaeological Center, 2002), 80, 7.15.7.

26 See PNA 2: 951, s.v. Nergal-nāṣir, 8 taking him at face value 'the Sutean'.

27 See R. Zadok, 'The Representation of Foreigners in Neo-and Late-Babylonian Legal Documents (Eighth through Second Centuries B.C.E.)', in *Judah and Judeans in the Neo-Babylonian Period* (ed. O. Lipschits and J. Blenkinsopp; Winona Lake: Eisenbrauns, 2003), 471–589, (506–507).

Ālu-ša-Qurab/matūa). It is a likely assumption that people from the towns situated on the itinerary of Nebuchadnezzar II's campaigns to the West (viz. Qurab/matu, Elumu, Neirab, Arqā, Išqallūnu and Hazatu) were settled in colonies in the Nippur region.[28] The same applies to Elammu near Uruk (originally a settlement near Carchemish).[29] The few West Semitic names in the archive of Bēl-eṭēri-Šamaš, almost all of which can be explained as Aramaic, occur in deeds issued in rural settlements.[30] A gentilic is contained in Ālu-ša-Nērebāya which refers to a colony of North-Syrians (from Neirab).[31] Ālu-ša-Addidāya, where a deed of the archive of Ninurta-mutīr-gimilli / Zēr-kitti-līšir // Absummu (534 B.C.E.) was issued, may also be based on the gentilic of a West Semitic group.[32]

A deed from Bīt *Za-bi-ni* (11.II.1 Cyr = 538/7 B.C.E.) has a co-creditor, a co-debtor and a witness (first out of three, the names of the remaining witnesses, being damaged, can be Akkadian-West Semitic) with Aramaic names, viz. *I-da-il*(DINGIR^{meš}), *Ta-a-ma-ke-e* / *Ú-ba*(or *ma*)*-de-e* and *Da-ki-ir-il*(DINGIR^{meš}) / *Ka-bar-il*(DINGIR^{meš}).[33] According to an unfinished five-year gardening contract (BE 8 132) datable to the late Chaldean or early Achaemenid period (found in Nippur), *Zab-di-ia*, servant of Mušallim-Illil / Bānīya was the lessee of palm groves on Nār-Sîn (the name of the settlement is broken, lessor: Illil-ittannu / Mannu-kī-Nanāya).[34]

---

28 For people there originating in upper Mesopotamia and Syria see Zadok, *On West Semites in Babylonia*, 11–13, 17, to which add, e.g., *Šam-nu-hu-kit-ri*/*Šamaš-ēṭir*, brother of Illil-hātin, 5.X.2 Dar II = 422/1 B.C.E. (Matthew W. Stolper, 'The *šaknu* of Nippur', *JCS* 40 [1988]: 127–155 [146–148]).

29 See Ran Zadok, 'Notes on the Historical Geography of Mesopotamia and North Syria', *Abr-Nahrain* 27 (1989), 154–169 (157–158). ^{uru}*Tap-su-hu*^{ki} is recorded in a Neo-Babylonian deed from 26.XI. 554/3 B.C.E. As was observed by Ran Zadok and Tikva Zadok, 'New/Late-Babylonian Geography and Documentation', *NABU* 2003/35, the name resembles biblical *Tpsḥ* (Tiphsah, Θαψακος), i.e. the strategic town on the Middle Euphrates. The phonological differences between the forms are minimal. The Hebrew form was erroneously printed '*Tps*" in my article in *NABU*. A year later the same identification was suggested by Laetitia Graslin and André Lemaire, 'Tapsuhu, "Thapsaque"?', *NABU* 2004/55. The judges in the deed are otherwise unknown. They are mentioned only with their given and paternal names and only the fourth and last also with his surname. This – as well as the use of the determinative *ki* at the end of the name (which is reserved to important locales) – strengthens the case for a peripheral settlement.

30 Cf. Michael Jursa, 'Das Archiv von Bēl-eṭēri-Šamaš', in *Approaching the Babylonian Economy: Proceedings of the START Project Symposium Held in Vienna, 1–3 July 2004* (ed. H. D. Baker and M. Jursa; AOAT 330; Münster: Ugarit-Verlag, 2005), 197–268.

31 Ran Zadok, *Geographical Names According to New- and Late-Babylonian Texts* (RGTC 8; Wiesbaden: Reichert, 1985), 18.

32 Zadok, *On West Semites in Babylonia*, 18.

33 Zadok and Zadok, 'New/Late-Babylonian Geography', 37–39. Ninurta-ahhē-bulliṭ, Banūnu and Ahhē-iddina were printed erroneously.

34 Jursa, *Economic History*, 416–417.

Altogether, outside the Murašû archive, no more than 40 individuals bearing West Semitic (mostly Aramaic) names are recorded in documents from the Nippur region dated in 744–359 B.C.E.[35]

3 The Late Achaemenid Period

All the source material from Late Achaemenid Nippur belongs to the Murašû archive, dated to the reigns of Artaxerxes I and Darius II (464–424 and 423–405 B.C.E. respectively) in the years 454–404 B.C.E., as the latest document is from the first year of Artaxerxes II. A possible post-Murašû deed is Veysel Donbaz and Matthew W. Stolper, *Istanbul Murašû Texts* (PIHANS 79; Leiden: Nederlands Historisch-Archaeologisch Instituut te Istanbul, 1997; henceforth: IMT) 108: 3–4 from 21.V.25 Art II? = 380/79? B.C.E.: *Da-la-ta-ni-'* / *Ha-an-*[*ni*]*-ia*, debtor, gardener (with a coparcener) of a palm grove situated on two canals whose names are severely damaged (creditor: Ninurta-uballiṭ / Libluṭ).

Unlike the other Babylonian temple cities, where the indigenous urbanites, being the only group bearing surnames, are easily identifiable, the almost complete lack of surnames in the Nippur documentation makes such a distinction difficult.[36] This is remedied to a limited extent by (1) the inclusion of repetitive lists of witnesses often with a fairly strict order in the compact prosopographical documentation of the Murašû archive (27 prominent individuals who belonged to the circle of friends and associates of the Murašû firm) and (2) the system of the *haṭru*-organisations.[37] Ethnic groups constitute just a quarter of the whole system

35 Zadok, 'Representation', 525: 3.1.3, 3–5; 526: 3.1.7.1.2, 3–4; 527: 3.1.7.3.1; 529: 3.1.16, 3–4; 530: 3.1.17.1.1.1, 3; 531: 3.1.17.2.1, 6; 532: 3.1.17.2.5; 3.1.17.3.1, 2; 534: 3.1.20.1, 1; 536: 3.1.26.1.1.1, 3; 538: 3.1.26.3.1, 1, 2; 542: 3.1.34, 3; 3.1.38.2.1, 2; 3.1.38.6; 549: 3.1.50.2; 550: 3.1.53; 552; Ran Zadok, 'West Semites in Administrative and Epistolary Documents from Northern and Central Babylonia', in *Shlomo: Studies in Epigraphy, Iconography, History and Archaeology in Honor of Shlomo Moussaieff* (ed. R. Deutsch; Tel Aviv-Jaffa: Archaeological Center, 2003), 255–271 (269–270).

36 See Zadok, *On West Semites in Babylonia*, 7; Nielsen, *Sons and Descendants*, 163–164.

37 Cf. Guillaume Cardascia, *Les archives des Murašû: Une famille d'hommes d'affaires babyloniens à l'époque perse (455–403 av. J.-C.)* (Paris: Imprimerie Nationale, 1951), 20; Linda B. Bregstein, *Seal Use in Fifth Century B. C. Nippur, Iraq: a Study of Seal Selection and Sealing Practices in the Murašû Archive* (Ph.D. Dissertation, University of Pennsylvania, 1993; Ann Arbor: University Microfilms, 1994; henceforth: SU), 197–205, 368–369. Aqar-aplu (KAL-A, previously read 'Danna') / Nādinu, a recurrent and frequent witness in the Murašû archive, was a descendant of Mannu-Illil-dāri (A. DUMU šá N. DUMU šá [sic] A., TuM 2/3 189: 18, first witness of 8; Matthew W. Stolper, 'Fifth Century Nippur: Texts of the Murašûs and from Their Surroundings', JCS 53 [2001], 83–132 [96–99: 7, 12], first witness of 11). His namesake, the son of Šuma-ukīn was a descendant of

of *haṭru*-organisations: only 15 (including Aruwāya, Scythians, Indians, Manneans, Carians, Urartians and Melitenians, Phrygians and Lydians[38]) out of over 60 such organisations were designated with ethnic names. Most *haṭru*-organisations (over 45) were of occupations and lower-status groups as well as households (mostly institutional) and estates. There are just five or six *haṭru*-organisations of West Semitic groups with only a handful of named individuals (see just below).[39] Such are the Tyrians, Arabians and the Aššeans. A sizable percentage of the numerous individuals of the Murašû archive either bore West Semitic names, had fathers with West Semitic names or had blood relatives with West Semitic names (altogether at least 464 such individuals). While the existence of such a collective is useful for our purpose here, it is hardly applicable on the level of the individual: to regard each bearer of an Aramaic name as an Aramean plain and simple oversimplifies the matter. The situation can be improved by keeping in mind that the sizable archive of Murašû is exceptionally relevant and resourceful, as it focuses on the countryside thereby allowing a rare glimpse at it – unlike most of the Neo-Babylonian / Late Babylonian archives which are urban-oriented. We can thus attain a significant socio-ethnic sample of the population of the Nippur region and certain rural settlements there. It should be stressed that the sample obtained is a minimum estimate of the Arameans. The long-established Babylonian urbanites as bearers of the dominant and prestigious culture influenced all the other population groups, whose members adopted Akkadian names, whereas the urbanites hardly borrowed non-Akkadian anthroponyms. In the absence of surnames in the Nippur documentation, there is good reason for thinking that also certain individuals with purely Akkadian filiations were of Aramean extraction (cf. the case of the Šarrabeans). Even this minimum Aramean sample is much larger than that of the handful of non-Aramean West Semites and non-indigenous Arameans (notably the Aššeans).

Indigenous Nippurean urbanites (*Nippurāya*) are a distinct group in the Murašû archive. Nippureans possessed fields in the countryside of Nippur,[40] notably on Nāru eššetu and in Bīt-ᶠṬābat-gabbi?-[x] (Stolper, 'Fifth Century Nippur', 96–99, 7: 1–2). Ālu-ša-Nippurāya (BE 8 69) 'the Nipureans' settlement'

Širiktu, same filiation format, tenth and last witness (BE 10 2: 16). The ancestor is presented as if he were the physical grandfather. Grandfathers are also recorded at Nippur.

38 A Lydian bore the name *Mi-da-'* (IMT 3: 3), which was common in Phrygia.

39 Cf. Matthew W. Stolper, *Entrepreneurs and Empire: The Murašû Archive, the Murašû Firm, and Persian Rule in Babylonia* (PIHANS 54; Leiden: NINO, 1985; henceforth: EE), 72–79. For a recent evaluation see Jursa, *Economic History*, 405–418, especially 413 on the land assigned to foreign population groups.

40 BE 9 65: 3: ˡᵘ́EN.LÍL$^{ki.meš}$; TuM 2/3 145, IMT 16: 5–6; 105 + EE 109; Stolper, '*šaknu*', 131.

was perhaps near Til-Gabbāri as one of the witnesses is mentioned in both settlements (BE 8 62 and 94). Nippureans formed part of Illil-šuma-iddina's retinue. They are listed after his household members, servants and commissioned agents (sg. *ālik našparti*) in BE 10 9: 3–4 and EE 109 (cf. IMT 105), which are about real property in the countryside, but they are absent in BE 9 69, possibly due to its urban setting (where such a specification would be redundant). Stolper suspects that there existed a *haṭru*-organisation of Nippureans, seeing that *šaknu* normally designates the overseer of such an organisation.[41] In addition to the explicit evidence for ethno-linguistic diversity at Nippur in the Sargonid period, it can be inferred that Arameans dwelt in late Achaemenid Nippur. Itti-Šamaš-balāṭu and *Za-ra-ah-*^{d}*Ta*$_{5}$*-míš* sons of Šamaš-iddina bought a house in Nippur on 6.IV.20 Art I (EE 106: 7–8). The Judean Udarna and *Ha-nun* / Bēlšunu, owner of considerable property (with a fingernail mark, 24$^{?}$.[I].41 Art I, BE 9 87: 1: [*Ha-nu*]*-nu*, 6, 8, 9, left edge), who brought their cases before the Nippurean assembly, presumably resided in Nippur. It cannot be established that *Ba-rik-ki-Bēl* / *Ba-rik-ki-*^{d}*Ta*$_{5}$*-míš*, who paid (together with ^{d}*Ta*$_{5}$*-míš-ba-rak-ku* / Bēl-ēṭir ($^{d+}$EN-SUR) and Bēl-ittannu / *Za-bi-na-'*) five minas of silver for two wooden doors (20.-.- Dar I, PBS 2/1 173: 3, 7, 10, 12), resided there.

The municipal authority of Nippur (e.g. the richly documented appointees of the quarters named after gates) included neither bearers of West Semitic names nor foreigners.[42] The office of the *šandabakku* existed as late as 73 B.C.E.[43] This reflects the continuity of the local cult and the Ekur temple. Western-Semites and foreigners are not represented among the brewers from Nippur.[44] Unlike the brewers with Akkadian filiations, who received *cassia* from a field of Bēl in Tīl-hurdi together with *Ag-gu-ba-'* / Bēl-eṭēru (household member$^{?}$ of Manuštānu, 29.III.40 Art I, IMT 40: 6–7), those led by the brewers' foreman Šuma-ukīn/Ispēšu were presumably non-prebendal ones (22.VIII.4 Dar II, TuM 2/3 184: 17).[45] The same may apply to *Hu-ú-ru* (Egyptian), the brewers' foreman on 25.VII.40 Art I (EE 40: 8–9), to *Ha-si-ma-'* / *A-qab-bi-il*(DINGIR^{meš}, 28.-.40 Art I, EE 99) and to *Qu-un-na-a* / Bēl-asû'a who together with Illil-kāṣir and anonymous partners received 200 vats of beer (3.VIII.2 Dar II, BE 10 59: 4, 5: -<*un*>, 9, 14). The deeds

41 See Stolper, '*šaknu*', 130, 137–138.

42 Cf. Stolper, '*šaknu*', 129 with nn. 8–9; Bregstein, SU, 170–174.

43 See Ran Zadok, 'Notes on Babylonian Geography and Prosopography', *NABU* 1997 § 6, on 5 (not 64 B.C.E.).

44 Cf. Paul-Alain Beaulieu, 'The Brewers of Nippur', *JCS* 47 (1995), 85–96 as well as BE 10 4 from 14.XII.41 Art I. Noteworthy is Kidin-Sîn / Lā-qīpu, brewer of Illil (cf. Bregstein, SU, 177–178).

45 In view of his paternal name Šuma-ukīn / Ispēšu was possibly of Iranian extraction. See also Stolper, EE, 95 ad PBS 2/1 135.

about beer vats of *Ba-rik-Illil*(^d+^EN.LÍL) / Ninurta-erība (co-debtor, 13.IX.30 Art I, BE 9 21: 4–5) and *Bēl-i-di-r*[*i-'*], (debtor, with a fingernail mark, Bīt-Gērāya, 20.IX.36 Art I, EE 98: 4, left edge: -*r*[*i-'*]) have no cultic background. Sealers of Murašû documents with Babylonian filiations preferred images with Babylonian motifs, whereas most such sealers with West Semitic names avoided Babylonian religious imagery.[46] Non-Nippurean Babylonians, i.e. urbanites not belonging to the same constituency, are referred to by their gentilics, e.g. 'Akkadian' (*Akkadû*, lúURIki, IMT 110: 2), i.e. 'from the land of Babylonia' (the alluvium)[47] or 'from the city of Baylon' (*Bābilāya*, lúTIN.TIRki, BE 10 95: 17; IMT 105: 11) in the Murašû archive. Nippureans were distinguished from residents of Babylon.[48] The only *haṭru*-organisation of Babylonian urbanites is – if taken at its face value – that of Māndērāya < *Mār-Dērāya*, i.e. people originating from the ancient temple city of Dēr. Its few members and people recorded in the homonymous settlement had a mixed Akkadian-Aramaic onomasticon.[49] Dērites resided in Ālu-ša-maqtūti 'the refugees' settlement'. The refugees (all bearing Akkadian names), who had their own *haṭru*-organisation, were possibly both indigenous and foreign. Their bow-properties were located in Ālu-ša-maqtūti, Bīt-Tabalāya and Galīya (2, d, 1'). Interestingly enough, the Lydians had the same geographical distribution (see just below). A Lydian refugee (lú*Lu-da*-A+A lú*ma-aq-tu*), recipient of oil rations, is recorded (after a Median refugee) in Babylon at the beginning of the 6th century B.C.E.[50]

The 'local milieu' refers here to the urbanite component of the long-established population, seeing that the clans of the Babylonian temple cities did not absorb foreigners, but as prestigious groups in Babylonia married daughters of

---

46 See Bregstein, SU, 370.

47 Cf. Eva von Dassow, 'On Writing the History of Southern Mesopotamia', *ZA* 89 (1999), 227–246 (241–242) who points out that Babylonia is a Greek notion corresponding to 'the land of Sumer and Akkad' in indigenous terminology. However, the component 'Sumer', being archaic, is typical of highly literary style. It is left out in concrete definitions, like in the list 'Akkad, Chaldea, Aram and the Sealand' in Assyrian royal inscriptions, and more tellingly in the adjective *Akkadû* for indigenous Babylonian items, like pieces of furniture, as opposed to imported or imitated products. The title of Gubaru, the satrap of Babylonia, is *pīhāt Akkadî*. In the late Parthian and Sasanian periods, *Bbl* in the Babylonian Talmud denotes the Babylonian alluvium without *Myšn* (Mesene, Sealand). Arabic *'Irāq* which goes back to Middle Persian 'lowland' likewise refers to the alluvium.

48 Cf. Donbaz and Stolper, IMT, 153 ad 105 and EE 109.

49 See Zadok, *On West Semites in Babylonia*, 18–20, especially on their bow-property in Ālu-ša-maqtūti, where their origin from Dēr is confirmed by the spelling DUMU.BÀD.ANki-A+A (CBS 5516 = EE 66).

50 Weidner, 'Jojachin', 934: C, i, 24.

the less prestigious groups.[51] Therefore the only non-Babylonian anthroponyms in the very rich prosopographical pool of the urbanite elite, are just a handful of female names, notably *Naq-qí-tu*$_4$ d. of Murašû (9.V.29 Art I, EE 40: 5, 7). It can be surmised that such Aramaic names were given by non-urbanite mothers. Foreigners assimilated to the Arameans who served as a vehicle for disseminating the Babylonian culture. This process was slower among the deportees, who were brought together with their families and settled in special settlements ('colonies'), than among soldiers who were single and married local women. Unlike the Assyrian rulers, the Neo-Babylonian empire did not encourage assimilation, but the circumstances, including the flat terrain and relatively good communication network of the alluvium, had their positive impact on this process. The result was that the relatively thin layer of foreign deportees (Levantines, Anatolians and Egyptians) did not maintain their culture into the post-Achaemenid period, except for the special case of the Judeans. This topological aspect resembles that of the Nile valley where the same process took place with the same result and exception. The Arameo-Arabians and to a lesser extent the Iranians became part of the local scene in Babylonia.

The only explicit Phoenicians in the Nippur region are Tyrians. This is expected in view of the long siege of Tyre by Nebuchadnezzar II, which probably resulted in deportation. Only a handful of individuals bore Phoenician names in the Nippur region during the Chaldean and Achaemenid periods.[52] There is no evidence for exiles from rebellious Sidon in late-Achaemenid Nippur.[53] The settlement of Bīt-Ṣūrāya on the Piqūdu canal was named after the Tyrians. It was also inhabited by other groups, notably Judeans and Lycians. The Tyrians had their own *haṭru*-organisation in the late-Achaemenid period. The only recorded member of this organisation is *Ha-az-zi-ia* / Bēl-ēṭir (with a ring seal, SU 287), whose name could be Phoenician, but is common West Semitic and therefore not exclusively so (PBS 2/1 197, 14.VIII.3 Dar II). His father, the explicit Tyrian Bēl-ēṭir

51 See Zadok, 'Representation' and Ran Zadok, *Catalogue of Documents from Borsippa or Related to Borsippa in the British Museum* vol. 1 (Nisaba 21; Messina: Dipartimento di Scienze dell'Antichità dell'Università degli Studi di Messina, 2009), 15.

52 See Ran Zadok, 'Phoenicians, Philistines and Moabites in Mesopotamia', *BASOR* 230 (1978), 57–65 (60–61), add ⌜*x-x-x-hu*⌝*-lu-ú-nu* with fingernail mark, 30.III.31 Art I (Stolper, 'Fifth Century Nippur', 93–97: 6, left edge), cf. perhaps *Ia-a-hu-lu-ú-nu* (< Phoenician).

53 Prominent Sidonians were deported to Susa after the revolt of Tennes in 351/0 B.C.E. (cf. Johann N. Strassmaier, 'Einige kleinere babylonische Keilschrifttexte aus dem Britischen Museum', in *Actes du huitième congrès international des Orientalistes tenu en 1889 à Stockholm et à Christiania*. Deuxième partie, section 1B, 281–283, pl. 1–35 (28 3: 6).

/ Ardi-Baba, has a purely Akkadian filiation.[54] The location of his field, as well as that which his father held (+x AC) on 25.VII.40 Art I (BE 9 77) is not reported. There is no proof that it was located in Bīt-Ṣūrāya 'the Tyrians' place'. *Ha-bi-i-si* held a bow property administered by the *simmāgir*-official (presumably belonging to his *haṭru*-organisation) in Bīt-Ṣūrāya.[55] *Am-ma-ši-'* had a field there on 27.IV.1 Dar II (BE 10 33: 11). Both names are West Semitic, but only *Am-ma-ši-'* may be Phoenician as the former is probably Arabian. *Am-ma-ši-'* was the neighbour of *Bēl-ia-a-da-ah* / Mannu-kī-Nanāya (an Aramaic filiation), who held a bow-property there (*haṭru*-organisation of alphabet scribes of the army) on 14.-.1 Dar II (PBS 2/1 27, 5), 2.VII.1 Dar II (BE 10 33: 2, lower edge) and 28.VIII.4 Dar II (PBS 2/1 89: 2). In the same manner, the individuals recorded in *Ar-qa-'* (BE 10 58: 5), which was also named after a Phoenician city, had purely Akkadian-Aramaic filiations, viz. Bēl-rāšil and Nabû-ittannu sons of *Bi-ba-nu*, 28.VII.2 Dar II (BE 10 58: 4–5). They held half of a bow-property, possibly belonging to the *haṭru*-organisation of the archers? (*māhiṣē*) of the left (flank; foreman: Bazuzu / Bēl-bullissu, servant of Artahšar).

Judeans dwelt or held real property also in Išqallūnu, which was named after deportees from Ashkelon in Philistia. The latter was destroyed after it had fiercely resisted the Syro-Palestinian campaign of Nebuchadnezzar II.[56] *Ia-di-'-im* and *Ha-ag-ga-a* sons of ^{d}*Ta*$_{5}$*-míš-ba-rak-ki* were lessees (with fingernail marks) of fields (their *bīt-ritti*) in Išqallūnu on 22.XII.40 Art I (IMT 17: 1, 13, reverse: -[*im*], *H*[*a-...*]). *Ha-ag-ga-a* and ^{d}*Ta*$_{5}$*-míš-ba-rak-ki* are Aramaic names whereas *Ia-di-'-im* may be a Canaanite anthroponym, perhaps a reminiscence of his Philistine extraction (the Philistines had long been Canaanised by then), but this is far from certain. The material from the Gazite colony is also unsatisfactory for our quest for continuity of onomastic tradition. All the filiations are Arameo-Akkadian: Bēl-iddina / *Šá-ge-e* held a field (with several coparceners bearing Akkadian names) in Hazzatūa (gentilic of *Ha-za-tu*, cf. BE 10 9 from 1.I.1 Dar II) on 5.V.34 Art I (IMT 71: 2: *Šá-*[*ge-e*], reverse). The deed, which was issued in Hazzatūa, is witnessed by Nidinti-Bēl / *Ab-di-ia* and *Nabû-ra-am-mu* / Ulūlāya (second and fifth of five witnesses).

Aššа was located in northwestern Osrhoene, i.e. in the northwestern edge of the vast Aramaic-speaking continuum. The two non-Akkadian names of the

54 See Zadok, 'Phoenicians', 60.

55 The other bow-property there was held by Šamaš-šarra-uṣur on 4.IX.40 Art I (according to BE 9 79: 4 from Huṣṣēti-ša-Nabû-nāṣir).

56 Sailors from Tyre and Ashkelon are recorded in the archive from Nebuchadnezzar II's palace, Weidner, 'Jojachin', 928–929.

Aššeans are also Aramaic: *Šá-la-ʾ-Bēl* / Ulūlāya, held a bow property (together with Nanâ-iddina / Bēlšunu +x AC) of the *haṭru*-organisation of the Aššeans (^{lú}*Áš-ši-'*-A+A) in Pandānu on 6.VII.2 Dar II (PBS 2/1 191: 6, 13: [EN]). It was administered by the foreman Bēl-[...] and his 'brother' (= colleague?) Ea-bullissu. The foreman of ^{lú}*Áš-ši-'* on 19.VI.3 Dar II was *Ha-an-na-ni-'* / Bēlšunu (fifth witness of eight, PBS 2/1 65: 24), perhaps brother of Nanāya-iddina.

Magullu and Ham-qadu are extant in the Late Babylonian gentilics ^{lú}*Ma-gul-la*-A+A and ^{lú}*Ha-am-qa-du-ú-a*.[57] The latter's foreman (with an Akkadian filiation) is the fifth and penultimate witness in BE 10 82 from 21.III.4 Dar II. The former (^{lú}*Ma-⌜gu⌝$^{?}$-la*-A+A) is perhaps recorded in PBS 2/1 126: 2 from 6.XI.6 Dar II about arable land in Bāb-Nār-Dērat and Bannēšu. Its *haṭru*-organisation held bow-properties in Hambanāyu on 18.-.3 Dar II (BE 10 81, cf. BE 10 84 from -.-.4 Dar II). Members' names are not mentioned (the foreman had an Akkadian anthroponym and an Egyptian paternal name). **Magullu* can be explained as Aramaic.[58] It is possible that Šumutkunāyu (see just below) refers to Western Semites. Bow properties of the *haṭru*-organisation of the Šarrabaneans (originally a West Semitic tribe residing in Babylonia) were located in the settlement of Šarrabānu on 13.VI.40 Art I. All five holders have Akkadian names (IMT 53; administered by their foreman Rēmanni-Bēl; cf. BE 9 60 = IMT 33: 4, 13 from 21.XII.37 Art I). The adoption of Akkadian names by tribesmen settled for generations next to a temple town is typical. If EE 13 (from -.III$^{?}$.38 Art I) joins IMT 14,[59] then it is an additional proof for the proximity of Šarrabānu to Larak (besides their juxtaposition in the Eponym Canon from 704 B.C.E., Allan Millard, *The Eponyms of the Assyrian Empire* [SAAS 2; Helsinki: The Neo-Assyrian Text Corpus Project, 1994], 49: 7) seeing that IMT 14 is about the Larak canal. It cannot be excluded that settlements named after Aramean tribes included *haṭru*-organisations of such colonized tribesmen: fields of five explicit Hatalleans (^{lú}*Ha-ṭal-ú-a*) were located in the settlement of *Ha-ṭal-ú-a*. All the seven Hatalleans bore Aramaic names (see below [345–350]).[60]

57 Cf. Stolper, EE, 75: 20, 79: 65.

58 It may derive from *g.l.l.*, i.e. /**magVll*/ as a formation of *g.l.l.* 'to roll' with *ma-* praeformative (-GUL- is a CVC sign which is indifferent to vowel quality). *G.l.l.* is productive in West Semitic toponymy, cf. *gall* 'heap of stones, terrace' and *galīl* 'district' in NorthWest Semitic (Aramaic and Hebrew possibly with a Ugaritic precursor).

59 A probable assumption according to Donbaz and Stolper, IMT, 90 ad 14.

60 For the restricted samples from Ibūlē and Gambūlāyu see Zadok, *On West Semites in Babylonia*, 183–191.

Arabians (^{lú}*Ar-ba*-A+A):[61] *[B]i-ru-qa-' / Kul-lu-ki-i-il*(DINGIR^{meš}), held a bow property (+x AC) of the *haṭru*-organisation of the Arabians in Hamb/mari on 25.IV.1 Dar II (IMT 82: 3). The fragmentary deed PBS 2/1 47 bearing the seal impression of Mušēzib-Bēl/Erībâ, the Arabians' foreman (his title is omitted), refers perhaps to members of his *haṭru*-organisation; these include: [Bē]l$^{?}$([^{d}+E]N$^{?}$)-ēṭir / *Šak-ku-hu, Ab-da-'* / Sîn-iddina and *[M]a$^{?}$-[r]e$^{?}$-' / Šá-ge-e* (the father is homonymous with an individual from Hazzatūa above) each held a share of a bow-property (another share was held by Šumāya and possibly by additional individuals, location not preserved) on 4.V.2 Dar II (PBS 2/1 47: 3–4). ^{d}*Ta*$_{5}$*-míš-ba-rak-ku* (upper edge, with an iron ring, SU 593) is listed before the foreman. The same foreman of the Arabians had a bow-property which belonged to the *haṭru*-organisation of the *šušānus* of *kirikēti* (13.V.2 Dar II, PBS 2/1 48).[62] The three deeds issued at Balšam (below [369–378]) contain mostly Aramaic names with a slight Arabian 'admixture'.[63] A comprehensive geographical distribution of the pertinent individuals and properties, amounting to a reconstruction of dossiers of small settlements wherever applicable is presented after the survey of the socio-economic distribution of the groups under discussion (below, Part III [302–464]).

All the West Semitic (practically: Aramaic) names in the nine mixed Iranian-West Semitic filiations refer to members of the second generation.[64] Taken together with the fact that second-third generation members of the multi-generational *haṭru*-organisation of the Iranian Aruwāyu bore Aramaic and Akkadian anthroponyms, this is a clear indication of acculturation of the Iranians to the local milieu (the slight Egyptian admixture is part of the process).[65] In the same manner, almost all the members of the *haṭru*-organisation of the Scythians bore Aramaic names in 417/6 B.C.E.[66] It is plausible that the Scythians were settled there several generations earlier, possibly shortly after the Achaemenid conquest of Babylonia. This conquest opened new horizons for long-distance slave trade.

---

61 E.g., IMT 82: 3, see Ran Zadok, 'On Early Arabians in the Fertile Crescent', *Tel Aviv* 17 (1990), 223–231 (224, 226–28).

62 For analogous cases see Stolper, EE, 85–86.

63 Cf. Ran Zadok, 'Arabians in Mesopotamia during the Late-Assyrian, Chaldean, Achaemenian and Hellenistic Periods Chiefly According to Cuneiform Sources', *ZDMG* 131 (1981), 42–84 (72–76).

64 Cf. Ran Zadok, *Iranische Personennamen in der Neu- und spätbabylonischen Nebenüberlieferung* (IPNB 7/1B; Vienna: Österreichische Akademie der Wissenschaften, 2009), 309, 392, 425, 476, 511, 553, 606, 641, with one exception only (557 a Judean; 517 is atypical).

65 Ran Zadok, 'Iranians and Individuals Bearing Iranian Names in Achaemenian Babylonia', *IOS* 7 (1977), 89–138 (115–120: 2, 15, 16, 20, 28).

66 TuM 2/3, 189, see Zadok, 'Iranians', 123–124 and Igor M. Diakonoff, 'The Cimmerians', in *Monumentum Georg Morgenstierne* 1 (ed. J. Duchesne-Guillemin and P. Lecoq; Acta Iranica 21; Leiden: Brill, 1981), 103–140 (121 with n. 39); The name *Ši-ka-ra-ku* can also be explained as Aramaic.

However, unlike infiltrations, deportations and mobilisations of workforce, such transactions had a very limited impact on the ethno-linguistic character of the Nippur region. *Bēl-na-tan-nu*, who was bought from *Bēl-ah-hi-ia-a-ni-'* / Mušēzib-Bēl in the cosmopolitan capital of Susa (on 3.XII.5 Dar II), was of mixed (Arameo-Egyptian) milieu and parentage (PBS 2/1 113: 2, 5). The female slave *Ha-an-na-ta-ᵈE-si-'* (PBS 2/1 65: 4, 9) had a hybrid (Arameo-Egyptian) name. Due to their very low percentage in the general population, almost all the non-Semitic ethnic groups, notably the Egyptians and Anatolians, show a considerable admixture of Aramaic and Babylonian names.

A brother of a second-generation Lydian adopted a typical Aramaic name: AH-*ba*(or *ma*)-*na-*ʾ / x[...] was brother of *Ba-rik-ki-ᵈBēl* (both with fingernail mark; cf. perhaps the paternal name AH?-*ba*(or *ma*)-*na* from Bīt-Zukkītu, below [312–314]). They held bow-properties (+x AC) in Galê and Bīt-Tabalāya (witnessed by the foreman of the Indians Bagazuštu / Bagapatu); [Nippur], 21.VII.1 Dar II (BE 10 53: 1, 14, upper edge). Another second-generation Lydian bore the Akkadian name Bēl-ittannu (/*Te-ma-*ʾ). He held a bow-property in Bīt-Tabalāya, very probably together with his son *Hu-ma-ni-hi-ia-a-'* (*Hu-ma-ni-'-ia-'*, with a fingernail mark) on 3+[x].VIII.40 Art I (EE 38). The latter bore a non-Babylonian, apparently Lydian, name, although he belonged to the third generation. Such non-linear naming tendencies were common among other foreign population groups, but on the long run they assimilated. In the same manner, the only recorded members of the *haṭru*-organisation of the Urartians and Melitenians have indigenous, i.e. Akkadian or mixed Arameo-Akkadian filiations, viz. *Ba-rik-ki-* Bēl / Bēl-šimanni, Bēl-zēra-iddina / Iddina-Bēl and *Ad-da-'* / Bēl-aba-uṣur, who held a bow property (+x AC) in Bīt-Iltehlāyi on 25.IV.1 Dar II (PBS 2/1 180: 3; the members dwelling in the settlement of Milidu, which was named after them, are anonymous). *ᵈTa₅-míš-ba-rak-ku* / Nidinti-Bēl, foreman of the Urartians and Melitenians (with a stamp seal, SU 184), -.V.6 Dar II (BE 10 107: 3, 6, lower edge), was himself a member of the *haṭru*-organisation of the boatmen.[67] All the three members and the foremen of the *haṭru*-organisation of *ˡúŠu-mu-ut-ku-na*-A+A (Aramaic *Šmtkny'* in Hattāya)[68] bore Babylonian names (9.-.6 Dar II, BE 10 115, witnessed by *Ahi-nūrī* / *Qu-da-a* and *Zab-di-ia* / *Na-ṭi-ru*, third and fourth of six, with a cylinder seal and a ring respectively, SU 320, 569, the latter recurs as *Za-bi-da-a*, 6.XI.6 Dar II, PBS 2/1 126: lower edge). The presence of Šumutkuneans in a settlement named after people

67 See Stolper, EE, 86.
68 See Zadok, *On West Semites in Babylonia*, 21 and Ran Zadok, *Geographical Names*, 296, s.v. Šumātakānu.

from eastern Anatolia or north Syria does not necessarily indicate that they originated from these regions.

Part II Occupation and Class

The aim of this second part is to present a preliminary overview of the various occupations and class categories attested for the Aramean population group represented in the Late Achaemenid Murašû archive from Nippur (as discussed in I.3 above). For the sake of clarity it would have been preferable to arrange the functionaries, professionals and occupations before classifying them by social status. However, the arrangement below is dictated by the nature of the material: functionaries and certain class categories (a-b) are not included in the system of the *haṭru*-organisations, whereas c-g are. Most organisations of that system refer to households (or estates) and classes in the first place: the occupational distribution is within the class. Many of these organisations consist of *šušānus*, a category of semi-free workmen, which is their most frequent common denominator and in addition each is defined by occupation. Individuals, whose organisational affiliation and domicile are unknown, are relegated to section h [198–229] (a few exceptions are listed in [230–239]), to be followed by those who are only attested as witnesses, unless they are related to the members of the socio-economic groups.

a Officialdom[69]

Some officials mentioned in the Murašû archive did not reside in Nippur. A case in point is Nahiš-ṭābu, appointee of Mitratu (with a ring, SU 510). He is recorded on 8.X.6 Dar II in Nippur (BE 10 114: 16, upper edge) and recurs as Nihistu-ṭābu in Borsippa on 21.V.10 Dar II.[70] The later occurrence is recorded in the archive of the satrap Bēlšunu (Belesys, *Dar.* 274). Royal officials generally resided in Babylon, which served as one of the Achaemenid capitals. Therefore it stands to

69 See Bregstein, SU, 114–161, 175–179.
70 *Nḥšṭb* (Ναάσταβος) meaning 'good omen' is very common among Arameans during the Hellenistic era (including the Mineans who – unlike other South Arabians – had intensive contact with Arameans, see O. Eissfeldt, '"Gut Glück!" in semitischer Namengebung', *JBL* 82 [1963], 195–200). *Nihistu-ṭābu*, referring to the same individual (*Dar.* 274: 4, 8), must be a secondary form with *interpretatio Akkadica* (for *nihistu* in Neo-Babylonian / Late Babylonian see CAD N/2, 219a) made by a sophisticated scribe of the Bēlšunu archive from Babylon.

reason that appointees and servants of prominent officials and princes (below [14, 34–36]) were itinerant. The case of *Šá-ma-ah-ta-ni-'*, the chief of herds of Prince Arsham (below [74]), whose master's estates were scattered over several regions, may be different: the presence of his brother among the shepherds active in the Nippur region may support *Šá-ma-ah-ta-ni-'*'s connection with Nippur. Foremen of *haṭru*-organisations and their aids (altogether 17) are listed below [34, 42–43, 52, 55, 88–89, 117, 125–126, 145–146, 149, 167, 186–187, 195].[71]

Important functionaries (6)

[1] *Na-ap-sa-nu* / Iddina-Nabû, prefect (*pīhātu*) of the left bank of the Nār-Sîn, [...], -.-.2 – 25.XI.3 Dar II (master of Ṭāb-ahu), was the highest official bearing a West Semitic name.[72]

[2] Bēl-ēreš / *Na-ti-na-'*, in charge of the rent (*sūtu*) of Nār-Sîn (with a cylinder seal, SU 32), 19.-.24 [Art I] (EE 43, 3', reverse: [...]).

[3] Bēl-ēṭir / *Šá-ra-ʾ -il*(DINGIR^{meš}), *ustarbar*-official (with a cylinder seal, SU 153), second witness of five; 16.VII.41 Art I (BE 9 102: 16).

[4] Šullumu / *Za-ab-ba-a*, summoner (*dēkû*; with an iron ring, SU 366), received the taxes of bow-properties of the *haṭru*-organisation of the archers (*māhiṣē*) of the left (flank) on 17.XI.1 Dar II (PBS 2/1 188: 10).[73] He acted as the sixth and last witness in a deed concerning a bow-property belonging to the same organisation on 28.VII.2 Dar II (BE 10 58: 15).

[5] Mīnu-<ana>-Bēl-dānu / *Da*(or *Ṭa*)*-ah-hu-ú-a*, *rab-ummi* functionary, second witness of nine (with a cylinder seal, SU 189), 18.VII.5 Dar II (BE 10 101: 24, lower edge).

[6] [*Na*]*bû-ha-qa-bi* / [...], probably a functionary, [Nippur], 9.XII.0 Dar II (IMT 105: 10).

For ^{lú}*pi-ti-pa-ba-ga* see below [109].

Judges (1)[74]

The only judge whose Aramean extraction is plausible is **[7]** *Ta-ta-'* / *Zab-di-ia* (of Nār-Sîn, -.V.3–10.VII.5 Dar II; Zadok, *Iranische Personennamen*, 517; with a stamp seal, SU 404). Bēl-ēreš / Ad-di-lu-uš-šú (with a cylinder seal, SU 299) and his colleague, *A-te-ia-na-'* / *Ba*(or *Ma*)*-qa-am-qa-am* (with a ring, SU 123) did not reside

71 Cf. Bregstein, SU, 161–69.

72 PBS 2/1 59: 4, 6; 72: 3, 6, 10; cylinder seal of his servant (SU 176); see Zadok, *On West Semites in Babylonia*, 191.

73 Cf. SAA 7 216a and EE 75: 22.

74 See Cardascia, *Les Archives*, 19–22.

in the Nippur region as they are described as judges of the Sealand (near Elam, 24.VII.40 Art I). The former has an Elamite paternal name[75] whereas the latter bears an Iranian anthroponym and possibly a West Semitic paternal name (BE 9 75: 16, reverse). The reason for the presence of these judges outside their territory of jurisdiction eludes us. Their colleague Bēl-aha-iddina witnessed a deed concerning the *haṭru*-organisation of the *šušānus* of the foremen (below [167–170]); the only localized bow-property of this organisation was in Abastanu, which like Kuzabatu, is recorded in BE 9 75 (see below [140–146]) where it is said to be located in the Nār-simmāgir district together with Hindāyu whose district is unknown.

Alphabet scribes (sg. *sepīru*; 3)

[8] Id-di-ia / *Za-bid-da-a*, of the treasurer (*mašennu*), third witness of 11; with a cylinder seal, SU 164), 25.VII.7 Dar II (PBS 2/1 193: 17, upper edge: [Id]-).

[9] *Aq-bi-il*(DINGIR^{meš}), of [...], fifth preserved witness of x+6, -.VII.6 Dar II (BE 10 113: 15).

[10] ^{d}*Ta*$_{5}$*-míš-ba-rak-ku* ^{lú}*se-p*[*i*$^{?}$*-ru*$^{?}$], fifth witness of nine preserved, 12.XII.4 Dar II (PBS 2/1 96: 20).

See also below [124–126] for *alphabet scribes of the army.*

Appointees (sg. *paqdu*; 5)

[11] *A-qu-bi-iá* (of Unnapar), no place, 4.-.26 [Art I] (EE 10: 4).

[12] *Bar-rik-ki-a* (of Parrinuš), 23.X.5 Dar II (BE 10 103: 8).

[13] *Ha-na-(an)-na* (of Lā-abâši), 4.IX.7 Dar II (BE 10 127).

[14] Nabû-ušēzib / *Ia-a-hab-bi-il*(DINGIR^{meš}), a functionary with a stamp seal (SU 625), brought a parchment letter from Lā-abâši, appointee of the crown prince's household, on 18.VII.5 Dar II (BE 10 101: 16: *i*[*a*]-, 20, upper edge).

[15] *Har-bat-ta-nu* (with one exception always with his title and stamp seal, SU 111), -.II.1 Dar II (BE 10 12: lower edge); *Har-ba-ta-nu*, 8.III.1 Dar II (BE 10 21: upper edge); *Har-bat-a-nu*, 5.IV.1 Dar II (PBS 2/1 177: right edge); 15.IV.1 Dar II (BE 10 28: lower edge); 20.IV.1 Dar II (BE 10 30: lower edge); 9.V.1 Dar II (BE 10 38: reverse); 10.VII.1 Dar II (PBS 2/1 187: left edge, cf. IMT 199); -.-.1 Dar II (PBS 2/1 190: reverse, cf. IMT 199); -.IX.- Dar II (PBS 2/1 161: reverse).[76]

---

75 Cf. *At-ta-lu-uš*, Ran Zadok, *The Elamite Onomasticon* (Supplemento agli Annali dell'Istituto Orientale di Napoli no. 40; Naples: Istituto Universitario Orientale, 1984), 18, 132.

76 See Bregstein, SU, 356 with n. 95, 504: 111, who lists also BE 10 13: upper edge to 5.II.1$^{?}$ Dar II and PBS 2/1 165: lower edge to -.-.-. Dar II, without indicating the spelling.

b Class Categories

Household members (sg. *mār-bīti*;[77] 6)

They were more prominent than servants (cf. the *cursus honorum* of Teri-kamu, Zadok, *Iranische Personennamen*, 525).

[16] *Ia-di-ih-il*(DINGIR^{meš}) / *Ha-na-ni-'* (of Artabara) in charge of the rent of Nār-Sîn (with a stamp seal, SU 426), 28.X. and 1.XI.28 Art I (BE 9 14:, 5, lower edge; 15: 10, 15).

[17] *Ba-rik-ki-il*(DINGIR^{meš}) / Atkallâ (with an iron ring, SU 157; of Ṣillāya, the foreman of the *haṭru*-organisation of the bowmen$^{?}$ of the left), concerning bow-properties on Nār-Māhiṣē in Arzuhinu on 17.XI.1 Dar II (PBS 2/1 188: 8–9, 12, right edge: *Ba-rik-*).

[18] *Ha-nun* / Bēl-kā[ṣir] (with a ring, SU 444), in a deed concerning bow-properties of the *haṭru*-organisation of the *šušānus*, makers of the levee$^{?}$, in settlements situated on Nār-simmāgir; 23.V.6 Dar II (PBS 2/1 120: upper edge); *Ha-nu-nu* / Bēl-kāṣir acted as proxy (with a ring, SU 444) for Harmahi, household member of the treasurer (*mašennu*) Hurumunapar (concerning fields on Nār-simmāgir) on 29.VI.9$^{?}$ Dar II (IMT 48: 7–8, right edge, cf. PBS 2/1 143).

[19] ^{d}*Ta*$_{5}$*-míš-li-in-ṭâr* (servant or household member of) Illil-šuma-iddina, 28.VI.1 Dar II (PBS 2/1 15: 3, 7: *-l*[*i*]-, 9: ^{d}*Ta*$_{5}$-).

[20] *Il*(DINGIR^{meš})*-na-ṭa-ri* (of Minū-<ana>-Bēl-dānu the *rab-ummi*) with an iron ring (SU 552), 10.VI.5 Dar II (PBS 2/1 207: 12, upper edge). He may be identical with his namesake, who – together with Illil-uballiṭ / *Ba-rik-ki-il*(DINGIR^{meš}) and *Ba-rik-Bēl* servant of Puhhurāya (with a ring, SU 384) – had to deliver dates from the chariot estate on Namgar-Dūr-Illil; 4.X.4 Dar II (PBS 2/1 209: 4, 8).

[21] *Ag-gu-ba-'* (see above, Part I.3).

Servants of the Murašûs (sg. *ardu* unless otherwise indicated; 12).

Of Illil-hātin:

[22] ^{d}*Ta*$_{5}$*-míš-ki-*⌜*i*⌝*-*[*ni*], *qallu*, 3.I.28 Art I (Stolper, 'Fifth Century Nippur', 89–92: 4, 5: *-ki*, copy DI-⌜*i*⌝-[*ni*], 9, 12).

Of Illil-šuma-iddina:

[23] *Ba-rik-*^{d}*Ta*$_{5}$*-míš*, 13.IX.30 Art I (BE 9 21: 3); *Ba-ri-ki-ta*$_{5}$*-míš*, 16.[...].35 Art I (BE 9 44: 20).

77 See Stolper, EE, 20–21; Bregstein, SU, 179–185.

[24] *Qâr-ha-an-ni* (with a fingernail mark), lessee of arable land on Nār-Sahidu, <Nippur>, 30.III.31 Art I. (Stolper, 'Fifth Century Nippur', 93–97: 6, 1, left edge: *Qâr-ha-nu*).

[25] *Ahi-li-ti-ia* had a rented field (*bīt-sūti*) on Nār-Sîn on 12.XI.37 Art I (BE 9 55: 8, 11, 21).

[26] *Ba-hi-il-ga-ad-du*, lessee of fields of the *simmāgir*-official in Bīt-Ṣababa-ēreš, 15.XII.34 Art I (IMT 8: 1); identical to [39]?

[27] ^{d}*At-tar-nu-ri-'*, lessee of palm groves of his master on Namgar-Dūr-Illil, 16.VII.41 Art I. (BE 9 101: 6).

[28] [...] / *Addu-ra-am-mu*, [^{lú} ... *šá*] (in broken context), [...], -.-.19 Art I (EE 48: 9).

[29] [^{d}*I*]*l-te-eh-ri-na-qi-*['], co-debtor (bricks; with a fingernail mark); [...], -.-.30+[x] Art I (EE 96: 3). He remained later in the service of Rēmūt-Ninurta; ^{d}*Il-te-eh-ri-na-aq-qí-'*, sixth and penultimate witness (with a cylinder seal, SU 532), -.VI.5 Dar II (PBS 2/1 106: 23, lefte edge).

Of Rēmūt-Ninurta:

[30] [*R*]*a-hi-im* / Bēl-aba-uṣur, fourth witness of six preserved, 6.-.1. Dar II (PBS 2/1 28: 14); *Ra-hi-im* (always with a cylinder seal, SU 55), lessee of fields and palm groves belonging to the *haṭru*-organisation of the *šušānus* of the treasury in Hattāya, *Imm*[*er*]*tu*$^{?}$ and Bīt-Nanāya-ēreš, -.III$^{?}$.5 Dar II (PBS 2/1 106: 1, reverse); first of eight witnesses, Tīl-Gabbāri, 11.X.5 Dar II (PBS 2/1 108: 7, upper edge); *Ra-h*[*i-im*], concerning a bow-property of the *šušānus* of the foremen in *Si-bi-ra-'-ni*; 4.II.6 Dar II (PBS 2/1 117: 7), concerning bow-property of the *šušānus* of the foremen, 6.VII.6 Dar II (BE 10 112: 1, lower edge); concerning bow-property of the *šušānus* of the treasury, Hašbāya (near Tīl-Gabbāri), 23.VIII.6 Dar II (PBS 2/1 123: 2, 21).[78]

[31] *Ni-il-la-ta-'*, principal acting in his master's name, 4.-.2 Dar II (PBS 2/1 56: 6).

[32] *Ha-an-na-ta-ni-'* (with a cylinder seal, SU 214), last witness, 20.IV.4 Dar II (PBS 2/1 83: 9, upper edge); ninth and last witness, 19.III.[6] Dar II (PBS 2/1 150: 26).

[33] *Za-bu-du* / *Nabû-ia-a-ha-bi* (with a fingernail mark, cf. IMT 202), 17.I.7 Dar II (PBS 2/1 222: 3–4).

---

78 See Stolper, EE, 89–90.

Servants of others (7)

Of Gubaru satrap of Babylonia:

[34] *Pa-qí-qí*, foreman of the household of the chief of the butchers and fifth witness of seven (with a cylinder seal, SU 146), 13.IV.4 Dar II (BE 10 84: 8, reverse; 85: 15, upper edge).

Of prince Manuštānu:

[35] *Man-ki-ia* / *Pa-qí-qí-i* (presumably the son of [34]), fourth witness of eight (with a ring, SU 549), 15.VIII.40 Art I (TuM 2/3 180: 9).

Of prince Artareme:

[36] *Da-la-ta-ni-'* / Ninurta-ēṭir, third witness of eleven (with a ring, SU 359), 15.VI.40 Art I (BE 9 72: 11, reverse).

Of *Ia-am-ma-'*:

[37] *Ba-rik-ki-il* (-DINGIR^{meš}, with a ring). His master owned a field in Huṣṣēti-ša-Nāṣiru on 20.VII.3 Dar II (BE 10 72: 4, upper edge).

Of Šuma-iddina and **[38]** *Za-bi-na-'*:

[39] *Ba-il-ga-ad-du*, 26$^{?}$.IV.1 Dar II (BE 10 32: 3); identical to [26]?

Of Liblut̩ / Lā-abâši:

[40] *Hi-in-nu-ni-'*, creditor, 3.XII.6 Dar II (PBS 2/1 129: 2, 8).

Of Rušundātu:

[41] *Hi-in-ni-'-Bēl* / *Da-la-ta-ni-'* (implicit dependent), cultivated fields of his master in Nāqidīni and other places, 15.VI.1 Dar II (BE 10 43: 1).

c Occupations

Pastry makers (*kaškadinē*; 1)[79]

[42] *Nabû-ra-am* / Nabû-aha-rēmanni, deputy (with a stamp seal, SU 191) of Ahūnâ, the foreman of their *haṭru*-organisation, 24$^{?}$.VII.4 Dar II (PBS 2/1 203: 6, obverse).

---

79 See Stolper, EE, 74: 15.

Carpenters (*naggārē*, Aramaic *ngry'*; 1)

[43] Their foreman, *Hi-'-du-ri-'* / Habaṣīru (with a stamp seal, SU 125), was servant of Balāṭu / *Ṣi-ha-'*, Hašbāya, 18.II.5 Dar II (BE 10 99: 4: [*Hi*]-, 9, upper edge, reverse: Aramaic *Ḥydwry* / *Ḥbṣyr*).[80]

Leather workers (8)

The bow properties of the *haṭru*-organisation of the leather workers were located in the homonymous settlement (Aškāpē, analogous to the location of the boatmen's properties; IMT 133).

[44] ^{d}*Ta*$_5$*-míš-ba-rak-ku* / Hašdāya brother of *Šá-lam-ahi* ([45]).

[45] *Šá-lam-ahi* (Akkadian – West Semitic) was their foreman (with an iron ring, SU 600), -.VIII.- Dar II (PBS 2/1 160: upper edge). Seven bow-properties in Aškāpē were administered by their foreman *Šá-lam-ahi* / Hašdāya according to BE 9 70: 2–8 from 13.XII.39 Art I. Three were held by bearers of Aramaic names:

[46] *Addu-na-tan-na* (together with Bēl-eṭēru)

[47] *Nabû-da-la-'* (with *Bi-ba-a*)

[48] *Ab-da-'* (together with Sîn-*ta-qu-nu*). All recur later. *Addu-na-tan-nu* / *Šak-ku-hu* (with a fingernail mark) held a bow-property in Aškāpē on 25.VI.41 Art I (IMT 74: 2–3, left edge) and *Nabû-da-la-'* / Bēl-ušēzib held a field there (25. VI.41 Art I, IMT 75 2: [^{d}+AG]-, left edge; same witnesses as in BE 9 98).

[49] Nādinu / *Ba-rik-ki-*^{d}*Ta*$_5$*-míš* (with a fingernail mark) and *Ab-da-'* / Sîn-iddina [48] held a bow-property (together with Illil-hātin / Bēlšunu +x AC) there (25.VI.41 Art I, IMT 76: 2; the fingernail mark of the former's father is also impressed, upper edge).

[50] *Zab-di-iá* / Sîn-nādin-ahi (with a fingernail mark) held a bow-property there (25.VI.41 Art I, BE 9 97: 2, left edge).

[51] *Ra-hi-im-il*(DINGIR^{meš}) / AH-ú-[...] (with a fingernail mark) held property there (25.VI.41 Art I, BE 9 98: 2, obverse: *Ra-hi-i*[*m-*...]).

Parchment-roll makers (*magallāta-karānu*; 3)

[52] *A-ra-ah* / Puhhuru, brother of Šamaš-nāṣir, was their foreman (with a stamp seal, SU 5) on 14.VIII.7 Dar II (PBS 2/1 136: 9, left edge).

[53] *Aha-a-bu-ú* / *Zab-di-ia* held (+x AC) a bow-property of their *haṭru*-organisation in Bannēšu on 3.IX.4 Dar II (BE 10 93: 4).

[54] ⌜*xx*⌝*-da-la-'* / Ninurta-gāmil held (with others) a bow-property of their organisation there on 14.VIII. 7 Dar II (PBS 2/1 136: 5).

---

80 For subordinate foremen see Stolper, EE, 88–89.

Horse-feeders (*aspastua, aspastūtu*; 4)[81]
Their foreman, *Gu-sur-ri*(-') / Lā-abâši (a royal *šušānu*), acted through his servants, notably:

[55] *Te-ri-hi-li-ia* (with a fingernail mark), assisted by an alphabet scribe on 14.XI.[3] Dar II (BE 10 80: 7, 10, lower edge: – *iá*).

[56] *Da-la-ta-ni-'* and

[57] *Ab-da-'* (+x AC) held a bow-property of their *haṭru*-organisation in Bāb-Nār-Šubat-Ea then. It is recorded with another bow-property, which was held there (+x AC) by Anu-ibni and

[58] *Za-bi-*[*n*]*a-'* on 24.XII.4 Dar II (PBS 2/1 95: 5).

Shepherds
Of the *haṭru*-organisation of the shepherds (3+1):

[59] *Man-nu-lu-ha-a* (Aramaic *Mn'*[...]) / *A-dar-ri-il*(DINGIR^{meš}),

[60] ^{d}*Ta*$_{5}$*-míš-nu-úr-ri-'* / *I-qu-pa-'* and

[61] *Ia-a-di-hu-il*(DINGIR^{meš}) / Ahūšunu held each a bow-property in Bīt-Arzāya on 2.VII.1 Dar II (BE 10 46: 2–4, left edge; with fingernail marks, cf. PBS 2/1 36), adjacent to the field of

[62] *Za-bu-da-'* with an additional plot in Bīt-Bahari.
Non-members (18): It is not known whether any of the following individuals was a member of a *haṭru*-organisation. All were engaged in small stock herding, except for two,

[63] *Za-bi-na-'* / Iddina-Illil (cattle); 19.VIII.36 Art I (IMT 34: 2: -[*bi-na*]-', 12; IMT 107).

[64] ^{d}*Na-na-a-id-ri-'* / *Sah-ma-'* leased a cow from Illil-šuma-iddina, presumably as a means of production; Bīt-māri-rubê, 1.VIII.30 Art I (BE 9 20: 5, 7: -[*i*]*d-r*[*i-'*], 10, 12: [....]-*id*, left edge: *Na-na-*[*a*]*-id- r*[*i-'*]). His brother,

[65] Nanāya-iddina / *Sa-ah-ma-'* is the seventh witness of nine, -.V.31 Art I (BE 9 27: 11).

[66] *A-qu-bu* / *Za-ab-di-ia* was probably employed as a guard of small stock by Illil-šuma-iddina (with a ring, SU 614) on 8.I.31 Art I (BE 9 24: 1, 3, 9, lower edge).[82] *A.* / *Zab-di-ia*, sixth witness of eight (with a ring, SU 614), 4.IX.40 Art I (BE 9 79: 13, lower edge; written by Ubāru / Nādinu). On the same day he acted as a witness (fifth of seven, with a ring) to a deed of the sale of

---

81 See Stolper, EE, 72–73.
82 See Cardascia, *Les Archives*, 184.

a slave by Tattannu / Aplāya, the *simmāgir*-official, to Illil-šuma-iddina in Huṣṣēti-ša-Nabû-nāṣir, written by a different scribe.[83]

[67] *Bi-ru-ha-'* and **[68]** *Ahi-li-te-'*, Illil-ašābšu-iqbi, time of Illil-šuma-iddina (EE 108). Witnesses 8 and 18 are explicitly described as shepherds, while witnesses 9–11, 13–17 were implicitly such (lessees of small stock, 7, 13–18 with fingernail marks):

[69] *Za-bid-*^{d}*Na-na-a / Ha-am-ba-ru-ru* (lessor: Rēmūt-Ninurta / Murašû via his servant Rībatu), no place, 10.III.6 Dar II (BE 10 106: 10, reverse: Aramaic *Zbdnn*').

[70] *Ab-da-'* (with a ring and a stamp seal), 10.III.6 Dar II (Stolper, 'Fifth Century Nippur,' 91–94: 5, 10, reverse);

[71] Bēl-ēṭir / Šamšāya (the paternal name is Akkadian-West Semitic), 10.III.6 Dar II (PBS 2/1 118: 9, reverse: Aramaic *Bl'ṭr*; with a ring, SU 372); ninth witness of eleven, followed by his brother [420] ^{d}*Ta*$_{5}$*-mīš-ba-r*[*ak-k*]*i*, Kapri-Lirīm, 14.VII.7 Dar II (PBS 2/1 226: 18).

[72] ^{d}*Il-te-ri-ia-a-ha-bi / Hi-in-nu-ni-'* (with a bronze ring, SU 631), 18.VI.11 Dar II (PBS 2/1 144: 1, 22, reverse: -[*ha-bi*]). ^{d}*Il-te-hi-ri-a-bi / H.*, eighth preserved and last witness, Hašbāya, 18.II.5 Dar II (BE 10 99: 16); ^{d}[*Il-t*]*e-hi-ri-a-bi / H.*, second witness of six, Titurru (near Hašbāya), 25.VI.5 Dar II (PBS 2/1 208: 16–17); ^{d}*Il-te-hi-ri-abi*(AD) / *H.*, tenth preserved and last witness, Hašbāya, 22.VIII.6 Dar II (PBS 2/1 123: 27). In all the witnesses' lists he occurs together (twice juxtaposed) with *Na-ṭi-ir / Ba-rik-ki-*^{d}*Ta*$_{5}$*-mīš* [403, see below].

[73] *Nabû-ra-am* / Nabû-ušēzib (with a stamp seal, SU 458), 3.III.- Dar II (PBS 2/1 227: 1: [^{d} +AG]-, upper edge).

[74] *Šá-ma-ah-ta-ni-'* / Isināya, chief of the herds *(rab būli*, with a ring, SU 560) of Aršama, 21.VI.11–29.II$^{?}$.13 Dar II (BE 10 130: 23, reverse; 131: 22, reverse; 132: 21, lower edge; PBS 2/1 146: 23; 147: reverse; 148: 23), was the most prominent functionary of livestock husbandry. He was the brother of

[75] *Bēl-na-tan-nu*, 21.VI.11 Dar II (PBS 2/1 147: 1, 22, reverse).

[76] ^{d}*Ta*$_{5}$*-mīš-nūrī*(ZÁLAG)*-'* / Ardi-Ninurta, 21.VI.11 Dar II (BE 10 130: 1: ⌜^{d}*Ta*$_{5}$-, 18, 21, reverse);

[77] *Da-hi-il-ta-'/Ha-za-'-il*(DINGIR^{meš}), Aramaic *Dḥlth / Ḥzh'l*, 21.VI.11 Dar II (PBS 2/1 145: 1).

---

83 Although Tattannu is mentioned without a title, he is probably identical with the homonymous and contemporary *simmāgir*-official (e.g. EE 117: 7', see Stolper, EE, 40 with n. 12 and 73–74; unfortunately, no seal is impressed after the caption implying that the tablet is a copy). Two of the remaining six witnesses are the seller's sons and one, the first, is his brother (IMT 104: 2, 7).

[78] *Bēl-za-bad-du* / *Bi-ṣa-a* and **[79]** *Ha-an-na-ni-'* (Aramaic *Ḥnny*) / Ṭābīya (DU_{10} GA-iá, Aramaic *Ṭby*, Akkadian – West Semitic), 29.II?.13 Dar II (BE 10 132: 1, 19).

[80] *dQu-su-ia-a-ha-bi* / *Ma-re-e*, 28.VII.1 Art II (BE 9 1: 1: *Q*[*u*]-, 23, 25: *Q*[*u-su-i*] *a*-, right edge). He is the latest of five individuals bearing Idumean-Arabian names in Neo-Babylonian / Late Babylonian sources.[84]

Boatmen (*malahhāni*; 4+1)

Of the Euphrates (implied by the location of their settlement Malahhāni on the Euphrates of Nippur):

[81] *dTa₅-mîš-ba-rak-ku* / Nidinti-Bēl held a bow-property of the *haṭru*-organisation of the boatmen in their settlement (Malahhāni) in -.II.1 Dar II (PBS 2/1 6: 2).

[82] *Kul-ki-i-il*(DINGIR*meš*) / Bēlāya, the brother of **[83]** Nidintāya, held a bow-property (together with that of Ubārīya / Kīnāya +x AC) of the same organisation there in -.-.1 Dar II (PBS 2/1 33: 2).

[84] Šamaš-ittannu / *Da-l*[*a-ta-ni-'*] (with a fingernail mark) held a bow-property possibly in Malahhāni on 17.[VII].41 Art I (EE 64: 2 from [Nippur]), but its organisational affiliation is not indicated. He recurs on 9.V.1 Dar II concerning a second mortgage of the bow-property of Aba-ul-īdi (+x AC, organisational affiliation unknown, BE 10 38: 2, left edge).[85]

Of the Tigris?

[85] *Hi-in-ni-'-Bēl* / Zitti-Nabû is recorded in a deed concerning a bow-property of the boatmen of the Tigris (PBS 2/1 135), *huṭāru*, *šušānus* makers of the levee?[86] and Indians from 6.VIII.7 Dar II (PBS 2/1 135: 3: *Hi-in-'-* [d+EN], 9).

Guards (sg. *kizû*; 2)[87]

[86] *Na-ah-ma-nu* and **[87]** *Ši-il-li-mu* (presumably Judeans) held (together with Bēl-ušallim) a bow-property of the *haṭru*-organisation of *kizû*-guards in Huṣṣēti-ša-*A-mu-qa-du*, 10.VII.5 Dar II (TuM 2/3 187: 4).

Gate guards (*maṣṣarē bābāni*; 2)

[88] *Ha-na-'-il*(DINGIR*meš*) / *Za-bad-du* held a bow-property of the *haṭru*-organisation of the gate guards (location not preserved) on 10.VIII.6 Dar II

84 See Ran Zadok, 'On the Prosopography and Onomastics of Syria-Palestine and Adjacent Regions', *UF* 32 (2000), 599–674 (602–603).
85 Cf. Stolper, EE, 106 with n. 11.
86 Cf. Stolper, EE, 77: 43.
87 Cf. Stefan Zawadzki, 'Miscellanea Sipparica', *NABU* 2002/55 (52).

(PBS 2/1 217: 6, reverse; with a cylinder seal, SU 65, cf. IMT 201). He was the foreman of the gate guards on 21.VI.7 Dar II (PBS 2/1 133: 25): *A-na-ʾ-il*(DINGIR*meš*) / *Z.* (without title, 22.-.7 Dar II; BE 10 128: 20, lower edge; in both deeds acting as the sixth and penultimate witness). His father, **[89]** *Za-bad-du* / Bēl-[...], was foreman of the gate guards on 9.V.29 Art I (EE 46: 6).

Third men of the right (flank) (*tašlīšāni*, functioning as guards; 1)[88]

[90] Bēl-ēṭir / *Ni-hu-ru* held (+x AC) a bow-property of the *haṭru*-organisation of the third men of the right (flank) in Larak on 2.V.1 Dar II (BE 10 36: 2). He turned up as the eighth and penultimate witness on the following day (PBS 2/1 181: 16). The deed is about another bow-property in Larak (belonging to a different *haṭru*-organisation).

d Lower status

Refugees (*maqtūtu;* 18)

[91] *Ha-ṣa-di-ni-*[ʾ] / Itti-Šamaš-balāṭu (+x AC) were under the jurisdiction of the refugees' foreman on 13.VI.23 Art I (location unknown, BE 9 5: 2).

[92] [Bēl-aba-uṣur] / *Nabû-qa-ta-ri* and **[93]** [*ᵈTa₅-míš-ra-hi-*ʾ/*-iá*] / *Ha-an-ṭa-šá-an-ni* each held a bow-property of the *haṭru*-organisation of the refugees on [x+]? 12.-.30 Art I (BE 9 23: 8,10', in Ālu-ša-maqtūti and Bīt-Tabalāya respectively, cf. below). *ᵈTa₅-míš-ra-hi-*ʾ / *Ha-an-ṭa-šú*, fifth and last witness, 18.VI.6 Dar II (PBS 2/1 214: 13) = *ᵈTa₅-míš-ra-hi-iá* / *Ha-an-ṭa-šú-an-na*, (tenth witness of twelve), 22.VIII.7 Dar II (BE 10 125: 20) = *ᵈTa₅-míš-ra-hi-*' / *Ha-an-ṭa-šú-an-na*, fourth and last witness, 18.VI.6 Dar II (EE 42: 13).

[94] [...] / [*B*]*a-rik-il*(DINGIR*meš*) held another bow-property of the same organisation possibly in Galê then (BE 9 23: 11').

[95] Ninurta-ibni / *Ahi-li-ti-*ʾ and **[96]** *Il-tar*-aha-iddina / Bēl-ēṭir held (with Illil-aha-uṣur / Nabû-uballiṭ +x AC and [93]) a bow-property of the same organisation in Bīt-Tabalāya on 7.III.1 Dar II (BE 10 20: 2–3; cf. below [106–108];

[97] *ᵈTa₅-míš-li-in-ṭár* / Marduka acted as the first witness of ten preserved ones).

---

88 See EE 78: 51, cf. A. C. V. M. Bongenaar, *The Neo-Babylonian Ebabbar Temple at Sippar: Its Administration and Its Prosopography* (PIHANS 80; Leiden: NINO, 1997), 45–46.

[98] *Il*(DINGIR^{meš})*-li-in-ṭár* / Bēl-ittannu (with a fingernail mark) held (+x AC) a bow-property of the same organisation in Bīt-Tabalāya then (BE 10 19: 4, witnessed by ^{d}*Ta*$_5$*-míš-li-in-ṭár* / Marduka, with a stamp seal, SU 537).

[99] [*Bi*?]-⌜*ṣa*⌝?-*a*, **[100]** Aha-iddina, **[101]** *Zab-di-ia* and **[102]** Nabû-re'ûšunu, sons of Nidinti-Bēl, as well as **[103]** *Za-bu-da-a* / Bēl-aha-iddina held (with an anonymous coparcener) a bow-property of the same organisation there, -.III.1 Dar II (BE 10 25: 2–3 with ^{d}*Ta*$_5$*-míš-li-in-ṭár* / Marduka acting again as the first witness of ten, see above, [95], like in PBS 2/1 25:15, left edge, where a bow-property of the same organisation in Bīt-ša-rēši is recorded on the same day; the coparceners have Akkadian filiations).[89]

[104] *Il*(DINGIR^{meš})*-ba-rak-ku* and **[105]** *Bi-ha-da-hi-'* sons of Ahūnu held a bow-property of the same organisation in Ālu-ša-maqtūti on [7].III.1 Dar II (PBS 2/1 176: 2; all the five deeds issued on the same day were written by the same scribe).

[106] ^{d}*Ta*$_5$*-míš-li-in-ṭár*, **[107]** Bēl-aha-iddina and **[108]** Tattannu, sons of Bēl-ēṭir (presumably brothers of the above-mentioned Iltar-aha-iddina [96]) held there a bow-property of the same organisation adjacent to the field of their above-mentioned colleague Bēl-aba-uṣur / *Nabû-qa-at-ri* on 29.-.1 Dar II (PBS 2/1 31: 2–3).

Gardu-workmen (8)[90]

[109] *Bi-ṣa-a* / Hašdāya, ^{lú}*pi-ti-pa-ba-ga* (with a fingernail mark; identical to [110]?), was in charge of the *gardu*-workmen of *bît kib/p-b/pu* (unexplained), as proxy of *Ia-di-ih-il* / *Ha-na-ni-'* on 1.XI.28 Art I (BE 9 15: 3, 8, 16, left edge).[91]

[110] *Bi-ṣa-a*, **[111]** *Šá-ra-'-il*(DINGIR^{meš}) / *In-za*-x-[...] (both with fingernail mark) and their colleagues were in charge of palm groves of the *gardu*-workmen on the Euphrates of Nippur and Namgar-Dūr-Illil (presumably in Bannēšu seeing that this settlement was situated on both canals; under the command of the *ahšadrapānu* Ṣihā and Ahūšunu, the foreman of the *gardu*-workmen), [...], 11.-.0 Dar II (PBS 2/1 2: 3, 5, 9, 12: *Šá*-[*r*]*a*-, left edge: [*Šá*]*-ra-*).[92]

---

89 ^{d}*Ta*$_5$*-míš-li-in-ṭár* / Marduka, first witness of 11, Illil-ašābšu-iqbi, 20.V.41 Art I (IMT 18: 26); second witness of 13, 28.VII.39 Art I (BE 9 67: 13).

90 See Stolper, EE, 55–59.

91 Cf. CAD K, 330a, s.v. *kibbu*.

92 See Stolper, EE, 58–59.

[112] Ea-ibni / *Ba-ri-ki-il*(DINGIR^{meš}, with a stamp seal, SU 374, about the fields of the crown prince's household, 3.XII.4 Dar II; BE 10 95: 8, lower edge) was a later *pitpabaga*-official of the *gardu*-workmen.

[113] *Šá-lam-ma-nu* / Hašdāya, of the *gardu*-workmen (with a ring, SU 304), held a field in Bannēšu on 27.IX.4 Dar II (PBS 2/1 91: 7, 9: both -<<*mu*>>-*ma*-, upper edge). There is no proof that he was brother of the above-mentioned *Bi-ṣa-a* seeing that the paternal name is common. It is not indicated to which household or estate these *gardu*-workmen belonged.

[114] This is also the case of *Il*(DINGIR^{meš})-*gab-ri* and **[115]** Nabûnāya, sons of Šūzubu (with rings), **[116]** as well in the case of [...]-x / *Nabû-im-me-e*, who all held bow-properties belonging to the *gardu*-workmen in Gammālē on -.V.- Dar II (IMT 32: 3–4, reverse with the impression of rings, cf. BE 10 92 from 13/23.IX.4 Dar II).

e Institutional households

The crown prince's household (*bīt mār šarri*; 4)[93]

[117] *Kul-la-'-Bēl*, servant of Artambari, was foreman of the butchers of the crown prince's household (with a cylinder seal, SU 49) on 21.VI.7 Dar II (PBS 2/1 133: 14, 16, lower edge).

[118] *Nabû-ra-hi-ia* and **[119]** Aplâ, sons of Ba-zu-zu (with fingernail marks), held a bow-property of the *haṭru*-organisation of the crown prince's household (their occupation is not indicated)[94] in Huṣṣēti-ša-Baba-ēreš on 26.IV.1 Dar II (BE 10 31: 2, lower edge).

[120] *Ga-ban-na-a* held (+x AC) a bow-property of the same organisation in Bīt-Zabīn (or in Bīt-Pirisāya or in Malahhāni) on 18.VII.5 Dar II (BE 10 101: 10).

Simmāgir's household (3)[95]

[121] *Zab-di-ia* and **[122]** Bēl-ēṭir, sons of *Ba-ri-ki-il*(DINGIR^{meš}), held (with two sons of Ṣababa-ēreš, all with fingernail marks) a bow-property of the *haṭru*-organisation of the *simmāgir*'s household in Bīt-Ṣababa-ēreš (apparently named after the coparceners' father) on 24.VI.41 Art I (BE 9 95: 2, left edge). The bow-property of Bēl-ēṭir there and that of

---

93 See Stolper, EE, 54, 59–62.

94 We happen to know of *girrisua-karānu* and *ālik mādakti* of the same household.

95 See Stolper, EE, 73–74.

[123] *Qar-ha-'*, perhaps son of Ahhē-lūmur, in Bīt-Taqbi-līšir of the same organisation are recorded on 19.VII.3 Dar II (BE 10 71). The latter's property is also mentioned in -.-.7 Dar II (PBS 2/1 142). *Za-ab-di-ia* / *Ba-rik-ki-il*(DINGIR^{meš}) acted as a witness to a deed about the same organisation on 22.VIII.7 Dar II (BE 10 125: 21).

Alphabet scribes of the army (5)[96]

[124] *Ba-rik-ki-Bēl* / Bēlšunu, messenger of Aba-ul-īdi, in charge of alphabet scribes (with a cylinder seal, SU 145), 5.I.1 Dar II (PBS 2/1 3: 11: [...], paternal name preserved, 16: [..-^{d}+E]N, upper edge); 16th and last witness (inserted), 2.I.1 Dar II (BE 10 7 = TuM 2/3 181: 18).

[125] Nabû-mīta-uballiṭ / Balāṭu, brother of the foreman *Za-bi-in*, initially assisted his brother:[97] 14.I$^{?}$.1 Dar II (PBS 2/1 27: 7, 12; 29: 7, 12); deputy (*šanû*) of **[126]** *Za-bi-ni*, Babylon, -.-.1 Dar II (PBS 2/1 34: 4, 9, lower edge); foreman of alphabet scribes, 2.I.1 Dar II (BE 10 7= TuM 2/3 181: 4, 7, left edge; all with a cylinder seal, SU 27); witness (without title, with another cylinder seal, SU 38), 25(or 26).XI.3 Dar II (PBS 2/1 72: 14, reverse). He is identical with *Za-bi-in* / Balāṭu, foreman of the *haṭru*-organisation of the alphabet scribes of the army, brother and master of Nabû-mīta-uballiṭ, 14.I$^{?}$.1 Dar II (PBS 2/1 27: 8, 14, lower edge; 29: 8, 13); Babylon, -.-.1 Dar II (PBS 2/1 34: 4, 9, lower edge: *Za-bi-ni*); foreman of the same organisation, 18.X.2 Dar II (*UCP* 9/3 271, 276: 19); *Za-bi-in* foreman of the same organisation, master of **[127]** Bēl-šuma-iddina (his brother and deputy with a seal), -.VI.3 Dar II (PBS 2/1 66: 15, upper edge; presumably identical with Bēl-šuma-iddina / Balāṭu, household member of Aba-ul-īdi with a golden ring, 20.IX.- Dar II, PBS 2/1 173: 17, upper edge, cf. SU 382); *Za-bi-ni* / Balāṭu, foreman of the same organisation, master of the appointee **[128]** Bēl-šuma-iddina / *Zi-im-ma-a* (with two cylinder seals, SU 51: 237), -.VI.3 Dar II and 21.VIII.5 Dar II (PBS 2/1 66: upper edge and BE 10 102: 6, 10, 12 respectively). *Za-bi-ni* / Balāṭu, ^{lú}*di-dak-ku* < Old Irananian **didī-ka-* 'supervisor, foreman' was a signatory (with a ring, SU 581) to a deed from 13.I.7 Dar II (BE 10 118: upper edge).[98] This is one of the rare cases in Late Babylonian, where an etymology is approved by prosopography.

---

96 See Stolper, EE, 76: 35.

97 See Stolper, EE, 85.

98 See J. Tavernier, *Iranica in the Achaemenid Period (ca. 550–330 B. C.): Lexicon of Old Iranian Proper Names and Loanwords in Non-Iranian Texts* (OLA 158; Leuven: Peeters, 2007), 419–20: 4.4.7.33.

[129] For *Bēl-ia-a-da-ah* see Part I.3.

Alphabet scribes of the household of the rab-un-qu-a-tú-official (1)[99]

[130] Bēl-ittannu / *Ug-ga-a* held (together with two Judean coparceners) a bow-property of the *haṭru*-organisation of the alphabet scribes of the household of this official in Bīt-Erība on 2.VII.1 Dar II (PBS 2/1 185: 3).

Garment storehouse (*bīt-talbultu*; 1)[100]

[131] One bow-property of the *haṭru*-organisation of *bīt-tabulti* in Bīt-ša-rēši was held by ^{d}*Ta*$_{5}$*-míš-li-in-ṭár* / Iddina-Illil (together with four named coparceners + x AC, with fingernail marks), 7.III.1 Dar II (BE 10 18: 1–4).

f Estates and Institutions

Bīt Itti-Šamaš-balāṭu (4)[101]

[132] *Du-gu-um-*[*x* ...]-x held a bow-property in Gabalīni, probably belonging to the *haṭru*-organisation of Itti-Šamaš-balāṭu's household on 25.VII.40 Art I (EE 40: 2).

[133] On 22.VIII.4 Dar II, *A-qu-bu* and **[134]** *Ha-am-ba*(or *ma*)*-nu* together held a bow-property in Bīt-Zabīn, and **[135]** *Hi-id-ra-a* had a bow-property in Bīt-Daddīya. Both properties belonged to the same organisation and were shared with anonymous coparceners, whose number is not indicated (TuM 2/3 184: 7–8).

Limītu 'fruit garden' (2)[102]

[136] *Il*(DINGIR^{meš})*-ba-na-'* / Nabû-ēreš and **[137]** Nanāya-iddina / *Qu-da-a* held (each +x AC) a bow-property of the *haṭru*-organisation of *limītu* in Kapri-Lirīm on -.-.4 Dar II (BE 10 98: 2, 3, 8) and 14.XI.6 Dar II (TuM 2/3 188: 3–4). The bow-property of *Il*(DINGIR^{meš})*-ba-na-'* (without filiation, +x AC) is also recorded on 17.XII.4 Dar II (BE 10 96: 4, 8) after bow-properties of the *haṭru*-organisation of *musahhirē* 'purchasing agents'.[103]

---

99 See Donbaz and Stolper, IMT, 82 ad 5: reverse 3.

100 See Stolper, EE, 74: 11.

101 See Stolper, EE, 95.

102 Cf. Michael Jursa, *Die Landwirtschaft in Sippar in neubabylonischer Zeit* (AfOB 25; Vienna: Institut für Orientalistik, 1995), 130.

103 Cf. Stolper, EE 75: 29.

Chariot estate or depot (*bīt narkabti*, 2)[104]

[138] *ᵈTa₅-míš-li-in-ṭár* held a bow-property in Bīt-Sîn-līšir and **[139]** Bēl-šuma-iddina / *Aḫḫē*(ŠEŠ^meš)-*ma-a* had a bow-property in Ḫuṣṣēti-ša-Addīya on 14.IX.4 Dar II. Both properties belonged to the *haṭru*-organisation under the jurisdiction of the foreman of *bīt narkabti* and were shared with anonymous coparceners, whose number is not indicated (BE 10 91: 4, 6).

g Semi-free Workmen (šušānus) Belonging to Households and Estates

Šušānus of households and estates

Perhaps the members of Simmāgir's household and Itti-Šamaš-balāṭu's estate ([121–123, 132–135]) were implicit *šušānus*.

Of the treasury (storehouse, [*bīt*] *nakkandi*; 9):[105] 3.5 bow-properties of the *haṭru*-organisation of the *šušānus* of the treasury were held on 24.VII.40 Art I by

[140] *Qa-ad-du-šú* / Lā-abâši (one, in Hindāyu) as well as by the following three members (all in Kuzabatu), viz. **[141]** Marduk-ēṭir / *Lu-la-'-Nabû* (one), **[142]** A+A-*na-a*/Bēl-kīna (one), and **[143]** Bēl-aba-uṣur together with **[144]** *Bīt-il-nūrī* (ᵈÉ.DINGIR-ZÁLAG-') sons of Nidinti-Bēl (half). These properties were administered by **[145]** *Ḫu-un-ṣa-ru-ru*, servant of Puḫḫurāya (with a stamp seal, SU 489), and the summoner **[146]** *Na-ma-ri-'* / *Šá-me-e-ra-mu* (BE 9 75, like his colleague who acted in the same capacity, above, a, 1', 4).

[147] Šiški-Bēl and **[148]** Tattannu-bullissu, sons of *Ha-da-an-nu* (both with fingernail marks), held a bow-property (+x AC) of the same organisation in Larak on 5.VI.1 Dar II (BE 10 41: 3).

Of the equerry's household (*bīt rab-urāti*; 17+1):[106]

[149] The foreman of their *haṭru*-organisation was Iddina-Amurru / *Ha-am-ba*(or *ma*)-*as-su* on 3.III.4 Dar II (TuM 2/3 183: 6–7).

[150] *Šu-ra-nu* held a quarter of a bow-property in Bīt-Ardīya on 20.I.35 Art I (IMT 4: 3, 10).

[151] *Ha-an-na-ni-'* / Ninurta-uballiṭ, grandson of Ardi-Ninurta, who together with his father, **[152]** *Aḫi-li-ti-'* / Nanāya-iddina and **[153]** Bēlet-ēṭir /

104 Cf. Stolper, EE 73: 8.

105 See Stolper, EE, 89–92.

106 See Stolper, EE, 73: 9, 95–96.

Dilbat-ittīya (brother of [154]) held a bow-property of the same organisation in Bīt-Ardīya on 10.VII.38 Art I (BE 9 63: 3, 6).

[154] *Ab-da-'* (brother of [153]) and **[155]** *Il*(DINGIR^{meš})*-ba-na-'* held (+x AC) two bow-properties of the same organisation there on 3.III.4 Dar II (TuM 2/3 183: 12: *-ba-<na>-*, 16). The former is the same as *Ab-da-'* / Dilbat-ittīya, who held (together with Ahūnu / Bēl-ēpuš +x AC) a bow-property of the same organisation there on 28.VIII.4 Dar II (TuM 2/3 124: 2).

[156] *Ia-a-di-hu-il*(DINGIR^{meš}) held a bow-property of the *haṭru*-organisation of *šušānus* of ^{lú}*mašāka*[107] in Bīt-Hadūru on 6.VIII.41 Art I (BE 9 107: 3). The field of *Ia-a-di-ih-il*(DINGIR^{meš}) was adjacent to bow-properties of the *haṭru*-organisation of the *šušānus* of the equerry's estate there on 12.IV.1 Dar II (PBS 2/1 178: 12).

[157] *Nabû-hi-in-ni-'* / Nurrašu, **[158]** *Za-bid-da-a* / Bēl-aha-iddina, **[159]** Bānīya / *A-dar-ri-il*(DINGIR^{meš}) and **[160]** Tattannu[108] / *Da-la-ta-ni-'* were holders (+x AC; with fingernail marks) of a bow-property of the same organisation in Bīt-Hadūru then (PBS 2/1 178: 2–4, lower edge).

[161] The brothers ^{d}*Ta*$_5$*-míš-ba-rak-ku* / Iqīšāya, **[162]** *Har-ra-ma-hi-'* and **[163]** Nabû-nādin held a bow-property (+x AC) of the same organisation there on 24.X.3 Dar II (PBS 2/1 198: 2; the first witness is the organisation's foreman).

[164] *Da-la-ta-ni-'* (father of [160]) held (+x AC) a bow-property there in -.VII.4 Dar II (PBS 2/1 88).

[165] *Ba-rik-ki-ta*$_5$*-míš* is also mentioned in PBS 2/1 88 in a broken context.

---

107 The identity of the *haṭru*-organisation of *ma-šá-a-ka/ma-šá-ku* with that of *rab-urāti*, "equerry", is argued by Stolper, EE, 95–96. This can be corroborated by the prosopography as [160], a member of the *haṭru*-organisation of the *rab-urāti* estate, is the son of [164], a member of the estate of *ma-šá-ku* (both situated in Bīt-Hadūru). *Ma-šá-a-ka/ma- šá-ku* is written with *ma-* at least in two Murašû documents (the reading is doubtful in a third document of the same archive, viz. IMT 2: 3). I argued that the reconstruction of *ma-šá-a-ka/ma-šá-ku* as Old Iranian **Važaka-* is not certain as Late Babylonian <*ma-*> does not render /*va-*/. For references and discussion see Tavernier, *Iranica*, 414: 4.4.68. Tavernier's (*Iranica*, 335: 4.2.1779 with n. 153, cf. 414) only example of <*ma-*> for /*va-*/, viz. *Ma-hi-a-ga-am-mu*, is extant in the fragment PBS 2/1 30: reverse 9'. It is preceded by DIŠ, which the editor interpreted as the *Personenkeil*. However, there is a long break before the DIŠ (room for at least five signs if one compares the damaged filiation of the next witness, *Ni-na-ak-ku*, on reverse 9'-10' with its preserved version in upper edge). This and a personal collation lead me to suspect that the DIŠ is the end of an Ú-sign, in which case the actual reading would be *Ú-ma-hi-a-ga-am-mu*, thereby resembling the intact spelling *Ú-he-e-ia-a-ga-am* for the same name (see Zadok, *Iranische Personennamen*, 570).

108 Written *Tat-TIN-nu* (the CVC-sign TIN being indifferent to vowel quality).

[166] The field of *Gu-sa*-A+A was adjacent to a bow-property of the same organisation in Bīštu-ša-rab-urāti (28.IV.1 Dar II; PBS 2/1 9: 11).

Of the foremen's household (*bīt/mārē šaknūti*; 5)[109]

[167] *Nabû-na-tan-nu* / *Aq-bi-il*(DINGIR^{meš}) was the foreman of the *haṭru*-organisation of the *šušānus* of the foremen (with a ring, SU 297) on 18.III.3 Dar II (BE 10 64: 6, upper edge).

[168] *Man-nu-ki-i-i-la-hi-i* / *A-qu-bu*, brother of **[169]** *Hi-in-nu-ni-'*, held (with his brother and others) a bow-property of the same organisation in Abastanu then (BE 10 64: 3) and on 10.VI.5 Dar II (PBS 2/1 207: 5: *Man-nu-ki-i-la-hi-'*).

[170] [...] / *Bēl-na-tan-nu* and *Nabû-na-tan-nu* [167] act as principals (in broken context) in a deed concerning the *šušānus* of the foremen, place and date lost (time of Rēmūt-Ninurta / Murašû, i.e. 429–415 B.C.E.). The deed is witnessed by Bēl-aha-iddina, judge of the Sealand (EE 52: 4, 6).

Of Hammatāyu's estate (5)

Ha-am-ma-ta-A+A (of *bīt*-~), being spelled with a *Personenkeil*, was probably an estate.[110] The bow-properties of the *haṭru*-organisation of its *šušānus* were concentrated mainly in Kār-Ninurta, its suburbs and neighouring settlements.

[171] *Nabû-ra-hi-ia* / [...] held (together with Illil-danu / [...], Hātinu / Ninurta-ibni as well as Bibāya and Ninurta-uballiṭ sons of Iddina-Illil +x AC, with fingernail marks) a bow-property of the same organisation in Bīt-Aplāya in -.-.2 Dar II (PBS 2/1 57).

[172] ^{d}*Ar-gu-ú-za-bad-du* / Lū-ahi held a bow-property together with Iddina-Illil / Bēlšunu and Bēl-ēṭir / Iddināya. The land belonged to the *haṭru*-organisation of the *šušānus* of Hammatāyu's estate in Āl-Bēl on 1.IV.4 Dar II (PBS 2/1 200: 2 from Illil-ašābšu-iqbi). *Ar-gu-ú-za-bad*-[*du*] held (together with Iddina-Illil +x AC) a bow-property of the *haṭru*-organisation of the *šušānus* of Zūzāya's estate (*bīt*-^{m}*Zu-za-a*) in Āl-Bēl on 8.-.3 Dar II (PBS 2/1 76: 3). See also [175] below.

[173] ^{d}*Ta*$_{5}$*-míš-li-in-ṭár* / *Il*(DINGIR^{meš})-*b*[*a-na-'*] and **[174]** Nabû-uballiṭ / *Ahi-li-ti-'* held (together with at least three bearers of Akkadian names +x AC) a share of a horse-property (cf. BE 10 51 below) of the same organisation in Bīt-Kīnāya then (PBS 2/1 76: 3, 13). This implies that the estate of Zūzāya was identical with that of Hammatāyu.[111]

109 See Stolper, EE 77: 41.
110 Cf. Stolper, EE 76: 40.
111 Cf. Stolper, EE 77: 42.

[175] *Nabû-ia-a-si-bi* / *Za-bid-^{d}Na-na-a*, *^{d}Ar-gu-ú-za-bad* [172], Iddina-Illil / Bēlšunu, Iddīya / Nabû-ibni, Hašdāya / Bēl-bullissu and Marduka / Mušēzib-Bēl held a bow-property together, but neither the location nor the affiliation are indicated (on 10.VI.6 Dar II; IMT 87; from Sîn-bēlšunu, witnessed by Ṭābīya /*Abi*(AD)-*li-te-'*). The bow-property of *Nabû-ia-[a-si-bi]* / *Za-bid-^{d}Na-na-a*, held with Iddīya / Nabû-ibni +x AC, is recorded in PBS 2/1 121. It was issued there on the same day and has several witnesses in common with IMT 87. Nabû-uballiṭ / *Ahu-li-ti-'* and *^{d}Ta$_{5}$-míš-li-in-ṭar* / *Il*(DINGIR^{meš})-*ba-na-'*, held (together with four named +x AC) a share of a horse-property in Bīt-Kīnāya (witnessed by the foreman of the *šušānus* of Zūzāya's estate) on 10.VII.1 Dar II (BE 10 51: 3–5).

Šušānus by occupations

Teamsters (*šādidē ša sisê*; 1)[112]

[176] *Lu-la-'-hi-ia* held a bow-property (together with Iddina-Nabû + x AC) of the *haṭru*-organisation of the teamsters of *šušānu*-status in Bît-Arzāya on 8.IX.6 Dar II (PBS 2/1 125: 4). Iddina-Nabû was *Lu-la-'-hi-ia*'s father according to IMT 92: 13–14, where *Lu-la-'-hi-ia* is the eighth and last witness (3.IX.39 Art I).

Bodyguards (*ṣāb-šepē*$^{?}$; 2+1)[113]

[177] *Bi-ṣa-a* / *Ba-rik-ki-^{d}Ta$_{5}$-míš* (with fingernail marks) held (+x AC) a bow-property of their *haṭru*-organisation in Hambanāyu. Implicitly: *Bi-ṣa-a* (Aramaic *Bṣy*) / *Ba-rik-ki-^{d}Ta[$_{5}$-míš]* (with fingernail mark), 6.X.4 Dar II (EE 114: 3, 5, 6, left edge).

Another bow-property of the same organisation was held there by

[178] *Il*(DINGIR^{meš})-*ha-da-ri* on 27.VIII.4 Dar II (BE 10 90: 2, 7, witnessed by their foreman). *Bît-il*(É.DINGIR^{meš})-*a-dar$^{!}$-ri* paid taxes via *Bi-ṣa-a* / *Ba-rik-ki-^{d}Ta$_{5}$-míš* (with FM), who had (+x AC) also a field there on 6.IV.7 Dar II (BE 10 122: 2, 4, 7, 10).

Makers of the levee (? IM):[114]

[179] *A-na-ni-'-il*(DINGIR^{meš}), concerning bow-properties belonging to the *haṭru*-organisation of the *šušānus* of makers of the levee$^{?}$ located in Abastanu,

---

112 See Stolper, EE 78: 49.

113 See Stolper, EE 77: 47.

114 See Stolper, EE 77: 43.

Kuzabatu and Hašbāya of the district of Nār-Simmāgir (preceded by Ardi-Nergal and followed by Ninurta-bani + x AC), 25.VII.2 Dar II (PBS 2/1 193: 8).

Šušānu field hands (*mārē ikkarāti*; 6)[115]
Four bow-properties of their *haṭru*-organisation in Ibūlē were held on 13.XII.40 Art I by

[180] *Ha-ma-da-'* / Sîn-iddina, **[181]** *Ia-a-da-hu-Nabû* / *Ba-rik-ki-il-ta$_5$-míš*, **[182]** *Nap-sa-an* / *Na-ad-bi-ia*, and **[183]** *Ia-a-da-hu-Nabû* / *Nabû-ha-qa-bi*.

[184] *A-qu-bu* / *Ha-ra-an-na* held a bow-property of the same organisation in Šappūtu then (BE 9 82 = IMT 54: 4–8).

[185] *Na-ṭi-ru* / *Ba-rik-il*(DINGIR^{meš}) is defined as *mār ikkari* (DUMU ^{lú}ENGAR, with a ring, SU 289) on 16.XIIb.40 Art I (royal field on Nār-šarri, BE 9 73: 3, 9, on lower edge; he recurs without title in PBS 2/1 123: 23 from Hašbāya, 22.VIII.6 Dar II).

Šušānu mārē hisanni (9)[116]
The pattern being analogous to that of *šušānu mārē ikkarāti* strongly suggests that *hisanni* / *hisāni* denotes an occupation. However, the interpretation of *hisanni* / *hisāni* as 'guardes' is etymologically unjustified and so far cannot be supported by the context.[117]

[186] *Ba-rik-ki-^{d}Ta$_5$-míš* was their foreman on 25.XIIb.29 Art I (IMT 52: 19: *Ba-rik-*[...], 22: *Ba-rik-k*[*i-*...]; also 55: 9, 11).

[187] *Ra-ʾ-bi-ìl* / Kalbi-Baba was deputy (with a cylinder seal, SU 152) of their foreman Šulum-Bābili on 16.-.35 Art I (BE 9 44: 16, left edge).

[188] Ninurta-ēṭir / *Ba-rik-^{d}Ta$_5$-míš* (his father may be identical with [186]) held (+x AC) a bow-property of the *haṭru*-organisation of the *šušānu mārē hisāni* in Hamb/mari on 19.X.26 and 12.VIII.27 Art I (BE 9: 7a, 2 and 8: 11–12 respectively). Ninurta-ēṭir (without a paternal name) held a bow-property of the same organisation in [Hamb/mari] on 4.VII.4 Dar II (PBS 2/1 87: 10) and in Hamb/mari in -.V.- Dar. II (PBS 2/1 63: 11).

[189] *^{d}Ta$_5$-míš-li-in-ṭár* / Bēlšunu held a bow-property (together with Kidinu and Illil-šuma-ibni sons of Ardi-Gula, with fingernail marks) of the same organisation in Bīt-Murānu on 20.IV.41 Art I (BE 9 94: 2–3, cf. PBS 2/1 63: 10–11).

---

115 See Stolper, EE 77: 46.

116 See Stolper, EE 77: 45.

117 Guillaume Cardascia, 'Le fief dans la Babylonie achéménide', in *Les liens de la vassalité et les immunités* (Recueils de la Société Jean Bodin 1; 2nd enlarged ed., Brussels 1958), 57–88 (59, n. 2).

[190] *Ha-an-na-ni-'* and **[191]** *Gu-ub-ba-a*, sons of Ninurta-ēṭir, held together with

[192] Nādinu and **[193]** Arad-Illil, sons of *Sa-'-ga-'*, a bow-property of the same organisation in Hamb/mari on 18.X.2 Dar II (BE 10 61: 2–3; cf. *Ha-an-na-ni-'* / Ninurta-ēṭir, third witness of six, almost all West Semitic, Bīt-Gērāya, 20.IX.36 Art I, EE 98: 13–14). A horse-property of Iddina-Amurru on the Piqūdu canal and the *šušānus mārē hisāni* are mentioned in a fragmentary deed in broken context (the bow-properties of Ninurta-ēṭir and *Sa-a-ga-'* are also recorded [+x AC]), [..,], 18.[...].1 Dar II (PBS 2/1 30: 12).

[194] *Hi-is-[da-nu]* / Kidinu held a bow-property of the same organisation in Bīt-Šulāya (on Namgar-Dūr-Illil) on 23.X.2 Dar II (PBS 2/1 194: 2, held by Kidinu in -.V.- Dar II, PBS 2/1 63: 12), cf. *Hi-is-da-a-nu* / Kidinu, seventh and last witness (preceded by a witness with an Aramaic name; deed about palm groves on Namgar-Dūr-Illil), 4.X.5 Dar II (PBS 2/1 209: 14), *Hi-is-da-nu* / Kidinu, eighth and penultimate witness (followed by Ṭābīya / *Abi-li-ti-'*), Qaštu, 16.V.6 Dar II (BE 10 39: 15).

Šušānu (of) *kirikēti* (perhaps performing an irrigational task, such as damming up; 3)[118]

[195] Bunānu / *Bēl-hi-im-me-e* was the foreman of their *haṭru*-organisation in -.-.4 Dar II (PBS 2/1 101: 11). According to the same deed, **[196]** *Il*(DINGIR^{meš})-*na-ta*[*n-n*]*u* held a bow-property of the *haṭru*-orgainisation in Zamburāyu and **[197]** Bēl-ēṭir / *Kul-la-'-la-ha-'* held (+x AC) a bow-property of the same organisation in Bīt-Zabīn. Bēl-ēṭir / *Kul-la-'-la-hu* held (with coparceners) a bow-property (location not indicated) of the same organisation as early as 13.VII.28 Art I (BE 9 12: 3).

h Other principals (32)

Brewers (2)

[198] *Ha-si-ma-'* and **[199]** *Qu-un-na-a* (see Part I.3 above).

---

118 See Stolper, EE 77: 44 with n. 33; CAD K, 313a, s.v. *kerku: ki-ri-ki*^{meš} interchanging with *ki-ri-ke-e-ti; ki-ir-ke-e-ti* (3x, twice in the same document), maybe with dropping of an unstressed vowel; cf. AHw. 468a, s.v. *kerku(m)*, with reference to *kiriktu* 'blocking' (of the water supply in a canal, CAD K, 405–406), both deriving from *karāku* 'to obstruct, dam' (CAD K, 199).

Creditors (2)

[200] Šuma-iddina / *Za-bu-da-a* (alias Ṣilli-Ninurta?), represented by the female (Aramaic *'ntt*) Rak-ku-su-nu who received the payment from the debtor, a slave of Illil-šuma-iddina, 6.XII.37 Art I (BE 8 126: 2).

[201] *dŠá-am-šá-nu* (with Bēlšunu, Tattannu and Na'id-Ninurta), 5.XI.38 Art I (BE 9 64: 6); identical with [280]?

Guarantors (2)

[202] *Ìl-li-in-ṭár* / Iddina-Illil (for a prisoner), 16.I.1 Dar II (BE 10 10: 1, 8, left edge: -<in>-).

[203] *Ha-an-ni-ia-'* / Ninurta-aha-iddina (co-guarantor), 10.V.30[+x] Art I (= 435–426 B.C.E.; EE 102: 2, 10).

Debtors (17)

[204] *dTa$_5$-míš-la-din-ni* / Damqāya, 2.XII.37 Art I (BE 9 56: 3).

[200] Šuma-iddina / *Za-bu-d*[*u*] (or –*d*[*a-*'?] and his wife Ahāssunu / Ahu-ēreš, 22.XII.37 Art I (BE 9 58: 4).

[205] *Za-bi-na-'* and **[206]** *dTa$_5$-míš-nu-ri–ia*, 10.V.30[+x] Art I (EE 102: 5, 9, 12: [d] *Ta$_5$-míš-nu-ri–'*).

[207] *fdNa-na-a-ta-hu-šà*, wife of Nidintāya and mother of **[208]** Hašdāya and **[209]** *Ab-di-da-'*, co-debtor (out of six including her sons and **[210]** *Bi-is-de-e* / Bēl-ittānnu), 13.XII.40 Art I (IMT 93: 3: *Bi-i*[*s-de-e*], 6, 11, 15).

[211] Members of a group of eight co-debtors on 12.I.41 Art I (BE 9 85): Iddina-Amurru / *Di-gir-di-la-an-nu* (l. 5; he acted as witness on 12.I.41 Art I, BE 9 86: 23);

[212] *dTa$_5$-míš-ba-rak-ku* / Mārē(DUMU^meš^)-iddina (l. 6),

[213] *Za-bi-ni* / Ninurta-aha-iddina (l. 8).

[214] *Zab-di-ia* / *Id-di-ri-ia-il*(DINGIR*meš*), first of seven co-debtors (12.I.41 Art I, BE 9 86: 3) and third witness of eleven on 12.I.41 Art I (BE 9 85: 19).

[215] *Zab-di-ia* / Bēl-zēra-ibni, 6.V.41 Art I (BRM 1 86: 3–4, outside the Murašû archive). Witness also in: *Zab-di-ía* / B., first of six, 21.VIII.39 Art I (BE 9 68: reverse 2); *Zab-di-ia* / B., ninth and last, 10.V.30+[x] Art I (EE 102: 18); fourth preserved and penultimate witness, 6.VII.2 Dar II (PBS 2/1 191: 16–17); fifth and penultimate witness, 3.III.4 Dar II (TuM 2/3 183: 21, upper edge); (with a cylinder seal, SU 35), eighth preserved and (ante-)penultimate, 12.XII.4 Dar II (PBS 2/1 96: left edge, cf. 22 where only the paternal name is preserved); *Zab-di-ia*/x [...], 6.VIII.7 Dar II (PBS 2/1 135: left edge, same seal); [*Zab*]-*di-ia* / B. (same seal, SU 35), 19.III.- Dar II (PBS 2/1 150: left edge). For more attestations see below, Part III.f ([356]).

[216] *Hi-in-nu-*[... (son of?)] Itti-Nabû-balāṭu, [..],13.-.- [Art I / Dar II] (EE 80: 2–3);

[217] *Ha-ag-ga-a* / [*Aq*]-*bi-il*(DINGIR^{meš}, with a fingernail mark), 3$^?$.II.1 Dar II (BE 10 12: 2: -*g*[*a-a*], upper edge);
[218] *Na-tin-na-'* / *Na-ṭi-ri*, 20.V.4 Dar II (PBS 2/1 85: 3, 7);
[219] *Nabû-ra-hi-i* / *Ha-an-na-ta-'*, 14.VI.6 Dar II (BE 10 109: 3);
[220] *Ha-an-ni-ia* / [...], husband of [f]x-x-Mulittu, 22.VII.- Dar II (IMT 101: 5).

Others (9)
[221] Ša-Sîn-ūdu / *Qa-ad-du-šú*, principal (partnership contract), place lost, 3.-.21 Art I (IMT 107 4);
[222] *<Ba>-rik-ki-Bēl* mentioned together with **[223]** [...]-*na-ti-'* in broken context, time of Illil-šuma-iddina (445-421 B.C.E.; EE 53: 7);
[224] *Bi-ṣa-a* (with a stamp seal?, SU 44), in broken context, place and date lost (445–421 B.C.E.; EE 57: 3', obverse);
[225] d?!*Ad-du-ia-at-tin*, principal (context broken), place and date lost (445–421 B.C.E.; EE 117: 3', sealed by the *simmāgir*-official);
[226] *Ra-hi-im* probably son of *Ba-rik-ki-il*(DINGIR^{meš}) and brother of **[227]** x⌟[...], concerning dates, probably assessed rent, -.-.6 Dar II (BE 10 116: 3–4); identical with [352]$^?$
[228] *Ga-a-'-du-ru*, principal (with a fingernail mark), -.-.-. Dar II (PBS 2/1 164: reverse).
[229] Illil-šuma-ibni / [d]*Ta*$_5$*-míš-li-in-ṭár* with a ring (deed damaged), place and date lost (IMT 88: left edge).

i Status

Slave owners (1)
[230] d*Ta*$_5$*-míš-li-in-ṭá*[*r*], master of Šuma-uṣur (debtor), 2.X.6 Dar II (PBS 2/1 219: 3).

Prisoners (6)
[231] *Ga-di-'* (together with another two individuals), 14.VI.41 Art I (IMT 103: 2, 7).
[232] *Il-lu-la-ta-'* and **[233]** *Il*(DINGIR^{meš})*-li-in-ṭar*, sons of Nabû-ēṭir, and **[234]** *Am-mat-*d*E-si-'*, wife of [232], 3.XI.1 Dar II (PBS 2/1 17: 5, 8, 10).
[235] The anonymous wives of Bēl-ibni / d*Na-na-a-du-ri-'* and **[236]** *Na-ṭi-ir* / Hašdāya, 28.I.2 Dar II (TuM 2/3 203: 4, 5, 9, 10, 12).

Slaves sold (3)
[237] fd*At-tar-ṭa-bat*, female singer, was sold together with **[238]** f*Bi-sa-ha-'*, **[239]** f*Šá-ak-ha-'* and another female singer, 4.IX.40 Art I (IMT 104: 1, 2, 6, 7).

Witnesses (108)
Principals acting as witnesses (above, passim) are not counted. Cases where witnesses with West Semitic filiations are juxtaposed (two, e.g. penultimate and last in IMT 4: 55, PBS 2/1 18: 209, seldom more, e.g. second to fourth in PBS 2/1 226 and ninth to eleventh in PBS 2/1 153 and in the dossiers of Balšam, Illil-ašābšu-iqbi, Kapri-Lirīm and Bīt-Zēru-līšir) are not rare in the Murašû archive. More such witnesses occur together, but not juxtaposed, in the same deed (cf. above and below, passim).

Recurrent (23):

[240] *Ha-ri-ba-<ta>-nu* / Zumbu, fifth witness of nine, 24.III.41 Art I (BE 9 87: 14, < *ha-ri*> proves that the initial polyphonic sign HAR in all the other occurrences has the value *har*); *Har-bat-a-nu* / Zumbu, thirteenth witness of 17, [...], -.-.-. Art I (BE 9 86a: 32); *Har-ba-ta-nu* / Zumbu, sixth witness of ten, 15.XI.0 Dar II (BE 10 2: 14); [*Har-ba-ta-nu*] / Zumbu, fourth witness of nine preserved; 15.XI.0 Dar II (BE 10 3: 14–15); [*Har-ba-t*]*a-nu* / Zumbu, fifth and penultimate witness, 20.VII.3 Dar II (BE 10 72: 15); *Har-ba-ta-nu* / Zumbu, fifth witness of seven, -.VII.4 Dar II (PBS 2/1 88: 19); eighth and last witness, 8.XI.4 Dar II (BE 10 94: 21); *Har-ri-ba-ta-nu* / Zumbu, seventh and last, 17.XI.4 Dar II (PBS 2/1 94: 14–15); *Har-ba-ta-nu* / Zumbu, fifth witness of nine, 4.VII.7 Dar II (EE 34: 14); sixth witness of 12, 22.VII.7 Dar II (BE 10 125: 18); last (out of eight, with a cylinder seal, SU 84), 4.IX.7 Dar II (BE 10 127: 17–18: [...], upper edge).

[241] *Har-bat-a-nu* / Šuma-iddina is followed by the homonymous appointee (above [15]), fourth to fifth (penultimate and last) witness, 10.VII.1 Dar II (PBS 2/1 187: 11–12); *Har-ba-ta-nu* / Šuma-iddina, third (last) witness, 11.XII.3 Dar II (BE 10 79: 14); *Har-bat-ta-n*[*u* ...], first of four preserved witnesses, place and date lost (time of Illil-šuma-iddina, IMT 25: 13; = 240 or 241).

[242] *Il*(DINGIR^{meš})-*za-bad-du* / Aplāya, seventh (penultimate) witness, [...], -.-.20+[x] Art I (EE 56: 20'); sixth witness of ten, 20.V.36 Art I (BE 9 45: 32); 13.VIII.37 Art I (possibly wife, with a stamp seal, SU 334, EE 12: right edge); sixth witness of 13, 24.VII.40 Art I (BE 9 75: 13); eighth (last) witness, 25.IV.1 Dar II (PBS 2/1 180: 18); seventh (last) witness, 26$^{?}$.IV.1 Dar II (BE 10 32: 19, lower edge); *Il*(DINGIR^{meš})-*z*[*a-bad*]-*du* / [Aplāya], third witness of ten preserved (with a cylinder seal, SU 323), 8$^{?}$.-.1 Dar II (PBS 2/1 32: 15); third witness of eight (with a ring, SU 563), 3.VII.3 Dar II (BE 10 70: 14, left edge).

[243] Aplāya / *Il*(DINGIR^{meš})*-na-tan-nu*, fourth (penultimate) witness, 28.XII.1 Dar II (BE 10 55: 14); first witness of five discernible ones, 26.IV 2 Dar II (PBS 2/1 46:10).

[244] *Zab-di-ia* / Bēl-asû'a, seventh witness of ten, juxtaposed with another two witnesses with Aramaic filiation, 27.IV.1 Dar I (BE 10 33: 18); ninth (last) witness, 27.IV.1 Dar I (BE 10 34: 21 || PBS 2/1 41).

[245] *Qar-ha-'* / Nabû-*za-bad*, sixth witness of eleven (BE 9 85: 21) and second preserved witness (out of seven), 12.I.41 Art I (BE 9 86: 18).

[246] *Ta*$_5$*-míš-li-in-ṭár* / *Ha-an-ṭa-šá-nu*, eighth (penultimate) witness (BE 10 34: 21 || PBS 2/1 41), ^{d}*Ta*$_5$*-míš-li-in-ṭár* / *Ha-an-ṭa-šá-nu*, eighth witness of ten, juxtaposed with another two with Aramaic filiation, 27.IV.1 Dar II (BE 10 33: 19).

Additional 16 recurrent witnesses are recorded mostly in the dossiers of Addiyāyu, Illil-ašābšu-iqbi, Balšam, and Bīt-Sîn-erība, as well as in the Nār-simmāgir and Namgar-Dūr-Illil districts (see below, Part III, 325–326, 332, 336, 375–380, 384, 402–404, 414, 435).

Non-recurrent (85):

1st witness (5)

Of five: **[247]** Ninurta-iqīša / *Ba-rik-Bēl*, 10.II.2 Dar II (PBS 2/1 45: 7). Of six: **[248]** *Bītāya*(É*-ta-a*) / Ahūšunu, 3.III.39 Art I (BE 9 66: 8). Of seven: **[249]** *Ha-na-ni-'* / Bēl-ittannu, 12.VIII.27 Art I (BE 9 8: 17); **[250]** *Ra-hi-i*[*m-*...], -.V.- Dar II (IMT 32: 16). Of nine: **[251]** Imbi-Sîn / *Sîn*(^{d}30)*-ra-mu*, 20.I.22 Art I (EE 3: 23).

1st & 2nd witness (2)

Of seven **[252–253]** Erībāya and *Ba-rik-ki-a*, sons of *Ag-ga-'*, 4.X.5 Dar II (PBS 2/1 209: 11).

2nd witness (4)

Of four: **[254]** Bēl-ēṭir / *Qar-ha-'*, 1.XI.38 Art I (BE 9 15: 18–19); **[255]** *Ha-an-na-ta-ni-'* / Nabû-ina-kāriši, 1.VI.41 Art I (BE 9 90: 7); **[256]** Šuma-uṣur / *Šá-ab-ba-a*, -.VII.7 Dar II (PBS 2/1 223: 11). Of eight preserved: **[257]** ^{d}*Ta*$_5$*-míš-*[...] / Tattannu, [...], -.-.20+[x] Art I (EE 56: 15').

2nd preserved witness (1)

[258] *Ra-hi-im-il*(DINGIR^{meš}) / [...], of at least six, -.-.7 Dar II (PBS 2/1 102: 13).

3rd witness (4)

Of five: **[259]** *Nu-ha-a* / Erībâ (SU-a), 28.VII.32 Art I (BE 9 4: 12). Of eight: **[260]** *Za-bi-na-'* / Ku-[x], 4.II.32 Art I (BE 9 31: 19). Of ten: **[261]** [...] / *Ba-rik-*

il(DINGIR^{meš}), place and date lost (EE 61: 9’). Of 11: **[262]** *Ba-ri-ki* / Iqīšāya (with a ring, SU 161), 13.XII.40 Art I (BE 9 82 = EE 55: 24, upper edge, cf. IMT 54: 24).

4th witness (8)

Last preserved: **[263]** *Šá-la-a-ma$^{!}$-a$^{?}$-nu*, 26.V.37 Art I (EE 94: 12). Last: **[264]** Ahūšunu / *Ga-mil-lu*, 14.XI.0 Dar II (IMT 22: 15). Penultimate: **[265]** Ahūšunu/ *Ga-ba-Bēl*, 11.XII.2 Dar II (PBS 2/1 55: 11). Of seven: **[266]** *Na-ah-ma-nu* / Mušēzib-Bēl, 4.X.5 Dar II (PBS 2/1 209: 12); **[267]** *Qu-da-a* / Iddīya, 23.VI.6 Dar II (PBS 2/1 215: 18). Of eight preserved: **[268]** *Ba-rik-ki* / [...], [...], -.-.20+[x] Art I (EE 56: 18’). Of 11: **[269]** *Hi-in-ni-ia* / Kīnāya, 12.I.41 Art I (BE 9 85: 20). Of 12: **[270]** *Abi*([AD)-*r*]*a-am* / Bēl-aba-uṣur, [...], -.X.- Art I (EE 59: 15).

4th-5th witness (2)

[271–272] *Da-di-ia* and *Addu-ga-šá-ri*-A+A-*lu-’*, sons of *Lu-la-’-Bēl*, penultimate and last witness, 13.I.40 Art I (IMT 53: 17–18).

5th witness (6)

Last: **[273]** *Da-hi-il-ta-’* / Bi-bi-bani(DÙ, for / *Bibānu* /), 9.XI.3 Dar II (BE 10 77: 15). Penultimate: **[274]** Ninurta-ēṭir / *Za-bu-du*, 13.IX.30 Art I (BE 9 21: 10). Ante-penultimate: **[275]** *Ra-hi-im-il*(DINGIR^{meš}) / Bulluṭāya (with a ring, SU 623), 23.VIII.4 Dar II (BE 10 89: 14, upper edge); **[276]** *Iq-ba-a* / Iddināya, 23.VI.6 Dar II (PBS 2/1 215: 19). Out of eight: **[277]** *Ba-rik-ki* / *Šá-lam$^{!}$-ahi*, 4.II.32 Art I (BE 9 31: 20); **[278]** *Nabû-id-ri-’* / Mušēzib-Bēl, 13.VI.3 Dar II (BE 10 67: 15).

6th witness (7)

Last: **[279]** Iddina-Illil / *Ba-rik-ki-^{d}Ta$_{5}$-míš*, 26.IV.2 Dar II (PBS 2/1 46: 14); **[280]** *Šá-am-šá-nu* / *Zi-im-ma-a*, [Nippur], 6.XI.6 Dar II (PBS 2/1 126: 18). Penultimate: **[281]** *A-qab-bi-il*(DINGIR^{meš}) / Aha-iddina, 3.III.28 Art I (BE 9 10: 29); **[282]** Bēl-iddina / *Ka-ṭi-nu*, 6.VIII.31 Art I (BE 9 28a: 13–14); **[283]** *Il*(DINGIR^{meš})-*li-in-ṭár* / Nidinti<<šá>>-Illil, -.V.- Dar II (IMT 32: 20); **[284]** *Za-bi-i-ni* / *Bil-te-e*, 4.XI.0. Dar II (BE 10 1 = TuM 2/3 29: 19). Out of 13: [**285**] *In-il*(DINGIR^{meš}), 28.VII.39 Art I (BE 9 67: 15).

7th witness (7)

Last: **[286]** *Zab-di-ia* / Bēl-ēṭir, 24.X.2 Dar II (BE 10 62: 18–19); **[287]** *^{d}Ta$_{5}$-míš-li-in-ṭár* / x-[...], 20.I.35 Art I (IMT 4: 15). Ante-penultimate: **[288]** Bibāya / *Ba-rik-ki-ta$_{5}$-míš* (with a ring, SU 398), 21.VI.11 Dar II (PBS 2/1 147: 30, upper edge);

[289] *Bi-ṣa-a* / Itti-Šamaš-balāṭu (with fingernail mark), 29.III.40 Art I (IMT 40: 7, right edge: -[*a*]); **[290]** *Ha-ba-ṣa-a* / Nidinti-Bēl, 25.VII.40 Art I (EE 40: 14). Out of nine preserved: **[291]** [(...-)]⌜x-*di-lu*?-*ú* / *Id-ra-ni-ʾ-il*(DINGIR*meš*) (the last witness is also non-Akkadian), [x+]?12.-.30 Art I (BE 9 23: 21'). Out of 13: **[292]** *Ìl-gab-ri* / *Na-tan-il*(DINGIR*meš*), 28.VII.39 Art I (BE 9 67: 15).

8th preserved witness (1)
[293] *Šá-am-ma-a* / *Ki-tir*?-*ri*?-*is*, penultimate, 17.II.0 Dar II (BE 10 5: 20).

9th witness (1)
Out of ten preserved: **[294]** *Man-nu-lu-ha-a* / Nabû-ēṭir, 6.VII.1 Dar II (BE 10 47: 20).

10th witness (2)
Penultimate: **[295]** *Aha-abu-ú* / Kīnāya, place of issue and date lost (IMT 55: 20); **[296]** Madānu-iddina / *Addu-ši-ki-in-ni-ʾ*, 25.VII.2 Dar II (PBS 2/1 193: 21–22).

11th witness (3)
Last: **[297]** *Šá-ra-ʾ-il*(DINGIR*meš*) / Bēl-ēṭir, 25.VII.2 Dar II (PBS 2/1 193: 22–23); **[298]** x-x-x-x / *B*[*a-r*]*ik-ki-*^{d}*Ta*$_5$*-míš*, place of issue and date lost (IMT 55: 21). Penultimate: **[299]** ^{d}*Ta*$_5$*-míš-nūrī*(ZÁLAG-ʾ) / Sîn-ēṭir, 5.VII.36 Art I (BE 9 49: 18).

12th witness (1)
[300] Rībatu / *Il*(DINGIR*meš*)*-na-ta-nu*, of 16 witnesses, 2.I.1 Dar II (BE 10 7 = TuM 2/3 181: 16).

14th witness (1)
[301] *Il*(DINGIR*meš*)*-id-ri-ʾ* / *Ap-pu-us-sa-ʾ*, of 22 witnesses, 4.VII.39 Art I (BE 9 69: 21).
Additional 31 witnesses are recorded in Part III ([337–338, 348–349, 351, 366–367, 381–383, 385–387, 400–401, 413, 417–421, (71), 427–432, 437–439]).

Part III Social Geography

This last part offers an overview of sources pertaining to the social geography of West Semites in the Nippur area. The list contains the names of those West Semites mentioned as property holders, or as otherwise active, in a particular village or district of the Nippur area. In this list, the figures following the geographical names refer to the number of West Semitic individuals attested in that place as holders, coparceners, witnesses and in other capacities. Bow-properties belonging to *haṭru*-organisations are followed by 'a' (e.g. 2a), bow-properties and other arable lands whose *haṭru*-organisation is not indicated, are followed by "b" and "AL" respectively. They might have belonged to such an organisation whose bow-properties were located in the same locale (such a possibility exists in at least six locales, viz. Bannēšu, Bīt-Hadīya, Kār-Ninurta, Bīt-Sîn-līšir, Abastanu, and Kuzabatu). Other individuals are followed by "c". Judeans, individuals with purely Arabian filiations and people of non-Aramean descent discussed in Part I above are not counted below.

a. Nippur and Nār-Šalla (very close to Nippur): 2b

[302] *Áh-ia-tal-la-'* / *Da-'-za-ak-ka* and **[303]** *Šá-ra-'-il*(DINGIR^meš^) / Šamaš-[x]-MU (with fingernail marks), 25.VII.27 Art I (IMT 35: 2, 6, left edge). *Áh-ia-a-tal-la-'* / [*Da*]-*'-za-'-ka-'* is the second of 11 preserved witnesses, 22.VII.34 Art I (IMT 37: 10); +3c: **[304]** Itti-Šamaš-balāṭu, **[305]** *Za-ra-ah-*^d^*Ta*$_5$*-míš* and **[306]** *Ha-nun* (Part I.3 above).

b. Euphrates of Nippur district (23)

Bannēšu (6)

5a: [see above 53, 54, 109, 110, 112]; + 1b: **[307]** *Nabû-za-bad-du* / Bēl-ēṭir (with a fingernail mark), 26.VII.1 Dar II (PBS 2/1 42: 2, left edge).

Bīt-Arzāya (8)

5a [see above 59, 60, 61, 62, 176]; + 2b: **[308]** *Ha-an-na-ni-'* / Iddina-Nabû, probably with **[309]** Bēlšunu / *Bi-ṣa-a*, 21.VII.1 Dar II (PBS 2/1 179: 2); + 1c: **[310]** *Ha-an-ni-ia* / Iddina-Bēl, debtor (dates), 26^?^.VI.18 Art I; debtor, 2.I.29 Art I (with a fingernail mark, Stolper, 'Fifth Century Nippur,' 86–87: 1, 5 and 86–88: 2, 4, right edge respectively).

Bīt-Hadīya (1)

1AL: **[311]** *Ad-gi-ši-ri-zab-du*/Bēl-erība, lessee (with a ring, SU 544), 28.XII.1 Dar II (BE 10 55: 2, 8: *-za-bad-du*).

Bīt-Zukkītu (3)

3b: **[312]** *Ia-a-si-bi-il*(DINGIR^meš^)/AH(?)-*ba* (or *ma*)-*na*, **[313]** Illil-ittannu / *Qu-da-a* and **[314]** *Nabû-di-li-in-ni-'* / Ninurta-ēṭir, debtors (followed by two Judean co-debtors from Bīt-Abi-ah), 13.XII.40 Art I (IMT 94).

Galê (1): 1a: [see above 94].
Malahhāni (3): 3a: [see above 81, 82, 84].
Bīt-Gērāya (1): 1c: **[315]** *Bēl-i-di-r*[*i-'*] (Part I.3 above).

c. Piqūdu district (58)
Piqūdu canal (4)
4AL: **[316]** *Ha-an-ba-ru-ru* / *Zab-di-ia* and **[317]** Kidinu / *Har-ra-a-ha-a*, 3.VII.7 Dar II (PBS 2/1 134: 3–4); **[318]** Ninurta-iddina / *A-qu-bu*, brother of **[319]** x [...] (with fingernail marks), -.VII.7 Dar II (PBS 2/1 223: 4).

Kār-Ninurta (3)
1b: (perhaps of Hammatāyu's estate, cf. above Part II.g) **[320]** *Man-nu-lu-ú-ha-ú-a* / Ninurta-ēṭir, place of issue not indicated, 13.VI.6 Dar II (PBS 2/1 213: 4); + 2AL: **[321]** Bi-ba-a / *Bil-ta-a* and **[322]** *Nabû-ra-hi-i* / Illil-(mu)kīn-apli, 13.VI.6 Dar II (PBS 2/1 212: 3–5).
Bīt-Aplāya: 1a (see above [171]).
Bīt-Murānu: 1a (see above [189]).
Bīt-Hadūru: 10a (see above [156–165]).
Bištu-ša-rab-urāti: 1a/b (see above [166]).
Addiyāyu (4)
2b: **[323]** *Da-la-ta-ni-'* / Ša-pī-kalbi (with another two people +x AC), 6.V.34 Art I (BE 9 38: 2); **[324]** [*A*]-*qu-bu* (with a fingernail mark), 5.[V.34] Art I (EE 74: lower edge); + 2c: recurrent witnesses (first and second respectively) **[325]** *La-ba-ni-'* / *Ra-hi-im-il* (DINGIR^{meš}, of six witnesses: BE 9 37: 10; 38: 10 of five witnesses: *La-ba-nu*, [5.V].34 Art I (EE 72: reverse 1') and **[326]** Bēl-ēṭir / *I-da-ri-nu-il* (DINGIR^{meš}, of five witnesses: BE 9 36: 12), Bēl-ēṭir / *Ia-da-ar-ni-'-il* (DINGIR^{meš}, of six witnesses: BE 9 37: 12; 38: 12).

Ālu-ša-maqtūti: 6a (see above [92, 104–108]).
Bīt-Tabalāya: 9a (see above [93, 95–103]).
Arzuhinu: 1a (see above [17]).
Bāb-Nār-Šubat-Ea: 4a (see above [55–58]).
Bīt-Ardīya: 6a (see above [150–155]).
Bīt-Erība: 1a (see above [130]).
Bīt-Iltehri-nūrī (1)
1AL: **[327]** ^{d}*Il-te-eh-ri-nūrī*(ZÁLAG-' the settlement's eponym), neighbour of members of the *haṭru*-organisation of the bowmen of the right (flank), [2]7.IV.1 Dar II (BE 10 34: 10 || PBS 2/1 41: 8); ^{d}*Il-te-eh-ri-* [...], -.-.1 Dar II (PBS 2/1 48: 8).

Bīt-Kīnāya: 2a (see above [173–174]).
Bīt-ša-rēši: 1a (see above [131]).
Bīt-Ṣūrāya: 1a (see at n. 55 above).
Nār-Šappūtu (1)
1b: **[328]** Ardi(?)-Sîn ([Ì]R$^{?}$-^{d}XXX) / *Zab-di-ia*, 22.XII.0 Dar II (PBS 2/1 1: 3, 7: [...]).
Šappūtu: 1a (see above [184]).

d. Namgar-Dūr-Illil district (13)

Namgar-Dūr-Illil (1)
1AL: **[329]** *Hi-li-ti-'* / In-na-Nabû, lessee, 7.IV.34 Art I (BE 9 34: 1).

Qaštu (3)
2b: **[330]** Illil-hātin and **[331]** Illil-ēṭir sons of *Zab-di-ia*, -.-.39 Art I (EE 79: 2–3); + 1c (witness): **[332]** Ṭābīya / *Abi*(AD)-*li-ti-'*, ninth and last witness, and second of eight witnesses, repeated as penultimate), Qaštu, 16.V.1 Dar II (BE 10 39: 16 and 40: 11, 15), Ṭābīya / *Abi-li-te-'*, third of five witnesses, Sîn-bēlšunu, 10.VI.6 Dar II (PBS 2/1 121: 13); Ṭābīya / *Abi-li-ti-'*, fourth of six witnesses, same place 10.VI.6 Dar II (BE 10 108: 13).

Bīt-Šulāya (2)
1a (see above [194]); + 1AL: **[333]** *Ahi-li-it-'*, 25.VII.40 Art I (EE 14: 5; 15: 5).

Bīt-Rihēti (2)
2b: **[334]** Bēl-ittannu / *Ba-rak-ki-*^{d}*Ta*$_5$*-míš*, Qaštu ša bīt mār-šarri, 17.V.1 Dar II (BE 10 40: 2). The same bow-property was held there by his brother, **[335]** Iddina-Marduk (/*Ba-rak-ku-*^{d}*Ta*$_5$*-míš*, with a fingernail mark, +x AC) according to a deed issued six days later (23.V.1 Dar II, PBS 2/1 10: 2, left edge).

Sîn-Bēlšunu (3)
3c (for witnesses attested there, see above [175]): **[336]** *Ba-ri-ki-il*(DINGIR^{meš}) / Bēl-iddina, fourth witness (PBS 2/1 121: 14); sixth and last (BE 10 108: 14); **[337]** Illil-iddina / *Lu-l*[*a*]*-'-hi-ia*, fifth and penultimate (10.VI.6 Dar II, 13–14); **[338]** *Na-ah-m*[*a-nu* ...], first of three, -.-.- Dar II (EE 89: reverse 2').

Pūṣāyu (2)
2AL: **[339]** *Ahi-ia-a-li-da* acted as lessee (+x AC), 25.VII.40 [Art I] (EE 14: 6); *Ahi-ia-li-du* / Ahūšunu (with fingernail mark), 2.XII.37 Art I (IMT 91: 3–4, left edge) with **[340]** *Bi-ṣa-*[*a*] (and Šulum-Bābili / Aplāya as well as [...] sons of Bēl-aha-iddina, +x AC) according to EE 16: 1 (*-l*[*i-da*]), lower edge (-[*da*]), reverse (Aramaic *ḥyl*[*d*]) from 20+[x].VI.34 Art I. *Ahi-ia-a-li-du* acted as co-guarantor

in EE 102: 3, 10 from 10.V.30[+x] Art I; *Ahi-ia-li-da* (+x AC, possibly = the three named ones in EE 16 six years earlier, EE 14: 6, 18: [ŠEŠ-*i*]*a-li-*[*da*]; 15, 6: [...]).

e. Cutha Canal district (19)

Gambūlāyu (2)

2b: **[341]** *Ha-an-na-ta-ni-'* / Ninurta-aba-uṣur and **[342]** *Ha-aṣ-ṣa-di-ni-'* / *Aq-qa-bi-il*(DINGIR^{meš}), [...], 13.VI.1 Dar II (PBS 2/1 12: 3, 6).

Bīt-Zabīn (6)

4a (see above [120, 133–134, 197],); + 2 AL: **[343]** *Id-ra-a* and **[344]** *Zab-di-ia* sons of Bēl-aha-iddina, 15.I.1 Dar II (PBS 2/1 4: 2).

Haṭallūa (7; suburb of Bīt-Zabīn)

4b: **[345]** *Gu-ra-'* / Līnuh-libbi-ilāni, 17.-.41 Art I (EE 69: 2, 5 ([*Gu-ra*]-'); **[346]** *Ha-nu-nu* / Ninurta-lukīn together with **[347]** *Za-bu-da-'* (both with fingernail marks) on 15.I.1 Dar II (PBS 2/1 174: 2, lower edge, cf. BE 10 8: 2); [344] *Zab-di-ia* / [Bēl-aha-iddina], 20.III.1 Dar I (the year number is preserved only in the main text, BE 10 24: 2, cf. PBS 2/1 153), *Zab-di-ia* / Bēl-aha-iddina, -.-.1 Dar II (in the text) (PBS 2/1 18: 2); + 3c: Both deeds are witnessed by **[348]** *Ha-an-na-ni-'* / Bēl-ēṭir, who is followed by **[349]** *Ba-rik-*^{d}*Ta*$_{5}$*-míš* / Nergal-iddina. *Zab-di-ia* / Bēl-aha-iddina had to deliver dates in nearby Bīt-Zabīn on 20.VI.1 Dar II (PBS 2/1 184: 2). *Zab-de-e* / Bēl-aha-iddina, ninth witness of 11, followed by [348] and [349]), 5.V.- Dar II (PBS 2/1 153: 14). **[350]** *Ha-an-ni-ia / Nabû-id-ri-'* worked (together with another three individuals bearing Akkadian names) for Ea-hātin in Haṭallūa on 25.IV.40 Art I (IMT 16: 21).

Gadimatu (4)

1b: **[351]** Na'id-Bēl / *La-ba-ni-'*, 15.IV.1 Dar II (BE 10 28: 3, left edge). Na'id-Bēl / *L*[*a-b*]*a-ni-iá* was lessee (with a stamp seal, SU 336) of fields in *Ha*$^{?}$*-še-bar*$^{?}$*-lu*$^{?}$,[119] 12.IX.41 Art I (BE 9 108: 1). Na'id-Bēl / *La-ba-ni-'*, third and penultimate witness, Kuzabatu, 24.VI.1 Dar II (BE 10 44: 11); + 3AL: [226] *Ra-hi-im* and **[352]** *Ha-an-na-ni-'* (= 227?) sons of *Ba-rik-ki-ìl* with **[353]** *Qu-da-a* / Ninurta-ibni, 23.VI.6 Dar II (PBS 2/1 215: 3); *An-na-ni-'* / *Ba-rik-ki-il*(DINGIR^{meš}), third witness of 11, 27.XIIb.32 Art I (BE 9 32: 16); *A-na-ni-'* / *Ba-rik-il*(DINGIR^{meš}), first witness of 17, 8.XI.34 Art I (IMT 3: 15) and third witness of seven, 20.I.35 Art I (IMT 4: 13–14).

119 Cf. Zadok, *Geographical Names*, 156.

f. Nār-Sîn district (54)

Aškāpē: 6a (see above [44–51]).

Bīt-Sîn-līšir (2)

1a: (see above [138]); + (probably) 1b: **[354]** *^{d}Ta$_5$-míš-na-ṭa-ri* / Bēl-ēṭir (together with Šulum-Bābili / Nabû-ittannu); 20.VI.41 Art I (BE 9 93: 3).

Gabalīni (2)

1a: (see above [132]); + 1AL: **[355]** *Ba-rik-^{d}Ta$_5$-míš* / Nanāya-ēreš, lessee (with a stamp seal, SU 192, field adjacent to the pass of Gabalīni), 15.XII.35 Art I (IMT 9 7: 9, 11: -[*Ta$_5$-míš*]), reverse; *Ba-rik-ki-* *^{d}Ta$_5$-míš* / Nanāya-ēreš, first witness of 16, 2.I.1. Dar II (BE 10 7 = TuM 2/3 181: 10, lower edge); *Ba-rik-ta$_5$-míš* / [Nanāya]-ēreš, ninth and penultimate witness, 20.III.1$^{?}$ Dar II (BE 10 24: 17–18).

Hambanāyu: 2a (see above [177–178]).

Huṣṣēti-ša-Addīya (2)

1a: (see above [139]); + 1AL: **[356]** *Ra-ab-bi-il*(DINGIR^{meš}) / Nabû-zēra-iddina, lessee, 22.IV.35 Art I (BE 9 40: 1: [*Ra*]-, 10); *Rab-bi-il*(DINGIR^{meš}) / Nabû-zēra-iddina, eighth witness of 11; followed by [215] *Za-ab-di-iá* / Bēl-zēra-ibni, 15.VI.40 Art I (BE 9 72: 14); ninth and last witness (preceded by *Zab-di-ia* / Bēl-zēra-ibni, 4.IX.40 Art I (BE 9 80: 16); sixth witness of ten, juxtaposed with *Zab-di-ia* / Bēl-zēra-ibni (fifth witness), 2.VII.1 Dar II (PBS 2/1 185: 19); seventh and last witness (the penultimate one is *Zab-di-ia* / Bēl-zēra-ibni), the preceding witnesses have Akkadian names, Illil-ašābšu-iqbi, 2.VII.1 Dar II (BE 10 54: 18); fourth witness (followed by *Zab-di-ia* / Bēl-zēra-ibni, out of eight), 3.VII.3 Dar II (BE 10 70: 15, lower edge: <^{meš}> unless the vertical trace underneath the DINGIR is the residue of MEŠ); principal (the paternal name is not preserved; with a stamp seal, SU 99), Illil-ašābšu-iqbi, 20.VII.[-] Dar II (PBS 2/1 158: 21, upper edge; *Zab-di-ia* with his seal and **[357]** [...] / [*Ba-ri*]*k-ki-il* acted as the last and penultimate witnesses respectively).

Huṣṣṣēti-ša-Nāṣiru (4)

3b: **[358]** *Gu-sa-*A+A with **[359]** *Zab-di-iá* / Ninurta$^{?}$-ēṭir$^{?}$ (^{d}MAŠ$^{?}$-SUR$^{?}$) (possibly brothers), Šulum-Bābili (? DI-E$^{\text{ki?}}$) / Nabû-uballiṭ, Balāṭu / Marduk-ēṭir, and **[360]** Šullumāya / *Zab-di-iá* (probably son of [359]), 20.VI.41 Art I (BE 9 92: 2–4); + 1AL: [see above 356] **[361]** *Ba-rik-ki-il*(DINGIR^{meš}; with a ring, SU 564), 20.VII.3 Dar II (BE 10 72: 4).

Til-hurdi (3)

1b: **[362]** [*Ba*]*-si-šú-a-na-ki* / *Gamillu*, 4.XII.32 Art I (BE 9 31: 2); + 2AL: **[363]** *Abi*(AD)*-la-hi-'*, 16.-.41 Art I (EE 118: 3); **[364]** *Nabû-šá-ra-'* / *Su-lum-ma-du* (with a stamp seal, SU 542), 27.XIIb.32 Art I (BE 9 32: 5, 6, 8, 10, reverse), Illil-ašābšu-iqbi, 7.X.5 Dar II (PBS 2/1 210: left edge).

Ham/bari on *Nār-šarri*: 5a (see above [188, 190–193]).
Nār-šarri: 1a/b/AL (see above [185]).
Āl-Bēl on *Nār-Bēl*: 1a (see above [172]).
Bīt-māri-rubê on *Nār-Bēl* (4)
1AL ([64]); + 1b: **[365]** *Amurru*(dKUR.GAL)*-na-tan-nu* / *Qu-da-a* (with Amurru-iddina); + 2c: the deed is witnessed by **[366]** Bēl-aba-uṣur / *Am-bu-ru* and **[367]** Šuma-iddina / *Šá-ra-ʾ-il*(DINGIR*meš*), fifth and sixth witness of seven, 25.XII.28 Art I (BE 9 16: 1 f., 15, 16); another witness is [64].

Bāb-Nār-Dērat and *Nār-Dērat* (1)
1AL: **[368]** *Ad-du-ra-am-mu* / Nabundu, lessee (with a ring, SU 597), 28.-.39 Art I (BE 9 67: 1, 2, 8, 11: *-ma*, edge); third witness of 11, 28.[VII].38 Art I (BE 9 65: 24); second witness of six, [...], time of Illil-šuma-iddina (IMT 100: 6').

Huṣṣēti-ša-Amuqqadu on *Nār-Nergal-dānu* (see above [86–87]).
Perhaps connected with the Nār-Sîn district
Balšam (10)
10c: 15–16.I.7 Dar II **[369]** *Ab-da-ʾ*, creditor (barley, BE 10 119: 2, 9; 120: 2; PBS 2/1 221: 2; co-creditor Bēl-ittannu). The same creditors recur in PBS 2/1 222, which was issued at Illil-ašābšu-iqbi one day later before another eight witnesses. Three of these witnesses with non-Akkadian names are juxtaposed. All the four deeds were written by the same scribe. **[370]** Ši-kin-il(DINGIRmeš) / *Nabû-za-bad-du*, debtor (barley; with a fingernail mark, BE 10 119: 3, 7); **[371]** *Ha-gi-gi-ʾ* (Arabian) / *Il*(DINGIRmeš)*-ia-a-ha-bi* (co-)debtor (BE 10 119: 8; PBS 2/1 221: 3: *-gu-ʾ*); **[372]** *Za-bad-da-a*, brother of *Ha-gi-gu-ʾ*, co-debtor (PBS 2/1 221: 4); **[373]** *Nabû-ra-pa-ʾ* / Baba-iddina, co-debtor (barley; with fingernail mark, BE 10 119: 8; 120: 3); **[374]** *Ha-an-ni-ia*, guarantor (BE 10 119: 9); **[375]** d*Ta*$_5$*-míš-ba-rak-ku* / *Ha-ri-im-ma-ʾ*, first witness (BE 10 119: 12: <*Ta*$_5$>; 120: 8; PBS 2/1 221: 9: -[*ma-ʾ*]); **[376]** *Da-la-ta-ni-ʾ* / *Su-lu-ma-da*, second witness (BE 10 119: 13; 120: 9; PBS 2/1 221: 10: *-ma-da*); **[377]** Mannu-kī-Nanāya (Akkadian-West Semitic hybrid) / Nidintāya, third witness (BE 10 119: 14; 120: 10; PBS 2/1 221: 11); *Ú-ma-ah-bu-ʾ* (Arabian) / Silim-Bēl, fourth witness (BE 10 119: 15; 120: 11; PBS 2/1 221: 12); **[378]** *Ba-ru-ha-ʾ* / *Ṭa-ab-ṭa-ba-ʾ*, fifth witness (BE 10 119: 16; 120: 12: *Ba-*; PBS 2/1 221: 13); and *Du-ú-ia-a-hab-be* / *Ah-da-ga* (both Arabian), sixth witness (BE 10 119: 17; 120: 13; PBS 2/1 221: 14).

Illil-ašābšu-iqbi (not far from Balšam; 9)[120]

9c: (witnesses) **[379]** *Ma-re-e* / Nidinti-Bēl, third witness of eleven, 20.V.41 Art I (IMT 18: 27) recurs in PBS 2/1 206: 11 from [...], 21.-.4 Dar II second witness of four. **[380]** *Ra-hi-im-il*(DINGIR^{meš}) / Rībatu, second witness of six (with a ring, SU 396), 17.VII.4 Dar II (TuM 2/3 147: 22, lower edge).[121] **[381]** Ṣilli-Nanāya / *Abi*(AD)-*nūri*(ZÁLAG)-', fourth witness of six, date lost (time of Illil-šuma-iddina, i.e. 445–421 B.C.E., EE 108: 20'); **[382]** *Nabû-za-bad-du* / Mušēzib-Nabû, fourth witness of eight, 17.I.7 Dar II (PBS 2/1 222: 10), is followed by a Judean and **[383]** *Bīt-il*(DINGIR^{meš})-*da-la-'* / Bēl-iddina (with a stamp seal, SU 480); **[384]** *Nabû-šá-ra-'* / Ina-Esagil-rāšil, fourth witness of eight, 12.II.7 Dar II (TuM 2/3 189: 19–20); recurs as second witness of six (with a stamp seal, SU 134), 28.VIII.7 Dar II, BE 10 126: 11, upper edge) followed by **[385]** Mušēzib-Bēl / *Addu-ra-am-mu*, fifth witness of fourteen; **[386]** Nabû-dayyānu / ^{d}*Ta*$_5$-*míš*-[*nū*]*rī* ([ZÁ]LAG-'), seventh and last witness, 7.X.5 Dar II (PBS 2/1 210: 20–21); **[387]** *Bi-ṣa-a* / Bēl-aba-uṣur, fourth witness of nine (with an iron ring, SU 628), -.V.6 Dar II (BE 10 107: 10, lower edge).

g. Nār-simmāgir district (32)

Abastanu (7)

2a: (see above [168–169]); + 5b: **[388]** Ardi-Nergal / *Ba-rik-ki-*^{d}*Ta*$_5$-*míš*, 20.VI.41 Art I (IMT 73: 3) and -.III.1 Dar II (PBS 2/1 151: 2: [ÌR-^{d}]U.GUR / *Ba-rik-ki-*^{d}<*Ta*$_5$>-*míš*). **[389]** Iddīya and **[390]** Šalam-ahi sons of x (with fingernail marks), 2.IV.1 Dar II (PBS 2/1 7: 2); **[391]** *Il*(DINGIR^{meš})-*li-in-ṭar* / Aššur-hamme-ibni, brother of **[392]** Iddina-Marduk, 12.IV.1 Dar II (PBS 2/1 8: 1).

Bīt-Nanâ-ēreš (see above [30]).

Bīt-Naṭir (1)

1b: **[393]** *Nabû*$^{?}$-*ra-am* / Iddinâ (together with [...] / x-x and Nabû-ušēzib / Nidinti-Nabû$^{?}$), place and date lost (time of Rībatu servant of Murašû, i.e. 428–415 B.C.E., EE 75: 2'-3').

---

120 See Zadok 'Nippur region', 316.

121 He recurs as witness with his paternal name: *Ra-hi-mu-il*(DINGIR^{meš}), fourth of ten, 11.VIII.1 Dar II (PBS 2/1 21: 16); *Ra-hi-im-il*(DINGIR^{meš}), first of five preserved (with a stamp seal, SU 211), 6.VII.2 Dar II (PBS 2/1 191, upper edge); first of seven (with a golden ring, SU 396), 17.XII.4 Dar I (BE 10 96: 13, left edge); third of five (with a ring, SU 396), 18.I.6 Dar II (PBS 2/1 211: 13, upper edge: [^{meš}]).

Hašbāya (11)

2b: **[394]** *Na-tan-ni-il*(DINGIR^{meš}) / ⸢x-lu-ba/ma-' and **[395]** *Za-bid-^{d}Na-na-a* / Rēmūt-Bēl (with another four individuals with Akkadian names +x AC) on 20.VII.5 Dar II (PBS 2/1 107: 2: -^{d}*N*[*a-na-a*], 11, witnessed by Tattannāya / Bagabigin, a foreman of unspecified *šušānus*); + 4AL: **[396]** *Ha-al-li-li-i / A-qa-bi-il*(DINGIR^{meš}), **[397]** ^{d}*Ta$_5$-míš-li-in-tár* and **[398]** *Ri-i-qàd-ilāni*(DINGIR^{meš}) sons of Bēl-aha-iddina had to deliver 300 water fowls according to a deed from Hašbâ, 17.XI.41 Art I (BE 9 109). According to another deed from there, **[399]** ^{d}*Ta$_5$-míš-nu-ri-'* / Bunene-ibni (together with Mušallim-Illil / Illil-šuma-iddina, with fingernail marks) was a lessee of an inundated area (*tāmirtu*) in Bīt-Dayyānatu for supplying fish on 18.XI.5 Dar II (PBS 2/1 112: 1, 9: *-míš-nu-ri-'*). Judean fishermen are recorded in nearby Titurru (PBS 2/1 208); + 5c (witnesses in deeds issued there): **[400]** *Zab-di-ia* / Lā-qīpu, sixth witness of eleven, -.VII.2 Dar II (PBS 2/1 53: 14); **[401]** *Ba-ri-ki-ìl* / Ahhē-iddina, first witness of nine (with a ring, SU 466), 27.V.7 Dar II (BE 10 123: 8, left edge); **[402]** *Illil*(^{d}+EN.LÍL)*-ia-a-hab-bi* / Na'id-Bēl, brother of Illil-ittannu (with a ring, SU 473), 18.II.5 Dar II (BE 10 99: right edge) is recorded on 8.VIII.1 Dar II as the fourth and penultimate witness in a deed concerning a field in nearby Abastanu (PBS 2/1 20: 14). **[403]** *Na-ṭi-ru / Ba-rik-ki-^{d}Ta$_5$-míš* is the sixth preserved witness of eight (with a ring, SU 586; PBS 2/1 20: 15, right edge: *-r*[*u*]); ninth and penultimate witness, 22.VIII.6 Dar II (PBS 2/1 123: 26); *Na-ṭi-ir / Ba-ri-ki-^{d}Il-ta$_5$-míš*, sixth witness of nine (with a ring), 27.V.7 Dar II (BE 10 123: 11). In three out of the four witnesses' lists he occurs together (twice juxtaposed) with [72]. The latter is recorded in deeds from there. *Na-ṭ*[*i*]*-r*[*u*]$^{?}$ / *Ba-rik-ki-^{d}ta$_5$-míš* witnessed a deed from nearby Titurru, third witness of six, 25.VI.5 Dar II (PBS 2/1 208: 17). **[404]** Šulum-Bābili / *Gu-sa-*A+A, first witness of four (with a ring, SU 400), Hašbāya, 18.XI.5 Dar II (PBS 2/1 111: 11; 112: 12; without paternal name in PBS 2/1 123, from there, 22.VIII.6 Dar I). He witnessed a deed from Kuzabatu, fourth and last witness, 24.VI.1 Dar II (BE 10 44: 12), and another one concerning a field in Abastanu, viz. PBS 2/1 20 (line 12: first of five, 8.VII.1 Dar II). Like Hašbāya, both settlements belonged to the district of Nār-simmāgir. Šulum-Bābili / *Gu-sa-*A+A, **[405]** ^{d}*Ta$_5$-míš-li-in-ṭár* and **[406]** Bēl-eṭēri-Šamaš, sons of Šamaš-šarra-uballiṭ, first, second and third witness of four respectively (the brothers have a ring and a seal respectively, SU 269, 526), Hašbāya, 18.XI.5 Dar II (PBS 2/1 111: 12, lower edge; 112: 12, upper edge). The brothers also witnessed a deed from Kapri-Lirīm (see below).

Hattāya (see above [30])

2c: **[407]** *Ahi-nūrī* and **[408]** *Zab-di-ia* (above, Part I.3).

Im-m[er]tu? (see above [30]).
Išqallūnu (see above Part I.3).

Kuzabatu (6)
5a: (at least; see above [140–144, 179]); + 1b: **[409]** *Da-la-ta-ni-'* / *A-qa-bi-il*(DINGIR^{meš}, with a fingernail mark, with Illil-hātin / Bēlšunu and Aplāya / Marduk-ēṭir, the former is homonymous with a coparcener of [49] above), 5.IV.1 Dar II (PBS 2/1 177: 3, left edge).

Tīl-Gabbāri (5)
1b: **[410]** *Ra-hi-im-il*(DINGIR^{meš}) and his sons, [...], -.-.-. Art I (BE 9 86a: 5, 7); + 2AL: **[411]** Bēlšunu / *Nabû-aq-qa-bi* (with a fingernail mark), -.VI.3 Dar II (PBS 2/1 79: 1, 12, left edge). He is recorded as a witness in two deeds issued in nearby Hašbāya: Bēlšunu / *Nabû-aq-bi*, sixth witness of eleven, -.VII.2 Dar II (PBS 2/1 53: 14) and Bēlšunu / *Nabû-a-qa-ab-bi*, eighth and penultimate witness, 27.V.7 Dar II (BE 10 123: 12). **[412]** *Hi-in-^{d}Na-na-a* / ^{d}[...], lessee with several partners (all with fingernail marks), Tīl-Gabbāri, -.-.5 [Dar II] (EE 23: 3); + 2c: **[413]** Šuma-iddina / *Nabû-a-qab-bi*, brother of [411], acted as the eighth and last witness, Tīl-Gabbāri, 11.X.5 Dar II (PBS 2/1 108: 12); **[414]** *A-qu-bu* / *Ṭa-ab-ṭa-ba-'*, probably the brother of [378] from Balšam, witnessed deeds from Tīl-Gabbāri, second witness of five, on 28.-.5 Dar II (PBS 2/1 115: 11) and from nearby Hašbāya, seventh of at least ten witnesses (with a ring, SU 381) on 22.VIII.6 Dar II (PBS 2/1 123: 25–26, left edge).

Nār-Sahtimanu and *Nār-Šanāya* (2)
2AL: **[415]** *Za-bu-du* / Tattannu, grandson of Ardīya, brother of **[416]** Bēl-bullissu, co-lessee (with members of his family), 1.III.38 Art I (EE 19: 2).

h. Old Tigris district (12)
Larak: 3a (see above [90, 147, 148])
Šarrabānu (above Part I.3)
Kapri-Lirīm (9)
2a: (see above [136, 137]); + 8c: **[417]** Bēl-ēṭir, [405] *^{d}Ta$_{5}$-mīš-li-in-ṭâr* and [406] Bēl-eṭēri-Šamaš, sons of Šamaš-šarra-uballiṭ, second, third and fourth witnesses, **[418]** Illil$^{?}$-[x] and **[419]** Bēl-šuma-iddina, sons of *Zab-di-ia*, seventh and eighth witness, [71] Bēl-ēṭir and **[420]** *^{d}Ta$_{5}$-mīš-ba-r[ak-k]i* sons of Šamšāya, ninth and tenth witness, and **[421]** Šamšāya (^{d}UTU-A+A) / *Ab-di-^{d}Iš-šâr* (Arameo-Assyrian), eleventh and last witness (with a cylinder seal, SU 156), 14.VII.7 Dar II (PBS 2/1 226: 13, 14, 17, 18, 19, left edge).

i. District unknown (46)
Nāqidīni on *Nār-Ahu-lē'* (see above [41]).
Arqā: 2a (**[422]** Bēl-rāšil and **[423]** Nabû-ittannu) (see above, Part I.3).
Bīt-Barēnā (1)
1AL: [270] *Abi*(AD)*-ra-am* / Bēl-aba-uṣur, Mušēzib-Bēl / Iššar-tarībi (Assyrian) and Bēl-eṭēru / *Ga-ag-gu-ú* (with a fingernail mark, Arabian paternal name); 2.V.33 Art I (EE 77: 2, left edge: [AD]-).

Bīt-Daddīya: 1a (see above [135]).
Bīt-Pirisāyu (see above [120], counted under Bīt-Zabīn).
Bīt-Sîn-ēreš (2)
2b: **[424]** *Ahi-im-mé-e* / *Ba-rik-il*([DINGIR]^{meš}), Aramaic *'ḥwm*[*y*] / [*B*]*rk*⌜'⌝*l*, brother of [122] Bēl-ēṭir (Aramaic *Bl'ṭr*, together with Ṣababa-šuma-iddina = Aramaic *Ṣbbšw*['[]*dn* / Ṣababa-ēreš +x AC), 17.VIII.29 Art I (EE 63: 3, lower edge).

Bīt-Sîn-erība (the field of ~; 9)
2b: **[425]** Ninurta-ibni and **[426]** *Na-dub*$^{?}$*-šu-nu*, sons of *Bi-ba-nu* (with another five people), Ridimhu$^{?}$, 12.IX.26 Art I (BE 9 7: left edge); + 7c: witnessed by **[427]** Bānīya / *Ba-rik-il*(DINGIR^{meš}), second witness of ten,[122] **[428]** *Ga-la-la-an* and **[429]** Bēl-ēṭir, sons of Lū-idiya, fifth to sixth witness, **[430]** *Bi-ru-ha-'* / *šá-ra-'-il*(DINGIR^{meš}), seventh witness, **[431]** Ninurta-ēṭir and **[432]** *Ba-rik-*^{d}*Ta*$_{5}$*-míš*, sons of Bēlet-taddin, ninth to tenth witness. Other: **[433]** Hašdāyu / *Zab-di-ia*, co-debtor.

Bīt-Ṣababa-ēreš (3)
2a: (see above [121, 122]); + 1AL: **[434]** *Bēl-id-ri-'*, 25.IV.40 Art I (IMT 16: 4).

Bīt-Taqbi-līšir: 1a (see above [123]).
Bīt-zēru-līšir (5)
2AL: **[435]** *Bēl-ba-rak-ki* / Bēl-ittannu, brother of **[436]** Marduk-ēṭir (the latter with a stamp seal, SU 131), concerning royal land administered by a deputy of the treasurer (*mašennu*), 5.V.33 Art I (BE 9 32a: 3, 7; *Bēl-ba-rak-ku* / Bēl-ittannu,

122 He recurs as witness: *Ba-né-e* / *Ba-ri-ki-il*(DINGIR^{meš}), first of 30 (with a cylinder seal, SU 497), 2.VII.36 Art I (BE 9 48 = TuM 2/3 144: 22, upper edge: *-rik-*; not a ranked list); Bānīya / *Ba-rik-il*(DINGIR^{meš}), first of six, <Nippur>, 30.III.31 Art I (BE 9 26: 15); first of six, 30.III.31 Art I (EE 17: reverse 5); first of seven, <Nippur>, 30.III.31 Art I (Stolper, 'Fifth Century Nippur', 93–97: 6, 21); brother of Nabû-bullissu, first and second of 5 or 6, 20.-.[31] Art I (EE 30: reverse 4'); third and penultimate, 12.V.32 Art I (BE 9 29: 26); third of six, 12.V.32 Art I (BE 9 30: 28); fifth of nine, -.V.31 Art I (BE 9 27: 10).

fourth witness of six preserved ones, -.-. 19 Art I, EE 48: 20); + 3c (all the witnesses, except for the only non-West Semitic one): **[437]** *Bi-ṣa-a* / *Ab-di-ia*, **[438]** *Ag-gi-ri-ia* / *Ha-ap-pa-as-su-a-'* and **[439]** *Za-bi-da-a* / Bēl-aba-uṣur.

Gammālē: 3a (see above [114–116]).
Hazzatu: 1AL (**[440]** Bēl-iddina) + 2c (**[441]** Nidinti-Bēl and **[442]** *Nabû-ra-am-mu* (above, Part I.3).
Hindāyu: 1a (see above [140]).
Huṣṣēti-ša-Baba-ēreš: 2a (see above [118–119]).
Huṣṣēti-ša-Zarūtu (2)
2AL: **[443]** *Ba-rik-*^{d}*Ta*$_5$*-míš* / Kiribti-Bēl, lessee (with partners, including **[444]** *Abi-*A+A*-qa-ri* / Napištu); 10.III.40 Art I (EE 11: 1–2). Cf. [*Abi*$^?$]*-ia-a-qa-ri* / Napištu, [x+?]6.-.1 Dar II (PBS 2/1 28: 1).

Ibūlē: 4a (see above [180–183]).
Qutānu (1)
1AL: **[445]** *Ra-hi-im* co-creditor (debtor: Bēl-eṭēri-Šamaš = Aramaic *Bl'ṭršwš* with fingernail mark), -.-.6 Dar I (BE 10 116: 3, 7).

Zamburāyu: 1a (see above [196]).
Nār-Balāṭu and *Tamirtu-*[*ša-Humāyi?*] (1)
1AL: **[446]** *Ha-na-ni-'* / *Da*(or *Ṭa*)*-ah-hu-ú-a* with a ring (place lost, time of Dar II, IMT 49: upper edge).

Nār-Ilīya (1)
1b: **[447]** *Ba-is-de-e* (Aramaic *By<s>dh*) / *Da-la-ta-ni-'* (with a ring, SU 127), 20.V.3 Dar II (TuM 2/3 146: 3: *Bi-*, 11).

Nār-Sahidu: 1AL (see above [24]).

j. Place not indicated (22)
5a (see above [88, 91, 170, 175, 197]); + 4b: **[448]** *Za-bi-da-a* and **[449]** Bēlšunu, sons of Iddināya (with fingernail marks, with Lā-abâši and Bēl-nādin sons of Aha-iddina), 3.III.28 Art I (BE 9 10: 2, 31); **[450]** Hašdāyu / *Za-bu-du* (with a fingernail mark, +x AC), 20.IV.1 Dar II (BE 10 30: 2). **[451]** *Na-ṭi-ru* (in broken context), place and date lost (time of Illil-šuma-iddina, i.e. 445–421 B.C.E., IMT 89: 5); + 9AL: **[452]** Illil-aha-iddina / *Ga-ah-la-'* (with a fingernal mark), 9.X.33 Art I (BE 9 33: 3). **[453]** *Da-hi-il-ta-ha-'* / Illil-ēṭir, lessee (with Arad-Egalmah / Ardi-Ninurta), 2.VI.36 Art I (IMT 11: 1, 10). **[454]** ^{d}*Ta*$_5$*-míš-*[*šú*]*-nu* (with Bēl-ēṭir), Nippur$^?$, 15.VII.- Art I (IMT 20: 6). **[455]** *Za-ba-du*, place lost,

-.-.22 Art I (EE 8: 3’: [*Za*]-, 5’). **[456]** *Šâ-ku-ú-hu* / *Hi-*ʾ-[*ra-an*] (Aramaic *Škwḥ* / *Ḥyrn*, with a fingernail mark), 21.VII.1 Dar II (BE 10 52: 1, 10, lower edge: *Šâ-ku-*[...], *Hi-*ʾ-[*ra-an*]). **[457]** *Da-di-i*[*a*] and **[458]** Illil-da-na sons of *Aha-ab-ú*, gardeners, 20.II.4 Dar II (PBS 2/1 81: 5, 14). **[459]** *Hi-in-ni-’* / ^{d}[x(x)]-ibni, co-lessee (with Nanâ-iddina, both with fingernail marks), 28.VI.1 Dar II (PBS 2/1 15: 1, 11); **[460]** *Ra-hi-im-il*(DINGIR^{meš}) / *Tad-di-’* (with a fingernail mark), debtor (dates), 2.VII.3 Dar II (BE 10 68: 2: *Ra-hi-*[...], 8, left edge, upper edge: Aramaic *Rḥym’l*). + 4c: **[461]** *Ba-rik-ki-Bēl*, **[462]** Bēl-ittannu, [**463**] ^{d}*Ta*$_{5}$*-míš-ba-rak-ku*/ Bēl-ēṭir and **[464]** *Ba-rik-Illil* (Part I. 3 above).

Part IV Some Conclusions

The continuity of Aramean presence in the Nippur countryside from the post-Kassite to the Achaemenid period can be shown by the persistence of settlements named after Aramean tribes, such as Haṭallu, Ibūlē, Gambūlu, Šarrabānu and Rabbilu. Aramaic toponymy is very common in the Nippur region during the period under discussion here. The adoption of Akkadian names with a Nippurean flavour by the Arameans is a slow process. Already in an early phase of their settlement in the Nippur region (mid-8th century B.C.E.) the Puqudeans were attracted by the Babylonian culture: it is reported that the whole tribe went to Nippur for the local festival.[123] They were influenced by the public cult of Enlil rather than by the cult performed within the temple precincts, access to which was severely restricted to anyone not from the local priesthood. The phenomenon of the impact of impressive cultic processions has numerous parallels in the anthropological record. The non-linear naming tendencies resulting in mixed Aramaic-Akkadian filiations continued as long as the traditional Babylonian cults persisted (i.e. until ca. 75 CE or the end of the Parthian period at the latest). By non-linear I mean the appearance of Akkadian anthroponyms with Aramaic paternal names and vice versa for several generations rather than the gradual disappearance of Akkadian anthroponyms. The phenomenon has an obfuscating effect on the level of the individual, since in view of the repetitive mixed Aramaic-Akkadian filiations we always have to reckon with ‘crypto-Arameans’. Mixed parentage is likely when non-Semitic names appear in filiations, notably Egyptians and Anatolians, but not necessarily Iranians, as adoption of Iranian names might

---

123 Cole, *Governor’s Archive*, 27.

have been motivated by their prestige. The Nippur region was totally Aramaicised by the late Parthian period.

Due to the absence of explicit Arameans in the Late-Babylonian record, we have to rely on a minimum sample of 464 Arameans (or 460 if four homonymous individuals, viz. 26 = 39, 109 = 110, 201 = 280 and 227 = 352, were physically identical), obtained according to the criteria described above (Part I.3). This is, admittedly, a torso, but a statistically significant one. It follows that these implicit Arameans are not a clear-cut and self-defined entity; they exist because we ascribe an Aramean identity to them. The latest occurrence of Aramean political entities (initially tribal) is from the beginning of the 6th century B.C.E. (in the Levant they disappeared from the political arena by c. 710 B.C.E. and they are not recorded as a group even in the rich Ptolemaic record of data on ethnic groups). Nothing is known about their self-awareness as a group whose culture was not the most prestigious in the wider Babylonian context, but what counts here is that the Arameans were demographically significant, and were becoming more and more dominant in the Nippur countryside over time. An explanation for the existence of such a distinct group, is the fact that 12.65 % of the sealers of the Murašû documents have Aramaic names (83 out of 656) compared with 71 % Babylonians and 7 % Iranians.[124] The prominent group of the Iranians is over-represented whereas that of the Arameans, placed basically on the opposite end of the social ladder, is under-represented.

The sample includes 356 individuals (76 %), whose occupations, roles and status are known. The remaining 108 (24 %) played the passive role of witnesses. The analysis below refers basically to the data presented in Part II and III above. It should be remembered that all the data are from a single archive (Murašû), which is a private one. Therefore they are inevitably biased, not devoid of incidental moments and with a high potential of accidents of documentation. The geographical distribution of the coparceners, holders and the other localized Arameans (altogether 213 = 46 %) by canal districts (seven with 61 locales, mostly settlements, percentage followed by number of locales), viz. Piqūdu 58 (27.2 % in 18), Nār-Sîn 54 (25.3 % in 15), Nār-Simmāgir 32 (15 % in 11), Euphrates-of-Nippur 23 (10.8 % in seven), Cutha 19 (8.9 % in four), Namgar-Dūr-Illil 13 (6.1 % in six), and Old Tigris 12 (5.6 % in three), conforms to that of the general population. In addition, 46 individuals are recorded in 21 locales whose district is unknown. It follows that the location of the majority of the Aramean principals within the Nippur

124 See Bregstein, *Seal Use*, 219–21, 225. My figure and percentage are obtained after deduction of the Judeans.

region can be established (but not that of most of the 108 witnesses). Here is their distribution in the 83 locales (individuals in each locale in descending order):

13 (6+7): Bīt-Zabīn with its suburb Haṭallūa (III.e);
11: Hašbāya (III.g);
10: Bīt-Hadūru (III.c), Balšam (III.f);
9: Bīt-Tabalāya (III.c), Illil-ašābšu-iqbi (III.f), Kapri-Lirīm (III.h), Bīt-Sîn-erība (III.i);
8: Bīt-Arzāya (III.b);
3+5: Kār-Ninurta with suburbs (III.c);
7: Abastanu (III.g);
6: Bannēšu (III.b), Ālu-ša-maqtūti (III.c), Bīt-Ardīya (III.c), Aškāpē (III.f), Kuzabatu (III.g);
5: Hamb/mari (III.f), Tīl-Gabbāri (III.g), Bīt-zēru-līšir (III.i);
4: Addiyāyu (III.c), Bāb-Nār-Šubat-Ea (III.c), Gadimatu (III.e), Huṣṣṣēti-ša-Nāṣiru (III.f), Ibūlē (III.i);
3: Bīt-Zukkītu (III.b), Malahhāni (III.b), Qaštu (III.d), Sîn-Bēlšunu (III.d), Til-hurdi (III.f), Larak (III.h), Bīt-Ṣababa-ēreš (III.i), Gammālē (III.i). Only one or two individuals are recorded in each of the remaining 50 locales.

Three *haṭru*-organisations had bow-properties in four locales.[125] One of them is that of the very important household in the hierarchy, that of the crown prince. The bow-properties of each of another six such organisations were scattered in three locales.[126] Each of the many remaining *haṭru*-organisations had bow-properties in one or two locales only. In the lack of contradictory evidence, it is possible that bow-properties of the same organisation in the same locale formed a block, but this can be demonstrated in one case only, where two such properties were adjacent to each other (see [153]). It can be surmised that leather workers were settled in a separate settlement or suburb due to the obnoxious smells of the tanning process. This assumption is enhanced by the archaeological finds from various sites (so far not from Nippur), where tanning installations are located outside settlements. The location of the boatmen of the Tigris and the Euphrates on the banks of the respective rivers is expected. The wide distribution of the bow-

125 The *haṭru* of the refugees (cf. [91–108]), of the *gardu* workmen (cf. [109–116]), of the crown prince's household (cf. [117–120]).

126 The *haṭru* of the *šušānus* of the treasury (cf. [140–148]), of the equerry's household (cf. [149–166]), of Hammatāyu's estate (cf. [171–175]), of the field hands (cf. [180–185]), of the *mārē hisanni* (cf. 186–194]), of Itti-Šamaš-balāṭu's household (cf. [132–135]); the members of these organisations were all *šušānus*, except for the latter (unless they were implicit *šušānus* in that case).

properties of the *šušānus* and *gardu*-workmen was perhaps in order to enhance the availability of these much-required manual workmen in as many locations as possible.

There is a fair representation of Arameans among the minor (almost lowest) functionaries, especially foremen of *haṭru*-organisations, many of whom were recruited from within their members, aided by relatives (it acquired almost a familial base) and in certain cases (apparently in organisations of ethnic groups) their office rotated among the organisation's clans (altogether 17 individuals, [34, 42–43, 52, Gu-sur-ri-' (see [55]), 88–89, 117, 125–126, 145–146, 149, 167, 186–187, 195]).

Just nine important royal functionaries, but not belonging to the higher echelons, can be considered Arameans with some degree of plausibility. No more than 20 acted as aides (appointees, scribes, household members and servants) of functionaries. Servants of the Murašû firm, despite being over-represented, include only 12 individuals with Aramaic names.

There is a fair representation of occupations (over 40 individuals). Most of them belonged to *haṭru*-organisations. It is, therefore, likely that the few brewers who had a supervisor also belonged to a *haṭru*. Occupations which clearly belonged to the palatial sector are, e.g. the pastry makers, who prepared food fit for the palace. Most of the shepherds in the Murašû archive bore West Semitic names. This is not surprising as Arameo-Arabians had a long tradition of small stock herding. Indeed, almost all of them dealt with sheep and goats. Documents about shepherds, especially in the Arsham dossier of the Murašû archive, have an impressive concentration of Aramaic notations. The range of recorded occupations in this rural-oriented archive is far from complete. In the same manner, people of lower status, such as refugees (18), as well as semi-free workmen, i.e. *gardu* (4) and *šušānus* (67), were also part of the *haṭru*-system. Like the people, whose occupations are reported, they were all coparceners of bow properties (altogether 110). In addition, there are 54 coparceners of bow-properties of unknown organisational affiliation, but it stands to reason that all the 164 coparceners were part of the *haṭru*-network. The same may apply to some of the 48 holders of fields. Much fewer were lessees of fields and very few were gardeners of palm groves. Most of these coparceners (their number can be fivefold or more by adding the anonymous unnumbered ones) pledged their bow-properties on behalf of the Murašû firm who financed their taxes, a process which inevitably led to a large-scale impoverishment of the cultivators.[127] To this large number of

127 See Jursa, *Economic History*, 409,

indebted cultivators are added more debtors (17) whereas the number of creditors (other than the Murašûs and their representatives) is negligent (two, [200, 201]). However, it should be remembered that indebted cultivators are inevitably over-represented due to the specialised activity of the Murašû firm. Among the known cases the most common cause of imprisonment of individuals were unpaid debts. The fact that a pair of brothers is involved ([232, 233]) strengthens this case: it can be surmised that they were indebted coparceners. This was the rationale behind their consignment to a prison (practically a workhouse, where their labour for their creditors would eventually cover the debts). The whereabouts of the imprisonment of two wives (of [235, 236]) elude us, but distress naturally comes to mind. The number of slaves and slave owners is negligent ([237–239; 230]) because the Murašû firm was hardly engaged in slave trade.

Non-recurrent witnesses in fully preserved lists ([247–301]) offer at best 'impressionistic' evidence on the relative social standing of individuals bearing Aramaic names, the more so since it is difficult to know whether such lists are arranged by rank. The most common position is that of the fourth witness (last and penultimate, but also placed closer to the beginning of the list preceding several others, viz. out of twelve, eleven and seven). The next common position is that of the seventh (mostly last and ante-penultimate, only once out of 13). Of the six in fifth position, four are last, penultimate or ante-penultimate and only two are out of eight. Each of the six witnesses in sixth position are also either last and penultimate. Three of the four second witnesses are antepenultimate. This position is common among the remaining witnesses. An exception are the four in third position, which are better placed (out of eight, ten and eleven). Only five witnesses are in first position.

The assumption that foreigners were settled mainly in outlying and marginal locales of the Nippur region[128] may be analogous to the situation in the documentation from Āl-Yāhūdu. However, regarding the Nippur region it must be relativised in view of the key position of Bannēšu.[129] This important colony of Carian prisoners of war close to Nippur was founded presumably by Nebuchadnezzar II, perhaps in order to neutralise those Nippureans, who opposed his father during his struggle against the Assyrians several decades earlier.

The presence of the few recorded guarantors reveals very little about social network other than the patronage of the Murašû firm. Two brothers were released

128 See Jursa, *Economic History*, 413.

129 See Ran Zadok, 'The Nippur Region during the Late Assyrian, Chaldean and Achaemenian Periods Chiefly According to Written Sources', *IOS* 8 (1978): 266–332, (291).

from prison after they had found three guarantors, namely the former's wife and two siblings whose relationship to the prisoners is unknown (cf. [232–234]). Members of the Murašû firm acted as guarantors in three cases. Two women were released from prison after they had found four guarantors of whom two were Rēmūt-Ninurta's servants ([235, 236]). A petition to release another prisoner was made by Nabû-ušēzib, servant of Illil-šuma-iddina ([231]). Tirakam, household member of Illil-šuma-iddina, assumed guarantee (on behalf of [444]) against wrongful demands (PBS 2/1 28). The same member of the Murašû firm released a prisoner who had found a guarantor ([202]). *Ha-an-ni-ia* from Balšam ([374]) was perhaps identical with the *Ha-an-ni-ia-'* who acted as co-guarantor 9–18 years earlier ([203]). *Ahi-ia-li-du* ([339]) acted in the same capacity. *Ia-šu-bu* / *Ha-ka-a*, probably a Judean, acted as a guarantor for *Na-tin-na-'* / *Na-ṭi-ri* ([218]).

Regarding interaction, some settlements had bow-properties of more than one *haṭru*-organisation. A member of the *haṭru*-organisation of the third men of the right (flank) witnessed a deed about the *haṭru*-organisation of the *šušānus* of the foremen in the same place ([90]). Not a few settlements had more than one *haṭru*-organisation and several ones had more than one population group. This strengthened the socio-ethnic intereraction. A deed from Hašbâ about the palm grove of a Lycian is witnessed not only by his two countrymen, but also by two Judeans and two Arameans in addition to bearers of Akkadian names (PBS 2/1 53). *A-qu-bu* / *Ṭa-ab-ṭa-ba-'* [414] witnessed a deed from Til-Gabbāri (second witness) together with three Judeans (*Ṭu-ub-ia-a-ma*'s sons, third to fifth witness of five, PBS 2/1 115). Recurrent witnesses may also convey interaction between neighbours and neighbouring settlements.

Compared with other groups, the Arameans are well-represented in the low echelon, with a modest presence in the middle one (contrast with the impressive number of Egyptians, who entered the ranks of the officialdom[130] despite being members of a group with a much narrower demographic base than that of the Arameans) and totally absent in the upper echelon (contrast with the ruling Persians). They were demographically dominant but lacked cultural prestige and generally did not rise from the bottom of the socio-economic ladder.

130 Cf. Hackl and Jursa in this volume.

Acknowledgment

The research for this paper is supported by the Ancient Israel (New Horizons) research program. I should like to thank the editors for their magnificent handling of a difficult manuscript and for patiently tackling the communicative challenges posed by the intricate material of this article.

Johannes Hackl and Michael Jursa

Egyptians in Babylonia in the Neo-Babylonian and Achaemenid Periods

1 Introduction

Egyptians are mentioned first in Babylonia in 676 B.C.E. and occasionally can be found also afterwards in Babylonian tablets of the Assyrian period.[1] However, more numerous attestations only appear in the Neo-Babylonian period, after the beginning of Nabopolassar's rebellion against the Assyrians. In the following discussion we distinguish the evidence from the 'long sixth century' (626–484 B.C.E.), with its abundant textual evidence, from later material. The general textual documentation from the period after the revolts against Xerxes, i.e. from 484 B.C.E. onwards, is far less abundant when compared with the earlier period. In view of the scarcity of the available sources, the number of attestations for Egyptians in the fifth and fourth centuries B.C.E. is considerable. It should be noted, however, that the evidence on Egyptians drawn from these sources is distributed unevenly in terms of institutional and private archives. The largest body of data stems from the Murašû archive from Nippur; additional attestations can be found in smaller archives from Northern Babylonia, particularly the Kasr and Tattannu archives, as well as in other tablets from Babylon and Borsippa. The largest institutional archive of the period, the Esagil archive with its substantial corpus of ration lists, on the other hand, yields no information on Egyptians working for the temple. The same holds true for the Zababa archive from Kiš, the second largest institutional archive from the late period.

The aim of this paper is to arrive at an understanding of the nature, and thus implicitly also of the quantitative dimension, of the Egyptian 'diaspora' in

1 See Ran Zadok, 'Egyptians in Babylonia and Elam during the 1st Millennium B. C.', *Lingua Aegyptia* 2 (1992): 139–146 (139); Melanie Wasmuth, 'Egyptians in Persia', in *Organisation des pouvoirs et contacts culturels dans les pays de l'empire achéménide* (ed. P. Briant and M. Chauveau; Persika 14; Paris: de Boccard, 2009), 133–141 (134, n. 7); Francis Joannès, 'Diversité ethnique et culturelle en Babylonie récente', in *Organisation des pouvoirs et contacts culturels dans les pays de l'empire achéménide* (ed. P. Briant and M. Chauveau; Persika 14; Paris: de Boccard, 2009), 217–236 (226, n. 37).

Johannes Hackl and Michael Jursa: University of Vienna

Mesopotamia in the period under discussion. We discuss in sequence the different socio-economic contexts in which these Egyptians can be found. Methodologically, we will use, but distinguish between, the cases in which Egyptians are explicitly designated as such and instances in which Egyptian origin must be inferred from the presence of an Egyptian name. Particular attention will be given to Egyptians who have connections with the royal administration, since state interference is ostensibly responsible for the presence of most of the Egyptians in Babylonia: links to the palace establishment are a feature determining the social and economic setting of the lives of many of these Egyptians.

Owing to the setting of our data in a predominantly Babylonian or at the most Babylonian and West-Semitic/Aramaic ethno-linguistic context, we consider Egyptian (and Iranian) names as 'marked' and thus as indicative of the origin, identity and/or aspirations of the name giver or the name bearer, while common Akkadian and West-Semitic names[2] are 'default' names in this society and thus not strongly indicative of the socio-economic and ethnic affiliation of the name bearer. Note that the evidence for members of the Miṣirāya clan, the descendants of 'the Egyptian', is not included here, as there is no real evidence apart from the name to prove that the bearers of this family name had maintained any real Egyptian background. We also do not deal with Egyptians documented in Akkadian (and Elamite) texts found in Iran, including Susa.[3]

2 Egyptians as Temple Slaves

The earliest body of data comes from Sippar and belongs to the context of the early Ebabbar archive.[4] There, from 13 Npl[5] (613 B.C.E.) onwards, a large(ish) group of Egyptians is attested as *širku*s, that is oblates, working for the temple.[6] The dossier of ration lists extends well into the reign of Nebuchadnezzar (16 Nbk), then it

---

2 This is, excluding 'Beamtennamen' and typical slave names.

3 Joannès, 'Diversité ethnique', 226–227 (n. 38).

4 See most recently Ira Spar, Thomas J. Logan and James P. Allen, 'Two Neo-Babylonian Texts of Foreign Workmen', in *If a Man Builds a Joyful House: Assyriological Studies in Honor of Erle Verdun Leichty* (ed. A.K. Guinan, M. deJong Ellis, A.J. Ferrara, S.M. Freedman, M.T. Rutz, L. Sassmannshausen, S. Tinney and M.W. Waters; CM 31; Leiden: Brill, 2006), 443–461.

5 I.e., from the thirteenth regnal year of Nabopolassar (Npl). Further abbreviations of this kind include: "Nbk" = Nebuchadnezzar; "Nbn" = Nabonidus, "Cyr" = Cyrus, "Camb" = Cambyses, "Dar" = (a) Darius; "Xer" = Xerxes; "Art" = (an) Artaxerxes.

6 BM 73261 (John MacGinnis, 'Servants of the Sun-God: Numbering the Dependents of the Neo-Babylonian Ebabbara', *BaghM* 35 [2004]: 27–38).

breaks off, even though individual *širku*s and other temple personnel of Egyptian origin are very occasionally also mentioned in later Sippar documents.[7] The early Sipparean *širku*s are attested as a collective as well as individuals; usually they are given the label 'Egyptian', but sometimes they can only be identified by their Egyptian names. While these *širku*s were kept distinct from the normal oblates or temple slaves of Ebabbar, they received the same provisions (food and occasionally textiles) as their non-Egyptian colleagues.[8] These men were undoubtedly gifted to the temple by the king. It should be noted that there is no evidence for women among them. Perhaps we are dealing with a group of males, which may explain the fact that we do not hear of such a group of Egyptian *širku*s after the second decade of Nebuchadnezzar – the original group may have died at this point, their possible descendants in any case would have been absorbed into the ranks of the common temple dependants. Occasionally, Egyptian temple slaves turn up also in other contexts. There is a sick (*marṣu*) Egyptian *širku* in 24 Nbk in Uruk, in the Eanna archive (*UCP* 9/1 29); and once in the reign of Nabonidus we hear of a *širku* of Nergal likewise active in the Uruk region (YOS 6 148, 9 Nbn).

The origins of these dependent groups of Egyptians must be sought in the military confrontations between the emerging Babylonian empire and the Egyptians in the Levant during the reign of Nabopolassar and early in the reign of Nebuchadnezzar. The date of the first attestation of this group is 13 Npl, that is, earlier than hitherto assumed. This must simply mean that the Egypto-Babylonian conflict began more or less at the moment when Babylonian influence first extended into Syria and the Levant in the wake of the crumbling Assyrian empire. The disappearance of the Sippar references to a coherent group of Egyptian temple slaves is explicable by the cessation of regular hostilities between the two states later in the Neo-Babylonian period and to the assimilation of the Egyptians into the normal workforce of the temples. The single reference to a collective of Egyptians from the reign of Cambyses (*Camb.* 313, 6 Camb) must refer to new arrivals – which, given Cambyses' engagement in Egypt in the second half of his reign, is entirely plausible. We have thus two 'waves' of 'incoming' Egyptians: one in the reign of Nabopolassar and in the early reign of Nebuchadnezzar, and one from the late reign of Cambyses onwards, owing to the Persian domination over Egypt.

---

7 E.g., *Dar.* 5 (522 B.C.E.); Michael Jursa, *Die Landwirtschaft in Sippar in neubabylonischer Zeit* (AfOB 25; Vienna: Institut für Orientalistik, 1995), 31 (a gardener, reign of Nabonidus).

8 A. C. V. M. Bongenaar and B. J. J. Haring, 'Egyptians in Neo-Babylonian Sippar', *JCS* 46 (1994): 59–72; Spar, Logan and Allen, 'Two Neo-Babylonian Texts'.

The Sipparean evidence for a temple estate bearing the name of 'settlement of Egyptians' (*bīt miṣirāya*) points into the same direction. It is first mentioned in the reign of Nabonidus, when the area in which it was situated was the site of extensive works on the irrigation infrastructure; clearly these Egyptians had been settled in a somewhat depopulated area of the Sipparean hinterland with a view towards its eventual development.[9] It is probable that groups of Egyptians that were settled as a collective in the hinterland of the cities could maintain their separate 'Egyptian' identity better than their colleagues who lived mostly in an urban context and were soon absorbed by Babylonian society.

In the period following the 'long sixth century', Egyptians are no longer attested in the temple sphere. The absence of references in the pertinent sources from the fifth century B.C.E. does not seem to be owed to mere accidents of recovery or archival composition. In view of the largely Babylonian onomasticon attested in the ration lists of the Esagil archive, there is reason to suppose that individuals with foreign names were given Babylonian names after they had been donated to the temple. Alternatively, and this seems more plausible, one might argue that the lack of Egyptian names is indicative of a well-advanced process of acculturation in the urban context whence these institutional texts originate.

3 Slaves of Egyptian Origin

Privately owned slaves of Egyptian origin are mentioned between the accession year of Nabonidus and the first year of Xerxes (555–485 B.C.E.). This is not necessarily indicative of the real number of Egyptian slaves in circulation, as the indication of their origin as 'Egyptian' must have been optional. Of the four slaves thus designated, one man (YOS 6 2, acc Nbn) and one woman (*Camb.* 334) bear Babylonian names, whereas the second man (Stol, *RA* 71, 96) and the second woman (NBC 6156) retained their Egyptian names. One slave woman is said to be her owner's booty, *hubut qaštišu*; her owner had served in the Persian army in Egypt (*Camb.* 334, 6 Camb). Incidentally, it should be noted that the slave woman [f]Tahhar who is sold in a document belonging to the Sipparean Ṣāhit-ginê B archive in 1 Xer is said to have had her name inscribed on her arm in Egyptian;

9 Michael Jursa, *Aspects of the Economic History of Babylonia in the First Millennium BC: Economic Geography, Economic Mentalities, Agriculture, the Use of Money and the Problem of Economic Growth.* With contributions by J. Hackl, B. Janković, K. Kleber, E. E. Payne, C. Waerzeggers and M. Weszeli (AOAT 377; Münster: Ugarit-Verlag, 2010), 330.

apparently there were scribes who could read Hieratic or Demotic in Babylon in this period.[10]

In the period after 484 B.C.E., privately owned slaves of Egyptian extraction do not only figure as the object of a transaction (e.g., in sales or transfers of ownership), but also as contracting parties and witnesses. The documentation on these slaves covers almost the entire fifth century B.C.E.; later attestations (from the reign of Artaxerxes II onwards) are rare. Here again, the number of Egyptian slaves identified in the texts either by name or gentilic cannot be regarded as representative of their real number. What is more, in the fifth century B.C.E. the indication of origin 'Egyptian' falls nearly out of use. Overall, the sources yield only two attestations postdating the revolts against Xerxes (*NABU* 1999/6a, 21 Xer and *AfO* 52 88 no. 9, 10 Dar II). Of the two individuals thus designated, only the Egyptian in the apprenticeship contract *AfO* 52 88 no. 9 is a slave. It is noteworthy that in this particular instance not only the apprenticed slave happens to be Egyptian, but also the kind of bread that is to be prepared by the apprentice (see below). The contract also mentions that the apprentice is a captive (*qallu ṣabtu*), a designation otherwise unattested in contemporaneous sources. Also this slave, like the female slave in *Camb.* 334 who is said to be her owner's booty, bears a Babylonian name.

Among the texts mentioning Egyptian slaves, there is only one contract in which slaves figure as the object of a transaction. PBS 2/1 65 (3 Dar II) from the Murašû archive records the sale of two slaves both bearing Egyptian names. It should also be noted that one of the previous owners of these slaves is of Egyptian extraction as well. In the remaining texts mentioning Egyptian slaves the latter are either party to the contract or listed among the witnesses. In addition to *AfO* 52 86 no. 8, in which the artisan concludes the apprenticeship contract with the owner of the slave, there are two debt notes in which Egyptian slaves appear as creditors (BM 82566, 11 Art I$^{?}$ and VS 3 189, 22 Art I). In another text (EE 27, 40 Art I) the tenant assumes warranty against legal claims that might be raised by a certain Harmahi who is referred to as a slave of the Persian Manuštānu. This is one of the many cases in this period in which men designated as *ardu* ("slave") of high-ranking Persians are actually rather agents than chattel slaves. Egyptian slaves acting as witnesses can be found in BM 82566 (11 Art I$^{?}$) and BE 10 129 (8 Dar II).

10 NBC 6156, cf. Matthew W. Stolper, 'Inscribed in Egyptian', in *Studies in Persian History: Essays in Memory of David M. Lewis* (ed. M. Brosius and A. Kuhrt; Achaemenid History 11; Leiden: Nederlands Instituut voor het Nabije Oosten, 1998), 133–143 (especially 142).

4 Free Men of Egyptian Origin

The data are not too rich, so we will simply give a catalogue and then try to draw some conclusions from the evidence. We find Egyptians in the following instances:

27 Nbk: Paṭ-Isiri (Egyptian name) is working as a free hireling for the Eanna temple on the building site of the North Palace in Babylon (YBC 4187);

reign of Nabonidus: Nabû-ēṭer, designated as 'Egyptian', buys a large quantity of dates from the Ebabbar temple for 72.5 shekels of silver (CT 57 342);

reign of Cyrus: Hašdāya son of Šamaš-ušēzib and Šamšāya son of Paṭ-Esu (Egyptian name) rent a large plot of land (rent: 50 kor barley) from the Ebabbar temple (BM 64697; *JEOL* 40 93–94, no. 2);

4 Dar: Harrimaha son of Huru-x (Egyptian name) is owed dates as *imittu* by several men with Babylonian names (written in Babylon, but the tablet may belong to a Borsippa archive; BM 103473);

11 Dar: (the Egyptian) Paṭmiustû son of Pir marries ^{f}Tahê-[...], daughter of Samannapir son of [...]; among the witnesses is a Qaus-yada$^{?}$ *ša rēš šarri* (courtier), Bagapātu son of Pisamiski – a man with an Iranian name and an Egyptian patronymic[11] – and the Egyptian Paṭniptēmu son of Amunu-tapunahti (*Dar.* 301);

21 Dar: (the Egyptian) Paṭ-Esu son of Panna$^{?}$ is listed as a witness for a silver debt note stating the credit of a slave of the Persian noble Baga$^{?}$apanu; the debtor is a Babylonian; the tablet was written in Babylon (NBC 4757);

3 Xer: two Egyptian witnesses, Nadhunzu son of Harsi-Esu and Padiarrasu son of Paṭ-Esu (not explicitly identified as Egyptians) are named in a sale document for a donkey, Babylon (BM 64155);[12]

3 Xer: Bēlšunu son of Paṭ-Esu (Egyptian name) appears as a witness in a debt note for dates; the creditor is a certain Bēl-iddin/Munahhem (8^{e} *Cong.* 20).

First, we should note naming patterns: in addition to men bearing Egyptian names, we have several Egyptians, or rather men of Egyptian origin, with Akkadian names, and also one such man with an Iranian name (Bagapātu son of Pisamiski). This Bagapātu almost certainly belongs to the royal administration in some way or another; otherwise the peculiar naming patterns (of a man living in Babylonia) would not be explicable. There are in fact other, clear cases of royal officials of Egyptian extraction who bear Iranian names, see below.

---

11 Martha T. Roth, *Babylonian Marriage Agreements, 7th–3rd Centuries B. C.* (AOAT 222; Kevelaer: Butzon und Bercker, 1989), 83.

12 Matthew W. Stolper, 'The Estate of Mardonius', *AuOr* 10 (1992): 211–221 (220).

The Egyptian Nabû-ēṭer who buys dates from Ebabbar during the reign of Nabonidus was a trader who worked either independently or for an institution (most likely the palace);[13] in any case, he could dispose of considerable funds: 72.5 shekels of silver would buy a male slave or the work of two hirelings for a year. Nabû-ēṭer, Šamšāya son of Paṭ-Esu from the reign of Cyrus, lessee of a large plot, and the land-owner Harrimaha son of Huru-x from the early reign of Darius are certainly to be situated on a higher rung of the social ladder than the free worker Paṭ-Isiri, who hired himself out to the Eanna temple to work on Nebuchadnezzar's North Palace.

Regarding the six Egyptian witnesses (or witnesses of Egyptian origin) who are mentioned in four tablets from the early Achaemenid period, it is significant that three of the four tablets are to be situated in an only partly Babylonian milieu also on account of other data: *Dar.* 301 is a marriage contract between Egyptians who probably also had a connection to the royal administration;[14] in the debt note NBC 4757, the creditor is the slave of a Persian noble, and in 8^{e} *Cong.* 20, the creditor is a man of West-Semitic origin. Most of the evidence comes from an urban setting, but some Egyptians were also involved in agriculture in the hinterland of the cities, both as lessee (BM 64697) and as landowner (BM 103473).

Textual evidence on free men of Egyptian origin is more abundant after 484 B.C.E., but biased to some extent owing to the clear preponderance of attestations from the Murašû archive. In the fifth century B.C.E., we find Egyptians in the following instances (note that stray tablets are either from Babylon or Borsippa):

4 Xer: In addition to the female guarantor who is identified as being Egyptian by her patronymic, the apprenticeship contract *AfO* 52 86 no. 8 discussed above also mentions several Egyptians (on account of their names or patronymics) acting as witnesses. The text clearly has a setting in a partly non-Babylonian environment;

10 Xer: In CT 4 34d both the creditor and debtor bear Egyptian names (Šanūmū and Pisusasmakāša). Note that the latter's patronymic is Persian;

21 Xer: In *NABU* 1999/6a, a lease contract from Dilbat (unknown archive), the field rented out borders on another field which belongs to a certain Paṭ-Esu. In addition to the Egyptian name, this man's Egyptian origin follows also from the presence of the ethnic label *miṣirāya*;

---

13 Jursa, *Aspects of the Economic History*, 583.

14 Among the witnesses is a courtier of (South-)West Semitic origin, Qaus-yada$^{?}$; this and the presence of men bearing Iranian names (one of whom has an Egyptian father) among the witnesses suggest placing the text in an 'international' environment that had links to the royal administration.

[...] Art I: VS 6 188 from the Tattannu archive records the adoption of a slave and his son for the performance of feudal services. The adopter bears a Babylonian name with the Egyptian patronymic Pattû;

33 Art I: Munnātu, son of Umahparê, appears as recipient and guarantor in EE 35 (Murašû);

34 Art I: Halabesu, son of Paṭ-Esu, is the lessor of a field (IMT 3; Murašû);

37 Art I?: *Iraq* 54 137 (unknown archive) is a rental contract including the obligation to perform construction works on the plot rented out. Both the name and patronymic of the lessor are Egyptian (Miṣirāya, son of Harsi-Esu);

39 Art I: BE 9 70 is a receipt concerning the payment of *ilku* (a kind of tax). Among the individuals involved, there is a certain Qahia, an Egyptian by name;

39 Art I: In PBS 2/1 113 (Murašû) Uqhappi, son of Nahtuhappi, is listed among the witnesses. Both names are Egyptian;

40 Art I: In BE 9 81 (Murašû) Harmahi, son Bēl-ēreš, appears as owner of the slave who constitutes one of the contracting parties. Note the Babylonian name of Harmahi's father;

40 Art I: In IMT 43 (Murašû) a certain Paṭ-Esu, son of Hungamu, is also addressed with his second name which happens to be Persian. Both his brothers bear Babylonian names;

0a Dar II: EE 109 (Murašû) mentions a certain Hūru who, if understood correctly, appears to be a party to a lawsuit;

0a Dar II: Aplāya, son of Harmahi, rents out a house (BE 10 1, Murašu);

1 Dar II: BE 10 23 is a debt note belonging to the Murašû archive. The debtor bears the Egyptian name Harmaṣu with the patronymic Na'sea which is probably Egyptian as well;

2 Dar II: Bēl-ittannu, son of Šammû, appears as contracting party in the fragmentary 'dialogue' record PBS 2/1 54 (Murašû).

2 Dar II: The name Harmahi, son of Ṣillāya, is found as seal caption in PBS 2/1 192 (Murašû). It is thus likely that he was a witness to the contract, even though the name is not given in the witness list;

3 Dar II: In PBS 2/1 198 (Murašû) Harmahi, son of Iqīšāya, appears as debtor. His brothers bear Babylonian names, as does his father; still, we should assume that the family was of Egyptian origin. Harmahi is probably identical with the man of this name who is mentioned in BE 10 66 without patronymic;

3 Dar II: PBS 2/1 65 is a slave sale mentioning several Egyptians. Kunuis, son of Nah-Esu, is said to be the former owner of the slave to be sold. Another Egyptian by name, Paṭ-Esu, son of *Na-an*-[x]-*ú-a*, is listed among the witnesses;

5 Dar II: PBS 2/1 113 (Murašû) records the sale of a slave who is said to have had the name of his former owner inscribed on his arm. The latter bears the Egyptian name Hūru;

4 Art II: According to his name (Hūru), the creditor of the debt note Stolper, *Fs. Biggs* no. 20, is Egyptian, yet his father bears the West-Semitic name Iltagubati.[15] The text stems from the Kasr archive.

It is not possible to reduce these data to a few socio-economic settings. Clearly, Egyptians were present and active in Babylonia in the fifth century B.C.E. in many walks of life: they were almost certainly more numerous than in the sixth century B.C.E.. It should be noted, however, that owing to the setting of the Murašû data in the realm of the land-for-service sector of the economy with its dependence on the crown, many of the Egyptians mentioned in these texts will have had links with the royal establishment even though these links may not be explicitly referred to in the sources. A considerable number of other Egyptians who are attested in the archive is demonstrably associated with the crown, as will be demonstrated below.

5 Egyptians Associated with the Royal Administration

The marriage document *Dar.* 301 with its Egyptians who have contacts to the royal administration is an illustration for the fact that the environment of the court and the royal administration in Babylonia under Achaemenid rule, but also earlier, was ethnically far more diverse than the realm of the temples and the social background of the majority of the Babylonian families whose archives have come down to us: urban Babylonians kept themselves segregated, rigorously so on the level of marriage and lineage and less distinctly, but still in a noticeable fashion, on the level of economic interchange, from their non-Babylonian surroundings. This is reflected by the fact that the Babylonian language and the cuneiform script, the traditional means of communication in Babylonia and especially in the urban context of the old cities of the alluvium, were increasingly replaced by Aramaic in the realm of royal administration already under the Babylonian monarchy and may have played a secondary role there as early as the reign of Neriglissar; it certainly did so under Persian rule.[16] It is surely significant that

15 Matthew W. Stolper, 'Kasr Texts: Excavated, but not in Berlin', in *Studies Presented to Robert D. Biggs* (ed. M. T. Roth, W. Farber, M. W. Stolper and P. von Bechtolsheim; AS 27; Chicago: The Oriental Institute of the University of Chicago, 2007), 241–281.

16 On these matters see e.g. Joannès, 'Diversité ethnique' and Michael Jursa, 'Ein Beamter flucht auf Aramäisch: Alphabetschreiber in der spätbabylonischen Epistolographie und die Rolle des

among the overall small number of attestations of Egyptians in the sixth century, there are several that associate Egyptians with the royal court, the royal army and the royal administration.

The presence in Babylonia of Egyptians serving in the Persian army is documented on the one hand by the presence of Carian or Egypto-Carian mercenaries in the region of Babylon and Borsippa who had been transferred there with their families from Egypt in the early Achaemenid period[17] and on the other hand by the remarkable document *Camb.* 85 (1 Camb). This document refers to a division of lots (*pūru*) of service land, that is land for which service as a royal soldier was owed (*bīt qašti*). According to the text, a pertinent decision was taken by a collective of Egyptian soldiers presided by the assembly of the elders of the Egyptians (*puhru ša šībūti ša miṣirāyī*). This evidence for the presence of to some extent self-governed military colonies of Egyptians in Babylonia already so early in the Persian period, before Cambyses' Egyptian campaign, strongly suggests that these Egyptians were 'survivors' of the first wave of Egyptians who had come to Babylonia under Nabopolassar and Nebuchadnezzar, some sixty to seventy years before the drafting of *Camb.* 85.

Individuals of Egyptian extraction working in the realm of the royal administration in the sixth century B.C.E. include the following. We name first personnel attested in the ration lists from Nebuchadnezzar's palace.[18] All these attestations date roughly to the second decade of Nebuchadnezzar's reign.

Harmaṣu, an Egyptian courtier (*ša rēši miṣirāyu*) who was responsible for a group of other Egyptians working in the palace in Babylon and who may also have worked as a measurer, *mandidu*;[19]

Aramäischen in der babylonischen Verwaltung des sechsten Jahrhunderts v. Chr.', in *Leggo! Studies Presented to Frederick Mario Fales on the Occasion of his 65th Birthday* (ed. G. B. Lanfranchi, D. Morandi Bonacossi, C. Pappi and S. Ponchia; Wiesbaden: Harrassowitz, 2012), 379–397.

17 Ran Zadok, 'On Anatolians, Greeks and Egyptians in "Chaldean" and Achaemenid Babylonia', *Tel Aviv* 32 (2005): 76–106; Caroline Waerzeggers, 'The Carians of Borsippa', *Iraq* 68 (2006): 1–22.

18 Olof Pedersén, *Archive und Bibliotheken in Babylon: Die Tontafeln der Grabung Robert Koldeweys 1899–1917* (ADOG 25; Saarbrücken: SDV, 2005), 111–127; Olof Pedersén, 'Foreign Professionals in Babylon: Evidence from the Archive in the Palace of Nebuchadnezzar II', in *Ethnicity in Ancient Mesopotamia: Papers Read at the 48th Rencontre Assyriologique Internationale, Leiden, 1–4 July 2002* (ed. W. van Soldt; PIHANS 102; Leiden: Nederlands Instituut voor het Nabije Oosten, 2005), 267–272.

19 Ernst F. Weidner, 'Jojachin, König von Juda, in babylonischen Keilschrifttexten', in *Mélanges syriens offerts à Monsieur René Dussaud par ses amis et ses élèves* (BAH 30; Paris: P. Geuthner, 1939), 923–935 (931, Pl. II 20).

Ape keepers bearing Egyptian names (*šušānê ša uqūpē*);[20]
Guardians (*maṣṣāru*):[21] eight Egyptians for the workshops of the palace (*bīt qīpūti*) and five Egyptians for the shipyard (*bīt sapīnāti*);
Boatmen (*mallāhu*; forty-six).[22]

These data reflect a situation similar to that found in the contemporary Ebabbar archive: Egyptians are present in considerable numbers in the institutional sphere. They are clearly prisoners, some are employed as specialists, such as the boatmen and the ape keepers. There is, however, also a courtier who is in charge of some of his countrymen: not all Egyptians who worked for the king were necessarily of a low rank. This fact is reflected also in data from other archives:
Reign of Nebuchadnezzar: Harmāṣu, the 'judge of the jail/work house', *dayyānu ša bīt kīli*; ROMCT 2 37 (the text is written in Babylon, the archive it belongs to may come from Nippur);
Late reign of Nebuchadnezzar to Nabonidus: Hardi-Esu, a high official of Egyptian extraction working in the royal administration, is mentioned as one of three officials (the others are a certain Amurru-rā[?]im-šarri and the *rab-dūri*) who put pressure on the Eanna temple with respect to the temple's work load and obligations vis-à-vis the royal administration (TCL 9 103);[23]
2 Camb: Šamaš-iddin, son of Huru-masutu, the Egyptian, is responsible for the share of the king in the offerings presented to Šamaš in Sippar (*ša kurummat šarri*; CT 57 133; *Camb.* 121);
26 Dar: Bagazuštu, son of Marharpu, the Egyptian chamberlain (*miṣirāyu ša rēš šarri wastarbara* [^{lú}*ú-ma-as-ta-ar-ba-ra-a*$^{?}$]);[24] this official is explicitly desig-

20 Weidner, 'Jojachin', 931, Pl. II 24.
21 Weidner, 'Jojachin', 930, Pl. V 27.
22 Weidner, 'Jojachin', 929, Pl. III 10.
23 This undated letter can be dated roughly because of its mention of building work in the region of Raqqat-Šamaš: Eanna was occupied in this area in the period between 23 Nbk and the first year of Cyrus (Kristin Kleber, *Tempel und Palast: Die Beziehungen zwischen dem König und dem Eanna-Tempel im spätbabylonischen Uruk* [AOAT 358; Münster: Ugarit-Verlag, 2008], 166).
24 Francis Joannès and André Lemaire, 'Contrats babyloniens d'époque achéménide du Bît-Abî râm avec une épigraphe araméenne', *RA* 90 (1996): 41–60 (48, no. 6; 26 Dar, Babylon). Regarding *ustarbaru* ('chamberlain'), see most recently Wouter F. M. Henkelman, 'An Elamite Memorial: the Šumar of Cambyses and Hystaspes', in *A Persian Perspective: Essays in Memory of Heleen Sancisi-Weerdenburg* (ed. W. F. M. Henkelman and A. Kuhrt; Achaemenid History 13; Leiden: Nederlands Instituut voor het Nabije Oosten, 2003), 101–72 (118–119, 122–126 and 162–165); Michael Jursa, 'Höflinge (*ša rēši, ša rēš šarri, ustarbaru*) in babylonischen Quellen des ersten Jahrtausends', in *Ktesias' Welt: Ctesias' World* (ed. J. Wiesehöfer, R. Rollinger and G. Lanfranchi; CleO 1; Wiesbaden: Harrossowitz, 2011), 159–173 (168–171); see also below.

nated as Egyptian even though he bears an Iranian name; his father's name is Egyptian. His high rank follows also from the fact that he owned a considerable estate (rented out in the present text);[25]

28 Dar: Harsi-Esu, a courtier, Egyptian, overseer over the millers (of the palace) (*ša rēš šarri miṣirāyu ša muhhi ararrī*) (BM 25660; 28 Dar, Borsippa): he is mentioned in the context of a receipt for agricultural dues levied on royal land by a scribe on his (the courtier's) behest;[26]

1 Xer: Bēl-iddin, the Egyptian, the tax collector (*rab miksi*), orders a payment of over four minas of silver to be made (VS 4 194; Borsippa).

These texts attest then, in the Chaldean period, one high-ranking Egyptian at Nebuchadnezzar's court and one middle-ranking official, as well as apparently numerous common workers of Egyptian descent employed in the realm of the palace administration. These are all representatives of the first wave of Egyptians that came as prisoners after the Egypto-Babylonian wars. From the Persian period, we have a courtier or chamberlain, another courtier working as a supervisor of the palace workforce, and a tax collector. All the officials attested as serving in the Chaldean administration happen to have kept their Egyptian names, while their Persian period successors either kept their Egyptian names, or shifted to Babylonian or Persian names. In the case of the changes in the linguistic affiliation of the names from generation to generation, the adoption of an Akkadian name can be seen as a sign of general integration into the Babylonian ethnolinguistic setting, while the choice of an Iranian name for a royal functionary of Egyptian origin is a very clear sign of an aspiration towards a more specific form of integration, viz. into the ranks of the Iranian administrative élite of the Achaemenid empire.

The later fifth and fourth century B.C.E. evidence for Egyptians in royal service include the following data:

40 Art I: EE 40 (Murašû) names a foreman of brewers (*šaknu ša sirāšê*) bearing the Egyptian name Hūru who is to clear receipts with his colleague;

25 Joannès and Lemaire, 'Contrats babyloniens', 48–50 and 54.

26 Michael Jursa, 'On Aspects of Taxation in Achaemenid Babylonia: New Evidence from Borsippa', in *Organisation des pouvoirs et contacts culturels dans les pays de l'empire achéménide* (ed. P. Briant and M. Chauveau; Persika 14; Paris: Éditions de Boccard, 2009), 237–269 (256); Caroline Waerzeggers, *The Ezida Temple of Borsippa: Priesthood, Cult, Archives* (Achaemenid History 15; Leiden: Nederlands Instituut voor het Nabije Oosten, 2010), 268.

41 Art I: *WZKM* 97 257–259, 279–281 (BM 120024)[27] is a legal record from the Tattannu archive concerning the resolution of a dispute. Among the witnesses, several of whom bear official titles, there is also a certain Unatta (Iranian) who appears to be Egyptian on account of his patronymic (Hūru). The same text mentions also a Ṣihā who bears the title *gardu ša*! *ambari*, 'storehouse overseer' or the like;[28]

acc Dar II: Ṣihā, the *ahšadrapānu* (lit. 'satrap'), is mentioned in the Murašû archive;[29]

1 Dar II: in BE 10 15 (Murašû) the *ustarbaru* Paṭan-Esu is listed among the witnesses. He is quite possibly identical with the *gardupatu* of that name attested in 4 Dar II (see below);

1–2 Dar II: a group of men among whom we find Hisdanu, son of Harmahi, is owed silver and food as *sūtu* by agents of the Murašû firm (PBS 2/1 13). Hisdanu figures as recipient. PBS 2/1 51 mentioning the same Hisdanu is a similar record;

3 Dar II: in BE 10 81 (Murašû) we find the foreman of the "scroll makers" (*magullāyya*) named Lābāši whose father bears the Egyptian name Umahparê.

4 Dar II: in PBS 2/1 91 (Murašû) two individuals with Babylonian names are to clear receipts with Paṭan-Esu who bears the Persian title *gardupatu*.[30] He is quite possibly identical with the *ustarbaru* of that name attested in 1 Dar II (see above);

4 Dar II: BE 10 88 (Murašû) is a receipt concerning the payment of *ilku* (a kind of tax). One of the parties involved is Pamunu, the foreman of the *šušānus* (semi-free workers who held grants of income-producing property[31]) of the storehouse/treasury (*nakkandu*);

5 Dar II: PBS 2/1 104 (Murašû) is a receipt in which Pamunu, the foreman of *ar*-[x x x], is listed among the witnesses;

6–7 Dar II: Harmahi, who is referred to as the major domus (*mār bīti*) of the high-ranking irrigation manager (*mašennu*) Harimunatu (probably also an

---

27 Michael Jursa and Matthew W. Stolper, 'From the Tattannu Archive Fragment', *WZKM* 97 (2007): 243–281 (265).

28 Emendation of the reading of the original edition courtesy Ran Zadok, after collation.

29 Jursa and Stolper, 'From the Tattannu Archive Fragment', 269–270.

30 On this title see Matthew W. Stolper, *Entrepreneurs and Empire: The Murašû Archive, the Murašû Firm, and Persian Rule in Babylonia* (PIHANS 54; Istanbul: Nederlands Historisch-Archaeologisch Instituut, 1985), 57.

31 A discussion of the term as employed during the Late Achaemenid and Seleucid periods can be found in Stolper, *Entrepreneurs and Empire*, 79–82.

Egyptian),[32] is attested as recipient of payments and as witness (PBS 2/1 130 and BE 10 123). In IMT 48 (= PBS 2/1 143+) he is to clear a receipt on behalf of his master. All texts belong to the Murašû archive;

7 Dar II: the Egyptian Hariṭabu who is also designated as bailiff (*paqdu*) of a certain Pappu[33] receives a rent (*sūtu*) payment made in silver (*FuB* 14 28–29 no. 21). The text belongs to the Kasr archive;

8 Dar II: Pitibirri, one of the two *ustarbaru*s bearing an Egyptian name, appears as contracting party in BE 10 129 (Murašû). One of his slaves or agents who witnesses the deed bears the Egyptian name Pānesi;

10 Dar II: in *FuB* 14 15 no. 4, Haršiku, the bailiff (*paqdu*) of *Ni-ki-ma*?-[x], is listed among the witnesses. The text belongs to the Kasr archive.

We have here several Egyptians employed on the lower rungs of the Achaemenid administrative hierarchy, such as foremen of professional groups (*šaknu*), agents of Iranian nobles and officials (the *paqdu*s, the *mār bīti* of the *mašennu*); in fact, the fifth century B.C.E. attestations of Egyptian 'slaves' (*ardu*) of high officials (see above) belong here too. Then we have two courtiers, *ustarbaru*, one of whom is probably also attested as *gardupatu*, i.e., as major domus of an Iranian aristocrat, and several middle- or even high-ranking officials: a high-ranking irrigation manager (*mašennu*; Hisdānu of PBS 2/1 13 has a similar role in agricultural management), an *ahšadrapānu*, a royal officer whose exact portefeuille is uncertain (Stolper, *Entrepreneurs and Empire*, 58), and finally the Egyptian 'storehouse overseer' and probably another witness to the important contract *WZKM* 97 257–259, 279–281, viz. Unatta, the son of an Egyptian bearing an Iranian name.

Given the fact that overall the documentation of the fifth and fourth centuries B.C.E. is much poorer than that of the sixth century B.C.E., the higher number of attestations of Egyptians who work for the royal administration, and the large

---

32 Cf. Elmar Edel, *Neue Deutungen keilschriftlicher Umschreibungen ägyptischer Wörter und Personennamen* (SÖAW 375; Vienna: Verlag der Österreichischen Akademie der Wissenschaften, 1980), 40–45 (no. 15); Ran Zadok, 'Review: Stolper, *Entrepreneurs and Empire*', *WO* 20–21 (1989–90): 273–276 (273). Both Ran Zadok, 'Review: Walther Hinz *et al.*, *Altiranisches Sprachgut der Nebenüberlieferungen* (Göttinger Orientforschungen III; Wiesbaden: Harrassowitz, 1975)', *BO* 33 (1976): 213–219 (215) and Muhammad A. Dandamayev, *Iranians in Achaemenid Babylonia* (Columbia Lectures on Iranian Studies 6; Costa Mesa, CA: Mazda Publishers, 1992), 83 reconstruct an Old Iranian name.

33 Probably to be connected with Iranian **papa*-; cf. Jan Tavernier, *Iranica in the Achaemenid Period (ca. 550–330 B. C.): Lexicon of Old Iranian Proper Names and Loanwords Attested in Non-Iranian Texts* (OLA 158; Leuven: Peeters, 2007), 263.

share of this group within the total of attested Egyptians,[34] is surely indicative of an increase in absolute figures of the number of Egyptians present in Babylonia in general, and of those involved in administrative tasks in particular. These Egyptians are identifiable as such only through their personal names; in contrast to the sixth century B.C.E., it is not common to designate Egyptians explicitly as such in the fifth and fourth centuries B.C.E.. This can be understood as an indication that Egyptians were not considered an 'oddity,' their ethnic origin was not understood to be sufficiently remarkable to serve as a distinguishing characteristic: another indication of their comparatively high numbers.

While precise quantifications are of course out of reach, we would suggest that it is virtually excluded that the frequency of Egyptians attested in Babylonian documents as working for the Great King reflects directly the share of Egyptians in the population of the country. We do not hear of settlements of Egyptians, we do not know of massive deportations from Egypt to Babylonia. Instead, we see, in all likelihood, traces of a system of administration that for its middle ranks relied heavily on the service of professional bureaucrats who were perhaps palace-trained (this is probably the case for the *ustarbaru*s who correspond to the Babylonian *ša rēši*s) and/or who had a cultural or intellectual background that made them seem suitable for administrative tasks, but who did not necessarily originate in the local population.

This hypothesis can be strengthened by an analysis of the evidence for individual offices. Thus, of the six *mašennu*s (high-ranking irrigation managers) attested in the Murašû archive, four have Babylonian names, one is Iranian, one is Egyptian.[35] More importantly, among the twenty-nine *ustarbaru*s attested in Babylonian texts from Babylonia, half bear Babylonian names, two Egyptian, and the rest have Iranian names (see the list given below, Appendix 2). No non-Akkadian Semitic names are present, even though Arameans (and to a lesser extent, Judeans, Phoenicians, Arabs and other West Semites) accounted for a significant part of the population of Babylonia. This is very unlikely to be a coincidence.

Observations on intergenerational naming patterns in the fifth and fourth centuries B.C.E. can be brought to bear on this matter. We find several cases of members of Egyptian families bearing Babylonian names: these are simple cases of acculturation. Thus we have, for example, the foreman Lābāši, son of Umahparê (BE 10 81). But Egyptian names could also reappear after a generation named in the Babylonian fashion: thus we have a Harmahi, son of Iqīšāya, in PBS

34 It bears repeating that many of the Egyptians mentioned without a title in the Murašû texts are most likely nevertheless linked to the royal administration.

35 Stolper, *Entrepreneurs and Empire*, 46–47.

2/1 198. His brothers bear Babylonian names, as does his father; nevertheless, we have to assume that the family was of Egyptian origin.[36] Then there are cases in which Persian names are adopted by Egyptian families. As stated in the introduction, this is a 'marked' onomastic choice that throws light on the socio-economic setting of the name bearer and name giver, for whom an association with the ruling Iranian élite was both desirable and achievable. Thus we have for example Paṭ-Esu, son of Hungamu, who is also addressed with his second, Iranian name in IMT 43 (Murašû).[37] There is Unatta, son of Hūru (*WZKM* 97 257–259, 279–281), and the bearer of a 'third generation' Egyptian name Harmahi, son of Bagadātu (PBS 2/1 84 and 104).[38] These Iranian names are 'prestige names' which were probably considered typical for members of the administration. It is thus highly significant and indicative of the strong Egyptian presence among the officials of the Empire that at least one powerful Babylonian family, the Tattannus, chose to give the Egyptian name Ṣihā to one, and perhaps two, of their offspring.[39] For them, this Egyptian name must have conveyed connotations that conformed well to their collective aspirations to acquire patronage and power in the satrapy of Babylonia. The Egyptian 'diaspora' in Babylonia under Achaemenid rule was thus of a particular kind, marked by a preponderance of specialists of administration whose (relative) frequency in the documentation reflects their importance for the royal administration, but not the absolute numbers of Egyptians in Babylonia.

6 Appendix 1: On the Presence of Egyptian Material Culture in Babylonia

Contacts with Egypt are occasionally documented by references to Egyptian products. In the sixth century B.C.E., the most frequently mentioned export good of Egypt is alum, *gabû ša miṣri*.[40] There are also two references to Egyptian pottery,

---

36 Note also Harmahi, son of Ṣillāya, in PBS 2/1 192, Harmahi, son Bēl-ēreš in BE 9 81, and the exceptional case of Hūru, son of Iltagubati (West Semitic) in Stolper, 'Kasr Texts: Excavated, but not in Berlin', no. 20 (Kasr archive).

37 Note that both his brothers bear Babylonian names.

38 It is much more likely that an Egyptian family adopted an Iranian name than the assumption that an Iranian family chose an Egyptian name for a child.

39 Jursa and Stolper, 'From the Tattannu Archive Fragment', 249.

40 YOS 6 168, 6 Nbn; BM 63984, 12 Nbn; *Nbn.* 214, 5 Camb?; YOS 3 20; NCBT 632 (13 <Nbn>).

viz. a lamp (*bīt nūri*, VS 6 314[41]) and a "wine jug with rim" (*šappatu ša ṣirê ša miṣri*; BM 65267, 12 Nbn), and to Egyptian linen (CT 2 2, 19 Dar).

From the fifth century B.C.E. and thereafter, the only text that yields pertinent information in this respect is the apprenticeship contract *AfO* 52 88 no. 9 that has already been mentioned above. According to this contract, the Egyptian apprentice is to be trained in the manufacturing of different types of bread among which we also find Egyptian bread. The overall scarcity of data notwithstanding, the fact that Egyptian bread was not only known in Babylonia at that time, but also prepared by specially trained bakers in an urban context, can be taken as evidence of the cultural identity of Egyptians within the Babylonian society.

7 Appendix 2: Fifth Century B.C.E. Data

[1] *ustarbaru* officials

Name	Writing	Archive	Date	Text
Ku-pi-ia-[x]	^{lú}*us-tar-ba-ri*	(?) (Babylon)	4 Xer	*AfO* 52 86 no. 8 (BM 40743)
Bēl-ībukaš	^{lú}*us-tar-ba-ri*	Murašû (Nippur)	1 Art I	BE 9 1
Bēlšunu	^{lú}*us-tar-ba-ri*	Tattannu(?) (Borsippa)	7 Art I	*AION* Suppl. 77 no. 1
Zababa-iddin	^{lú}*us-tar-bar-ru* ^{lú}*us-tar-ba-ri*	Murašû (Nippur)	31 Art I	BE 9 28 and duplicate TuM 2/3 179
Bagamihi	^{lú}*us-tar-ba-ri*	Murašû (Nippur)	36 Art I	BE 9 50
Bēl-bullissu	^{lú}*us-tar-ba-ri*	Murašû (Nippur)	41 Art I	BE 9 102
Bēl-ēṭer	^{lú}*us-tar-ba-ri*	Murašû (Nippur)	41 Art I	BE 9 102
Enlil-šumu-ibni	^{lú}*us-tar-ba-ri*	Murašû (Nippur)	34 Art I	IMT 3
Tiridata (= Nabû-kāṣir)	^{lú}*us-tar-ba-ri*	Bēl-ittannu/ Nidintu (Babylon)	12 Art I	BM 54205[42]
Bēl-ittannu	^{lú}*us-tar-ba-ri*	Murašû (Nippur)	[...]	EE 52
	^{lú}*us-tar-ba-ri*		0a Dar II	EE 109; IMT 105
	^{lú}*us-tar-ba-ri*		3$^{?}$ Dar II	BE 10 80
	^{lú}*us-tar-ba-ri*		3 Dar II	PBS 2/1 63
	^{lú}*us-tar-ba-ri*		3 Dar II	PBS 2/1 65

41 The text is undated, but probably belongs to the early Ebabbar archive and thus dates to the reign of Nabopolassar or Nebuchadnezzar.

42 Wilhelm Eilers, *Iranische Beamtennamen in der keilschriftlichen Überlieferung, Teil 1* (Abhandlungen für die Kunde des Morgenlandes 25, 5; Leipzig: F. A. Brockhaus, 1940), pl. 3.

Name	Writing	Archive	Date	Text
	^{lú}*us-tar-ba-ri*		[3] Dar II	PBS 2/1 76
	^{lú}*us-tar-ba-ri*		5 Dar II	PBS 2/1 104
	^{lú}*us-tar-ba-[ra*^{meš}]		7 Dar II	PBS 2/1 224
Bagadātu	^{lú}*us-tar-ba-ri*	Murašû (Nippur)	1 Dar II	BE 10 9
Paṭan-Esu[43]	^{lú}*us-tar-bar*	Murašû (Nippur)	1 Dar II	BE 10 15
Kiribti-Bēl	^{lú}*us-tar-ba-[ri]*	Murašû (Nippur)	4 Dar II	BE 10 89
Līnuh-libbi-ilāni	^{lú}*us-tar-ba-ri*	Murašû (Nippur)	4 Dar II	BE 10 91
Nanāya-iddin	^{lú}*us-tar-ba-ri*	Murašû (Nippur)	5 Dar II	BE 10 102
	^{lú}*us-tar-ba-ri*		5 Dar II	BE 10 103
Ipradatunā	^{lú}*us-tar-ba-ri*	Murašû (Nippur)	6 Dar II	BE 10 114
Pitibibiri[44]	^{lú}*us-tar-ba-ri*	Murašû (Nippur)	8 Dar II	BE 10 129
Nināku[45]	^{lú}*us-tar-ba-ri*	Murašû (Nippur)	1 Dar II	PBS 2/1 30
Siamu[46]	^{lú}*us-tar-ba-ri*	Murašû (Nippur)	[2] Dar II	PBS 2/1 38
Šibbû[47]	^{lú}*us-tar-ba-ri*	Murašû (Nippur)	2 Dar II	PBS 2/1 43
Tabtanu-bullissu	^{lú}*us-tar-ba-ri*	Murašû (Nippur)	2 Dar II	PBS 2/1 48
Parmuš, Parniš[48]	^{lú}*us-tar-ba-ri*	Murašû (Nippur)	[3] Dar II	PBS 2/1 70
			[4] Dar II	PBS 2/1 102
Bēl-tattannu-	^{lú}*us-tar-ba-ri*	Murašû (Nippur)	4 Dar II	PBS 2/1 96
bullissu	^{lú}*us-tar-bar*^{meš}	Murašû (Nippur)	6 Dar II	PBS 2/1 126
Rībat	^{lú}*us-tar-ba-ri*	Murašû (Nippur)	6 Dar II	PBS 2/1 128
Hašdāya	^{lú}*us-tar-ba-ri*	Murašû (Nippur)	7 Dar II	PBS 2/1 135
Bagāzuštu[49]	^{lú}*us-tar-bar-ra*	(?) ([Babylon$^{?}$])	Dar II(?)	VAT 15608
Bagapātu[50]	^{lú}*us-tar-ba-ri*	Tattannu (Borsippa)	19 Art II	*WZKM* 97 252–253, 278 (HSM 1931.1.11)
Gūzanu	^{lú}*us-tar-ba-ri*	(?) (Babylon$^{?}$)	~ Art II/III	*AfO* 52 90 no. 11 (BM 37939+)

43 Cf. Hermann Ranke, *Keilschriftliches Material zur altägyptischen Vokalisation* (APAW/II; Berlin, 1910), 40.

44 Cf. Muhammad A. Dandamayev, 'Egyptians in Babylonia in the 6th–5th Centuries B.C.', in *La circulation des biens, des personnes et des idées dans le Proche-Orient ancien*: *Actes de la* XXXVIIIe *Rencontre Assyriologique Internationale, Paris*, 8–10 *juillet* 1991 (ed. D. Charpin and F. Joannès; Paris: Éditions Recherche sur les Civilisations, 1992), 321–325 (323).

45 Cf. Tavernier, *Iranica*, 260.

46 Cf. Tavernier, *Iranica*, 316.

47 Cf. Tavernier, *Iranica*, 319.

48 Cf. Tavernier, *Iranica*, 264.

49 Cf. Bagazuštu/Bagadātu in PBS 2/1 192 who is given without title.

50 For the reading of the name, see now Jan Tavernier, 'A note on ^{Id}Hu-'-a-pa-a-tu$_{4}$ (HSM 8414)', *NABU* 2004/3 (*pace* Ran Zadok, 'Foreigners and Foreign Linguistic Material in Mesopotamia', in *Immigration and Emigration within the Ancient Near East*: *Festschrift E. Lipiński* [ed. K. Van Lerberghe and A. Schoors; OLA 65; Leuven: Peeters, 1994], 431–448 [442] and 'Some Iranian Anthroponyms and Toponyms', *NABU* 1997/7 [no. 5]).

[2] Egyptians identified by gentilic (and personal name)

Name		Archive	Date	Text
Bēl-iddin, *rab miksi*, *miṣirāya*	*ina našparti* BI (receipt)	(?) (Susa)	1 Xer	VS 4 194
Paṭ-Esu, *miṣirāya*	owner of adjacent plot (rental contract)	(?) (Nippur)	21 Xer	*NABU* 1999/6a (CBS 10059)
Bēl-ēdu-uṣur, *qallu ṣabtu*, *miṣirāya*?	apprentice	Minû-ana-Bēl-dān, son of Belbullissu (Babylon)	10 Dar II	*AfO* 52 88 no. 9 (BM 16656)

[3] Egyptians identified by personal name

Name		Archive	Date	Text
Ha-ku-um-me-en-na(?), son of ***Ha-re-en-na-a'***	witness	(?) (Babylon)	4 Xer	*AfO* 52 86 no. 8 (BM 40743)
Halabesu(?), son of **Paṭ-Esu**	lessor (lease)	Murašû (Nippur)	34 Art I	IMT 3
Halabesu(?), son of Mukēšu	lessor (lease)	Murašû (Nippur)	34 Art I	IMT 3
Ha-re-en-na-a'(?) (father of ***Ha-ku-um-me-en-na***)	patronym	(?) (Babylon)	4 Xer	BM 40743
Harimunatu,[51] *ikkaru*, *mašennu*	affiliated with Harmahi (*mār bīti*)	Murašû (Nippur)	6 Dar II 7 Dar II [7 Dar II]	PBS 2/1 130 BE 10 123 IMT 48 (= PBS 2/1 143+)
Hariṭabû,[52] *paqdu ša* PN	recipient (receipt)	Kasr (Babylon)	7 Dar II	*FuB* 14 28–29 no. 21
Harmahi[53] (father of Aplāya)	patronym	Murašû (Nippur)	0a Dar II	BE 10 1
Harmahi, slave of Manuštānu	contestant (warranty clause)	Murašû (Nippur)	40 Art I	EE 27

51 See note 34.
52 Cf. Ran Zadok, 'On some Foreign Population Groups in First-Millennium Babylonia', *Tel Aviv* 6 (1979): 164–181 (173).
53 Cf. Edel, *Neue Deutungen*, 37–40 (no. 14).

Name		Archive	Date	Text
Harmahi, *mār bīti* of **Harimunatu**	witness recipient (receipt) *ina našparti* H. (receipt)	Murašû (Nippur)	6 Dar II 7 Dar II 7 [Dar II]	PBS 2/1 130 BE 10 123 IMT 48 (= PBS 2/1 143+)
Harmahi (father of Hisdanu)	patronym	Murašû (Nippur)	1 Dar II 2 Dar II	PBS 2/1 13 PBS 2/1 51
Harmahi, son of Bagadātu (and father of Puhhurāya)	witness	Murašû (Nippur)	4 Dar II 4 Dar II	PBS 2/1 104 PBS 2/1 84
Harmahi, son of Ṣillāya	witness? (seal caption)	Murašû (Nippur)	2 Dar II	PBS 2/1 192
Harmahi, son of Iqīšāya	debtor (debt note)[54]	Murašû (Nippur)	3 Dar II	PBS 2/1 198
Harmahi	debtor (receipt)	Murašû (Nippur)	3 Dar II	BE 10 66
Harmahi, son of Bēl-ēreš	slave owner (receipt)	Murašû (Nippur)	40 Art I	BE 9 81
Harmaṣu[55]	debtor (debt note)	Murašû (Nippur)	1 Dar II	BE 10 23
Har-ri-hi-bi-i'(?) (father of Mušēzib)	patronym	Dahhū'a (Babylon)	3 Dar II	BM 46687
Haršiku,[56] *paqdu* of *Ni-ki-ma*?-x	witness	Kasr (Babylon)	10 Dar II	*FuB* 14 15 no. 4
Hūru,[57] slave of PN	witness	(?) ([Borsippa?])	11 Art I/II	BM 82566
Hūru (father of ***Tu*?*-ri-ti-am-mu-û***)	patronym	(?) (Babylon)	4 Xer	*AfO* 52 86 no. 8 (BM 40743)
Hūru, *šaknu ša sirāšê*	debtor (receipt)	Murašû (Nippur)	40 Art I	EE 40
Hūru, slave of PN[58]	slave (slave sale)	Murašû (Nippur)	3 Dar II	PBS 2/1 65
Hūru	former owner (slave sale)	Murašû (Nippur)	5 Dar II	PBS 2/1 113

54 The debt is owed by Harmahi and his two brothers who bear non-Egyptian names.
55 Cf. Edel, *Neue Deutungen*, 25–28 (no. 7).
56 Cf. Dandamayev, 'Egyptians in Babylonia', 323 n. 28.
57 Cf. ÄPN 1 245 (no. 18).
58 Hūru is sold together with his sister who bears the hybrid name Hannat-Esu.

Name		Archive	Date	Text
Hūru	party(?) to a lawsuit	Murašû (Nippur)	0a Dar II	EE 109
Hūru, son of *Il-ta-gu-ba-ti*	creditor (debt note)	Kasr (Babylon)	4 Art II	Stolper, *Fs. Biggs* no. 20
Hūru (father of Unatta,[59] *rab kāṣirī*)	patronym (legal protocol)	Tattannu (Borsippa)	41 Art I	*WZKM* 97 257–259, 279–281 (BM 120024)
Kunuis(?),[60] son of **Nahesi**	former owner (slave sale)	Murašû (Nippur)	3 Dar II	PBS 2/1 65
Miṣrāya, son of **Harsiesi**	lessor (rental contract)	(?) (Dilbat)	37? Art I/II	*Iraq* 54 137
Nadhunzu, son of **Harsiesi**	witness	Mardonios (Babylon)	[x] Xer	*AuOr* 10 219
Nahesi (father of Kunuis)	patronym	Murašû (Nippur)	3 Dar II	PBS 2/1 65
Nahtuhappi[61] (father of **Uqhappi**)	patronym	Murašû (Nippur)	39 Art I	PBS 2/1 113
Napūnahhu[62] (father of **Šanūmū**)	patronym	(?) (Babylon)	10 Xer	CT 4 34d
Padâ(?) (father of Lābāši)	patronym	Esagil (Babylon)	35 Art II 1 Art II/III	BM 87228 BM 87250
Padiyā[63] (father of **Paṭanesi**)	patronym	Dahhū'a (Babylon)	10 Dar II	BM 46691
Pahhē, *mār bīti* of Bagapidū	recipient (receipt)	Bēl-ittannu, son of Nidintu (Babylon)	0a Dar II	*JEOL* 34 45–46
Pamunu, *šaknu ša šušanê ša nakkandi*	recipient (receipt)	Murašû (Nippur)	4 Dar II	BE 10 88
Pamunu, *šaknu ša Ar*-[x-x]	witness	Murašû (Nippur)	5 Dar II	PBS 2/1 104
Pānesi, slave of **Pitibirri**	witness	Murašû (Nippur)	8 Dar II	BE 10 129

59 Probably Old Iranian, cf. Dandamayev, *Iranians in Achaemenid Babylonia*, 137 and Tavernier, *Iranica*, 337.
60 Cf. Dandamayev, 'Egyptians in Babylonia', 322.
61 Cf. Edel, *Neue Deutungen*, 45 (no. 16).
62 Cf. Ran Zadok, 'On some Egyptians in First-Millennium Mesopotamia', *Göttinger Miszellen* 26 (1977): 63–68 (64, no. 10).
63 Cf. ÄPN 1 121 (no. 17) and Zadok, 'On some Egyptians', 64–65, no. 13.

Name		Archive	Date	Text
Pattû[64] (father of Bēl-šumu-iddin, adopter)	patronym	Tattannu (Borsippa)	[7+] Art I	VS 6 188
Paṭanesi, *gardupatu*[65]	*ina našparti* P (receipt)	Murašû (Nippur)	4 Dar II	PBS 2/1 91
Paṭanesi, son of **Padiyā**	witness	Dahhū'a (Babylon)	10 Dar II	BM 46691
Paṭanesi	witness, *ustarbaru*	Murašû (Nippur)	01 Dar II	BE 10 15
Paṭasiri,[66] slave of PN	creditor (debt note)	(?) ([Borsippa?])	11 Art I/II	BM 82566
Paṭemun,[67] slave of P[N] (*ustarbaru*)	master (apprenticeship contract)	(?) (Babylon)	4 Xer	*AfO* 52 86 no. 8 (BM 40743)
Paṭ-Esu (father of **Halabaesu**)	patronym	Murašû (Nippur)	34 Art I	IMT 3
Paṭ-Esu,[68] son of *Na-an-*[x]*-ú-a*	witness	Murašû (Nippur)	3 Dar II	PBS 2/1 65
Pisamiṣki,[69] son of ***Sa-am-mu-hu-nu-ú-ru***	witness	(?) (Babylon)	4 Xer	*AfO* 52 86 no. 8 (BM 40743)
Pisusasmakāša, son of Patnāšu	creditor (debt note)	(?) (Babylon)	10 Xer	CT 4 34d
Pitibirri	slave owner, *ustarbaru*	Murašû (Nippur)	8 Dar II	BE 10 129
Qahia[70]	recipient (receipt)	Murašû (Nippur)	39 Art I	BE 9 70
Sa-am-mu-hu-nu-ú-ru(?) (father of **Pisamiṣki**) patronym	(?) (Babylon)		4 Xer	*AfO* 52 86 no. 8 (BM 40743)

64 Cf. ÄPN 1 112 (no. 4) and Zadok, 'On some Egyptians', 64, no. 11.
65 On this title see Stolper, *Entrepreneurs and Empire*, 57.
66 Cf. ÄPN 1 123 (no. 1).
67 Cf. Zadok, 'On some Egyptians', 64–65, no. 13.
68 Cf. ÄPN 1 121 (no. 18) and Zadok, 'On some Egyptians,' 64–65, no. 13.
69 Cf. Edel, *Neue Deutungen*, 36–37 (no. 13).
70 Cf. ÄPN 1 336 (no. 24)

Name		Archive	Date	Text
Ṣihā,[71] [son of Tattannu]	buyer (slave sale)	Tattannu (Borsippa)	[39+] Art I	VS 5 141
	owner of slaves		39 Art I	VS 6 184
Ṣihā (father of ᶠ*A-sa-ri*-DA[?]-*tu*, guarantor)	patronym	(?) Babylon	4 Xer	*AfO* 52 86 no. 8 (BM 40743)
Ṣihā, son of Bēl(?)-rēhtu-ēreš	witness	Dahhū'a (Babylon)	0a Dar	BM 46687
Ṣihā, son of Bagadādu (and brother of Attaluš)	recipient (receipt)	Esagil (Babylon)	[26?] Art II	CT 44 81
Ṣihā (father of Nabû-šumu-uṣur)	patronym	Esagil (Babylon)	[x] Art II/III	BM 87264
Šammû, son of Bagahaja	witness	Mušallim-Bēl, son of Nidintu (Hursagkalama)	4 Art I	OECT 10 192
Šammû, slave of AS-*ba*/*ma-a*	creditor (debt note)	(?) (Borsippa)	22 Art I	VS 3 189
Šammû (father of Bēl-ittannu)	patronym	Murašû (Nippur)	2 Dar II	PBS 2/1 54
Šanūmū(?),[72] son of **Napūnahhu**	debtor	(?) (Babylon)	10 Xer	CT 4 34d
Šīšuya[73]	slave (slave sale)	Murašû (Nippur)	3 Dar II	PBS 2/1 65
Tu*[?]*-ri-ti-am-mu-ú(?), son of **Hūru**	witness	(?) (Babylon)	4 Xer	*AfO* 52 86 no. 8 (BM 40743)
Umahparê[74] (father of Munnātu)	patronym	Murašû (Nippur)	33 Art I	EE 35
Umahparê (father of Lābāši, *šaknu ša magullāyya*)	patronym	Murašû (Nippur)	3 Dar II	BE 10 81
Uqhappi,[75] son of **Nahtuhappi**	witness	Murašû (Nippur)	39 Art I	PBS 2/1 113

71 Cf. ÄPN 1 411 (no. 12).
72 Cf. Zadok, 'On some Egyptians', 64, no. 10, and note 7.
73 Cf. ÄPN 1 405 (no. 21) and Tavernier, *Iranica*, 525.
74 Cf. Zadok, 'Review: Stolper', 274.
75 Cf. Edel, *Neue Deutungen*, 45 (no. 16).

Acknowledgment

This paper was written under the auspices of the project 'Official Epistolography in Babylonia in the First Millennium BC' that is financed by the FWF (Vienna). J. Hackl provided the sections on the fifth and fourth centuries B. C.E data in sections 1, 2, 3, 4 and 6, the entirety of section 7 and the list of fifth century B.C.E. attestations of Egyptians in section 5; the rest, in particular the overall conception of the paper and the conclusions drawn from the data are by M. Jursa; J. Hackl should not be held responsible for shortcomings in this respect.

Caroline Waerzeggers

Babylonian Kingship in the Persian Period: Performance and Reception

The Persian conquest of Babylon set in motion a chain of events that eventually led to the partial return of Judah's exilic community and to the rebuilding of the temple of Jerusalem. Despite Cyrus' prominent role in the biblical narrative about these events – and despite the historical reality of Yehud's place within the Persian Empire – the Hebrew Bible constructs the context of the return as a kingless arena which required a profound reworking and re-interpretation of the traditional alignments between the Davidic king and Yahweh.[1] In this paper, I will contextualize these reflections by asking how Babylonian audiences responded to *their* loss of indigenous kingship following the Persian conquest – for, even though the institution of 'King of Babylon' with its rituals and symbols survived into the Persian period, there is evidence of profound change during the Empire's two hundred years of existence. After an introduction, the first part of my paper will deal with contemporary responses to Persian rule in Babylonia; the second part then moves on to a discussion of the reception of Persian period kingship by later generations of Babylonians.

1 A New King for Babylon

In 539 B.C.E., the Persian conquest of Mesopotamia brought a new and unexpected king to the throne of Babylon: Cyrus the Great of Persia. He was unexpected, not in the eyes of bystanders (his army had been advancing for years), but in view of Babylonia's long-term history. Foreign invaders had taken the throne before, but they had left quickly, struggled fruitlessly, or assimilated entirely.[2] By

1 See recently on this topic Joseph Blenkinsopp, *David Remembered: Kingship and National Identity in Ancient Israel* (Grand Rapids: Eerdmans), 2013; and also the essay by Madhavi Nevader in this volume.

2 E.g. see on the Assyrians in Babylonia John A. Brinkman, 'Babylonia under the Assyrian Empire, 745–627 BC', in *Power and Propaganda: A Symposium on Ancient Empires* (ed. M. T. Larsen; Mesopotamia 7; Copenhagen: Akademisk Forlag, 1979), 223–50 and Grant Frame, 'Babylon: Assyria's Problem and Assyria's Prize', *JCSMS* 3 (2008): 21–31. On the Kassites in Babylonia, see John A. Brinkman, 'The Monarchy in the Time of the Kassite Dynasty', in *Le palais et la royauté:*

Caroline Waerzeggers: Leiden University

contrast, Cyrus and his successors did not only keep Babylonian kingship for two hundred years with limited local resistance, they also combined the office with other regional titles (e.g. pharaoh of Egypt) and integrated it within a new articulation of Achaemenid kingship centered on Iran.[3] Nowadays, the Persian hold of Babylonian kingship is described as a continuation of the local tradition.[4] But given the novelty of the dynastic, ethnic, geopolitical and institutional context, how likely is this?

The throne of Babylon never reverted to an indigenous king after 539 B.C.E. There were sporadic attempts by rebels to win it back, but eventually it was a Macedonian who claimed the prize from Persia in 331 B.C.E. and passed it on to his Greek successors. For this reason, the Persian conquest of 539 B.C.E. constitutes a major break in the history of southern Mesopotamian kingship. Defining this break in terms of an opposition between foreign (Persian) and native (Babylonian) kingship does not, however, do justice to the complex history of this institution, nor to the nature of Babylonian society in the mid-first millennium B.C.E. Not long before Cyrus, a man of Aramean descent had occupied the throne of Babylon (Neriglissar, 559–556 B.C.E.) and at no point was his reign

---

XIXe Rencontre Assyriologique Internationale (ed. P. Garelli; Paris: Librairie Paul Geuthner, 1974), 395–408 and Susanne Paulus, 'Foreigners under Foreign Rulers: The Case of Kassite Babylonia (2nd Half of the 2nd Millennium BC)', in *The Foreigner and the Law: Perspectives from the Hebrew Bible and the Ancient Near East* (ed. R. Achenbach, R. Albertz and J. Wöhrle; BZABR 16; Wiesbaden: Harrassowitz, 2011), 1–15.

3 On Achaemenid kingship ideology, see Margaret Cool Root, *The King and Kingship in Achaemenid Art: Essays on the Creation of an Iconography of Empire* (Leiden: Brill, 1979); Pierre Briant, *From Cyrus to Alexander: A History of the Persian Empire* (Winona Lake: Eisenbrauns, 2002), 204–54; Margaret Cool Root, 'Defining the Divine in Achaemenid Persian Kingship: The View from Bisitun', in *Every Inch a King: Comparative Studies on Kings and Kingship in the Ancient and Medieval Worlds* (ed. L. Mitchell and C. Melville; Rulers and Elites 3; Leiden: Brill, 2013), 23–66; Mark B. Garrison, 'Royal Achaemenid Iconography', in *The Oxford Handbook of Ancient Iran* (ed. D. T. Potts; Oxford: Oxford University Press, 2013), 566–95.

4 Amélie Kuhrt, 'Usurpation, Conquest and Ceremonial: From Babylon to Persia', in *Rituals of Royalty: Power and Ceremonial in Traditional Societies* (ed. D. Cannadine and S. Price; Cambridge: Cambridge University Press, 1987), 20–55; Susan Sherwin-White, 'Seleucid Babylonia: A Case-Study for the Installation and Development of Greek Rule', in *Hellenism in the East: The Interaction of Greek and Non-Greek Civilizations from Syria to Central Asia after Alexander* (ed. A. Kuhrt and S. Sherwin-White; Berkeley: University of California Press, 1987), 1–31 (9); Amélie Kuhrt, 'The Persian Empire', in *The Babylonian World* (ed. G. Leick; New York and London: Routledge, 2007), 562–76 (567); Robert Rollinger, 'Das teispidisch-achaimenidische Großreich: ein 'Imperium' avant-la-lettre?', in *Imperien und Reiche in der Weltgeschichte: Epochenübergreifende und globalhistorische Vergleiche* (ed. M. Gehler and R. Rollinger; Wiesbaden: Harrassowitz, 2014), 149–92 (156).

judged negatively for it. If not for the careful detective work of modern scholars, Neriglissar's Aramean descent would never have been revealed.[5] There is also a lot of uncertainty about the origins of Nabonidus, the king from whom Cyrus took the throne of Babylon in 539 B.C.E.;[6] arranging these two men in a simple opposition of 'native' against 'foreign', or even 'Babylonian' against 'Persian', is at least problematic. Nabonidus came to be remembered as the founder, and only representative, of the unpopular Dynasty of Harran by some later traditions.[7] It is probably correct that he hailed from this city outside Babylonia proper;[8] but the negative memory of his reign was based on his deeds, not on his non-local origin. In fact, no individual at that time, except for the inhabitants of the city of Babylon proper, would have referred to himself or herself as 'Babylonian'.[9] Scholarly discussions of 'Babylonian' society in the first millennium B.C.E. struggle to describe what that society was like. A quadruple make-up is usually put forward (Arameans, Chaldeans, Babylonians, minorities) but how these groups may be identified in text, image or material culture, and how they related to each other in society is very much unclear.[10] In this context, it is not surprising that there was no straightforward connection between foreign and improper kingship: some Assyrians who ruled as king of Babylon were recognised as fully legitimate holders of this office, others were not.[11] When Cyrus took the throne of Babylon in

5 On Neriglissar's Aramean background, see most recently Paul-Alain Beaulieu, 'Arameans, Chaldeans, and Arabs in Cuneiform Sources from the Late Babylonian Period', in *Arameans, Chaldeans, and Arabs in Babylonia and Palestine in the First Millennium B. C.* (ed. A. Berlejung and M. P. Streck; LAOS 3; Wiesbaden: Harrassowitz, 2013), 31–55 (35–36) and Rocío Da Riva, *The Inscriptions of Nabopolassar, Amēl-Marduk and Neriglissar* (SANER 3; Berlin: de Gruyter, 2013), 14.

6 Paul-Alain Beaulieu, *The Reign of Nabonidus, King of Babylon, 556–539 B. C.* (YNER 10; New Haven: Yale University Press, 1989), 67–86.

7 *Dynastic Prophecy* II: 12 (A. K. Grayson, *Babylonian Historical-Literary Texts* [Toronto Semitic Texts and Studies 3; Toronto: University of Toronto Press, 1975], 28–37).

8 Beaulieu, *The Reign of Nabonidus*, 67–86.

9 Eva von Dassow, 'On Writing the History of Southern Mesopotamia', *ZA* 89 (1999): 227–46 (241–42).

10 See among the more recent studies of the multi-ethnic nature of Babylonian society in the first millennium B.C.E., Frederick Mario Fales, 'Moving around Babylon: On the Aramean and Chaldean Presence in Southern Mesopotamia', in *Babylon: Wissenskultur in Orient und Okzident* (ed. E. Cancik-Kirschbaum, M. van Ess and J. Marzahn; Topoi 1; Berlin: de Gruyter, 2011), 91–112; Beaulieu, 'Arameans'; Grant Frame, 'The Political History and Historical Geography of the Aramean, Chaldean, and Arab Tribes in Babylonia in the Neo-Assyrion Period', in *Arameans, Chaldeans, and Arabs in Babylonia and Palestine in the First Millennium B. C.* (ed. A. Berlejung and M. P. Streck; LAOS 3; Wiesbaden: Harrassowitz, 2013), 87–122.

11 Cf. Frame, 'Babylon'.

539 B.C.E., his non-Babylonian origin would not have rendered his rule improper. On the contrary, the viewpoint of the *Cyrus Cylinder*, which was written shortly after the conquest and which probably represents a consensus opinion within literate Babylonian society at the time, is that Marduk summoned Cyrus from abroad to dispel the incompetent indigenous king, Nabonidus, and set things straight.[12]

A problematic dimension of the new situation did emerge soon, however. Cyrus invaded Babylonia on the crest of a wave of conquests, and this wave soon carried him further, towards new territory and more victory.[13] He disappeared almost as fast from the Babylonian realm as he had entered it. His first steps as the ruler of Babylonia were necessarily experimental; there was no model to be followed, no precedent to be recreated. Due to unexpected circumstances, Cyrus could not partake in the New Year festival of 538 B.C.E.; instead, his son Cambyses was crowned 'King of Babylon', while Cyrus himself took the imperial title of 'King of the lands'.[14] This improvised co-regency of father and son was abandoned after one year, and both titles ('King of Babylon, King of the lands') were then conferred upon Cyrus. The next years, a system of royal representation was set in place. Cyrus' empire now stretched from Sardis to Iran and from the Caspian Sea to the Persian Gulf, too large a territory to maintain a personal

---

12 For the text of the *Cyrus Cylinder*, see Hanspeter Schaudig, *Die Inschriften Nabonids von Babylon und Kyros' des Großen samt den in ihrem Umfeld entstandenen Tendenzinschriften: Textausgabe und Grammatik* (AOAT 256; Münster: Ugarit-Verlag, 2001), 550–62; a recent translation, with new additions, is offered by Irving Finkel, 'The Cyrus Cylinder: The Babylonian Perspective', in *The Cyrus Cylinder: The King of Persia's Proclamation from Ancient Babylon* (ed. I. Finkel; London: I. B. Taurus, 2013), 4–34 (4–7). Some key studies are: J. Harmatta, 'Les modèles littéraires de l'édit babylonien de Cyrus', *Acta Iranica* 1 (1974): 29–44; Amélie Kuhrt, 'The Cyrus Cylinder and Achaemenid Imperial Policy', *JSOT* 25 (1983): 83–97; Amélie Kuhrt, 'Nabonidus and the Babylonian Priesthood', in *Pagan Priests: Religion and Power in the Ancient World* (ed. M. Beard and J. North; London: Duckworth, 1990), 119–55; Amélie Kuhrt, *The Persian Empire: A Corpus of Sources from the Achaemenid Period* (London and New York: Routledge, 2007), 70–74; Amélie Kuhrt, 'Cyrus the Great of Persia: Images and Realities,' in *Representations of Political Power: Case Histories from Times of Change and Dissolving Order in the Ancient Near East* (ed. M. Heinz and M. H. Feldman; Winona Lake: Eisenbrauns, 2007), 169–91; R. J. van der Spek, 'Cyrus the Great, Exiles, and Foreign Gods: A Comparison of Assyrian and Persian Policies on Subject Nations', in *Extraction and Control: Studies in Honor of Matthew W. Stolper* (ed. M. Kozuh, W. F. M. Henkelman, Ch. E. Jones, and Ch. Woods; SAOC 68; Chicago: The Oriental Institute of the University of Chicago, 2014), 233–64.

13 Briant, *From Cyrus to Alexander*, 31–50.

14 The use of these titles in the first year of Persian rule was rather complex; a detailed study is offered by Gauthier Tolini, *La Babylonie et l'Iran: les relations d'une province avec le coeur de l'empire perse* (PhD thesis, Université Paris I – Panthéon-Sorbonne, 2011), 135–45.

presence everywhere. Satraps were appointed to see to judicial, administrative, military, and fiscal tasks by royal proxy.[15] The satrap of Babylon was put in charge of the entire former territory of the Babylonian kingdom. This allowed for territorial continuity within the new provincial structure of the Empire, but Babylon's integration in a foreign imperial sphere did mean a dramatic change of perspective.

Mesopotamia had always had porous boundaries and groups had entered the fertile plain, peacefully as well as forcefully, for as long as our evidence stretches. However, until now, hegemonic ambitions had pulsated from Mesopotamian royal centres (Babylon, Assur, and others) towards neighbouring regions. Such interference by political outsiders that did exist, like that of the Elamites in Babylonian and Assyrian politics in the first half of the first millennium B.C.E., had never materialized in stable, lasting submission. In that sense, the inclusion of Mesopotamia in the Persian Empire, with its ideological and political heartland in Elam and Persia, represents a radical change. Contrasting Nebuchadnezzar's and Darius' visions of territory aptly captures the geo-political shift.

> Nebuchadnezzar, *Hofkalender*[16]
> (These are) the territorial leaders of the land of Akkad: Ea-dayyān, the governor of the Sealand; Nergal-šarru-uṣur, the Simmagir official; Nādin-ahi, of the country of Tupliyaš; Bēl-šumu-iškun, of the country of Puqūdu; Bibea, the Dakūrean; Nādin-ahi, the *šangû* of Dēr; Marduk-šarru-uṣur, of the country Gambūlu; Marduk-šarrani, the provincial governor of Sumandar; Bēl-lū-dārû, the Amūkean; Rēmūt the governor of Zamê; Nabû-ēṭir-napšāti, the governor of Yapṭiru.

> Darius, *Apadana foundation tablets*[17]
> This (is) the kingdom which I hold, from the Saca who are beyond Sogdiana, from there as far as Kush, from the Indus as far as Sardis, which Auramazda, the greatest of the gods, bestowed upon me.

> Darius, *Inscription on the south wall of the Persepolis terrace*[18]
> By the favour of Auramazda, these (are) the countries of which I took possession together

---

15 For a recent discussion of the military, fiscal, and administrative duties of satraps, focused on Anatolia, see Elspeth R. M. Dusinberre, *Empire, Authority, and Autonomy in Achaemenid Anatolia* (Cambridge: Cambridge University Press, 2013), 33–49. On the origins and creation of the satrapal system, see Thierry Petit, *Satrapes et satrapies dans l'empire achéménide de Cyrus le Grand à Xerxès Ier* (Bibliothèque de la Faculté de Philosophie et Lettres de l'Université de Liège 254; Paris: Société d'Édition "Les Belles Lettres", 1990).

16 *Hofkalender* vi*:19'–32' (Beaulieu, 'Arameans', 34 [translation]; Rocío Da Riva, 'Nebuchadnezzar II's Prism (EŞ 7834): A New Edition,' ZA 103 (2013): 196–229 [edition]).

17 DPh § 2 (Kuhrt, *The Persian Empire*, 476).

18 DPe § 2 (Kuhrt, *The Persian Empire*, 486).

> with these Persian people; these feared me (and) brought me tribute: Elam, Media, Babylonia, Arabia, Assyria, Egypt, Armenia, Cappadocia, Lydia, Ionians of the mainland and (those) by the sea, and the countries beyond the sea, Sagartia, Parthia, Drangiana, Areia, Bactria, Sogdiana, Chorasmia, Sattagdyia, Arachosia, India, Gandara, Scythians, Maka.

The creation of the Persian Empire led to a growing distance between king and population. In purviewing their territory, both Nebuchadnezzar and Darius emphasized its composite nature, but the level of social and geographical detail provided by Nebuchadnezzar, who acknowledged the personal involvement of minor regional leaders, greatly differs from Darius' sweeping overview by ethnicity and compass point. Of course, these texts belong to different discursive and functional frameworks and they are therefore not directly comparable. However, I still want to draw on these texts as a point of entry into the main issue of this paper, which relates to the problem of scale in the new imperial setting. Even if Cyrus was recognized as legitimate king of Babylon, Babylonia's political space was devoid of royal presence most of the time after 539 BC. The Persian Empire was simply too large for its kings to establish a regular presence in each of their major satrapies. The report of seasonal migrations of the Persian court by classical authors, who lent equal importance to Babylon as to Ecbatana, Susa and Persepolis in the annual scheme, is far too optimistic.[19] It does not at all tally with the evidence of cuneiform sources drafted 'on the ground' which show that Persian royal visits were very infrequent and far between.[20] Most of the time, there was no king physically present in the Mesopotamian realm during two centuries of Persian rule. As Babylonian kingship was highly performative in nature,

---

19 On the seasonal migration of the Persian kings as reported by Greek and Latin authors see Christopher Tuplin, 'The Seasonal Migration of Achaemenid Kings: A Report on Old and New Evidence', *Achaemenid History* 11 (1998): 63–114; Briant, *From Cyrus to Alexander*, 186–95.

20 The evidence has been gathered by Tolini, *La Babylonie et l'Iran*; this reveals that in two hundred years of Persian history, Babylon and its region received only a dozen recorded royal visits. Some occasions will certainly have gone unrecorded, but even so the picture that arises from the cuneiform texts is a far cry from the annual winter holidays postulated by ancient Greek authors and uncritically restated by modern historians (e.g. Ernie Haerinck, 'Babylon unter der Herrschaft der Achaemeniden', in *Das wieder erstehende Babylon* [ed. R. Koldewey; 5th edition edited by B. Hrouda; München: Beck, 1990], 372). For instance, in the reign of Darius the Great only one royal visit is attested, in 497 B.C.E.; for a detailed study of this event, see Gauthier Tolini, 'Les ressources de la Babylonie et la table de Darius le Grand (520–486 av. J. C.)', in *Le banquet du monarque (Proche-Orient, Grèce, Rome)* (ed. C. Grandjean, Ch. Hugoniot and B. Lion; Table des Hommes; Rennes: PUR and Tours: PUFR, 2013), 145–62.

the question arises how the lack of involvement was perceived among local audiences.

The aim of this article is to investigate the experience and reception of Persian rule in Babylonia. By necessity, the social place where this will be tested is that of cuneiform literate society, and in particular that of the temple communities who monopolized text production relevant to the issue and who played an important role as audience as well as source of kingship ideology.[21] In recent years, historical and assyriological scholarship has emphasized the continuity of the office of King of Babylon under Persian rule. The transfer of the institution and symbols of Babylonian kingship to the Persian rulers is considered a satisfactory arrangement for both parties, as it enabled the accommodation of existing (Babylonian) and recently gained (Persian) prerogatives in a mutually supported political framework and symbolic system. However, the institutional, ethnic and geopolitical conditions under which Persian rulers exercised Babylonian kingship did not compare to those that prevailed under Nabonidus and his predecessors who ruled an independent state, and the issue therefore merits closer scrutiny.

2 Setting the Scene: Babylonian Kingship Ideology at the Time of Cyrus' Conquest

As this paper deals with the perception and evaluation of Babylonian kingship under Persian rule, it is necessary to first outline the ideological framework within which this experience took place.[22] Babylonian kings derived their legitimacy from divine appointment, particularly by Marduk, and from normative con-

---

21 On literacy in Babylonian temple communities, see Michael Jursa, 'Cuneiform Writing in Neo-Babylonian Temple Communities', in *The Oxford Handbook of Cuneiform Culture* (ed. K. Radner and E. Robson; Oxford: Oxford University Press, 2011), 184–204; on the role of these communities as retainers and producers of kingship ideology, see Caroline Waerzeggers, 'The Pious King: Royal Patronage of Temples', in *The Oxford Handbook of Cuneiform Culture* (ed. K. Radner and E. Robson; Oxford: Oxford University Press, 2011), 725–51.

22 On Babylonian kingship ideology in the first millennium B.C.E., see Kuhrt, 'Usurpation'; Beate Pongratz-Leisten, 'Das "negative Sündenbekenntnis" des Königs anläßlich des babylonischen Neujahrsfestes und die *kidinnūtu* von Babylon', in *Schuld, Gewissen und Person: Studien zur Geschichte des inneren Menschen* (ed. A. Assmann and T. Sundermeier; Studien zum Verstehen fremder Religionen 9; Gütersloh: Mohn), 83–101; David S. Vanderhooft, *The Neo-Babylonian Empire and Babylon in the Latter Prophets* (HSM 59; Atlanta: Scholars Press, 1999), 9–59; Rocío Da Riva, *The Neo-Babylonian Royal Inscriptions: An Introduction* (GMTR 4; Münster: Ugarit-Verlag, 2008), 26–31; Kristin Kleber, *Tempel und Palast: Die Beziehungen zwischen dem König und dem*

secration, *in concreto* by priests. They were expected to be pro-active in a number of domains: the ideal king upheld justice and established peace and security, maintained cultic order and respected religious traditions, honored civil rights and refrained from unlawful taxation. Multiple texts and ceremonies assume a triangular relationship between king, gods, and temples: the king extended his generosity towards the gods through the patronage of their tempels; the gods in turn lent him their authority and empowered his rule; the priests, finally, intermediated between these two levels of sovereignty by taking care of the gods' needs, by means of regular temple worship under royal protection, and by installing the king on behalf of the gods. The protection of citizen's rights, *kidinnūtu*, provided a fourth dimension to this triangular relationship.[23]

This ideology is reflected in two texts that were central to the performance of Babylonian kingship at the time of Cyrus' conquest. The *Enūma Eliš* was read out, and perhaps enacted, during the New Year festival, when the human king, a priestly agent, and their divine lord, Marduk, engaged in a complex ritual of re-investment.[24] The poem explains how the ordered world came into being by Marduk's combative and creative power; on a secondary level, it spells out the conditions of acceptable kingship.[25] By subtle and less subtle allusions, Marduk plays the part of the human king, while the other gods declare their willingness to obey on condition that he takes care of their temples. The god Anšar puts it as follows:[26]

> When he [Marduk] speaks, we will all do obeisance,
> At his command the gods shall pay heed.
> His word shall be supreme above and below,
> The son, our champion, shall be the highest.

Eanna-Tempel im spätbabylonischen Uruk (AOAT 358; Münster: Ugarit-Verlag, 2008); Waerzeggers, 'The Pious King'.

23 For this last aspect, see in particular Pongratz-Leisten, 'Sündenbekenntnis'.

24 Jeremy A. Black, 'The New Year Ceremonies in Ancient Babylon: "Taking Bel by the Hand" and a Cultic Picnic', *Religion* 11 (1981): 39–59; Annette Zgoll, 'Königslauf und Götterrat: Struktur und Deutung des babylonischen Neujahrsfestes', in *Festtraditionen in Israel und im Alten Orient* (ed. E. Blum and R. Lux; Veröffentlichungen der Wissenschaftlichen Gesellschaft für Theologie 28; Gütersloh: Gütersloher Verlagshaus, 2006), 11–80; Walther Sallaberger and Katharina Schmidt, 'Insignien des Königs oder Insignien des Gottes? Ein neuer Blick auf die kultische Königskrönung beim babylonischen Neujahrsfest', in *Stories of Long Ago: Festschrift für Michael D. Roaf* (ed. H. D. Baker, K. Kaniuth and A. Otto; AOAT 397; Münster: Ugarit-Verlag, 2011), 567–94.

25 Thorkild Jacobsen, *The Treasures of Darkness: A History of Mesopotamian Religion* (New Haven: Yale University Press, 1976), 167–91.

26 *Enūma Eliš* VI: 101–13 (translated by Benjamin R. Foster, *Before the Muses: An Anthology of Akkadian Literature* [3rd edn; Bethesda: CDL, 2005], 472–73).

> His lordship shall be supreme, he shall have no rival,
> He shall be the shepherd of the people of this land, his creatures.
>
> They shall tell of his ways, without forgetting, in the future.
> He shall establish for his fathers [the old gods] great food offerings,
> He shall provide for them (*zanānu*), he shall take care of their sanctuaries.
> He shall cause incense burners to be savored, he shall make their chambers rejoice.
> He shall do the same on earth as what he brought to pass in heaven,
> He shall appoint the people of this land to serve him.

The verb *zanānu* is the key word here. It describes the benevolent act of showering (literally, raining) gifts upon the temples of the land. The Babylonian kings used its derivate *zāninu* ('provider') as a much-beloved official title.[27] Earlier in the poem, Marduk had already taken upon himself the task of assigning the 'watch' (i.e. temple service) to the gods, each one according to his share (i.e. prebend, *isqu*). He also liberated them by assigning the work of the gods to humankind. At the end of the poem, all gods exclaim joyfully 'Our provider, we will exalt his name!'[28] Among Marduk's fifty ceremonial names, several refer to his interactions with temples and priests: the ninth name Asaralimnunna is explained as 'he who is their provider, who assigns their prebends, whose tiara increases abundance for the land,' the 33rd name Zulum is explained as 'grantor of prebends and food offerings, tender of sanctuaries'.[29] In *Enūma Eliš* the world on high mirrors the world below: at creation, Marduk and the gods agreed to participate in the same reciprocal interaction that defined the relationship between the human king and the priests.

The second text informing us about the ideology of kingship at the time of Cyrus' conquest is a speech delivered by the king during the ceremony of the New Year festival, when he denied a set of accusations in a negative confession to the chief priest of Babylon.[30] Here too, the focus is on the king's role as protector of cult and temple, but city and citizens also feature in the confession:[31]

> I did not commit any sins, lord of the lands [Marduk]. I did not neglect your divinity. I did not destroy Babylon. I did not order its dispersal. I did not make the Esagil tremble, I did not forget its rites. I did not strike the privileged citizens' cheeks, I did not humiliate them. I took care of Babylon, I did not tear down its walls.

---

27 Da Riva, *The Neo-Babylonian Royal Inscriptions*, 99–107.
28 Foster, *Before the Muses*, 475.
29 Foster, *Before the Muses*, 476, 480.
30 Pongratz-Leisten, 'Sündenbekenntnis'.
31 *Ritual of the New Year Festival at Babylon* (François Thureau-Dangin, *Rituels accadiens* [Paris: Leroux, 1921], 144: 423–8).

3 A New Beginning: Cyrus and the Babylonians

The first months and years after the conquest were necessarily experimental: the expansion of the Empire was in full swing and Cyrus needed to delegate power in Babylonia to a representative. As we have seen, the co-regency with his son Cambyses lasted not much more than a year. After this episode, a defected former governor of Nabonidus (*šākin-māti*) became the highest representative of the new regime in Babylonia, until a new provincial system was set up headed by a Persian satrap of Babylon-and-Across-the-River.[32] Throughout this unsettled period, an effort was made to aid continuity of local institutions and stabilize the region. This can be seen throughout the cuneiform text corpus surviving from this period, for instance in the wholesale adoption of administrative hierarchies and practices, and in the prosopographical continuities in offices of all ranks.[33] The intention to honour established traditions of kingship transpires from the *Cyrus Cylinder*, an important official document endorsed by the Persian victors of Mesopotamia. The text contains a report of the building work that Cyrus undertook in Babylon shortly after the defeat of Nabonidus. It is written in the Babylonian language and script, it uses the conventional style and ideology of Babylonian royal inscriptions, and it has the shape of a traditional foundation deposit. Although its functionality implies a limited readership, the recent discovery of a library copy in the British Museum shows that the text enjoyed a considerably wider circulation than the foundation of the wall of Babylon where the original was (to all likelihood) deposited.[34] As a result, the *Cylinder* may well have been an important vehicle of communication between conquerors and conquered.[35]

32 Matthew W. Stolper, 'The Governor of Babylon and Across-the-River in 486 B.C.', *JNES* 48 (1989): 283–305; Tolini, *La Babylonie et l'Iran*, 27–28.

33 A. C. V. M. Bongenaar, *The Neo-Babylonian Ebabbar Temple at Sippar: Its Administration and its Prosopography* (PIHANS 80; Istanbul: Nederlands Historisch-Archaeologisch Instituut, 1997); Michael Jursa, 'The Transition of Babylonia from the Neo-Babylonian Empire to Achaemenid Rule', in *Regime Change in the Ancient Near East and Egypt: From Sargon of Agade to Saddam Hussein* (ed. H. Crawford; PBA 136; Oxford: Oxford University Press, 2007), 73–94; Kleber, *Tempel und Palast*; Caroline Waerzeggers, *The Ezida Temple of Borsippa: Priesthood, Cult, Archives* (Achaemenid History 15; Leiden: Nederlands Instituut voor het Nabije Oosten, 2010).

34 The library copy is discussed by Finkel, 'The Cyrus Cylinder' (see note 12 above). As to the findspot of the Cyrus Cylinder, Jonathan Taylor concludes in a recent study that 'the Imgur-Enlil wall [w]as the more likely place of deposition in antiquity' (Jonathan Taylor, 'The Cyrus Cylinder: Discovery', in *The Cyrus Cylinder: The King of Persia's Proclamation from Ancient Babylon* [ed. I. Finkel; London: I. B. Taurus, 2013], 35–68 [59]).

35 Finkel, 'The Cyrus Cylinder'.

The text of the *Cylinder* is drawn up in two parts. The first part is a condemnation of Nabonidus' reign, the second a celebration of Cyrus' accomplishments as new king of Babylon.[36] Both parts make use of the conventional imagery of the just king; in Nabonidus' case that image is reversed into an account of bad kingship. In this sense, the text may serve as a testimony of the expectations that lived in Babylon at the start of the Persian era. As pointed out by A. Kuhrt, the *Cyrus Cylinder* 'reflects the pressure that Babylonian citizens were able to bring to bear on the new royal claimant more than it casts light on the character of the potential king-to-be.'[37] Seen in this light, one may read the *Cyrus Cylinder* as a manifesto of conditional collaboration by the vanquished, rather than a charter of goodwill by the victor, the unilateral view of more traditional interpretations.[38] The process of negotiation is reflected in the following passage of the *Cylinder*:[39]

> All the people of Tintir (Babylon), of all Sumer and Akkad, nobles and governors, bowed down before him and kissed his feet, rejoicing over his kingship and their faces shone. The lord through whose help all were rescued from death and who saved them all from distress and hardship, they blessed him sweetly and praised his name. I am Cyrus, (...) When I went as harbinger of peace i[nt]o Babylon I found my sovereign residence within the palace amid celebration and rejoicing. Marduk, the great lord, bestowed on me as my destiny the great magnanimity of one who loves Babylon, and I every day sought him out in awe. My vast troops were marching peaceably in Babylon, and the whole of [Sumer] and Akkad had nothing to fear. I sought the safety of the city of Babylon and all its sanctuaries. As for the population of Babylon [..., w]ho as if without div[ine intention] had endured a yoke not decreed for them, I soothed their weariness; I freed them from their bonds(?).

Anšar could not have hoped for a better king when he joyfully exclaimed his wish to be given a 'provider' (*zāninu*) in *Enūma Eliš*.[40] And indeed, a reference to *Enūma Eliš* further down in the *Cyrus Cylinder* suggests that the new contract stipulated in the present time between Cyrus and the Babylonians was but a continuation of the contract that had been made between Marduk and the gods at the beginning of the created world.[41]

---

36 Finkel, 'The Cyrus Cylinder', 23–24 proposes a tripartite structure.

37 Kuhrt, 'Cyrus the Great of Persia', 175.

38 Most recently, for instance, Eric van Dongen ('Propaganda im frühen Perserreich, ca. 550–500 v. Chr.', in *Inszenierung des Sieges – Sieg der Inszenierung: Interdisziplinäre Perspektiven* [ed. M. Fahlenbock, L. Madersbacher and I. Schneider; Innsbruck: StudienVerlag, 2011], 173–180 [175]) described the *Cyrus Cylinder* as an instance of 'Persian propaganda'.

39 *Cyrus Cylinder*: 18–26 (Finkel, 'The Cyrus Cylinder', 6).

40 Anšar's speech is quoted above, 188–9.

41 Line 36 of the *Cyrus Cylinder* refers to *Enūma Eliš* V: 115 in labelling Cyrus and his son Cambyses as the providers (*zāninū*) of Babylonian temples. Cf. Irving Finkel, 'Transliteration of the

4 Frustrations

The message of the *Cyrus Cylinder* was one of political hope: hope of Cyrus – that he would be (and stay) accepted as king of Babylon – and hope of at least some Babylonians, that the Persians would respect the balancing-act between king and temple, and preserve the privileged position of priests and citizens within that relationship. But on both sides, this hope dissipated within decades. Twenty years after Cyrus' conquest, the Babylonians revolted against Persian rule, taking advantage of a wave of rebellions that broke out everywhere in the empire after Cambyses' death and the murder of his brother Bardiya. Darius the Great managed to take control of the situation, but not without huge effort.[42] Whereas the social, economic, cultural and institutional history of Babylonia under Persian rule had so far been characterized by continuity, change now set in.[43] The rebels, who had named themselves after the revered Babylonian king Nebuchadnezzar, were put to death.[44] The fact that they both claimed to be sons of Nabonidus goes to show that loyalties were more complex than the liberation rhetoric of the *Cyrus Cylinder* admits. A stela depicting the humiliation of these rebels at the hands of Darius was erected in the processional road of Babylon as a powerful reminder of the futility of opposition.[45] In Babylonia's temple communities, Darius replaced people who had supported the rebels with trusted protégés, causing a significant shift in the social landscape of urban centres and ending the prosopographical continuities that had marked the transition from Nabonidus to Cyrus.[46] Darius also founded a new capital in Elam (Susa) which had the long-term effect of

---

Cyrus Cylinder Text', in *The Cyrus Cylinder: The King of Persia's Proclamation from Ancient Babylon* (ed. I. Finkel; London: I. B. Taurus, 2013), 134–135.

42 For the troubled accession of Darius the Great, see e.g. Briant, *From Cyrus to Alexander*, 107–38.

43 Jursa, 'The Transition of Babylonia' describes the process of initial continuity under Cyrus and the ensuing change under Darius. Some of the changes heralded by Darius' reign will be discussed in greater detail below.

44 The unfolding of the events is reconstructed by Jürgen Lorenz, *Nebukadnezar III/IV: Die politischen Wirren nach dem Tod des Kambyses im Spiegel der Keilschrifttexte* (Dresden: ISLET, 2008).

45 Ursula Seidl, 'Ein Relief Dareios' I. in Babylon', *AMI* 9 (1976): 125–30; Ursula Seidl, 'Ein Monument Darius' I. aus Babylon', *ZA* 89 (1999): 101–14; Ursula Seidl, 'Eine Triumphstele Darius' I. aus Babylon', in *Babylon: Focus mesopotamischer Geschichte, Wiege früher Gelehrsamkeit, Mythos in der Moderne* (ed. J. Renger; CDOG 2; Saarbrücken: SDV, 1999), 297–306.

46 Jursa, 'The Transition of Babylonia'; Kleber, *Tempel und Palast*, 343; Caroline Waerzeggers, *Marduk-rēmanni: Local Networks and Imperial Politics in Achaemenid Babylonia* (OLA 233; Leuven: Peeters, 2014).

diminishing the status of Babylon as imperial capital, and the short-term effect of draining manpower and resources from Mesopotamia that were summoned to assist the building project in Susa.[47] Herodotos' depiction of Darius as tax collector and tax innovator is corroborated by the Babylonian evidence, which shows a marked increase in the detail and use of tax terminology during his reign.[48] Administrative reforms included splitting up the satrapy of Babylon and Across-the-River in two units of more manageable size, and probably also abolishing the post of city governor in some cities (*šākin-ṭēmi*) towards the end of his reign, thus delivering a further blow to the career possibilities of local elites.[49] A diminished importance of Babylon in representations of imperial geography is reflected in Darius' inscriptional works.[50] Another innovation attributed to Darius is the issuing of new laws (*dātu*) to complement existing legal practice in Babylonia.[51]

It is of course impossible to look into the minds of the Babylonians to see how these various changes were perceived, but growing frustration is apparent

---

47 Francis Joannès, 'Les relations entre Babylonie et Iran au debut de la période achéménide: quelques remarques', in *Approaching the Babylonian Economy* (ed. H. D. Baker and M. Jursa; AOAT 330; Münster: Ugarit-Verlag, 2005), 183–96; Caroline Waerzeggers, 'Babylonians in Susa: The Travels of Babylonian Businessmen to Susa Reconsidered,' in *Der Achämenidenhof – The Achaemenid Court* (ed. B. Jacobs and R. Rollinger; CleO 2; Wiesbaden: Harrassowitz, 2010), 777–813; Tolini, *La Babylonie et l'Iran*; Tolini, 'Les ressources de la Babylonie'; Pierre Briant, 'Susa and Elam in the Achaemenid Empire', in *The Palace of Darius at Susa: The Great Royal Residence of Achaemenid Persia* (ed. J. Perrot; London: I. B. Tauris, 2013), 3–25.

48 Michael Jursa (with a contribution by Caroline Waerzeggers), 'On Aspects of Taxation in Achaemenid Babylonia: New Evidence from Borsippa', in *Organisation des pouvoirs et contacts culturels dans les pays de l'empire achéménide* (ed. P. Briant and M. Chauveau; Persika 14; Paris: de Boccard, 2009), 237–69; Michael Jursa, 'Taxation and Service Obligations in Babylonia from Nebuchadnezzar to Darius and the Evidence for Darius' Tax Reform', in *Herodot und das Persische Weltreich – Herodotus and the Persian Empire* (ed. R. Rollinger, B. Truschnegg and R. Bichler; CleO 3; Wiesbaden: Harrassowitz, 2011), 431–48.

49 Stolper, 'The Governor of Babylon'; senior posts in the Persian administration were reserved for Persians: Pierre Briant, 'Ethno-classe dominante et populations soumises dans l'empire achéménide: le cas de l'Égypte', in *Achaemenid History III: Method and Theory* (ed. A Kuhrt and H. Sancisi-Weerdenburg; Leiden: Nederlands Instituut voor het Nabije Oosten, 1988), 137–73. On the disappearance of the Governor of Babylon, see Caroline Waerzeggers, 'The Babylonian Revolts Against Xerxes and the 'End of Archives', *AfO* 50 (2004): 150–73 (161).

50 A. Leo Oppenheim, 'Babylonian Evidence of Achaemenian Rule in Mesopotamia', in *The Cambridge History of Iran, Volume 2: The Median and Achaemenian Periods* (ed. I. Gershevitch; Cambridge: Cambridge University Press, 1985): 529–87 (531 n. 5); Bruce Lincoln, *'Happiness for Mankind': Achaemenian Religion and the Imperial Project* (AcIr 53; Leuven: Peeters, 2012), 43–44.

51 Kristin Kleber (with a contribution by Johannes Hackl), '*Dātu ša šarri*: Gesetzgebung in Babylonien unter den Achämeniden', *ZABR* 16 (2011): 49–75.

from the fact that a second double revolt broke out soon after Darius' death.[52] The nature of Xerxes' reprisals is debated,[53] but their repercussions were widespread.[54] In the northern region of the land, where the rebels had been most active, numerous priestly archives and temple administrations were brought to an end as a result of these reprisals. Compared to Darius' intervention in local elite politics, the effect of Xerxes' actions was more far-reaching. In Babylon, the prebendary economy of the Esagil temple was abolished, bringing about a disruption of the priestly way of life and an explicit denial of the basic royal task of protecting the legal rights of the servants of the gods.[55] In the south, families with roots in the north disappeared, paving the way for a renaissance of local traditions, most aptly seen in cultic life at Uruk.[56]

By 484 B.C.E., the atmosphere of goodwill that had informed the redaction of the *Cyrus Cylinder* had dissipated on both sides. The question what caused

---

52 Waerzeggers, 'The Babylonian Revolts'.

53 Heather D. Baker, 'Babylon in 484 BC: The Excavated Archival Tablets as a Source for Urban History', *ZA* 98 (2008): 100–16; Amélie Kuhrt, 'Xerxes and the Babylonian Temples: A Restatement of the Case', in *The World of Achaemenid Persia* (ed. J. Curtis and St. J. Simpson; London: I. B. Tauris, 2010), 491–94; Wouter F. M. Henkelman, Amélie Kuhrt, Robert Rollinger and Josef Wiesehöfer, 'Herodotus and Babylon Reconsidered', in *Herodot und das Persische Weltreich – Herodotus and the Persian Empire* (ed. R. Rollinger, B. Truschnegg and R. Bichler; CleO 3; Wiesbaden: Harrassowitz, 2011), 449–70; Walter Kuntner, Sandra Heinsch and Wilfrid Allinger-Csollich, 'Nebuchadnezzar II., Xerxes, Alexander der Große und der Stufenturm von Babylon', in *Inszenierung des Sieges – Sieg der Inszenierung: Interdisziplinäre Perspektiven* (eds. M. Fahlenbock, L. Madersbacher and I. Schneider; Innsbruck: StudienVerlag, 2011), 263–68; Walter Kuntner and Sandra Heinsch, 'Die babylonischen Tempel in der Zeit nach den Chaldäern', in *Tempel im alten Orient* (ed. K. Kaniuth, A. Löhnert, J. L. Miller, A. Otto and W. Sallaberger; CDOG 7; Wiesbaden: Harrassowitz, 2013), 219–62; Amélie Kuhrt, 'Reassessing the Reign of Xerxes in the Light of New Evidence', in *Extraction and Control: Studies in Honor of Matthew W. Stolper* (ed. M. Kozuh, W. F. M. Henkelman, Ch. E. Jones, and Ch. Woods; SAOC 68; Chicago: The Oriental Institute of the University of Chicago, 2014), 163–69.

54 Karlheinz Kessler, 'Urukäische Familien versus babylonische Familien: Die Namengebung in Uruk, die Degradierung der Kulte von Eanna und der Aufstieg des Gottes Anu', *AoF* 31 (2004): 237–62; Waerzeggers, 'The Babylonian Revolts'; Baker, 'Babylon in 484 BC'; Michael Jursa, 'Epistolographic Evidence for the Trips to Susa by Borsippean Priests and for the Crisis in Borsippa at the Beginning of Xerxes' Reign', *ARTA* 2013/003.

55 On the abolishment of the prebendary system in Babylon, see Johannes Hackl, *Materialien zur Urkundenlehre und Archivkunde der spätzeitlichen Texten aus Nordbabylonien* (PhD Dissertation, University of Vienna, 2013). On the priestly way of life at the time of the revolts, see Waerzeggers, *The Ezida Temple*; Michael Jursa, 'Die babylonische Priesterschaft im ersten Jahrtausend v. Chr.', in *Tempel im alten Orient* (ed. K. Kaniuth, A. Löhnert, J. L. Miller, A. Otto and W. Sallaberger; CDOG 7; Wiesbaden: Harrassowitz, 2013), 151–66.

56 Kessler, 'Urukäische Familien'.

the Babylonian frustrations with their Persian overlords is of course extremely complex: dissatisfaction with increasing tax pressures, 'nationalist' feelings, thwarted elite dynamics, discontent over increasing control on temple affairs, neglect of traditional royal tasks may all have played a role in the revolts against Darius and Xerxes.[57] One way to approach this complex issue is by reference to the triangular diagram of interaction that underlay the ideology of kingship in Babylonia. For although Cyrus adopted the language and symbols of traditional Babylonian kingship in the wake of conquest, the exchange relationships that made obedience to the king worthwile appear to have been neglected by him and his successors in the following years and decades.

Compared to the dozens of inscriptions that commemorate building projects of the Neo-Babylonian kings those that honor Persian initiative are very marginal.[58] Only three projects can be assigned to the Persians and they all date to the very first years of Cyrus' rule. In Babylon, the city walls and the embankment were strengthened (and some other, unidentifiable, buildings refurbished) shortly after the conquest, as reported in the *Cyrus Cylinder* (lines 38–42). In the cities of Uruk and Ur, bricks stamped with the name and royal titulature of Cyrus were discovered.[59] The *Cylinder* and the bricks bear witness to his attempt to respect the routines of Babylonian kingship.[60] However, in all these inscriptions, imperial titles and foreign genealogies were used: by listing three Anšanite ances-

57 Matthew W. Stolper, '"No-One Has Exact Information Except for You": Communication between Babylon and Uruk in the First Achaemenid reigns', in *A Persian Perspective: Essays in Memory of Heleen Sancisi-Weerdenburg* (ed. W. Henkelman and A. Kuhrt; Achaemenid History 13; Leiden: Nederlands Instituut voor het Nabije Oosten, 2003), 265–87 (266) argued that control on temple affairs was tightened in the early Achaemenid period; I will take up this issue later in this paper.

58 Da Riva, *The Neo-Babylonian Royal Inscriptions*, 116–27 (catalogue) and Da Riva, *The Inscriptions of Nabopolassar*. Numerous inscriptions of Assyrian rulers and their viceroys attest to equally fervent building activities: Grant Frame, *Rulers of Babylonia: from the Second Dynasty of Isin to the End of Assyrian Domination (1157–612 BC)* (Royal Inscriptions of Mesopotamia, Babylonian Periods 2; Toronto: University of Toronto Press, 1995).

59 Bricks from Uruk: Christopher B. F. Walker, *Cuneiform Brick Inscriptions in the British Museum, the Ashmolean Museum, Oxford, the City of Birmingham Museum and Art Gallery, the City of Bristol Museum and Art Gallery* (London: British Museum, 1981), no. 115 and Schaudig, *Die Inschriften*, 548 (K1.1) with edition and older literature. Bricks from Ur: Walker, *Cuneiform Brick Inscriptions*, no. 116 and Schaudig, *Die Inschriften*, 549. Note that the attribution of a cylinder fragment from Ur to Cyrus (e.g. Kuhrt, 'The Cyrus Cylinder', 89) is disputed, cf. Schaudig, *Die Inschriften*, 480–81.

60 Bricks stamped with the names of Nabopolassar, Nebuchadnezzar, Amēl-Marduk, Neriglissar and Nabonidus have been found in abundance on Babylonian sites, see Walker, *Cuneiform Brick Inscriptions* and Da Riva, *The Neo-Babylonian Royal Inscriptions*.

tors, the *Cylinder* appeals to a process of legtitimation foreign to the Babylonian tradition;[61] in the Uruk bricks 'king of the lands' was put before the more traditional title 'lover of the Esagil and the Ezida' and followed by the military title 'strong king';[62] in the Ur bricks Cyrus' Anšanite roots and his conquest and pacification of the lands were emphasized without using any of the traditional Babylonian royal titles;[63] and the *Cylinder* puts Cyrus forward as a new Assurbanipal quite explicitly, following a revived interest in the legacy of the Assyrian Empire that began under Nabonidus.[64] In short, while the bricks respect the *format* of Babylonian brick inscriptions, neither of these texts can really be said to be true to the Babylonian spirit of piety. They rather celebrate Cyrus' imperial program and drive home Babylonia's submission.

No building inscriptions have been found from the remaining two hundred years of Persian rule in Babylonia.[65] It is highly unlikely that this silence can be fully explained as an accident of discovery. Even an ephemeral Babylonian king like Amēl-Marduk, who reigned less than two years, left his mark on Babylonia's urban heritage.[66] I should like to stress that, while the lack of advertisement of royal patronage is striking, this does not imply that all temples of Babylonia were hopelessly left to deteriorate during the two centuries of Persian rule. A recent reconsideration of the archaeological evidence by Walter Kuntner and Sandra Heinsch argues that Babylonian temples were not all in ruin by the time Darius III was expelled from Mesopotamia by Alexander the Great.[67] Especially in the last decades of Achaemenid rule, some building activity seems to be recorded. However, there is no reason to assume that the initiative and the funding for these

---

61 Robert Rollinger, 'Thinking and Writing about History in Teispid and Achaemenid Persia', in *Thinking, Recording, and Writing History in the Ancient World* (ed. K. A. Raaflaub; Malden: Wiley Blackwell, 2014), 187–212 (189).

62 'Cyrus, king of the lands, who loves Esagil and Ezida, son of Cambyses, the mighty king am I' (Kuhrt, *The Persian Empire*, 74).

63 'Cyrus, king of the world, king of Anšan, son of Cambyses, king of Anšan. The great gods filled my hands with all lands and I caused the land to dwell in tranquility' (Kuhrt, *The Persian Empire*, 75).

64 Harmatta, 'Les modèles littéraires'; Kuhrt, 'The Cyrus Cylinder'; Piotr Michalowski, 'Biography of a Sentence: Assurbanipal, Nabonidus, and Cyrus', in *Extraction and Control: Studies in Honor of Matthew W. Stolper* (ed. M. Kozuh, W. F. M. Henkelman, Ch. E. Jones, and Ch. Woods; SAOC 68; Chicago: The Oriental Institute of the University of Chicago, 2014), 203–10; Beaulieu, *The Reign of Nabonidus*, 139–40; Rollinger, 'Das teispidisch-achaimenidische Großreich', 164–65.

65 See also Paul-Alain Beaulieu, 'Agade in the Late Babylonian Period', *NABU* 1989/66, p. 46.

66 Da Riva, *The Inscriptions of Nabopolassar*.

67 Kuntner and Heinsch, 'Die babylonischen Tempel'.

projects derived from the Persian administration and not, for instance, from the local population or the temple treasuries.

A similar lack of visible engagement can be observed in two related areas of patronage: the provisioning of the sacrificial cult and the gifting of cultic objects. Entirely conforming to Babylonian tradition, Cyrus claims in his *Cylinder* to have ordered an increase of offerings (presumably in the Esagil temple; lines 37–38). No records from the Esagil temple survive that allow us to confirm or dismiss this statement, but according to one text from Akkad, steps were indeed taken in Cyrus' fourth year to restore in the temple of Ešnunna the cultic practice of Nebuchadnezzar's reign, while another text from the same city shows that governor Gubāru undertook an investigation into a matter involving (cultic) jewels of the Eulmaš temple of Akkad. These events are in line with the policy announced in the *Cylinder*. Both Akkad and Ešnunna are listed among the cities 'across the Tigris' that Cyrus promised to re-invigorate in the *Cylinder*.[68] However, from the very beginning of Persian rule there are some signs of change as well. In the Eanna temple archive from Uruk evidence for sacrifices sponsored by the king (*niqê šarri*) stops abruptly when Cyrus enters the scene.[69] This meant a decrease in the offerings of about 200 to 400 sheep, and several dozen head of oxen, birds and eggs, per year.[70] The only secure reference to royal offerings in a Babylonian temple under Persian rule comes from a prebend text (written in a private context) in standard formulary.[71] There is no record of Persian donations of chariots, jewels, vessels or other cultic paraphernalia, which constituted an impor-

68 Beaulieu, 'Agade', 45; Michael Jursa, 'Akkad, das Eulmaš und Gubaru', *WZKM* 86 (1996): 197–211.

69 YOS 7 8 contains the last reference to this type of offering in Eanna. Interestingly the last offering of the king was presented in the 16th year of Nabonidus; the remainder of the text, which extends into the second month of Cyrus' first full regnal year, does not mention the *niqê šarri* anymore. See Kleber, *Tempel und Palast*, 281–5 for the *niqê šarri* in the reign of Nabonidus; note that Kleber's claim that the practice was continued by the Achaemenids (p. 281) is not substantiated, it is based on the mention of royal offerings in the Seleucid ritual text TCL 6 38 (p. 281 n. 797) but this text was written as a conscious attempt to recreate the Neo-Babylonian offering practice in the Seleucid period; it does not bear on the intervening, Persian period.

70 This estimate is based on the figures of the *niqê šarri* during some well-documented years of Nabonidus' reign (Kleber, *Tempel und Palast*, 283).

71 'Ana-Bēl-ēreš voluntarily sold his butcher's prebend in the ox and sheep from the royal offerings, the offerings of the worshipper (*kāribu*), the regular offerings (*ginû*), the festive offerings (*guqqû*), the *eššēšu* festivals, the *bayyātānu* festivals, the greeting-of-the-temple festivals', Heather D. Baker, *The Archive of the Nappāhu Family* (AfOB 30; Vienna: Institut für Orientalistik der Universität Wien, 2004) no. 60: 1–5 (Babylon, 26th year of Darius I).

tant area of patronage under Babylonian and Assyrian rule.[72] An unexplained confiscation of temple vessels by the Persian authorities rather amounted to an inversal of the expected gift pattern.[73] The tithes (*erbu*) that members of the Neo-Babylonian royal households occasionally gave to the temples, ceased to be paid in the Persian period.[74] There are also three instances of cultic innovation that do not tally well with the traditional role of the king as restorer and protector of tradition. The first of these innovations was the introduction of a sacrificial cult for a statue of Darius in the Ebabbar temple of Sippar shortly after his death.[75] The second was the inclusion of a Persian queen among the beneficiaries of sacrificial remainders.[76] The third was the introduction of a cult for 'Sîn-of-Heaven' in the temples of Sippar and Uruk, apparently as part of a re-thinking of the state cult that constituted an intriguing contradiction with what public statements had to say about Nabonidus' hated Sîn worship.[77]

According to the *Cyrus Cylinder* and the *Nabonidus Chronicle*, the Persian army took care not to interrupt the cultic procedures of the Esagil temple at the time of conquest. As worship continued, so persisted the need of expert personnel. In general, one observes broad continuities of human resources in Babylonian temples under the new Persian rulers, not just in administrative posts but also in their priestly ranks. We find ample evidence of this in countless archives of priests and temples that cover the critical moment of transition.[78] However, a case can be made for changes affecting the conditions of priestly life under Persian rule, some more subtle than others. One of these changes is the distancing of the

---

72 The inventories from the Eanna temple show that the number of vessels in use remained static between Nbn 06 and Camb 06 (Francis Joannès, 'Un inventaire de mobilier sacré d'époque néobabylonienne', *RA* 77 [1988]: 143–50 [146–47]).

73 ROMCT 2 5 (Uruk, Cyr 06).

74 Michael Jursa, *Der Tempelzehnt in Babylonien von siebenten bis zum dritten Jahrhundert v. Chr.* (AOAT 25; Münster: Ugarit-Verlag, 1998), 65–67; Kleber, *Tempel und Palast*, 342–43.

75 Caroline Waerzeggers, 'A Statue of Darius in the Temple of Sippar', in *Extraction and Control: Studies in Honor of Matthew W. Stolper* (ed. M. Kozuh, W. F. M. Henkelman, Ch. E. Jones, and Ch. Woods; SAOC 68; Chicago: The Oriental Institute of the University of Chicago, 2014), 323–29.

76 Ran Zadok, 'An Achaemenid Queen', *NABU* 2002/65; Ran Zadok, 'Updating the Apammu Dossier (cf. NABU 2002/65)', *NABU* 2003/33.

77 In Sippar, worship of Sîn-of-Heaven was performed together with that of the Statue of Sargon, which had been part of the state cult of Marduk until the end of Nabonidus' reign (see Waerzeggers, 'A Statue of Darius'). In Eanna, the cult of Sîn-of-Heaven was also newly introduced in the beginning of the Persian period (Joannès, 'Un inventaire de mobilier sacré', 147).

78 Hans M. Kümmel, *Familie, Beruf und Amt im spätbabylonischen Uruk: Prosopographische Untersuchungen zu Berufsgruppen des 6. Jahrhunderts v. Chr. in Uruk* (ADOG 20; Berlin: Mann, 1979); Bongenaar, *The Neo-Babylonian Ebabbar Temple*; Waerzeggers, *The Ezida Temple*.

figure of the king from state – temple interactions. Due to the absence of the king, the New Year festival and other ceremonies of kingship were suspended. These rituals were important moments of engagement between royalty and priesthood and served as a public confirmation of their mutual dependence. Certain duties that were traditionally performed by kings of Babylon were delegated to the satrap or to local dignitaries. For instance, Persian kings did not issue calendrical adjustments as their Babylonian predecessors had done.[79] In the temples, not only high-end criminal activities came under the scrutiny of the satrap. Gubāru (Gobryas), the first satrap of Babylon and Across-the-River, launched a large-scale investigation into financial and administrative malpractice in Babylonian temples. All areas of the temple economy were controlled, from sheep and cattle breeding (notoriously, the Gimillu case) to thefts of temple property. In the latter category, several priests (sometimes entire priestly colleges) were accused and held responsible for objects that had gone missing.[80] Overzealous inspection of temple affairs in combination with attempts to press a restrictive legislation onto the activities of the priesthood may well have affected the initial willingness of the priests to co-operate with their new rulers, especially if one considers that the Persian government at the same time neglected its duty of protecting the rights of the priests.[81] Tax exemption, traditionally granted to the citizens of major towns, was tampered with: Darius conscripted even priests in the rotational workforce of his new capital of Susa.[82] This was, if not a deliberate, at least an effective degradation of local elites, who had enjoyed such prerogatives for a long time. As we have seen, during the New Year festival, the Babylonian king promised not to humiliate the 'privileged citizens', or *ṣābē kidinni* (those granted *kidinnu* status).[83] Granting *kidinnu* was as much part of the package of being a just king as ordering sacrifices and building temples.[84] In the words of Assurbanipal:[85]

---

79 Kleber, *Tempel und Palast*, 268.

80 Stolper, 'Communication'.

81 The *Craftsmen's Charter* dates from the fourth year of Cyrus' reign and attempts to restrict the work of temple craftsmen to temple assignments; see David B. Weisberg, *Guild Structure and Political Allegiance in Early Achaemenid Mesopotamia* (YNER 1; New Haven: Yale University Press, 1967) and the new edition and additional evidence presented by, Elizabeth E. Payne, 'New Evidence for the 'Craftsmen's Charter'', *RA* 102 (2008): 99–114.

82 Waerzeggers, 'Babylonians in Susa'.

83 Pongratz-Leisten, 'Sündenbekenntnis'.

84 Kuhrt, 'Usurpation'.

85 Translation by Frame, *Rulers of Babylonia*, B.6.32.1: 10–14.

> During my reign, ... Marduk entered Babylon amidst rejoicing and took up his residence in the eternal Esagila. I reconfirmed the regular offerings for Esagila and the gods of Babylon. I re-established the privileged status of Babylon (*kidinnūtu*) and appointed Šamaš-šumu-ukīn my brother to the kingship.

The early Neo-Babylonian wisdom text *Advice to a Prince* warns that Marduk will turn the land over to the enemy if a king abolishes the privileged status of the citizens of Sippar, Nippur and Babylon.[86] Royal protection of *kidinnu* status, and related tax exemption terminology, was particularly relevant for the priesthood, as freedom from taxes enabled them to dedicate themselves entirely to the service of the gods; it was the king's duty to guarantee that freedom and it was a matter of pride for the priests who advertised this right at places that symbolised their unique status. For instance, a doorframe in the Egishnugal temple of Ur was inscribed with the following commemorative text of Nabonidus:[87]

> I am Nabonidus, king of Babylon, fearful of Sîn and Nergal. I built Egipar, the house of the highpriestess in Ur, for my lord Sîn. I have established the *kidinnu*-status of the priests ('washed ones') of the Egishnugal temple and fixed their *šubarrû* (exemption).

In short, Darius' conscription of priestly delegations as corvée gangs in his Elamite building project was nothing short of the slap in the face of the privileged people – one of the very sins that any rightful king was eager to deny during the ritual of confirmation at the New Year festival. Documentary evidence from priestly archives shows that the tax burden created acute financial difficulties among priestly families; some were even unable to maintain their inherited prebendary titles as a consequence.[88] Shortly before the outbreak of the revolts against Xerxes, the prebendaries of Borsippa were driven to despair as they had to bargain their titles for what they were still worth; whether the Persian authorities were to blame for this crisis is, admittedly, unknown.[89] In any event, there is anecdotal evidence that Persian corvée demands on Babylonian temples were at times experienced as being excessive, and that hardship was – rightly or wrongly – directly blamed on the Persian administrators whose task it was to extract such control.[90]

---

86 Wilfred G. Lambert, *Babylonian Wisdom Literature* (Oxford: Clarendon, 1960), 112–4; Steven W. Cole, *The Early Neo-Babylonian Governor's Archive from Nippur* (OIP 114; Chicago: The Oriental Institute of the University of Chicago, 1996), no. 128: 24–29.

87 UET 1 187; Schaudig, *Die Inschriften*, 344 (line 12).

88 Waerzeggers, *Marduk-rēmanni*.

89 Jursa, 'Epistolographic Evidence'.

90 Stolper, 'Communication'; Jursa, 'Taxation and Service Obligations', 434–35.

Finally, a word about the New Year festival is in order. It is sometimes suggested that the Persians restored the celebration of the New Year festival after Nabonidus' protracted absence due to his stay at Teima.[91] However, of all Persian kings, only Cambyses participated with reasonable certainty in the New Year festival and only in his father's first year as ruler of Babylonia.[92] As reported in the *Nabonidus Chronicle*, the celebration was an act of imperial drama: either Cambyses or (less likely) Cyrus himself appeared in traditional Elamite dress at the most important festival of the Babylonian religious year. As with the stamped bricks, a traditional Babylonian medium was used, but the message was one of conquest. It is possible that Cyrus and his successors visited the New Year festival from time to time, but the annual cycle of de- and enthronement was broken.[93]

In conclusion, already after the first years of Persian rule it was clear that Babylonian kingship was transformed. In the *Cylinder*, Cyrus was portrayed as a traditional Babylonian monarch and there is corroborative evidence that the words of the *Cylinder* were indeed translated into policy: he undertook building work in the cities of Babylon, Uruk and Ur; his satrap restored the sacrificial practice of the time of Nebuchadnezzar in the city of Akkad; he and/or his son Cambyses participated in the New Year festival in his first year of reign. All these activities were part of the traditional understanding of kingship in Babylonia. However, scratching below the surface, certain details of Cyrus' performance did not match the expected pattern. His advertisement of pious patronage used

---

91 Kuhrt, 'Usurpation,' 52.

92 This is reported in the *Nabonidus Chronicle* (Albert Kirk Grayson, *Assyrian and Babylonian Chronicles* [TCS 5; Locust Valley: J. J. Augustin, 1975], no. 7). The passage about the celebration of the New Year festival in Cyrus' first year of rule is damaged and its reading contested; see Andrew R. George, 'Studies in Cultic Topography and Ideology', *BO* 53 (1996): 363–95 and Tolini, *La Babylonie et l'Iran*. Moreover, the fact that the only surviving copy dates, to all likelihood, to the fourth century B.C.E. or later (Paul-Alain Beaulieu, 'Nabonidus the Mad King: A Reconsideration of His Steles from Harran and Babylon', in *Representations of Political Power: Case Studies from Times of Change and Dissolving Order in the Ancient Near East* [ed. M. Heinz and M. H. Feldman; Winona Lake: Eisenbrauns, 2007], 137–66) casts doubt on its acquired status in scholarship as 'the sole reliable document' about the conquest of Babylon in 539 B.C.E. (Kuhrt, *The Persian Empire*, 47).

93 This is mostly based on an argument from silence. However, there is positive evidence that the New Year festival was *not* celebrated in those years when the court sojourned at Susa: Darius I, years 13, 16, 17, 24, 28, 30, 31, and Xerxes year 2 (Waerzeggers, 'Babylonians in Susa', 780–5). Note also that business document BM 30235 (Kathleen Abraham, *Business and Politics under the Persian Empire: The Financial Dealings of Marduk-nāṣir-apli of the House of Egibi (521–487 B.C.E.)* [Bethesda: CDL, 2004], no. 5) is dated to Dar 05-I-26, i.e. to the crucial fifth day of Nisan, only weeks after Darius had made a rare (but protracted) appearance in Babylon. The fact that Darius left only weeks before the New Year festival shows its insignificance in Babylonian-Persian relations at that point. For Darius' visit in his 25th year, see Tolini, 'Les ressources de la Babylonie'.

unfamiliar, imperial language (as seen in the bricks) and his (or Cambyses') participation in the New Year festival was used as an opportunity to stage imperial drama (as seen in the Elamite robes). Cyrus' successors remained passive at best in executing the duties of traditional Babylonian kingship. No more building work was undertaken or advertised by royal initiative; certain types of royal offerings were interrupted; no tithes of the Persian royal family were received; and new beneficiaries were added to those who enjoyed the leftovers of the meals of Babylonian gods. Some new policies may have thwarted local sensitivities rather more actively, like conscripting priests in corvée gangs and sending them to Elam, or overzealously controlling and legislating the activities of the priesthood while failing to protect their rights effectively. Babylonian resistance against Persian rule erupted at least twice, in 522 and 484 B.C.E.[94] These revolts were supported by the temples and priesthoods on whose archives our knowledge of historical events and of the ideological framework is based. How widely this discontent resonated within the society at large is difficult to say. Taking the abandonment of archives at the time of Xerxes' suppression of the revolts as an indicator, it is clear that not all groups within society, and not even all groups within the temple communities, supported the rebels. Care-takers and managers of Persian estates, for instance, remained loyal to their overlords, and in Uruk, local families managed to assert their independence from Babylon-based families who dominated the senior offices in Eanna.[95] It should thus be clear that the traditional understanding of kingship as intimately tied to the cult of Marduk was an ideology not necessarily shared by all 'Babylonians' (a problematic category to begin with, as we have seen); as a consequence, the breakdown of the relationships underlying that model will not have been perceived as problematic by all 'Babylonians' either. Moreover, as many of the adherents of this traditional model were unable to survive Xerxes' repercussions after the revolts of 484 BC, some of the most vocal opponents of Persian rule disappeared from the very positions that had led to their visibility in records and archives so far. This is important to keep in mind as we turn to the question of how Persian rule was remembered by later generations of Babylonians.

---

94 A possible third rebellion is debated, see below note 99.

95 Kessler, 'Urukäische Familien'; Waerzeggers, 'The Babylonian Revolts'; Baker, 'Babylon in 484 BC'.

5 In Retrospect

When later generations of Babylonian scholars looked back on the history of Babylonian monarchy, they pictured a long and uninterrupted succession of kings, from the Assyrians down to the Seleucids. The inclusion of Persian kings in this chronographic tradition was uncontested, and there can be no doubt that the Persians were recognized as *de facto* rulers of Babylon. This emerges clearly in the Hellenistic period, from cuneiform as well as Greek sources. A well-known testimony is found in Ptolemy's *Royal Canon*. Compiled in the second century CE, this work lists a continuous succession of kings of Babylon from Nabonassar to Alexander, including the Persian holders of this office.[96] The Babylonian origin of this section of the *Canon* is widely accepted, and it is therefore unproblematic to take it as evidence of an earlier Babylonian viewpoint, despite the *Canon*'s late date and Alexandrian location. The *Uruk King List* offers the most prominent testimony of this tradition in cuneiform, at a much earlier date than the *Canon*. This much-damaged, one-column tablet from the late third century B.C.E. presents a largely correct enumeration of Kings of Babylon until Seleucus II (246–226 B.C.E.).[97] Because the top is broken off it is unclear with whose reign the tablet began, but as it mentions Kandalānu (647–627 B.C.E.) and suppresses the name of his Assyrian overlord (Assurbanipal, 668–627 B.C.E.), we may safely conclude that the list was designed to represent specifically the history of the kingship of Babylon, from at least the seventh century B.C.E. onward.[98] In this respect it is significant that the Persian kings appear fully integrated in the list. No notification of their non-Babylonian origin is made, nor did the author deem it necessary to indicate the true extent of their massive empire. The text propagates a purely local view on the history of Babylonian kingship, oblivious of the imperial context in which the institution survived for two centuries, from Cyrus to Darius III. The

---

96 Leo Depuydt, '"More Valuable than All Gold": Ptolemy's Royal Canon and Babylonian Chronology', *JCS* 47 (1995): 97–117.

97 Albert Kirk Grayson, 'Assyrian and Babylonian King Lists: Collations and Comments', in *Lišān mithurti: Festschrift Wolfram Freiherr von Soden zum 19.VI.1968 gewidmet von Schülern und Mitarbeitern* (ed. W. Röllig; AOAT 1; Kevelaer: Butzon & Bercker / Neukirchen-Vluyn: Neukirchener Verlag des Erziehungsvereins, 1969), 105–18 (Plate III); Albert Kirk Grayson, 'Königslisten und Chroniken', *RlA* 6 (1983): 86–135 (97–98).

98 Based on an estimate of the size of the missing piece at the top of the tablet, Jan van Dijk ('Die Tontafeln aus dem rēš-Heiligtum', in *XVIII. Vorläufiger Bericht über die von dem Deutschen Archäologischen Institut und der Deutschen Orient-Gesellschaft aus Mitteln der deutschen Forschungsgemeinschaft unternommenen Ausgrabungen in Uruk-Warka, Winter 1959/60* [ed. H. J. Lenzen; ADOG 7; Berlin: Mann, 1962], 53–61) suggested that the text may have commenced in c. 700 BC.

author employed the same template when inserting the reign of Cambyses as he did when treating the reigns of Nabonidus and Alexander. The result is a coherent vision of Babylonian kingship, expressing long-term unity and constancy rather than actual dynastic change. Within this construct, the Persian period figured as an integral and unquestionable bridge between the ancient kings who reigned half a millennium ago and the present king in office at the time of writing (perhaps Antiochus III). A peculiar inconsistency of the text nonetheless draws our attention: in the pre-Persian portion of the list, the scribe displays knowledge of 'messy' intervals of Babylon's royal history (mentioning Sîn-šumu-līšir, Sîn-šarru-iškun, and Lâbâši-Marduk), whereas in the Persian portion he offers a polished version of the accession of Darius I (skipping over Bardiya, Nebuchadnezzar III and Nebuchadnezzar IV) while at the same time acknowledging an otherwise unattested rebel (Nidin-Bēl) immediately before the reign of Darius III.[99] The inconsistent redaction may derive from the use of different chrono- and historiographic traditions, an issue to which I will return below.

Ptolemy's *Royal Canon* and the *Uruk King List* remind us that the Persian period was an accepted episode in the political memory of later Babylonia. However, in view of their chronographic nature and practical function, these texts are hardly the kind of place where interpretations of Persian rule were likely to be voiced. We stand a better chance to capture retrospective evaluations in historical narrative writing, a literary activity that flowered in Hellenistic Babylonia. We will have occasion in this paper to visit a number of these texts. As we will see, Hellenistic Babylonian authors used a wide cast of historical kings as a resource to reflect on issues of regal governance, creating a literary space removed in time from contemporary politics. Nabopolassar, Nebuchadnezzar and Nabonidus were favorite characters in this literature, but other, less well-known royal figures, like the obscure eighth century B.C.E. king Nabû-šumu-iškun, were also revisited as exemplary cases of proper and improper royal conduct. Given the deeply negative sentiments about Xerxes and his successors in Greek historiography and literature,[100] there would have been few inhibitions for these Hellenistic Babylonian authors to vent their criticism of Persian rulers in such literature if they so wanted – as indeed happened in Egypt[101] – but no discourse of explicit

---

99 On the figure of Nidin-Bēl, see Oppenheim, 'The Babylonian Evidence', 533.

100 Heleen Sancisi-Weerdenburg, 'The Personality of Xerxes, King of Kings', in *Archaeologia Iranica et Orientalis: Miscellanea in honorem Louis Vanden Berghe* (ed. L. De Meyer and E. Haerinck; Gent: Peeters, 1989), 549–61; Briant, *From Cyrus to Alexander*, 515–68.

101 Günter Vittmann, *Ägypten und die Fremden im ersten vorchristlichen Jahrtausend* (Kulturgeschichte der Antiken Welt 97; Mainz: von Zabern, 2003), 140–41; Michel Chauveau and Christophe Thiers, 'L'Égypte en transition: des Perses aux Macédoniens,' in *La Transition entre*

anti-Persian sentiment developed in Babylonia. Rather, the Persian kings are conspicuous by their limited presence in the new historical literature created in the Hellenistic period.

6 The Dynastic Prophecy and the Babyloniaca of Berossos

Two Hellenistic Babylonian texts offer a long-term history of Babylonia that includes the Persian period: the *Dynastic Prophecy* and the *Babyloniaca* of Berossos. Both texts exceed the purely factual of the *Uruk King List* and the *Royal Canon*, and comment extensively on past events. In both texts, the evaluation of Persian rule has been difficult for modern readers to assess. According to Haubold, Berossos' critique of Persian rule is encapsulated in his unconventional claim that Cyrus destroyed the walls of Babylon during the conquest of 539 B.C.E.[102] In the *Dynastic Prophecy*, by contrast, both an anti-Persian *and* a pro-Persian author may have been at work during its very complex redaction process.[103] Here, I want to take a step back and draw attention to a less complicated, but in my mind crucial, issue that affects the understanding of both texts.

The *Prophecy* and the *Babyloniaca* include the Persian period in their long narratives of Babylonian history, but it is debatable just how much their authors told or knew about this period and, on a related note, which episodes of that long

l'empire achéménide et les royaumes hellénistiques (ed. P. Briant and F. Joannès; Persika 9; Paris: de Boccard, 2006), 375–404 (378).

102 Johannes Haubold, *Greece and Mesopotamia: Dialogues in Literature* (New York: Cambridge University Press, 2013), 163–4.

103 The evaluation of Cyrus' reign in the *Prophecy* is ambivalent, but most modern readers interpret it as a negative verdict (see below n. 151). The faulty prediction of Alexander's downfall at the hands of Darius III's army may reflect anxieties during the last years of the Empire's existence (Matthew Neujahr, 'When Darius defeated Alexander: Composition and Redaction in the Dynastic Prophecy', *JNES* 64 [2005]: 101–07; Matthew Neujahr, *Predicting the Past in the Ancient Near East: Mantic Historiography in Ancient Mesopotamia, Judah, and the Mediterranean World* [BJS 354; Providence: Brown Judaic Studies, 2012], 58–63), but the entire passage is marred by damages and other difficulties (cf. R. J. van der Spek, 'Darius III, Alexander the Great and Babylonian Scholarship', in *A Persian Perspective: Essays in Memory of Heleen Sancisi-Weerdenburg* (ed. W. F. M. Henkelman and A. Kuhrt; Achaemenid History 13; Leiden: Nederlands Instituut voor het Nabije Oosten, 2003), 289–346 [311–24]). Wildly differing interpretations have been put forward (cf. lately by M. Rahim Shayegan, *Arsacids and Sasanians: Political Ideology in Post-Hellenistic and Late Antique Persia* [Cambridge: Cambridge University Press, 2011], 137–40).

period attracted their interest. This issue can be approached from two angles: by looking at the texts themselves and by looking at the cultural realm in which these compositions were produced. Both texts are only partially preserved and it remains uncertain how representative of the original composition current reconstructions are. It is therefore important to pay attention not only to what is in the texts, but also to their context.

The *Dynastic Prophecy* starts with the overthrow of Assyria by Nabopolassar and ends at some point after the arrival of Alexander in Mesopotamia; the Persian section of the extant copy only treats the reigns of Cyrus (539–530 B.C.E.), Arses (337–336 B.C.E.) and Darius III (335–331 B.C.E.).[104] Whether or not the intervening reigns were included in the original composition is a matter of uncertainty: the clay tablet is broken in such a way that both reconstructions are possible. If they were not included, the author(s) skipped 193 years of Persian history without further comment. This is how A. K. Grayson, the original editor, understood the text.[105] In this case, the main theme of the text would be regime change. If the intervening reigns were included, the section from Cambyses to Artaxerxes III would have filled no less than two columns (both now lost), implying a reasonably detailed knowledge of these reigns. This is how the text has been understood since W. G. Lambert objected, based on common sense, to Grayson's reconstruction.[106] In this case, the focus of the text would not be on regime change but on individual histories of Babylonian kingship. Given the text's poor state of preservation, and the general disregard of the cultural context of Hellenistic Babylonian literature in assyriological scholarship at the time of Lambert's writing, some caution is warranted. The missing text of the *Dynastic Prophecy* would be the *only* surviving testimony that detailed historical knowledge about the early and mature Persian Empire was used and reworked by authors engaged in historical fiction in Hellenistic Babylonia.[107] The only other testimony is the *Babyloniaca* of Berossos, but our understanding of this text is marred by exactly the same kind of uncertainty.

104 First edition by Grayson, *Babylonian Historical-Literary Texts*, 24–37. New editions by van der Spek, 'Darius III', 311–24 and Neujahr, *Predicting the Past*, 58–63.
105 Grayson, *Babylonian Historical-Literary Texts*, 25–26, 32–35.
106 Wilfred G. Lambert, *The Background of Jewish Apocalyptic* (London: Athlone, 1978), 13. Lambert's reconstruction is generally accepted (e.g. Susan Sherwin-White, 'Seleucid Babylonia', 11; Matthijs de Jong, *Isaiah Among the Ancient Near Eastern Prophets: A Comparative Study of the Earliest Stages of the Isaiah Tradition and the Neo-Assyrian Prophecies* [VTSup 117; Leiden: Brill, 2007], 429–30; van der Spek, 'Darius III', 311–24); Neujahr remains agnostic ('When Darius Defeated Alexander', 102 n. 7).
107 This point is further elaborated below.

The transmission of the text of the *Babyloniaca* is infamously lacunal.[108] The third book, which interests us here, offers a monarchical history of Babylonia from (after) Nabonassar to Alexander the Great.[109] The temporal scope suggests a continuous narrative, but the transmitted text covers the period unevenly. The accent is on Assyrian and Babylonian history until the fall of Babylon to Cyrus. Whatever Berossos told of subsequent Persian history did not make it into the work of later historians.[110] Eusebius' summary is schematic: 'Cyrus ruled Babylonia for nine years. Then, after having been engaged in another war on the Daas Plain, he died. After him Cambyses ruled eight years, and after him Darius for thirty-six years. Then Xerxes ruled and the rest of the Persian kings'.[111] Is the shallow historical depth of this summary due to Eusebius' disinterest in Persian history, or to Berossos' cursory treatment of it? This question is impossible to answer because we do not know how Berossos' text looked like or how Eusebius represented it. The summary reflects the chronographic format of the Babylonian king list, so perhaps it is closer to the actual text of Berossos than assumed. In that case, Berossos would have switched from a narrative history to a chronographic list after the reign of Cyrus. It is of course utterly impossible to be certain of any of this, but it is worthwile to ponder the question of Berossos' coverage of Persian history a bit longer. One brief detail of Berossos' Persian history did make it into the work of later historians. This passage concerns the cult of Anahita, an episode set in the reign of Artaxerxes II (404–359 B.C.E.).[112] How does this passage relate to the rest of Berossos' work on the Persian period? Should it be awarded broad relevance as a sign of the rich history that has been lost? Or should it be given narrow relevance as a sign that Berossos was better informed about some parts of the Persian period than about others?

---

108 Amélie Kuhrt, 'Berossus's *Babyloniaca* and Seleucid Rule in Babylonia', in *Hellenism in the East: The Interaction of Greek and Non-Greek Civilizations from Syria to Central Asia after Alexander* (ed. A. Kuhrt and S. Sherwin-White; Berkeley: University of California Press, 1987), 32–56; Johannes Haubold, Giovanni Lanfranchi, Robert Rollinger and John M. Steele, eds. *The World of Berossos* (CleO 5; Wiesbaden: Harrassowitz, 2013).

109 Geert De Breucker, *De Babyloniaca van Berossos van Babylon: Inleiding, editie en commentaar* (Ph.D. diss., Groningen University, 2012; http://irs.ub.rug.nl/ppn/352625899), 421–569; Giovanni B. Lanfranchi, 'Babyloniaca, Book 3: Assyrians, Babylonians and Persians', in *The World of Berossos* (ed. J. Haubold, G. Lanfranchi, R. Rollinger and J. M. Steele; CleO 5; Wiesbaden: Harrassowitz, 2013), 61–74.

110 With the exception of the Anahita episode, see below.

111 F10b; translation by Gerald P. Verbrugghe and John M. Wickersham, *Berossos and Manetho, Introduced and Translated: Native Traditions in Ancient Mesopotamia and Egypt* (Ann Arbor: The University of Michigan Press, 1996), 61.

112 Kuhrt, *The Persian Empire*, 566–7.

With this last question in mind, let us return to the *Dynastic Prophecy*. As preserved, the text presents a selective discussion of the Persian period, focused on its very beginning (Cyrus) and very end (Arses and Darius III). In the *Babyloniaca*, coverage of the post-Cyrus period is equally shallow; apart from a general chronographic outline, the transmitted version of the text offers concrete detail only for one solitary episode in the reign of Artaxerxes II. In brief: as preserved, both texts share an interest in Cyrus and display a better understanding of the last phase of the Persian Empire than of the intermittent period – but as substantial parts of both texts may be missing, the validity of these observations is questionable.

We may gain a new angle on this issue by consulting the wider cultural context in which the *Dynastic Prophecy* and the *Babyloniaca* were produced. Although their exact dates are not known, both texts may with reasonable certainty be assigned to the early part of the third century B.C.E.[113] Their authors did not only inhabit the same time but also the same space: the Esagil temple of Babylon. This is the place where Berossos worked as a priest, and it is also the place where the copy of the *Dynastic Prophecy* was found.[114] As shown by R. J. van der Spek and others, there are many points of similarity between the two texts and it is highly likely that Berossos and the authors of the *Prophecy* were familiar with each other's writings.[115] Other literary texts were found in the archive of the Esagil temple, and these allow us to gain an insight in the ideas that circulated in the cultural world of Berossos and his colleagues.

113 For the date of composition of the *Babyloniaca*, see Geert De Breucker, 'Berossos: His Life and His Work', in *The World of Berossos* (ed. J. Haubold, G. Lanfranchi, R. Rollinger and J. M. Steele; CleO 5; Wiesbaden: Harrassowitz, 2013), 15–28. Johannes Bach, 'Berossos, Antiochos und die Babyloniaca', *Ancient West & East* 12 (2013): 157–80 proposes a slightly later date. For the date of the *Dynastic Prophecy*, see the works cited in n. 103 above. These all concur on a date in the early Hellenistic period, except for Shayegan, *Arsacids and Sasanians*, 137–40 who suggests a much later date in the Arsacid period.

114 Berossos' social and intellectual location in the Esagil temple of Babylon has been discussed by R. J. van der Spek, 'Berossus as a Babylonian Chronicler and Greek Historian', in *Studies in Ancient Near Eastern World View and Society Presented to Marten Stol on the Occasion of his 65th Birthday* (ed. R. J. van der Spek; Bethesda: CDL, 2007), 277–318; Paul-Alain Beaulieu, 'Berossus on Late Babylonian Historiography', in *Special Issue of Oriental Studies: A Collection of Papers on Ancient Civilizations of Western Asia, Asia Minor and North Africa* (ed. Y. Gong and Y. Chen; Beijing, 2007), 116–49; Geert De Breucker, 'Berossos Between Tradition and Innovation', in *The Oxford Handbook of Cuneiform Culture* (ed. K. Radner and E. Robson; Oxford: Oxford University Press, 2011), 637–57; De Breucker, *De Babyloniaca van Berossos*.

115 van der Spek, 'Berossus as a Babylonian Chronicler'; Beaulieu, 'Berossus on Late Babylonian Historiography'; De Breucker, *De Babyloniaca van Berossos*, 86.

7 Historical Literature in Babylon and Uruk in the Late First Millennium B.C.E.

The Esagil temple boasted a history of about 1,500 years at the time when Berossos and his peers conducted their research in its library. The origins of this library, although of a respectable age, did not reach as far back in time as the temple's first foundations. It is generally assumed that the Esagil library (that is, the one consulted by Berossos and his peers, and excavated in the 19th century CE) enjoyed an active lifespan of three to four centuries from the reign of Artaxerxes II to circa 60 B.C.E.[116] During this time its collections grew organically as a result of the activity of scholars like Berossos who consulted its holdings and added new works to it. The collections grew at their quickest pace in the second century B.C.E.[117] Some older texts (pre-400 B.C.E.) were available, but these had been transferred from an earlier collection and as such they are not indicative of the library's active lifespan.[118]

The library's shelves were mostly stacked with technical texts produced by astronomers, diviners, exorcists, and cultic and medical experts. Transposing today's fashionable language to the ancient world, the Esagil temple may be characterized as an institution that fostered 'excellence in science': its members did not only maintain and preserve received scholarship, they also engaged in original research and achieved great advances doing so. A number of cultural and social conditions stimulated their creativity, such as a fixed income, standards of training and career development, professional associations, etc.[119] Within

---

116 For the lifespan of the library, see Francis Joannès, 'De Babylone à Sumer: le parcours intellectuel des lettrés de la Babylonie récente', *Revue Historique* 302 (2000): 693–717 (703). The library received detailed study by Philippe Clancier, *Les bibliothèques en Babylonie dans la deuxième moitié du Ier millénaire av. J.-C.* (AOAT 363; Münster: Ugarit-Verlag, 2009).

117 Clancier, *Les bibliothèques*.

118 The key barometer that is used to test the vitality of the library is the corpus of *Astronomical Diaries*. These texts only began to be composed with notable regularity in the reign of Artaxerxes II (Abraham Sachs and Hermann Hunger, *Astronomical Diaries and Related Texts from Babylonia, Vol. I: Diaries from 652 B. C. to 262 B. C.* [Vienna: Österreichische Akademie der Wissenschaften, 1988]). Less than a handful of older exemplars are preserved in the library; these indicate, on the one hand, that the 'new' activity was in fact a continuation of older practice, but on the other hand, that there was a break in the archival practice underlying this corpus.

119 Francesca Rochberg, *The Heavenly Writing: Divination, Horoscopy, and Astronomy in Mesopotamian Culture* (Cambridge: Cambridge University Press, 2004); Paul-Alain Beaulieu, 'The Astronomers of the Esagil Temple in the Fourth Century BC', in *If A Man Builds A Joyful House: Assyriological Studies in Honor of Erle Verdun Leichty* (ed. A. K. Guinan, M. deJong Ellis, A. J. Ferrara, S. A. Freedman, M. T. Rutz, L. Sassmanshausen, S. Tinney and M. W. Waters; CM 31; Leiden:

this environment the Esagil's scholarly community achieved an unprecedented leap forward in mathematical astronomy, optimized existing fields of study and invented new ones.[120] Compared to these innovations in science, the fixity and marginality of literature has troubled Assyriologists. The Esagil library contains remarkably few items of classical literature, the *Gilgamesh Epic* and the *Enūma Eliš* being among the few exceptions. Did literary creativity not thrive in this world of scientific excellence?

It has been overlooked that one type of literary activity did florish beyond earlier achievements. This activity consisted of 'historical writings', i.e. texts about historical events.[121] The subject of this literature was the nature of regal governance, a topic that was explored by reference to examples from Babylonia's past. Because none of these texts can be dated exactly, we do not know precisely how this literature emerged and developed. It is particularly unclear whether all or some of these compositions were new creations (made between c. 400–60 B.C.E.) or copies of older (now lost) originals. The presence of these texts in the Esagil library is by itself proof of their relevance and actuality to the library's users, so even if they were not written at the time, they still tell us something about the interests and concerns of their readership. Nevertheless, I consider the first scenario more likely, and below I will offer some arguments in its support.

Compared to the massive corpus of practical texts kept at the Esagil temple, the number of historical writings is admittedly modest, but judged within the parameters of this particular genre the labels 'creative' and 'productive' certainly apply. The production of historical royal narratives was an activity driven by curi-

Brill, 2006), 5–22; Paul-Alain Beaulieu, 'De l'Esagil au Mouseion: l'organisation de la recherche scientifique au IVe siècle avant J.-C.', in *La Transition entre l'empire achéménide et les royaumes hellénistiques* (ed. P. Briant and F. Joannès; Persika 9; Paris: de Boccard, 2006), 17–36.

120 Francesca Rochberg, *Babylonian Horoscopes* (TAPS 88; Philadelphia: American Philosophical Society, 1998); David Brown, *Mesopotamian Planetary Astronomy-Astrology* (CM 18; Groningen: Styx, 2000); Eleanor Robson, *Mathematics in Ancient Iraq: A Social History* (Princeton: Princeton University Press, 2008), 214–62; Mathieu Ossendrijver, *Babylonian Mathematical Astronomy: Procedure Texts* (New York: Springer, 2012).

121 My remarks here are preliminary. Only individual compositions and certain subgroups have been described so far (cf. Benjamin R. Foster, *Akkadian Literature of the Late Period* [GMTR 2; Münster: Ugarit-Verlag, 2008), e.g. fictional royal letters of the late period (Eckart Frahm, 'On Some Recently Published Late Babylonian Copies of Royal Letters', *NABU* 2005/43), chronicles and related literature (cf. Grayson, *Babylonian Historical-Literary Texts*, van der Spek, 'Berossos as a Babylonian Chronicler' and De Breucker, *De Babyloniaca van Berossos*). In the next pages I will argue that epics, letters, (fake) royal inscriptions, and (post-factum) chronicles were all part of a single corpus of historical literature, consulted and created at the Esagil temple of Babylon and connected to similar efforts in other centers of Babylonian learning.

osity and the will to know, as it combined original research of primary sources, archives and sites with received historiographic traditions and ideologies.[122] It used established genres in an experimental way, recasting narratives in various formats for the sake of effect.[123] It was part of an active research field, characterized by emergent conventions of subject matter, and responsive to events and interests in the contemporary world.[124] And it was part of a larger development, affecting not just the home community at the Esagil temple, but also centres of learning in other Babylonian cities, notably Uruk.

I will discuss these features at various points below, but the last observation merits our attention first. Like the library of the Esagil temple, the priestly archives discovered at Uruk (and roughly from the same period) predominantly consist of practical and professional literature, with only a sprinkling of literary works.[125] Within this last category, historical writings are rare, but they share with the material from the Esagil library their subject matter and general orientation (the examination of proper/improper kingship through historical examples). Nevertheless, in their details these local traditions differed. In Babylon, historical texts were mostly concerned with the drama and trauma of Babylonian kingship as it confronted the larger world. The stories are about conquest, defeat, liberation, revenge, diplomacy, rebellion and dynastic change. In Uruk, the outlook was much more provincial. Here, the primary concern was with the king as an actor within the local community: his role as protector of ritual propriety and cultic continuity, his obligation to respect established rights of citizens and priests, his duty to maintain and deliver justice, and his task to extend and preserve the material prosperity of temple, town and countryside.[126] Both traditions share an

122 Cf. van der Spek, 'Berossus as a Babylonian Chronicler'; Beaulieu, 'Berossus on Late Babylonian Historiography'; De Breucker, *De Babyloniaca van Berossos.*

123 We will encounter a number of examples below.

124 The emergence of conventions of subject matter is explored below; reactions to contemporary events, a. o. Frahm, 'On Some Recently Published Late Babylonian Copies of Royal Letters'; Foster, *Before the Muses*, 369; Beaulieu, 'Berossus', 125–126, 132; Paul-Alain Beaulieu, 'The Historical Background of the Uruk Prophecy', in *The Tablet and the Scroll: Near Eastern Studies in Honor of William W. Hallo* (ed. M. E. Cohen, D. C. Snell and D. B. Weisberg; Bethesda: CDL, 1993), 41–52; Antoine Cavigneaux, 'Shulgi, Nabonide, et les Grecs', in *An Experienced Scribe Who Neglects Nothing: Ancient Near Eastern Studies in Honor of Jacob Klein* (ed. Y. Sefati, P. Artzi, Ch. Cohen, B. L. Eichler and V. Hurowitz; Bethesda: CDL, 2005), 63–72 (these last two titles are about texts from Uruk).

125 Clancier, *Les Bibliothèques*, 400–409.

126 *The Sacrileges of Nabû-šuma-iškun* (Steven W. Cole, 'The Crimes and Sacrileges of Nabû-šuma-iškun', *ZA* 84 [1998]: 220–52), the *Uruk Prophecy* (Beaulieu, 'The Historical Background') and the *Shulgi Chronicle* (Cavigneaux, 'Shulgi, Nabonide, et les Grecs').

outspoken preference for pre-539 B.C.E. kings as resources to explore their respective issues: in Uruk, no Persian era subjects are attested, in Babylon only three texts (the *Dynastic Prophecy*, the *Babyloniaca*, and the *Nabonidus Chronicle*) treat Persian reigns. The larger scope of the writings from the Esagil temple renders these texts more suitable for the purpose of the present article than the materials from Uruk, and I will therefore focus the remainder of my discussion on the former.

Historians at the Esagil were above all interested in the dynastic struggles that punctuated the history of Babylonian kingship. This theme is approached in two broadly different ways. On the one hand there are texts that espouse a bird's eye view on the matter: they discuss the long succession of dynasties that ruled over Babylonia, in enumerative lists or in richer narratives. The *Dynastic Prophecy*, books 2 and 3 of the *Babyloniaca*, the *Babylonian King List A* and the *Babylonian King List B* all belong in this category.[127] On the other hand there are texts that espouse a 'microscopic' view on the matter: they focus on one particular episode of transition and comment in detail on the actions of the kings involved. As we will see, this usually involved singling out a pair of kings who were constructed as each other's ideological opposites (oppressor/liberator, foreign/Babylonian, unlawful/legitimate) and who had in fact been opponents in history. Neither of these approaches is in itself innovative; in the first category, one may think of the 21st-17th century B.C.E. *Chronicle of the Single Monarchy*, better known as the *Sumerian King List*, and in the second, of the Old-Babylonian composition *Naram-Sin and the Lord of Apišal* among many other examples.[128] What is new is the weaving together of a complex historical subject matter in a variety of texts, genres and plots, all concerned with the ideology of kingship in its various concrete manifestations in history. Particularly noteworthy is that this literature selected from Babylonia's long regal history a new cast of figures to serve as protagonists of its narratives. Sargon and Naram-Sin, though certainly not forgotten by the learned community of the Esagil temple, did not serve as active and productive *exempla* in their writings, as they had done before.[129] Neither do we

127 For the *Babylonian King List A* and *B*, see Grayson, 'Assyrian and Babylonian King Lists', 106–09 (Plate I and II); Grayson, 'Königslisten und Chroniken', 90–96, 100.

128 For the former, see Jean-Jacques Glassner, *Mesopotamian Chronicles* (SBLWAW 19; Atlanta: Society of Biblical Literature, 2004), 117–26; for the latter, see Joan Goodnick Westenholz, *Legends of the Kings of Akkade: The Texts* (Mesopotamian Civilizations 7; Winona Lake: Eisenbrauns, 1997), text 12.

129 For these royal figures in earlier historiography, see Marc van de Mieroop, *Cuneiform Texts and the Writing of History* (New York: Routledge, 1999), 59–75; Marc Van De Mieroop, 'Literature and Political Discourse in Ancient Mesopotamia: Sargon II of Assyria and Sargon of Agade', in

find stories about Hammurabi, Samsu-iluna, Shulgi, or Kurigalzu – all significant figures in historical literature represented in the earlier, Neo-Babylonian Ebabbar library.[130] The development of a new cast of protagonists is one of the most striking innovative features of late Babylonian historical writing.

A popular royal figure in this history was Nabopolassar, the king who liberated Babylonia from the Assyrians in the seventh century B.C.E. As 'avenger of Akkad', his life served as a model for reflecting on the nature of foreign domination, the hope of retaliation, the belief in dynastic independence, and the role of Marduk as mover of history. The language of vengeance and divine providence was inspired on original inscriptions of Nabopolassar and Nabonidus, to which scholars of the Esagil temple probably had access.[131] Original texts from the Neo-Babylonian period were still present in Babylon's cityscape: they were displayed, for instance, on architectural parts of temples and palaces, and buried (and hence rediscoverable) in their foundations.[132] Chronicles about the reign of Nabopolassar may also have been available. A large multi-tablet chronicle covering the period from Nabû-nāṣir to after Šamaš-šuma-ukīn (and almost certainly including the reign of Nabopolassar) circulated in Babylon at the time of Darius I and copies may have been around in the fourth century and beyond, even if

Munuscula Mesopotamica: Festschrift für Johannes Renger (ed. B. Böck, E. Ch. Cancik-Kirschbaum and T. Richter; AOAT 267; Münster: Ugarit-Verlag, 1999), 327–39; Seth Richardson, 'The First "World Event": Sennacherib at Jerusalem', in *Sennacherib at the Gates of Jerusalem: Story, History, and Historiography* (ed. I. Kalimi and S. Richardson; CHANE 71; Leiden: Brill, 2014), 433–505 (488).

130 Cf. *Letter of Samsu-iluna* (Farouk N. H. al-Rawi and Andrew R. George, 'Tablets from the Sippar Library III: Two Royal Counterfeits', *Iraq* 56 [1994]: 135–48; Beaulieu, 'Nabonidus the Mad King', 142–3); *Weidner Chronicle* (Farouk N. H. al-Rawi, 'Tablets from the Sippar Library I. The "Weidner Chronicle": A Suppositious Royal Letter Concerning a Vision', *Iraq* 52 [1990]: 1–13); *Letter of Kurigalzu* (David J. Wiseman, 'A Late Babylonian Tribute List?', *BSOAS* 30 [1967]: 495–504; al-Rawi and George, 'Tablets from the Sippar Library III', 135 n.2); copy of the prologue of the *Codex of Hammurabi* (Abdulillah Fadhil, 'Der Prolog des Codex Hammurapi in einer Abschrift aus Sippar', in *XXXIVème Rencontre Assyriologique Internationale* [ed. H. Erkanal, V. Donbaz, and A. Uğuroğlu; Ankara: Türk Tarih Kurumu, 1998], 717–29).

131 For the theme of vengeange in Nabopolassar's inscriptions and its application in the *Declaration of War*, see Da Riva, *The Inscriptions of Nabopolassar*, 6. The *Declaration of War*'s dependance on the *Basalt Stele of Nabonidus* has been discussed by Pamela Gerardi, 'Declaring War in Ancient Mesopotamia', *AfO* 33 (1986): 30–38. Berossos used original inscriptions of Nebuchadnezzar in his account of the palace of Babylon: van der Spek, 'Berossus as a Babylonian Chronicler', 296–300; Beaulieu, 'Berossus', 121–6, and Ronald H. Sack, *Images of Nebuchadnezzar: The Emergence of a Legend* (Selinsgrove: Susquehanna University Press, 1991), 25.

132 Cf. Beaulieu, 'Berossus', 121.

these have not been discovered so far.[133] These various materials – some original, others borrowed from historiographic traditions – were reworked into a variety of literary compositions at the Esagil between c. 400 and 60 B.C.E. Four texts bear witness to this creative activity: the *Letter of Sin-šarra-iškun to Nabopolassar*, the so-called *Declaration of War*, the *Nabopolassar Epic*, and a fragmentary text of unknown genre.[134] It has been suggested that some or all of these texts are copies of earlier originals (composed at the time of Nabopolassar or shortly thereafter), but this seems unlikely.[135] The texts were produced in a cultural world that was aware, not only of the relative power of the Babylonian king, but of the possibility of world domination.[136] Moreover, the stories about Nabopolassar are one strand in a wider discursive framework that also included stories about other kings whose reigns marked transitional moments in the history of Babylonian kingship.

One of these other characters is Nebuchadnezzar I, a Babylonian king who achieved victory over invading Elamites in the late 12th century B.C.E. and who had been a popular subject of historical literature at least since the Neo-Assyrian period.[137] The 'invasion-liberation' plotline underlying his reign offered an occasion for Esagil's scholars to explore issues of foreign domination, self-rule and providence. The *Elamite Attack on Nippur* describes Kudur-nahhunte's destruction of Nippur, Babylon, Borsippa and Uruk as an episode of absolute terror,

133 ABC 1.

134 For the *Letter of Sîn-šarra-iškun to Nabopolassar*, see Ira Spar and Wilfred Lambert, *Literary and Scholastic Texts of the First Millennium* (CTMMA 2; New York: Metropolitan Museum of Art, 2005) no. 44; Frahm, 'On Some Recently Published Late Babylonian Copies of Royal Letters'. For the *Declaration of War*, see Gerardi, 'Declaration'; Da Riva, *The Inscriptions of Nabopolassar*, 6. For the *Nabopolassar Epic*, see Grayson, *Babylonian Historical-Literary Texts*, 78–86; Hayim Tadmor, 'Nabopolassar and Sîn-šum-līšir in a Literary Perspective', in *Festschrift für Rykle Borger zu seinem 65. Geburtstag am 24. Mai 1994* (ed. S. M. Maul; CM 10; Groningen: Styx, 1998), 353–57. Note that Berossos' *Babyloniaca* and the *Dynastic Prophecy* also include sections about Nabopolassar and his adversary Sîn-šarra-iškun.

135 Spar and Lambert, *Literary and Scholastic Texts*, 203–07.

136 Nabopolassar's claim that he was selected by Marduk to serve as lord of all the lands (Da Riva, *The Inscriptions of Nabopolassar*, 6) recalls the justification and scope of Cyrus' rule in the *Cyrus Cylinder*: 11–12, where Marduk is said to have 'inspected and checked all the countries, seeking for the upright king of his choice' (Finkel, 'The Cyrus Cylinder', 5). In Nabopolassar's original inscriptions, the scope of his dominion seems to have been limited to 'the land and the people' (cf. Da Riva, *The Inscriptions of Nabopolassar*, 6), i.e. Akkad.

137 Cf. Richardson, 'Sennacherib', 488–89. For the historical literature about Nebuchadnezzar I in the earlier first millennium BC, see Wilfred G. Lambert, 'Enmeduranki and Related Matters', *JCS* 21 (1967): 126–38 (*Seed of Wisdom*); Foster, *Before the Muses*, 381–3 and Frame, *Rulers of Babylonia*, 19–21 (*War with Elam*); Foster, *Before the Muses*, 385 (*Nebuchadnezzar and Marduk*).

while *Marduk and the Elamites* explains how Marduk helped to overturn this threat.[138] The *Correspondence of Kudur-nahhunte and the Babylonians* and the *Letter of an Elamite King* deal with conflicting claims to the throne of Babylon based on maternal descent (by the Elamite king) and indigeneity (requested by the Babylonians).[139] Here the opinion that foreign rule equates illegitimate rule is voiced straightforwardly.[140] Nebuchadnezzar's nativity in Babylon is also picked up in the *Letter of Nebuchadnezzar to the Babylonians*.[141] Most of these compositions were kept at, and presumably written in, the library of the Esagil in the late Achaemenid, Hellenistic or early Parthian periods.[142] A fragmentary text about an Elamo-Babylonian conflict in the late Kassite period, eventually resolved by the elimination of the Elamite threat, tells about a comparable episode.[143]

The pairing of two rivals – the one an unwanted and foreign oppressor, the other a liberator-king of Babylon – was a common narrative strategy in this historical literature. We already encountered it with the Assyrian Sîn-šarra-iškun and Nabopolassar, and with the Elamite Kudur-nahhunte and Nebuchadnezzar I. A similar pair was Tukulti-Ninurta I and Adad-šuma-uṣur (late 13th century BC). Tukulti-Ninurta I was the first Assyrian king to capture the throne of Babylon and to combine the kingship of Babylon with his existing office. *Chronicle P* describes his reign as an episode of particular wickedness, involving the destruction of Babylon, an attack on its citizens, the confiscation of sacred property, and the kidnapping of Marduk's statue.[144] The situation was resolved by Adad-šuma-uṣur with the aid of the leaders of Akkad. As with the literature about Nabopolassar,

---

138 W. G. Lambert, 'The Fall of the Cassite Dynasty to the Elamites: An Historical Epic', in *Cinquante-deux Réflexions sur le Proche-Orient ancien offertes en hommage à Léon De Meyer* (ed. H. Gasche; Mesopotamian History and Environment Occasional Publications 2; Leuven: Peeters, 1994), 67–72; Foster, *Before the Muses*, 371–4, 374–5.

139 *Correspondence of Kudur-nahhunte and the Babylonians*: Foster, *Before the Muses*, 370–1; W. G. Lambert, 'The Enigma of Tukulti-Ninurta I', in *From the Upper Sea to the Lower Sea: Studies on the History of Assyria and Babylonia in Honour of A. K. Grayson* (ed. G. Frame; Leiden: Nederlands Instituut voor het Nabije Oosten, 2004), 197–202 (200–2). *Letter of an Elamite King* (VS 24 91): Jan van Dijk, 'Die dynastischen Heiraten zwischen Kassiten und Elamern: eine verhängnisvolle Politik', *Or* 55 (1986): 159–70.

140 Lambert, 'Tukulti-Ninurta I', 200.

141 VS 24 87 (van Dijk, 'Die dynastischen Heiraten', 170; Foster, *Before the Muses*, 386–87 with references).

142 Note however that it is unclear how the texts from Berlin (VS 24 87 and 91) connect to the Esagil library.

143 Grayson, *Babylonian Historal-Literary Texts*, 47–55.

144 Grayson, *Assyrian and Babylonian Chronicles*, 175–76; Pongratz-Leisten, 'Sündenbekenntnis', 86–87.

the date of composition of *Chronicle P* is debatable.[145] The text is known from a single manuscript preserved in a museum collection that also contains material from the Esagil library, so it is likely (but not certain) that it was part of the library's holdings. The text uses original historical details and terminology, but the accusations against Tukulti-Ninurta I are of such generic nature that they may easily have been crafted from ideology rather than from historical reality.[146] Literary texts are among the chronicle's sources, and its arrangement of certain historical materials betrays a rationalizing effort to group periods of foreign domination in Babylonia (Assyrian, then Elamite).[147] It is therefore very well possible (but not proven beyond doubt) that *Chronicle P* was a new creation by the Esagil's scholarly community. In any event, the figure of Tukulti-Ninurta I was part of a larger narrative fabric that was, if not actually being created at the Esagil, at least in active use there. This fabric includes a literary 'epic' about the trials of his adversary and victor, Adad-šuma-uṣur. Like *Chronicle P*, the *Epic of Adad-šuma-uṣur* is only known from a single manuscript held at the Esagil temple of Babylon, so similar problems of dating apply.[148] Whereas *Chronicle P* focuses on the terror of Tukulti-Ninurta I's reign, the *Epic* tells a moralizing tale about Adad-šuma-uṣur, casting him first in the role of sinner against Marduk, and then, after an episode of isolation and penitence, as an enthusiastic supporter of his cult. Because this 'conversion' theme is more widely found in late Babylonian regal literature – for instance in the *Epic of Amēl-Marduk*, the *Lament of Nabû-šuma-ukīn*, the *Shulgi Chronicle* from Uruk, and outside of the Babylonian cultural realm, in the Jewish *Prayer of Nabonidus* – we may speculate that the *Epic of Adad-šuma-uṣur* was a late creation as well.[149]

The next pair of kings who feature in the Esagil's historical literature are Nabonidus and Cyrus. In contrast to Tukulti-Ninurta I / Adad-šuma-uṣur, Kudurnahhunte / Nebuchadnezzar I, and Sîn-šarra-iškun / Nabopolassar the evalua-

---

145 Grayson, *Assyrian and Babylonian Chronicles*, 56.

146 Cf. John A. Brinkman, *A Catalogue of Cuneiform Sources Pertaining to Specific Monarchs of the Kassite Dynasty* (Materials and Studies for Kassite History 1; Chicago: The Oriental Institute of the University of Chicago, 1976), 18–19; Pongratz-Leisten, 'Sündenbekenntnis'.

147 Grayson, *Assyrian and Babylonian Chronicles*, 57; Brinkman, *Materials*, 19.

148 Grayson, *Babylonian Historical-Literary Texts*, 56–77.

149 *Epic of Amēl-Marduk*: Grayson, *Babylonian Historical-Literary Texts*, 87–92; Schaudig, *Die Inschriften*, 589–90. *Lament of Nabû-šuma-ukīn*: Irving Finkel, 'The Lament of Nabû-šumu-ukīn', in *Babylon: Focus mesopotamischer Geschichte, Wiege früher Gelehrsamkeit, Mythos in der Moderne* (ed. J. Renger; Saarbrücken: SDV, 1999), 323–41. *Shulgi Chronicle*: Cavigneaux, 'Shulgi, Nabonide, et les Grecs'. *Prayer of Nabonidus*: Reinhard G. Kratz, 'Nabonid in Qumran', in *Babylon: Wissenskultur in Orient und Okzident* (ed. E. Cancik-Kirschbaum, M. van Ess and J. Marzahn; Topoi 1; Berlin: de Gruyter, 2011), 253–70.

tion of their reigns is ambiguous. In the other examples, the oppressive reign of a foreign king is followed by an act of liberation by a Babylonian king with the help of Marduk. In the case of Nabonidus and Cyrus this qualification did not apply unless modified. Texts composed soon after Cyrus' victory cast Nabonidus in the role of oppressor while hailing Cyrus as liberator helped by Marduk (the *Cyrus Cylinder*, the *Verse Account*), but they do not paint over Cyrus' foreign origin; on the contrary, the *Cyrus Cylinder* draws attention to this fact in several ways (e.g. by mentioning his Anšanite roots and genealogy; by locating Marduk's search for Cyrus in all the lands). Literary texts from the Esagil library (considerably later in date) are not unanimous about the wicked nature of Nabonidus' reign. In the *Dynastic Prophecy*, Nabonidus is criticized as a 'rebel prince' and the founder of the 'dynasty of Harran'.[150] Was this an attempt to fit his reign into the expected model by casting him in the role of evil outsider? Perhaps, but things were certainly more complicated than that: Cyrus – who should play the role of native liberator in this scheme – was positioned outside Babylonia as 'King of Elam' and his rule was evaluated in the same terms as that of Nabonidus, both being 'stronger than the land'.[151] It would seem that the *Dynastic Prophecy* remains undecided, uninterested, or deliberately ambiguous about the relative quality of these reigns. What is important, however, is that not all literature about Nabonidus and Cyrus produced in the late period shares this ambivalence. A fragmentary composition about Nabonidus praises his rule and rehabilitates him as a pious supporter of the state cult of Marduk and Nabû, in what can only be interpreted as an explicit criticism of the polemics waged against him in the *Cyrus Cylinder* and the *Verse Account*.[152] The *Royal Chronicle*, also known as the *Nabonidus Epic*, also offers a positive evaluation of his reign.[153] A completely different, utterly negative opinion about Nabonidus is found in the *Verse Account*, a copy of which was perhaps kept

150 *Dynastic Prophecy* II: 11–12.

151 *Dynastic Prophecy* II: 22–24; for the interpretation of these lines, see Kuhrt, *Persian Empire*, 81 with literature; most recently R. J. van der Spek, 'Cyrus the Great, Exiles, and Foreign Gods', restated his opinion that the *Prophecy* judged Cyrus' reign positively (251).

152 Schaudig, *Die Inschriften*, 474–75 (text 2.20). The text is fragmentary and resembles a royal inscription.

153 W. G. Lambert, 'A New Source for the Reign of Nabonidus', *AfO* 22 (1969): 1–8; Peter Machinist and Hayim Tadmor, 'Heavenly Wisdom', in *The Tablet and the Scroll: Near Eastern Studies in Honor of William W. Hallo* (ed. M. E. Cohen, D. C. Snell and D. B. Weisberg; Bethesda: CDL, 1993), 146–151; Schaudig, *Die Inschriften*, 590–95 (new edition); Peter Machinist, 'Mesopotamian Imperialism and Israelite Religion: A Case Study from the Second Isaiah', in *Symbiosis, Symbolism and the Power of the Past: Canaan, Ancient Israel, and Their Neighbors from the Late Bronze Age through Roman Palaestina* (ed. W. G. Dever and S. Gitin; Winona Lake: Eisenbrauns, 2003), 237–64 (248–9).

in the Esagil library.[154] What we see emerge here, then, are the traces of a historical 'debate': different opinions on the same events were put forward in different narrative formats. It is impossible to reconstruct the interplay between these texts, but it seems likely that they react, or answer, to each other. One text that, in my opinion, also features in this dialogue is the *Nabonidus Chronicle*. Modern historians usually take the *Nabonidus Chronicle* at face value, as a product of contemporary chronicle writing and a 'reliable document' about the conquest of Babylon.[155] However, the text is known from a single manuscript held in the Esagil temple and, in keeping with my observations about the embedded nature of the Nabopolassar stories in the historical literature of the Esagil, I suggest that the *Nabonidus Chronicle* too fits within a larger group of texts about Nabonidus and Cyrus. The fact that we are dealing with a chronicle does not necessarily mean that it was written at the time of the events reported therein. Molding historical matter into narratives of a variety of genres, including that of the chronicle, is one of the key features of the historical literature found at the Esagil.[156] Moreover, the text's concern with Nabonidus' persistent absence from the New Year festival and its overall sparse coverage of his reign are features that contrast sharply with the rich commentary it delivers on the celebration of the festival by Cambyses (and Cyrus?) in 538 B.C.E. This suggests that the *Chronicle*'s contents are the result of a careful process of redaction and not the outcome of 'objective' observation of the events. The author(s)'s ultimate verdict on either reign is unclear in the *Chronicle*. The Elamite dress episode at the New Year festival of 538 may be a covert criticism of Persian imperialism. The absence of Nabonidus and his failure to celebrate the New Year Festival may be equally critical of that king's reign. In its ambiguity, the *Nabonidus Chronicle* resembles the *Dynastic Prophecy*, where we noticed a similar lack of distinction in the evaluation of these two reigns. Ambivalence thus may have been an intended effect of both texts, quite contrary to the explicit judgements found in the *Royal Chronicle*, the literary fragment about Nabonidus, and the *Verse Account*.

There is much more to be said about the historical literature of the Esagil library, but the general remarks outlined so far suffice for my present purposes. One point worth emphasizing before moving on, however, is that not *all* works

154 Text: Schaudig, *Die Inschriften*, 563–78; for the late date of the copy, see Beaulieu, 'Nabonidus the Mad King', 137. The consensus is that our present manuscript is a late copy of a much earlier original, drafted not long after the fall of Babylon, see e.g. Machinist and Tadmor, 'Heavenly Wisdom', Schaudig, *Die Inschriften*, 563. Our present manuscript is located in the 80-11-12 collection of the British museum, which holds some material from the libraries associated to Esagil.
155 See note 92 above.
156 See my discussion of *Chronicle P* above.

in this literature focused on transitional moments of Babylonia's dynastic past. Kings located within dynastic lines were also studied and the evaluation of their reigns did not necessarily depend on dynastic affiliation. For instance, in the Neo-Babylonian dynasty of Nabopolassar, his son Nebuchadnezzar II is an (perhaps, the) example of a good king, whereas his grandson Amēl-Marduk received mixed judgement as a sinner who eventually repents.[157] Assurbanipal was a beloved figure as patron of the scribal arts, despite being an Assyrian; in the same literary tradition his predecessor Sîn-šarru-iškun is paired with Nabopolassar, the 'Avenger of Akkad', as we have seen.[158] The Elamites of the 13th and 12th centuries B.C.E., however, were unanimously cast as enemies of Akkad, without nuance.

8 Practical Constraints

Let us now return to the *Dynastic Prophecy* and the *Babyloniaca*. Their long narrative histories of Babylonian kingship, bracketing the Persian period, are exceptional when placed within their cultural context. The question how much detail these texts offered of the Persian period remains unanswered. In their present state of preservation, their content is well in keeping with the general picture: Cyrus was a subject of historical debate, not his successors. How faithfully this reflects the original state of these texts, is of course speculative, but the point I want to make here is that neither of these texts provides evidence of a sustained interest in the Persian period. This may have been due to practical reasons, rather than ideological ones. Information about late Achaemenid reigns was available in the products of chronicle writing, a practice that blossomed at the Esagil alongside historiogrpahy.[159] In keeping with the library's active lifespan, it is in the reign of Artaxerxes II that we first find regular evidence of chronicle writing, at first in the context of the *Astronomical Diaries* and then also as

---

157 *Epic of Amēl-Marduk*: Grayson, *Babylonian Historical-Literary Texts*, 87–92; note that Finkel, 'Lament', 336–37 and Schaudig, *Die Inschriften*, 589–90 interpret the tribulations of Amēl-Marduk differently. The *Lament of Nabû-šuma-ukīn* also deals with Amēl-Marduk according to Irving Finkel, 'The Lament'; it is a tablet from the Esagil library and is preserved in the same collection as the *Dynastic Prophecy*. Berossos delivers a negative verdict on Amēl-Marduk; De Breucker, *De Babyloniaca van Berossos*, 541–44.

158 BM 45642; Grant Frame and Andrew R. George, 'The Royal Libraries of Nineveh: New Evidence for King Ashurbanipal's Tablet Collection', *Iraq* 67 (2005): 265–84.

159 For the practice of contemporary chronicle writing (about on-going rather than past events), see R. Pirngruber, 'The Historical Sections of the Astronomical Diaries in Context: Developments in a Late Babylonian Scientific Text Corpus,' *Iraq* 75 (2013): 197–210.

an independent genre. Material about earlier Persian reigns was probably hard to come by. The Neo-Babylonian chronicles had been buried in Borsippa since at least 484 B.C.E., if not several decades earlier.[160] Copies may have circulated but this is unproven. The *Babylonian Chronicle*, which at one point was available and redacted in Babylon, did not stretch beyond the early reign of Darius (c. 500 B.C.E.).[161] Primary texts (royal inscriptions such as cylinders, prisms, inscribed architectural parts, steles), which were eagerly studied by Berossos and his peers for earlier swaths of history, were not available for the majority of Persian kings, as explained above. These factors combined must have made it virtually impossible for historians in the Hellenistic period to write a continous, narrative history of the Persian period. Eusebius' kinglist-like summary of the early Persian period and the laconic treatment of the early Persian period in the *Uruk King List* might suggest that they did, in fact, not write a fuller prose history.

9 The Persian Period in Retrospect

The preceeding pages introduced a rich cast of kings of Babylon who feature as subjects in the Esagil's historical texts. This cast consisted of kings from the Kassite, early Neo-Babylonian and Neo-Babylonian periods, contrapointed by characters who threatened or destroyed Babylon's autonomy from abroad. Some of these figures had been productive subjects in earlier historiographic traditions, in particular Nebuchadnezzar I in stories about his defeat of the Elamites; other figures were newcomers to the genre, like Nabopolassar who had featured in chronicles before but who now became a subject of historical enquiry. The introduction of new characters shows the vivacity and relevance of the royal past to a particular contemporary audience. I have situated that audience in 'late' Babylon, in the literate community of scholars and priests associated with the Esagil library. The active lifespan of that library is c. 400–60 B.C.E., which means that these stories may have developed at any point between the Persian Empire's last decades and the Parthian period.

When quizzed about their experience of Persian rule, these texts are, on the surface, mute. The Persian kings were marginal characters in this literature. The only exceptions are Cyrus in the *Dynastic Prophecy*, the *Babyloniaca*, and

160 Caroline Waerzeggers, 'The Babylonian Chronicles: Classification and Provenance', *JNES* 71 (2012): 285–98.
161 ABC 1.

the *Nabonidus Chronicle*, and Arses and Darius III in the *Dynastic Prophecy*. As explained above, the *Dynastic Prophecy* and the *Babyloniaca*, both bracketing the Persian period, may originally have covered the reigns of other Persian kings as well, but this remains uncertain in view of their lacunal state of transmission and preservation. In their wider literary context we find no evidence of such an interest. There are no narratives about Cambyses, Darius or Xerxes. Of the Nabonidus-Cyrus pair, the reign of Nabonidus was subject to far more intense debate than that of Cyrus. Looking for prototypes of royalty, the Esagil's literate community visited the pre-Persian past. In this sense, one may conclude that, within this specific socio-cultural setting, the experience of Persian rule was irrelevant in the history of Babylonian kingship.

But this conclusion requires modification. The recurring motifs of competitive dynastic struggle, external threat, and the rise of an Akkadian avenger are all indicative of a world where Babylon's status as navel of the world had been deeply challenged. While Babylonia had experienced such decentering during the Assyrian period, the imperial background on which these stories are premised seems more specifically related to the Persian Empire. First, there is the probable date of composition of these stories. Though for each individual story its date is unfixable, there is collective weight in the group as a whole – based on its unity of protagonist type, thematic orientation and generic experimentation – to place all of them in the same period, i.e. in the active lifespan of the library. The allusion to the *Cyrus Cylinder* in the Nabopolassar cluster provides a terminus post quem pointing in the same direction. More speculatively, the popular vilain figure of the Elamite invader may have served as a historical parallel, a covert allusion, or a reference to contemporary (or recent) Persian kings.[162] The use of the anachronistic title 'king of Elam' in the *Dynastic Prophecy* should have triggered a whole baggage of allusions to the horrible role played by those other 'kings of Elam' in stories set in the 13th and 12th centuries. Such evocation may have served as a foil of the inevitable: Babylonian vengeange and liberation. If this is correct, the long sequence of royal pairs, constructed in each other's mirror image (oppressor/liberator, foreign/internal) and going back to the Kassite period, offers a long prelude to the predictable restitution of the Babylonian throne to a 'seed of Babylon'.[163]

162 Cf. Foster, *Before the Muses*, 369. Note that the creation of subtexts through the substitution of historical protagonists was a known narrative device in late Babylonian literature and in Hellenistic literature more broadly. Nabonidus was disguised as Shulgi in the *Shulgi Chronicle* (Cavigneaux, 'Shulgi, Nabonide, et les Grecs'), and as Nebuchadnezzar in certain stories in Daniel (Reinhard Kratz, *Translatio imperii: Untersuchungen zu den aramäischen Danielerzählungen und ihrem theologiegeschichtlichen Umfeld* [WMANT 63; Neukirchen-Vluyn: Neukirchener Verlag, 1991]).
163 Quote from VS 24 87: 3.

The fact that the application of this model to Nabonidus and Cyrus was deemed to be problematic shows that Cyrus, though hailed as a liberator by certain contemporary audiences at the time of the conquest, did not continue to enjoy this reputation among their descendants. Also, it shows that the establishment of Persian rule was experienced as an ambivalent event, at odds with the regularities discovered in earlier episodes of contestation. In short, the interest in distant episodes of Elamite oppression and Babylonian victory may have spoken to deep-seated hopes of liberation from Persian imperial control, or from the imperial pretext they set for Greek and Parthian successors. The Nabonidus-Cyrus episode constituted a hermeneutic problem that authors writing at that time (c. 400–60 B.C.E.) were struggling to answer. What we should not conclude from all this, however, is that all retrospective judgement of Persian rule was necessarily and unanimously negative. On the contrary, evaluations were nuanced. By being called 'King of Elam', the *Dynastic Prophecy* cast Cyrus, if not as the impersonator, then at least as the institutional heir of a feared and hated dynasty. Triggering the memory of this heritage also evoked the certain knowledge of retribution that was part and parcel of the stories told about that dynasty. That same text, however, modifies this very judgement by erasing the contrast with Cyrus' predecessor (Nabonidus and Cyrus are both qualified as being 'stronger than the land') as demanded by the model. In the *Nabonidus Chronicle*, Cyrus appears without that loaded royal title but with the more historically correct 'King of Anšan' and 'King of Parsa'; at the same time, judgement of his rule was milder as the lavish description of the New Year celebrations of 538 B.C.E. is a foil to Nabonidus' grave neglect of that same festival. Looking beyond Cyrus, Darius III also has a presence in this historical literature. Famously, he is predicted in the *Dynastic Prophecy* to achieve victory over the Hanean army; regardless whether this is a genuine prediction or a manipulation of history, it shows that Persian rulers were not subject to wholesale, collective evaluations. Just as the Neo-Babylonian dynasty features positive and negative examples of kingship, so did rulers of the Persian dynasty offer the possibility of divergent opinions.

Acknowledgment

This paper was written and researched within the framework of the ERC Starting Grant project 'Babylon'. I wish to thank Jonathan Stökl and Bert van der Spek for their valuable comments to an earlier draft of this paper.

Jonathan Stökl

"A Youth Without Blemish, Handsome, Proficient in all Wisdom, Knowledgeable and Intelligent": Ezekiel's Access to Babylonian Culture

dedicated to the memory of
Friedrich-Christoph von Bismarck
(1934–2013)

1 Introduction

The book of Ezekiel is a very special text and the prophet described in it has an intense personality. The book is also known for containing a vast number of allusions to and borrowings from Mesopotamian culture; it is likely the biblical text with the highest density of material that is directly owed to Mesopotamian culture. In this essay I will focus on one aspect of Ezekiel-scholarship, namely the attempts to identify the social location of its author (or authors). It is quite common to read that Ezekiel was a priest who lived in exile in Babylonia. Whether or not that was the case, however, does not explain where he would have had access to the kind of information that is reflected in the book bearing his name.

I am not the first to argue for what David Vanderhooft has recently called an 'acculturated' Ezekiel, but I am, as far as I know, the first to argue for the particular route by which 'Ezekiel' may have acquired access to the knowledge displayed in the book: cuneiform scribal school.[1] Moshe Greenberg and others have argued that Ezekiel was a well educated priest.[2] If we accept the implied author's image as a priest we are relatively safe in assuming that he would have had a comparatively

1 David S. Vanderhooft, 'Ezekiel in and on Babylon', in *Bible et Proche-Orient: Mélanges André Lemaire* (Supplements to Transeuphratène; ed. J.-M. Durand and J. Elayi; Paris: Gabalda, 2014), 99–119.
2 See Moshe Greenberg, *Ezekiel: A New Translation with Introduction and Commentary 1–37* (AB 22; 2 vols.; New York: Doubleday, 1983, 1997), who often links themes and images in the book to the traditions of ancient Israel and the priesthood in particular; see also Daniel I. Block, *The Book of Ezekiel: Chapters 1–24* (NICOT; Grand Rapids: Eerdmans, 1997), 9; Baruch J. Schwartz, 'A Priest out of Place: Reconsidering Ezekiel's Role in the History of the Israelite Priesthood',

Jonathan Stökl: King's College London

good education in Judean sacred tradition and related fields such as alphabetic writing. However, cuneiform and alphabetic scribal traditions were carried out by separate classes of specialists in Mesopotamia, and their training did, as far as we can see, not overlap. I will be arguing that Ezekiel went to cuneiform scribal school, possibly learned to read and write in cuneiform, and was familiarised with the traditions that he went on to use in his own writing. That means that my argument is not focused on reading and writing cuneiform as such, but on the access to special knowledge with which cuneiform schooling would have provided him.[3]

As is in the nature of suggestions such as this one, it is impossible to be proven correct, unless we find a cuneiform tablet with a colophon indicating that it was written by a certain scribe Ezekiel, the prophet. Instead, the argument I am making is cumulative in nature; indeed, it does not sit easily with our understanding of the divulgation of learning in Mesopotamia in the first millennium B.C.E. However, to my mind it is currently the best explanation for the evidence as we have it.

1.1 Judeans in Babylonia

References and allusions to Babylonian culture abound in Ezekiel; it is mostly set there which suggests that it is written and edited so that it is read as a text conceived of by someone living there. It seems reasonable, therefore, to assume that the core of the composition of the original book happened in Babylonia some time after 587 B.C.E. Since we know that Judeans remained in Babylonia as a distinct and recognisable group the text may have been written in the sixth or the fifth century or even later.[4] But we must allow sufficient time for the book to

---

in *Ezekiel's Hierarchical World: Wrestling with a Tiered Reality* (SBLSymS 31; ed. S. L. Cook and C. L. Patton; Atlanta: Society of Biblical Literature, 2004), 61–71 (63).

3 It is possible that the overlap between cuneiform and alphabetic writing was greater than portrayed here. As Philippe Clancier, 'Cuneiform Culture's Last Guardians: The Old Urban Notability of Hellenistic Uruk', in *The Oxford Handbook of Cuneiform Culture* (ed. K. Radner and E. Robson; Oxford: Oxford University Press, 2011), 752–773 has shown, at least some commentaries of canonical cuneiform scribal education appear to have existed on scrolls written in alphabetic writing. Seth Sanders (personal communication) will argue that this overlap was far larger than previously assumed; if Sanders is correct in his analysis this would make the late Hellenistic and early Parthian eras the most productive for the exchange of traditional Mesopotamian knowledge not only into Greek, through the work of Berossus, but also into Aramaic and Hebrew.

4 The logic presented in Stephen Garfinkel, 'Of Thistles and Thorns: A New Approach to Ezekiel ii 6', *VT* 37 (1987): 421–437 fails to take account of the continued Babylonian setting of part of the Jewish/Judean community. See now Clancier, 'Last Guardians', for a summary of cuneiform

develop and grow after the first Babylonian 'edition' until the wider Ezekiel tradition is attested.

If the authors of the book were physically located in Babylonia, it follows that we can make an attempt at understanding the social location of Judeans in Babylonia. Until recently the evidence for Judeans in Babylonia was relatively scanty: there are the so-called Weidner Ration Lists that prove that Jehoiachin was regarded as the King of Judah by the Babylonians and that he, his family and his retinue were well cared for at the Babylonian court.[5] The lists do not provide much detailed information but they indicate that there was a community of upper class Judeans living at the Neo-Babylonian royal court.

The scholarly community owes much to Ran Zadok for his work identifying members of ethnic minorities in Neo-Babylonian texts, in particular Judeans.[6] The majority of people identified by Zadok are agricultural producers, low-level

---

scribes and their exchange with alphabetic scribes in Hellenistic and early Parthian Uruk. Clancier (p. 761–764) argues that in Hellenistic Uruk the choice of writing material implies a value judgement and choice of the character of the text. According to him scholarly texts are virtually exclusively written in Akkadian on clay tablets. He points to two references of scholarly texts on scrolls (*magallatu*) as a curious exception to this rule. For legal material such a distinction does not appear to have been operating. Due to their different material aspects wax writing boards served for either script and for a variety of text genres including scholarly texts. Having said that, Philippe Clancier ('Les scribes sur parchemin du temple d'Anu', *RA* 99 [2005]: 85–104), shows how alphabetic scribes had been integrated into the temple administration in Hellenistic Uruk. It is not entirely clear when alphabetic scribes acquired this role in Babylonian temples. The evidence discussed in Mladen Popović, 'The Emergence of Aramaic and Hebrew Scholarly Texts: Transmission and Translation of Alien Wisdom', in *The Dead Sea Scrolls: Transmission of Traditions and Production of Texts* (STDJ 92; ed. S. Metso, H. Najman and E. M. Schuller; Leiden / Boston: Brill, 2010), 81–114, also tentatively points to the possibility that Akkadian to Aramaic to Hebrew transmission of knowledge may have happened at a later than normally assumed date. On this issue see also the contributions to Popović, ed. *Jewish Cultural Encounters in the Ancient Mediterranean and Near Eastern World* (Leiden / Boston: Brill, forthcoming).

5 See Ernst F. Weidner, 'Jojachin, König von Juda, in babylonischen Keilschrifttexten', in *Mélanges syriens offerts à monsieur René Dussaud: secrétaire perpétuel de l'Académie des Inscriptions et Belles-Lettres, par ses amis et ses élèves. Tome II* (Bibliothèque archéologique et historique 30; Paris: Paul Geuthner, 1939), 923–935.

6 See, e.g., Ran Zadok, *On West Semites in Babylonia During the Chaldean and Achaemenian Periods: An Onomastic Study* (Jerusalem: H. J. & Z. Wanaarta, 1977); Ran Zadok, 'Phoenicians, Philistines, and Moabites in Mesopotamia', *BASOR* 230 (1978): 57–65; Ran Zadok, 'Geographical, Onomastic, and Lexical Notes', *AfO* 46–47 (1999): 208–212; Ran Zadok, 'The Representation of Foreigners in Neo- and Late-Babylonian Legal Documents (Eighth through Second Centuries B.C.E.)', in *Judah and the Judeans in the Neo-Babylonian Period* (ed. O. Lipschits and J. Blenkinsopp; Winona Lake: Eisenbrauns, 2003), 471–589; Ran Zadok, 'The Onomastics of the Chaldean, Aramean, and Arabian Tribes in Babylonia during the First Millennium', in *Arameans, Chal-*

administrators or local traders, but there are also some merchants and craftsmen living in the cities of Babylonia.

Recently, the evidence for Judeans in Babylonia has improved considerably thanks to the *āl Yāhūdu* tablets. According to the texts the Judeans lived in *Bīt-našar* ('Eagleton'), *Bīt-rē'i* ('Shepherdham'), and most notoriously, a town called *āl Yāhūdāya* ('town of the Judeans') in the earliest text and *āl Yāhūdu* ('Judah-ville') later on.[7] These texts are the remnants of private archives and they contain the vast majority of our evidence about Judean exiles in Babylonia. Unlike king Jehoiachin and the royal family, these people appear to have been settled by the Babylonians in the Nippur region.[8] Indeed, there appears to have been a concerted programme by the Babylonians to resettle and redevelop this area which had suffered badly from the Assyrian and Elamite conquests of Babylonia earlier in the first millennium B.C.E. While it is impossible to be entirely certain before the final publication of the texts, it appears that the Judeans lived a relatively modest live as subsistence farmers and low level officials. All the scribes mentioned in these texts bear Babylonian names. There is the curious case of an individual in the *āl Yāhūdu* texts called *Yahū-šar-uṣur* ('May Yahu protect the king!') whose name is once spelled as *Bēl-šarra-uṣur* ('May Bēl / Marduk? protect the king!').[9] Normally, modern scholars would identify the bearer of the first name as Judean on the basis of the theophoric element 'Yahu', and the second as Babylonian. Grammatically, both names are Akkadian. The second name is of a form often referred to as *Beamtenname* – a name a civil servant might adopt. This raises the possibility

---

deans, and Arabs in Babylonia and Palestine in the First Millennium B. C. (LAOS 3; ed. A. Berlejung and M. P. Streck; Leipzig: Harrassowitz, 2013), 261–336.

7 *Āl Yāhūdu* is usually translated as '(New) Jerusalem' by scholars, and it is true that uru *ya-a-hu-du* is used in ABC 5: rev. 12' in order to refer to Jerusalem. However, this is the only time that the city is spelled like that and it seems to me to refer to the 'town (= capital) of Judah', not Jerusalem by name. This is also indicated by the reading of uru as a determinative and not part of the name by Jean-Jacques Glassner, *Mesopotamian Chronicles* (SBLWAW 19; Atlanta: Society of Biblical Literature, 2004), 230, i.e. [uru]*ya-a-hu-du*. Elsewhere, Jerusalem is spelled *uru-sa-lim-ma*. Laurie Pearce and Cornelia Wunsch have recently published the texts in *Documents of Judean Exiles and West Semites in Babylonia in the Collection of David Sofer* (CUSAS 28; Bethesda: CDL Press, 2015). On the community see also Cornelia Wunsch, 'Glimpses on the Lives of Deportees in Rural Babylonia', in A. Berlejung and Michael P. Streck (eds), *Arameans, Chaldeans, and Arabs in Babylonia and Palestine in the First Millennium B.* C. (LAOS 3; Wiesbaden: Harrassowitz, 2013), 247–260.

8 The region is described as the 'Nippur-Kesh-Karkara triangle' by Laurie E. Pearce, '"Judean": A Special Status in Neo-Babylonian and Achemenid Babylonia?', in *Judah and the Judeans in the Achaemenid Period: Negotiating Identity in an International Context* (ed. O. Lipschits, G. N. Knoppers and M. Oeming; Winona Lake: Eisenbrauns, 2011), 267–277 (270).

9 On this and the following see the discussion by Laurie Pearce in this volume.

that there may have been more non-Babylonians among cuneiform scribes, but even if this were the case, numbers surely would not have been very large.[10]

The image that we get from the *āl Yāhūdu* texts fits rather well with that gained from the archive of the Babylonian entrepreneurial family Murašû in which Judeans are recorded as borrowing money, etc.[11] What makes the *āl Yāhūdu* texts so important is that they are from archives by Judean exiles, rather than Babylonian bankers who interacted with Judeans among other clients, and they represent an internal view of the economic and legal ongoings in the community.

There is, thus, evidence for at least three kinds of communities of Judean exiles in Babylonia: 1) upper class Judeans at the royal court in Babylon, 2) traders throughout the Babylonian cities, and 3) subsistence farmers in the Nippur region.[12] To which did the author of Ezekiel belong?[13] Which is the most likely location for the kind of learning that he appears to have had access to?

---

10 Paul-Alain Beaulieu ('Official and Vernacular Languages: The Shifting Sands of Imperial and Cultural Identities in First Millennium BC Mesopotamia', in *Margins of Writing: Origins of Cultures* [OIS 2; ed. S. L. Sanders; Chicago: Oriental Institute of the University of Chicago, 2006], 185–215 [194]) speculates that most *sēpirus* were likely Aramaic speakers and that the prevalence of Babylonian names among them reflects the adoption of Babylonian names for official purposes.

11 H. V. Hilprecht and Albert T. Clay, *Business Documents of Murashû Sons of Nippur Dated in the Reign of Artaxerxes I (464–424 B. C.)* (The Babylonian Expedition of the University of Pennsylvania: Series A. Cuneiform Texts 9; Philadelphia: University of Pennsylvania, Department of Archaeology and Palaeontology, 1898); Matthew W. Stolper, *Entrepreneurs and Empire: The Murašû Archive, the Murašû Firm, and Persian Rule in Babylonia* (PIHANS 54; Istanbul: Nederlands Historisch-Archaeologisch Instituut te Istanbul, 1985); Matthew W. Stolper and Veysel Donbaz, *Istanbul Murašû Texts* (PIHANS 79; Istanbul: Nederlands Historisch-Archaeologisch Instituut te Istanbul, 1997); Matthew W. Stolper, 'Fifth Century Nippur: Texts of the Murašûs and from Their Surroundings', *JCS* 53 (2001): 83–132.

12 See Caroline Waerzeggers, 'Locating Contact in the Babylonian Exile: Some Reflections on Tracing Judean-Babylonian Encounters in Cuneiform Texts', in *Encounters by the Rivers of Babylon: Scholarly Conversations between Jews, Iranians and Babylonians in Antiquity* (TSAJ 160; ed. U. Gabbay and S. Secunda; Tübingen: Mohr Siebeck, 2014), 131–46.

13 The book itself identifies Ezekiel as living by the Kebar canal (Ezek 1:1). This may very well have been true for the historical person Ezekiel, but whether that is true for the people who wrote and compiled the book under his name is a different question.

1.2 Alphabetic Scribes in Babylonia

Scholars have long suggested that some Judeans underwent scribal training in Babylonia as indicated by Daniel 1:3–4:

> (3)Then the king ordered Ashpenaz, his chief officer, to bring some Israelites of royal descent and of the nobility – (4)youths without blemish, handsome, proficient in all wisdom, knowledgeable and intelligent, and capable of serving in the royal palace – and teach them the writings and the language of the Chaldeans.

The problem with this thesis is that so far not a single cuneiform scribe with a Judean name has come to light for the entire Neo-Babylonian period. However, the evidence presented here suggests that it is likely that the Babylonians – or, perhaps, more likely, the Persians – granted access to scribal training of the highest level to some members of the Judean community. It is important to note in this context that it is likely that the training and status of cuneiform scribes and alphabetic scribes differed. In Mesopotamia, Aramaic writing scribes are attested in the eighth century in the wall-panels of Neo-Assyrian palaces.[14] A little later a certain Quqû'a witnesses a land sale contract – to my knowledge the earliest attestation of a named *sēpiru*.[15] In the Neo-Babylonian and then later in the Hellenistic period the term is attested fairly widely, considering that most of the surviving evidence was produced by cuneiform and not by alphabetic scribes.[16]

---

14 See e.g. a stone panel from Tiglath-Pileser III's central palace in Nimrud (BM ME 118882), dated to ca. 730 B.C.E. There are also the products of the scribe's labour. Thus there are, e.g., the famous bronze lion weights from Calḫu inscribed in both Hebrew and Aramaic. For a discussion of Aramaic in the Neo-Assyrian empire see F. M. Fales, *Aramaic Epigraphs On Clay Tablets of the Neo-Assyrian Period* (Studi Semitici 2 / Materiali per il lessico Aramaico 1; Rome: Università degli studi di Roma "La Sapienza", 1986); Frederick M. Fales, Karen Radner, Cinzia Pappi and Ezio Attardo, 'The Assyrian and Aramaic Texts from Tell Shiukh Fawqani', in *Tell Shiukh Fawqani 1994–1998* (HANEM 6/2; ed. L. Bachelot and F. M. Fales; Padova: SARGON, 2005), 595–694.

15 VAT 9763: rev. 8, see Jaume Llop, 'Quqû'a', in *The Prosopography of the Neo-Assyrian Empire: vol 3/I: P-Ṣ* (ed. H. D. Baker, S. Parpola, K. Radner and R. M. Whiting; Helsinki: Neo-Assyrian Text Corpus Project, University of Helsinki, 2000), 1018–1019.

16 On the *sēpiru* see Laurie E. Pearce, '*Sepīru* and LÚA.BA: Scribes of the Late First Millennium', in *Languages and Cultures in Contact: At the Crossroads of Civilizations in the Syro-Mesopotamian Realm; Proceedings of the 42th RAI* (OLA 96; ed. K. Van Lerberghe and G. Voet; Leuven: Peeters, 1999), 355–368; Laurie E. Pearce and L. Timothy Doty, 'The Activities of Anu-bēlšunu, Seleucid Scribe', in *Assyriologica et Semitica: Festschrift für Joachim Oelsner anläßlich seines 65. Geburtstages am 18. Februar 1997* (AOAT 252; ed. J. Marzahn and H. Neumann; Münster: Ugarit-Verlag, 2000), 331–341; David S. Vanderhooft, '*'el mědînâ ûmědînâ kiktābāh*: Scribes and Scripts in Yehud and in Achaemenid Transeuphratene', in *Judah and the Judeans in the Achaemenid Period: Ne-*

There are alphabetic and Persian scribes with West Semitic, Persian and Egyptian names, indicating that different ethnic groups had access to different scribal training. It is possible that the occasional cuneiform scribe with a Babylonian name may have been of a non-Babylonian background, but cuneiform culture appears to have been preserved mostly among the Babylonian elite.[17]

The first *sēpiru* with a Judean name I am aware of is Gedalyaw ben Banna-Ea who is attested on a tablet written in 486 B. C.E, just before the second Babylonian revolt and the changes in Babylonian society associated with that.[18] Like the vast majority of the available evidence for Judeans in Babylonia, this text comes from a good 50 years after the fall of the Neo-Babylonian empire and attests to the continuing existence of Judeans in Mesopotamia.

2 Learning in Ezekiel

The learning reflected in the book of Ezekiel can be allocated into different categories. There is priestly and (Judean) legal knowledge, knowledge of iconographic traditions, and allusions to Mesopotamian literary and scholarly traditions.

It is likely that as a priest Ezekiel would have had access to considerable amounts of legal and scholarly training, which his father or another male relative would have imparted.[19] While important for the interpretation of the texts and

gotiating Identity in an International Context (ed. O. Lipschits, G. N. Knoppers and M. Oeming; Winona Lake: Eisenbrauns, 2011), 529–544; Clancier, 'scribes sur parchemin'; Clancier, 'Last Guardians,' 764–766; Michael Jursa, 'Ein Beamter flucht auf Aramäisch: Alphabetschreiber in der spätbabylonischen Epistolographie und die Rolle des Aramäischen in der babylonischen Verwaltung des sechsten Jahrhunderts v. Chr.', in *Leggo! Studies Presented to Frederick Mario Fales on the Occasion of His 65th Birthday* (ed. G. B. Lanfranchi, D. M. Bonacossi, C. Pappi and S. Ponchia; Wiesbaden: Harrassowitz, 2012), 379–397. *Sēpiru* (sometimes, particularly in earlier publications, normalised as *sepīru*, see CAD S 226) is cognate with Hebrew *sōp̱ēr* ('scribe').

17 From Hellenistic Uruk we know that the Urukean elite used both Akkadian and Greek names, but only the Babylonian elite kept cuneiform writing and culture alive (Clancier, 'Last Guardians,' 760).

18 Vanderhooft, '*'el mĕdînâ ûmĕdînâ kiktābāh*'. The tablet in question was published by Matthew W. Stolper, 'The Governor of Babylon and Across-the-River in 486 B. C.', *JNES* 48 (1989): 283–305. On the effects of the revolt on Babylonian archives in the second year of Xerxes (484 B. C.E), see Caroline Waerzeggers, 'The Babylonian Revolts Against Xerxes and the "End of Archives"', *AfO* 50 (2003): 150–173.

19 Greenberg, *Ezekiel 1–20; 21–37*; Moshe Greenberg, Moses Aberbach, Stephen G. Wald, Abraham Ben-Yaacob and Haïm Z'ew Hirschberg, 'Ezekiel', in *Encyclopaedia Judaica 6* (ed. M. Berenbaum and F. Skolnik; Detroit: Macmillan / Keter, 2007), 635–646 (643).

traditions in the book, the Judean learning does not appear, therefore, to point the modern scholar to where 'Ezekiel' acquired his Mesopotamian learning.

Different forms of iconographic traditions have been identified in the text. To some scholars Mesopotamian traditions in the book abound, others find only traces. In his work on Ezekiel Daniel Bodi identifies many such borrowings.[20] Moshe Greenberg attempts to trace most of the iconographic references to West Semitic traditions allowing for them to be written in Mesopotamia.[21] Christoph Uehlinger argues that there are allusions to Mesopotamian iconographic traditions but that they have undergone a West Semitic transformation.[22] This kind of knowledge could either be transmitted through seeing some of the iconography on palace and temple walls, or, indeed, through the wider stream of tradition. In interpreting the influence of iconographic traditions it is important to be aware that the vast majority of the iconographic programme in Babylonia would not have been easily accessible to the casual observer, since the inside of temples and palaces were only accessible to the religious and / or political elites. Guests of the king (otherwise known as 'hostages') may have had access to parts of the palace, at most they would not have been allowed to more than the public gardens and forecourts of the temples but even that is uncertain.

Finally, there is scholarly knowledge, such as astronomy or the knowledge of rituals, word-lists, and other material that would not be accessible to anyone who did not have the training as a scribe. There are some examples in the text of Ezekiel which suggest that this kind of information can be found, and that suggests that the transmission took place through contact initiated in a school.

2.1 Scribal Schools

Before I discuss some examples for knowledge transfer it is necessary to give a brief overview of scribal schools in first millennium Mesopotamia. Following the work of Niek Veldhuis and Herman Vanstiphout who focussed mostly on Sumerian in Old-Babylonian scribal schools, Petra Gesche has recently presented

---

20 See, e.g., Daniel Bodi, *The Book of Ezekiel and the Poem of Erra* (OBO 104; Fribourg: Universitätsverlag / Göttingen: Vandenhoeck & Ruprecht, 1991); Daniel Bodi, *Commentary on the Book of Ezekiel* (Zondervan Illustrated Bible Backgrounds Commentary 4; Grand Rapids: Zondervan, 2009).

21 Greenberg, *Ezekiel*.

22 See, e.g., Christoph Uehlinger, 'Virtual Vision vs. Actual Show: Visualizing Strategies in the Book of Ezekiel', *WO* (forthcoming). M. Greenberg, *Ezekiel 1–20*, 58, derives everything from internal Israelite traditions 'supplemented by neighboring iconography'.

an in-depth study of scribal education in first millennium Babylonia.[23] When discussing ancient schools most modern scholars have (tacitly) assumed that schools would have been relatively large enterprises. Gesche's work makes it clear that such an image is wrong; instead we should conceive of much smaller groups, usually a father with three to four sons and other male relatives.[24] The tri-partite curriculum appears to have been fairly standardized by the middle of the 5th century, including testing by exams: a basic training which one could finish in three years, a secondary phase, which took another three years, and then further studies, as desired and required.

Mesopotamian students started their scribal career by copying the three basic signs of cuneiform writing: the vertical wedge, the horizontal wedge and the *winkelhaken*. Once mastered, all cuneiform signs can be written with these. Once the student had mastered these they would start copying excerpts from standard word-lists. The lists with which first millennium scribal students started are the Syllabary S^{a}, the vocabulary lists S^{b} A and S^{b} B, as well as Weidner's list of gods, and, significantly, the lexical list ur$_{5}$.ra = *ḫubullum*, in particular tablets I-III. Ur$_{5}$.ra = *ḫubullum* is interesting in our case as the first two tablets consist mostly of terms from the juridical and mercantile spheres, as do many of the loanwords in Ezekiel.

As students progressed, ever more complicated texts were included in the curriculum. In the second stage of the elementary scribal training, students wrote canonical myths, such as the *Enūma eliš*, incantations and prayers; but further lists, such as lú = *ša*, *malku* = *šarru*, etc. were also copied. The most complicated and/or secret texts were left for what Gesche has dubbed the *Fachausbildung*, which allowed scribes to work in a particular profession needing further training, such as the *āšipu* ('exorcist').[25] The incantation list *maqlû* ('burning'), which

23 Petra D. Gesche, *Schulunterricht in Babylonien im ersten Jahrtausend v. Chr.* (AOAT 275; Münster: Ugarit-Verlag, 2000); see also the review by Niek Veldhuis, 'On the Curriculum of the Neo-Babylonian School', *JAOS* 123 (2003): 627–633.

24 Michael Jursa, 'Cuneiform Writing in Neo-Babylonian Temple Communities', in *The Oxford Handbook of Cuneiform Culture* (ed. K. Radner and E. Robson; Oxford: Oxford University Press, 2011), 184–204 (191). Yoram Cohen's study of the Emar scribes shows this well for the Western periphery of the Akkadian writing world in the Late Bronze age (Yoram Cohen, *The Scribes and Scholars of the City of Emar in the Late Bronze Age* [HSS 59; Winona Lake: Eisenbrauns, 2009]).

25 On the concept of the secret, see Alan Lenzi, *Secrecy and the Gods: Secret Knowledge in Ancient Mesopotamia and Biblical Israel* (SAAS 19; Helsinki: Neo-Assyrian Text Corpus Project University of Helsinki, 2008); on the *āšipu* in particular, see Cynthia Jean, *La magie néo-assyrienne en contexte: Recherches sur le métier d'exorciste et le concept d'āšipūtu* (SAAS 17; Helsinki: Neo-Assyrian Text Corpus Project University of Helsinki, 2006). See also Ulla Susanne Koch, *Secrets of Extispicy: The Chapter Multābiltu of the Babylonian Extispicy Series and Niṣirti bārûti Texts Mainly*

contains an anti-witchcraft ritual, does not appear in the first or second stage education and it can therefore be safely assumed that it is part of the professional training of the *āšipu*.

Students who wanted to work in administration or as self-employed scribes could leave school after the first part of the training; it is likely that they would have joined a professional scribe as an apprentice (*šamallû ṣeḫru* – 'young apprentice'; *ṭupšarru ṣeḫru* – 'young scribe') to work and learn the ropes of their trade. Students who aspired to become 'professionals', scholars or to join the upper levels of the administration would go on to complete the second phase and in many cases also further professional training.

It is important to note that reading and writing was not quite as restricted as sometimes assumed. Many priests, but also other professionals, would have a basic control of reading and possibly some writing.[26] But, it is important to separate the ability to read and write from the access that scribal training may have provided to the scholarly tradition(s) of Mesopotamia. Ezekiel's ability to read and write as such is not our concern here. It is his access to traditions, access to which would have been severely limited outside the social groups connected to scribal schools and temples.[27]

3 Ezekiel's Learning

This section will assess the kind of Mesopotamian learning that Ezekiel appears to have been familiar with. Not all examples for direct Mesopotamian influence that have been suggested are convincing. I will start with some examples that do not appear to be as strong as others, which, I hope, will nonetheless build a cumulative case.

---

from Aššurbanipal's Library (AOAT 326; Münster: Ugarit-Verlag, 2005); Netanel Anor, 'Secret of Extispicy Revealed', in *Esoteric Knowledge in Antiquity* (ed. M. Geller and K. Geus; Berlin: Max-Planck-Institut für Wissenschaftsgeschichte, 2014), 7–19.

26 Dominique Charpin, 'Lire et écrire en Mésopotamie: Une affaire de spécialistes?', *CRAI* 148 (2004), 481–508; Dominique Charpin, *Lire et écrire à Babylone* (Paris: Presses universitaires de France, 2008); Dominique Charpin, *Reading and Writing in Babylon* (Cambridge, MA: Harvard University Press, 2010).

27 Lenzi, *Secrecy*.

3.1 Contested Examples

Isaac Gluska has suggested that the weeping for Tammuz in Ezekiel 8 is an example of a Babylonian cultural trait that made its way into the text of the Hebrew Bible.[28] Ezekiel 8 contains a vision of the Jerusalem temple in which women are said to weep for Tammuz. Unless we accept the history of the religion of ancient Judah as presented in the Hebrew Bible as entirely accurate, there is no reason to assume that a cult similar to that of Dumuzi and Ištar was not common in pre-exilic Judah.[29] It appears more likely to me that the adherence to the ritual of weeping for Tammuz in Jerusalem predated the Babylonian invasion.

The second example is also taken from Gluska and regards the activity of king Nebuchadnezzar in Ezekiel 21:26:

> For the king of Babylon stood at the parting of the way, at the head of the two ways, to use divination: he shook his arrows, he consulted *teraphim*, he inspected the liver.

According to Gluska, hepatoscopy, divination by means of the inspection of the liver, usually of a sheep, was unknown in Israel. In my view, the clay liver model from Hazor, admittedly from the late second millennium B. C.E., militates against Gluska's view.[30] The fact that Ezekiel does not explain what Nebuchadnezzar is doing here further suggests that his readers would have been familiar with hepatoscopy.

Daniel Bodi suggested that the image of the two rivers in Ezekiel 47 is a direct borrowing from a Mesopotamian original.[31] Bodi's examples include the

---

28 Isaac Gluska, 'Akkadian Influences on the Book of Ezekiel', in *"An Experienced Scribe Who Neglects Nothing": Ancient Near Eastern Studies in Honor of Jacob Klein* (ed. Y. Sefati, P. Artzi, C. Cohen, B. L. Eichler and V. A. Hurowitz; Bethesda: CDL, 2005), 718–737 (725–726).

29 See, e.g., Izaak de Hulster, 'Figurines from Persian Period Jerusalem', *ZAW* 124 (2012): 73–88, for evidence that a female deity played a role in Judah before, during and after the exile. For the continued relevance of a cult centered on Dumuzi in Mesopotamian religion after the Old-Babylonian period, see Michael M. Fritz, *„... und weinten um Tammuz": Die Götter Dumuzi-Ama'ušumgal und Damu* (AOAT 307; Münster: Ugarit-Verlag, 2003), 236–238 and 339–341.

30 Hazor 2–3. For convenient access to these texts see Wayne Horowitz, Takayoshi Oshima and Seth L. Sanders, *Cuneiform in Canaan: Cuneiform Sources from the Land of Israel in Ancient Times* (Jerusalem: Israel Exploration Society, 2006), 66–68. See also Frederick H. Cryer, 'Der Prophet und der Magier: Bemerkungen anhand einer überholten Diskussion', in *Prophetie und geschichtliche Wirklichkeit im alten Israel: Festschrift für Siegfried Herrmann zum 65. Geburtstag* (ed. R. Liwak and S. Wagner; Stuttgart: Kohlhammer, 1991), 79–88; Frederick H. Cryer, *Divination in Ancient Israel and its Near Eastern Environment: A Socio-Historical Investigation* (JSOTSup 142; Sheffield: JSOT Press, 1994).

31 Bodi, *Commentary on the Book of Ezekiel*, 495–498.

painting of the investiture of the king of Mari with the two streams, as well as the wall panels of the 14th century B. C.E. Ištar temple at Uruk. The very impressive Mari painting – one of the few surviving examples of 2nd millennium wall painting – is, at the very youngest, from the 18th century B. C.E., if not significantly older, and none of the examples given by Bodi are younger than the 9th century B.C.E. This is not to deny that Bodi is correct that the Mesopotamian and the Ezekelian imagery draw on the same common ancient Near Eastern tradition. But how would the Judean exiles in Nippur or in Babylon have seen the image of the double stream at the temple if the artifacts in question had been covered by earth and other buildings for centuries?[32] They were, after all, only excavated in the 20th century CE. Thus, there is no direct mode of transmission between the Mesopotamian idea and Ezekiel. Indeed, I would argue that rather than dealing with a specifically Mesopotamian idea, we are dealing with a common ancient Near Eastern tradition that the temple (and the garden of the gods) had several (often, but not always, two) rivers and trees. That Ezekiel reflects this is only to be expected, even if I would agree that much of the description of the new utopian temple in Ezekiel 40–48 is owed to the Etemenanki ('temple of the foundation of Heaven and Earth'), the Ziggurat of the Esagil ('temple of the raised head'), Marduk's temple in Babylon.[33]

Driver suggested that the term איל (*ʔayil*) as it occurs in Ezek 17:13, 31:11 and 32:21 (and elsewhere in the Hebrew Bible) is at times not a metaphorical use of the word 'ram', but rather refers to noblemen and is derived from Akkadian *awīlum*/*amēlu* ('[free] man').[34] While the meaning of noble- or freeman would certainly fit these three texts, the metaphorical meaning 'hero, ruler' fits just as nicely. Additionally, as Mankowski points out, the one time that the Hebrew text transcribes the Akkadian word *amēlu* with certainty, in its transcription of the name Amēl-Marduk, it does so with the expected י (yod) in the middle: אויל־מרדך. If איל could be a transcription of *amēlu* into Hebrew, it would be the only word with a long -ī/ē vowel that does not indicate it with *mater lectionis*.[35] It thus seems rather unlikely that Driver's suggestion can be followed here.

32 It is true that some early ancient monuments were available for onlookers in the second half of the first millennium (see, e.g., Caroline Waerzeggers in this volume), but to my knowledge this does not apply to the objects identified by Bodi.

33 Michael Konkel, *Architektonik des Heiligen: Studien zur zweiten Tempelvision Ezechiels (Ez 40–48)* (BBB 129; Berlin: Philo, 2001).

34 G. R. Driver, 'Studies in the Vocabulary of the Old Testament V', *JTS* 34 (1933): 33–34.

35 Paul V. Mankowski, *Akkadian Loanwords in Biblical Hebrew* (HSS 47; Winona Lake: Eisenbrauns, 2000), 28–29. As noted by Mankowski, Stephen A. Kaufman (*The Akkadian Influences on the Aramaic and the Development of Aramaic Dialects* [AS 19; Chicago: Oriental Institute of the

3.2 More Secure Examples

Let us now look at some examples which I think are better for our current enterprise. I will start by discussing some suggested Akkadian loanwords in Hebrew. For the purposes of this discussion, I understand as loanwords such words that are technical terms in Akkadian which appear to be used in Hebrew with the same meaning. For obvious reasons, their usage and semantics in Neo-Babylonian Akkadian and in Biblical Hebrew are important.[36]

The first two examples can be found in Ezek 13:18. They are the two terms כְּסָתוֹת and מִסְפָּחוֹת.

> וְאָמַרְתָּ כֹּה־אָמַר אֲדֹנָי יְהוִה הוֹי לִמְתַפְּרוֹת כְּסָתוֹת עַל כָּל־אַצִּילֵי יָדַי וְעֹשׂוֹת הַמִּסְפָּחוֹת עַל־רֹאשׁ כָּל־קוֹמָה לְצוֹדֵד נְפָשׁוֹת הַנְּפָשׁוֹת תְּצוֹדֵדְנָה לְעַמִּי וּנְפָשׁוֹת לָכֶנָה תְחַיֶּינָה׃
>
> [[17]Prophesy against them] [18]and say: Thus said the Lord YHWH: Woe to those who sew pads on all arm-joints and make bonnets for the head of every person, in order to entrap! Can you hunt down lives among My people, while you preserve your own lives?

University of Chicago, 1974], 34) possibly undermines an important part of Driver's argument. Kaufman notes that after collating the tablet he considers the *lamed* in the Aramaic docket on DEA 91 as uncertain. This would render the reading *ʔwlt* impossible. However, upon renewed collation of the tablet the *lamed* appears to me relatively certain. For DEA 91 (79–4-19, 3=BM 33091) see James Henry Stevenson, *Assyrian and Babylonian Contracts with Aramaic Reference Notes* (Vanderbilt Oriental Series; New York: American Book Company, 1902), 94–95 (text 32) with a drawing on page 193 and, with regard to the Aramaic, Louis Delaporte, *Épigraphes araméens: Étude des textes araméens gravés ou écrits sur des tablettes cunéiformes* (Paris: Paul Geuthner, 1912), 76–77.

36 This is not a discussion of the understanding of loanwords as such. For the purposes of this paper, 'loanwords' are not distinguished from other forms of transfer of words from one language to another. For recent discussion of loaning words as part of the general evolution and change of languages see Peter Koch, 'Lexical Typology from a Cognitive and Linguistic Point of View', in *Language Typology and Language Universals: An International Handbook / Sprachtypologie und sprachliche Universalien: Ein internationales Handbuch / La typologie des langues et les universaux linguistiques: Manuel international* (Handbücher zur Sprach- und Kommunikationswissenschaft 20; ed. M. Haspelmath, E. König, W. Oesterreicher and W. Raible; Berlin / New York: de Gruyter, 2001), 2:1142–1178. See also Martin Haspelmath, 'Loanword Typology: Steps Toward a Systematic Cross-Linguistic Study of Lexical Borrowability', in *The Use of Databases in Cross-Linguistic Studies* (Empirical Approaches to Language Typology 41; ed. M. Everaert, S. Musgrave and A. Dimitriadis; Berlin: de Gruyter Mouton, 2008), 283–300; Martin Haspelmath, 'Lexical Borrowing: Concepts and Issues', in *Loanwords in the World's Languages: A Comparative Handbook* (ed. M. Haspelmath and U. Tadmor; Berlin: de Gruyter Mouton, 2009), 35–54; Joachim Grzega, 'Borrowing as a Word-Finding Process in Cognitive Historical Onomasiology', *Onomasiology Online* 4 (2003): 22–42 and Haspelmath and Tadmor, eds. *Loanwords in the World's Languages: A Comparative Handbook* (Berlin: de Gruyter Mouton, 2009) for loanwords in many of the world's languages but in spite of their promising cover not a single Semitic language was chosen.

Due to its vocalisation the first of the two terms, כְּסָתוֹת, is usually derived from כֶּסֶת.[37] This word is likely to be derived from Akkadian *kasû* A ('bind') or (more likely) *kasītu* ('[magical] constraint'). *Kasītu* appears to be something of the 'odd one out' in this discussion of possible Akkadian loan words in Classical Hebrew in that it is not contained in any of the standard lexical lists, but it can be found in texts used by exorcists such as Šurpu IV: 70.[38]

The second peculiar word from this verse, מִסְפָּחוֹת ('veil'), could have been discussed in the previous section. It is normally linked to the Arabic term *safīḥ* ('robe of course material').[39] I am not aware of any Akkadian term that is a direct cognate to the noun. Stephen Garfinkel discusses the suggestion that מספחה might be the result of a metathesised form of מסחפה*, which could then be linked to one of the many Akkadian words for 'net', *musaḫḫiptu*.[40] Garfinkel is likely correct when he denies this possibility. Thus, while the Hebrew term itself is unclear it is unlikely to be a direct loan from Akkadian.

---

37 See, e.g., HALOT; Hayim ben Yosef Tawil, *An Akkadian Lexical Companion for Biblical Hebrew: Etymological-Semantic and Idiomatic Equivalents with Supplement on Biblical Aramaic* (Jersey City: Ktav, 2009), 171; Stephen Garfinkel, 'Studies in Akkadian Influences in the Book of Ezekiel', unpublished PhD thesis, Columbia University, 1983, 94; Chaim Rabin, 'Hittite Words in Hebrew', *Or* 32 (1963): 113–139 (126 n.2). See also Walther Zimmerli, *Ezechiel 1–24* (BKAT 13/1; Neukirchen-Vluyn: Neukirchener Verlag, 1969), 296–297; Greenberg, *Ezekiel 1–20*, 239; Block, *Ezekiel 1–24*, 413; Jonathan Stökl, 'The מתנבאות of Ezekiel 13 Reconsidered', *JBL* 132 (2013): 61–76 (64–65). It could, of course, also be derived from a word כִּסְתָה.

38 The vocalisation suggests that the Akkadian word loaned into Hebrew was stressed on the first syllable which would suggest a form *kāsitu* rather than *kasītu*. In Mishnaic and later Hebrew כֶּסֶת refers to 'pillow'. This is also reflected in the Septuagint of Ezekiel which has προσκεφάλαιον. Origen translates φυλακτήρια, which suggests that he understood כֶּסֶת as related to a form of *kasû* (cited in Zimmerli, *Ezechiel 1–24*, 297).

39 Tawil, *Lexical Companion*, 266 only discusses the verbal root ספך and not the noun(s) derived from it. Greenberg, *Ezekiel 1–20*, 239 links מספחה to the מספחת in Lev 13:6–8. GES[18]: 897 links the latter to ספחת in Lev 13:2 and 14:56. It is fairly clear that Hebrew ספך (G 'asscociate with') and שׁפך (meaning disputed) are both cognates to Akkadian *sapāḫu* ('scatter, disperse'), but that does not give us any indication with regard to either the meaning of מספחה or whether it is a loaned word. Garfinkel, 'Akkadian Influences,' 104–105 wants to dissociate מספחה from Akkadian *sapāḫu* but because both Hebrew roots are likely cognates of the Akkadian term he – and, e.g., Block, *Ezekiel 1–24*, 414 – is only partially successful.

40 Garfinkel, 'Akkadian Influences,' 104–105. The suggestion goes back to H. W. F. Saggs, '"External Souls" in the Old Testament', *JSS* 19 (1974): 1–12.

There can be little doubt that the expression אֲמֻלָה לִבָּתֵךְ in Ezek 16:30 is cognate to the expression *libbāti malû*.[41] The expression is also known from Aramaic texts so that it is impossible to know whether the idiom was loaned directly from Akkadian or via the intermediary Aramaic.[42]

Like Akkadian, Hebrew and Aramaic share the somewhat peculiar construction of the target of the anger being expressed by the suffix on *libbātu*.[43] Depending on the context, the preceding form of *malû* can be either finite or not. Hebrew – according to the Masoretic text – appears to have understood it as a

41 Mankowski, *Akkadian Loanwords*, 77–80. Mankowski describes the expression as a calque, but according to Haspelmath, 'Lexical Borrowing: Concepts and Issues,' 38–40 the term 'loanblend' may be more appropriate, as the loan combines loaned elements with aspects already existing in the language prior to the loan. As Mankowski notes, the suggestion itself can be found first in D. H. Baneth, 'Bemerkungen zu den Achikarpapyri', *OLZ* 17 (1914): 248–252, 295–299, 348–353 (251 n.1). G. R. Driver, 'Some Hebrew Words', *JTS* 29 (1928): 390–396 (393); G. R. Driver, 'Studies in the Vocabulary of the Old Testament III', *JTS* 32 (1931): 361–366 (366), following A. E. Cowley, *Aramaic Papyri of the Fifth Century B. C.* (Oxford: Clarendon Press, 1923), who in turn followed Baneth, came to the same conclusion, which indicates that Driver's ideas here were not quite independent. Curiously, the idiom is missing from Tawil, *Lexical Companion*. As Block, *Ezekiel 1–24*, 496–497, points out, the LXX of this verse (τί διαθῶ τὴν θυγατέρα σου ['how shall I circumcise your daughter']) misunderstands אמלה and derives it from the verb מול ('to circumcise') and לבתך from בַּת ('daughter'). Zimmerli, *Ezechiel 1–24*, 331–341, follows F. Stummer, 'אֲמֻלָה (Ez. XVI 30 A)', *VT* 4 (1954): 34–40 and derives אמלה from Arabic *mll* 'to be shaken with fever' (see also Franz Zorell, *Lexicon Hebraicum Veteris Testamenti* [Rome: Pontifical Biblical Institute, 1984], 62).

42 See Kaufman, *Akkadian Influences*, 66. Compared to Hebrew the idiom is relatively well attested in Aramaic. According to the Comprehensive Aramaic Lexicon, it occurs at least in lines 19–20 of the Aššur ostracon (=KAI 233), Mark Lidzbarski, *Altaramäische Urkunden aus Assur* (WVDOG 38; Leipzig: Hinrich, 1921), 8, as well as at least 4 times in texts from Egypt: TAD A2.3: rev. 6, A3.3: 10, A3.5: rev. 4 and A4.2: 11. See also Jacob Hoftijzer and Karel Jongeling, *Dictionary of the North-West Semitic Inscriptions* (HO 21; Leiden: Brill, 1995), 563. Paul-Alain Beaulieu, 'Aspect of Aramaic and Babylonian Linguistic Interaction in First Millennium BC Iraq', *Journal of Language Contact* 6 (2013): 358–378.

43 The use of a suffigal pronoun to express the object of the emotion expressed by a noun is attested also with the noun אהבה (Gen 29:20, 1 Sam 18:3, 20:17, 2 Sam 1:26, Is 63:9, Zeph 3:17, Ps 109:4–5, Prov 5:19 and Eccl 9:6). Constructs can express either objective or subjective (possessive) genitives, see GK § 128h. There, Gesenius-Kautzsch give the example of מֵחֲמַס אָחִיךָ ('your brother's violence', i.e. 'the violence done to your brother', Ob 10) and also list Ezek 12:19 where מֵחֲמַס is followed by כָּל־הַיֹּשְׁבִים בָּהּ, which expresses not the violence done to Jerusalem's inhabitants, but the violence committed by them, i.e. a subjective genitive. I would like to thank Hugh G. M. Williamson, Kevin Cathcart and John Huehnergard (unbeknownst to him) for discussing this issue with me.

passive G-participle,[44] while in Egyptian Aramaic the expression uses an active G-participle.[45]

The term *libbātu* itself occurs in Erimḫuš V: 176,[46] Antagal D 136[47] and the so-called appendix to Ea = *nâqu* iv: 3.[48] Of these Erimḫuš is a reasonably well-known schooltext, which opens the possibility that the loan could have been through schooling, but the fact that the expression also occurs in Aramaic – and is more widespread there than in Hebrew, leads us to the assumption that the expression was first loaned – or loanblended – into Aramaic, before it entered Hebrew. The fact that the loan into Aramaic had taken place already by the time of the Aššur ostracon in the middle of the seventh century B. C.E. makes it likely that contact with the administrative practises of the Neo-Assyrian empire led to the loanblend in Aramaic before the idiom is attested also in Hebrew.

One of the most famous words in Ezekiel in this regard is נדניך in Ezek 16:33. The entire verse runs:

44 Hebrew does not decline its suffixes and they are usually understood as possessive (genitive) suffixes. This suffix, however, may better be understood as an accusative suffix with directional force: my anger against you. Like in other cases, G. R. Driver, 'Some Hebrew Verbs, Nouns, and Pronouns', *JTS* 30 (1929): 371–378; Driver, 'Studies in the Vocabulary of the Old Testament III', suggest alternative vocalizations: אִמָּלֶה (N-PC 1cs) and אֶמְלֶה (G-PC 1cs). Chaim Cohen, *Biblical Hapax Legomena in the Light of Akkadian and Ugaritic* (SBLMS 37; Missoula: Scholars Press, 1978), 47, 90 n. 230 parses אֻמְלָה as a *pu'al* perfect (D-SC 3fs), presumably repointing אֻמְּלָה.

45 See, e.g., TAD A4.2:11 (=CAP 37:11): מילין לבתכם.

46 Antoine Cavigneaux, Hans G. Güterbock and Martha T. Roth, *The Series Erim-ḫuš = anantu and An-ta-gál = šaqû* (MSL 17; Rome: Pontifical Biblical Institute, 1985), 74.

47 Cavigneaux, Güterbock and Roth, *Erim-ḫuš*, 205.

48 These are to be found on one Neo-Assyrian copy, CT 11 28; See Miguel Civil, *Ea A = nâqu, Aa A = nâqu with their Forerunners and Related Texts* (MSL 14; Rome: Pontifical Biblical Institute, 1979), 519. The line is equivalent to Ea III: 121 but the tablet is broken where the Akkadian equivalent to mur-gu$_4$ would have been; see Civil, MSL 14, 308. According to CAD L: 163, Aa = *nâqu* VIII/2: 230 has the entry [*ta-a*]*b* GÍR = *lib-ba-tu*. Civil, MSL 14, 503, more cautiously, reads line 230 as [*ta-a*]*b* GÍR = ⌜x⌝-*ma-tu*. Obviously, this leaves open the reading *libbātu*. In either case, it is unlikely that a student would have copied line 230 of tablet 40 (!) of Aa = *nâqu*. Ea = *nâqu* does not have an equivalent of that particular line.

> לְכָל־זֹנוֹת יִתְּנוּ־נֵדֶה וְאַתְּ נָתַתְּ אֶת־נְדָנַיִךְ לְכָל־מְאַהֲבַיִךְ וַתִּשְׁחֳדִי אוֹתָם לָבוֹא אֵלַיִךְ מִסָּבִיב בְּתַזְנוּתָיִךְ׃
> All prostitutes are given 'gifts'[49] but you give your bride-money to all your lovers as a bribe so that they come to partake in your whoring!

This verse is part of Ezekiel's oracle against Jerusalem. In it, YHWH compares Jerusalem to an adulterous wife who acts as a sex-worker, and announces his punishment of Jerusalem in graphic sexualised language of a sexual assault against her, which has led to its description as a 'text of terror' by modern interpreters.[50] For our current enterprise, however, the nature of the context of our verse is of little further importance. In his discussion of the term Mankowski follows Kaufmann in explaining the somewhat surprising י after the base of the word in analogy to loans of Akkadian words with a long final vowel resulting from the reduction of two vowels (i.e. *-û*) into Aramaic with a final *-ê* vowel spelled with a *yod*.[51] The

49 The word נֵדֶה is commonly derived from the Aramaic root *ndy* ('to give'). Jonas C. Greenfield, 'Two Biblical Passages in the Light of Their Near Eastern Background – Ezekiel 16:30 and Malachi 3:17 [Hebrew]', *ErIsr* 16 (1982), derives נֵדֶה from Akkadian *nidnu* ('a groom's gift to the bride'), but cf. CAD N/2: 208–209 which translates it generically as 'gift'. In either case it is clear that the text is playing with words for 'gift' here.

50 Phyllis Trible, *Texts of Terror: Literary-Feminist Readings of Biblical Narratives* (OBT 13; Philadelphia: Fortress Press, 1984). The potential for double entendre of the 'dowry' / 'gift' to refer also to the woman's genitalia is noted in Tawil, *Lexical Companion*, 233, who also suggests a potential word-play with נְדָן ('sheath') which is used as a euphemism for female genitalia in the Genesis Apocryphon (1Q20 II 10; Joseph A. Fitzmyer S. J., *The Genesis Apocryphon of Qumran Cave 1 [1Q20]: A Commentary* [BibOr 18/B; Rome: Pontifical Biblical Institute, 2004], 68–69, 131).

51 Mankowski, *Akkadian Loanwords*, 100–101. As Mankowski notes, the loan was first proposed by Delitzsch and Zimmern (Friedrich Delitzsch, *Assyrisches Handwörterbuch* [Leipzig: Hinrichs'sche Buchhandlung, 1896], 451; Heinrich Zimmern, *Akkadische Fremdwörter als Beweis für babylonischen Kultureinfluss* [Leipzig: Hinrichs'sche Buchhandlung, 1915], 146). For examples of the same sound-change in Akkadian loanwords in Aramaic see Kaufman, *Akkadian Influences*, 149. Against the possibility noted by Mankowski, *Akkadian Loanwords*, 162–163 that long vowels in Late Babylonian are reduced to short vowels, which, in turn, do not normally survive the transmission into Hebrew, we have to note that the evidence for this transition in Akkadian comes from Hellenistic texts, and we can assume that Akkadian continued to evolve during the Neo-Babylonian and Late Babylonian periods – they were, after all, among the most productive periods for cuneiform writing. For a first attempt to systematise the evidence see Johannes Hackl, 'Language Death and Dying Reconsidered: The Rôle of Late Babylonian as a Vernacular Language', forthcoming [a draft version is available at http://iowp.univie.ac.at/sites/default/files/IOWP_RAI_Hackl.pdf; last accessed 19 July 2014]. The discussion in Garfinkel, 'Akkadian Influences,' 111–112 is too unspecific to be helpful. Greenberg, *Ezekiel 1–20*, 285 understands the terms as 'morphological variants', but reports that Greenfield, 'Two Biblical Passages in the Light of Their Near Eastern Background – Ezekiel 16:30 and Malachi 3:17 [Hebrew]' connects the word to Akkadian *nidnu*.

possibility cannot, of course, be ruled out that the word was loaned from a form *nudinnû* as cited by von Soden in volume 2 of his *Handwörterbuch.*[52]

It is, in fact possible, that Hebrew נָדָן II (*nāḏān*) was not loaned directly from Akkadian *nudunnû*, but rather indirectly via the conduit of Aramaic *ndwnyh*. Following the *communis opinio* that the Hebrew and Akkadian words are related we have to explain the sound-changes from the Akkadian to the Hebrew. To me, this appears an unsurmountable problem that could potentially be solved by the assumption of an Aramaic intermediate stage, as it seems that in Aramaic the quality of the second vowel is preserved and, as already mentioned, the final *yod* is also explicable in a loan from Akkadian to Aramaic to Hebrew. However, the problem remains that Aramaic *ndwnyh* is only attested in Jewish Palestinian (ca. 100–1,200 CE) and Jewish Babylonian Aramaic (ca. 400–1,100 CE).[53] The Aramaic marriage contracts from the Achaemenid era tend to use the root *prn* for 'dowry'.[54] The semantics make it clear that the Hebrew term is ultimately derived from the Akkadian, but its vocalization also make it relatively clear that it is unlikely to have been a direct loan.

Further, neither do the Aramaic marriage contracts from the Persian period use the *ndwnyh* nor do any of the currently known Akkadian marriage contracts

---

52 See Wolfram von Soden, *Akkadisches Handwörterbuch: Unter Benutzung des lexikalischen Nachlasses von Bruno Meissner (1868–1947)* (Wiesbaden: Harrassowitz, 1972), II: 800.

53 See The Comprehensive Aramaic Lexicon (CAL), online at http://cal1.cn.huc.edu (accessed on May 17th, 2013). See also the standard entries in Morris Jastrow, *A Dictionary of the Targumim, the Talmud Babli and Yerushalmi, and the Midrashic Literature* (London: Luzac & Co; New York: G. P. Putnam's Sons, 1903), 878; Michael Sokoloff, *A Dictionary of Jewish Babylonian Aramaic of the Talmudic and Geonic Periods* (Ramat-Gan: Bar Ilan University Press; Baltimore: Johns Hopkins University Press, 2002), 730b; Shelomo Morag and Yechiel Kara, *Babylonian Aramaic in Yemenite Tradition: The Noun* (Jerusalem: Hebrew University, 2002), 212. On dowry giving according to biblical traditions and Jewish / Judean wedding contracts see T. M. Lemos, *Marriage Gifts and Social Change in Ancient Palestine: 1200 BCE to 200 CE* (Cambridge: Cambridge University Press, 2010). For dowries in the Genizah documents see Mordechai Akiva Friedman, *Jewish Marriage in Palestine: A Cairo Geniza Study* (Tel Aviv: Tel Aviv University; New York: Jewish Theological Seminary of America, 1980), 1:288–311. On the Elephantine marriage contracts see Reuven Yaron, 'Aramaic Marriage Contracts from Elephantine', *JSS* 3 (1958): 1–39; Reuven Yaron, 'Aramaic Marriage Contracts: Corrigenda and Addenda', *JSS* 5 (1960): 66–70; Edward Lipiński, 'Marriage and Divorce in the Judaism of the Persian Period', *Transeuphratène* 4 (1991): 63–71. Sadly, Samuel Greengus, 'The Aramaic Marriage Contracts in the Light of the Ancient Near East and the Later Jewish Materials' (unpublished MA Dissertation, University of Chicago, 1959) was unavailable to me. See also the Maresha Edomite marriage contract: Esther Eshel and Amos Kloner, 'An Aramaic Ostracon of an Edomite Marriage Contract from Maresha, Dated 176 B.C.E.', *IEJ* 46 (1996): 1–22.

54 E.g. פרנא, פורן, פרונה, פרנון. See Jastrow, *A Dictionary of the Targumim*, 1230; Morag and Kara, *Babylonian Aramaic*, 93 attests that in the Yemenite tradition of Aramaic the form פרנא survives.

that involve individuals with Judean and other West Semitic names use *nudunnû*.[55] As Abraham notes, the most likely reason for this is that a *nudunnû* is given only by parties who can afford it and the Judean communities for whom we have marriage contracts were not sufficiently wealthy to afford such a gift.

The normal location for the transfer of a technical term such as *nudunnû* would be in the context in which it is used, in this case the writing of marriage contracts.[56] As we have just said, however, it is peculiarly absent in Akkadian from those marriage contracts involving individuals with West Semitic names, as well as from any Persian period Aramaic marriage contracts. This suggests that either the available evidence is simply incomplete in this question, or that the loan happened elsewhere. The casual use of the word in Ezek 16:33 suggests that it does not require any further explanation and was well-known among Ezekiel's readers.[57] If it is true that Ezekiel and his audience come from a wealthier background than the farmers of *āl Yāhūdu*, we could speculate that they may have given *nudunnû* during their marriage negotiations, and therefore been familiar with them. In either case, the route of transmission from Akkadian to Hebrew must remain an open question at this point in time.

Outside of marriage contracts, the term *nudunnû* also occurs in a number of lexical lists. We find the term on ur_5.ra = *ḫubullu* 13: 146,[58] Erimḫuš III: 39[59] and *ana ittišu* 3, III: 5.[60] However, as a direct loan from Akkadian into Hebrew seems

---

55 For a discussion of these texts, see Kathleen Abraham, 'West Semitic and Judean Brides in Cuneiform Sources of the Sixth Century BCE', *AfO* 51 (2005): 198–219; Cornelia Wunsch, *Urkunden zum Ehe-, Vermögens- und Erbrecht aus verschiedenen neubabylonischen Archiven* (Babylonische Archive 2; Dresden: ISLET, 2003), 21–24. See also Kathleen Abraham's contribution to this volume.

56 On this question see e.g. Haspelmath, 'Loanword Typology'; Haspelmath, 'Lexical Borrowing'.

57 It would be possible to speculate that Ezekiel uses a word of recognizably Akkadian origin to indicate to his readers that he is referring to Judah's pre-Exile betrayal of their Babylonian overlords by siding with Egypt. This suggestion, however, would seem to me to rest on rather shaky grounds due to the peculiar vocalization of the Hebrew term נדניך. We could go on to speculate that the Masoretic vocalization is incorrect and that there was a u-vowel between the second and third root letter, but there is absolutely no evidence to suggest that. LXX translates נדניך with μισθώματα, accusative plural of μισθός ('wages'), thereby misunderstanding the direction of Ezekiel's accusation in any case.

58 See Benno Landsberger, *The Fauna of Ancient Mesopotamia: First Part, Tablet XIII* (MSL 8/1; Rome: Pontifical Biblical Institute, 1960), 19.

59 Cavigneaux, Böck and Roth, *The Series Erim-ḫuš*, 68; According to Cavigneaux (p. 5), there are Neo-Babylonian school-tablets excerpting Erimḫuš.

60 Benno Landsberger, *Die Serie ana ittišu* (MSL 1; Rome: Pontifical Biblical Institute, 1937), 42.

unlikely for phonetic reasons, it appears more plausible that this technical term was not acquired in a school setting.[61]

Derivations from the root חבל (*ḫbl*) are attested in Ezek 18:7, 12, 16 and 33:15. The root חבל has traditionally been linked to Akkadian *ḫabālu* B ('to acquire on credit').[62] Kaufmann followed by Mankowski derives it instead from *ḫabālu* A ('to oppress, wrong, ravage').[63] Both allow that the two nominal forms חֲבֹל and חֲבֹלָה are 'Masoretic assimilation[s] to the Aramaic word *ḥ(y)bwl*, 'interest', which is demonstrably a loan from Akkadian (<*ḫubullu*, NA *ḫabullu*).'[64] חֲבֹל and חֲבֹלָה thus join the growing number of Akkadian words which end up in Hebrew through the intermediation of Aramaic.[65]

The term סוּגַר in Ezek 19:9 is usually taken as a loanword from Akkadian *šigaru* ('lock, neck-stock').[66] It is a relatively common Akkadian word and occurs in a great number of lexical lists.[67] As has been pointed out by many interpreters, the imagery used in the Ezekelian verse fits well with Assyrian practice.[68] While the Hebrew word's derivation from Akkadian seems plausible, the change in vocali-

61 Thus also von Soden, *Akkadisches Handwörterbuch* II: 800; Kaufman, *Akkadian Influences*, 79.

62 See e.g. HALOT; Zimmern, *Akkadische Fremdwörter als Beweis für babylonischen Kultureinfluss*, 18; von Soden, *Akkadisches Handwörterbuch* I: 302. As pointed out by Tawil (*Lexical Companion*, 98), Shalom Paul (*Amos: A Commentary on the Book of Amos* [Hermeneia; Minneapolis: Fortress Press, 1991], 85), had already indicated that Hebrew lexicons give a wrong meaning for *ḫabālu* B as 'to take a pledge'.

63 Kaufman, *Akkadian Influences*, 56 n.122; Mankowski, *Akkadian Loanwords*, 55–56.

64 Mankowski, *Akkadian Loanwords*, 56 relying on Kaufman, *Akkadian Influences*, 71.

65 For discussions of the curious expression and suggestions for emendations, etc. חבלתו חוב see Zimmerli, *Ezechiel 1–24*, 405; Greenberg, *Ezekiel 1–20*, 329; Block, *Ezekiel 1–24*, 570.

66 As first suggested by Friedrich Delitzsch, 'Prefatio et Specimen glossarii Ezechielico-Babylonici', in יחזקאל ספר – *Liber Ezechielis: Textum Masoreticum accuratissime expressit, e fontibus masorae varie illustravit, notis criticis confirmavit* (ed. S. Baer; Leipzig: Tauchnitz, 1884), xv. I follow the normalisation in CAD Š/2. In older publications the word is usually cited as *šigāru*. The meaning 'neck-stock' rather than 'cage' was established by Edmund I. Gordon, 'Of Princes and Foxes: The Neck-Stock in the Newly-Discovered Agade Period Stele', *Sumer* 12 (1956): 80–84. For this word see also Mankowski, *Akkadian Loanwords*, 108; Tawil, *Lexical Companion*, 258; Garfinkel, 'Akkadian Influences,' 116. For further discussions see also Zimmerli, *Ezechiel 1–24*, 426–427; Greenberg, *Ezekiel 1–20*, 352; Block, *Ezekiel 1–24*, 597 n.35.

67 CAD lists ur_5.ra = *ḫubullu* V 294–295, VI 199–200, VI 205–6, XI 282, XXIII v 12 (MSL 11 148 ii 57), idem = *ḫubullu* Forerunner 35 ff., Antagal C 41 ff., Erimḫuš II 45 ff., Erimḫuš Excerpt B r. 5'ff. (MSL 17 28 note to II 45 and 56–48) and Igituḫ I 342.

68 See e.g. Cohen, *Biblical Hapax Legomena*, 48.

zation is striking (/i/ > /ū/). The Hebrew vocalization also occurs in Aramaic, but it is attested only in Syriac and Late Jewish Literary Aramaic.[69] The word may have entered Hebrew through Assyrian propaganda – in which case it is surprising that we find it in Ezekiel and not in Isaiah – through everyday use, or through training in a scribal school. The first possibility seems unlikely, and there is not enough data to decide whether it is more likely to have influenced Ezekiel from a literary context in copying an Assyrian text in his proposed Babylonian school, which might explain the current context; or whether everyday contact of a relatively common word in an agricultural environment can explain its existence in Biblical Hebrew. The latter possibility would not explain the literary use, but the use to which it is put in the expression is not that particular that it needs explaining.

The relatively rare word שָׁשַׁר is attested only in Jer 22:14 and in Ezek 23:14. According to Mankowski it is a clear loan from Akkadian *šaršerru*.[70] Whatever the material on which it is based, it clearly represents some reddish colour – CAD translates 'reddish clay or paste'. The word is attested in ur_5.ra = *ḫubullu* XI 316 which would open it up for potential transfer through scribal training.[71] According to Mankowski the loan is most likely to have occurred in Neo-Babylonian, while von Soden prefers Neo-Assyrian. As Hebrew שָׁשַׁר is attested in pause both times we cannot be sure what the absolute form of the noun would have been, whether שָׁשַׁר or שָׁשֵׁר. If the former is the absolute form, the loan is more likely to have come via Neo-Babylonian, and conversely, if the absolute form is שָׁשֵׁר with the -*ē*-vowel under the second שׁ, the vocalisation would support a derivation via Neo-Assyrian. However, since Neo-Assyrian *šaššeru* is likely to have been pronounced *sasseru* we would be left without being able to explain the *š* in Hebrew.[72]

69 CAL [accessed September 06 2013]. It is possible that the term existed before its Syriac attestations, but its absence in the Targum to Ezekiel make that unlikely; conversely it is possible that Biblical Hebrew influenced Syriac and Late Jewish Literary Aramaic.

70 Mankowski, *Akkadian Loanwords*, 149. Above, I cite the form as it appears in CAD Š/II. Mankowski cites the noun as *šaršaru*. Interestingly, Greenberg, *Ezekiel 21–37*, 479 derives it from Neo-Assyrian *šaššeru* following the lead of von Soden (*Akkadisches Handwörterbuch* III: 1191). See also Tawil, *Lexical Companion*, 424.

71 Benno Landsberger, *The Series ḪAR-ra = ḫubullu Tablets VIII-XII* (MSL 7; Rome: Pontifical Biblical Institute, 1959), 140, 316.

72 For the pronunciation of š in Neo-Assyrian see Simo Parpola, 'The Alleged Middle / Neo-Assyrian Irregular Verb **naṣṣ* and the Assyrian Sound Change š > s', *Assur* 1 (1974): 1–10.

In Ezek 23:44 we find אשת (*ʔiššōṯ*) a peculiar plural form of אִשָּׁה (*ʔiššā*, 'woman').[73] Following Driver's lead, Mankowski interprets this as a likely case in which Akkadian *aššātu* has entered the Hebrew text.[74] It may be possible to regard this as an unconscious influence, with the author unwittingly using a form that has the same meaning but that is not, strictly speaking, Hebrew.[75] It is well known that the Septuagint reads an infinitive of the root עשה ('to do') here, as it is wrestling with the same unusual plural of אשה.[76]

The Hebrew noun מַלָּח (*mallāḥ*, 'sailor'), attested only in Ezek 27:9, 27, 29 and in Jonah 1:5, is undoubtedly a loanword. Mankowski derives it directly from Akkadian, while Wagner regards it as a loan into Hebrew from Aramaic.[77] Both ultimately derive the term from Sumerian malaḫ which is attested in Akkadian as *malāḫu*. While Wagner argues that the doubling of the middle radical in Hebrew indicates that it has been loaned into Hebrew via Aramaic, Mankowski holds that it is also possible that when being loaned into Hebrew from Akkadian the noun was assimilated to the North-West Semitic nominal pattern *qattal* with a lengthening of the second vowel. Unsurprisingly, the term is well represented in the various versions of lú = *ša*, which means that both routes for the loan are conceivable.[78]

73 Normally, the word forms the plural נָשִׁים (*nāšīm*) in Classical Hebrew.

74 G. R. Driver, 'Linguistic and Textual Problems: Ezekiel', *Bib* 19 (1938): 60–69, 175–187 (175); Mankowski, *Akkadian Loanwords*, 45–46; Tawil, *Lexical Companion*, 38; Garfinkel, 'Akkadian Influences,' 46–47. See also Zimmerli, *Ezechiel 1–24*, 536 who reports the suggestion to emend אשת into לעשת on the basis of the Septuagint. Block, *Ezekiel 1–24*, 758 n.168 notes that the Phoenician amulet from Arslan Taš (AT1 = KAI 27:18) has *ʔšt*; but there it is usually interpreted as a singular construct, rather than the plural.

75 See Dong-Hyuk Kim, *Early Biblical Hebrew, Late Biblical Hebrew, and Linguistic Variability: A Sociolinguistic Evaluation of the Linguistic Dating of Biblical Texts* (VTSup 156; Leiden / Boston: Brill, 2013), 85–89 for a good description of some theories of loaning with regard to whether or not they are conscious.

76 Greenberg, *Ezekiel 21–37*, 487 refers to this as 'an attractive emendation of MT', while Zimmerli, *Ezechiel 1–24*, 535–536 only gives a list of commentators who have followed the MT, while himself following Driver's lead.

77 Mankowski, *Akkadian Loanwords*, 93; Max Wagner, *Die lexikalischen und grammatikalischen Aramaismen im alttestamentlichen Hebräisch* (BZAW 96; Berlin: Töpelmann, 1966), 76–77, 152. See also Tawil, *Lexical Companion*, 214.

78 See CAD M/I: 149–150 for details.

Another example is the אֶשְׁכָּר in Ezek 27:15 and Psalm 72:10.[79] It is used in parallel with the מִנְחָה ('gift, tribute') paid by the kings of Taršiš, and its meaning should therefore be sought in that semantic field. Normally, it is translated as 'tribute' (thus HALOT). The word is a loan from Akkadian *iškaru* which itself is loaned into Akkadian from Sumerian (éš-gàr). The Akkadian *iškaru* covers the semantic field of 'corvée work', 'manpower', 'equipment', and their 'monetary' equivalent (whence the Aramaic meaning 'field'); it is from this latter meaning that Ezek 27:15 takes its cue; the coastlands paid in ivory and ebony instead of providing manpower. We, thus, see the use of a Neo-Babylonian technical term being borrowed into West Semitic languages.

Another example is גַּלָּב ('barber') – from Akkadian *gallābu*. Ezekiel is commanded to shave his head and beard in Ezek 5:1 in order to produce the hair that he needs for a slightly enigmatic sign-act in which he is to burn a third of his hair, throw a third in the air and hit it with a sword, and to scatter a third in the wind. Out of this last group the prophet is to take some hair symbolising the survivors. Then the prophet is to throw some more of that last lot into the fire. It is possible that the word גַּלָּב would have been more common than it seems to us – after all, we do not have access to a comprehensive corpus of Classical Hebrew literature or every-day speech but only to the small and selected group of texts in the Hebrew Bible.[80] It is sometimes argued, that the word occurs in Ugaritic, as it does in later Phoenician, Nabatean, and other more recent Semitic languages, but the term *gulbumu*, related to Akkadian *gulbūtu*, is translated as 'barley' by more recent lexical studies, so that there is no pre-Ezekielian attestation in any West Semitic language. As it stands, גַּלָּב is a *hapax legomenon* and the links with Akkadian *gallābu* are fairly uncontroversial.[81] While the Akkadian word is the standard word for any barber, it features large in the world of the Babylonian priesthood,

---

79 See, e.g., Mankowski, *Akkadian Loanwords*, 42; Greenberg, *Ezekiel 21–37*, 555; Tawil, *Lexical Companion*, 39.

80 According to Kaufman, *Akkadian Influences*, 51, '[e]vidence to determine whether these terms [sic] are borrowed or merely cognate is lacking.' He quotes Heinrich Zimmern, *Akkadische Fremdwörter als Beweis für babylonischen Kultureinfluss* (Leipzig: Hinrichs'sche Buchhandlung, 1917), 28; Carl Brockelmann, *Lexicon Syriacum* (Halle: M. Niemeyer, 1928), 117; von Soden, *Akkadisches Handwörterbuch* I: 274. While Zimmern's 1915 doctoral thesis is a remarkable piece of work for the time it is now obviously outdated. See also Greenberg, *Ezekiel 1–20*, 108 who supports the theory of a loan from Akkadian.

81 Tawil, *Lexical Companion*, 65; Cohen, *Biblical Hapax Legomena*, 134; Hayim ben Yosef Tawil, 'Late Biblical Hebrew-Aramaic ספר, Neo-Babylonian *sirpu/sirapu*: A Lexicographical Note IV', *Beit Mikra* 154–155 (1998): 343–342[sic!].

as they were shaven before entering the temple precinct. The shaving in Ezekiel 5 is not linked to priestly shaving – instead it is linked to mourning rites. Ezekiel's awareness of priestly shaving can be seen in chapter 44 where he argues vociferously against it.

The term *gallābu* is contained on lú=*ša* I: 152b,c-153, and would, thus, have been part of the basic scribal training. Considering the importance of the profession this does not surprise.[82] As the word is so common, it seems prudent not to decide whether the word entered Hebrew through spoken Aramaic or Akkadian or whether it would have been picked up through scribal training, as either path of transmission would have been very likely.

Ezek 27:24 contains a well-known *hapax legomenon*, בְּרֹמִים (*bĕrōmīm*), which is usually derived from Akkadian. Due to its vocalisation, Cohen's suggestion to derive it from *birmu* ('multi-coloured') is rather unlikely to be correct.[83] HALOT suggests a derivation from *burummu* ('multi-coloured piece of clothing'), pointing to an Assyrian dialect form *barummu*, both of which would nicely explain the Hebrew vocalization. The verb *barāmu* ('to be variegated') and its derivatives often refer to multi-coloured items, in particular a kind of bird (*burummu*) and clothing (*barmu*).

There can be little doubt that Hebrew מָנֶה (*mānā*) in Ezek 45:12 is a Hebrew version of the Akkadian word *manû* ('mina').[84] As Mankowski admits, the term seems to be a normal Hebrew reflex of the Hebrew root *mny* ('to count'). However, he follows Kaufman's argument that the absence of the term from Ugarit, and its presence in Biblical Hebrew no earlier than the exilic period indicates that it is a loan from Akkadian, in spite of the fact that the word is vocalised מָנֶה and not מָנוּ as would be expected if it were a loan. In my view, to call the term a loanword is imprecise; it appears to be what Hapelmath refers to as a 'loanshift', and more precisely as a semantic borrowing, as it seems to be a Hebrew formation inspired by the Akkadian term.[85] Looking for a possible social location for the borrowing therefore appears to be futile.

---

82 Miguel Civil, *The Series lú = ša and Related Texts* (MSL 12; Rome: Pontifical Biblical Institute, 1969), 100.

83 Cohen, *Biblical Hapax Legomena*, 48–49.

84 Mankowski, *Akkadian Loanwords*, 94; Kaufman, *Akkadian Influences*, 69; Tawil, *Lexical Companion*, 217.

85 Haspelmath, 'Loanword Typology' classifies this kind of loan as a 'loan translation'.

The last example that I will look at is דרור (*děrōr*) in Ezek 46:17, which is also attested in Lev 25:10, Isa 61:1, Jer 34:8, 15 and 17. Most of the dictionaries list it as an Akkadian loanword in Hebrew from the word (*an*)*durāru* ('remission of debts').[86] Mankowski hesitates to identify it as a direct loan on account of the loss of the /*an*/ prefix as well as the change of the long /*ā*/ in *andurāru* to a long /*ō*/ in Hebrew דרור. According to Lemche, the dropping of the prefix /*an-*/ can best be explained through the Neo-Assyrian by-form *durāru*, but as Mankowski points out, this does not explain the vocalisation with an /*ō*/.[87] On the basis of the vocalisation Mankowski suggests that it is explained most easily as a loan-adaptation.[88]

Christoph Uehlinger recently presented a study of the evolution of the imagery in Ezekiel 1 and 10 from a basically Mesopotamian image of the four beasts with indistinct faces into a Mesopotamian-Judean hybrid in which the four beasts are individualised.[89] His view depends on a redaction-critical reading of both chapters that he has argued for elsewhere, but it paints a persuasive picture of how an image may have been used in an exilic text, and when that text was transported back into a Judean context, it was changed and evolved further. Once chapter 1 was added to chapter 10, the קרובים of chapters 8–11 started to be equated to the חיות of chapter 1 for scroll-internal consistency. The *Wirkungsgeschichte* of the חיות goes from Mesopotamia and Ain Dara right into most western Christian churches, where the four animals have changed again, now representing not angelic beings but the four Evangelists.

3.3 Structural Examples

These are just some of the many examples of uses of Akkadian loanwords and iconography in Ezekiel. According to David Vanderhooft, they indicate that the author of the book was thoroughly acculturated into Babylonian society.[90] Indeed, all of the examples of loanwords in the book of Ezekiel can be found on the standard word-lists that form part of the material for the basic part of scribal

---

86 Thus also Tawil, *Lexical Companion*, 81.

87 Niels Peter Lemche, '*Andurārum* and *mīšarum*: Comments on the Problem of Social Edicts and their Application in the Ancient Near East', *JNES* 38 (1979): 11–22 (22); Mankowski, *Akkadian Loanwords*, 51.

88 Mankowski, *Akkadian Loanwords*, 50–51.

89 See Uehlinger, 'Virtual Vision vs. Actual Show'.

90 Vanderhooft, 'Acculturation in Ezekiel'.

training. Most of them could also be learned through cultural contact with trained scribes through professional dealings, such as contracts, sales, debt-notes, inheritance, etc., as we can see from the Murašû archive and the *āl Yāhūdu* texts. Many of the loanwords here are likely to have been transmitted to Hebrew via Aramaic, which could mean that they are evidence of the divulgation and internationalisation of legal and scribal language in general rather than cuneiform schooling for Ezekiel.

The next three examples will go deeper than the mere existence of loanwords and iconography that may have been picked up through less intensive contact. Two of these are literary structures, and the third shows the use of Mesopotamian hermeneutic principals to explain a difficult passage.

The first example is that of a common motif in Ezekiel and the well-known Mesopotamian myth *Erra and Išum*: the preservation of the city. Erra and Išum was widely distributed and we can assume that a high level Judean in Babylon, as opposed to a low level Judean farmer in Nippur, would have had access to it at least in oral form. The links between Erra and Išum on the one hand and on the other the book of Ezekiel have long since exercised scholars' minds. Frankena already pointed to some of them in his 1965 inaugural lecture in Utrecht, and Daniel Bodi has presented a fuller analysis and continues to study this field.[91] The first example is the theme of preservation from the flood. The text of Erra IV: 50 has

> Even Sippar, the eternal city, which the Lord of
> Lands did not allow the Flood to overwhelm,
> because it was so dear to him.[92]

According to Bodi, Ezek 22:24 contains the same theme:

> O mortal, say to her: You are an uncleansed land, not washed with rain on the day of indignation.

The intention of the two expressions is different – the preservation of Sippar is positive, while Ezekiel describes the preservation of Jerusalem as causing the city not to have been purified of human transgression during the great flood.[93]

---

91 R. Frankena in his inaugural address published as *Kanttekeningen van een Assyrioloog bij Ezechiël* (Leiden: E. J. Brill, 1965); Bodi, *Ezekiel and Erra*; Bodi, *Commentary on Ezekiel.*

92 Luigi Cagni, *The Poem of Erra* (Malibu: Undena Publications, 1977); Luigi Cagni, *Das Erra-Epos: Keilschrifttext* (Studia Pohl 5; Rome: Päpstliches Bibelinstitut, 1970).

93 Bodi (*Ezekiel and Erra*, 306–320) also identifies other themes, such as that of the intercessor, and that of the deity who departs the sanctuary thereby causing catastrophe – in the case of the Hebrew Bible this catastrophe is the exile, in the case of *Erra and Išum* the catastrophe is the

The second example is Ezekiel's famous exhortation against male and female prophets in chapter 13. The pericope is replete with Akkadian loanwords, mostly in connection with either magical practices or the underworld. Additionally, the feminine participle plural in the Dt-stem (hitpael) of the root נ.ב.א occurs only here in the Hebrew Bible. Some time ago, Nancy Bowen suggested that the second half of the chapter – the pericope on female prophets – follows the basic structure of the anti-witchcraft ritual *Maqlû* ('the burning').[94] The basic structure of *Maqlû* as identified by Bowen on the basis Tzvi Abusch's analysis is the following:

1. Judgement and execution of the witch
2. Release of the effects of witchcraft, burning of the witch (hence the name of the ritual)
3. Extinguishing the fire and life of the witch
4. Disposal of the body of the witch

The second half of Ezekiel 13 follows a similar pattern. Part one: in vv. 18–19(, 22) the women are judged for their harmful activities. Part two: Yhwh judges them (vv. 20–21[, 23]). As Ezekiel 13 does not advocate burning, the third and fourth parts fall into one: there is no need to extinguish any fire. In verses 21–23 the deity imposes a ban on the women whose power has previously been neutralized and they are removed from society. The first half of Ezekiel 13 (vv. 3–17), addressed against male prophets also follows a similar structure.[95] If Bowen's interpretation that Ezekiel 13 was aware of *Maqlû* or at least a text very much like it is correct, the author or editor of the chapter would have had to have access either to an *āšipu* willing to explain the procedure, Alternatively, taking into account the appeal of secrecy as a virtue among Babylonian scholars, the authors / editors could have undergone some training themselves.

flood. Bodi's study argues that the parallels he identifies indicate that it is likely that the author of Ezekiel was aware of *Erra and Išum* and inspired by it in his own literary creation. In this form Bodi's bold thesis has not found many supporters – for skeptical reviews of Bodi's work, see, e.g., Nicholas Postgate (*VT* 43 [1993]: 127–129) and Michael S. Moore (*JBL* 112 [1993]: 519–520), and I would agree that it is unlikely that Ezekiel wrote with a copy of *Erra and Išum* in front of him. But that does not mean that individual examples are impossible.

94 Nancy R. Bowen, 'The Daughters of Your People: Female Prophets in Ezekiel 13:17–23', *JBL* 118 (1999): 417–433. On Ezekiel 13 see also Stökl, 'Ezekiel 13'. Additionally, Garfinkel, 'Of Thistles and Thorns', 435–437, links Ezek 2:6 to *Maqlû* III: 150–157. See I. Tzvi Abusch and Daniel Schwemer, *Corpus of Mesopotamian Anti-Witchcraft Rituals: Vol. I* (Ancient Magic and Divination 8.1; Leiden / Boston: Brill, 2011), for related texts.

95 There are natural similarities in both texts to the order of legal procedure of accusation, judgement of the accused, and carrying out of the judgement.

The third example is taken from Avraham Winitzer's recent study of the connections between Gilgameš and Ezekiel.[96] It illustrates that Ezekiel could have had access also to and introduction to Mesopotamian textual hermeneutic.

Ezek 4:4–6 reads:

> 4"Then lie on your left side, and let it bear the punishment of the House of Israel; for as many days as you lie on it you shall bear their punishment. 5For I impose upon you three hundred and ninety days, corresponding to the number of the years of their punishment; and so you shall bear the punishment for the House of Israel.
> 6When you have completed these, you shall lie another forty days on your right side, and bear the punishment of the House of Judah. I impose on you one day for each year.

Interpreters have wrestled with the question why Ezekiel is to lie 390 days on his left and 40 on his right in the Masoretic text. The Septuagint of Ezekiel preserves the same text with the difference that Ezekiel only needs to lie on his left side for 150 days instead of 390. What on first sight may only change the number of days lying on one side may be explained as the result of learned exegesis, following the rules of Mesopotamian hermeneutics.[97]

As Winitzer notes, 150 corresponds to a learned spelling of the word *šumēla* ('left') in cuneiform. It is usually spelled as 2, 30 with the 2 representing 2 × 60 in the Mesopotamian base 60 system. The 40 days on the right (Akkadian *imitta*) are less immediately obvious but could be the result of a sophisticated mathematical-hermeneutical procedure. The reciprocal of 150 in a base 60 system would be 0.4 (1/150 × 60).[98] The number 0.4 would be graphically realised as a 40 in cuneiform. If Winitzer's analysis of this reference is correct the use of the numbers with left and right would correspond to learned exegesis and hermeneutics in the text production of Ezekiel 5. While such analysis may sound somewhat suspect to the modern scientific mind, we can find numerous cases of *gematria*-like interpretation in Akkadian commentary literature, showing that it was regarded as a valid form of interpretation.[99] It is but one form of the normal Akkadian exegetical

---

96 Abraham Winitzer, 'Assyriology and Jewish Studies in Tel Aviv: Ezekiel among the Babylonian *literati*', in *Encounters by the Rivers of Babylon: Scholarly Conversations between Jews, Iranians and Babylonians in Antiquity* (ed. U. Gabbay and S. Secunda; TSAJ 160, Tübingen: Mohr Siebeck, 2014), 163–216.

97 Eckart Frahm, *Babylonian and Assyrian Text Commentaries: Origins of Interpretation* (GMTR 5; Münster: Ugarit-Verlag, 2011).

98 The reciprocal of a number is calculated by dividing 1 by it. Expressed mathematically, the reciprocal of a number n is 1/n (e.g., in a base 10 system, the reciprocal of 5 is 1/5 = 0.2).

99 On the use of *gematria* as a hermeneutic principal, see Frahm, *Commentaries*, 76–79. Winitzer notes the esoteric text i.NAM.giš.ḫur.an.ki.a as an example for mathematic-based hermeneutics.

principle to read a different value for the signs out of which a word or sentence is composed in order to arrive at a different meaning, which is then put (sometimes forced) into some form of a connection to the original word.

4 Conclusions

What can we conclude from the preceding? It appears that some of the texts in the book of Ezekiel show evidence of not only the priestly lore of Israel and Judah but also to some of the *niṣirtu*, the secret knowledge, to which only people had access who had undergone a certain amount of training.[100] On first glance it seems that it is unlikely that the Babylonians or Persians would have granted access to a Judean to cuneiform school.[101] And each of the references on their own could possibly be explained in other ways. But together they do form a reasonably strong cumulative case.

Three models for the path by which Ezekiel acquired the Babylonian culture in his book come to mind. In a first scenario we assume that simple every-day contact, 'acculturation' in Vanderhooft's terminology, is sufficient for this.[102] But how would Ezekiel have got access to secret knowledge? A second possibility is that he may have had access to someone who explained everything to him. While that is theoretically possible, it is unlikely. Divulging secret knowledge to anyone

---

For the text, see Alasdair Livingstone, *Mystical and Mythological Explanatory Works of Assyrian and Babylonian Scholars* (Oxford: Clarendon, 1986), 17–52.

100 There appear to be some structural similarities between the Akkadian *niṣirtu* and the Qumran רז ('secret'), in that both can refer to special knowledge not available to those not initiated in their respective scholarly interpretative tradition. On רז, and its Aramaic equivalent רזא, at Qumran see, e.g., Esther Eshel, 'The *Genesis Apocryphon* and Other Related Aramaic Texts from Qumran: The Birth of Noah', in *Aramaica Qumranica: The Aix en Provence Colloquium on the Aramaic Dead Sea Scrolls* (STDJ 94; ed. K. Berthelot and D. Stökl Ben Ezra; Leiden / Boston: Brill, 2010), 277–297 (289–294); Jonathan Ben-Dov, 'Scientific Writings in Aramaic and Hebrew at Qumran: Translation and Concealment', in *Aramaica Qumranica*, 379–402 (397–399).

101 According to Mladen Popović ('Network of Scholars: The Transmission of Astronomical and Astrological Learning between Babylonians, Greeks and Jews', in *Ancient Jewish Sciences and the History of Knowledge* [ed. J. Ben-Dov and S. L. Sanders; New York: New York University Press, 2014], 153–194), mathematical, astronomical and astrological knowledge that can be found in the Qumran scrolls is several centuries out of date in comparison with its Babylonian counterparts. It may be possible to speculate that the Persians organised their own Akkadian cuneiform schools for administrative reasons but that their access to material was somewhat restricted compared to the training for Babylonians themselves. This might explain the time-delay noticed by Popovič.

102 Vanderhooft, 'Acculturation in Ezekiel'.

who was not a member of the Babylonian scribal elite but a foreigner seems implausible. Caroline Waerzeggers has recently mapped the connection between individual Judeans and Babylonians attested in the Neo-Babylonian corpus from Borsippa. Not a single Judean was in direct contact with a priest or a scholar of sufficient standing. While the data is not complete this does indicate that the transfer of knowledge is likely to have taken another route.[103]

The third possibility for the transfer of information is through cuneiform education. This is where Ezekiel could have picked up the information, training and contacts that would explain the amount of knowledge, its quality, and the literary, theological and hermeneutic skill with which it is used in the book of Ezekiel. The structural and especially the hermeneutic parallel in conjunction with knowledge of cuneiform script otherwise seem coincidental. On their own, the loanwords can be explained by cultural immersion; at most, they indicate primary scribal training. Together with the structural parallels and the hermeneutic one, however, they might serve an indication that the author(s) of Ezekiel had access to secondary or even higher level scribal training. Our data currently indicate that the Babylonians did not provide access to cuneiform scribal training to people of non-Babylonian origin. My suggestion therefore appears to contradict what we already know. This forces me to question the results of my study. But until a better explanation is found to explain the data that we have, cuneiform scribal schooling appears to be the best model for the book of Ezekiel.

Acknowledgment

A first draft of this paper was presented to the annual meeting of the British Association for Jewish Studies in London in 2012 and then in the joint session of the Prophetic Texts in their Ancient Contexts and the Theology in the book of Ezekiel groups at the annual meeting of the SBL later that year. I would like to thank the panelists and audience of both session for the discussions. I would particularly like to thank Jonathan Ben Dov, Mladen Popović and Caroline Waerzeggers for their comments and questions. The research for this paper was carried out under the auspices of the ERC project 'Babylon' directed by Caroline Waerzeggers at Leiden University.

103 Waerzeggers, 'Locating Contact in the Babylonian Exile'.

H. G. M. Williamson

The Setting of Deutero-Isaiah: Some Linguistic Considerations

The geographical setting of any piece of writing that appears to include propagandistic elements is naturally of considerable importance. Without such knowledge, the questions of who is being addressed, what the rhetorical force of the writing may be, and the desired outcome of the writer all remain uncertain.

The place of composition of Isaiah 40–55 was hardly a topic of concern for much of the past two and a half millennia because it was assumed that it had all been written by the eighth-century Judean prophet Isaiah; anything that might appear to relate to the circumstances of what we call the Neo-Babylonian period was the result of divinely inspired prophecy. Curiously, for our current quest this could mean that the writing was as good as something written in Babylon at that later time, so that one might relate text to historical setting in a seamless manner. Although a few very conservative scholars still hold to this position,[1] there would be general agreement that their motivation derives from a religious presupposition with regard to the nature of the Bible, making it difficult to engage with their arguments in the form of normal scholarly discourse.

By contrast, over the past two centuries the view has gradually come to well-nigh universal agreement that these chapters are the product of a later writer or writers roughly contemporary with the period of transition from the Neo-Babylonian to the Achaemenid empire. Unfortunately, however, that is far from being the end of our difficulties. A general consensus that had been reached by the middle of the past century has now been challenged in several different ways, leading us back into uncertainty over several of the basic questions I mentioned at the outset.

The consensus was that these chapters were written more or less in their entirety in Babylon shortly before the arrival there of Cyrus. The path to that consensus was not quite as straightforward as might be supposed from the textbooks, and the elements which led to it have been well documented by Barstad.[2]

---

1 E.g. John N. Oswalt, *The Book of Isaiah Chapters 1–39* and *Chapters 40–66* (NICOT; Grand Rapids: Eerdmans, 1986 and 1998); Alec Motyer, *The Prophecy of Isaiah* (Leicester: Inter-Varsity, 1993); Kenneth A. Kitchen, *On the Reliability of the Old Testament* (Grand Rapids: Eerdmans, 2003), 378–80.
2 Hans M. Barstad, *The Babylonian Captivity of the Book of Isaiah: "Exilic" Judah and the Provenance of Isaiah 40–55* (Oslo: Novus, 1997).

H. G. M. Williamson: University of Oxford

There were two major steps in the process. First, the definition of the extent of the work under discussion was largely resolved by Bernhard Duhm's commentary of 1892. He argued against the previous opinion that Isaiah 40–66 as a whole should be ascribed to a single author.[3] For reasons that seem obvious to most of us as soon as they are presented, he demonstrated that chapters 40–55 address the situation in Babylon whereas chapters 56–66 presuppose a setting in Judah and Jerusalem. Although the composition history of 56–66 (and perhaps of 40–55) now appears more complicated than a simple two-staged work might suggest, the number of those who still hold to a unified composition of 40–66 as a whole is now marginal, and I do not intend to engage further with them.[4] The previous consensus was agreed in ascribing chapters 40–55 to a single author separate from the material before and after it.

The location of this author was also variously identified at first, Duhm himself, for instance, favouring Phoenicia, and other suggestions including Egypt (and perhaps Syene in particular), and Palestine.[5] Babylon was also always preferred by some commentators, however, and over the course of time this became the almost unanimous view.

Both elements of this consensus have been challenged in recent years. In the first place, two scholars in particular, while generally still referring comfortably to 'Deutero-Isaiah', have argued strongly for a Palestinian setting. Barstad, already mentioned, is one, in a lengthy series of interrelated studies,[6] and most recently Tiemeyer has published a substantial monograph dedicated entirely to this question.[7] If they are right this will inevitably have significant implications for our

---

3 Bernhard Duhm, *Das Buch Jesaia* (HKAT 3/1; Göttingen: Vandenhoeck & Ruprecht, 1892).

4 E.g., Benjamin D. Sommer, *A Prophet Reads Scripture: Allusion in Isaiah 40–66* (Stanford: Stanford University Press, 1998); Shalom M. Paul, *Isaiah 40–66: Introduction and Commentary* (2 vols., Hebrew; Mikra LeYisrael; Tel Aviv: Am Oved, and Jerusalem: Magnes, 2008); from an earlier generation, see especially Charles C. Torrey, *The Second Isaiah: A New Interpretation* (Edinburgh: T & T Clark, 1928).

5 See Barstad, *Babylonian Captivity*, 23–33.

6 In addition to *Babylonian Captivity*, see *inter alia* Hans M. Barstad, 'Lebte Deuterojesaja in Judäa?', in *Veterotestamentica: Donum natalicium Aruido S. Kapelrud a collegis et amicis XIV lustra complenti* (*NTT* 83/2, ed. S. A. Christoffersen and Hans M. Barstad; Oslo: Universitetsforlaget, 1982), 77–87; idem, 'On the So-Called Babylonian Literary Influence in Second Isaiah', *SJOT* 1:2 (1987): 90–110; idem, *A Way in the Wilderness: The 'Second Exodus' in the Message of Second Isaiah* (JSSM 12; Manchester: University of Manchester, 1989); idem, 'Akkadian "Loanwords" in Isaiah 40–55 and the Question of the Babylonian Origin of Deutero-Isaiah', in *Text and Theology: Studies in Honour of Prof. Dr. Theol. Magne Saebø* (ed. A. Tångberg; Oslo: Verbum, 1994), 36–48.

7 Lena-Sofia Tiemeyer, *For the Comfort of Zion: The Geographical and Theological Location of Isaiah 40–55* (VTSup 139; Leiden: Brill, 2011).

understanding of a number of central topics in these chapters. Of major concern to the theme of the present volume are, of course, those several passages which have previously been understood to relate to the return from exile as a journey through the desert under the guise of a second exodus. Two or three studies have appeared recently which have sought to reinterpret these passages metaphorically in different directions.[8] It is not that these chapters are completely devoid of material relevant to exile and return, but things clearly look very different if the standpoint adopted is that of the home territory rather than the exilic setting. Second, the famous anti-idol polemics will also need re-evaluation, for though we need not doubt that idolatry was known in Judah, it will have had a somewhat different theology from that which is more specific to and distinctive of Mesopotamia. Third, the presentation of Cyrus and his arrival in Babylon would need to be rethought if it did not address the immediate needs of the Judeans who were living close at hand. And finally, given that the whole purpose of these chapters seems to have as one of its major concerns the encouragement to faith of a community which is presented as having lost all confidence in God's ability or willingness to aid them, it will be inevitable that the general circumstances in which the target audience was living will need to be rethought if it applies to people in Judah rather than in Babylon.

The other challenge to the previous consensus is that a number of significant studies have appeared which challenge the authorial unity of these chapters. These studies differ among themselves over many significant points of detail, but they are united in adopting a fairly radical redaction-critical approach. Going beyond the relatively common, though not universal, opinion that some of the idol passages and the four servant songs might represent late additions to the basic text, these studies argue for several layers of composition throughout these chapters.[9] Only a limited amount could possibly belong to the Neo-Babylo-

---

8 Barstad, *Way*; Øystein Lund, *Way Metaphors and Way Topics in Isaiah 40–55* (FAT, 2. Reihe 28; Tübingen: Mohr Siebeck, 2007); Bo H. Lim, *The "Way of the Lord" in the Book of Isaiah* (LHBOTS 522; NewYork / London: T & T Clark, 2010).

9 E.g., Klaus Kiesow, *Exodustexte im Jesajabuch: literarkritische und motivgeschichtliche Analysen* (OBO 24; Freiburg: Universitätsverlag, and Göttingen: Vandenhoeck & Ruprecht, 1979); Rosario P. Merendino, *Der Erste und der Letzte: Eine Untersuchung von Jes 40–48* (VTSup 31; Leiden: Brill, 1981); Reinhard G. Kratz, *Kyros im Deuterojesaja-Buch: Redaktionsgeschichtliche Untersuchungen zu Entstehung und Theologie von Jes 40–55* (FAT 1; Tübingen: Mohr [Paul Siebeck], 1991); Odil Hannes Steck, *Gottesknecht und Zion: Gesammelte Aufsätze zu Deuterojesaja* (FAT 4; Tübingen: Mohr [Paul Siebeck], 1992); Jürgen van Oorschot, *Von Babel zum Zion: Eine literarkritische und redaktionsgeschichtliche Untersuchung* (BZAW 206; Berlin: de Gruyter, 1993); Ulrich Berges, *Das Buch Jesaja: Komposition und Endgestalt* (HBS 16; Freiburg: Herder, 1998), 322–413 (in his more recent commentary he ascribes much of the basic composition to a circle of writers who

nian period; much was added in successive stages over the following decades. Although this new phase of research has not attended so much to the issue of geographical location, it is obvious that it is theoretically related and one might well suppose that different locations might be posited for different layers.

In considering what part, if any, linguistic factors might contribute to a discussion of the first challenge to the consensus it is obvious that I need to take some sort of position on the second in order to know with what material I should be dealing. First, as will be seen below, I accept the possibility that, as with many other biblical texts, there may be shorter or longer additions of an explanatory, updating or correcting nature. It is in the nature of the case that each has to be discussed and identified on an individual basis and, against what I regard as a widespread misuse of terminology, these should not be called a redaction or redactional layer. If the latter implies the need for complete reworking of a scroll, these *Fortschreibungen* or *relectures* (both in a strict sense rather than the misapplication that again has become all too common) can, by contrast, be easily accommodated as scribal additions to an existing scroll and so may be treated as more 'random' from a compositional perspective.[10]

Second, I am in agreement with those who find the distinction between chapters 40–48 and 49–55 more impressive than the bases on which horizontal redactional layering throughout these chapters is posited. To summarize the case that has been made more fully elsewhere, the following characteristic elements occur regularly in the first part but not at all in the second:[11] material related to Cyrus, references to Babylon, anti-idol polemic, trial scenes, and the contrast between

were close to the temple Levitical singers: *Jesaja 40–48* [HThKAT; Freiburg: Herder, 2008]); Jürgen Werlitz, *Redaktion und Komposition: Zur Rückfrage hinter die Endgestalt von Jesaja 40–55* (BBB 122; Berlin: Philo, 1999); for reflections on some of these works in a generally sympathetic manner, see Hans-Jürgen Hermisson, 'Einheit und Komplexität Deuterojesajas: Probleme der Redaktionsgeschichte von Jes 40–55', in *The Book of Isaiah* (BETL 81; ed. J. Vermeylen; Leuven: University Press and Peeters, 1989), 287–312 (repr. in *Studien zu Prophetie und Weisheit: Gesammelte Aufsätze* [FAT 23; Tübingen: Mohr Siebeck, 1998], 132–57); Rainer Albertz, *Die Exilszeit: 6. Jahrhundert v. Chr.* (Biblische Enzyklopädie 7; Stuttgart: Kohlhammer, 2001), 283–323 (ET, *Israel in Exile: The History and Literature of the Sixth Century B.C.E.* [Studies in Biblical Literature 3; Atlanta: SBL, 2003]).

10 See my 'The Vindication of Redaction Criticism', in *Biblical Interpretation and Method: Essays in Honour of John Barton* (ed. K. Dell and P. Joyce; Oxford: Oxford University Press, 2013), 26–36.

11 See, for instance, Menahem Haran, 'The Literary Structure and Chronological Framework of the Prophecies in Is. xl–xlviii', in *Congress Volume: Bonn 1962* (VTSup 9; Leiden: Brill, 1963), 127–55; Peter Wilcox and David Paton-Williams, 'The Servant Songs in Deutero-Isaiah', *JSOT* 42 (1988): 79–102; Joseph Blenkinsopp, *Isaiah 40–55: A New Translation with Introduction and Commentary* (AB 19A; New York: Doubleday, 2002), 59–61 *et passim*.

the 'former things' and 'the new (or coming) things'. In addition, the names of the addressees in 40–48 are regularly Jacob/Israel, but this does not occur at all in 49–55 except in the opening verses of chapter 49 which itself tells of a transition in the work of the servant precisely in regard to whom he is to address in his ministry. This latter point underlines the clear distinction between the two parts and also indicates that it is consciously planned.[12] In chapters 49–55 the addressees are generally Jerusalem or Zion, suggestive of a different vantage point. These names occur only occasionally in 40–48, and then primarily in places which are likely to be part of the final shaping of the material, such as the introductory 40:1–11. In the light of these observations it is clear that it would be prudent to restrict the corpus for investigation to chapters 40–48 if we are seeking to ascertain whether any of this material can be securely located in Babylon rather than Judah.

The role that language in general can play in this discussion is open to challenge. The Hebrew of the Old Testament is a comfortable member of the North-West Semitic family, although some elements of its orthography, grammar, and syntax are complicated by the fact that the text itself has been transmitted over many centuries by a living community and that it received major attention in the middle of the first Christian millennium in a way that has affected all of us who come later to learn it. The Dead Sea Scrolls, at least, give us insights into the form of the text around the turn of the eras (which is long before the representation of vocalization was added to the written text), but even so they remain considerably later than the main period of composition. Given the paucity of inscriptions or other samples of writing contemporary with the composition of the biblical text, our knowledge of ancient Hebrew remains limited and spasmodic. Despite a good deal of recent discussion[13] it remains far from clear to what extent, if at all, we can distinguish regional variations or dialects, and diachronic conclusions, with which we are familiar and which still seem cogent to me within certain limitations, have recently been forcefully challenged.[14] So the first problem we face is the limited scope of secure knowledge on which to proceed.

12 See my 'Jacob in Isaiah 40–66', in *Continuity and Discontinuity: Chronological and Thematic Development in Isaiah 40–66* (FRLANT; ed. Hans M. Barstad and Lena-Sofia Tiemeyer; Göttingen: Vandenhoeck & Ruprecht, 2014), 175–94.

13 See, for example, Gary A. Rendsburg, *Linguistic Evidence for the Northern Origin of Selected Psalms* (SBLMS 43; Atlanta: Scholars Press, 1990); Ian Young, *Diversity in Pre-Exilic Hebrew* (FAT 5; Tübingen: Mohr [Paul Siebeck], 1993); Scott B. Noegel and Gary A. Rendsburg, *Solomon's Vineyard: Literary and Linguistic Studies in the Song of Songs* (Ancient Israel and its Literature 1; Atlanta: Society of Biblical Literature, 2009), 3–55.

14 For a wide range of essays that represent different points of view on this topic, see Ian Young (ed.), *Biblical Hebrew: Studies in Chronology and Typology* (JSOTSup 369; London: T & T Clark

In addition, however, it has to be acknowledged that the lexical stock is so small that it becomes difficult to assert with any confidence whether an obscure item of vocabulary is obscure because it has been borrowed from elsewhere (Ugaritic, Aramaic, Akkadian or other) or simply because it happens not to occur elsewhere in the corpus even though it was a perfectly common Hebrew word in all other respects. We have to be cautious not to assume that our modern philological brilliance in unearthing ancient meanings on comparative bases may not mislead us into thinking that we have at the same time stumbled across anything that would have seemed unlikely to a native speaker.

For these reasons it has to be accepted that whatever linguistic evidence is brought to bear on the question of geographical location can be met with the rejoinder that it is all just a matter of chance, the accident of survival, and so on. Nevertheless, some lines of argument may be more persuasive than others, and what I propose to do now is to take one example from each of the three main categories of material that I mentioned earlier as those for which geographical setting might be of particular importance for interpretation (i.e. the return journey from exile, anti-idol polemics, and Cyrus and Babylon; I shall deal with these in reverse order). Each example will focus on a word which appears to have been misunderstood in later tradition (or at least in major parts of it), as we can tell from unexpected vocalization, to go no further, and which can now be most reasonably understood in the light of Akkadian as attested in the Neo-Babylonian period. Given that each of the three is a hapax legomenon and that common Hebrew alternatives could have been used in their place, and given also that each of the three relates in some distinctive manner to matters of Babylonian concern, I suggest that the most reasonable explanation for this is that it shows influence from its geographical environment at the time of writing.[15] I need hardly add that the identification of these words is not original to me here, but I hope that this manner of juxtaposing them may reinforce their relevance for our present concern in a new and more forceful manner.

International, 2003). Beyond that it is sufficient to refer here to the two volumes of Ian Young, Robert Rezetko and Martin Ehrensvärd, *Linguistic Dating of Biblical Texts* (London: Equinox, 2008). Volume 2 includes a lengthy survey of previous research.

15 See the somewhat comparable line of argument in David S. Vanderhooft, *The Neo-Babylonian Empire and Babylon in the Latter Prophets* (HSM 59; Atlanta: Scholars Press, 1999), 169–88. While we both discuss Isa 40:20, he does not attend to either 45:2 or 44:4, so that to that extent my analysis may be said to supplement his.

(1) Isaiah 45:2. This verse is part of the main Cyrus oracle (44:24–45:7), which prophecies (among other things) his triumphal arrival at Babylon. Most of it implies that it will be taken by violent attack:

> Thus says the Lord to his anointed, to Cyrus,
> whose right hand I have grasped
> to subdue nations before him
> and strip kings of their robes ...
> I will go before you
> and level the mountains.
> I will break in pieces the doors of bronze
> and cut through the bars of iron ... (Isa 45:1–2, NRSV)

As has been fully explained by Kratz,[16] however, there is a sharp contrast here with the portrayal in the last line of verse 1: 'to open doors before him – and the gates shall not be closed', which corresponds in a much closer manner with the historical reality of Cyrus's mainly peaceful entry, if not welcome, into Babylon.[17] This distinction may be further underlined by the use of the third person in verse 1 by contrast with the expected second person address in verse 2.[18] This contrast is most easily explained as an example of a prophecy, which expected a violent capture of Babylon, being corrected by a later scribe in the light of historical experience in such a manner as to invite a rereading of verse 2 in its wake.

That conclusion itself seems to me to make a Babylonian setting extremely probable, as one might wonder whether such concerns for detail would have affected the community in Judah. Be that as it may, there is one word in the earliest layer which has caused difficulty since ancient times which has now been satisfactorily explained in the light of our relatively recent knowledge of Akkadian.

The second clause of verse 2 reads וַהֲדוּרִים אֲוַשֵּׁר. The first word is of uncertain meaning but, vocalized as it is, it has been taken to be a plural passive participle of *hdr* ('swell [?], honour, adorn'), hence either 'swelling places' such as hills (cf. BDB, 213B; RV: 'rugged places'), or 'crooked ways, paths' (so Rashi and Kimchi),

---

16 Kratz, *Kyros im Deuterojesaja-Buch*, 26.

17 There is evidence that soon after Cyrus's entry into Babylon some repairs to a gate and the city wall were required; see Gauthier Tolini, 'Quelques éléments concernant la prise de Babylone par Cyrus (octobre 539 av. J.-C.)', *ARTA* 2005.003 [http://www.achemenet.com/ressources/enligne/arta/pdf/2005.003-Tolini.pdf]. The reasons are unknown, so that it is difficult to be sure to what extent this evidence may qualify the later recollection of a peaceful entry in terms of some degree of conflict. Either way, this cannot by itself overcome the obvious tension in the way these events are portrayed in the biblical text.

18 Does this then also involve the middle lines of v. 1 in the addition?

or perhaps of people, 'haughty ones'.[19] This is hardly convincing, however, and it is not very suitable in the immediate context. An alternative reading is attested in antiquity, namely והררים ('and mountains') in 1QIsa[a], and this may possibly be also presupposed as the LXX's *Vorlage*.[20] This involves only the slight and frequently attested confusion of ד and ר, and it has been favoured by quite a number of commentators, but again it may be considered contextually unsuitable. Beside Deutero-Isaiah elsewhere always uses the form הרים as the plural for mountain (40:12; 41:15; 42:11, 15; 44:23; 49:11, 13; 52:7; 54:10; 55:12). More conjecturally the older suggestion of Houbigant to read הדרכים ('the ways') has been favoured by a number of scholars,[21] and it has the advantage of occurring with the same verb in verse 13 just below, but it enjoys no direct textual support and it is further from the received form of the text.

In view of the difficulties with MT as it stands and the proposed alternatives, a wholly satisfying alternative approach has been independently argued by Hoffmann and Southwood,[22] namely to find here an exact Hebrew equivalent of (the definite article plus) 'a common Akkadian word *dūru* as a loan word, of a semi-technical kind, with the meaning "city walls", and more specifically the inner ring of Babylon's defences' (Southwood, p. 802). Hoffmann provides many examples of the use of *dūru* in similar contexts. It naturally fits the context perfectly, preceding the references to doors and bars, and in reference to the envisaged fall of Babylon it may well have been thought more suitable than standard Hebrew חומה. Interestingly, the Targum renders שוריה ('walls'). Given the final redaction, at least, of Targum Jonathan in Babylon, we might wonder whether the memory of the word's meaning somehow lived on there;[23] but even if not, it serves as a powerful indication of what would have been contextually more appropriate.

---

19 See, for instance, Menachem Cohen (ed.), *Isaiah* (Mikra'ot Gedolot 'Haketer'; Ramat Gan: Bar Ilan University, 1996), 294.

20 We may note the curiously mixed form והרורים in 1QIsa[b]; Karl Elliger, *Deuterojesaja*: 1: *Jesaja 40,1–45,7* (BKAT XI/1; Neukirchen-Vluyn: Neukirchener Verlag, 1978), 482, suggests that this is a deliberately mixed form, which would indicate that there was conscious knowledge of the variants in antiquity. The word is not preserved in any of the manuscripts from cave 4.

21 E.g. Claus Westermann, *Das Buch Jesaja, Kapitel 40–66* (ATD 19; 4th ed., Göttingen: Vandenhoeck & Ruprecht, 1981), 124 (ET, *Isaiah 40–66: A Commentary* [OTL; London: SCM, 1969], 153).

22 Charles H. Southwood, 'The Problematic *h*ª*dūrîm* of Isaiah xlv 2', *VT* 25 (1975): 801–2; A. Hoffmann, 'Jahwe schleift Ringmauern – Jes 45, 2a*b*', in *Wort, Lied und Gottesspruch: Beiträge zu Psalmen und Propheten: Festschrift für Joseph Ziegler* (ed. Josef Schreiner; FzB 2; Würzburg: Echter Verlag, 1972), 187–94. His suggestion that the word occurs also in Isa 29:3 is not contextually satisfying, however, as one would hardly build such a wall as an attacking siege element.

23 The possibility that *dūru* may lie behind the Biblical Aramaic place name Dura in Dan 3:1 is explored by, for instance, Louis F. Hartman and Alexander A. Di Lella, *The Book of Daniel: A New*

I conclude that Isa 45:2 provides evidence of a conscious use of an Akkadian word that was in common use in the Neo-Babylonian period for something relevant to Cyrus's capture of Babylon and that it occurs in a passage which was probably written in advance of his actual arrival there.

(2) Isaiah 40:20. This verse occurs in one of the classic anti-idol polemical passages. Because 40:(18)19–20 is similar in some respects with 41:6–7 (note, for instance, the fact that both end with לא ימוט, and in other respects with 46:5–7 and the longer 44:9–20 (see too Jer 10:1–16), and because it can be argued that some of these passages, at least, seem to be intrusive or unexpected in their present locations, it has long been held by many that they comprise a separate series of additions to the earliest form of the text. If that is correct (and one should acknowledge that strong arguments have also been advanced in favour of retaining them as original parts of the basic composition[24]), then we should have to conclude that this was a genuine redactional layer, as the passages' length in some cases is too great for mere *Fortschreibungen* or the like. As it happens, I have argued for a similar collection of anti-idol polemical passages in Isaiah 1–39, again interrelated though not, so far as I can see, sharing the same distinctive elements that unite the passages in Deutero-Isaiah.[25] It seems strange that both parts of the book have such passages which in some respects appear to be out of context and which yet must have been a topic of major concern to the author(s). It would be attractive to speculate that the similarities between them all are to be explained as due to a pressing concern of a redactor of the whole work and at the same time that the obvious differences between the presentation of detail in the two halves reflect different places of origin – the one, I assume, Judean, and perhaps written directly by the redactor, and the other Babylonian, incorporating for later use some polemical material that he had inherited and which had been

Translation with Introduction and Commentary (AB 23; Garden City, NY: Doubleday, 1978), 160, Donald J. Wiseman, *Nebuchadrezzar and Babylon* (The Schweich Lectures of the British Academy 1983; Oxford: Oxford University Press, 1985), 110–11, and most fully Edward M. Cook, '"In the Plain of the Wall" (Dan 3:1)', *JBL* 108 (1989): 114–15. If it had become a standard loan word in Aramaic (and the LXX of Daniel at this point suggests it may), it would help explain the Targum rendering in Isaiah.

24 For an introductory survey of opinions, see Knut Holter, *Second Isaiah's Idol-Fabrication Passages* (BET 28; Frankfurt am Main: Peter Lang, 1995), 15–25.

25 See Hugh G. M. Williamson, 'A Productive Textual Error in Isaiah 2:18–19', in *Essays on Ancient Israel in Its Near Eastern Context: A Tribute to Nadav Na'aman* (ed. Yairah Amit *et al.*; Winona Lake, IN: Eisenbrauns, 2006), 377–88; idem, 'Isaiah 30:1', in *Isaiah in Context: Studies in Honour of Arie van der Kooij on the Occasion of his Sixty-Fifth Birthday* (VTSup 138; ed. Michaël N. van der Meer *et al.*; Leiden: Brill, 2010), 185–96.

circulated separately before his time. But this is mere speculation and need not directly affect the case that I am trying to make here, even though it fits my case very well.

The passage has long been a puzzle to translators and I wrote about it extensively many years ago.[26] The conclusion I favoured built upon a much older proposal for the identification of the first word in the verse. I sought to bolster that identification a bit, to discuss and dismiss alternative proposals, and to explain in a fresh way how one or two other items in the verse might be better related to it. There have been several textual and linguistic studies of the passage since,[27] but, although they do not all agree with the solution that I defended, there has not, I believe, been any convincing challenge to the rendering of the first word that I favoured and it remains the overwhelmingly majority opinion. It is not, therefore, necessary to go over all the ground again here; I shall content myself with summarizing the problems of MT as it stands and then indicating briefly the better solution. This will allow us finally to reflect a little further on the matter in the context of our wider discussion here.

In addition to considerable textual uncertainty in the tradition, indicating that the first word in the verse was a puzzle for many readers already in antiquity, the solution that the Masoretes appear to have worked with is certainly unsatisfactory. They seem to want to read the word as the definite article followed by a puʿal participle of *skn* to mean 'the poor man'. Their view is thus that verse 19 describes the idol-making practice of a rich man who used silver and gold, whereas the poor man in verse 20 could afford only wood. However, verse 19 does not refer explicitly to a rich man, and the subject of verse 20 is apparently able to afford the services of a 'skilled craftsman' (חרש חכם). Furthermore, a reference to

---

26 Hugh G. M. Williamson, 'Isaiah 40,20 – A Case of Not Seeing the Wood for the Trees', *Biblica* 67 (1986): 1–20.

27 In addition to the commentaries, see, for instance, Israel Eph'al, 'Isa 40:19–20: On the Cultural and Linguistic Background of Deutero-Isaiah', *Shnaton* 10 (1986): 31–35 [Hebrew]; Manfred Hutter, 'Jes 40,20 – kulturgeschichtliche Notizen zu einer Crux', *BN* 36 (1987): 31–36; Aloysius Fitzgerald, 'The Technology of Isaiah 40:19–20 + 41:6–7', *CBQ* 51 (1989): 426–46; Marjo C. A. Korpel, 'Soldering in Isaiah 40:19–20 and 1 Kings 6:21', *UF* 23 (1991): 219–22; Holter, *Second Isaiah's Idol-Fabrication Passages*, 34–59; Kees van Leeuwen, 'An Old Crux: הַמְסֻכָּן תְּרוּמָה in Isaiah 40, 20', in *Studies in the Book of Isaiah: Festschrift Willem A. M. Beuken* (BETL 132; ed. J. van Ruiten and M. Vervenne; Leuven: University Press and Peeters, 1997), 273–87; Angelika Berlejung, *Die Theologie der Bilder: Herstellung und Einweihung von Kultbildern in Mesopotamien und die alttestamentliche Bilderpolemik* (OBO 162; Freiburg: Universitätsverlag, and Göttingen; Vandenhoeck & Ruprecht, 1998), 370–75; Michael B. Dick, 'Prophetic Parodies of Making the Cult Image', in *The Making of the Cult Image in the Ancient Near East* (ed. Michael B. Dick; Winona Lake, IN: Eisenbrauns, 1999), 1–54.

an inferior idol in verse 20 would completely contradict the implications of the overall rhetoric, which is challenging people to produce some likeness for the incomparable God (v. 18). Finally, if the author wished to refer to a poor man, why did he not use some standard word to express the point? From the same root, the adjective and noun מִסְכֵּן occurs four times elsewhere, for instance, whereas we are presented here with a hapax legomenon that is based on a puʿal of a verb whose use is not attested anywhere else at all. Moreover, among ancient witnesses not one appears to have understood the word in this way. The search for an alternative explanation thus seems more than justified.

The solution usually favoured now, and the one with which I agree, was first proposed by Zimmern in 1894.[28] He proposed that this is the name of a tree, namely the equivalent of Akkadian *musukkannu*, which, by good detective work but without reference to our particular occurrence, has since been identified by Gershevitch as *dalbergia sissoo* roxburgh, this displacing other suggested identifications which had been proposed in the meanwhile.[29] The possibility that the word refers to a tree was known already in antiquity. Jerome explained it this way in his commentary on Isaiah, the Targum renders it as אורן, probably 'fir' or 'pine', and Saadia proposed 'oak'. In my view, this approach is strengthened by my observation that the words עץ לא ירקב ('a tree that will not rot') intrude into the otherwise very regular line length of verses 19–20 and so should almost certainly be construed as the incorporation of an early marginal comment on the rare word, indicating both that it was a hardwood tree of some sort and that it was not widely known in the location in which the text was subsequently transmitted.[30] Since this was certainly Judah (as the subsequent addition of chapters 56–66, to go no further, indicates), this supports the view that the word was not known there.

A further indication that the word was less probably known in Judah derives from the known locations where the tree grew in antiquity. The full study of this matter by Maxwell-Hyslop points clearly to the tree's native origin substantially to the East, in northern India, and that it spread to areas moving west from there and that it grew also especially in Oman. In historical times it occurs regularly in Mesopotamian texts, initially, no doubt, supplied by sea trade from the Gulf, though this is not explicitly stated anywhere. From Ashurnasirpal II's time, at

28 Heinrich Zimmern, '*mesukkân* Jes. 40,20 = ass. *musukkânu* "Palme"', *ZA* 9 (1894): 111–12.

29 Ilya Gershevitch, 'Sissoo at Susa', *BSOAS* 19 (1957): 317–20.

30 We may note as an alternative the suggestion of Vanderhooft, *The Neo-Babylonian Empire*, 174, that this is the equivalent of the frequent Akkadian comment on *musukkannu* that it is *iṣṣu dārû*, 'lasting, durable wood.'

least, it was also being grown in Assyria and Babylonia itself, and we may safely assume that this continued in the Neo-Babylonian and Persian periods as well.[31]

Less certainly, the word that follows מסכן in Isa 40:20 could also be an Akkadian loanword of a technical nature. Traditionally, תרומה has been identified with a sacrificial term for an offering of some sort, but that is hardly appropriate in the present setting. Millard and Snook proposed that it might refer to the base, plinth or podium on which the image was set.[32] While possible (based on the root רום, 'to be high'), it is awkward in that words of this formation are usually passive in meaning (GK § 84ᵃ*m*). Given that we have firm evidence that sissoo wood was used, *inter alia*, as an item of tribute, the possibility that תרומה is here an otherwise unattested cognate of *tarīmtu*(*m*) ('levy, gift') is attractive[33] and would strengthen the conclusion that this polemic on idol manufacture was firmly based on vocabulary for which we have no evidence of knowledge in Judah. To speculate that scribes there could have known of it is an appeal to a conclusion for which there is no direct evidence in order to support a theory to which this verse is an embarrassment.[34]

---

31 K. R. Maxwell-Hyslop, '*Dalbergia Sissoo* Roxburgh', *Anatolian Studies* 33 (1983): 67–72; see too J. Nicholas Postgate, 'Trees and Timber in the Assyrian Texts', *BSA* 6 (1992): 177–92, who comments on p. 183 that etymologically *musukkannu* may mean *mes*-tree of Makkan, referring to Oman, but not thereby excluding an ultimate origin in the Indus, and Vanderhooft, *The Neo-Babylonian Empire*, 172–75. Other studies surveying its particular usages in antiquity include Hutter, 'Jes 40,20', and G. van Driel, 'Woods, Reeds and Rushes: A Note on Neo-Babylonian Practical Texts', *BSA* 6 (1992): 171–76.

32 Alan R. Millard and I. R. Snook, 'Isaiah 40:20, Towards a Solution', *Tyndale House Bulletin* 14 (1964): 12–13.

33 Godfrey R. Driver, 'Three Technical Terms in the Pentateuch', *JSS* 1 (1956): 97–105; W. von Soden, '*Mirjam*-Maria "(Gottes-) Geschenk"', *UF* 2 (1970): 269–72. In his Lexikon, von Soden gives 'Geschenkgegenstand'.

34 Simon Sherwin, '*Hammsukkan* in Isaiah 40:20: Some Reflections', *TynB* 54 (2003): 145–59, followed by Tiemeyer, *For the Comfort of Zion*, 112, seems to me to come perilously close to falling into this trap. He accepts that 'there is no direct textual evidence for the presence of *musukkannu*-wood west of Mari' and that (apart from our passage) it is not known in any West Semitic or Egyptian language of the relevant period, so that 'available evidence favours a Babylonian setting'. Nevertheless, he concludes that at the same time 'the possibility cannot be ruled out that the wood was also known in the west as a luxury item back into the second millennium BC', this on the basis that it occurs in a Mesopotamian lexical text, a fragment of which (missing the relevant section) has been found in Canaanite Ashkelon. At the most this could only indicate that the word might have been known, but direct evidence even for this is lacking, and it would be a big leap from that to knowledge of the word in Iron Age Judah. While of course any conclusions currently held may be overturned by future discoveries, it seems better methodologically to proceed on the basis of available evidence rather than hypothetical alternatives.

As a final comment on this example, it is worth noting that the other anti-idol passages, especially 44:9–20, also include some unusual vocabulary, but it does not seem to fall into the same diagnostic category as the present example.

(3) Isaiah 44:4. The received text of the first half of the verse is more or less impossible to construe convincingly. The first word, וצמחו ('and they will spring up') is fine in the context and works well with the second half of the line as a complementary comparison: 'like willow-trees beside the watercourses'. In between, however, we have בבין חציר, which is usually rendered 'among grass', or the like. However, בין is never used with the preposition ב in front of it, and in any case it is difficult to see what 'between grass' means.[35] Delitzsch's guess that the grass is a reference to the land is unsupported and has no parallel elsewhere, and in any case it fails to deal with the initial grammatical problem.[36]

It is hard to escape the conclusion, therefore, that we should adopt the reading of 1QIsa[a], which is found also in several medieval manuscripts and which seems to enjoy some versional support, namely that the initial letter is a כ, not a ב, just as at the start of the second half of the line.

What kind of comparison might this be introducing, however? Several emendations have been suggested, but they all seem to face difficulties which make them implausible. For instance, in partial dependence on the LXX, the most widely canvassed has been כבין מים חציר, and this was adopted by, *inter alia*, the RSV, 'like grass amid waters'.[37] However, the proposal is itself not good Hebrew, for there is no evidence that the comparative particle כ can be separated from the noun that it qualifies (חציר), and in any case it is far from clear what 'grass amid waters' means. The only advantage of an emendation, from the point of view of method, is that it should neatly eliminate problems, not lead to further ones.

Others have adopted the philological approach, but two of these, at least, are also open to other serious objections.[38] A third, however, seems to me entirely

---

35 *Contra* Dominique Barthélemy, *Critique textuelle de l'Ancien Testament*, 2: *Isaïe, Jérémie, Lamentations* (OBO 50/2; Fribourg: Éditions universitaires and Göttingen: Vandenhoeck & Ruprecht, 1986), 322–24, followed by Berges, *Jesaja 40–48*, 291.
36 Franz Delitzsch, *Commentar über das Buch Jesaia* (4th edn; Leipzig: Dörffling & Franke, 1889), 450 (ET, *Biblical Commentary on the Prophecies of Isaiah* [Edinburgh: T & T Clark, 1894], ii, 190).
37 According to Elliger, *Deuterojesaja*, 1, 363, this proposal reaches back as far as Houbigant (1753), and he lists a number of relatively recent commentators who have adopted it.
38 Alfred Guillaume, 'A Note on the Meaning of בין', *JTS* ns 13 (1962): 109–11, but see the objections of James Barr, *Comparative Philology and the Text of the Old Testament* (Oxford: Clarendon Press, 1968), 165, and Harris H. Hirschberg, 'Some Additional Arabic Etymologies in Old Testa-

plausible, as it retains the text (excepting only the confusion of ו and י, which is wholly understandable once the original sense had been forgotten and further confused by the reading of the כ as a ב). The proposal came from John Allegro back in 1951,[39] and after relative neglect it seems now to have gained a wider currency. He suggested that בין (vocalized with *ī* rather than *ē*) should be understood as the equivalent of Akkadian *bīnu* (with cognates also in Arabic and Aramaic), which all the Akkadian lexicons gloss now as 'tamarisk'. This, of course, provides excellent parallelism.

In taking this forward, we should note next that on every one of its few occurrences in the Hebrew Bible ערבים is linked with water, which is why 'willow' is an attractive identification even if the older 'poplar' is also possible: Lev 23:40 and Job 40:22 both talk of ערבי נחל (NRSV 'willows of the brook/wadi'; see comparably Isa 15:7), while Ps 137:2 has them by the 'rivers of Babylon'. The use in our present verse with יבלי מים is thus similar, though it may refer more narrowly to the well-known canals in the region of Babylon. In view of this reference to the well-watered nature of the supposed setting, it is attractive to revocalise חציר as חצור, so that the first half of the line reads 'and they will spring up like the green ben tree'.

The difficulty which now confronts us, however, is that it is virtually impossible to identify the specific species of tree in question. There are over fifty species of tamarisk alone, so that there is unlikely to be progress along that front. Allegro thought that *Moringa oleifera* was more likely, and it certainly has some features that fit the present context better. However, his main conclusion was that it was likely the same as the 'willows' in the second half of the line, and if this is correct it would suit our present considerations well, a rare word being effectively 'explained' by a more familiar word in parallel. While it cannot be so securely affirmed that this is an Akkadian loan word, given its occurrence in some forms of Aramaic, to go no further, I submit that there is a greater likelihood that the verse speaks of a tree that was known from Babylon, where its use is well attested, and that the author was conscious of the need to parallel it with a more familiar term. As with מסכן in Isa 40:20, the text seems to have preserved a word whose meaning became forgotten and tried to accommodate it to a later understanding by means of a variant form of vocalization.

ment Lexicography', *VT* 11 (1961): 373–85 (375), but his suggestion depends upon the methodologically dubious procedure of combining textual emendation with philological conjecture.

39 John M. Allegro, 'The Meaning of בין in Isaiah xliv, 4', *ZAW* 63 (1951): 154–56.

As already indicated, these three examples (of which I regard the first two as virtually certain and the third as highly probable) seem to me to be most easily explained as reflections of words that would have been familiar in Babylon but which, as their alternative vocalization shows, were clearly forgotten in the later Judean context of textual transmission. The assertion that they could have been known in Judah from the start is impossible to disprove, of course, but far less likely. Given that they refer to three separate but central elements of Deutero-Isaiah's oeuvre, it therefore follows that this work was most likely originally composed there.

As my main interest here has been methodological, I have not trawled further to see if additional examples could be added. I agree entirely that many examples which have been canvassed in the past have no probative value. Tiemeyer lists many of these and has no difficulty in showing that they could as easily have a Judean as a Babylonian origin.

Furthermore, I have limited myself to strictly linguistic arguments whereas a decision about the geographical setting of Deutero-Isaiah (or of Isaiah 40–48 in particular) needs to take many other factors into consideration. To give just one example, Schaudig has recently made a strong case for the view that Isa 46:1–2 reflects first-hand knowledge of a specific element in the Babylonian New Year festival.[40] However powerful his arguments, there is nothing in the language of these two verses to help decide the issue, and so I have not taken it into consideration here. Methodologically, the questions an analysis such as his raises are of a different order from those I have tried to illustrate here.

What I hope may have become apparent, however, is that, if we are to move forward from the current impasse, we need to think far more systematically than has been done in the past about how the limited evidence at our disposal can be more effectively and rigorously deployed to answer questions which the text we have inherited does not set out to answer.

40 Hanspeter Schaudig, '"Bel Bows, Nabû Stoops!" The Prophecy of Isaiah xlvi 1–2 as a Reflection of Babylonian "Processional Omens"', *VT* 58 (2008): 557–72; cf. Vanderhooft, *The Neo-Babylonian Empire*, 175–80. Similar comments might be made about his treatment of Isaiah 47 on pp. 181–88.

Madhavi Nevader

Picking Up the Pieces of the Little Prince: Refractions of Neo-Babylonian Kingship Ideology in Ezekiel 40–48?

The ubiquitous shadow of Babylon dominates many of texts that will become the sacred scriptural tradition of 'Israel'. Where, for example, would our Yahwist be without a Babel to bamboozle; our Second-Isaiah without a servant to subvert; P without a creation tradition to co-opt? That the Book of Ezekiel is part of the textual community hovering in this (protective?) shadow is widely recognized,[1] not least because the narrated author, in distinction to many of his contemporary writers, openly places himself there.[2] But the influence goes well beyond the narrative pretext of the book. Indeed, a life lived in or around Babylon impacts virtually every level of the text from vocabulary and language to internal dating markers and structure. Rarely, however, is the final Temple Vision (Ezek 40–48),[3]

1 E.g. Daniel Bodi, *The Book of Ezekiel and the Poem of Erra* (OBO 104; Freiburg: Universitätsverlag, 1991); Isaac Gluska, 'Akkadian Influence on the Book of Ezekiel', in *An Experienced Scribe Who Neglects Nothing: Ancient Near Eastern Studies in Honor of Jacob Klein* (ed. Y. Sefati; Bethesda: CDL, 2005), 718–737; David S. Vanderhooft, 'Ezekiel in and on Babylon' in *Bible et Proche-Orient: Mélanges André Lemaire* (Transeuphratène 46; ed. J.-M. Durand and J. Elayi; Paris: Gabalda, 2014), 99–119.

2 For ease of discussion I will refer both to the singular author and Ezekiel in what follows. This is not to imply that a single hand is responsible for the book.

3 The five Ws of Ezek 40–48 are, of course, heavily contested. Moshe Greenberg remains the benchmark for reading the vision as a unified whole ('The Design and Themes of Ezekiel's Program of Restoration', *Int* 38 [1984]: 181–208; though see already Menahem Haran, 'The Law Code of Ezekiel XL-XLVIII and its Relation to the Priestly School', *HUCA* 50 [1979]: 45–71). Other important studies have treated Ezek 40–48 as a thematic whole (cf. Jon D. Levenson, *Theology of the Program of Restoration of Ezekiel 40–48* [HSM 10; Missoula: Fortress Press, 1976]; Susan Niditch, 'Ezekiel 40–48 in a Visionary Context', *CBQ* 48 [1986]: 208–224; Kalinda R. Stevenson, *Vision of Transformation: The Territorial Rhetoric of Ez 40–48* [SBLDS 154; Atlanta: Scholars Press, 1996]), but they largely disagree on the purpose of the single unit. Levenson, for example, reads Ezek 40–48 as an apolitical, eschatological programme of restoration (*Theology of the Program*), while Stevenson reads the unit as a rhetorical work, explicitly political in nature (*Vision of Transformation*). The standard for a heavily redacted Ezek 40–48 is Harmut Gese, *Der Verfassungsentwurf des Ezechiel (Kap. 40–48) traditionsgeschichtlich untersucht* (BHT 25; Tübingen: J. C. B. Mohr, 1957), from which follow Walther Zimmerli, *Ezekiel 2: A Commentary on the Book of the Prophet Ezekiel, Chapters 25–48* (Hermeneia; Philadelphia: Fortress Press, 1983; ET of *Ezechiel 2* [BKAT 13/2; Neu-

Madhavi Nevader: University of St. Andrews

with which the book concludes, marshalled as evidence of Ezekiel's Babylonian context.[4] In part, its absence in discussions can be explained theologically – many scholars see the restoration in Ezek 40–48 as some sort of Pentateuchal

kirchen-Vluyn: Neukirchener Verlag, 1969]), Meindert Dijkstra, *Ezechiël II* (Kampen: Kok, 1989), Thilo A. Rudnig, *Heilig und Profan: Redaktionskritische Studien zu Ez 40–48* (BZAW 287; Berlin: de Gruyter, 2000), Michael Konkel, *Architektonik des Heiligen: Studien zur zweiten Tempelvision Ezechiels (Ez 40–48)* (Berlin: Philo, 2001), and Karl-Friedrich Pohlmann, *Der Prophet Hesekiel (Ezechiel) Kapitel 20–48* (ATD 22/2; Göttingen: Vandenhoeck & Ruprecht, 2001). Works that take a lighter approach to issues of redaction include George A. Cooke, *Ezekiel* (ICC; Edinburgh: T & T Clark, 1936) and more recently Ronald M. Hals, *Ezekiel* (FOTL 19; Grand Rapids: Eerdmans, 1989); Leslie C. Allen, *Ezekiel 20–48* (WBC; Dallas: Word Books, 1994); Daniel I. Block, *The Book of Ezekiel: Chapters 25–48* (NICOT; Grand Rapids: Eerdmans, 1998); Rainer Albertz, *Israel in Exile: The History and Literature of the Sixth Century B.C.E.* (SBL Studies in Biblical Literature 3; trans. D. Green; Atlanta: Society of Biblical Literature, 2003; ET of *Die Exilszeit: 6. Jahrhundert v. Chr.* [Biblische Enzyklopädie 7; Stuttgart: W. Kohlhammer, 2001]), 345–375; Paul M. Joyce, *Ezekiel: A Commentary* (LHBOTS 482; London: T & T Clark International, 2007); Steven S. Tuell, *Ezekiel* (NIBC; Peabody: Hendrickson, 2009). As to 'whom', since Zimmerli (*Ezekiel 2*) one often finds reference to an Ezekiel school or to circles of his disciples, though this does assume that there is an Ezekiel to refer to in the first place, an assumption not shared by all (e.g. Joachim Becker, 'Ez 8–11 als einheitliche Komposition in einem pseudepigraphischen Ezechielbuch', in *Ezekiel and His Book: Textual and Literary Criticism and their Interrelation* [BETL 74; ed. J. Lust; Leuven: Leuven University Press and Peeters, 1986], 136–50; Frank-Lothar Hossfeld, 'Die Tempelvision Ez 8–11 im Licht unterschiedlicher methodischer Zugänge', in ibid., 151–65; but already Charles C. Torrey, *Pseudo-Ezekiel and the Original Prophecy* [New Haven: Yale University Press, 1930]). The distinct *golah orientierten* in Rudnig (*Heilig und Profan*) speaks to his Marburg training (see Jörg Garscha, *Studien zum Ezechielbuch: Eine redaktionskritische Untersuchung von 1–39* [Europäische Hochschulschriften 23; Bern: Herbert Lang, 1974]; Pohlmann, *Ezechielstudien: Zur Redaktionsgeschichte des Buches und zur Frage nach den ältesten Texten* [BZAW 202; Berlin: de Gruyter, 1992]). Above all, Rudnig's *golah-* and diaspora-redactions leave the text's authors/redactors (of which there are at least eleven) in Babylon through the 4th century. Redactional assessments of those passages addressing the *nāśī'* remain heavily influenced by Gese's proposed *nasi-Schicht* (*Verfassungsentwurf*, 110). Though scholars have largely moved away from his exact proposal, it remains the case that for many the legislation concerning the *nāśī'* is part of a secondary rewriting of the Vision (e.g. Tuell, *The Law of the Temple in Ezekiel 40–48* [HSM 49; Atlanta: Scholars Press, 1992]; Rudnig, *Heilig und Profan*; Konkel, *Architektonik*), though again there seems to be little agreement on the 'why' of the Vision's rewriting.

4 Some have looked at Mesopotamian elements – theological or literary – in Ezek 40–48; cf. Niditch, 'Ezekiel 40–48'; Victor Hurowitz, *I Have Built You an Exalted House: Temple Building in the Bible in Light of Mesopotamian and Northwest Semitic Writings* (JSOTSup 115; Sheffield: JSOT Press, 1992), 326–327; David H. Engelhard, 'Ezekiel 47:13–48:29 as Royal Grant', in *"Go to the Land I Will Show You": Studies in Honor of Dwight W. Young* (ed. J. E. Coleson and V. H. Matthews; Winona Lake: Eisenbrauns, 1996), 45–56; Diane M. Sharon, 'A Biblical Parallel to a Sumerian Temple Hymn? Ezekiel 40–48 and Gudea', *JANES* 24 (1996): 99–109; Margaret S. Odell, *Ezekiel* (Smyth & Helwys Bible Commentary; Macon: Smyth & Helwys, 2005), 483–485.

renaissance;[5] in part, it can also be explained historically – many believe that the text is too late to be affected by Babylon.[6] My direct concern will be with neither. Instead, I wish to engage the vision's infamous *nāśī'* in conversation specifically with Neo-Babylonian royal ideology.[7] The hope in doing so is firstly to provide some lines of clarity for the interpretation of this problematic figure. Secondly, for the wider discussion of the present volume, I think that a text such as Ezek 40–48 can illustrate not simply *that* Judah chose to engage with Babylon, but the magisterial level to which some chose to do so.

1 Ezekiel's 'Little Prince'

The description of the person and functions of the *nāśī'* in Ezek 40–48 is a precarious mix of acclaim and criticism. From even a cursory reading of these nine chapters, it is apparent that the immediate background against which the *nāśī'* is set is the temple, the impact of which is felt by all institutions through systematic legislation that maps out the relationship of each to the imposing building complex, a temple turned divine military fortress.[8] The importance of the

5 E.g. Levenson, *Theology of the Program*, and Block, *Book of Ezekiel.*

6 Though it follows along similar scholarly lines to the 'who' of Ezek 40–48, the 'when' remains largely unresolved, varying on a rolling trajectory from the early 6th century B.C.E. (Greenberg, 'Design and Themes') to the 2nd (famously Charles C. Torrey, *Pseudo-Ezekiel*). Wellhausen's interpretation of the vision as the springboard for the priestly *coup* of the Second Temple period has had long lasting ramifications for the text. Interpreting it as some sort of Zadokite fantasy, much scholarship on the vision tends to place it in the Persian period looking forward. But as the Cyrus Cylinder so clearly illustrates, it is entirely possible for something to be written in the early Persian period whilst retaining a Babylonian flavor.

7 Iain M. Duguid, *Ezekiel and the Leaders of Israel* (VTSup 56; Leiden: Brill, 1994); Rudnig, *Heilig und Profan*, 137–164; Sunwoo Hwang, 'נשׂיא in Ezekiel 40–48', *SJOT* 23 (2009): 183–194.

8 For architectural or spatial readings of Ezek 40–48, see Jonathan Z. Smith, *To Take Place: Towards Theory in Ritual, Chicago Studies in the History of Judaism* (Chicago: University of Chicago Press, 1987), 47–73; Stevenson, *Vision of Transformation*; Hanna Liss, "'Describe the Temple to the House of Israel": Preliminary Remarks on the Temple Vision in the Book of Ezekiel and the Question of Fictionality in Priestly Literatures', in *Utopia and Dystopia in Prophetic Literature* (ed. E. Ben Zvi; Publications of the Finnish Exegetical Society 92; Helsinki: The Finnish Exegetical Society; Göttingen: Vandenhoeck & Ruprecht, 2006), 122–143; Hugo Antonissen, 'Architectural Representation Technique in New Jerusalem, Ezekiel and the Temple Scroll', in *Aramaica Qumranica: Proceedings of the Conference on the Aramaic Texts from Qumran in Aix-en-Provence, 30 June – 2 July 2008* (STDJ 94; ed. K. Bertholet and D. Stökl Ben Ezra; Leiden: Brill, 2010), 485–513.

nāśīʾ to the running of the vast temple cult is such that some have labelled him the temple's cult patron.[9] At all annual festivals, the *nāśīʾ* provides the daily materials required for the sacrifices for the seven-day duration of each festival legislated (Ezek 46:11);[10] a protocol that similarly exists for the celebration of the New Moon and the weekly Sabbath (Ezek 46:4–7). In addition, the *nāśīʾ* is expected to provide a young bull as a purification offering at Passover for himself and the laity (Ezek 45:22), to present his personal offering (Ezek 46:12) and to supply the priesthood with a burnt and a cereal offering each day as the *tāmīḏ* (Ezek 46:13–14). To this wealth of sacrificial offerings, the laity adds nothing save for a requisite contribution to what we must assume is a national offering (Ezek 45:16).[11] The *nāśīʾ* alone provides the materials for all national acts of cult (Ezek 45:17), the quantity of which once tabulated is staggering.[12] As the sole source of material for the state cult, it is no surprise then that the remaining functions and possessions of the *nāśīʾ* stem from this obligation.

The first of these is no doubt his unique allotment of land. To him is given two sizeable pieces of land[13] that span the width of the Israelite borders, save for the square holy portion (*tĕrūmaṯ haqqōḏeš*) that houses the temple and city at the centre of his land (Ezek 45:7–8a). There can be little doubt regarding the purpose of the *nāśī*'s land possession. Commensurate with the material contribution that he is expected to make to the cult, the *nāśīʾ* possesses a quantity of land that enables him to rear or produce the materials required for the maintenance of said cult. Requirements for cult provision may also explain the location of the land, which is in close proximity to the sanctuary. In a system governed entirely by the sanctuary, the leader is positioned both through physical location and wealth to fulfil the sacrificial requirements of the temple institution.

---

9 Tuell, *Law of the Temple*.

10 The cultic calendar in Ezek 40–48 shares a number of aspects with those in the Covenant Code and Deuteronomy. Passover (Ezek 45:21; cf. Ex 23:15; Deut 16:1–8) and a seven-day festival in the seventh month, which while unnamed in Ezekiel appears to coincide with Sukkoth (Ezek 45:25; cf. Ex 23:16; Deut 16:13–15), are present. Missing, however, is the festival of First Fruits (Ex 23:16; Deut 16:13–15) and the Day of Atonement (Lev 16), though a festival legislated on the seventh day of the first month in the Temple Vision is set in place in order to purify anyone who has sinned unintentionally and consequently to purify the Temple (Ezek 45:19).

11 Though presented in the format of a sacral offering, many have explained the sacrificial תרומה (*tĕrūmā*) more as a secular tax, effectively allowing the *nāśīʾ* to levy some form of official taxation system (see especially Tuell, *Law of the Temple*, 109; Albertz, *Israel in Exile*, 372).

12 For the cult, the *nāśīʾ* annually provides 725 lambs, 158 rams, 14 goats and 113 bulls with accompanying grain and oil condiments (Ezek 45:18–46:15).

13 The portion is 25,000 cubits long and covers the width of the Israelite territory save for the sacred portion and that of the city that bifurcate the *nāśī*'s land (Ezek 45:7; 48:21).

A further dividend of the *nāśī*'s patronage of the cult, or perhaps a position held in tandem with it, is his standing in the sacrificial cult itself. The legislation appears to establish the *nāśī'* as the foremost Israelite in all cultic activities involving the laity, charging him at times with unique responsibilities and granting him privilege of access to certain locations within the temple complex.[14] In a rehearsal of ritual movements, Ezek 46:1–15 states that on the cultic occasions of Sabbath and New Moon, the otherwise closed inner east gate will be opened in the morning, and the *nāśī'* will enter to present the required sacrifices to the priesthood (Ezek 46:2). He is allowed to enter by way of the vestibule (*'ūlām*) and to stand at the podium (*mĕzūzāh*) of the gate,[15] a process ritualised in such a way that many claim the inner gate is effectively turned into the *nāśī*'s own cultic stage.[16] Furthermore, whereas the *nāśī* may repeat the procedure by returning to the inner east gate to offer his free-will sacrifice whenever he so wishes, the laity is not granted the same privilege, the gate on these occasions being immediately shut upon the *nāśī*'s exit (Ezek 46:12). The distinction between access rights granted to the people and those granted to the ruler, as well as the latter's posited role as cultic head of a sacral procession (Ezek 46:10), has contributed to a scholarly consensus that the *nāśī'* stands at the pinnacle of the worshipping community, the figure through whom all sacrificial activity is consummated.[17]

The *nāśī*'s most exalted cultic privilege by far, however, involves the consumption of a sacred meal (*'aḵāl lipnēy* YHWH)[18] in the otherwise restricted outer

14 Zimmerli, *Ezekiel 2*, 68, 245; Tuell, *Law of the Temple*, 108; Duguid, *Ezekiel and the Leaders*, 51; Block, *Book of Ezekiel*, 615, 744.

15 Odell makes a strong case for reading *mĕzūzāh* as 'podium' rather than the usual 'doorpost' ('"The Wall is No More": Temple Reform in Ezekiel 43:7–9', in *From the Foundations to the Crenellations: Essays on Temple Building in the Ancient Near East and the Hebrew Bible* [AOAT 366; ed. M. J. Boda and J. Novotny; Münster: Ugarit-Verlag, 2010], 339–356 [349]).

16 Zimmerli, *Ezekiel 2*, 490; Tuell, *Law of the Temple*, 108; Deborah W. Rooke, *Zadok's Heirs: The Role and Development of the High Priesthood in Ancient Israel* (OTM; Oxford: Oxford University Press, 2000), 115; John W. Wright, 'A Tale of Three Cities: Urban Gates, Squares and Power in Iron Age II, Neo-Babylonian and Achaemenid Judah', in *Second Temple Studies III: Studies in Politics, Class and Material Culture* (JSOTSup 340; ed. P. R. Davies and J. M. Halligan; London: Sheffield Academic Press, 2002), 19–50 (39); Odell, 'Temple Reform in Ezekiel', 350.

17 Zimmerli, *Ezekiel 2*, 490; Allen *Ezekiel 20–48*, 266–267; Tuell, *Law of the Temple*, 108; Duguid, *Ezekiel and the Leaders*, 52; Block, *Book of Ezekiel*, 674, 677, 745; Rooke, *Zadok's Heirs*, 116–119.

18 For royal dining in the Mesopotamian context, see Paul-Alain Beaulieu, 'Cuts of Meat of King Nebuchadnezzar', *NABU* 1990/93; David B. Weisberg, '"Dinner at the Palace" during Nebuchadnezzar's Reign', in *Homeland and Exile: Biblical and Ancient Near Eastern Studies in Honour of Bustenay Oded* (VTSup 130; ed. G. Galil, M. Geller, and A. Millard; Leiden/Boston: Brill, 2009), 261–268. Much, if not all, of such dining, would most likely have taken place at the royal palace rather than the temple (cf. Kristin Kleber, *Tempel und Palast: Die Beziehungen zwischen dem*

east gate (Ezek 44:3),[19] closed because it is through this gate that YHWH first enters the temple precinct upon returning to residence (Ezek 44:2; cf. 43:2–4). This unique dispensation leads many to conclude that the outer east gate loses its function as such and instead becomes yet another cultic room for the private use of the *nāśī'*.[20] If the inner east gate has been given to the *nāśī'* as the stage on which to enact his cultic drama, the outer gate then comes to serve as his exclusive green room for this most distinguished member of the lay congregation.[21]

Given the stated functions and possessions of the *nāśī'*, then, he is above all servant to the sanctuary. From this perspective his character is defined and his functions are dictated. Though charged with other responsibilities, the *nāśī'*'s foremost role is to be the sanctuary's patron, which results in a system that most will argue is essentially a state-supported cult. The distinctive allocation of a sizable piece of land provides the *nāśī'* with wealth and rich resources, thus ensuring his ability to provide for the sacrificial institution. As material provider for the sacrificial cult, the *nāśī'* is the chief Israelite, a status that allows him special access to the inner gate complex, denied to the common Israelite, and gives him an exclusive location in which to eat the fruit of his own sacrifices in the otherwise forbidden east gate. Integral to the cult as he is, the intended perpetuity of the restored sacrificial institution would be impossible without the figure. When all is said and legislated, it appears that the *nāśī'*, granted privileges otherwise withheld from the nation at large, is the most exalted member of Israel restored.

Nonetheless, clouds of hesitancy hover above the character. He is a far cry from the glorious Cyrus intoned in Deutero-Isaiah (Isa 41:2–3; 45:1–4); gives off nothing of the perfume of restoration promised in Jeremiah (e.g. Jer 23:5–6; 33:16) or indeed in earlier sections of Ezekiel (Ezek 34:23–24; 37:24–25);[22] seems not to

---

König und dem Eanna-Tempel im spätbabylonischen Uruk [AOAT 358; Münster: Ugarit-Verlag, 2008], 292–310).

19 Many suggest that the verse allowing the *nāśī* to enter the outer east gate has been secondarily added; see classically Gese, *Verfassungsentwurf*, 86, followed in suit by Zimmerli (*Ezekiel 2*, 439), and now Tuell (*Law of the Temple*, 109). In defence of the verse's originality, Block (*Book of Ezekiel*, 615) points to the prophet's propensity for resumptive exposition by which he is able to zigzag from topic to topic often without introduction, only later to return to them with full attention. What is intimated here, argues Block, is addressed fully in Ezek 45:21–46:12.

20 Zimmerli, *Ezekiel 2*, 441; Block, *Book of Ezekiel*, 615; Albertz, *Israel in Exile*, 372.

21 The promotion of the *nāśī* to prime Israelite goes as far back as the early decades of last century (see Gustav Hölscher, *Hesekiel, der Dichter und das Buch: eine literarkritische Untersuchung* [BZAW 39; Giessen: Töpelmann, 1924], 211) and has remained an almost *verbatim* refrain in the analysis of the figure to the present (e.g. Albertz, *Israel in Exile*, 372).

22 The relationship between Ezek 34, 37 and 40–48 is complicated at best. It is common to treat Ezek 34 and 37 as earlier texts to Ezek 40–48 because of their placement in the book, but there

attract language associated with traditional Judahite royal ideology (particularly that from militaristic and judicial spheres); is denied the explicit title of *meleḵ*; and above all is not a scion of David. Moreover, in contrast both to the Judahite kings who came before him (cf. 1 Kgs 9:25; 12:29; 2 Kgs 16:10–16; Ps 110:4) and his Jeremian alter ego who returns to such a position immediately (Jer 30:21), the *nāśī'* does not have an obvious role in the sacrificial cult. While he has the foremost duty to provide materials for the cult (e.g. Ezek 46*), he has only a small role to play in its rituals, unable as he is to approach the altar. Thus the perceived disparity between responsibility and presentation leaves the *nāśī'* as something of a puzzling figure, with the pendulum of scholarship swinging wildly in its evaluation of him as 'the representative of the divinity'[23] to 'a mock king as in some saturnalian role reversal.'[24]

A common, if not axiomatic, explanation is that the *nāśī'* is somehow a natural by-product of the priestly worldview that dominates the Vision. In negative renditions, the conversation between the binary pairs of sacred-profane and pure-impure that govern the theological and institutional structure of the Vision are used to demote the status of the *nāśī'* in light of the new claims of the work's priestly author(s). In attempting to implement a reform that granted the priesthood prime of place and complete independence, the priestly writers subjected the *nāśī'* to an innate hierarchical ordering of the cult. And so, as a necessary consequence, the royal figure is relegated to a secondary, inferior status.[25]

But the cultic or sacral orientation of the Vision has been marshalled with the same ease to interpret the figure in a positive light. For both Jon D. Levenson[26] and Daniel I. Block,[27] the cultic perspective of Ezek 40–48 allows them to construct an apolitical and sacral *nāśī'*, who is situated very much at the centre (if not *as* the centre) of the restored nation.[28] If in the pre-exilic period the king stood

are compelling reasons to understand both as additions to the text that post-date Ezek 40–48 (cf. Anja Klein, *Schriftauslegung im Ezechielbuch: Redaktionsgeschichtliche Untersuchungen zu Ez 34–39* [BZAW 391; Berlin/New York: de Gruyter, 2008]).

23 Wright, 'Tale of Three Cities', 39.

24 Smith, *To Take Place*, 61.

25 Smith, *To Take Place*; Albertz, *Israel in Exile*.

26 Levenson, *Theology of the Program*.

27 In addition to the various positions taken in Block, *Book of Ezekiel*, see further ibid., 'Bringing Back David: Ezekiel's Messianic Hope', in *The Lord's Anointed: Interpretation of Old Testament Messianic Texts* (ed. R. S. Hess, P. E. Satterthwaite, and G. J. Wenham; Carlisle: Paternoster Press, 1995), 167–188; Block, 'Transformation of Royal Ideology in Ezekiel', in *Transforming Visions: Transformations of Text, Tradition, and Theology in Ezekiel* (PTMS 127; ed. W. A. Tooman and M. A. Lyons; Eugene: Pickwick, 2010), 208–246.

28 Cf. Duguid, *Ezekiel and the Elders*.

as the zenith of the political, the Vision's *nāśī'* stands as the fulcrum of the sacral, confirmed, as was David, in a position of power, albeit by a new set of criteria in the form of 'apolitical', Sinaitic Law. Block writes:

> In this vision (and only here), with its radically theocentric portrayal of Israel's future, the *nāśī'* emerges as a religious functionary, serving the holy community of faith, which itself is focused on the worship of the God who dwells in their midst.[29]

Both interpretive variations seem to be flawed on the level of logic, each in its own way suffering from positing an assumed priestly necessity that is far from given. Against the larger positive interpretation, it remains unclear how a sacral (or even a priestly!) concern makes a text or its ruling figures necessarily apolitical.[30] As we will see in due course, the Neo-Babylonian royal inscriptional corpus is concerned almost entirely with the king in relation to the sacral in the form of his relationship with the great Babylonian temples. It would be veering towards the absurd to claim as a consequence that the texts, the royal position vis-à-vis the temple or the theological underpinnings of this element of royal ideology are apolitical.[31] Precisely the same line of reasoning is applicable, in my mind, to the negative interpretation of the sacrally or priestly rendered *nāśī'*. A world organized according to a priestly hierarchy need not necessarily disadvantage a ruler.[32] All is dependent upon the ruler's standing with respect to the priestly office. If, as in Neo-Assyrian royal theology, the king acted as *the* priest with the larger

29 Block, 'Bringing Back David', 187; Block, *Book of Ezekiel*, 746.

30 One could pose the question to Block whether this was ever not the case regarding the royal figure. To be king was to emerge as a religious functionary in one capacity or another and to serve one's subjects, who themselves were focused on the worship of their god(s) who dwelt in their midst. Even the prototypical *Unheilsherrscher* functions as such (e.g. 1 Kgs 12) and in acting as cultic functionary to a god (albeit in an apostate manner), fulfils one of the primary royal prerogatives.

31 Written by priests and serving an explicitly political function, the Nabonidus Verse Account is the obvious counter example (Amélie Kuhrt, 'Nabonidus and the Babylonian Priesthood', in *Pagan Priests: Religion and Power in the Ancient World* [ed. M. Beard and J. North; London: Duckworth, 1990]; 117–156; for the text and further discussion, see Hanspeter Schaudig, *Die Inschriften Nabonids von Babylon und Kyros' des Großen samt den in ihrem Umfeld entstandenen Tendenzschriften: Textausgabe und Grammatik* [AOAT 256; Münster: Ugarit-Verlag, 2001], 563–578). As such, it is entirely unjustified to conclude that because the Temple Vision is concerned above all with the restoration of YHWH in his temple that the text or the figure of a human ruler within it is apolitical. As soon as a god is enthroned, as YHWH is in Ezek 43:7, a text becomes political whether we read it this way or not.

32 *Pace* Smith, *To Take Place*.

institution deriving therefrom,[33] the ruler would be at the very top of a priestly hierarchy. The *nāśīʾ* clearly is not in the restoration envisioned by Ezek 40–48, but one cannot explain his status by an appeal to priestly logic or bias. Neither necessitates royal demotion.

Eschewing a more theological explication, the second major approach to the *nāśīʾ* has been to examine him in relation to the presumed historical setting of the text, which is overwhelmingly determined as the (early) restoration period.[34] Steven Tuell's sensitive analysis of Ezek 40–48 is a fine example of this line of thought. For Tuell, the vision reflects in its entirety the historical realities of Judean socio-political hierarchies under the reign of Darius I, making the *nāśīʾ* none other than the governor (*peḥāh*) of Persian-period Yehud.[35] Tuell suggests that we should look to Sheshbazzar, himself called both *nāśīʾ* and *peḥāh* (Ezra 1:8; 5:14), as the historical model for the figure found in the Temple Vision.

> We have already seen in Sheshbazzar the use of the title נשיא [*nāsīʾ*] for a Persian governor. Moreover, we know that Sheshbazzar, as leader of the first returnees to the land following the edict of Cyrus, was given a cultic charge: the return of the sacred Temple vessels to Jerusalem. Finally, we know that state support of the cult was Persian policy. These parallels strongly suggest that the נשיא of the Law of the Temple was the Judean governor, under Persian hegemony.[36]

---

33 Peter Machinist, 'Kingship and Divinity in Imperial Assyria', in *Text, Artifact, and Image: Revealing Ancient Israelite Religion* (BJS 346; ed. G. M. Beckman and T. J. Lewis; Providence: Brown Judaic Studies, 2006), 152–188; Hanspeter Schaudig, 'Cult Centralization in the Ancient Near East? Conceptions of the Ideal Capital in the Ancient Near East', in *One God – One Cult – One Nation: Archaeological and Biblical Perspectives* (BZAW 405; ed. R. G. Kratz and H. Spieckermann; Berlin: de Gruyter, 2010), 144–168 (156–159).

34 There are more supporters of this line of argumentation than one might expect, even if they do not claim that it is the governing principle of either the Temple Vision as a whole or their reconstruction of the *nāśīʾ*. The primary example of this is in all likelihood Gese (*Verfassungsentwurf*) with his *nasi-Schicht*, which he argued was inserted by writers initially favourable to a restored monarch (see variations in Rudnig, *Heilig und Profan*, and Konkel, *Architektonik)*. The difference between Tuell's line of arguing and the recent Gesian variations most likely has to do with intention. The likes of Rudnig and Konkel would say that it is the hopes of the early post-exilic period that have inspired changes (good or bad), whereas Tuell argues that the legislation is written to codify practice, not hope.

35 The *peḥāh* is attested in Hag 1:1, 14; 2:2, 21; Mal 1:8; Esther 3:12; 8:9; 9:3; Dan 3:2, 3, 27; 6:8; Ezra 5:3, 6, 14; 6:6, 7, 13; 8:36; Neh 2:7, 9; 3:7; 5:14, 15, 18; 12:26; 2 Chron 9:14.

36 Tuell, *Law of the Temple*, 116.

The smaller elements of Tuell's argument will elicit various responses.[37] Of more concern is the degree to which this type of argument is contingent upon our ability to reconstruct the 'historical reality' of a period that sadly remains shrouded by a veil of uncertainty. For example, though almost axiomatic when he was writing, the theory of Persian imperial authorization is now on less solid ground, if not denied outright,[38] making the very 'historical' premise from which Tuell launches untenable. Could the *nāśīʾ* in Ezek 40–48 reflect the role played and responsibilities held by the Persian period governor in the rebuilt Jerusalem temple? Yes, one supposes. But given how little we know about said temple and what we do know is that it was not that envisioned in Ezek 40–48, the answer could just as easily be no. This is by no means to question the value of historical reconstruction. It is simply to warn that in this specific case the knowledge of 'historical reality' needed to assume as much is far from our grasp. For an interpretation of the *nāśīʾ* directly, it means that the oddities of his character in the Temple Vision are not explained by the historical realities of the Persian period, largely because we do not know *what* those realities were.

It appears then that both roads down which scholars have variously travelled with the Temple Vision's *nāśīʾ* seem to lead to dead ends of one description or another, too often being based on 'givens', 'necessities' or 'historical realities' that not only need not be the case, but more importantly rarely are. As a new fork in the road, what I would like to propose here is that the presentation of the *nāśīʾ* has its structural grounding in Neo-Babylonian royal ideology, a suggestion that to the best of my knowledge no one has thus far offered up on the altar of scholarly discussion. It may be that looking at the Temple Vision as a musing of sorts on or perhaps with Babylonian political theology of the long 6th century BCE will bring us closer to an explanation for a prince who has otherwise eluded exegetical resolution.

37 In particular, I have concerns with Tuell's conflation of titles based on the figure of Sheshbazzar. Though Sheshbazzar is indeed called *hannāśīʾ līhūdā* in Ezra 1:8, his status as leader of the single tribe does not make him the governor of the returned community, nor the titles synonymous. As for Sheshbazzar's cultic charge to return the Temple vessels, however historically certain it may be, it reflects nothing of the Temple in the vision, which otherwise empties the sanctuary of the accoutrements of the traditional Jerusalem Temple (cf. Robert Kasher, 'Anthropomorphism, Holiness and Cult: A New Look at Ezek 40–48', *ZAW* 110 [1998]: 192–208).

38 Cf. Lisbeth S. Fried, *The Priest and the Great King: Temple-Palace Relations in the Persian Empire* (Biblical and Judaic Studies from the University of California San Diego 10; Winona Lake: Eisenbrauns, 2004).

2 Neo-Babylonian Kingship Ideology

David Vanderhooft[39] and Caroline Waerzeggers[40] have each in their own way laid the foundation to illuminate a particular Neo-Babylonian articulation of royal ideology such that it can now be identified beyond the otherwise sticky malaise that we refer to as 'Mesopotamian kingship ideology'.[41] The portrait to emerge from their work is an ideology that, on the one hand, is built on a deliberately archaized royal rhetoric intended to show the new empire as the legitimate heir to Babylon's ancient tradition,[42] while on the other, seeks to present an image of the ideal king that is overwhelmingly anchored by the king's relationship to the gods, to their respective residences and the temple cults fundamental thereto. Towards this end, the inscriptional corpus highlights time and again the king's obligations to the gods, which manifests primarily in his dual roles as humble temple servant and wise shepherd.[43]

One of Nebuchadnezzar II's early call narratives illustrates the trajectory of Neo-Babylonian royal ideology beautifully. Recounting his divine commission, Nebuchadnezzar iterates the *raison d'être* of the royal office:

> ^{d}AMAR.UTU ... KUR *šú-te-šú-ru ni-šim re-e-a-am / za-na-an ma-ḫa-zi ud-du-šú eš-re-e-tim / ra-bi-iš ú-ma-'e-er-an-ni*
>
> Marduk sublimely commanded me to lead the land aright, to shepherd the people, to provide for cult centres, (and) to renew temples.[44]

---

39 David S. Vanderhooft, *The Neo-Babylonian Empire and Babylon in the Latter Prophets* (HSM 59; Georgia: Scholars Press, 1999); Vanderhooft, 'Babylonian Strategies of Imperial Control in the West: Royal Practice and Rhetoric', in *Judah and the Judeans in the Neo-Babylonian Period* (ed. O. Lipschits and J. Blenkinsopp; Winona Lake: Eisenbrauns, 2003), 235–262.

40 Caroline Waerzeggers, 'The Pious King: Royal Patronage of Temples', in *The Oxford Handbook of Cuneiform Culture* (ed. K. Radner and E. Robson; Oxford: Oxford University Press, 2011), 725–751.

41 See also John A. Brinkman, 'The Early Neo-Babylonian Monarchy', in *Le Palais et la Royauté* (ed. P. Garelli; Paris: Geuthner, 1974), 409–415; Rocío Da Riva, *The Neo-Babylonian Royal Inscriptions: An Introduction* (GMTR 4; Münster: Ugarit-Verlag, 2008).

42 For a full discussion of the Neo-Babylonian titular, see Vanderhooft, *Neo-Babylonian Empire*, 16–23. For the sake of the exercise, I will make broad a variegated royal titular that changes from Nabopolassar to Nabonidus. Vanderhooft provides a nuanced treatment of the changes the royal presentation undergoes (ibid., 33–59).

43 We are always speaking of degrees here. To deny that (Neo-)Assyrian monarchs were not concerned with temple building or justice is silly. There is simply a particular emphasis on these two concerns in the Neo-Babylonian royal corpus.

44 VAB 4 Nbk 1 i 11–14.

The first two royal obligations – to lead the land aright (*māta šutēšuru*) and to shepherd the people (*nišī rē'û*) – emphasize the king's terrestrial responsibilities. The shepherd metaphor has a pedigree within the royal rhetoric of Sumero-Mesopotamian kings as old as Enlil himself[45] and does not in and of itself indicate a reinterpretation of royal ideology. Nonetheless, it highlights a Neo-Babylonian preoccupation with the outcome of the royal office, namely that the king as shepherd benevolently safeguard the welfare of his subjects at all cost.[46] A subject-orientation also underpins the command to lead the land aright, which has a close parallel in the divine commission of Hammurabi:

> *i-nu-ma* ᵈAMAR.UTU *a-na* <u>*šu-te-šu-ur ni-ši*</u> <u>KALAM</u> *ú-si-im šu-ḫu-zi-im ú-wa-e-ra-an-ni ki-it-tam ù mi-ša-ra-am i-na* KA *ma-tim aš-ku-un ši-ir ni-ši ú-ṭi-ib*
>
> When the god Marduk commanded me to set the people of the land aright in order to attain appropriate behaviour, I established truth and justice as the declaration of the land, I enhanced the wellbeing of the people.[47]

The evidence may not be strong enough to propose a genetic link between the two texts, but there is an undeniable 'air of Hammurabi' to the rhetoric of the Neo-Babylonian kings. The connection is particularly strong with Nebuchadnezzar, which suggests that the king sought to present himself as Hammurabi *Redivivus*,[48] but Nabopolassar and Nebuchadnezzar alike utilize the royal title *šar mīšari* ('King of Justice') first coined by Hammurabi.[49]

---

45 All Neo-Babylonian royal titles and epithets are tabulated in Da Riva, *Neo-Babylonian Royal Inscriptions*, 99–107. For *rē'û*, 'shepherd', see pages 99 (Nabopolassar), 101 (Nebuchadnezzar), 105–106 (Nabonidus). The term's use in the wider Mesopotamian canon is collated by Marie-Joseph Seux, *Épithètes royales akkadiennes et sumériennes* (Paris: Letouzey et Ané, 1967), 244–250. For a discussion of the royal presentation, see Joan G. Westenholz, 'The Good Shepherd', in *Schools of Oriental Studies and the Development of Modern Historiography: Proceedings of the Fourth Annual Symposium of the Assyrian and Babylonian Intellectual Heritage Project Held in Ravenna, Italy, October 13–17, 2001* (Melammu Symposia 4; ed. A. Panaino and A. Piras; Milan: Università di Bologna & IsIao, 2004), 281–310.

46 Whether the king shepherds the one or the many changes with Nebuchadnezzar. His father makes a point of eschewing imperial language when referring to the extent of his kingdom. With the advent of empire, the rhetoric will subtly change from the king's rule over the *nišī* ('peoples') to the *nišī rapšātim* ('widespread peoples') (cf. Vanderhooft, *Neo-Babylonian Empire*, 34–41).

47 CH v 14–24.

48 Wilfred G. Lambert, 'Nebuchadnezzar King of Justice', *Iraq* 27 (1965): 1–11 (3); Vanderhooft, *Neo-Babylonian Empire*, 44, 50–51.

49 Da Riva, *Neo-Babylonian Royal Inscriptions*, 99 (Nabopolassar), 102 (Nebuchadnezzar). The title is overwhelmingly Babylonian and is largely confined to the royal inscriptional corpus of

A return of the judicious king to the royal project underscores two tendencies in the Neo-Babylonian inscriptional corpus already identified. First and foremost, it rearticulates the ideal of the king as supreme guardian. Whether his responsibility is for Babylon alone or for the 'widespread peoples' (*nišū rapšātu*) as the growing demands of empire will necessitate,[50] the king is placed in office by the gods to safeguard the welfare of his land and its inhabitants. Secondly, it is indicative of the Neo-Babylonian penchant for the antiquarian.[51] Purposefully resurrecting archaic royal titles from the Ur III and Old Babylonian periods as well as building literary links to this past, the scribal enterprise became one of innovative transformation by returning to a time when Babylon experienced its first flirtation with empire. This exercise was by no means cosmetic. The three centuries prior to the rise of the new Babylonian dynasty were dominated by the wax and wane of Assyrian hegemony, which, at least with the case of Sennacherib, had had devastating consequences for Babylon. In conformity to the broad strokes of traditional disaster theology, Babylon's misfortune was interpreted as the result of divine anger. But the ideological link forged in the royal inscriptions between the first and newest Babylonian empires reinterprets history such that the entire intervening period is understood as a protracted state of chaos.[52] By presenting themselves as the initiators of a second *pax babyloniaca* that overturns temporal chaos, the Neo-Babylonian kings were able to claim custodianship of Babylon's illustrious past.[53] More fundamental, the weight placed on the king as just ruler points in my opinion to a re-imagining of the royal institution wherein the dynasty itself comes to function as a long-awaited *mīšarum* for the land.

Babylon (Nebuchadnezzar I [RIMB B.2.4.1; B.2.4.8; B.2.4.11]; Simbar-Šipak [RIMB B.3.1.1]; Erība-Marduk [RIMB B.6.13]). Nabonidus claims that he *rā'im mīšari* ('loves justice'; Da Riva, *Neo-Babylonian Royal Inscriptions*, 105), which likely implies a similar sentiment. The idiom is Assyrian (Seux, *Épithètes royales*, 236–237), but this fits the rhetorical flavour of Nabonidus, who chooses the Assyrian over the Babylonian for political reasons his own (Vanderhooft, *Neo-Babylonian Empire*, 57–58).

50 Vanderhooft, *Neo-Babylonian Empire*, 35–36.

51 Paul-Alain Beaulieu, 'Antiquarianism and the Concern for the Past in the Neo-Babylonian Period', *Bulletin of the Canadian Society of Mesopotamian Studies* 28 (1994): 37–42.

52 Da Riva, *Neo-Babylonian Royal Inscriptions*, 114. Not all texts present the time of Assyrian domination in a negative light. The Neo-Babylonian Chronicles, for example, narrate the succession of kings, as well as the transfer of power from Assyria to Babylonia, in a dispassionate manner. For the texts, see Jean-Jacques Glassner, *Mesopotamian Chronicles* (SBLWAW 19; Atlanta: Society of Biblical Literature, 2004), 218–238.

53 Nabonidus, as intimated already, consciously elides himself with the Sargonid kings (Vanderhooft, *Neo-Babylonian Empire*, 57–59). Without rejecting the literary milieu of Babylonia entirely, he nonetheless seeks to present himself as the imperial heir of Assyria.

The wellbeing of any land large or small was directly proportionate to the contentedness of its gods. Maintaining such contentedness was a responsibility that fell to the king. How a royal ideology incorporated the obligation varied both geographically and temporally, but the Babylonian articulation planted it firmly in the context of its temple system. Over and above the king's call to shepherd the people, perhaps even to its exclusion in some cases, the king is positioned as reverent guardian of the temple cult, assiduously devoted to its continuation and proper performance. Narrating the circumstances of his rise to the throne of Babylon, Nabopolassar recounts the piety of his youth:

> *i-nu-um i-na mé-eṣ-ḫe-ru-ti-ia* / DUMU *la ma-am-ma-na-ma a-na-ku-ma* / *áš-rat* ᵈAK *ù* ᵈAMAR.UTU EN*-e-a* / *áš-te-né-'e-a ka-a-a-nim* / *šá ku-un-ni pa-ar-ṣi-šu-nu* /*ù šu-ul-lu-mu ki-du-de-e-šu-nu* / *i-ta-ma-a ka-ba-at-tì*
>
> When in my youth – although I was the son of a nobody – I constantly sought the sanctuaries of my lords Nabû and Marduk, my mind was preoccupied with the establishment of their cultic ordinances and the complete performance of their rituals.[54]

Where Assyrian kings tend to legitimate their rule by means of divine commission in the womb or at a young age,[55] Nabopolassar establishes his right by appealing to a pious character that has governed his behaviour from childhood.[56] Such piety in turn leads to divine election and thereafter is expressed through the king's tireless commitment to the continuation of the cult by means of construction. The prerogative and task of (re)building temples belonged to all kings,[57]

54 A Babylon II i 7–13; text in Farouk N. H. Al-Rawi, 'Nabopolassar's Restoration Work on the Wall "Imgur-Enlil" at Babylon', *Iraq* 47 (1985): 1–13. Note how the inscription continues on: *a-na kit-ti ù mi-ša-ri ba-ša-a uz-na-a-a*, 'my attention was directed towards justice and equity' (line 14).
55 E.g. Aššur-rēša-iši I (RIMA 1 A.0.86.1); Šamši-Adad V (RIMA 3 A.0.103.1); Adad-nirari III (RIMA 3 A.0.104.1); Esarhaddon (Ash. § 27); Assurbanipal (ARAB II § 765). A similar idiom appears in Nabonidus' rehearsal of his commission (VAB 4 Nbn 1 i 4–5), which further aligns him with a Neo-Assyrian ideology rather than with that of the Babylonian throne he has usurped.
56 There is no such appeal to youthful piety in Nebuchadnezzar's inscriptions, but this is only because he is the legitimate heir to the throne. In an almost Job-like manner, Nabopolassar records his son's piety as a child when he accompanied his father in his building projects (VAB 4 Npl 1 ii 61–iii 18). The twin appearance of father and son acts to justify the current throne, he who will hold it next, and the dynasty to come (Hanspeter Schaudig, 'The Restoration of Temples in the Neo- and Late Babylonian Periods', in *From the Foundations to the Crenellations: Essays on Temple Building in the Ancient Near East and the Hebrew Bible* [AOAT 366; ed. M. J. Boda and J. Novotny; Münster: Ugarit-Verlag, 2010], 141–164 [153]).
57 Arvid S. Kapelrud, 'Temple Building, a Task for Gods and Kings', *Or* 32 (1963): 120–132; Hurowitz, *I Have Built*, 332–334; Schaudig, 'Restoration of Temples'.

but the function dominates the entire Neo-Babylonian royal corpus. Indeed, what little militaristic rhetoric appears in the inscriptions serves to further this goal.[58]

> *e-nu-ma i-na qí-bí-a-tim* / ^{d}*na-bi-um ù* ^{d}AMAR.UTU / *na-ra-am šar-rù-ti-ia* / *ù* GIŠ.TUKUL ZI.DA KALAG / *šà* ^{d}*gìr-ra ra-šú-ub-bu* / *mu-uš-tab-ri-qu za-à-ri-ia* / *su-ba-ru-um a-na-ru* / KUR-*su ú-te-ir-ru* / *a-na* DU_6 *ù ka-ar-mi* / *í-nu-mi-šú è-temen-an-ki*
>
> When on the command of Nabû and Marduk, who love my kingship, and by the true and strong weapon of the awe-inspiring Erra, which strikes down my foes, I smashed the Subaraean and turned his land into ruin hills and wasteland, then (Marduk entrusted me with building) Etemenanki ...[59]

The *inūma-inūšu* ('when-then') structure on which the introduction of Nabopolassar's Etemenanki cylinder turns establishes a clear link between military victory and temple restoration. Nabû and Marduk command Nabopolassar to defeat the Assyrians and only once successfully completed is he entrusted with the task of rebuilding Marduk's temple. Viewed from one angle, the relationship between royal action and divine commission runs along traditional lines – through successful battle the monarch erects the platform necessary to play king. However, the *inūšu* clause foregrounds a concern particular to Neo-Babylonian ideology – most, if not all, royal activity is aimed at ensuring the continuation of the temple cult. Thus, in this instance, the age-old image of the warrior king is both subordinated to and rendered in service of the larger initiative to present the king as temple builder.[60]

Whilst much of the royal task was devoted to guaranteeing the physical stability of the cult through building and renovation, the overarching principle of the king as servant of the gods was furthered by means of his role as principal

---

58 Vanderhooft places special emphasis on the non-militaristic tone of the early Neo-Babylonian royal inscriptions. The rhetoric of Nabopolassar's inscriptions rends any connection between Neo-Assyrian and Neo-Babylonian rule (*Neo-Babylonian Empire*, 32–33). The trend continues with Nebuchadnezzar, whose scribes reformulate the *šibirru* ('royal scepter') into an emblem that protects the king's many subjects in contradistinction to its terrifying implications of destruction in Neo-Assyrian rhetoric (ibid., 42–43).

59 VAB 4 Npl 1 i 23–31. New edition by Rocío Da Riva, *The Inscriptions of Nabopolassar, Amēl-Marduk and Neriglissar* (Studies in Ancient Near Eastern Records 3; Berlin: de Gruyter, 2013), 77–92.

60 Nebuchadnezzar's Wadi Brisa inscriptions, which recount his successful campaigns in Lebanon, should be read along similar lines. All that the king endeavors to achieve militaristically is done for the exaltation and betterment of Babylon (Da Riva, *Neo-Babylonian Royal Inscriptions*, 108–109; cf. Vanderhooft, *Neo-Babylonian Empire*, 45–49; Schaudig, 'Cult Centralization', 159–163).

provider for the sacrificial cult. The king's largesse towards the cult is emphasised through the royal titulary, especially with the recurring title *zānin Esagil u Ezida* ('provider of Esagila and Ezida'), which is second in attestation only to the generic title *šar Bābili* ('king of Babylon').[61] Consequently, the extant corpus, such that it is, is littered with accounts of royal munificence befitting the actions and intentions of an attentive king.

> I [Nebuchadnezzar] strove to provide for them [Nabû and Nanāja] more lavishly than before with their great regular offerings: every day one fattened "unblemished" *gumāhu*-bull whose limbs are prefect, whose body [has no] white spot; 16 fattened sheep, fine *zuluhhû*-breed; in addition to what (pertains) to the gods of Borsippa: 2 ducks; 3 doves; 20 *murratu*-birds; 2 ducklings; 3 bandicoot rats; a string of Apsû fish, the best things of the marsh; profuse vegetables, the delight of the garden; rosy fruits, the bounty of the orchards; dates; Dilmun-dates; dried figs; raisins; finest beer-wort; ghee; *muttāqu*-cake; milk; the best oil; honey; beer; purest wine; (all of this) I provided more lavishly than before for the table-spread of my lords Nabû and Nanāja.[62]

Similar in some ways to the Late Sumerian and Old Babylonian law collections, which sought to illustrate through the compendium of numerous laws the just character of the kings to whom they were ascribed, Nebuchadnezzar's rehearsal of provisions for the cult at Borsippa illustrates to a divine audience that he is a worthy king and a superlatively generous one at that. 'Striving' (*aštēma*) to increase daily the provision for the table spread of Marduk's son, Nabû, and his consort, Nebuchadnezzar paints himself the *zānin Ezida* extraordinaire.[63] Though Nebuchadnezzar is most grandiloquent in this regard, the sentiment is not confined to his rule. The royal title is used by Nabopolassar and Nabonidus, and appears too in the rhetoric of Neriglissar.[64] Even if Nabonidus is posthumously

61 Da Riva, *Neo-Babylonian Royal Inscriptions*, 94.
62 WBA vii 1–20; translation from Rocío Da Riva, *The Twin Inscriptions of Nebuchadnezzar at Brisa (Wadi esh-Sharbin, Lebanon): A Historical and Philological Study* (AfOB 32; Wien: Institut für Orientalistik, 2012), 51.
63 Nebuchadnezzar is particularly fond of the title *zānin Esagil u Ezida*, which he uses no less than fifty-two times (Da Riva, *Neo-Babylonian Royal Inscriptions*, 103). Though occurring with less frequency, two further titles *zānin kal māḫāzīka* ('provider of all your shrines') and *zānin māḫāz ilāni rabûti* ('provider of the shrine of the great gods') convey a similar sentiment.
64 Nabopolassar uses the titles *zānin Esagil u Bābili* and *zānin Esagil u Ezida* (Da Riva, *Neo-Babylonian Royal Inscriptions*, 100). The preferred title of Nabonidus is *zānin Esagil u Ezida*, but *zānin Ur* appears once, as does *zānin ešrēti* ('provider of the chapels'; Da Riva, *Neo-Babylonian Royal Inscriptions*, 107). The title is not attested to in Neriglissar's inscriptions, but an explanation may be his short reign rather than a change of ideology. Nonetheless, he does praise himself as *mu-ṭa-aḫ-ḫi-id sa-at-tu-uk-ku / mu-uš-te-ši-ru šú-lu-uḫ-ḫe-šú-un* ('one who makes the daily offerings

castigated for doing so, we should read his efforts to bolster the cult of Sîn as following on in logical order from the cultic rationale of his predecessors.

The king's divine commission to act as guardian of the cult established a firm relationship between himself and the priestly institution, over which he acted as protector and judge to ensure correct behaviour, further guaranteeing divine blessing for his personal dynasty,[65] as well as the land at large. But royal oversight did not – in contrast to the prerogative of his Assyrian counterpart[66] – translate into a priestly role for the king.[67] Though he played a unique role in the *akītu* festival[68] and will have been well represented in the most sacred precincts of a given temple by means of his cult statue,[69] the king did not act as altar priest nor could he independently approach the divine cult image, privileges strictly reserved for the highest category of priest, the *ērib-bīti* ('temple-enterer').[70] Nevertheless, as overseer of the priestly prebendary system, which allowed the king (at least in theory) to appoint and depose priestly actors, and as sole builder, the king remained in a position of significant power with respect to the temple institution and the priesthoods attached to it. Where the Neo-Babylonian material leads us is not to a picture of the king as Atlas bound, limited by the demands of Babylonia's great temples and associated priesthoods, but to a symbiotic relationship between monarch and priest, which sought to ensure the livelihood of both households alike.[71]

Scholarly appraisals of the Neo-Babylonian royal corpus at times exhibit a tendency to overemphasize the pious elements of the ideology, suggesting that all other royal prerogatives cower under the looming silhouette of the devout king. The stance is not entirely without justification. Virtually every articulation of Neo-Babylonian royal ideology in the corpus that we possess derives from a text that recounts a given king's success at religious and civic building or the restoration of cults and rituals putatively long forgotten.[72] Here the emphasis on *res-*

---

abundant and ensures that their ritual is correctly observed'; VAB 4 Ngl 2 i 9–10 cf. Da Riva, *The Inscriptions of Nabopolassar*, 116).

65 E.g. VAB 4 Npl 1 iii 43–61.

66 See note 33 above.

67 Schaudig, 'Cult Centralization', 158–159; Waerzeggers, 'Pious King', 733–737.

68 Waerzeggers, 'Pious King', 731–732.

69 Ibid., 745; cf. Irene J. Winter, '"Idols of the King": Royal Images as Recipients of Ritual Action in Ancient Mesopotamia', *JRitSt* 6 (1992): 13–42; Machinist, 'Kingship and Divinity'.

70 Waerzeggers, 'Pious King', 735.

71 Waerzeggers, 'Pious King', 745–746.

72 See the two appendices in Da Riva, *Neo-Babylonian Royal Inscriptions*, 116–131.

toration and *re*building is purposeful,[73] allowing each king in turn to establish links with a past otherwise denied by the previous two centuries of Neo-Assyrian hegemony (so the Nabopolassar dynasty) or lack of royal filiation (so Neriglissar and Nabonidus). On a theological course not dissimilar to Gilgameš, who through trial [*ni*]-*ṣir-ta i-mur-ma ka-ti-im-ta ip-tu / ub-la ṭè-e-ma šá la-am a-bu-bi* ('found out what was secret and uncovered what was hidden, brought back a tale of times before the Flood'),[74] the Neo-Babylonian kings tirelessly sought to unearth a sacred past that would somehow reverse the misfortunes of Babylon's recent history. As ever, royal ideology came to play a decisive role in this process, rooting the power of the king in his humble obligation to the divine realm. As builder, the king guaranteed that the gods were correctly housed and attended to according to divinely established protocol. As shepherd, he guaranteed that his nation lived in a requisite state of order to promote the correct worship of the gods.

3 Ezekiel the Copy Cat?

But what does Babylon have to do with Israel restored, the *zāninu* to do with the *nāśī'*? Without underplaying or ignoring the fundamental differences between the Babylonian royal inscriptions and Ezek 40–48, it appears to me that Ezekiel's *nāśī'* comes into sharper focus only when set against a particular Neo-Babylonian backdrop. Suggesting that the authors of the Temple Vision have adopted the broad contours of a Neo-Babylonian royal ideology to present the *nāśī'* explains precisely those enigmatic elements that have preoccupied scholarly debates over the figure. Immediately, the Neo-Babylonian corpus acts a model for an ideology that reads in an apolitical manner, providing a precedent for a royal rhetoric that excludes militaristic overtones. But it is particularly the cultic orientation of Neo-Babylonian royal ideology that acts as the cypher for unlocking the Temple Vision's *nāśī'*. Anomalous if set against a Judahite royal ideology,[75] the *nāśī'*'s active, but non-priestly role in temple ritual, his copious patronage of the cult,[76] and his sacred meal read to perfection if seen through the Babylonian lens. It may even be that we can explain Ezekiel's distinct royal title *nāśī'* as a purposeful

73 Da Riva, *Neo-Babylonian Royal Inscriptions*, 115.
74 SBV I i 7–8; Andrew R. George, *The Babylonian Gilgamesh Epic: Introduction, Critical Edition and Cuneiform Texts* (Oxford: Oxford University Press, 2003), 538–539.
75 Cf. 1 Kgs 9:25; 2 Kgs 16:10–16; Ps 110:4.
76 In total, the *nāśī'* provides one thousand and ten animals per annum.

archaization in conformity with the Neo-Babylonian tendency,[77] though I appreciate that this may be a step too close towards the dangerous waters of *parallelomania*. Regardless, if we can lead Ezek 40–48 by the hand down a Neo-Babylonian road, it allows for a fuller reading that exculpates the text from the charge of being nothing more than a thinly veiled priestly *coup d'état*.

Two roles central to Neo-Babylonian royal ideology are, however, conspicuously absent in Ezek 40–48, hinting that the dawn of restoration is not as rosy tipped as some would like. The first is the responsibility of the king to act as judge, which in Ezek 40–48 is a prerogative given to the priesthood.[78] Within a long exposition on the priestly task (Ezek 44:15–31), which includes the expected precautions regarding dress, appearance, marriage and contact with the contagious dead incumbent upon a priest to take, the remit of the priestly occupation is laid out, which includes acting as judge in controversies according divine judgment (*běmišpātay*; Ezek 44:24a). Some have difficulty with the shift in judicial authority from royal to priest. If the passage is not excised altogether as part of a secondary or tertiary Zadokite stratum,[79] an argument is offered that the sanctuary bias of the author or redactors of the Temple Vision leads them to ignore the minutiae of secular politics, which includes the judicial functions of the *nāśī'*.[80] This does start to sound like special pleading however. If judicial authority as a topic were entirely missing from the vision, I would be happier to leave it unad-

---

77 Gen 17:20; 23:6; 25:16; 34:2; Ex 16:22; 22:28; 34:31; 35:27; Lev 4:22; Num 1:16, 44; 2:3, 5, 7, 10, 12, 14, 18, 20, 22, 25, 27, 29; 3:24, 30, 32, 35; 4:34, 46; 7:2–3, 10–11, 18, 24, 30, 36, 42, 48, 54, 60, 66, 72, 78, 84; 10:4; 13:2; 16:2; 17:2, 6; 25:14, 18; 27:2; 31:13; 32:2; 34:18, 22–28; 36:1; Josh 9:15, 18–19, 21; 13:21; 17:4; 22:14, 30, 32; 1 Kings 8:1; 11:34; Ezra 1:8; 1 Chr 2:10; 4:38; 5:6; 7:40; 2 Chr 1:2; 5:2. This grouping of references should be treated with care. It is not clear that the appearances in 1 Chronicles are any later than, say, those in Numbers. What the distribution of the term does indicate is that it is used to describe an 'old' or archaized political figure in most instances, lending in most instances an element of authority through antiquity.

78 The issue of priesthood in the Temple Vision is vexed (cf. Joachim Schaper, *Priester und Leviten im achämenidischen Juda: Studien zur Kult- und Sozialgeschichte Israels in persischer Zeit* [FAT II/31; Tübingen: Mohr, 2000]; Steven L. Cook and Corrine L. Patton, eds., *Ezekiel's Hierarchical World: Wrestling with a Tiered Reality* [SBLSymS 31; Atlanta: Society of Biblical Studies, 2004]). Putting aside the Zadokite/Levite conundrum, the descriptions of priesthood otherwise falls nicely into a Neo-Babylonian milieu. To be sure it does not begin to reflect the complexity that is in evidence at the likes Borsippa, but priestly rank is determined by task and access. Thus the two types of priests to which the legislation refers are שמרי משמרת המזבח ('those who keep the service of the altar'; Ezek 40:46) and שמרי משמרת הבית ('those who keep the service of the house; Ezek 40:45).

79 E.g. Gese, *Verfassungsentwurf*, 111; Pohlmann, *Prophet Hesekiel*, 591–593.

80 Duguid, *Ezekiel and the Leaders*. E.g. 'In a theocracy, one need devote no attention to the mechanics of government' (Levenson, *Theology of the Program*, 113).

dressed.[81] But since it is not given to the *nāśī'* as a royal prerogative *and* instead is allocated to another institution,[82] it must come to bear in any final reckoning we make of the political restoration envisioned in these chapters whether against a Neo-Babylonian backdrop or not.

The second royal prerogative absent in the Temple Vision is that of the king as temple builder/administrator. The absence is acute, especially so since it is the function consistently attested to in all Near Eastern royal ideologies (including Judahite) irrespective of changes in religious ideology, regime or imperial control. That noted, identifying who, in contrast to the *nāśī'*, is responsible for building the temple is not straightforward. To begin with, the temple cannot actually be built, lacking as it does any vertical measurements. Nevertheless Ezekiel is escorted through a physical space and an already constructed one at that, so we must assume that YHWH is the builder of his restored temple.[83] While YHWH's role as temple builder may be a little too amorphous for some, his singular control of the administration of the restored temple is clear as day. YHWH appoints the workforce (Ezek 44:9–16), establishes cultic protocol in designating the festivals that will take place in the temple (Ezek 45:18–25; 46:13–15), reconfigures the procedures of worship (Ezek 46:1–12) and the temple's very structure (Ezek 40–42; 43:13–17), establishes the national weights (Ezek 45:10–12), and indeed determines the priestly prebend (Ezek 44:28–30). YHWH even moves the temple to a new location, separating it from the city that lies to the south![84] The level of agency one ascribes to YHWH will largely determine the importance of these changes, but undeniable is the fact that the restoration of this temple is the only one in which the earthly ruler does not play a pivotal role.

Given that two integral royal prerogatives have been removed from the ideological foundation supporting the *nāśī'* in Ezek 40–48, perhaps in the positive elements of his presentation too are hints of a realignment of power. By way of example, I will have the discussion in relation to the access the *nāśī'* enjoys

81 As one might if reading a *Grundschicht* that includes only Ezek 40:1–43:10* (e.g. Tuell, *Law of the Temple*, 18–35; Konkel, *Architektonik*, 244–270). Ultimately, a shorter text does little to rehabilitate the *nāśī'*.

82 This is not to assert that two different institutions could not simultaneously hold judicial authority (e.g. 2 Chron 19:8–11). Indeed, the widely attested practice of seeking YHWH in complicated judicial situations, presumes the presence of a priest 'as judge'. Ez 44 and Deut 17 are, however, the only two texts in the Hebrew Bible to legislate a judicial protocol for state (re)formation that does not include the royal figure as the institution's ultimate arbiter.

83 Stevenson, *Vision of Transformation*.

84 Odell, *Ezekiel*.

within the temple proper. But what emerges for the particular in this instance can be equally applied to his relationship to the cult, land and people.[85]

As long acknowledged, the Temple Vision is an unparalleled map of a restored nation and sanctuary, formulated according to divinely ordained symmetry. In a system based on concentric areas of holiness, decreasing from YHWH's throne room to the outer limits of the Israelite territory through a masterfully devised conversation between constructed shapes and boundary markers,[86] access and orientation determine the status of the figures and institutions associated with the temple. As Susan Niditich reminds us, 'One's place in this society is defined not only by one's job per se but also by the location one is allowed to occupy in the temple-as-cosmos'.[87]

It is precisely in relation to temple-as-cosmos that the status of the *nāśī'* begins to deteriorate in relation to a Neo-Babylonian ideal. Though permitted to stand in the inner east gate, the *nāśī'* cannot under any circumstance breach the inner court, let alone approach the altar or the inner sanctum. In this divine house, the *nāśī'* is restricted to public space, banned from the sacred centre that serves as home both to the deity and to the primary object through which the purity of Israel is maintained, the altar. If the temple was a king's to traverse as its guardian, even if babysat by a priest for safety, in Ezekiel's reformulation, the *nāśī'* has been banished to the outer regions of the temple. Nowhere is this more obvious than in the enactment of official ceremony. During national festivals, the movements of the *nāśī'* are constrained, his movement within the temple court being dictated entirely by those of the people:

> When the people of the land come before YHWH at the appointed festivals, whoever enters by the north gate to worship shall go out by the south gate; and whoever enters by the south gate shall go out by the north gate: they shall not return by way of the gate by which they entered, but shall go out straight ahead. When they come in, the *nāśī'* shall come in with them; and when they go out, he shall go out. (Ezek 46:9–10)

From the supposed rights of movement enjoyed by the *nāśī'*, one might be inclined to conclude that his special mention is evidence of privilege.[88] Yet legislated movement in this instance only restricts freedom of access. Not only is the

85 For the fuller discussion, see chapter four in Madhavi Nevader, *Yhwh versus David: The Eclipse of Monarchy in Deuteronomy and Ezekiel 40–48* (OTM; Oxford: Oxford University Press, forthcoming).

86 Stevenson, *Vision of Transformation*, 137–148; cf. Smith, *To Take Place*, 48–75.

87 Niditch, 'Ezekiel 40–48', 218.

88 Tuell, *Law of the Temple*, 108; Duguid, *Ezekiel and the Leaders*, 53.

nāśī' confined to prescribed locations whenever in the temple, but the legislation further holds him to set patterns of movement from which he cannot deviate, in effect putting him on a conveyor belt of processional duty.

The constraint placed upon the movement of the *nāśī'* likely affects the evaluation of his most privileged prerogative of all – exclusive access to the outer east gate in which he consumes a sacred meal (Ezek 44:3). Located at the eastern-most point of the East-West axis, the outer gate lies at the bottom of the axis of holiness and thus is the structure farthest removed from YHWH's throne room and the Holy of Holies. While possessing exclusive entrance rights to the gate, the *nāśī'* is nonetheless spatially removed from the locus of divine presence and cut off from the remainder of the sanctuary. If location does determine importance, the banishment of the *nāśī'* to the outermost recesses of the temple complex places him precariously between the sacred and profane.[89] Jonathan Z. Smith is correct that hierarchies of power are realised in many instances by means of movement and access. Ezek 40–48 is no exception. However, the spatial hierarchy at play in the Temple Vision relegates the *nāśī'* to a position of relative powerlessness, thus standing out from any tradition (Judahite or Neo-Babylonian) upon which it might be based.

The spatial realignment of the *nāśī'* in relation to the temple is illustrative of a more pervasive tendency in the Temple Vision to reconceptualise the nature of royal power. Ingeniously, the author creates a platform out of the temple, which had traditionally acted as the very foundation of royal ideology,[90] to recast the ideal king according to rubrics entirely new. Utilizing Neo-Babylonian royal ideology to create a humble prince, the legislator separates the image of monarchy restored from the ideology of Judahite kings. But the limitations put on the *nāśī'* go far beyond the humble presentation of the pious Neo-Babylonian king. He is denied those roles intrinsic to the basic conceptualizations of monarchy and is oriented within the temple by a new logic of holiness that renders him mundane.[91]

89 A further problem with the outer east gate is its status. Because it is structurally integral to the sanctuary wall, the gate is integral to a structure the purpose of which is to separate what is holy from what is mundane (Ezek 42:20). In entering this gate from the outer court, the *nāśī'* therefore enters a space that is oddly less sacred than that from which he entered. As such, the Vision locates its royal in a space that is as structurally mundane as can be determined by its own system of conferring status, closer in proximity to the common than any other functional location permitted within the temple complex.

90 Keith W. Whitelam, 'The Symbols of Power: Aspects of Propaganda in the United Monarchy', *BA* 49 (1986): 166–173.

91 Albertz, *Israel in Exile*, 369.

By means of this particular formulation, the legislation has fundamentally redefined the understanding not only of the *nāśī'*, but of the royal institution itself.[92]

4 Picking Up the Pieces

Addressing the value of reading the book within its exilic context, John F. Kutsko concluded that 'the Babylonian setting of Ezekiel offers critical avenues of investigation ... for considering the ideological arguments presented in the book of Ezekiel'.[93] I have suggested that one of these ideological arguments is with the nature of Judahite monarchy, particularly as it is debated through the figure of the *nāśī'* in Ezek 40–48. The restored royal has bewildered many an interpreter, the complexities of his presentation more often than not being resolved by appeal to the supposed priestly milieu behind the nine chapters or to the historical demands of the Persian period. Wishing to deny neither a priestly tendency to the text or a possible Persian provenance, I have suggested that there are a number of similarities between the *nāśī'* in Ezek 40–48 and the ideal monarch according to Neo-Babylonian kingship ideology, which are particularly fruitful for understanding Ezekiel's prince. Chief amongst these is the *nāśī'*'s standing as sole provider for the sacrificial cult, a role that situates him in a position of importance but denies him the priestly prerogative afforded by normative Judahite royal ideology. The muted nature of Neo-Babylonian royal ideology may also provide a standard for understanding that found in Ezek 40–48. Formulated in reaction to a humiliating past under the yoke of the Neo-Assyrian empire, the ideology of Babylon's new dynasty portrays the king as a servant whose diligent work makes manifest the supremacy of the Babylonian gods. Thus Nebuchadnezzar concludes the summary of his lifelong Babylon project *ka-la e-ep-še-ti-ia šá i-na* NA_4.NA.RÚ.A *aš-ṭu-ur mu-da-a li-ta-am-ma-ar-ma ta-nit-ti* DINGIR.DINGIR *li-iḫ-ta-as-sa-as*, 'all of my deeds that I have inscribed on this document, let the learned read, and let him understand the excellence of the gods'.[94] Ironically, Ezek 40–48 appears to adopt a similar approach in the hopes of reversing the devastation wrought by Nebuchadnezzar, suggesting perhaps that the authors were amongst the 'learned' called to task by the king.[95]

---

92 *Pace* e.g. Rooke, *Zadok's Heirs*, 104–119; Block, 'Bringing Back David'.

93 John F. Kutsko, *Between Heaven and Earth: Divine Presence and Absence in the Book of Ezekiel* (Biblical and Judaic Studies 7; Winona Lake: Eisenbrauns, 2000), 23.

94 VAB 4 Nbk 20 iii 61–64.

95 See the essay by J. Stökl in this volume on the possibility that Ezekiel may have had some

Despite the many similarities, Ezekiel's *nāśī'* does not comply entirely with the Neo-Babylonian model. Though an endemic interpretation, the differences should *not* be explained as an adaptation of foreign ideology to Biblical sensibilities.[96] 'Biblical sensibilities' regarding the monarchy are admittedly problematic, but it is clear enough that Judahite royal ideology conformed to that typical of small Levantine states of the first millennium before being retrospectively reworked to account for the institution's ultimate failure.[97] On a rudimentary level, then, we should see the variance in presentation between Ezek 40–48 and the Neo-Babylonian corpus as an example of ideology used to different effect. The Neo-Babylonian dynasty employs its ideology in cautious sanguinity over independence-cum-imperial rule. The authors of the Temple Vision employ it to situate their theologically disastrous present by reimagining a provocative future. Put simply, Babylon uses it to rule, Judah to account for being ruled.

However, neither the similarities nor the differences fully account for the masterful reinterpretation of royal power in the vision, wherein the sacrality of the Judean monarchy is comprehensively dismantled. This is the masterful achievement of the vision's theologian alone. Exploiting a natural check on power inherent to Babylonian royal ideology, Ezekiel disassembles the power superstructures of the past by undoing the royal thread by which Israel's identity and relationship with YHWH was held together. On account of this, it seems unlikely to me that by using the particular Neo-Babylonian tradition that Ezekiel is necessarily constructing a polemic against Babylon or the Babylonian king. We know that the author of Ezekiel is well aware of the literary traditions dear to Babylonia and very happy to use them when it serves his purpose, even if that purpose is entirely different from that intended by the Babylonian *Ur*-tradition. It may be that we should understand Ezek 40–48 as an example of a theo-political thought experiment utilizing the intellectual tools afforded by the author's Babylonian location. Irrespective, it is clear that Babylon loomed large, its potency in the Judean imagination lasting long after some sat by its rivers and reinvented Zion.

---

schooling in cuneiform reading and writing.

96 So Abraham Winitzer, 'Assyriology and Jewish Studies in Tel Aviv: Ezekiel among the Babylonian *Literati*', in *Encounters by the Rivers of Babylon: Scholarly Conversations between Jews, Iranian, and Babylonians: Proceedings from the Conference Held at The Hebrew University, Jerusalem, May, 23–25, 2011* (TSAJ; ed. U. Gabbay and S. Secunda; Tübingen: Mohr Siebeck, 2014), 163–216.

97 For a reasoned treatment of Levantine royal ideology, see Gösta W. Ahlström, 'Administration of the State in Canaan and Ancient Israel', in *Civilizations of the Ancient Near East* (ed. J. M. Sasson; Peabody: Hendrickson, 2000), 587–603.

Lester L. Grabbe

The Reality of the Return: The Biblical Picture Versus Historical Reconstruction

The exile and return remain abiding concerns in biblical scholarship, partly because the idea became such a pivotal symbol in the history of Judaism. The theme already made its mark on a good deal of biblical literature – and not just that talking about post-exilic events. The whole thrust of narrative from Genesis to 2 Kings is to lead up to exile and then return. What follows is my attempt at a synthesis: asking what we can know and prove, or at least reasonably infer. It thus goes over some basic material and primary sources, but it aims to be comprehensive within the limits of a short paper.

1 The 'Biblical Picture'

When we talk about the 'biblical picture', the fact is that there is more than one biblical picture. Yet the abiding image is the one found in the first few chapters of Ezra. This has tended to canalize the image of the return from exile, with other biblical passages interpreted to fit this scheme.[1] Yet the books of Haggai and Zechariah 1–8 give a somewhat different picture when read on their own, and while their dating is disputed, they seem closer to the events than Ezra 1–6.

Thus, while we could say that the 'biblical picture' is derived from all the biblical texts, the book of Ezra actually tends to be the perspective followed, with the other biblical texts fitted into that outline. According to Ezra, Cyrus issued a decree for the people to return and sent the temple vessels back immediately (ch. 1). Then some 40,000 people immigrated, led by Zerubbabel and Joshua (ch. 2). There is a certain awkwardness, because this return journey is dated to the reign of Darius, putting it more than fifteen years after Cyrus' decree, yet this lengthy chronological gap is ignored by the text. The altar is first built and the cult reinstated, before the formal rebuilding of the temple takes place (ch. 3). Then

1 An exception to this perspective is Peter R. Ackroyd, *Exile and Restoration* (OTL; Philadelphia: Westminster; London: SCM, 1968).

Lester L. Grabbe: University of Hull, England

follows a rather confused account of opposition and the stopping and restarting of the temple building (chs 4–6). If the contradictory details are ignored, the impression that emerges is that opponents got the temple building stopped for a period of time but that it was resumed, eventually with Persian approval, and finished after about six years, still early in Darius' reign. Then some sixty years later – another chronological gap that the text quietly ignores – Ezra comes with his book of the law and enforces separation from the 'peoples of the land' (chs 7–10), followed by Nehemiah (entire book) a few years later. Apart from the question of when to date Ezra (some put him in 398 BCE rather than 458), this is the historical outline given widely in commentaries and histories.[2]

2 Sources and Synthesis

2.1 Overview of Demographics

We begin our story with the last days of Judah and the fall of Jerusalem under the Babylonians. According to the biblical texts, fewer than 10,000 people were deported in the fifteen years between 597 and 581 BCE (Jer 52:27–30; cf. 2 Kings 24:14–16). The statement that 'all but the poorest of the land' (2 Kings 24:14; 25:12) were deported contradicts these passages. Yet the archaeology indicates that the population fell drastically between the end of the Iron II and the Persian period.[3] The cause of this was evidently not primarily deportation but other factors: war, especially, but perhaps famine and disease that often accompanied war. These factors could have drastically affected the birth rate or at least the infant mortality rate. Also, some regions evidently ceased to be within the boundaries of Judah, there was some movement of population, and Jerusalem itself seems to have been uninhabited during the rest of the Neo-Babylonian period.[4]

2 The data in Lester L. Grabbe (*A History of the Jews and Judaism in the Second Temple Period 1: Yehud: A History of the Persian Province of Judah* [LSTS 47; London: T & T Clark International, 2004]) are assumed throughout this paper. If a statement is made without a reference, further information or discussion can usually be found there.

3 Oded Lipschits, 'Demographic Changes in Judah between the Seventh and the Fifth Centuries B.C.E.', in *Judah and the Judeans in the Neo-Babylonian Period* (ed. Oded Lipschits and Joseph Blenkinsopp; Winona Lake, IN: Eisenbrauns, 2003), 323–76.

4 Oded Lipschits, *The Fall and Rise of Jerusalem: Judah under Babylonian Rule* (Winona Lake, IN: Eisenbrauns, 2005), 211, 218. He proposes that the Babylonians may have interdicted settlement in the city after its destruction, a quite reasonable suggestion.

What appears to be the case is that there was a population in Judah of about 110,000 at the end of the Iron II (i.e., about 600 BCE).[5] During the Babylonian period, much of the population was concentrated in the area of Benjamin. It appears that Mizpah was the Babylonian 'capital' of the province (cf. Jer 40:6–41:3; 2 Kings 25:23, 25), and settlement patterns for 6th century Benjamin seem to be focused on Mizpah.[6] A number of sites there (Tell en-Naṣbeh [Mizpah], Tell el-Fûl [Gibeah], Beitin [Bethel], el-Jib [Gibeon]) show no evidence of destruction by the Babylonians.

The problem with archaeological surveys is that they characterize only a period. We can guess whether the population rose or fell only by applying other known factors to the data. When we look at the survey statistics for the Persian period, we are probably seeing the situation as it stood about the middle of the 5th century BCE. Any development over the entire period requires the use of other factors that may indicate fluctuations in population for different regions. When we take those into account, the following picture emerges:

First, Jerusalem itself is re-inhabited with a population of up to about 3000. The region around Jerusalem becomes an area of relatively dense population. There was evidently a corresponding decline in population in the area of Benjamin, probably in the late 6th and early 5th century BCE (though there was some recovery later on in the Persian period). If so, the archaeology supports two features of the text. One of these is a return of Jerusalem to the position of a regional centre once more, which is the general picture of the biblical texts, certainly Ezra and Nehemiah but also Haggai and Zechariah (on these see below). The other is a possible influx of population from abroad. A simple increase in population in an area does not prove that these new settlers were immigrants, but the situation allows for that possibility. The name of Zerubbabel the governor indicates an immigrant from Babylonia, and the references to Joshua/Jeshua the high priest show him to be a returnee as well.

The Persian king was no doubt interested in all members of his empire, but some regions were of more value than others. Looked at from the perspective of the Persian capital, the cities of the coast were very important. Not only did they contain valuable resources and also serve as sites of trade and commerce. They also had strategic worth because they could be used to launch military operations against Egypt or the Aegean. Things were different for the province of Judah up

5 Following Lipschits, 'Demographic Changes'. Diana Edelman, *The Origins of the "Second" Temple: Persian Imperial Policy and the Rebuilding of Jerusalem* (London/Oakville, CT: Equinox, 2005), 327, has been critical of Lipschits, yet she seems to draw similar sorts of conclusions.
6 Lipschits, 'Demographic Changes', 346–51.

in the hill country. It had little strategic use and its revenue potential was mainly a matter of limited agricultural produce. The central government wanted all the agricultural production it could harness, and Judah thus had its benefits, but the province was not as fertile or resource-rich as some.

The population of Judah was small but seems to have been sufficient for the task (the population was probably only 20,000 to 30,000 at its height). At least, there is no evidence that the Persians were trying to import further settlers, in spite of some hypotheses to that effect.[7] Thus, although any immigrants would have been permitted and even welcomed by the Persian administration, the actual number of those coming in from Babylonia seems to have been relatively small. The question is, how much was the province worth in terms of tribute? We have no direct data, but the figure of 20 silver talents per year for the middle of the third century BCE may not be far wide of the mark.[8]

According to 2 Kings 15:19–20, the land owners contributed 50 sheqels each in the eighth century BCE. Since the amount given to the Assyrian king was 1000 talents of silver, with a talent generally worth 3000 sheqels, this would be three million sheqels. If the Israelites of substance contributed the full amount, that would make 60,000 'men of substance' in Israel at the time. The sum of 20 talents mentioned by Josephus in the third century BCE would be 60,000 sheqels or 240,000 drachmas. If one reckoned a population of 30,000 as representing 6000 family units, this would require an annual contribution of 10 sheqels or 40 drachmas per family. That may be too high but perhaps this gives us something near the actual figure. The point is that Judah made its contribution to the economy of the Persian empire, but it was a relatively modest one, though if the total contribution of Ebir-nari to the Persian coffers was 350 talents, this 20 talents was not negligible.[9]

Judah was primarily a rural agricultural settlement: 'There are no architectural or other finds that attest to Jerusalem as an urban centre during the Persian Period.'[10] It was not a Persian fortress: nothing indicates that Persian soldiers were stationed in Jerusalem, and there are no strategic reasons for it to be part of

---

7 Cf., e.g., Kenneth G. Hoglund, *Achaemenid Imperial Administration in Syria-Palestine and the Missions of Ezra and Nehemiah* (SBLDS 125; Atlanta: Scholars Press, 1992), 57–60.

8 According to Josephus, *Ant.* 12.4.1 §§ 158–59. See the discussion in Grabbe, *A History of the Jews and Judaism in the Second Temple Period 2: The Coming of the Greeks: The Early Hellenistic Period (335–175 BCE)* (LSTS 68; London: T & T Clark, 2008), 220–21.

9 According to Herodotus (*Hist.* 3.91), the satrapy of Transeuphratene (Ebir-nari) contributed 350 silver talents per year.

10 Oded Lipschits, 'Achaemenid Imperial Policy, Settlement Processes in Palestine, and the Status of Jerusalem in the Middle of the Fifth Century B.C.E.', in *Judah and the Judeans in the Persian*

any Persian line of defence.[11] Persia was not being threatened by Egypt; on the contrary, it was Persia which was threatening Egypt and, under Cambyses, Egypt was conquered by the Persians. Over the next two centuries, Egypt managed to break away several times but was also reconquered several times. The invasion of Egypt was generally mounted from the Phoenician area. The coast was a vital interest for the Persians but not the interior hill country of Palestine.

2.2 Cyrus' Decree

We have evidence that Cyrus gave permission for certain peoples, who had been brought to Babylonia shortly before the Persian conquest, to be repatriated, along with their gods. This is found in the *Cyrus Cylinder*, which states:

> 30 … From [Shuanna] I sent back to their places to the city of Ashur and Susa,
> 31 Akkad, the land of Eshnunna, the city of Zamban, the city of Meturnu, Der, as far as the border of the land of Guti – the sanctuaries across the river Tigris – whose shrines had earlier become dilapidated,
> 32 the gods who live therein, and made permanent sanctuaries for them. I collected together all of their people and returned them to their settlements,
> 33 and the gods of the land of Sumer and Akkad which Nabonidus – to the fury of the lord of the gods – had brought into Shuanna, at the command of Marduk, the great lord …[12]

This is only a limited repatriation, focusing on gods from regions to the east of Babylonia. What it suggests in the light of the biblical information is that Cyrus issued a more encompassing decree allowing more general repatriation of peoples. If so, this actual decree from Cyrus was more likely a shorter, more informative and more pragmatic statement in the standard language of the bureaucracy. This is all that would be needed to allow deported peoples to return to their ancestral homes, if they wished. Not surprising is the lack of mention specifically of Judah

---

Period (ed. Oded Lipschits and Manfred Oeming; Winona Lake, IN: Eisenbrauns, 2006), 19–52 (31).

11 Grabbe, 'Was Jerusalem a Persian Fortress?', in *Exile and Restoration Revisited: Essays on the Neo-Babylonian and Persian Periods in Memory of Peter R. Ackroyd* (LSTS 73; ed. Gary N. Knoppers and Lester L. Grabbe, with Deirdre Fulton; London: T & T Clark, 2009), 128–37.

12 *Cyrus Cylinder*, lines 30–33; translation from Irving Finkel (ed.), *The Cyrus Cylinder: The King of Persia's Proclamation from Ancient Babylon* (London: I. B. Tauris, 2013), 6–7; see also COS 2.315. Text in Finkel, *Cyrus Cylinder*, 132; also Hanspeter Schaudig, *Die Inschriften Nabonids von Babylon und Kyros' des Groben samt den in ihrem Umfeld entstandenen Tendenzschriften: Textausgabe und Grammatik* (AOAT 256; Münster: Ugarit-Verlag, 2001), 553.

or Judahites, but the statement of the *Cyrus Cylinder* fits generally with what looks like later Judahite propaganda, most notably Ezra 1:2–4:

> Thus says Cyrus, the king of Persia, 'Yhwh, the God of the Heavens, has given all the kingdoms of the earth to me, and he charged me to build for him a House in Jerusalem which is in Judah. Whoever among you from all his people – let his God be with him and let him go up to Jerusalem which is in Judah, and let him build the House of Yhwh the God of Israel – he is the God who is in Jerusalem. Everyone remaining from every place where they sojourn – let the men of their place support them with silver and gold and goods and cattle, with free-will offerings, for the House of the God who is in Jerusalem.'

Although this has been defended as authentic by no less a person than E. J. Bickerman,[13] the propagandistic nature of the decree in its present form seems obvious.[14] It is unlikely that in his first year Cyrus was so concerned about an obscure province on the edge of his empire that he issued a specific decree on their behalf, but if he did, it would not have taken this form. More likely is a general decree (with more practical and specific wording than the *Cyrus Cylinder*, as noted above) which the Jews could have taken advantage of.

Cyrus would have been concerned about his whole empire, and the Mediterranean coast would have been of considerable importance, because of Greece and because of Egypt. This made Phoenicia very important throughout Persian rule. But, as already noted, Judah was a small and not very prosperous province up in a mountainous area of Palestine and of less strategic concern. All provinces would have been important, but we need to consider the nature of the Persian administration. The first concern of the king was governance of the large satrapies, which were usually given to a trustworthy member of the Persian ruling family. At times, especially in later periods, some of these satraps saw themselves as rivals to the Persian king, but mainly the king was concerned to govern the empire through them. The satraps had a great deal of power and autonomy, even if in time the king sought means of keeping an eye on them and their activities.

This meant that the satrapy of Babylon and Ebir-nari (Transeuphratene) was given to a high-ranking Persian to govern. It is he who would have dealt with any specifics to do with the province of Yehud, including issuing decrees on its behalf. This would have included the appointment of a governor over Judah,

---

13 Elias J. Bickerman, 'The Edict of Cyrus in Ezra 1', in *Studies in Jewish and Christian History* (AGJU 9, 1; Leiden: Brill, 1976), 72–108 (= partial revision of *JBL* 65 [1946]: 244–75), followed by such later commentators as H. G. M. Williamson, *Ezra, Nehemiah* (WBC 16; Waco, TX: Word Books, 1985), 6–7, 11–14.

14 Cf. the discussion in Grabbe, *A History of the Jews and Judaism: vol. 1*, 273–74.

which was likely to have been done in most cases by the satrap rather than the emperor (Nehemiah might have been an exception). There is much we do not know about the administration of the Persian empire under Cyrus nor of its development subsequently. Yet we do have evidence that the office of governor was an important one.

2.3 The Office of Governor

When we talk about the office of 'governor' in the Persian empire, we run into an immediate problem: there is no consistent terminology in our sources. For modern scholars 'satrap' and 'satrapy' have fairly well-defined meanings, but neither the Greek nor the Persian words were used so consistently in the original sources. The word appears in Greek as σατράπης, and Aramaic and Hebrew as אחשדרפן (Ezra 8:36; Esther 3:12; 8:9; 9:3; Daniel 3:2, 3; 6:2, 5, 7, 8); it also appears in Neo-Babylonian, Syriac, Palmyrene, Armenian, and other languages. The word 'satrap' comes from Avestan *xšaθrapāvan* = Old Persian *xšaçapāvan* 'protector of the empire'. It is thus up to the modern reader to try to determine whether a satrap over a large region is in question or a provincial governor. It is ironic that perhaps as much direct information on Persian provincial governorship is found in Jewish sources as in Persian or Greek. These Jewish sources tend to be biblical ones.[15]

2.4 Zechariah and Haggai

Although the prophetic texts considered in this section are often combined with Ezra to produce a fuller 'biblical picture' in many commentaries and histories, I cover them separately as more likely primary sources than Ezra. This includes noting how they both correspond with and differ from the standard 'biblical picture' of Ezra.

The interest of Haggai and Zechariah is a religious one. Their concern is to make certain theological points relating to worship, religious leadership, and

15 For further information, see Lester L. Grabbe, 'The Terminology of Government in the Septuagint – in Comparison with Hebrew, Aramaic, and Other Languages', in *Jewish Perspectives on Hellenistic Rulers* (ed. Tessa Rajak, Sarah Pearce, James Aitken, and Jennifer Dines; Berkeley: University of California Press, 2007), 225–37. To this might be added Jan Tavernier, *Iranica in the Achaemenid Period (ca. 550–330 B.C.): Lexicon of Old Iranian Proper Names and Loanwords, Attested in Non-Iranian Texts* (OLA 158; Leuven: Peeters, 2007).

purifying the effects of the destruction of Jerusalem and the exile. For example, Zechariah 3 is devoted to the theological problem of removing the guilt of the high priest so that he could be installed in his office. Yet although religious or theological writings, these are the materials that the historian often has to work with, and within the theological prophetic statements are indications of the social and historical situation.

A major theme of Zechariah is the rebuilding of Jerusalem the city. Yhwh will return to Jerusalem and the city would be rebuilt (1:16–17). The city that was cursed for seventy years has now been pardoned (1:12). There will be so many people in the city that Jerusalem will be an unwalled city like the open country (2:8). Curiously, this statement about Jerusalem seems to coincide with the picture at the beginning of Nehemiah, with no city wall; however, one must reluctantly admit that the statement in Zechariah 2:8 is probably a general metaphor for the city's expansion rather than an actual description. In any case, people old and young will crowd the squares (8:4–5). Haggai says little or nothing about Jerusalem as a whole being rebuilt.

A second theme is that God's house would be rebuilt in the city, and here Haggai is more emphatic than Zechariah. This is overwhelmingly Haggai's message, with its taking up most of the short book in one form or another. Yet Zechariah does have several references to the rebuilding of the temple, beginning with the brief statement in 1:16. Zerubbabel is proclaimed as the one who will bring the temple to completion: the foundations of the temple had been laid (4:9; 8:9), now the hands of Zerubbabel will complete it (4:9–10). He seems to be identified with the figure referred to as the Branch who would build the temple (6:12–13).

Both prophets dwell on the current economic and social situation: the people have been experiencing agricultural difficulties (Hag 1:9–11). Now the lean times will be over; prosperity will return (Zech 8:10–13). The skies have withheld precipitation and the earth has curbed its agricultural yield, but if only the temple will be rebuilt, new wine, oil, and grain will rain down on them (Hag 1:9–11). The produce has been cursed, but now that the foundations are laid, this will all change (Hag 2:15–19).

These passages suggest that two events dominated the thinking of at least some of the people: the settlement and population of Jerusalem and the building of the temple. But when was this? Diana Edelman has argued for the middle of the 5th century BCE.[16] I have argued against this elsewhere.[17] Granted that

---

16 Edelman, *The Origins of the "Second" Temple.*

17 Grabbe, '"They Shall Come Rejoicing to Zion" – Or Did They? The Settlement of Yehud in the Early Persian Period', in *Exile and Restoration Revisited: Essays on the Neo-Babylonian and Per-*

most scholars have little faith in the accuracy of the prefaces to prophetic books, Haggai and Zechariah give some rather precise dates – unusual in itself. Zechariah also refers to the '70 years' of desolation (Zech 1:12), which hardly fits with a mid-5th century date but goes well with one toward the beginning of Persian rule. The assignment of the books to the reign of Darius seems as reasonable as any other date. If so, this makes the general picture at the beginning of Ezra correct: Jerusalem was being inhabited once again and the temple was being rebuilt. This is hardly surprising, however, since Ezra 1–6 probably uses Haggai and Zechariah as major sources.[18]

2.5 Travellers Afar: the Return of Babylonian Jews

One of the gaps in our knowledge of the ancient Near East is information on how groups travelled, whether under their own volition or under forced conditions. We have some iconographic images of peoples being deported by the Assyrians, and we would assume that travel under normal conditions involved wheeled vehicles, animals (horses and donkeys), walking, and even boats. What we do not know is the arrangements for those journeying from Babylonia to Judah on their own initiative. This has to be considered in the context of statements about roads and travelling found in widely scattered passages in our literature.[19]

It has been alleged that no one could travel on the Persian roads without an official permit; however, I have been unable to confirm this. It is true that anyone travelling on the royal road and receiving provisions seems to have needed an official travel permit.[20] Many documents from the Persepolis Treasury Tablets and the Persepolis Fortification Tablets indicate this, which is hardly surprising since drawing on government supplies would have needed proper authorization. The royal roads were built primarily for official travel and the movement of armies. Most of our information on these roads relates to Persian and foreign officials and both Persian and hostile armies.

---

sian Periods in Memory of Peter R. Ackroyd (LSTS 73; ed. Gary N. Knoppers and Lester L. Grabbe, with Deirdre Fulton; London: T & T Clark, 2009), 116–27.

18 Cf. Hugh G. M. Williamson, 'The Composition of Ezra i-vi', *JTS* 34 (1983): 1–30.

19 The following comments have been informed by the discussion on roads in Pierre Briant, *From Cyrus to Alexander: A History of the Persian Empire* (transl. Peter T. Daniels; Winona Lake, IN: Eisenbrauns, 2002), 357–83 (ET of *Histoire de l'empire perse de Cyrus à Alexandre: Volumes I-II* [Achaemenid History 10; Leiden: Nederlands Instituut voor het Nabije Oosten, 1996; originally published by Librairie Arthème Fayard, Paris]).

20 Briant, *From Cyrus to Alexander*, 364–65, 368.

What we do not have information on is the use of these roads by other people, ordinary inhabitants of the Persian empire and others who were private individuals. The suggestion is that the royal roads had regular checkpoints and travel could be monitored (e.g., Herodotus, *Hist.* 1.123–24; 5.35; 7.239). This by itself would not have prevented private individuals from travelling on the royal roads, but there may have been a desire to keep them free from any but official traffic. We simply do not know. Yet we do have a statement by Xenophon (with regard to Cyrus the Younger) that suggests the use of roads by ordinary travellers, both Persian and foreign, as if there was no hindrance from Persian officials as long as they were obeying the law:

> Yet, on the other hand, none could say that he permitted malefactors and wicked men to laugh at him; on the contrary, he was merciless to the last degree in punishing them, and one might often see along the travelled roads people who had lost feet or hands or eyes; thus in Cyrus' province it became possible for either Greek or barbarian, provided he were guilty of no wrongdoing, to travel fearlessly wherever he wished, carrying with him whatever it was to his interest to have. [*Anab.* 1.9.11–12, LCL translation]

Yet there are references here and there to other roads and routes where people could escape the potential surveillance of government agents. Plutarch states with regard to Themistocles,

> Now as he was going down to the sea on his commission to deal with Hellenic affairs, a Persian… satrap of Upper Phrygia, plotted against his life.… But while Themistocles was asleep at midday before, it is said that the Mother of the Gods appeared to him in a dream.… Much disturbed, of course, Themistocles, with a prayer of acknowledgment to the goddess, forsook the highway, made a circuit by another route, and passing by that place, at last, as night came on took up his quarters. [*Them.* 30.1–2, LCL translation]

It is of course possible that some sort of travel permit was issued to those who wanted to return to their ancestral homeland. As noted above, an individual decree might have been issued on behalf of specific peoples, most likely by administrative officials, following a more general decree of Cyrus. But the few hints in our sources suggest that ordinary people could use the secondary routes, if not the main roads, without need of applying to the government, though they presumably did so at their own risk.

The case seems to be that from the heartland of Babylonia, Judean returnees would not have needed to take the royal road (which passed through Arbela in the north), but they could follow the Euphrates route, which had been used for centuries before them. It allowed Syrians and others from the West to reach such cities as Sippar, Babylon, and others further south in the riverine network of Mesopotamia. These Euphrates routes would have been open to everyone.[21]

In sum, there is a lot we do not know about the condition and situation with the travel of those Jews wanting to return from Babylonia to Yehud. It seems possible, though, that they could come singly or in small groups and did not have to have official caravans or formal permits beyond Cyrus' general declaration.

2.6 Building Jerusalem and a New Community

If there were organized caravans of Jewish groups returning, we are not aware of it. In any event, the archaeology suggests a slow but gradual growth, such as would be the result of natural population increase and perhaps a small amount of immigration. This would be best explained not by large groups of immigrants returning to the land and attempting to be absorbed into the community but, rather, a trickle of people returning individually or in small groups. The picture of Ezra 2 and Nehemiah 7 of a large community of more than 40,000 people returning at once looks complete fantasy. Indeed, as long recognized, the structure of the lists suggests a possible census list of settled peoples at some point. Yet even the numbers do not inspire confidence, since the archaeology suggests a settlement figure closer to 30,000 or so, even at its height (see above).

As noted above, the resettlement of Jerusalem at the beginning of the Persian period, after decades without habitation under Babylonian rule, might suggest – or at least allow for – a small amount of immigration. If Zerubbabel and Joshua were sent from Babylonia, as seems the case, they might have brought a number of immigrants with them: priests, bureaucrats, officials, along with some others. But these would have been a couple of thousand at most, and might have been only a few hundred.

Commentators have frequently pointed out the problems with large groups of immigrants trying to establish themselves among a settled population of some size, especially if the immigrants were claiming ownership of land that had already long been occupied by families who had not been deported but remained in the land after the destruction of Jerusalem in 586 BCE.[22] Given the assump-

---

21 E.g. Michael Jursa, *Aspects of the Economic History of Babylonia in the First Millennium BC. Economic Geography, Economic Mentalities, Agriculture, the Use of Money and the Problem of Economic Growth* (AOAT 377; Münster: Ugarit-Verlag, 2010), 76–7.

22 E.g., Morton Smith, *Palestinian Parties and Politics That Shaped the Old Testament* (London: SCM, 1987; corrected reprint of New York: Columbia, 1971), 110.

tions made in such discussions, the conclusions seemed logical and could even be supported by the internal conflicts pictured in Ezra 1–6. Yet a closer look at the text makes the opponents of the Jewish community all outsiders, which also seems to be the significance of the designation 'people(s) of the land(s)' (Ezra 3:3; 4:4; 9:1–2, 11, 14; 10:2, 11). This has been recognized but put down to the hostility of the book's author to the native Jews living in the land, and this sort of hostility surfaces later in the Ezra story in chs 7–10 where various Jews, even the leaders, supposedly marry 'foreigners'. Yet elsewhere in biblical texts and also in rabbinic literature, the 'people of the land' are Israel, not foreigners.[23] It seems to me that any supposed 'intermarriage' was not usually with non-Jews but with elements of the Jewish community not favoured by the author.[24]

If there was not a large immigrant population, though, is this proposed intra-community conflict likely? We know that with small numbers of migrants, there can still be tensions. If there were claims of land ownership, this could create some legal challenges and bad feelings. Yet there seems to have been plenty of available land, and tensions between individuals would not have occasioned major crises within the community overall. Since some of the returnees were most likely priests, conflicts between them and the priests not deported might well have taken place. A distinction between altar priests and lower clergy (Levites, gatekeepers, etc.) was already in existence by this time, apparently.[25] Yet this might still have been working itself out.

One area of potential conflict might well have been with the leadership of the community in general. It seems clear that Ezra makes the *golah* the legitimate community. Although in my view Ezra was written rather late in the Persian period or even in the Hellenistic period, it may reflect an attitude on the part of some of the community. A number of sources indicate that the leadership at the beginning of the Persian period was made up of returnees. First, we have the 'Sheshbazzar fragment' (Ezra 1:8–11; 5:13–16). The writer of Ezra tries to make light of Sheshbazzar's place but seems embarrassingly stuck with a tradition that does not fit his story. What little information we have makes Sheshbazzar the first governor of Judah. It also associates him with a theme to be discussed below, the reconstitution of the Jerusalem temple cult and the rebuilding of the temple.

---

23 A. H. J. Gunneweg, 'עם הארץ – A Semantic Revolution', *ZAW* 95 (1983): 437–40; Aharon Oppenheimer, *The 'Am ha-Aretz: A Study in the Social History of the Jewish People in the Hellenistic-Roman Period* (ALGHJ 8; Leiden: Brill, 1977).

24 Cf. Grabbe, *A History of the Jews and Judaism: vol. 1*, 285–88.

25 Cf. ibid., 225–30.

How long Sheshbazzar was governor and his accomplishments apart from the temple are unknown. Yet he did journey from Mesopotamia during Cyrus' reign. The next information comes in the reign of Darius – a considerable gap of time covering the reigns of Cyrus, Cambyses, and the first two years of Darius, or the best part of twenty years (538 to 520). It may be that Sheshbazzar governed for a number of years, and one or more other governors might have been in office during this period. Yet in the eyes of the author of Ezra nothing significant happened.

When the veil lifts in the second year of Darius, Zerubbabel's governorship is just getting underway, and he has an associate in the person of Joshua the high priest. Whether they were bosom buddies remains to be discovered, but the books of Zechariah and Haggai both throw them together as partners of a sort. Again, we have individuals who seem to be journeying from Babylonia to take up their roles. Ezra 2 and Nehemiah 7 have them lead a group of settlers to the Promised Land. While that may not be entirely wrong, it would have been a much smaller group than the 40,000+ envisaged in the list accompanying their name.

As noted above, the governor's job was not primarily to build temples or lead religious activities. He was to see that the fertile land was cultivated and taxes made their way to Damascus or Babylonia or Persepolis or wherever they were collected. Yet the biblical text is primarily interested in the temple, whether the prophets Zechariah and Haggai or Ezra 1–6. It seems likely that temple building was on the agenda, at least for some Jews, though not necessarily for all Jews or the Persian administration. Zechariah and Haggai both make it clear that there were agricultural problems, with poor harvests or other problems, and most Jews would have been focused on problems of sustaining themselves and their families. It was prophets, who had nothing better to do, that were agitating for the temple to be rebuilt. Zechariah and Haggai do not recognize the work of Sheshbazzar, but it seems possible to reconcile their statements with the picture of Sheshbazzar's beginning work on the temple a couple of decades earlier, work that did not progress beyond laying some foundations.

Joshua, with the temple as his power base and home, would have been very interested in having it rebuilt. Whether Zerubbabel was equally enthusiastic is unknown, in spite of Haggai and Zechariah's enthusiasm on his behalf. If we are sceptical of the story in Ezra 1–6, as I am, tracing the events leading from Haggai's and Zechariah's pronouncements to the completed temple is impossible. How the temple building progressed and when it was finished are unknown. Ezra paints us a picture of a building work to some extent comparable to Solomon's, even if its magnificence is admittedly not comparable (Ezra 3:12–13; cf. Haggai 2:2–9): e.g., Phoenician workmen help, and logs are collected from the Lebanese cedar forests (Ezra 3:7). Haggai, on the other hand, thinks local timber will do (1:8). The text also makes the completion and dedication as early as Adar in the sixth year of Darius or March 516 BCE (Ezra 6:15). But this date is not found in any base text of Ezra, only the framework. It seems unlikely that, even with a more limited construction, there would have been the resources available to finish it in less than four years, especially considering the small population.

There is also another possible indication of dating that, to the best of my knowledge, has not been commented on up to now. Darius I had a long reign, 522–486 BCE. The letter in Ezra 5:6–17 is addressed to Darius, but the letter does not bear a date. The satrap over Babylon and Ebir-nari in the early years of Darius was Uštānu who held the office apparently from about 521–516 BCE.[26] We also have some information on Tattenai (Babylonian Tattannu) who was governor of Ebir-nari in 502 BCE.[27] The assumption is that he was deputy to Uštānu, but we actually have no information to this effect. It is not impossible that he held the office for nearly twenty years, but it seems more likely that any interaction with Judah was closer to 502 BCE.

The absence of Zerubbabel at the dedication of the temple has often been remarked upon. Yet Joshua is also absent. Either the author of Ezra knows something we do not and suppresses it, or he simply had no information. Of course, if the completion was long after 520 BCE, neither Zerubbabel nor Joshua would have been around. Speculation about Zerubbabel being declared a messianic figure is exciting, but such an interpretation is not necessary to explain his absence. If the temple was not finished until some time around 500 BCE, the original instigators were likely to have been off the scene by that time.

What about relations with Samaria and other provinces? This could have been retrojected from the time of Nehemiah. There is no reason why the governors of Samaria and Judah should be on bad terms with each other on a permanent basis. More likely is a personal conflict on the part of Nehemiah and Sanballat, or even on the part of Nehemiah alone. Nehemiah himself admitted with regret that the Judahite nobles maintained good relations with Tobiah and others outside Judah, even while Nehemiah was doing his damnedest to shut them out (Neh 6:17–19). Jedadiah of the Elephantine Jewish community wrote to both Bagohi, the governor of Judah, and Sanballat's sons Shelamiah and Delaiah. Bagohi and Delaiah (governor of Samaria?) then wrote a joint memorandum to the Elephantine com-

---

26 Matthew W. Stolper, 'The Governor of Babylon and Across-the-River in 486 B.C.', *JNES* 48 (1989): 283–305 (290–91).
27 Ibid.

munity.[28] This was about 407 BCE, only a few years after Nehemiah's conflict with Sanballat. It argues against a permanent conflict between the governors of Judah and Samaria. Also, I cannot imagine that the satrap of Ebir-nari would have tolerated very much outward conflict between governors of neighbouring provinces.

Finally, what about the alleged crisis on intermarriage described in Ezra 9–10? There are several reasons to doubt the reality of the story: (1) the situation in Ezra 9–10 looks remarkably parallel to Nehemiah 9–10 and might be modelled on that passage.[29] (2) A number of the names in the list in Ezra 10:18–43 seem to be borrowed from the list in Ezra 2//Nehemiah 7. (3) The wives in question seem more likely to be the descendants of Jews who were not deported rather than actual foreigners. (4) The men named, including a number of priests, were not likely to submit quietly to being forced to give up their wives and families. (5) Such a situation would almost certainly come to the attention of the Persian administration who would not be pleased with the potential instability being created.

Yet in what might be a part of the Nehemiah Memorial, Nehemiah talks about Jews who had married inhabitants of Ashdod, Ammon, and Moab (Neh 13:23–27). He intervened, though it is not clear that he broke the marriages up, but he did drive out the son of the high priest who had married a daughter of Sanballat (Neh 13:28). This looks much more realistic. The marriages described are with individuals outside the Judahite community, and it fits Nehemiah's personality to intervene vigorously. Thus, there was probably some intermarriage with outsiders on the margins of society, but it was unlikely to have been a major issue. But most of the 'foreign wives' inveighed against by the book of Ezra seem to be Jews in reality, just not *golah* Jews.

---

28 For the documents, see especially Bezalel Porten and Ada Yardeni, *Textbook of Aramaic Documents from Ancient Egypt* (4 vols; Jerusalem: Hebrew University, Department of the History of the Jewish People, Texts and Studies for Students, 1986–99), documents A4.6–10.
29 See the discussion in Grabbe, *History of Jews and Judaism*, 1:313–16.

3 Conclusions

The results of this study can be best summed up by a comparison between the picture of the text and the results of the reconstruction suggested above:

Ezra 1–6	Reconstruction
Cyrus issued a personal decree on behalf of the Jews, commanding the return and the rebuilding of the temple	Cyrus issued a general decree, which the Jews could take advantage of
	Temple rebuilding was a Jewish initiative
Sheshbazzar brought back temple vessels	Sheshbazzar was probably the first governor of Judah
A large group of 40,000+ returned under Zerubbabel and Joshua	The numbers returning were small, probably a trickle of individuals or small groups
Zerubbabel and Joshua began the temple construction	Sheshbazzar began the temple construction
The temple was completed quickly	The temple probably took a generation
The 'people(s) of the land(s)' were foreigners who hindered the Jews in their rebuilding	Those called 'peoples of the land(s)' were probably descendants of Jews never deported
There was opposition, especially from Samaria	Relations with Samaria were probably good most of the time
Intermarriage with foreigners was a major problem that had to be resolved (Ezra 9–10)	Some instances of marriage with outsiders no doubt arose, but the situation described in Ezra 9–10 is very problematic to credit

Jason M. Silverman

Sheshbazzar, a Judean or a Babylonian? A Note on his Identity

Sheshbazzar has been a bit of a mystery in discussions of Persian Period Yehud. He is only mentioned four times in the Hebrew Bible, each in Ezra. Ezra 1:8 calls him "the Prince of Yehud" (הנשיא ליהוד); 1:11 credits him with bringing the temple vessels back to Yehud along with the exiles; 5:14 calls him governor (פחה); and 5:16 claims he laid the foundations of the temple. He is then mentioned in the derivative traditions of *1 Esdras* and Josephus's *Antiquities*.[1] Although almost always accepted as historical,[2] the sparse attestation (including lack of patronymic), the apparent disjunction in titles, and an overlap in responsibilities with Zerubbabel have led to numerous scholarly theories on who Sheshbazzar was and what his role was.[3]

The discussions of the identity of Sheshbazzar have largely been concerned with whether he was of the Davidic dynasty.[4] Most scholars understand him as

1 For a discussion of the latter two, see Sara Japhet, 'Sheshbazzar and Zerubbabel: Against the Background of the Historical and Religious Tendencies of Ezra-Nehemiah II', *ZAW* 95 (1983): 218–229.

2 E.g., Lester L. Grabbe, *Ezra-Nehemiah* (London: Routledge, 1998), 135, who notes he is mentioned within a more genuine Aramaic document. On the documents and their authenticity see, e.g., Lester L. Grabbe, 'The "Persian Documents" in the Book of Ezra: Are They Authentic?', in *Judah and the Judeans in the Persian Period* (eds. O. Lipschits and M. Oeming; Winona Lake, IN: Eisenbrauns, 2006), 531–570. Richard C. Steiner, 'Bishlam's Archival Search Report in Nehemiah's Archive: Multiple Introductions and Reverse Chronological Order as Clues to the Origin of the Aramaic Letters in Ezra 4–6', *JBL* 125 (2006): 641–685 is more positive about their authenticity based on comparisons with Imperial Aramaic archival practices.

3 The majority consider him to be a Davidic governor, although Kurt Galling, 'Serubbabel und der Wiederaufbau des Tempels in Jerusalem', in *Verbannung und Heimkehr: Beiträge zur Geschichte und Theologie Israels im 6. und 5. Jahrhundert v. Chr.* (ed. A. Kuschke; Tübingen: Mohr Siebeck, 1961), 75 considered him a "commissar for the temple" and I. Milevski, 'Palestine's Economic Formation and the Crisis of Judah (Yehud) during the Persian Period', *Transeuphratène* 40 (2011): 152 a temple official. For other views, see below.

4 E.g., Jacob M. Myers, *Ezra Nehemiah: Introduction, Translation, and Notes* (The Anchor Bible; Garden City, New York: Doubleday, 1965), 9; Antti Laato, *The Servant of YHWH and Cyrus: A Reinterpretation of the Exilic Messianic Programme in Isaiah 40–55* (CBOTS 35; Stockholm: Almqvist & Wiksell, 1992), 223; Gabriele Boccaccini, *Roots of Rabbinic Judaism: An Intellectual History from Ezekiel to Daniel* (Grand Rapids, MI: Eerdmans, 2001), 50; Paolo Sacchi, *History of the Second*

Jason M. Silverman: Leiden University

Judean and Cyrus's first gubernatorial appointee.[5] Although the lack of specific evidence makes certainty impossible, the present note argues for an alternative, simpler understanding: that the nature of the evidence for Sheshbazzar (present but sparse and vague) relates to his unimportant role in (later) Judean eyes as the last Neo-Babylonian governor of the province.[6] This is preferable to speculative attempts to identify Sheshbazzar with other figures, whether Shenazzar, Shealtiel, Zerubbabel, or Nehemiah.[7]

Temple Period (London: T & T Clark, 2004), 60; Andrew E. Steinmann, 'A Chronological Note: the Return of the Exiles under Sheshbazzar and Zerubbabel (Ezra 1–2)', *JETS* 51 (2008): 519.

5 E.g., Loring W. Batten, *A Critical and Exegetical Commentary on the Books of Ezra and Nehemiah* (ICC; Edinburgh: T & T Clark, 1913), 70; Sara Japhet, 'Sheshbazzar and Zerubbabel: Against the Background of the Historical and Religious Tendencies of Ezra-Nehemiah I', *ZAW* 94 (1982): 98; Joseph Blenkinsopp, *Ezra-Nehemiah: A Commentary* (OTL; Louisville, KY: Westminster John Knox, 1988), 62; cf. Blenkinsopp, *David Remembered: Kingship and National Identity in Ancient Israel* (Grand Rapids, MI: Eerdmans, 2013), 71; Tamara C. Eskenazi, 'Sheshbazar', in *Anchor Bible Dictionary* (ed. D. N. Freedman; Garden City, NY: Doubleday, 1992): 1208; John Kessler, *The Book of Haggai: Prophecy and Society in Early Persian Yehud* (VTSup 91; Leiden: Brill, 2002), 68; H. G. M. Williamson, *Studies in Persian Period History and Historiography* (FAT 38; Tübingen: Mohr Siebeck, 2004), 13, 84; Steinmann, 'A Chronological Note', 519.

6 This opinion was already briefly offered by J. Maxwell Miller and John H. Hayes, *A History of Ancient Israel and Judah* (London: SCM, 1986), 446 and Gösta W. Ahlström, *The History of Ancient Palestine* (Minneapolis, MN: Fortress Press, 1994), 838–839, in neither case elaborated or defended. Rainer Albertz, *Israel in Exile: the History and Literature of the Sixth Century BCE* (SBL Studies in Biblical Literature 3; trans. D. Green; Atlanta: SBL, 2003), 123 is willing to see Sheshbazzar as either the Neo-Babylonian governor or a new appointee by Cyrus. Already in 1895 Kosters averred Sheshbazzar was a Persian, but with little argumentation (W. H. Kosters, *Die Wiederherstellung Israels in der persischen Periode: Eine Studie* [trans. A. Basedow; Heidelberg: J. Hörning, 1895], 27–29). Welch thought Sheshbazzar was a Babylonian, but this is based on an argument for his sitting at Samaria, Adam C. Welch, *Post-Exilic Judaism* (Baird Lecture for 1934; Edinburgh: William Blackwood & Sons, 1935), 98–101.

7 Proposing Shenazzar, e.g., Batten, *A Critical and Exegetical Commentary*, 70; William F. Albright, 'The Date and Personality of the Chronicler', *JBL* 40 (1921): 108–110; John Bright, *A History of Israel* (London: SCM, 1981), 343; Boccaccini, *Rabbinic Judaism*, 50; James C. Vanderkam, *From Joshua to Caiaphas: High Priests After the Exile* (Minneapolis, MN: Fortress, 2004), 6–8. Nevertheless, this is linguistically untenable: P.-R. Berger, "Zu den Namen ששבצר und שנאצר," *ZAW* 83 (1971): 98–100; Eskenazi, 'Sheshbazar', 1208; Laato, *Servant of YHWH and Cyrus*, 223.

Proposing Shealtiel, e.g., Aaron Demsky, 'Double Names in the Babylonian Exile and the Identity of Sheshbazzar', in *These are the Names: Studies in Jewish Onomastics* (ed. A. Demsky; Ramat-Gan: Bar Ilan University Press, 1999), 34–39; Nadav Na'aman, 'Royal Vassals or Governors? On the Status of Sheshbazzar and Zerubbabel in the Persian Empire', *Hen* 22 (2000): 35–44 (here 37). Proposing Zerubbabel, e.g., M. Saebø, 'The Relation of Sheshbazzar to Zerubbabel – Reconsidered', *SEÅ* 54 (1989): 168–177.

Even granting the accuracy of Ezra 1:8–11, the term "prince" (נשיא) need not imply a royal status or Davidic heritage for Sheshbazzar, despite many commentators so claiming; it certainly does not imply a vassal kingdom status for Judah.[8] The term seems to have denoted a variety of different kinds of leadership roles.[9] Blenkinsopp has noted that the word is used for tribal heads in Chronicles,[10] and Williamson has pointed to the resonances the term has with the exodus.[11] Moreover, the designation "prince of Judah" is no more necessarily indicative of Judean *identity* than the modern "Prince of Wales" denotes Welsh identity – it could merely denote a geographic area.[12] Whether or not the compiler of Ezra 1–6 may have used the word נשיא as a way of implicitly identifying him with the Davidic dynasty, the temple administration,[13] and/or the exodus, the Aramaic document in Ezra 5 only uses the much clearer term "governor" (פחה).

Ezra 1:11b says Sheshbazzar "brought back [the vessels] when the exiles came back from Babylon to Jerusalem" (הכל העלה ששבצר עם העלות הגולה מבבל לירושלם). There are two reasons why this phrase need not be taken to mean that Sheshbazzar's imperial career began with Cyrus. First, the temple vessels incident is itself dubious: the number of vessels is huge (5400!), the document doubtful or at least confused, and the editor clearly tendentious.[14] Second, even assuming a histori-

---

Proposing Nehemiah, e.g., Luc Dequeker, 'Nehemiah and the Restoration of the Temple after the Exile', in *Deuteronomy and Deuteronomic Literature. Festschrift C. H. W. Brekelmans* (BETL 133; ed. M. Vervenne and J. Lust; Leuven: Peeters, 1997), 547–567.

8 Contra F. Bianchi, 'Le Rôle de Zorobabel et de la dynastie davidique en Judée du VIe siècle au IIe siècle av. J.-C.', *Transeuphratène* 7 (1994): 153–165 and Sacchi, *History of the Second Temple Period*, 60, and in agreement with Na'aman, 'Royal Vassals or Governors?'.

9 Used for a variety of foreign leaders (e.g., Gen 34:2, Num 25:18, Josh 13:21, Ezek 26:16, 30:13, 32:29) and with a variety of meanings in cognate languages as well, J. Hoftijzer, et al., *Dictionary of Northwest Semitic Inscriptions* (HO; Leiden: Brill, 1995), 2:763. Numbers, Kings, and Chronicles use it for Israelites too. At Qumran it appears to have been used for angels (DCH 5:772).

10 Blenkinsopp, *Ezra-Nehemiah: A Commentary*, 79.

11 H. G. M. Williamson, *Ezra, Nehemiah* (WBC 16; Waco, TX: Word Books, 1985), 18–19; Williamson, *Studies*, 255.

12 As noted by Japhet, 'Sheshbazzar and Zerubbabel I', 96–98.

13 Jon Douglas Levenson, *The Theology of the Program of Restoration of Ezekiel 40–48* (HSM 10; Missoula, MT: Scholars Press, 1976), 57–67 argues that the term should be understood as a liturgical role in the Second Temple Period.

14 For a study of the passage as controlled by communal *tendenz*, see e.g., Tamara C. Eskenazi, *In an Age of Prose: A Literary Approach to Ezra-Nehemiah* (SBLMS 36; Atlanta, GA: Scholars, 1988), 40–41, 48–53. Note, however, that Williamson, *Ezra, Nehemiah*, 7, thinks there is an actual source behind the inventory, due to loanwords and *hapax legomena*. This of course does not mean it was originally relevant to Sheshbazzar. Beyond the issue of numbers, however, there is a real historical problem with the survival of the vessels themselves. See Peter Ackroyd, 'The

cal return of people or vessels, the language used, “go up” (עלה, twice, *hiph‘il* and *niph‘al* construct)[15] does not require it to be *either* Sheshbezzar’s inaugural trip *or* a trip of his at all. The fact that the causative (*hiph‘il*) is used is consonant even with Sheshbazzar not being in Babylon in person, but rather with the transportation from Babylon falling under his jurisdiction or authority.[16] Alternatively, it could be understood in relation to Sheshbazzar needing to travel to Babylon to have his position *re*confirmed. Certainly the much later Aršama archive shows peripatetic officials going to Babylon. Neither must his naming as governor in 5:14 require that Sheshbazzar have had no previous Neo-Babylonian position. Therefore, even under the assumption of the reliability of Ezra 1, there is no need for Sheshbazzar to be considered either to have been a Judean or to have been first appointed by Cyrus. Since the meager information in Ezra does not require a Judean identity, is there a probable identity in light of the historical context?

Nebuchadnezzar II installed several vassal kings in Palestine during his campaigns, including Mattaniah, whom he renamed Zedekiah.[17] After the failure of the (second) vassal arrangement under Zedekiah, the Neo-Babylonians installed

---

Temple Vessels: A Continuity Theme’, in *Studies in the Religion of Ancient Israel* (VTSup 23; ed. H. Ringgren; Leiden: Brill, 1972); Isaac Kalimi and James D. Purvis, ‘King Jehoiachin and the Vessels of the Lord’s House in Biblical Literature’, *CBQ* 56 (1994): 679–688.

15 *BHS* recommends emending the second usage from *niph‘al* to *qal* construct, but presumably this is intended to make the exiles’ “going up” sound more voluntary than enforced. A case could be conceivably made that, in relation to the occasional use of עלה for corvée labor (2 Kgs 5:27, 9:15, 21, see Ludwig Koehler and Walter Baumgartner, *The Hebrew and Aramaic Lexicon of the Old Testament* [trans. M. E. J. Richardson; 2 vols.; Leiden: Brill, 2001], 830), the return in 1:11 was an enforced bout of service to the imperial realm, as attested in the Persian heartland, e.g., Wouter Henkelman and Kristin Kleber, ‘Babylonian Workers in the Persian Heartland: Palace Building at Matannan in the Reign of Cambyses’, in *Persian Responses: Political and Cultural Interaction with(in) the Achaemenid Empire* (ed. C. Tuplin; Swansea: Classical Press of Wales, 2007), 163–176. While this might be an adventurous interpretation, it is also certainly true that the word could carry connotations of the exodus (e.g., Exod 32:1, Deut 20:1), as noted by Williamson, *Ezra, Nehemiah*, 17–19. If either connotation is true, it gives no firm indication for the historical identity of Sheshbazzar and does not require his originating among the Babylonian exiles.

16 There is certainly precedence for seeing multiple layers of administrative responsibility within Persian administration. For a recently published example, see Joseph Naveh and Shaul Shaked, *Aramaic Documents from Ancient Bactria from the Khalili Collections* (London: Khalili Family Trust, 2012), 112–113 (A6), where the presumed satrap orders a governor to have buildings repaired, presumably not himself doing the building.

17 2 Kgs 24; Jer 37. Cf. A. K. Grayson, *Assyrian and Babylonian Chronicles* (TCS 5; Locust Valley, NY: JJ Augustin, 1975), no. 5; Jean-Jacques Glassner, *Mesopotamian Chronicles* (SBLWAW 19; Atlanta, GA: Society of Biblical Literature, 2004), 226–231.

a leader of the region, Gedaliah, as reported in 2 Kgs 25//1 Chron 25 and Jer 38–43, likely a governor.[18] Although this first incumbent was assassinated, one must presume that a new governor would have been appointed by Babylon. Since Gedaliah was likely of the Judean nobility,[19] one would not be overly surprised if Babylonian policy shifted to appointing Babylonians instead of local leaders, given the Babylonians' dismal track record at pacification in Judah – two rebellious vassal kings and an assassinated governor. This might even explain why Gedaliah continued to be commemorated in later tradition, being the last native ruler.[20] Be that as it may, there is no indication of a break in the Neo-Babylonian period at Mizpah, the presumed provincial capital, during the Neo-Babylonian period.[21] Although David Vanderhooft argues that there was no Neo-Babylonian administration in Judah,[22] it would be illogical and unlikely for an empire to

---

18 Although the texts give him no title. See, e.g., David S. Vanderhooft, 'Babylonian Strategies of Imperial Control in the West: Royal Practice and Rhetoric', in *Judah and the Judeans in the Neo-Babylonian Period* (eds. O. Lipschits and J. Blenkinsopp; Winona Lake, IN: Eisenbrauns, 2003), 235–262 (244). The evidence for Gedaliah is caught up in the redaction of the Jeremiah and DtrH and its complex, and thus not dealt with here. For a discussion see Arthur J. Nevins, 'When Was Solomon's Temple Burned Down? Reassessing the Evidence', *JSOT* 31 (2006): 3–25.

19 The family of Shaphan appears as a pro-Babylonian noble family (2 Kgs 22//2 Chron 34; Jer 36; 40; Ezek 8:11). The suggestion of local family connections to Mizpah certainly does not need to imply the creation of a freewill religious organization preceeding the "Bürger-Tempel-Gemeinde" as claimed by Joel Weinberg, 'Gedaliah, the Son of Ahikam in Mizpah: his status and role, supporters and opponents', *ZAW* 119 (2007): 356–368 (367).

20 E.g. Zech 7:5 and Tosefta Soṭah 6:10. cf. Christopher T. Begg, 'The Gedaliah Episode and its Sequels in Josephus', *JSP* 6 (1994): 21–46.

21 E.g., Kenneth G. Hoglund, *Achaemenid Imperial Administration in Syria-Palestine and the Missions of Ezra and Nehemiah* (SBLDS; Atlanta, GA: Scholars Press, 1992), 5. Some useful overviews over the general situation are available in Oded Lipschits, *The Fall and Rise of Jerusalem: Judah under Babylonian Rule* (Winona Lake, IN: Eisenbrauns, 2005); Yigal Levin, 'Judea, Samaria, and Idumea: Three Models of Ethnicity and Administration in the Persian Period', in *From Judah to Judaea: Socio-Economic Structures and Processes in the Persian Period* (ed. J. U. Ro; Sheffield: Sheffield Phoenix, 2012), 4–53; and Avraham Faust, 'Social, Cultural and Demographic Changes in Judah during the Transition from the Iron Age to the Persian Period and the Nature of the Society during the Persian Period', in *From Judah to Judaea: Socio-Economic Structures and Processes in the Persian Period* (ed. J. U. Ro; Sheffield: Sheffield Phoenix, 2012), 106–132. On Mizpah, see Jeffrey R. Zorn, 'Mizpah: Newly discovered Stratum Reveals Judah's Other Capital', *BAR* 23 (1997): 28–38, 66; Jeffrey R. Zorn, 'Tell en-Nasbeh and the Problem of the Material Culture of the Sixth Century', in *Judah and the Judeans in the Neo-Babylonian Period* (eds. O. Lipschits and J. Blenkinsopp; Winona Lake, IN: Eisenbrauns, 2003), 413–450.

22 Vanderhooft, 'Babylonian Strategies of Imperial Control', based on rejecting a continuation of Neo-Assyrian polity; David S. Vanderhooft, 'New Evidence Pertaining to the Transition from Neo-Babylonian to Achaemenid Administration in Palestine', in *Yahwism After the Exile: Per-*

completely ignore a subject area, especially when intended to prevent Egyptian machinations. There are several elusive hints that Neo-Babylonian strategy in the Levant used both vassal kings and governors. The setting up of some governorships may be implied by the Letter of Adon, in which an Egyptian vassal seems to complain that Nebuchadnezzar will replace him with a governor.[23] Several cuneiform texts from the 19th year of Nebuchadnezzar mention a governor of Arpad.[24] Moreover, an inscription of Nebuchadnezzar in the Etemenanki mentions kings, governors, and officials of the Levant.[25] This sort of litany is repeated by Nabonidus in his enumeration of officials who mourn the death of this mother[26] and who celebrate the rebuilding of the temple in Harran.[27] The latter two references are in the context of the empire as a whole, and thus are not specific enough to know whether these mentioned governors are governors of the heartland or the periphery. The most complete extant source for Neo-Babylonian administration, the so-called Court Calendar, breaks off after a list of seven vassal kings, therefore unfortunately not clarifying the issue.[28] The sources certainly allow Neo-Babylonian governorships, and the successors of Gedaliah must have been governors,

spectives on Israelite Religion in the Persian Era (ed. R. Albertz and B. Becking; Assen: Van Gorcum, 2003): 219–236 (227–228).

23 As noted by Hoglund, *Achaemenid Imperial Administration*, 19. A transcription and translation is available in James M. Lindenberger, *Ancient Aramaic and Hebrew Letters* (SBLWAW 14; Atlanta, GA: Society of Biblical Literature, 2003), 23–24, and an English translation only in William W. Hallo, ed., *The Context of Scripture* (Leiden: Brill, 2002), 132–134 (3.54).

24 Francis Joannès, 'Une visite du governeur d'Arpad', *NABU* 1994/1 (1994): 21–22.

25 Text given in Friedrich Wetzel and F. H. Weissbach, *Das Hauptheiligtum des Marduk in Babylon, Esagila und Etemenanki* (Ausgrabungen der deutschen Orient-Gesellschaft in Babylon 7; Leipzig: Hinrichs, 1938), 44–49, relevant sections 46–47. Discussed by Vanderhooft, 'Babylonian Strategies of Imperial Control', 245, who nevertheless thinks it shows lack of Babylonian administration over the region, at least not modeled on Assyrian administration.

26 Adad-Guppi Stele III: 18–24; James B. Pritchard, ed., *Ancient Near Eastern Texts Relating to the Old Testament* (3rd ed.; Princeton: Princeton University Press, 1969), 560–562; Hanspeter Schaudig, *Die Inschriften Nabonids von Babylon und Kyros' des Grossen samt den in ihrem Umfeld entstandenen Tendenzschriften: Textausgabe und Grammatik* (AOAT 256; Münster: Ugarit-Verlag, 2001), 500–513. Cf. Amélie Kuhrt, *The Ancient Near East c. 3000–330 BC* (Routledge History of the Ancient World; 2 vols.; London: Routledge, 1995), 2:608.

27 The Sippar Cylinder I: 36; William W. Hallo, ed., *The Context of Scripture* (Leiden: Brill, 2000), 310–313; Schaudig, *Die Inschriften Nabonids*, 409–440.

28 See Kuhrt, *Ancient Near East*, 2:605–607; Michael Jursa, *Neo-Babylonian Legal and Administrative Documents: Typology, Contents, and Archives* (GMTR 1; Münster: Ugarit-Verlag, 2005), 51; Michael Jursa, 'Der neubabylonische Hof', in *Der Achämenidenhof/The Achaemenid Court* (CleO 2; ed. B. Jacobs and R. Rollinger; Wiesbaden: Harrassowitz, 2010), 67–106.

too.[29] The continuity of the governorship must be considered to last until the conquest of Babylon by Cyrus (539 BCE).

Cyrus inherited the lordship of Syria-Palestine when Babylon fell. In the process of taking over the empire, Cyrus seems to have both replaced some key officials with his own men (e.g., Gobryas, briefly even his son Cambyses)[30] and reconfirmed some existing officials (e.g., Nabû-aḫḫē-bulliṭ, Nabû-mukīn-zēri, and Širikti-Ninurta).[31] The governorship of Yehud would therefore have needed either to be reconfirmed or replaced. Although Cyrus's activities between 539 and his death in 530 BCE are sparsely attested outside Greek sources at present,[32] he

---

29 Even Blenkinsopp, who argues that Gedaliah was a non-Davidic, Benjaminite client king, thinks the Babylonians would have had to revert to a governor after his assassination, Blenkinsopp, *David Remembered*, 53, 59.

30 Texts for Cambyses given in Jerome Peat, 'Cyrus "King of Lands", Cambyses "King of Babylon": the Disputed Co-Regency', *JCS* 41 (1989): 199–216. Cf. Amélie Kuhrt, 'Babylonia from Cyrus to Xerxes', in *Cambridge Ancient History* (ed. J. Boardman, et al.; Cambridge: Cambridge University Press, 1988): 122–126; Muhammad A. Dandamaev, *A Political History of the Achaemenid Empire* (trans. W. J. Vogelsang; Leiden: Brill, 1989), 56–58; Pierre Briant, *From Cyrus to Alexander: A History of the Persian Empire* (trans. P. T. Daniels; Winona Lake, IN: Eisenbrauns, 2002), 71.

31 See Mariano San Nicolò, *Beiträge zu einer Prosopographie neubabylonischer Beamten der Zivil- und Tempelverwaltung* (SBAW 141.2.2; Munich: Verlag der Bayerischen Akademie der Wissenschaften, 1941), 13, 16; Briant, *From Cyrus to Alexander*, 71. Dandamaev, *A Political History of the Achaemenid Empire*, 55, sees most officials as maintaining their positions; cf. Michael Jursa, 'The Transition of Babylonia from the Neo-Babylonian Empire to Achaemenid Rule', in *Regime Change in the Ancient Near East and Egypt from Sargon of Agade to Saddam Hussein* (ed. H. Crawford; *Proceedings of the British Academy* 136; Oxford: Oxford University Press, 2007), 73–94; Kristin Kleber, 'Zēria, *šatammu* von Esangila, und die Entstehungszeit des "Strophengedichts"', *NABU* 2007/52 (2007); Caroline Waerzeggers, 'Very Cordially Hated in Babylonia? Zēria and Rēmūt in the Verse Account', *AoF* 39 (2012): 316–320.

32 The issue is complicated by legends concerning Cyrus's death. Herodotus I.201, 205–6, 208 has Cyrus die in an invasion against the Massagetae. Nevertheless, it is worth noting that this is claimed to be an attempt to go beyond the Syr Darya, implying Cyrus already held extensive eastern lands prior. The extant Ctesias has Cyrus conquer Bactria before Asia Minor and also has Cyrus die campaigning east, but against the Derbices. Fragment 11 of Berossos preserved in the Armenian version of Eusebius also mentions his death in the east in the plain of Daas, after a reign of nine years (Geert De Breucker,*De Babyloniaca van Berossos van Babylon* [PhD Groningen, 2012]: 559–60, available http://dissertations.ub.rug.nl/faculties/arts/2012/g.e.e.de.breucker/). In contrast, Xenophon, *Cyropaedia* VIII.7 has Cyrus die at home. Yet Xenophon appears to be unaware of the eastern areas at all, as they receive no satraps in *Cyr.* VIII.6.1–8, and he has Cyrus conquering Syria and Egypt after Babylon, but naught else (*Cyr.* VIII.6.19–21). For a convenient collection of some of these, see Amélie Kuhrt, *The Persian Empire: a Corpus of Sources from the Achaemenid Period* (London: Routledge, 2009), 99–102. For Ctesias see Loyd Llewellyn-Jones and James Robson, *Ctesias' History of Persia: Tales of the Orient* (Routledge Classical Translations; London: Routledge, 2010), 171–173.

must have largely campaigned east, since the eastern satrapies appear as already held in the Behistun inscription of Darius.[33] There is a possible attestation of Cyrus travelling from roughly Borazjan to Uruk at the end of his reign,[34] but this only highlights the multiple priorities of the Great King which kept him away even from Babylonia. In this light, it is reasonable to see very little Persian intervention in Syria-Palestine during this period. Indeed, in Gauthier Tolini's interpretation, unforeseen circumstances even prevented Cyrus from personally participating in the Akītu festival in 538 BCE.[35] The Cyrus Cylinder (and Ezra 1) should not be taken to mean that there was a wide-spread repatriation at the beginning of Cyrus's reign to which Sheshbazzar can be attached. Though merely an assumption, it would make sense to understand the majority of Neo-Babylonian officials as merely reconfirmed in the west at this time.[36] Indeed, even in Babylonia itself, few administrative changes seem to have been undertaken before Cyrus's fourth year, when Ēbir-nāri appears in titles.[37] In this context it is unlikely that Yehud would have been important enough at such a point in time to merit administrative reform. Presumably loyalty and collaboration rather than ethnic ties were the key consideration, especially in the early days of Cyrus's reign while he was still formulating how to control his new vast territories.[38]

Thus the distinct possibility exists that Cyrus, at least initially, merely reconfirmed the Neo-Babylonian governor of Yehud in his position. There is a reasonable case for understanding Sheshbazzar as this Neo-Babylonian governor. First, he appears early on in Cyrus's reign as governor, so on the above assumption, he

---

33 E.g., DB I § 6; II § 21, where the eastern countries rebel, implying they were previously held (and indeed, they already have satraps).

34 Discussion based on provisions for the king's table in 531/530 BCE. Reconstructed by Gauthier Tolini, *La Babylonie et l'Iran: les relations d'une province avec le coeur de l'empire perse* (PhD thesis, Université Paris I – Panthéon-Sorbonne, 2011), 147–150; cf. 151–173. The author is grateful to Tolini for forwarding a copy of his dissertation for consultation.

35 See Tolini, *La Babylonie et l'Iran*, 135–145. As is well noted by him, the lacunose nature of the Chronicle at this point makes restorations hazardous.

36 Although he is rather agnostic on knowledge of this period in Palestine, Briant also allows for aspects of Darius's satrapal reforms to predate his reign. See Briant, *From Cyrus to Alexander*, 48–49, 64.

37 Matthew W. Stolper, 'The Governor of Babylon and Across-the-River in 486 B.C.', *JNES* 48 (1989): 283–305 (289); Jursa, *Neo-Babylonian Legal and Administrative Documents*, 54.

38 Even much later a Babylonian is attested as the Satrap of Across the River (Bēlšunu), rather than a West Semite. See, e.g., Stolper, 'The Governor of Babylon and Across-the-River'; Briant, *From Cyrus to Alexander*, 61–62; Muhammad A. Dandamaev, 'Neo-Babylonian and Achaemenid State Administration in Mesopotamia', in *Judah and the Judeans in the Persian Period* (ed. O. Lipschits and M. Oeming; Winona Lake, IN: Eisenbrauns, 2006), 373–398 (392, 395).

would have been the pre-existing governor. Second, he has an explicitly Babylonian name. If he was a Babylonian official, this removes the need for any speculation over the translation of names, second names, or cryptic identifications. Of course names do not determine ethnicity, but they are certainly consonant with it. Third, the absence of a patronymic suggests a lack of local familial ties (at least ones of interest to Judeans).[39] Such a shortage of family could have many causes, yet a particularly plausible reason would be a Babylonian, and thus non-Judean, provenance. Indeed, in the analysis of Jursa, high Babylonian royal officials typically did not use family names.[40] Lastly, being the last Neo-Babylonian governor is a role unlikely to be memorable to the local populace: neither a Davidide, nor associated with the liberating Persians, nor presiding over a renewed cult. His brief mention in Ezra must surely be due to mention in source materials used by the author; he is certainly mentioned in a way which suggests all-but-forgotten remoteness.[41] The latter is strengthened when one realizes that the second pair of references to Sheshbazzar as governor appear in what might have been an authentic administrative Aramaic document, while the first pair, calling him a prince, is the compiler's own reconstruction.[42]

In addition to the reappointment/reconfirmations of Neo-Babylonian officials within the Babylonian heartland noted above, there is a potential parallel for Cyrus retaining a Neo-Babylonian official in an extra-Babylonian territory, though it is, like Sheshbazzar, uncertain. An economic receipt from Nippur in the 5th year of Cyrus mentions a certain Sîn-šarru-uṣur, a "deputy" of Qedar (BE 8 65).[43] Sîn-šarru-uṣur has no patronymic or other identifier beyond the title in this receipt. Beaulieu interprets this individual as a Babylonian official installed over

---

39 What Goswell calls "a studied disinterest in his family connections," Gregory Goswell, 'The Absence of Davidic Hope in Ezra-Nehemiah', *TJ* 33 (2012): 19–31 (20).

40 Michael Jursa, 'Families, Officialdom and Families of Royal Officials in Chaldean and Achaemenid Babylonia. Version 01,' Imperium and Officium Working Papers (IOWP), Last Updated Date 2012. Available from http://iowp.univie.ac.at/node/254.

41 As noted by Japhet, 'Sheshbazzar and Zerubbabel I', 92.

42 Opinions of Grabbe, *Ezra-Nehemiah*, 135; Albertz, *Israel in Exile*, 121–122.

43 Paul-Alain Beaulieu, *The Reign of Nabonidus King of Babylon 556–539 B.C.* (YNER 10; New Haven, CT: Yale University Press, 1989), 180, n. 23 transliterates the title as ^{lú}MIN-*u šá* ^{uru}*qé-da-ri*, while Michael Jursa, *Aspects of the Economic History of Babylonia in the First Millennium BC: Economic Geography, Economic Mentalities, Agriculture, the Use of Money, and the Problem of Economic Growth* (Veröffentlichungen zur Wirtschaftsgeschichte Babyloniens im 1. Jahrtausend v. Chr. 4; AOAT 377; Münster: Ugarit-Verlag, 2010), 191 transliterates as ^{uru}Qiṭāru and Israel Eph'al, *The Ancient Arabs: Nomads on the Borders of the Fertile Crescent in the 9th–5th Centuries BC* (Jerusalem: Magness Press, 1982), 190 as ^{uru}*Qi-da-ri*.

Qedar by Nabonidus.[44] However, Eph'al understands Sîn-šarru-uṣur to have been an official over a "town of the Arabs" in Babylonia, analogous to the now known "town of the Judeans."[45] Jursa merely sees him as a royal official.[46] The lack of patronymic makes identifying this individual difficult and precarious.

There are at least three separate individuals attested with the name Sîn-šarru-uṣur in the Neo-Babylonian and Achaemenid cuneiform record.[47] One was active in the region of Uruk and is attested in Weisberg no. 4[48] and in Joannès no. 47,[49] whom they think was identical to the *ša rēš šarri bēl-piqitti* of Eanna known in a text from the 5th year of Cambyses.[50] Sîn-šarru-uṣur also appears in a receipt dating from 11/IX/6th Cambyses (from Uruk?).[51] He seems to have been active at least from the 5th year of Cambyses until the 11th year of Darius I,[52] and is likely to be the Sîn-šarru-uṣur mentioned as a recipient in three undated letters from Uruk.[53] There seems to have been a homonymous person in the region; in YOS 7

44 Beaulieu, *Reign of Nabonidus*, 180, n. 23.

45 Eph'al, *The Ancient Arabs*, 190–191. On the Arabian settlements in Babylonia, see Muhammad A. Dandamaev, 'Twin Towns and Ethnic Minorities in First Millennium Babylonia', in *Commerce and Monetary Systems in the Ancient World: Means of Transmission and Cultural Interaction* (Melammu Symposia 5; Oriens et Occidens 6; ed. R. Rollinger and C. Ulf; Munich: Franz Steiner, 2004), 137–151 (138, 145). The so-called "āl-Yāhūdu" texts are not yet published. For some advance information see Laurie E. Pearce, 'New Evidence for Judeans in Babylonia', in *Judah and the Judeans in the Persian Period* (ed. O. Lipschits and M. Oeming; Winona Lake, IN: Eerdmans, 2006), 399–412, as well as the contribution of Pearce in this volume.

46 Jursa, *Aspects of the Economic History*, 192, n. 1081.

47 Arch Tremayne, *Records from Erech: Time of Cyrus and Cambyses* (YOS 7; New Haven, CT: Yale University Press, 1925), 36.

48 David B. Weisberg, *Guild Structure and Political Allegiance in Early Achamenid Mesopotamia* (YNER 1; New Haven, CT: Yale University Press, 1967), 21–22.

49 Francis Joannès, *Textes Économiques de la Babylonie Récente* (Étude des textes de TBER 6; Paris: Étude Recherche sur les Civilisations, 1982), 206–207.

50 AnOr 8 76; cf. Karlheinz Kessler, *Uruk: Urkunden aus Privathäusern 1: Die Archive der Söhne des Bēl-ušallim, des Nabû-ušallim und des Bēl-supê-muḫur* (AUWE 8; Mainz-am-Rhein: Philipp von Zabern, 1991), 45–47.

51 Ronald H. Sack, *Cuneiform Documents from the Chaldean and Persian Periods* (London: Associated University Presses, 1994), text no. 45. Note that the index (p. 80) reads Sin-šar-uṣur but the translation (p. 102) reads Šamaš-šarra-uṣur. The transliteration is ^{id}30-LUGAL-ŠEŠ. The author is grateful to Tero Alstola and Rieneke Sonnevelt for discussing this matter.

52 Joannès, *Textes Économiques de la Babylonie Récente*, 206–207; San Nicolò, *Beiträge zu einer Prosopographie neubabylonischer Beamten*, 20. Kleber sees him in office until the rebellion of Nebuchadnezzar IV, Kristin Kleber, *Tempel und Palast: die Beziehungen zwischen dem König und dem Eanna-Tempel im spätbabylonischen Uruk* (AOAT 358; Münster: Ugarit-Verlag, 2008), 37.

53 YOS 3 77, 82, 126: Albert T. Clay, *Neo-Babylonian Letters from Erech* (YOS 3; New Haven, CT: Yale University Press, 1919), 17; Erich Ebeling, *Neubabylonische Briefe aus Uruk 1.–4. Heft* (Bei-

106 appears a Sîn-šarru-uṣur who was a *šatammu* of a town near Uruk.[54] Another text from the accession year of Cambyses mentions a Sîn-šarru-uṣur and Gobryas.[55]

A presumably different individual from the Uruk administrator is also attested in Uruk: in YOS 7 65, dated to the 8th year of Cyrus, a Sîn-šarru-uṣur, son of Kinā, grandson of Dannu-Nergal appears as a bowman.[56] Kozuh thinks this person was replacing another member from a family of herdsmen,[57] and is therefore unlikely to be the same individual as the important Eanna official.

Finally, a text dated 13/X/10th Nabonidus mentions a Sîn-šarru-uṣur, "head of the king's merchants."[58] This individual has no further identifiers, so it is not possible to know whether this merchant was the same as the one associated with Qedar. It would be reasonable to see an official stationed in Northwest Arabia to have had important economic and trading duties for the king, and the "Chief of the King's merchants" was an important official in the Neo-Babylonian Empire.[59]

---

träge zur Keilschriftforschung und Religionsgeschichte des Vorderen Orients 1–4; Berlin: Ebeling, 1930–1934), 64–67, 70–71, 103–104.

54 Treymayne, *Records from Erech*, 36; Muhammad A. Dandamaev, *Slavery in Babylonia: From Nabopolassar to Alexander the Great (626–331)* (trans. V. A. Powell; DeKalb, IL: Northern Illinois University Press, 1984), 236–238.

55 BIN 2 114; James B. Nies and Clarence E. Keiser, *Historical, Religious, and Economic Texts and Antiquities* (BIN 2; New Haven, CT: Yale University Press, 1920), xii, 73. I have been unable to find a transliteration or translation of this text.

56 Tremayne, *Records from Erech*, 36; Michael Kozuh, *The Sacrificial Economy: On the Management of Sacrificial Sheep and Goats at the Neo-Babylonian/Achaemenid Eanna Temple of Uruk (c. 625–520 BC)* (PhD, University of Chicago, 2006), 214–217. Cf. Hans Martin Kümmel, *Familie, Beruf und Amt im spätbabylonischen Uruk: Prosopographische Untersuchungen zu Berufsgruppen des 6. Jahrhunderts v. Chr. in Uruk* (ADOG 20; Berlin: Mann, 1979), 74.

57 Kozuh, *The Sacrificial Economy*, 217.

58 *Nbn.* 464. Text transliterated and translated in Muhammad A. Dandamaev, 'Die Rolle des *tamkārum* in Babylonien im 2. und 1. Jahrtausend v. u. Z.'," in *Beiträge zur Socialen Struktur des Alten Vorderasien* (Schriften zur Geschichte und Kultur des Alten Orients 1; ed. H. Klengel; Berlin: Akademie Verlag, 1971), 69–78 (74). Cf. A. C. V. M. Bongenaar, *The Neo-Babylonian Ebabbar Temple at Sippar: Its Administration and Its Prosopography* (Istanbul: Nederlands historisch-archaeologisch Instituut te Istanbul, 1997), 138–139.

59 Listed in the so-called "Court Calendar." For discussion, see Jursa, 'Der neubabylonische Hof', 90. For the King's Merchant, cf. Michael Jursa, 'Grundzüge der Wirtschaftsformen Babyloniens im ersten Jahrtausend v. Chr.', in *Commerce and Monetary Systems in the Ancient World: Means of Transmission and Cultural Interaction* (Melammu Symposia 5; Oriens et Occidens 6; ed. R. Rollinger and C. Ulf; Munich: Franz Steiner, 2004), 115–136 (129); Kuhrt, *Ancient Near East*, 2:607; Maria Brosius, 'New Out of Old? Court and Court Ceremonies in Achaemenid Persia', in *The Court and Court Society in Ancient Monarchies* (ed. A. J. S. Spawforth; Cambridge: Cambridge University Press, 2007), 17–57 (23); Dandamaev, 'Die Rolle des *tamkārum* in Babylonien'; Muhammad A. Dandamaev, 'The Neo-Babylonian *tamkārū*', in *Solving Riddles and Untying Knots: Bibli-*

However, should the figure in BE 8 65 be understood as the same as Nabonidus's chief merchant, there would be reason to suspect he might have been of non-Babylonian ethnicity.[60] Under Nebuchadnezzar the chief merchant was a Phoenician, and other West Semitic merchants are known.[61] Though it is impossible to know whether the officials in BE 8 65 and *Nbn.* 464 were the same individual, it is likely that trade was a significant aspect to the Neo-Babylonian royal interest in Arabia.[62]

That the Neo-Babylonians installed officers in "Arabian" provinces is indicated by a receipt from the 11th year of Nabonidus, which mentions Kinā, the brother of the governor of Dilmun (*bēl pīḫāti Dilmun*, VS 6 81).[63] A fragmentary inscription from near Dedan mentions a governor, but the king's name is lost.[64] Several other Arabian inscriptions mention various officials who came with Nabonidus.[65] These include an unclear term *hlm* and several individuals with non-Babylonian names.[66] Unfortunately, the status and administration of Arabia

---

cal, Epigraphic, and Semitic Studies in Honor of Jonas C. Greenfield (ed. Z. Zevit, et al.; Winona Lake, IN: Eisenbrauns, 1995), 523–530; Dandamaev, 'Twin Towns and Ethnic Minorities ', 142.

60 See, e.g., Michael Jursa, 'Kollationen', *NABU* 2001/102; Jursa, 'Grundzüge der Wirtschaftsformen Babyloniens', 131.

61 Dandamaev, 'The Neo-Babylonian *tamkārū*', 527; Jursa, 'Grundzüge der Wirtschaftsformen Babyloniens', 131. On the trade system in general, see A. Leo Oppenheim, 'Essay on Overland Trade in the First Millennium B. C.', *JCS* 21 (1967): 236–254.

62 The reasons for Nabonidus's decade-long stay in Northwest Arabia are contested, but the lucrative trade route was certainly a significant factor. See F. V. Winnett and W. L. Reed, *Ancient Records from North Arabia* (Near and Middle Eastern Studies 6; Toronto: University of Toronto Press, 1970), 88–93; Eph'al, *The Ancient Arabs*, 179–191; Beaulieu, *Reign of Nabonidus*, 149–232; Paolo Gentili, 'Nabonidus' Friends in Arabia', *NABU* 2001/90; Jan Retsö, *The Arabs in Antiquity: Their History from the Assyrians to the Umayyads* (London: RoutledgeCurzon, 2003), 181–192; Ricardo Eichmann, et al., 'Archaeology and Epigraphy at Tayma (Saudi Arabia)', *Arabian Archaeology and Epigraphy* 17 (2006): 163–176; Bradley L. Crowell, "Nabonidus, as-Sila', and the Beginning of the End of Edom," *BASOR* 348 (2007): 75–88.

63 Mariano San Nicolò and Arthur Ungnad, *Neubabylonische Rechts- und Verwaltungsurkunden I* (Leipzig: Hinrichs, 1935), text 641 (pp. 550–551). Cf. D. T. Potts, *The Arabian Gulf in Antiquity I: From Prehistory to the Fall of the Achaemenid Empire* (Oxford: Clarendon, 1990), 349–350.

64 Eph'al, *The Ancient Arabs*, 204; Winnett and Reed, *Ancient Records from North Arabia*, 115.

65 See André Lemaire, 'Nabonidus in Arabia and Judah in the Neo-Babylonian Period', in *Judah and the Judeans in the Neo-Babylonian Period* (ed. O. Lipschits and J. Blenkinsopp; Winona Lake, IN: Eisenbrauns, 2003), 285–298 (289); Yaakov Gruntfest and Michael Heltzer, 'Nabonid, King of Babylon (556–539 B.C.E.) in Arabia in Light of New Evidence', *BN* 110 (2001): 26–28; Hani Hayajneh, 'First Evidence of Nabonidus in the Ancient North Arabian Inscriptions from the Region of Taymā'', *Proceedings of the Seminar for Arabian Studies* 31 (2001): 81–95.

66 Gruntfest and Heltzer, 'Nabonid, King of Babylon', 27, 29; Gentili, 'Nabonidus' Friends in Arabia'; Hayajneh, 'First Evidence of Nabonidus', 82, 91. The latter thinks these attested officials were Arabians from Babylonia.

in the Achaemenid era is unclear, even more so for the transition from Nabonidus to Cyrus.[67] All of this means that Sîn-šarru-uṣur, official of Qedar, can plausibly be understood as a Neo-Babylonian administrator (whether merchant or not) retained from Nabonidus to Cyrus, but it cannot be proved. It is thus in many respects analogous to the evidence available for Sheshbazzar.

Whatever the reality behind the decree of Cyrus to repatriate the temple vessels and the Judeans,[68] the earliest most likely context for direct Persian interest in southern Palestine was the preparation for the invasion of Egypt. This may have begun late in Cyrus's reign, but more likely began with Cambyses.[69] The reign of Cambyses is noticeably absent from biblical tradition. Josephus's addition of Cambyses to the account in *1 Esdras* does nothing to ameliorate this lacuna.[70] The lead-up to invasion would be a more logistically logical time for the Persian administration to replace the governorships in southern Palestine than previously, since it would relate to the preparations for war as well as the fact that Cambyses would have personally passed through at the start of the campaign. Again, no evidence for this is available.[71] Nevertheless, it would explain why

---

67 See, e.g., Eph'al, *The Ancient Arabs*, 201–205; David F. Graf, 'Arabia during Achaemenid Times', in *Centre and Periphery* (Achaemenid History 4; ed. H. Sancisi-Weerdenburg and A. Kuhrt; Leiden: Nederlands Instituut voor het Nabije Oosten, 1990), 131–148; Retsö, *The Arabs in Antiquity*, chs. 7 and 9; Björn Anderson, 'Achaemenid Arabia: A Landscape-Oriented Model of Cultural Interaction', in *The World of Achaemenid Persia: History, Art and Society in Iran and the Ancient Near East* (ed. J. Curtis and S. J. Simpson; London: I. B. Tauris, 2010), 445–456.

68 An extensively debated topic which is not addressed here. See, e.g., Grabbe, 'The "Persian Documents" in the Book of Ezra', 541–544.

69 John Kessler, 'Prophecy at the Turning of the Ages: Imminent Crisis and Future Hope in Hag 2:6–9; 20–23 and Zech 2:10–17 [ET 6–13]', *Transeuphratène* 40 (2011): 97–134 (104) is also of this opinion. Cf. Briant, *From Cyrus to Alexander*, 48–49. Note, however, Oded Lipschits, 'Achaemenid Imperial Policy, Settlement Processes in Palestine, and the Status of Jerusalem in the Middle of the Fifth Century B.C.E.', in *Judah and the Judeans in the Persian Period* (eds. O. Lipschits and M. Oeming; Winona Lake, IN: Eisenbrauns, 2006), 25, doubts there was any change even during Cambyses's invasion, with all interest or intervention waiting until Darius I.

70 Josephus, *Antiquities* XI, knows Cambyses, but probably from Herodotus, since Josephus repeats Herodotus's characterization of Cambyses as a madman. On Josephus, see Louis H. Feldman, 'Restoration in Josephus', in *Restoration: Old Testament, Jewish, and Christian Perspectives* (SJSJ 72; ed. J. M. Scott; Leiden: Brill, 2001), 223–264.

71 Almost the only Palestinian trace of Cambyses appears to be a still unpublished Neo-Babylonian tablet from Tel Mikhmoret dated to the 10th of Ab, fifth year of Cambyses, and even this has been argued to have been brought to Palestine from Babylonia. See Yosef Porath, et al., 'Mikhmoret, Tel', in *The New Encyclopedia of Archaeological Excavations in the Holy Land* (eds. E. Stern, et al.; Jerusalem: Israel Exploration Society, 1993), 1044–1045; Ephraim Stern, *Archaeology of the Land of the Bible Vol. 2: The Assyrian, Babylonian, and Persian Periods: 732–332 BCE*

Sheshbazzar remained in the records used by the later compilers of Ezra despite not being of much interest to them; he had not been removed too long beforehand not to exist within the Persian administrative records available to the compiler of Ezra.

Although no new hard evidence is presently available to clarify the issue, understanding Sheshbazzar as the last Neo-Babylonian governor (who was reconfirmed as the first Persian governor) removes the difficulty created when scholars postulate a direct relationship with the Davidic dynasty, and it needs not make recourse to (even more speculative) onomastics. More importantly, it explains why the name appeared in the official records available to the compilers (i.e., Ezra 5), but had faded from Judean memory at the time Ezra 1–6 was compiled. In line with Occam, then, this solution would seem to be simplest and therefore most preferable. Moreover, if this identity is accepted, it gives a new, potential locus for the influence of Babylonian temple practices on the restored practices within the Second Temple in Jerusalem, in the person of an (ex-) Neo-Babylonian governor present at its re-founding.

Acknowledgment

This research was conducted as part of the ERC funded project "By the Rivers of Babylon," which explores the relationships between the Neo-Babylonian and Second Temple priesthoods. The principle investigator is Caroline Waerzeggers. The BABYLON project's aim is to engage in a comparative study between the Second Temple of Jerusalem and the Babylonian temple cult as evidenced by the recently disclosed cuneiform records. The project in its final stage addresses the question of possible, direct or indirect, influence of Babylonian models on Judean practices. The rebuilding of the Jerusalem temple, however, occurred under the Achaemenid kings, and the author's research, from which this paper derives, attempts to explore how the new Persian context informs and contextualizes the Mesopotamian-Judean interactions.

(Anchor Bible Reference Library; New York: Doubleday, 2001), 361, 404; Wayne Horowitz, et al., *Cuneiform in Canaan: Cuneiform Sources from the Land of Israel in Ancient Times* (Jerusalem: Israel Exploration Society, 2006), 109.

Katherine Southwood

The Impact of the Second and Third-Generation Returnees as a Model for Understanding the Post-Exilic Context

By using the framework of return migration, and its common effects on ethnic identity, as a heuristic analytical tool through which to achieve a more sophisticated level of dialogue with Ezra's intermarriage crisis, it may be possible to address the return from exile with fresh insight. As will be demonstrated, it seems that once religious identity is factored into the equation, migration becomes a powerful variable which has a drastic impact on the constructions of ethnic identities.

Before examining and analysing the evidence at stake, some brief comments regarding the choice of applying a social-scientific method to the text are necessary. Although this issue has been discussed in detail elsewhere,[1] it is nevertheless important to re-iterate a number of key points which are often overlooked, forgotten, or simply misunderstood regarding the use of the social sciences for understanding the exilic and post-exilic contexts and for understanding the biblical text. First, the use of the later-generations return model is not being applied to the material as if it were ontologically 'true'.[2] Rather, material taken from a continually growing field of research into generations of returnees is being applied in order to gain a new perspective on the material and to assess the extent to which the model assists us in this task. We are not attempting to validate the model

1 A vast array of material exists concerning this discussion. Much of it is referenced in Katherine Southwood, *Ethnicity and the Mixed Marriage Crisis in Ezra 9–10: An Anthropological Approach* (Oxford Theological Monographs; Oxford: Oxford University Press, 2012), 9–15; and Katherine Southwood, 'Ethnicity and Ethnography', in *The Oxford Encyclopedia of the Bible and Ethics* (ed. Robert L. Brawley; Oxford: Oxford University Press, 2014), 238–243. For a general overview, refer to Philip F. Esler (ed.), *Ancient Israel: The Old Testament in Its Social Context* (Minneapolis: Fortress Press, 2006) and to Robert R. Wilson, 'Reflections on Social-Scientific Criticism', in *Method Matters: Essays on the Interpretation of the Hebrew Bible in Honor of David L. Petersen* (SBLRBS 56; ed. Joel M. LeMon and Kent H. Richards; Atlanta: Society of Biblical Literature, 2009), 505–522. Also, for an excellent example of the application of the approach refer to Philip F. Esler, *Sex, Wives, and Warriors: Reading Biblical Narrative with its Ancient Audience* (Eugene, OR: Cascade Books, 2011).

2 Refer to note 21 for a discussion of the problems concerning the term 'generation'.

Katherine Southwood: University of Oxford

itself, neither is application of the model an attempt to 'validate' some reconstructed version of 'the Bible's historicity'. Second, we are not forcing the biblical and extra-biblical evidence to fit into the model's schema, nor is the material concerning later generations of migrants chosen to mirror the biblical material. Instead, the aim of using this model is as a heuristic analytical tool with which to discern any patterns within the evidence that may before have gone unnoticed with the use of traditional methods.

For example, rather than imagining the 'exiles in Babylon' the use of modern studies shows us the *complexity* of exile. It is very unlikely that all exiles would have been in the same place and still less likely that they all returned at once. Instead, we should consider the many different contexts of exile. Most notably, we realise that not all communities in exile would have acculturated at the same pace; those who were in rural settlements may, in fact, have resisted assimilation.[3] Likewise, careless use of terms drawn from the social sciences are clarified and sharpened through greater reference to the on-going work of ethnographers, anthropologists, and sociologists. Rather than using intuitive, value-laden, language such as 'actual foreigners', reference to such research allows us not to take such terminology for granted, but to ask more perceptive questions such as 'how might Judean ethnic identity be understood? In what sense is Judean ethnic identity measurable for later generations in exile'? Effectively, by using models drawn from a variety of modern studies we are attempting to avoid projecting ethnocentric and anachronistic perspectives on to the text.[4] Hence, what we are trying to

3 Liisa H. Malkki, *Purity and Exile: Violence, Memory and National Cosmology among Hutu Refugees in Tanzania* (Chicago: Chicago University Press, 1995); Southwood, *Ethnicity*, 41–48. Note that the later Murašû documents from Nippur show individuals with Yahwistic names who are reasonably well-assimilated into the economic system as smallholders, petty officials, tax-collectors and witnesses. Similarly, the later documents from Elephantine, despite a plea to the Jerusalem temple, never actually allude to any desire to move to Yehud. Therefore, it is reasonable to suggest that not all people with Yahwistic beliefs and/or culture maintained a desire to 'return' and that different experiences of exile existed.

4 The criticism of 'anachronism' which is often levelled against social scientific models is one of the main things such models actually aim to avoid. Rather than attempting to force the biblical text and ancient evidence into any one model, a model is instead constructed carefully through compiling evidence which is taken from the accumulation of data. The aim is, therefore, to reach a culturally consistent model or set of analytical questions through which to analyse the biblical data. It is important not to treat such models as definitive, but instead to attempt to think of them as offering plausible suggestions which inform our broader understanding. It must be acknowledged that the two sets of data being compared are very different. However, anthropologists on fieldwork research sometimes face similar challenges to the biblical scholar using anthropology in terms of a mismatch of the data available and the questions being asked. For example, the

achieve is a guide designed to direct us to the most pertinent questions regarding the data – biblical and extra-biblical – which we have. That is, through increased use of material within subjects such as, in this case, social anthropology, we are looking for the connections between ideas and concepts and for the increased awareness, precision, and comprehension of the analytical language which we apply to the data.

It takes little more than a glance through the literature to recognize the lack of terminological clarity regarding 'return migration'; some of the terms used to describe the phenomena include repatriation, counter-stream migration, reflex migration, retro-migration, and U-turn migration. Perhaps this lack of concrete definition mirrors the problematic nature of the term 'return' itself. The literature on, what will for convenience's sake be loosely termed, 'return migration' occurs within the broader parameters of research into ethnicity, a phenomenon which is itself contentious and difficult to define. Thus against the context of ethnicity, migrations and return migrations have a vast impact on migrants, and those who do not move away.[5] The problematic nature of 'return' migration is intricately connected to the complexities surrounding the notion of a homeland. In the imaginations of many Diaspora communities,[6] the homeland not only con-

---

emic interpretation of a behaviour as tradition, or custom, may differ considerably from the etic questions about how, and in what context, certain behaviours emerged. I have discussed this problem at length elsewhere (Southwood *Ethnicity*, 9–16).

5 Barth's seminal study, which was brutally challenged by Cohen, provoked a renewed interest within the field of social anthropology into ethnicity. Barth illustrates how ethnic identities are experienced the strongest (as both dividing and uniting factors) in times of threat; see Fredrick Barth, *Ethnic Groups and Boundaries: The Social Organization of Culture Difference* (Oslo: Universitetsforlaget, 1969) and Anthony P. Cohen, *The Symbolic Construction of Community* (Key Ideas; Chichester: Ellis Horwood, 1985). However, the term ethnic identity is 'so vague, and so variously used' (Cohen, *The Symbolic Construction*, 107) that it is to some extent 'still on the move' (Nathan Glazer and Daniel P. Moynihan, eds., *Ethnicity: Theory and Experience* [London: Harvard University Press, 1975], 1), hence referring to 'ethnic movements' rather than identities may be more practical (Marcus Banks, *Ethnicity: Anthropological Constructions* [London: Routledge, 1996], 136). Although there is not enough space to sufficiently address the complexities of the vast literature concerning ethnicity, it is worth acknowledging that debates within social anthropology and sociology regarding ethnicity can be divided into various methodological camps, most prominently, primordialism and instrumentalism. For further discussion, refer to Southwood, *Ethnicity*, 19–72.

6 Defining the term 'diaspora' is also problematic. Cohen produces a five-fold typology of the topic to include (Robin Cohen, *Global Diasporas: An Introduction* [London: UCL Press, 1997]): Victim diasporas (Jews, Armenians, slave diasporas); Labour diasporas (Indian indentured labour, Italians, and Filipinos); Imperial/colonial diasporas (Ancient Greek, British, Portuguese); Trade diasporas (Lebanese, Chinese); Cultural diasporas (Caribbean). A more productive way of

tinues to be relevant, but is also imbued with a renewed level of significance for such communities.[7]

In her influential book, *Cartographies of Diaspora*, Avtar Brah illustrates the multi-local perceptions of 'home' among diasporas through underlining the difference between 'home as where one is' and home as 'where one comes from'. Home, Brah argues, is the 'lived experience of locality, its sounds and smells', yet it is also a 'mythic place of desire in the diasporic imagination ... a place of no return, even if it is possible to visit the geographical territory that is seen as the place of origin'.[8] This gives way to the 'myth of home' which emerges as a result of

---

defining diasporas can be found through examining the priorities and ideals of Diaspora communities themselves, rather than imposing external descriptive categories on certain Diaspora communities. For example, Safran shows that diasporas are 'expatriate minority communities' whose notable characteristics include (William Safran, 'Diasporas in Modern Societies: Myths of Homeland and Return', *Diaspora* 1/1 [1991]: 83–84): Diasporas, or their ancestors, were dispersed, (through persecution and genocide), from a specific original centre to two or more distant, foreign locations; diasporas maintain a collective memory, *which may be mythical*, about their homeland; diasporas may believe that they are not fully accepted by their host country and this may lead to isolation; diasporas understand their ancestral home as their 'authentic, pure' home and as a place of eventual return; diasporas are committed to the maintenance and restoration of their homeland; the diaspora's consciousness and solidarity are importantly defined by their on-going relationship to their homeland.

7 This is unsurprising in light of some of the observations regarding the development and articulation of ethnic identity. As Harre comments, 'People typically form their identities within the context of their ethnic backgrounds and the socio-political contexts in which they are socialised. Moreover people often construct autobiographies to place themselves in the social order and seek out settings and situations for confirmation' (Rom Harre, 'Language Games and Texts of Identity', in *Texts of Identity* [ed. John Shotter and Kenneth J. Gergen; London: Sage, 1989], 20–35). This is also reflected in the many security risks that can be associated with the homeland, as stated in Amnesty International's journal *Refugee*, 'Despite the bitter memories most victims must have of their expulsion or flight, many refugees and displaced people are determined to return. Their greatest concern appears to be the security and the political situation in their home areas ....' (Amnesty International, 'Who's living in My House?': Obstacles to the Safe Return of Refugees and Internally Displaced Peoples. (Bosnia-Herzegovina) *Refugee* [*AI Index: EUR 63/ 01/ 1997*]: 4).

8 Avtar Brah, *Cartographies of Diaspora: Contesting Identities* (London / New York: Routledge, 1996), 192. It is important to realise at this point that the concept of a homeland is also, to some extent, ideological since it is socially constructed in the imaginations of those who perceive themselves as having been separated from it. For example, for some migrants, or indeed later generations of migrants whose parents and grandparents successfully integrate in their host societies, their new circumstances quickly become their home. This is more likely for those who have chosen, rather than been forced, to migrate. This paper uses the term homeland with the assumed context of those who perceive themselves as exiles from the land.

the fact that the rose-tinted illusion of the homeland experience is frozen in space and time, an ossified relic of a past existence.

This longing for the mythical homeland is easily discerned through the material relating to the Babylonian exile. The place name 'the city of Judah' (*āl-Yāhūdu*) is represented on cuneiform tablets referring not to Jerusalem, but to a place in Babylonia.[9] This name reflects the geographic and ethnic origin of its population since onomastic examination of the tablets reveals numerous West Semitic and Yahwistic names.[10] The Babylonian practice of grouping ethnic communities together may have facilitated an increased awareness of ethnicity since the custom of naming a settlement according to the origins of the exiles living there is well attested.[11] However, in light of the evidence concerning return migration, it is possible that the name may also betray a degree of emotional attachment to the homeland and would also function as a constant reminder of ethnic origins.[12]

Alongside the epigraphic evidence, a variety of biblical texts attest the sense of ideological attachment to the pre-exilic homeland and attempts at conformity with past cultural and religious practice. Numerous examples of this sentiment occur in prophetic literature, which Blenkinsopp has aptly designated 'projections of a restored past in post disaster prophecy.'[13] However, the narrative within the book of Ruth may also provide an example of ethnic change in relation to the homeland. Some scholars have already noted the change for Ruth herself who, given the epithet 'the Moabite' appears not to be a returnee. For example, Lau argues that Ruth subordinates and overrides her own identity since kinship is

---

9 Francis Joannès and André Lemaire, 'Trois tablettes cunéiformes à onomastique ouest-sémitique', *Transeuphratène* 17 (1999): 17–33.

10 See Cornelia Wunsch and Laurie E. Pearce, *Documents of Judean Exiles and West Semites in Babylonia in the Collection of David Sofer* (CUSAS 28; Bethesda, MD: CDL Press, 2015). These studies supersede some of the details given in the preliminary, but nevertheless instructive, articles: Laurie Pearce, 'New Evidence for Judeans in Babylonia,' in *Judah and Judeans in the Persian Period* (ed. Manfred Oeming and Oded Lipschits; Winona Lake: Eisenbrauns, 2006), 399–411, and Laurie Pearce, '"Judean:" A Special Status in Neo-Babylonian and Achaemenid Babylonia?', in *The Judeans in the Achaemenid Age: Negotiating Identity in an International Context* (ed. Manfred Oeming and Oded Lipschits; Winona Lake: Eisenbrauns, 2011), 267–277.

11 Israel Eph'al, 'On the Political and Social Organization of the Jews in the Babylonian Exile' ZDMGSup 5 (1980): 106–112.

12 For a more extensive study of mirror names, refer to Dominique Charpin, 'La "toponymie en miroir" à l'époque amorrite', *RA* 97 (2003), 3–34, and see the contribution of Gauthier Tolini in the present volume.

13 Joseph Blenkinsopp, *Judaism, The First Phase: The Place of Ezra and Nehemiah in the Origins of Judaism* (Grand Rapids, MI: Eerdmans, 2009), 122–125.

her priority.[14] Likewise, Glover emphasizes the transformation in Ruth's ethnic identity by the end of the narrative, noting that 'Ruth's ethnic transformation is mysterious because at the last the text abandons its obsession with Ruth's ethnicity.' Indeed, Ruth is continually called a Moabite (Ruth 1:4, 22; 2:2, 6, 21; 4:5, 10). 'However, in the text's final reference, Ruth is given no ethnic identifier. She is no longer "Ruth the Moabite", neither is she "Ruth the Israelite"; rather she is simply "Ruth".'[15] However, attention is seldom given to the idea of, and effects of, migration within the text. At the outset, we are informed that Naomi

> Wherefore she went forth out of the place where she was, and her two daughters in law with her; and they went on the way to return (לשוב) unto the land of Judah. (Ruth 1:7)

Furthermore, a few verses later, we are reminded that Naomi intends not just to travel, but to return, as the daughters-in-law claim that 'we will return (נשוב) with you' (Ruth 1:10). This is emphasized again at the end of the chapter when we are told that Naomi 'returned' and Ruth 'returned' with her (Ruth 1:22). It is interesting that when famine and death occur Naomi's reaction is to return to the homeland. Perhaps such a move can be interpreted as evidence of Naomi's perception of Bethlehem, the place to which Naomi returns, as a place of safety and refuge. However, as Matthews notes, 'Naomi faces the uncertainty on her return to Bethlehem of how to maintain control of Elimelech's property and to keep his name alive, and this may contribute to her labelling herself as "Mara" (bitter) when the women exclaim "Is this Naomi?" (1:19–20).'[16] Effectively, upon return to the homeland, Naomi is perceived differently to the extent of being unrecognizable and the realization of the return leads to a new set of problems in the homeland. What is interesting about this new relationship between Naomi and Bethlehem is the effect it has on Ruth's relationship to the 'homeland'. As noted, the text makes it clear from the start that Ruth is a Moabite. However, through returning with Naomi, her mother in law, Ruth can be understood as a later-generation returnee. Although Ruth is not returning in the strict sense, she is nevertheless incorporated within Naomi's homeland community by virtue of the generations and family link between herself and Naomi.

---

14 Peter H. W. Lau, *Identity and Ethics in the Book of Ruth: A Social Identity Approach* (*BZAW* 416; Berlin / New York: de Gruyter, 2011).

15 Neil Glover, 'Your People, My People: An Exploration of Ethnicity in Ruth', *JSOT* 33 (2009): 293–313, and Katherine Southwood, 'Will Naomi's Nation be Ruth's Nation?: Ethnic Translation as a Metaphor for Ruth's Assimilation within Judah', *Humanities* 3 (2014): 102–131.

16 Victor H. Matthews, 'The Determination of Social Identity in the Story of Ruth', *BTB* 36 (2006): 49–54, citation page 52.

The most obvious example is Psalm 137 which not only highlights the dissonance of living in a 'foreign land' (אדמת נכר) but also centralizes the religious culture of the homeland (singing the 'songs of Yahweh'), and emphasizes remembering and not forgetting Jerusalem as the 'capital' (ראש) joy (Ps 137:1–6).[17] The emotionally charged repetition of, and balance between, the polarized terms remember/forget in Hebrew may be an indication of the increased significance of the homeland.

By the rivers of Babylon we sat and wept
when we *remembered* Zion ....
If I *forget* you, O Jerusalem,
may my right hand *forget* ...
May my tongue cling to the roof of my mouth
if I do not *remember* you

Effectively, we have a classic example of the greater symbolic significance of the homeland and the desire to move back to what may have been seen by exiles as a sort of glorious pre-exilic 'golden age'. This concept is intimately linked to the development of ethnicity through the forging of 'home-from-home' collective diasporic identities wherein the 'nation' and 'homeland' are conflated. Thus, it may be that the attempt to preserve past cultural practices – perhaps resistance to intermarriage among them – and a sense of 'homeland' despite being in exile represent the development of a stronger awareness of foreignness.[18] Similarly, the representations of the experiences of exiles within later texts attest the consciousness of being 'foreign' and consequent resistance to cultural and ethnic assimilation.

However, one complication connected to the return migration model, which is particularly significant for the postexilic context, is the possibility that part of the returning population were 'ancestral return migrants' who were born in exile. To clarify, that is, the 'return' to the 'homeland' of the later generations of exiles. Of course, this concept is an oxymoron. Such so-called return migrants are not return migrants, but are born in a host society of migrant parents. Hence they are not return migrants in the strict sense, but first-time emigrants to their parents' country of origin. As a result, King nominates the category 'counter-diasporic

17 The end of verse 137:5 is missing in Hebrew: ... אם אשכחך ירושלם תשכח ימיני. Translations often insert an object, such as 'its work'.

18 It must be noted that this is not a model for all Judeans living outside Jerusalem. For example, intermarriage occurs without comment in marriage contracts from Elephantine, TAD B2.4, 2.6, 3.3, 3.6, 3.7, 3.8, 6.1, 6.2, 6.3 and 6.4.

migration' to describe the return to the diasporic hearth of descendants of the original migrants who were scattered. According to King, the people 'returning' are the children of the original exiles, or the link can be more historically remote (return to the land of the ancient ancestors).[19] If this is the case, then to what extent can we maintain that the difference between the returnee and 'stayee' populations is an intra-Jewish matter, as Smith-Christopher states in '... some of these "mixed" marriages ... were probably not "mixed" at all in any truly racial/ethnic sense of the term.'[20] Although this, in many ways, brings us back to the complex, perhaps irresolvable, question of what ethnic movements are, and how ethnicity might be defined and measured, some further research into the effects of modern ancestral return movements is clearly warranted.

One way of looking at this rather broad category of migrants is to narrow the boundaries slightly by examining research concerned with second- and third-generation migrants.[21] This focus has the advantage of being slightly more

---

19 Russell King, 'Generalizations from the History of Return Migration', in *The Mediterranean Passage: Migration and New Cultural Encounters in Southern Europe* (Liverpool Studies in European Regional Cultures 9; ed. R. King; Liverpool: Liverpool University Press, 2001), 7–55.

20 Daniel L. Smith-Christopher, 'Between Ezra and Isaiah: Exclusion, Transformation and Inclusion of the "Foreigner" in Post-Exilic Biblical Theology', in *Ethnicity and the Bible* (Supplements to Biblical Interpretation 19; ed. Mark G. Brett; Leiden: Brill, 1996), 123; Daniel L. Smith-Christopher, 'The Mixed Marriage Crisis in Ezra 9–10 and Nehemiah 13: A Study of the Sociology of the Post-exilic Judean Community', in *Second Temple Studies 2: Temple and Community in the Persian Period* (JSOTSup 175; ed. T. C. Eskenazi and K. H. Richards; Sheffield: Sheffield Academic Press, 1994), 257. I have discussed the problems associated with failing to distinguish between race, ethnicity, and nationalism elsewhere (Southwood, *Ethnicity*, 31–41). It should be noted that since ethnicity and race are socially constructed, it might be difficult to refer to a 'true' sense of the term.

21 The use of second- *and* third-generation migrants is chosen here because of the difficulty of defining clearly what is meant by 'generation'. There is some degree of debate about the usefulness of the very notion of "generation" as a demographic and sociological concept (Susan Eckstein, 'On Deconstructing and Reconstructing the Meaning of Immigrant Generations', in *The Changing Face of Home: Transnational Lives of the Second Generation* [ed. Peggy Levitt and Mary C. Waters; New York: Russell Sage Foundation, 2002], 211–215; Peter Loizos, 'Generations in Forced Migration: Towards Greater Clarity', *Journal of Refugee Studies* 20 [2007]: 193–209). Kertzer identifies four meanings (David I. Kertzer, 'Generation as a Sociological Problem', *Annual Review of Sociology* 9 [1983]: 129–149: Generation as a principle of kinship descent: here it is a relational, genealogical concept used to define patterns within the larger universe of kinship; generation as life-stage, often referring to a particular life-course segment (infancy, childhood, adolescence, adulthood, middle age, elderly etc.) or to more generalised contrasts (younger generation, older generation, college generation etc.) where there may or may not be a genealogical relation such as parent–child; generation as cohort: a set of similar-age people moving through the life-course, for instance based on a birth cohort; generation as historical period: the mean-

relevant as a heuristic tool for building a picture of post-exilic Yehud than, for example, ancestral return movements with gaps of several centuries.

What is interesting about this research is the number of defining characteristics which mark the language and imagery connected with ancestral return movements. Initially, as Cohen points out, a strong agricultural or gardening trope is evident in the semantics and discourse of diasporas.[22] Diaspora members frequently talk of 'roots', 'ancestral soil' and 'family trees' to the extent that some anthropologists, during fieldwork, have adopted this language, classifying the concept as a whole as 'roots return'.[23] This indicates a special awareness of kinship at an emic level when kinship and land are very closely connected. Although an individual rather than a group example, the experience of Rebecca as recorded within King and Christou's fieldwork, is a classic example of this conceptual connection.[24] Rebecca, a returnee to Greece, responds thus when quizzed about why she decided to return and what it meant for her identity:

> ... I'd been working all over the place and also ignored the fact that I have Greek roots ... and then it was an identity crisis of ... 'Who are you?' This is when I started to discover that it's to do with – not where I'm coming from, not where I was born – but with my ancestors.[25]

Thus, there is another dimension involved in the second-generation's 'return' to the 'homeland'; not only is the journey evidence of their embracing a particular

---

ing used by Eckstein above, where generation is linked to some historical event or to people living/moving in a particular historical period. Further problems occur when we begin to relax these definitions. For example, what about children with one immigrant parent? How do we view children brought to a host country when they are very small? Given the problematic nature of defining this term clearly, second- *and* third-generations are included in order to give an impressionistic portrait of the situation. Such an impressionist portrait is preferred over enforced systematization between generations, such as can be found in other nevertheless commendable studies of later generations: John J. Ahn, *Exile as Forced Migrations: A Sociological, Literary, and Theological Approach on the Displacement and Resettlement of the Southern Kingdom of Judah* (BZAW 417; Berlin: de Gruyter, 2011).

22 Cohen, *Global Diasporas*, 177–178.

23 E.g. Paul Basu, 'Route metaphors of "roots-tourism" in the Scottish Highland diaspora', in *Reframing Pilgrimage: Cultures in Motion* (ed. Simon Coleman and John Eade; London: Routledge, 2004), 150–174.

24 Russell King and Anastasia Christou, *Cultural Geographies of Counter-Diasporic Migration: The Second Generation Returns 'Home'* (Sussex Migration Working Paper 45; Sussex: University of Sussex, 2008), reprinted as 'Cultural Geographies of Counter-Diasporic Migration: Perspectives from the Study of Second-Generation "Returnees" to Greece', *Population, Space and Place* 16 (2010): 103–119.

25 King and Christou, *Cultural Geographies*, 17. The citation is not included in the reprint.

myth of the homeland, created by their parents or grandparents, and an attempt to rediscover and reclaim its sacred sites, it is also the discovery of and search for what Blunt terms 'grounded attachment'.[26] However, from the perspective of those who never left the land the roots metaphor may be interpreted as an expression of a 'darker purpose'. It becomes self-certifying and ends up being emphasized over and above the empirical facts of migration, geography and genealogy to the extent that second- and third-generation returnees often end up being overly keen to emphasize survival narratives of the ancestors.

A good illustration of this idea of roots return are the narratives relating to the lists in Ezra 2:59–63 // Neh 7:61–65. These lists question the authenticity of claims to the land through emphasizing the importance of ancestral roots. Only those who can claim direct genealogical descent can forge an entitlement to the land. As such the sons of the priests whose genealogy was not found are treated as though they are defiled (גאל). This brief narrative taps into an important aspect of roots return: the role of the ancestors. One important aspect about claims to the land, and indeed about emotional attachment to the land, is the perceived link between those who return, the land itself, and the land's connection to the ancestors. This issue has recently been explored in detail with regard to anthropological theory relating to burial. As Stavrakopoulou argues, 'Persian-period incomers ... appropriated traditional land-claiming strategies, thus "indigenizing" themselves by textually re-mapping and re-placing the ancestral dead'.[27] As such, ideas about the territorial dead play a serious role in forging connections with the land. However, the material relating to the idea of roots return reveals another dimension to this link with the land. Not only is it a connection on a political and social level, it is also an emotionally important connection. Ancestors are not simply used to stake a claim in the land, they form part of a larger network of ideas about ethnic identity. As such, making claims to connection with the land through ancestors reveals what Blunt refers to as grounded attachment. Although the results of such ideas about return to, and bonds with, the land are open to manipulation (especially if such ideas are challenged by a perceived ethnic Other on the land), the degree of emotional attachment to the land through ancestors is nevertheless a powerful motivating factor for return, and one which is not necessarily intentionally exclusive from the outset.

---

26 Alison Blunt, 'Cultural Geographies of Migration: Mobility, Transnationality and Diaspora', *Progress in Human Geography* 31 (2007): 684–694 (687).

27 Francesca Stavrakopoulou, *Land of Our Fathers: The Roles of Ancestor Veneration in Biblical Land Claims* (LHBOTS 473; New York / London: T&T Clark, 2010), 136.

A narrative which illustrates the concept of grounded attachment effectively is that of Jacob's death (Gen 47:29–31).

> bury me not (קבר), please, in Egypt:
> But I will lie (שכב) with my fathers,
> and thou shalt carry me out of Egypt,
> and bury me (קבר) in their burying place (Gen 47:30c-31).

Jacob's request that he is buried back in the land is particularly interesting. If some degree of parallelism can be assumed, then the aged plea of the dying man appears to conceptualize burial as unification with the ancestors since the verbs 'bury' and 'lie with' both appear in the second stich. The verb שכב is particularly revealing, usually referring to the death and burial of kings (1 Kgs 2:10; 11:43; 14:20, 31; 15:8, 24; 16:6, 28). Just as a royal line is not broken, so too the narrator suggests that a grounded attachment to the land through ancestral inheritance should not be broken.

If we assume that among those who returned to Yehud, there may have been second- or third-generation individuals who underwent ancestral return migration, then these observations are particularly interesting. Ezra's intermarriage incident is introduced using terminology which explicitly connects the community with the land through what might be termed 'roots metaphors'. The introductory self-ascription of those who returned from the exile, the בני הגולה, is the 'Holy Seed' (זרע הקדש; Ezra 9:2). Moreover, it is reported that the Holy Seed have 'intermingled' (התערב) a metaphoric expression of intermarriage (התחתן) with the 'people of the land' (Ezra 9:2). Of course, it is clear that at this point, the semantic range of the noun 'seed' is being exploited in quite a sophisticated manner to give the metaphoric self-ascription multivalent levels of significance. However, the implication is clear: holy seed and holy soil belong together, or put another way, bad seed will pollute good soil. That is to say, the presence of the ironically named – since it implies possession – 'people of the land' on the land itself defiles the land. This sentiment is especially clear through the powerfully derogatory statement of Ezra 9:11:

> The land you are entering to possess is a land polluted (ארץ נדה) by the corruption (נדה) of its peoples. By their detestable practices (בתועבתיהם) they have filled it with their impurity (בטמאתם) from one end to the other.

Much has been written about this statement, especially with regard to the purity terminology. However, against the context of second and third-generation ancestral return migration, it is especially interesting. We noted how the homeland becomes a sort of mythical place, and how this myth manifests itself in terms of survival narratives and roots metaphors which can be used coercively. When viewed from this perspective the conceptual link between the land and the seed becomes a rallying cry for justifying the Holy Seed's existence on the land, and for denigrating the so-called people of the land in terms of their rights to remain living there. Thus, the author depicts a world where those who have claims to the land are those who can claim ancestral inheritance, rather than those who live there.

A trend reported by many second- and third-generation return migrants, or ancestral return migrants, is the experience of a hybridized identity. In many ways this is a more extreme version of the 'foreign homeland' experienced by returning migrants, just with the additional complication that the "homeland" was always an imagined placed, constructed by parents and grandparents who experienced exile. Since diasporas partake in a 'triangular' relationship with the host society and the homeland it is not surprising that notions of 'home' and 'belonging' for the later generation are likely to be highly ambiguous and multi-layered.[28] King and Christou illustrate how for the second generation, the search for 'belonging' and 'home' is often an extremely powerful, emotional, and even life-changing experience through using the example of Greek-Americans returning to Greece. For these ancestral return migrants, the search for the homeland is 'also a search for ontological security from a world which is otherwise confusing or perceived as moving too fast or in the wrong direction'.[29] That is to say, the second and third-generations may be understood as searching for a final 'resting place' in order to ease the cognitive dissonance, or existential anxiety of half-belonging/not belonging. In many ways such an emotion is comparable to the 'homeland myth' among first-generation returning exiles.[30] In both cases, the 'return' is a loaded nexus of ideas orbiting around an imagined stability and coherence, that is, an attempt to relocate an identity which has been dislocated by experience of exile (or the parents' and grandparents' experiences of exile). This experience is illustrated most profoundly in the case studies by Potter and Phillips concerning people who are casually referred to as 'Bajan-Brits'.[31] The studies illustrated that some Bajan-Brits felt that they did not 'belong' anywhere. As a consequence, they expressed their status of living in the plural world of their parents' origin, after

28 William Safran, 'Diasporas in Modern Societies: Myths of Homeland and Return', *Diaspora* 1/1 (1991): 83–99.
29 King and Christou, *Cultural Geographies*, 16.
30 Southwood, *Ethnicity*, 48–49.
31 Robert B. Potter and Joan Phillips, '"Mad Dogs and International Migrants?" Bajan-Brit Second-Generation Migrants and Accusations of Madness', *Annals of the Association of American Geographers* 96 (2006): 586–600. 'Bajan' is a contraction referring to British citizens who were originally from Barbados or whose ancestors come from there.

having been raised in the colonial 'mother country', as one of 'liminal, hybrid, and in-between positionality'. Thus, the complexity of identity for the second generations mirrors cross-cutting issues connected with ethnicity, class, and age.[32]

In light of these observations, the evidence suggesting a prolonged return movement from exile to postexilic Yehud is particularly significant. Many returnees were probably second-generation descendants. This adds a further level of significance to the self-ascription בני הגולה. In this case, the noun גולה is being used not only to refer to the sustained period of existence away from Yehud, but also to refer to the group who were initially exiled. The observation that ancestral return movements provoke the sense of being an 'outsider,' or of having a hybridized identity, is also interesting in light of the title. It is remarkable that throughout Ezra 9 and 10, the preferred expression of identity is 'Children of the Exile,' rather than 'Holy Seed' or 'Israel.' The paradoxical retention of this title while in the ancestral homeland could, at some level, be understood as a reflection of the on-going consciousness of being 'outsiders', alongside a boundary-marking, self-isolation device. When confronted with the cross-cutting issues of land ownership and tenure, class, and possibly, differences in religious practice, such problematic relationship with the so-called homeland could only have been exacerbated. Thus, as well as referring to a collective 'imagined diaspora', the term בני הגולה also functions as an assertion of ethnic kinship. The בני הגולה are the only group who can claim authentically to be Israel since their ancestry can be traced to pre-exilic times, and as a consequence of this belief they, or at least our author, perceive the necessity for endogamous 'ethnic' barriers.

Conclusions

It is widely acknowledged that the exile was a traumatic event which had a powerful, long-standing, impact upon the religious and social dimensions of Yahwism. However, it must also be acknowledged that the return from exile was just as, if not more, of an ordeal for those who returned. Both events could have, and given the treatment of 'foreign women' within the text, clearly did give rise to a greater consciousness of ethnicity, of its boundaries, of its components, and of its instrumental utility for gaining land and influence. Yet, in light of the case-studies connected to return migration, it seems that the return from exile was potentially *more* devastating than the exile itself; the on-going emotional signifi-

32 Potter and Phillips, 'Mad dogs', 586–592.

cance of the homeland and artificial preservation of the 'old homeland' could only have given rise to disappointment, an emotion all the more pronounced for the ancestral return migrants of later generations. In light of these observations, the simplistic application of the 'exile and return' paradigm which often occurs within scholarship should be dispensed with. Instead, what appears to be the case is a long-standing development of religious and ethnic identities in light of the prevailing complex social forces that often accompany migratory movements. The poignant and ironic consequences of modern return migration movements, which, as has been demonstrated, are that those who stayed in the homeland, now Yehud, are *perceived*, as ethnically and religiously foreign. That is to say, that although they may not be different in what we would term a 'racial' sense, the perception of ethnicity is nevertheless strong enough to manifest itself in the types of behaviours that accompany ethnic difference. As noted, in many ways, this observation brings us back to the challenge of defining and describing ethnicity. In light of the literature relating to the effects of return migration on ethnicity, it is likely that what we find within many accounts concerning return to the land in postexilic literature was more deep-seated than legitimization politics. What emerges is a greater recognition of the social significance of various migrations, even across the generations, which the group responsible for the text are a product of. The consequent sense of dislocation, most palpable through the expressions of diasporic identity, which emerged through returning to Yehud invoked the perception of foreignness. Likewise the sense of vulnerable ethnic identity provoked by such circumstances is likely to have played a pivotal role in the group's emphasis of boundaries and on authenticity. Therefore, ethnic differences progress from being perceived, to being created, and even exacerbated upon return to the homeland.

Peter R. Bedford

Temple Funding and Priestly Authority in Achaemenid Judah

How was the rebuilding of the Jerusalem temple funded, and how were its ongoing expenses met? What does the funding of a shrine tell us about its place in society and the status of those that served there? In keeping with the chronological interests of the volume, this paper attempts to draw out some issues regarding these questions by focusing on the early and middle Persian periods (down through the governorship of Nehemiah, say, ca. 430 BCE).

In the monarchic period, the temple building was funded by the crown and much of the ongoing expenses were met by the crown since the temple functioned to legitimate the kingdom and its ruler, with its functionaries being state officials (funding: 1 Kgs 5–7, 12:26–33; state functionaries: 2 Sam 8:17, 1 Kgs 2:26–27, 4:2–4, 12:31–32, 2 Kgs 12:1–8, 23:4).[1] In the monarchic period the people made freewill donations to the temple (2 Ki 12: 4–16, 22:4); they do not appear to were not required to make payments in the form of a temple tax or other enforced payments to the temple. Tithes and other income (offerings, vows) for the central Jerusalem temple, as well as for local temples, should be construed as voluntary donations, although there were attempts to make their payment obligatory through divine sanction (Deut 12:6, 14:22–29, 18:4, 26:1–15).[2]

---

1 Gösta W. Ahlström, *Royal Administration and National Religion in Ancient Palestine* (SHANE 1; Leiden: Brill, 1982); Carol Meyers, 'Kinship and Kingship: The Early Monarchy', in *The Oxford History of the Biblical World* (ed. Michael D. Coogan; Oxford/New York: Oxford University Press, 1998), 221–271 (256–264); Patrick D. Miller, *The Religion of Ancient Israel* (Library of Ancient Israel; Louisville: Westminster John Knox, 2000), 87–89, 189–197; Rüdiger Lux, 'Der König als Tempelbauer: Anmerkungen zur sakralen Legitimation von Herrschaft im Alten Testament', in *Die Sakralität von Herrschaft: Herrschaftslegitimierung im Wechsel der Zeiten und Räume* (ed. Franz-Reiner Erkens; Akademie Verlag, 2002), 99–122; Detlef Jericke, *Regionaler Kult und lokaler Kult: Studien zur Kult- und Religionsgeschichte Israels und Judas im 9. und 8. Jahrhundert v. Chr.* (Abhandlungen des deutschen Palästina-Vereins 39; Wiesbaden: Harrassowitz, 2010), 37–47, 182–185. I leave aside here questions of dating the building of the first temple.

2 Roland de Vaux, *Ancient Israel: Its Life and Institutions* (trans. John McHugh; London: Darton, Longman & Todd, 1961), 139–142; Marty K. Stevens, *Temples, Tithes, and Taxes: The Temple and the Economic Life of Ancient Israel* (Peabody: Hendrickson, 2006), 93–96, 108–113, 116–118, although Stevens does not usually distinguish between sources pertaining to the monarchic and

---

Peter R. Bedford: Union College, New York

The destruction of the Jerusalem temple attended the demise of the kingdom of Judah. Hopes for Judean restoration featured a rebuilt temple, but with the temple's royal patron lost how would its rebuilding be funded and its ongoing financial needs met? Identifying a patron to oversee funding for the post-monarchic temple is a recurring issue in exilic/post-exilic period biblical texts. Without seeking to be exhaustive, some proposals can be readily noted:

1. Replace the indigenous monarch with the emperor/great king and have that king fulfil the role of benefactor – Deutero-Isaiah seems to do this, at least in respect to temple rebuilding (Cyrus in Isa 44:27–28); as does Ezra in respect to rebuilding and on-going support (Cyrus: Ezr 1:1–11, 6:2–5; Darius: Ezr 6:8–10; Artaxerxes: 7:15, 21–24, 8:25), and Nehemiah with regard to supporting the rebuilding of Jerusalem (Neh 2:1–11). Note that Ezra and Nehemiah both include a role for the wider Jewish community in support of the temple (Ezr 1:6, 2:68–69, 3:7, 7:16, 8:25 [emphasis on diaspora]; Neh 10:1–40 [ET 9:38–10:39] [emphasis on those residing in Judah]) along with the support offered by the imperial rulers.[3]
2. Expect an indigenous monarch, perpetuating monarchic royal ideology, but initial funding for temple rebuilding comes from the community, soon to be supplemented by the international wealth Yahweh controls (community: Hag 1:8; Yahweh's beneficence using international wealth: Hag 2:7–9; Zerubbabel as royal figure: Hag 2:23).[4]

later periods; Oded Lipschits, 'On Cash-Boxes and Finding or Not Finding Books: Jehoash's and Josiah's Decision to Repair the Temple', in *Essays on Ancient Israel in Its Near Eastern Context: A Tribute to Nadav Na'aman* (ed. Yairah Amit *et al.*; Winona Lake: Eisenbrauns, 2006), 239–254 (243–249); Moshe Weinfeld, *Deuteronomy and the Deuteronomic School* (Oxford: Clarendon Press, 1972; repr. Winona Lake: Eisenbrauns, 1992), 213–217. As I consider P and H to be post-monarchic texts, they are included in the ensuing discussion.

3 On Cyrus as temple builder in Deutero-Isaiah, see, e.g., Reinhard G. Kratz, *Kyros im Deuterojesaja-Buch* (FAT 1; Tübingen: Mohr Siebeck, 1991), 183–191; Antti Laato, *The Servant of YHWH and Cyrus: A Reinterpretation of the Exilic Messianic Programme* (CBOTS 35; Stockholm: Almqvist & Wiksell, 1992), 177–187; Lisbeth Fried, 'Cyrus the Messiah? The Historical Background to Isaiah 45:1', *HTR* 95 (2002): 373–393. On the Ezra-Nehemiah texts, an orientation to the issues they raise can be obtained from H. G. M. Williamson, *Ezra, Nehemiah* (WBC 16; Waco: Word Books, 1985); Joseph Blenkinsopp, *Ezra-Nehemiah: A Commentary* (OTL; Philadelphia: Westminster, 1988); Christiane Karrer, *Ringen um die Verfassung Judas: Eine Studie zu den theologisch-politischen Vorstellungen im Esra-Nehemia-Buch* (BZAW 308; Berlin/New York: de Gruyter, 2001).

4 Peter R. Bedford, *Temple Restoration in Early Achaemenid Judah* (SJSJ 65; Leiden/Boston: Brill, 2001), 140–152, 237–254.

3. Institute a diarchy of indigenous royal figure and high priest, with responsibilities for funding unclear; some contributions made by diaspora (Hag 1:1, 12, 2:2, 4; Zech 6:10–11, 15).[5]
4. Dispense with royal patron in favour of Yahweh providing for the temple from the wealth of the nations who are coming to Zion and from donations given by repatriates/diaspora (Isa 60).[6]
5. Dispense with royal patron in favour of another indigenous leader who assumes responsibility for ensuring that the community supports the temple (*nasî'* in Ezek 45:13–17; governor in Neh 10, 13:4–14, 13:31; prophet in Mal 1:14, 3:6–12.[7]
6. Dispense with royal patron in favour of a putative pre-monarchic model in which another figure, sanctioned by divine authority, ensures that the community takes responsibility for funding (Moses: Ex 25:1–9, 30:11–16, 35:4–29; Priests: Lev 25, Lev 27).[8]

---

5 So, e.g., Carol L. Meyers and Eric M. Meyers, *Haggai, Zechariah 1–8* (AB 25B; Garden City: Doubleday, 1987); Bernard Gosse, 'Le governeur et le grand prêtre, et quelques problèmes de fonctionnement de la communauté postexilique: Au sujet des rapports entre les charismatiques et l'autorité religieuse et civile dans le cadre de l'empire perse', *Transeuphratène* 21 (2001): 149–173.
6 Jacques Vermeylen, *Jérusalem centre du monde: Développements et contestations d'une tradition biblique* (Lectio divina; Paris: Cerf, 2007), 166–180; Shalom M. Paul, *Isaiah 40–66: Translation and Commentary* (Eerdmans Critical Commentary; Grand Rapids: Eerdmans, 2012), 514–535.
7 On the *nasî'* in Ezekiel, see, e.g., Iain M. Duguid, *Ezekiel and the Leaders of Israel* (VTSup 56; Leiden: Brill, 1994), 50–57; Brian Boyle, 'The Figure of the *nasî'* in Ezekiel's Vision of the New Temple (Ezekiel 40–48)', *ABR* 58 (2010): 1–16; and Madhavi Nevader in this volume. On the governor in Nehemiah, see, e.g., Michael Heltzer, 'The Social and Fiscal Reforms of Nehemia in Judah and the Attitude of the Achaemenid Kings to the Internal Affairs of the Autonomous Provinces', in *The Province Judah and Jews in Persian Times: (Some Connected Questions of the Persian Empire)* (ed. Michael Heltzer; Tel Aviv: Achaeological Center Publication, 2008), 71–93; Ran Zadok, 'Some Issues in Ezra-Nehemiah', in *New Perspectives on Ezra-Nehemiah: History and Historiography, Text, Literature, and Interpretation* (ed. Isaac Kalimi; Winona Lake: Eisenbrauns, 2012), 160–170. On Malachi, see, e.g., Rainer Kessler, 'Die Theologie der Gabe bei Maleachi', in *Das Manna fällt auch heute noch: Beiträge zur Geschichte und Theologie des Alten, Ersten Testaments: Festschrift für Erich Zenger* (ed. Frank-Lothar Hossfeld and Ludger Schwienhorst-Schönberger; Freiburg: Herder, 2004), 392–407, esp. 403–404. Both the *nasî'* and Nehemiah have been thought by some commentators to exhibit royal roles. In addition to the studies above see also, for Nehemiah, Isabelle de Castelbajac, 'Les sources deutéronomistes de la figure royale de Néhemie', *Transeuphratène* 30 (2005): 65–76.
8 On Moses, see, e.g., Eckart Otto, *Die Tora des Mose: Die Geschichte der literarischen Vermittlung von Recht, Religion und Politik durch die Mosegestalt* (Berichte aus den Sitzungen der Joachim Jungius-Gesellschaft der Wissenschaften e. V., Hamburg 19/2; Göttingen: Vandenhoeck & Ruprecht, 2001), which links the development of Moses' royal roles to the Assyrian period; Danny Mathews, *Royal Motifs in the Pentateuchal Portrayal of Moses* (LHBOTS 571; London: T & T

7. Recognize that the monarchic period models how the community has historically taken financial responsibility for the temple along with the king, and that now without a king the community is positioned to assume that role (Chronicles).[9]

These various models, which of course do not exhaust the diversity of scholarly interpretations, raise issues for the ideology of the temple in the post-monarchic setting. Without indigenous kingship and political autonomy, what does the temple symbolize? Does it still legitimate ruler and polity, with the expectation of the ruler's responsibility to support and superintend the temple? How are 'ruler' and 'polity' to be defined? In respect to funding, in short, if the Jerusalem temple is no longer a Judean royal shrine, who has responsibility for its funding? The answer is not clear in the texts.

Equally unclear is exactly what is due to the temple from the community. To rehearse the texts mentioned above: in Ezek 45:13–17 a levy is placed on wheat, barley, oil, and sheep; in Hag 1:8, 14 mention is made only of cutting beams for the temple and labouring to build it; Zech 6:10–11 mentions only contributions in silver and gold from the diaspora; Mal 1:14 and 3:6–12 identify sacrifices that are vowed and tithes that are required to be paid; Ezr 1:6, 2:68–69, 3:7, 7:16 and 8:25 note contributions from the diaspora in silver and gold; Ex 30:11–16 introduces a half shekel poll tax and contributions of various kinds (*tĕrūmā* including metals, fabrics, spices, gems, jewellery, and other items; Ex 25:1–9, 35:4–29); Leviticus lists tariffs for vows and the redemption of consecrated objects (Lev 27) and perhaps the reclamation of lands (Lev 25); 2 Chronicles 31 emphasizes the payment of tithes; and Nehemiah has a list that includes one third of a shekel poll tax, first fruits and first born animals, tithes paid to Levites, and wood consignment for altar sacrifices (Neh 10:33–40 [ET 32–39]), with the imposition and collection of tithes mentioned again in Neh 13:10–12, 31 (wood consignment also in v. 31). Many of these are arguably free-will donations, including the contribu-

Clark, 2012). On priests, see, e.g., Rainer Albertz, *A History of Religion in the Old Testament Period* (2 vols; trans. John Bowden; London: SCM Press, 1994) 2.459–464; Gabriele Boccaccini, *Roots of Rabbinic Judaism: An Intellectual History, from Ezekiel to Daniel* (Grand Rapids: Eerdmans, 2002), 43–82; James C. VanderKam, *From Joshua to Caiaphas: High Priests after the Exile* (Minneapolis: Fortress Press, 2004), 1–111.

9 So, Roddy L. Braun, 'The Message of Chronicles: Rally "Round the Temple"', *Concordia Theological Monthly* 42 (1971): 502–514; William Riley, *King and Cultus in Chronicles: Worship and the Reinterpretation of History* (JSOTSup 160; Sheffield: Sheffield Academic Press, 1993). Other readings of Chronicles promote the central role of priestly authority, so, for example, Jonathan E. Dyke, *The Theocratic Ideology of the Chronicler* (BIS 33; Leiden/Boston: Brill, 1998).

tions from the diaspora. And some of the tariffs in Leviticus 27 also pertain to free-will offerings. In addition to community contributions, Persian rulers are said to make donations and give tax breaks to temple personnel (Cyrus: Ezr 1:1–11, 6:2–5; Darius: Ezr 6:8–10; Artaxerxes: 7:15, 21–24, 8:25).[10]

I am suspicious of claims that the Achaemenid Persian administration stepped into the role vacated by indigenous kingship to ensure that the Jerusalem temple was funded.[11] The contention has been made that the temple and its personnel served as an arm of the imperial administration. Local taxes for the empire, as well as state sanctioned taxes for the upkeep of the temple, were housed in the temple and overseen by its personnel, thus ensuring a reliable income stream and a central role for the temple and its personnel. Contemporary Babylonian temples are sometimes adduced as models for the Jerusalem temple in the Persian period in this regard. However, the former were never largely dependent on royal largesse, so under foreign political control they could keep their long-standing funding models, which were based on agriculture and manufacturing, connecting leading urban families to the temple through land allotments and prebends.[12] This does not appear to be an applicable model for the Jerusalem temple in the Achaemenid

10 On payments to the temple in the Achaemenid Persian period, see Melody D. Knowles, *Centrality Practiced: Jerusalem in the Religious Practice of Yehud and the Diaspora in the Persian Period* (Archaeology and Biblical Studies 16; Atlanta: Society of Biblical Literature, 2006), 105–120, who highlights modes of funding for the temple without drawing out the issue of who takes responsibility to ensure the funding; see also Herbert Niehr, 'Abgaben an den Tempel im Yehud der Achaimenidenzeit', in *Geschenke und Steuern, Zölle und Tribute: Antike Abgabenformen in Anspruch und Wirklichkeit* (CHANE 29; ed. H. Klinkott, S. Kubisch and R. Müller-Wollerman; Leiden/Boston: Brill, 2007), 141–157.

11 The nature of this relationship between the Achaemenid imperial administration and the Jerusalem temple has been modeled in various ways; see, e.g., Meyers and Meyers, *Haggai, Zechariah 1–8*; Joseph Blenkinsopp, 'Temple and Society in Achaemenid Judah', in *Second Temple Studies, Vol. 1: Persian Period* (JSOTSup 117; ed. Philip R. Davies; Sheffield: Sheffield Academic Press, 1991), 22–53; Joel P. Weinberg, *The Citizen-Temple Community* (trans. Daniel L. Christopher; JSOTSup 151; Sheffield: Sheffield Academic Press, 1992); Joel P. Weinberg, *Der Chronist in seiner Mitwelt* (BZAW 239; Berlin/New York: de Gruyter, 1996); Joachim Schaper, 'The Jerusalem Temple as an Instrument of the Achaemenid Fiscal Administration', *VT* 45 (1995): 528–539; Joachim Schaper, 'The Temple Treasury Committee in the Times of Nehemiah and Ezra', *VT* 47 (1997): 200–206; Joachim Schaper, *Priester und Leviten im achämenidischen Juda: Studien zur Kult- und Sozialgeschichte Israels in persischer Zeit* (FAT 31; Tübingen: Mohr Siebeck, 2000); Stevens, *Temples, Tithes, and Taxes*; Kyong-Jin Lee, *The Authority and Authorization of the Torah in the Persian Period* (CBET 64; Leuven: Peeters, 2010), 177–195.

12 Caroline Waerzeggers, *The Ezida Temple of Borsippa: Priesthood, Cult, Archives* (Achaemenid History 15; Leiden: Nederlands Instituut voor het Nabije Oosten, 2010).

Persian period.[13] Recent studies by Lipschits and Vanderhooft on the Yehud stamp impressions from Ramat Rahel further bear out how the Jerusalem temple, and arguably the city itself, was not the economic and administrative hub some have supposed. Ramat Rahel, not Jerusalem, was the main administrative centre from the late sixth through third centuries BCE, based on the corpus of Yehud stamps.[14] By the end of the Persian period, when the High Priest in Jerusalem obtained authority to mint small denomination coins, one could say that the temple was undertaking an administrative role.[15] Before then such a claim is problematic.

The Persian empire was not interested in implementing and administering a taxation system in support of local cults. It was interested in meeting the costs for its imperial administration and shifting wealth to satrapal and imperial capitals and to the ruling elite. Most of the texts reviewed above ostensibly claim that funding for the temple was actually on the basis of voluntary donation, not formal taxation. Texts from the early Persian period, such as Haggai and Malachi, show that the community had to be cajoled into making the donations. The prospect of divine blessing or (the continuation of) divine curse was the incentive held out to an agricultural-based community on the edge of economic survival. Nehemiah 10, perhaps relating to the middle Persian period, looks like a formal arrangement for funding the temple, assuming this text reflects an historical event, but in this instance also people make a choice to participate in the 'binding agreement' (Neh 10:1 [ET 9:38]). In both the early and middle Persian period examples moral obligation to support the temple is emphasized rather than administrative

---

13 Peter R. Bedford, 'The Economic Role of the Jerusalem Temple in Achaemenid Judah: Comparative Perspectives', in *Shai le-Sara Japhet: Studies in the Bible, its Exegesis and Language* (ed. M. Bar-Anbar *et al.*; Jerusalem: Bialik Institute, 2007), 3*–20*.

14 Oded Lipschits, 'Persian-Period Judah: A New Perspective', in *Texts, Contexts and Readings in Postexilic Literature: Explorations into Historiography and Identity Negotiation in Hebrew Bible and Related Texts* (FAT 53; ed. Louis Jonker; Tübingen: Mohr Siebeck, 2011), 187–211; Oded Lipschits and David S. Vanderhooft, *The Yehud Stamp Impressions: A Corpus of Inscribed Impressions from the Persian and Hellenistic Periods in Judah* (Winona Lake: Eisenbrauns, 2011). Alexander Fantalkin and Oren Tal, 'The Canonization of the Pentateuch: When and Why?', *ZAW* 124 (2012): 1–18, 201–212 (17 n. 49), contend, against Lipschits and Vanderhooft, that the "most logical assumption" is that these stamps are connected to the Jerusalem temple, providing for "cultic needs and method of income".

15 Peter B. Machinist, "The First Coins of Judah and Samaria: Numismatics and History in the Achaemenid and Early Hellenistic Periods," in *Achaemenid History VIII: Continuity and Change* (ed. Heleen Sancisi-Weerdenburg, Amélie Kuhrt, Margaret C. Root; Leiden: Nederlands Instituut voor het Nabije Osten, 1994), 365–379, esp. 376: "the hints suggest a connection between the change from governor to priestly rule and closeness to, or independence from, the central Achaemenid administration"; Bedford, *Temple Restoration*, 204–206.

injunction. The exception is Nehemiah 13 where, as governor, Nehemiah demands reforms in respect to the temple (including the funding of Levites through tithes) and also to social and economic practices.

It would appear from the discussion so far that one point emerges quite clearly: the Jerusalem temple priesthood did not have the authority to extract payments from the community in support of the temple (formal taxes, if you like). If authority to tax is a clear sign of political power, then the priesthood did not have it. The community may impose payments on themselves (Neh 10) and have the governor police them (Neh 13), assuming the narrative flow of Nehemiah reflects historical events, but this still underlines the fact that the priesthood lacked the power to demand them.

Allow me to touch on two episodes from the history of Achaemenid Judah which I believe highlight the relative political weakness of the priesthood. The first concerns the rebuilding of the Jerusalem temple which took place in the reign of Darius I between 520–515. I have argued at length elsewhere that the rebuilding is not an initiative of the Persians reflecting an empire-wide administrative policy towards the cults of subjugated peoples nor does the rebuilt temple serve as an arm of the Persian provincial administration.[16] This is significant since it means that political authority was not devolved by the Persians to the Jerusalem priesthood. The Persians relied on governors to rule on their behalf, the earliest ones being Sheshbazzar and Zerubbabel, the latter serving at the time of the rebuilding of the temple. Their appointment reflects the Persian predilection to draw on local elites to serve in administrative posts, but it is noteworthy that in this context 'local' does not mean someone necessarily living in the district in which they take up their post. It can mean, as it does here and with Ezra and Nehemiah and perhaps others, that the appointee lives elsewhere in the empire but has kin in or some historic cultural connection to the district.

What was the authority of the Jerusalem priesthood? At the time of the temple rebuilding the authority of the Jerusalem priesthood was limited to their brief to re-establish that cult as a legitimate enterprise. They had social status related to their roles and responsibilities in the temple, but that did not translate into political power.[17] Notions of a temple-state headed by the high priest, or a diarchy

---

16 Peter R. Bedford, 'Early Achaemenid Monarchs and Indigenous Cults: Toward the Definition of Imperial Policy', in *Religion in the Ancient World: New Themes and Approaches* (ed. Matthew Dillon; Amsterdam: Hakkert, 1996), 14–39; Bedford, *Temple Restoration*, 132–157, 183–230; Bedford, 'Economic Role'.

17 Deborah W. Rooke, *Zadok's Heirs: The Role and Development of the High Priesthood in Ancient Israel* (OTM; Oxford: Oxford University Press, 2000), 125–239; Bedford, *Temple Restoration*, 202–206.

in which power was shared between the governor and the high priest, or the temple as a center for taxation and the administration of law with the temple personnel supervising such matters are problematic, basically because the evidence adduced in their support is commonly drawn from supposed parallels elsewhere in the Achaemenid Persian empire.[18] The parallels are predicated on the premise that the imperial administration pursued empire-wide policies in respect to temples and their personnel or at least drew on administrative models that successfully made use of temples elsewhere in the empire. In my opinion neither is likely to be true. The Persians were keen to develop relevant local administrative practices, thus permitting variation, and they distinguished between important provinces, such as Babylonian and Egypt, and relatively unimportant districts, such as Judah, in governing the empire.[19] Such diversity is arguably an important factor in the durability of the empire. Attempts to use comparative administrative practices to aid our understanding of what was happening in Judah is understandable, but it is misleading if the supposed parallels turn out to be inaccurate. The proposed economic role of the Jerusalem temple based on parallels with Babylonian temples is a good case in point.[20]

So the political power of the Jerusalem priesthood was circumscribed, arguably limited to affairs directly related to the temple, although not including a means to guarantee funding for these affairs. Zerubbabel's remit is difficult to determine precisely, although I expect that it did not initially include a brief for the rebuilding of the temple. That this emerged during his tenure is telling for Judean perceptions of legitimate political authority. The restoration of the temple was seen as marking the end of the divine ire with the people, which had resulted in the destruction of the kingdom and the temple. The rebuilt temple would allow Yahweh to return to Jerusalem, manifest his kingship, and restore Judah and its people to political and religious normalcy. Zerubbabel's arrival was a catalyst to this goal since he was from the Judean royal family. As in the monarchic period, it was expected that the king would take responsibility for temple building. The prophets Haggai and Zechariah were careful to couch their call for rebuilding in terms that would not be politically threatening to the Persian imperial authorities, but they both reflect an understanding that political authority and its concomitant responsibilities are in continuity with the monarchic period.

18 See the discussion in Bedford, *Temple Restoration*, 183–207; Bedford, 'Economic Role', 14*–20*.

19 See the discussion in Bedford, *Temple Restoration*, 132–152.

20 I have in mind in particular here the supposed roles of the temple in (i) legitimating land holding and (ii) serving fiscal administration; see the discussion in Bedford, *Temple Restoration*, 207–230; Bedford, 'Economic Role'.

For the second episode we move forward in time some seventy years after the rebuilding of the Jerusalem temple to consider the authority of the Jerusalem priesthood under the governorship of Nehemiah. It has already been mentioned that the temple did not supervise the collection of taxes and, concomitantly, it did not have the authority to tax. Who did have the authority to tax? This is clearly a central question in reflecting on political power. In monarchic Judah, it was a right exercised by the king. Obviously the Persian empire exercised this right to extract taxes from its subjugated territories, and its oversight would have been one of the main responsibilities of the governor. In the Nehemiah Memoir (Neh 1–7, 12:27–43, 13:4–31), we can garner some important information about political power reflected through forms of taxation, even while recognizing the self-serving character of the narrative. (Of a number of actions Nehemiah recounts he petitions: 'Remember for my good, O my God, all that I have done for this people' Neh 5:19; 13:14, 21, 30.)

Ezra 4:13 mentions that Judeans had to pay taxes of three types: *mindā/middā*, *belō*, and *hălāḵ*, conventionally taken to refer to tribute, poll tax, and land tax respectively. These are due to the empire. There is a further tax imposed by the Persians to support their local administration. This is 'the food allowance of the governor', which Nehemiah mentions he generously revoked to ease the tax burden on Judeans (Neh 5:14–15). This means that while Nehemiah had no authority to adjust *middā*, *belō*, and *hălāḵ*, he could claim authority over the governor's tax. What of other imposts? The Nehemiah memoir makes mention of payments due to the temple in support of the Levites (Neh 13:5, 10–14). These are annual tithes. It is notable that while they are related to the temple, it is Nehemiah the governor who claims the authority to demand their payment by Judeans and have them disbursed to the Levites, not anyone representing the temple. In this way Nehemiah exercises responsibilities earlier held by Judean kings (note the episodes recounting the refurbishment of the temple and the paying of tithes in 2 Kings 12 [Jehoash] and 2 Chr 29–31 [Hezekiah]). It is worth pointing out in this context that when it came to pressuring upper-class Judeans to relieve the debts of their fellow Judeans who had borrowed from them to meet tax obligations (Neh 5:1–13), Nehemiah depends on moral suasion to move them rather than command them by right of office. He had no political authority to do the latter. But he did have the political authority to abrogate the governor's tax and to demand payment of tithes to the temple by Judeans.

Nehemiah's authority to demand payment of the tithes can be contrasted with the lack of political power held by the Jerusalem priesthood. In the book of Malachi, conventionally dated to just before the time of Nehemiah, the prophet remonstrates with his fellow Judeans, priests and people, for their sub-standard offerings and provision of only partial tithes. The prophet can threaten divine punishment for those who fail to meet their responsibilities to the temple (Mal 1:14, 3:10–11), but neither priests nor prophet has the political power to make the community conform to their demands.

Nehemiah's authority also extended to demanding corvée labour, another form of taxation. On his arrival in Judah to take up his appointment as governor, Nehemiah informs 'the Judeans, the priests, the nobles, the officials and the rest that were to do the work' (Neh 2:16) that they would be restoring the walls of Jerusalem (Neh 3). Nehemiah does not attempt to garner their support by means of a lengthy speech persuading them of their moral obligations as he later does in chapter 5 regarding debt remission. Rather, the Judean leaders, including the priests, accept the imposition of the work detail after few words, and accept Nehemiah's direction on organizing the work groups and assigning them their stations.[21]

Nehemiah's authority over the Jerusalem temple was not limited to ensuring that tithes were paid. In Nehemiah chapter 13 he evicts from the temple precinct Tobiah the Ammonite, who had taken up residence there thanks to his relative Eliashib the (high?) priest. He appoints treasurers over the temple storehouses, he enforces observance of the Sabbath by halting trading, he commands the

21 On the wall rebuilding as corvée labour, see Aaron Demsky, '*Pelekh* in Nehemiah 3', *IEJ* 33 (1983): 242–244; Hayim Tadmor, 'Judah', in *The Cambridge Ancient History, Vol. 6* (2nd ed.; ed. David M. Lewis *et al.*; Cambridge: Cambridge University Press, 1994), 262–296 (279); Lisbeth S. Fried, *The Priest and the Great King: Temple-Palace Relations in the Persian Empire* (Biblical and Judaic Studies 10; Winona Lake: Eisenbrauns, 2004), 200; André Lemaire, 'Administration in Fourth-Century B.C.E. Judah in Light of Epigraphy and Numismatics', in *Judah and the Judeans in the Fourth Century B.C.E.* (ed. Oded Lipschits, Gary N. Knoppers and Rainer Albertz; Winona Lake, IN: Eisenbrauns, 2007), 53–54 (61). H. G. M. Williamson, 'The Family in Persian Period Judah: Some Textual Reflections', in *Symbiosis, Symbolism, and the Power of the Past: Canaan, Ancient Israel, and Their Neighbors from the Late Bronze Age through Roman Palaestina* (ed. William G. Dever and Seymour Gitin; Winona Lake: Eisenbrauns, 2003), 469–485 (476 n. 4), rightly notes that the use of *pelek̲* in Neh 3 does necessary mean 'corvée labor', although Zadok, 'Some Issues', 164, affirms that the *śr plk* were functionaries that 'controlled teams of workmen'. While I view Nehemiah's purpose in rebuilding Jerusalem to be the establishment of the city as the provincial capital, thus making the wall rebuilding an undertaking of the imperial administration, it must be recognized that the evidence can be construed otherwise; so, Lester L. Grabbe, *A History of the Jews and Judaism in the Second Temple Period* (LSTS 47; 2 vols.; London: T & T Clark, 2004), 1.298: '... we cannot rule out some sort of Persian imperial project, but we also cannot rule out that Nehemiah was primarily carrying out his own personal mission, compelled by his own vision of how things should be in Judah and Jerusalem. Nor can we rule out a combination of the two, but the text gives little support to such an idea'. If Nehemiah was not acting in this matter as a state official, then his organization of labour for rebuilding the wall may need to be considered in other terms; see below n. 25.

Levites to purify themselves, he disciplines those who have married 'foreign' women, including the son of the high priest, and, to quote him directly 'established the duties of the priests and Levites, each in his work; and I provided for the wood offering, at appointed times, and for the first fruits' (Neh 13:30–31). In short, Nehemiah the governor had authority over the temple. The authority of the high priest is quite limited relative to this.

Nehemiah may well represent the forms of authority exercised by governors in Achaemenid Judah. It is undeniable, and hardly surprising, that this Persian administrative appointee, while a 'local' in that his kin and cultural connections were in Judah, dutifully exercises his authority in submission to his Achaemenid Persian overlords. His authority comes from the Persians, and he governs on their behalf. But from a Judean perspective, at least in respect to taxation and the Jerusalem temple, he fulfils royal responsibilities (cf. the report cited by Sanballat of Samaria that 'you [Nehemiah] wish to become their king', Neh 6:6).

Nehemiah's memoir is by no means the final word on the authority of the high priest in Achaemenid Judah, not the least given its self-serving purpose. It does seem, though, that the authority of the high priest perhaps develops only after the governorship of Nehemiah in circumstances that are less than clear. The letter written from the Judean community in Elephantine in 407 petitioning Bagavahya, the governor of Judah, to lend his political support to the rebuilding of their temple mentions an earlier missive sent to 'Je(ho)ḫanan the high priest and his colleagues the priests'.[22] It was expected that the priests in Jerusalem had political influence they could exercise on behalf of their fellow Judeans in Egypt. Notably, the response in support of rebuilding the temple arguably comes from the governor, since his is the office with authority.[23] As already noted, the minting of coins stamped with the name of the high priest is arguably a sign of growing political authority. The earliest examples, one with the name Yoḫanan, another with the name Yaddua, are dated by Cross to the early fourth century, although some others (Spaer, Barag) date the Yaddua coin to c. 420.[24] It must be admitted

22 TAD A4.7 = CAP 30:18–19.

23 TAD A4.9 = CAP 32.

24 Frank Moore Cross, 'A Reconstruction of the Judean Restoration', in *From Epic to Canon: History and Literature in Ancient Israel* (Baltimore: The Johns Hopkins University Press, 1998), 151–172 (153–154), revised and expanded edition of *JBL* 94 (1975); Arnold Spaer, "Jaddua the High Priest?" *Israel Numismatic Journal* 9 (1986–87): 1–3; Dan Barag, "A Silver Coin of Yohanan the High Priest and the Coinage of Judea in the Fourth Century B. C.," *Israel Numismatic Journal* 9 (1986–87): 4–21.

that the dating of the coins to the Achaemenid Persian period and their significance are contested.[25]

It appears that among Nehemiah's actions as governor were formalizing certain payments for the temple, and as such this contradicts my earlier claim that temple funding was basically a voluntary undertaking. In Nehemiah 13 (Nehemiah 10 will be discussed below), tithes in support of the Levites and the wood consignment (for sacrifices, one expects) are specifically mentioned (Neh 13:10–14, 31). Up until this point in time they must not have been mandatory. They may have been *expected* to be paid, as befitting a member of the Judean community, but Nehemiah uses his political authority to ensure their payment. He makes community members pay what they are morally obligated to pay. That is to say, given that the payments are morally obligated, they are not formal taxes. They are contributions that are socially prescribed, but that have for whatever reason fallen from being a priority.

It is worthwhile teasing out something more on the nature of these contributions. Economists have recently been studying 'informal taxation' in developing economies whereby local communities have an expectation of contributions of labour or money from families, according to their relative means, to support communal projects that have been introduced by the government.[26] (One example: in Central Java, Indonesia the district government delivered 29 drums of raw asphalt to resurface a road. Leaders of the local community assigned households an expected contribution in labour or money to complete the project).[27] There is a powerful social expectation that a contribution will be made in order to ensure the successful completion of the project for the public good. The government needs to know the nature of local 'informal taxation' so that it spares itself sending resources to a community that has a developed expectation that its

---

25 See the discussion in Machinist, "The First Coins of Judah"; L. Mildenberg, "*yehud* und *smryn*. Über das Geld der persischen Provinzen Juda und Samaria im 4. Jahrhundert," in *Geschichte-Tradition-Reflexion. Festschrift für Martin Hengel zum 70. Geburtstag* (2 vols; ed. Hubert Cancik, Hermann Lichtenberger and Peter Schäfer; Tübingen: Mohr Siebeck, 1996), 1.119–46; Schaper, *Priester und Leviten*, 153–161; Joachim Schaper, "Numismatic, Epigraphik, alttestamentliche Exegese und die Frage nach politischen Verfassung des achämenidischen Juda," *ZDPV* 118 (2002): 150–168.

26 Benjamin A. Olken and Monica Singhal, "Informal Taxation," *American Economic Journal: Applied Economics* 3 (2011): 1–28. "We define informal taxation as a system of local public goods finance coordinated by public officials but enforced socially rather than through the formal legal system" (p. 2).

27 Olken and Singhal, "Informal Taxation," 4–5.

members will provide certain goods and services themselves, thus freeing up that money to be expended elsewhere on other projects.

The focus here is on projects instigated by government. Regarding the Jerusalem temple, I would contend that while it was officially sanctioned by the Persian administration, it was not instigated by them.[28] Nevertheless, this arguably amounts to much the same thing in respect to 'informal taxation'. The temple was a government-sanctioned public work for local good, much of whose costs (for rebuilding and ongoing maintenance, and for its personnel) the government expected the local community to meet. The local community had responsibility for organizing how these costs were to be met. In short, the government was either financially unable or unwilling to fund these local projects, either instigated by them or desired by the local community, and so sought payments in support of the project. The means of payment, the amounts contributed by various community members, and the sanctions for non-compliance are handled by the local community. There are other examples to suggest that the Achaemenid Persian empire was conscious of the place of 'informal taxation' in the imperial economy, with local communities taking financial responsibility for projects which might receive some support from the imperial administration, and which were certainly conducted under the monitoring eye of the state.[29] Contributions to the temple may have been expected in a context of strong social sanction, so that while technically they can be described as 'donations', they more realistically can be considered 'informal taxation'.[30]

---

28 This is a central contention of Bedford, *Temple Restoration.*

29 See the examples taken from Babylonia, Egypt, and Asia Minor, specifically regarding temples, discussed in Fried, *The Priest and the Great King*; a number of these examples are also discussed in Sebastian Grätz, *Das Edikt des Artaxerxes. Eine Untersuchung zum religionspolitischen und historischen Umfeld von Esra 7,12–26* (BZAW 337; Berlin/New York: de Gruyter, 2004). At the symposium Caroline Waerzeggers drew my attention to a likely example from Borsippa in the Neo-Babylonian period in which the priests of the Ezida temple undertook construction of a temple wall commissioned by Neriglissar and continued under Nabonidus. She discusses this project in Waerzeggers, *The Ezida Temple of Borsippa*, 337–345. In this example there is a strict requirement for payment since the government has imposed the project on the temple personnel, while the means of payment are worked out locally. Nehemiah's wall building project (Neh 2:11–3:32) might also be an example of informal taxation if the requisite payments, largely in terms of labour on the wall, were determined by the members of the community rather than by the government (here represented by Nehemiah). The matter is complicated by the fact that Nehemiah views himself as a member of the local Judean community as well as the official representative of the imperial administration.

30 Olkin and Singhal, 'Informal Taxation', 19–27, discuss four 'non-mutually exclusive' explanations for informal taxation, one of which is 'altruistic voluntary contributions'. These are 'contri-

Who, then, was part of the community that saw itself as 'connected' to the Jerusalem temple, on whom such informal taxes could be levied? We might expect they would be persons or families or extended kin groups that sufficiently identified themselves with the Jerusalem temple to accept the social demands for such payments. But is that a matter of self-identification, or is there a mechanism or an authority for determining who is among the group that should pay?

Here we enter the debate regarding the marking of the boundaries in the post-exilic Judean community.[31] I have argued elsewhere that in the early Persian period the repatriates were open to accepting Judeans who had never gone into exile and that the distinction between repatriates and non-repatriates was introduced later after Nehemiah by Judeans who had remained in the Babylonian-Elamite diaspora, in order to solidify their connection to the homeland, through the repatriates that lived there, and to legitimate the experience of exile.[32] Rejection of 'foreigners', defined to include Judeans who had never gone into exile, Samarians, and any other non-exiled Yahwists in the region, was fundamental to

butions [that] may be purely voluntary, reflecting "warm glow" in the provision of public goods' (26). The other three explanations are: informal taxation as a response to legal restraints on formal taxes ('local communities are unable to raise formal taxes to fund their preferred level of public goods, and informal taxation is therefore the only funding mechanism available to them', 25); informal taxation as an optimal response to information and enforcement constraints ('informal taxation reflects the desire of communities to impose more redistributive [socially enforced] tax schedules than are feasible under formal taxation, by taking advantage of local information about income within the community that is observable but not verifiable', 26); informal taxation as user fees ('informal taxation may also represent pre-paid user fees, particularly for goods that are excludable', 26).

31 An extensive scholarly literature has developed around this topic in recent years, especially in respect to intermarriage (Ezr 9–10, Neh 13), see, e.g., by way of orientation to the key issues, Jörn Kiefer, *Exil und Diaspora: Begrifflichkeit und Deutungen im antiken Judentum und in der hebräischen Bibel* (Arbeiten zur Bibel und ihrer Geschichte 19; Leipzig: Evangelische Verlagsanstalt, 2005); David Goodblatt, *Elements of Ancient Jewish Nationalism* (Cambridge: Cambridge University Press, 2006); Joseph Blenkinsopp, *Judaism: The First Phase: The Place of Ezra and Nehemiah in the Origins of Judaism* (Grand Rapids: Eerdmans, 2009); Christian Frevel (ed.), *Mixed Marriages: Intermarriage and Group Identity in the Second Temple Period* (LHBOTS 547; London/New York: T & T Clark, 2011); Oded Lipschits, Gary N. Knoppers and Manfred Oeming (eds.), *Judah and the Judeans in the Achaemenid Period: Negotiating Identity in an International Context* (Winona Lake: Eisenbrauns, 2011); Katherine E. Southwood, *Ethnicity and the Mixed Marriage Crisis in Ezra 9–10: An Anthropological Approach* (OTM; Oxford/New York: Oxford University Press, 2012); Ralf Rothenbusch, *"... abgesondert zur Tora Gottes hin": Ethnische und religiöse Identitäten im Esra/Nehemiabuch* (Herders Biblische Studien 70; Freiburg: Herder, 2012); Jeremiah W. Cataldo, *Breaking Monotheism: Yehud and the Material Formation of Monotheistic Identity* (LHBOTS 565; London/New York: Bloomsbury T & T Clark, 2012).

32 Peter R. Bedford, 'Diaspora-Homeland Relations in Ezra-Nehemiah', *VT* 52 (2002): 147–65.

the later, narrower view of defining the Judean community and thus who rightly should be responsible for supporting the temple. That is why in Ezra 3, anachronistically in my opinion, the overtures of support to Judeans in rebuilding the temple offered by Samarians are rejected. Support from the Persian authorities can be accepted, in part because they fulfil the role of royal benefactors, and in part because they do not lay claim to actually being Judeans.

For Judeans, both in the diaspora and in the homeland, funding the temple was a mechanism to distinguish between who was in the community and who was not. But the boundary lines were drawn in different places by different groups at different times. The 'collection text' at Elephantine can be construed as reflecting a very open attitude by one group of diaspora Jews in Egypt towards both those who could contribute and the cults they could support.[33] In Judah, as well as in the Babylonian-Elamite diaspora as represented by the book of Ezra, they may not have been quite so accommodating.

Of all the texts noted above Neh 10 is the most pointed on the topic of temple funding (Neh 10:40 [ET 39]: 'We will not neglect the temple of our God'), and it connects temple funding with another agent for community definition, a prohibition on exogamy. So it must already presume to know who is outside the group in order to avoid marrying them. Elsewhere in Nehemiah, the Nehemiah Memoir identifies as 'enemies' members of the ruling elites of neighbouring districts, suggesting that for Nehemiah the demarcation between Judean and non-Judean was political. Notably, in Nehemiah 13 (Neh 13:4–5), much to Nehemiah's consternation the priest Eliashib has no problem with opening the temple to the tenancy of Tobiah the Ammonite, who with his son had married into Judean families. And the family of the High Priest intermarries with the family of Sanballat of Samaria (Neh 13:28). So the Judean priests do not share Nehemiah's view of who is acceptable to marry and where the boundaries of the community lie. Neither do Judeans more generally, given that Judean men marry 'women from Ashdod, Ammon and Moab' (Neh 13:23 cf. Ezra 9–10 for a similar episode). Nehemiah's political authority outweighs that of the priests and people, so they had to acquiesce to his rulings.

Nehemiah 10 is an answer to both weak funding for the temple and weak community boundaries. The two issues are tackled in tandem. A community whose identity focused on the repudiation of marriage with 'the peoples of the land' and a commitment to temple funding would seem to address my question regarding who should pay the 'informal taxes' in support of the temple. And a 'binding agreement' would offer the strong social expectation that the commitments be

33 TAD C3.15 = CAP 22.

met. But I am suspicious as to the historical veracity of this pact, not least because while it claims that both the leading citizens and 'the rest of the people' agreed to adhere to it, the list of names inserted at its beginning seems short and selective, and therefore contrived, and I suspect the text says more about the perception of problems in the community than how they were actually resolved. If the Books of Chronicles are later than Nehemiah 10, then they show that the temple continues to struggle to find its place in the community. Chronicles is conventionally dated to around 400. It can be read as an attempt to give particular prominence to the Jerusalem temple and its personnel in the history of monarchic Judah. This serves as the basis for a plea for a renewed community commitment to the temple in the late Persian period, which belies a claim that Nehemiah 10 resolved the issue. Nehemiah's actions in Nehemiah 13, if connected to Nehemiah 10 at all, are at best a short-term solution to the problem of temple funding; a solution, by the way, which promoted Nehemiah's authority and interests in the district.

The initial questions with which this paper began were: How was the rebuilding of the Jerusalem temple funded, and how were its ongoing expenses met? What does the funding of a shrine tell us about its place in society and the status of those that served there? I would contend that funding the Jerusalem temple was not resolved in the early and middle Persian period. It was funded by 'informal taxation', but the social expectation for contributing was not always strong enough to ensure payments were made. The Jerusalem priesthood lacked the political authority to demand payments, and they also lacked the authority to implement formal taxes. Connection to the temple could be a source of community identity, but the boundaries of the community continued to be contested. In the context of post-monarchic Judah the temple arguably had an ambivalent status which it struggled to overcome.

Abbreviations

8ᵉ Cong.	J. N. Strassmaier, 'Einige kleinere babylonischen Keilschrifttexte aus dem Britischen Museum', in *Actes du 8e Congrès International des Orientalistes*, Leiden, 1893, 2–35
AB	Anchor Bible
ABC	*Assyrian and Babylonian Chronicles*. A. K. Grayson. TCS 5. Locust Valley, New York, 1975
ABL	*Assyrian and Babylonian Letters Belonging to the Kouyunjik Collections of the British Museum*. Edited by R. F. Harper. 14 vols. Chicago, 1892–1942
ABR	*Australian Biblical Review*
AcIr	*Acta Iranica*
ADOG	Abhandlungen der deutschen Orientgesellschaft
AfO	*Archiv für Orientforschung*
AfOB	Archiv für Orientforschung: Beiheft
AGJU	Arbeiten zur Geschichte des antiken Judentums und des Urchristentums
AHw	*Akkadisches Handwörterbuch*. W. von Soden. 3 vols. Wiesbaden, 1965–1981
AION	*Annali dell'Istituto Orientale di Napoli*
ALGHJ	Arbeiten zur Literatur und Geschichte des hellenistischen Judentums
AMI	*Archäologische Mitteilungen aus Iran*
AnOr	Analecta Orientalia
AnOr 8	*Neubabylonische Rechtsurkunden aus den Berliner Staatlichen Museen*. A. Pohl. AnOr 8. Rome, 1933
AOAT	Alter Orient und Altes Testament
AoF	*Altorientalische Forschungen*
APAW	Abhandlungen der (Königl.) Preußischen Akademie der Wissenschaften
ÄPN	*Die Ägyptische Personennamen*. H. Ranke. 3 vols. Glückstadt, 1935–1977
ARAB	*Ancient Records of Assyria and Babylonia*. D. D. Luckenbill. Chicago, 1926–1927
ARTA	*Achaemenid Research on Texts and Archaeology*
AS	Assyriological Studies
Ash.	*Die Inschriften Asarhaddons Königs von Assyrien*. R. Borger. Graz, 1956
ATD	Das Alte Testament Deutsch
AuOr	*Aula Orientalis*
AUWE	Ausgrabungen in Uruk-Warka, Endberichte
BA	*Biblical Archaeologist*
BaAr 2	*Urkunden zum Ehe-, Vermögens- und Erbrecht aus verschiedenen neubabylonischen Archiven*. C. Wunsch. Babylonische Archive 2. Dresden, 2003

BaAr 6	*Judeans by the Waters of Babylon. New Historical Evidence in Cuneiform Sources from Rural Babylonia. Texts from the Schøyen Collection.* C. Wunsch with contributions by L. Pearce. Babylonische Archive 6. Dresden, forthcoming
BaghM	*Baghdader Mitteilungen*
BAH	Bibliothèque archéologique et historique
BAR	*Biblical Archaeology Review*
BASOR	*Bulletin of the American Schools of Oriental Research*
BBB	Bonner biblische Beiträge
BE	The Babylonian Expedition of the University of Pennsylvania: Series A. Cuneiform Texts
BE 8	*Legal and Commercial Transactions Dated in the Assyrian, Neo-Babylonian and Persian Periods, Chiefly from Nippur.* A. T. Clay. BE 8. Philadelphia, 1908
BE 9	*Business Documents of Murashû Sons of Nippur Dated in the Reign of Artaxerxes I (464–424 B.C.).* H. Hilprecht and A. T. Clay. BE 9. Philadelphia, 1898
BE 10	*Business Documents of Murashû Sons of Nippur Dated in the Reign of Darius II (424–404 B.C.).* A. T. Clay. BE 10. Philadelphia, 1904
BETL	Bibliotheca Ephemeridum Theologicarum Lovaniensium
BHS	*Biblia Hebraica Stuttgartensia.* Edited by K. Elliger and W. Rudolph. Stuttgart, 1983
BHT	Beiträge zur historischen Theologie
Bib	*Biblica*
BIN	Babylonian Inscriptions in the Collection of James B. Nies
BIN 2	*Historical, Religious, and Economic Texts and Antiquities.* J. B. Nies and C. E. Keiser. BIN 2. New Haven, CT, 1920
BIS	Biblical Interpretation Series
BJS	Brown Judaic Studies
BKAT	Biblischer Kommentar, Altes Testament
BMA	*Babylonian Marriage Agreements 7th – 3rd Centuries B.C.* M. T. Roth. AOAT 222. Neukirchen-Vluyn, 1989
BN	*Biblische Notizen*
BO	*Bibliotheca Orientalis*
BSA	*Bulletin on Sumerian Agriculture*
BSOAS	*Bulletin of the School of Oriental and African Studies*
BTB	*Biblical Theology Bulletin*
BZABR	Beihefte zur Zeitschrift für Altorientalische und biblische Rechtsgeschichte
BZAW	Beihefte zur Zeitschrift für die alttestamentliche Wissenschaft
CAD	*The Assyrian Dictionary of the Oriental Institute of the University of Chicago.* Edited by I. J. Gelb et al. Chicago, 1956–2010
CAL	Comprehensive Aramaic Lexicon
Camb.	*Inschriften von Cambyses, König von Babylon (529–521 v. Chr.).* J. N. Strassmaier. Babylonische Texte 8–9. Leipzig, 1890
CAP	*Aramaic Papyri of the Fifth Century.* A. E. Cowley. Oxford, 1923
CBET	Contributions to Biblical Exegesis and Theology

CBOTS	Coniectania Biblica. Old Testament Series
CBQ	*Catholic Biblical Quarterly*
CDCPP	*Cuneiform Documents from the Chaldean and Persian Periods.* R. H. Sack. London, 1994
CDOG	Colloquien der deutschen Orientgesellschaft
CHANE	Culture and History of the Ancient Near East
CleO	Classica et Orientalia
CM	Cuneiform Monographs
COS	*The Context of Scripture.* Edited by W. W. Hallo. 3 vols. Leiden, 1997–2002
CRAI	Comptes rendus des séances de l'Académie des Inscriptions et Belles-Lettres
CT	Cuneiform Texts from Babylonian Tablets in the British Museum
CTMMA	Cuneiform Texts in the Metropolitan Museum of Art
CUSAS	Cornell University Studies in Assyriology and Sumerology
CUSAS 28	*Documents of Judean Exiles and West Semites in Babylonia in the Collection of David Sofer*. L. E. Pearce and C. Wunsch. CUSAS 28. Bethesda, 2014
Dar.	*Inschriften von Darius, König von Babylon (521–485 v. Chr.)*. J. N. Strassmaier. Babylonische Texte 10–12. Leipzig, 1890
DEA	*Épigraphes araméens: Étude des textes araméens gravés ou écrits sur des tablettes cunéiformes*. L. Delaporte. Paris, 1912
EE	*Entrepreneurs and Empire: The Murašû Archive, the Murašû Firm, and Persian Rule in Babylonia*. M. W. Stolper. PIHANS 54. Leiden, 1985
ErIsr	*Eretz-Israel*
FAT	Forschungen zum Alten Testament
FOTL	Forms of the Old Testament Literature
FRLANT	Forschungen zur Religion und Literatur des Alten und Neuen Testaments
FuB	*Forschungen und Berichte, Staatliche Museen zu Berlin*
FzB	Forschung zur Bibel
GK	Gesenius, H. F. Wilhelm and Emil Friedrich Kautzsch, *Gesenius' Hebrew Grammar: As Edited and Enlarged by the Late E. Kautzsch*. Translated by A. E. Cowley. Oxford, 1946
GMTR	Guides to the Mesopotamian Textual Record
HALOT	Hebrew and Aramaic Lexicon of the Old Testament
HANEM	History of the Ancient Near East Monographs
HBM	Hebrew Bible Monographs
HBM 8	*New Seals and Inscriptions, Hebrew, Idumean, and Cuneiform*. Edited by M. Lubetski. HBM 8. Sheffield, 2007
HBS	Herders Biblische Studien
Hen	*Henoch*
HKAT	Handkommentar zum Alten Testament
HO	Handbuch der Orientalistik
HSM	Harvard Semitic Monographs
HSS	Harvard Semitic Studies
HThKAT	Herders Theologischer Kommentar zum Alten Testament

HTR	*Harvard Theological Review*
HUCA	*Hebrew Union College Annual*
ICC	International Critical Commentary
IEJ	*Israel Exploration Journal*
IMT	*Istanbul Murašû Texts*. Veysel Donbaz and Matthew W. Stolper. PIHANS 79. Leiden, 1997
Int	*Interpretation*
IPNB	*Iranische Personennamen in der Neu- und spätbabylonischen Nebenüberlieferung*. R. Zadok. Iranische Personennamenbuch 7/1B. Vienna, 2009
JANES	*Journal of the Ancient Near Eastern Society*
JAOS	*Journal of the American Oriental Society*
JBL	*Journal of Biblical Literature*
JCS	*Journal of Cuneiform Studies*
JCSMS	*Journal of the Canadian Society for Mesopotamian Studies*
JEOL	*Jaarbericht van het Vooraziatisch-Egyptisch Gezelschap (Genootschap) Ex oriente lux*
JESHO	*Journal of the Economic and Social History of the Orient*
JETS	*Journal of the Evangelical Theological Society*
JNES	*Journal of Near Eastern Studies*
JRitSt	*Journal of Ritual Studies*
JSJ	*Journal for the Study of Judaism in the Persian, Hellenistic, and Roman Periods*
JSOT	*Journal for the Study of the Old Testament*
JSOTSup	Journal for the Study of the Old Testament: Supplement Series
JSP	*Journal for the Study of the Pseudepigrapha*
JSS	*Journal of Semitic Studies*
JSSM	Journal of Semitic Studies Monographs
JTS	*Journal of Theological Studies*
JTVI	*Journal of the Transactions of the Victoria Institute*
KAI	*Kanaanäische und aramäische Inschriften*. H. Donner and W. Röllig. Wiesbaden, 1962–1964
LAOS	Leipziger Altorientalische Studien
LCL	Loeb Classical Library
Levant	*Levant: Journal of the Council for British Research in the Levant*
LHBOTS	Library of Hebrew Bible/Old Testament Studies
LSTS	Library of Second Temple Studies
MSL	Materialien zum Sumerischen Lexicon
NABU	*Nouvelles Assyriologiques Brèves et Utilitaires*
NBDM	*Neo-Babylonian Documents in the University of Michigan Collection*. E. W. Moore. Ann Arbor, 1939
Nbn.	*Inschriften von Nabonidus, König von Babylon*. J. N. Strassmaier. Babylonische Texte 1–4. Leipzig, 1889
NIBC	New International Biblical Commentary
NICOT	New International Commentary on the Old Testament
NTT	*Norsk Teologisk Tidsskrift*
OBO	Orbis Biblicus et Orientalis

OBT	Overtures to Biblical Theology
OECT	Oxford Editions of Cuneiform Texts
OIP	Oriental Institute Publications
OIS	Oriental Institute Seminars
OLA	Orientalia Lovaniensia Analecta
OLZ	*Orientalistische Literaturzeitung*
Or	*Orientalia* (NS)
OTL	The Old Testament Library
OTM	Oxford Theological Monographs
PBA	*Proceedings of the British Academy*
PBS	Publications of the Babylonian Section, University of Pennsylvania
PBS 2/1	*Business Documents of Murashû Sons of Nippur Dated in the Reign of Darius II.* A. T. Clay. Publications of the Babylonian Section 2/1. Philadelphia, 1912
PIHANS	Publications de l'Institut historique et archéologique néerlandais de Stamboul
PNA	*Prosopography of the Neo Assyrian Empire*. Edited by S. Parpola, H. D. Baker, K. Radner and R. M. Whiting. 3 vols. Helsinki, 1998–2012
PTMS	Pittsburgh Theological Monograph Series
RA	*Revue d'assyriologie et d'archéologie orientale*
RAcc.	*Rituels Accadiens*. F. Thureau-Dangin. Paris, 1921
RB	*Revue Biblique*
RGTC	Répertoire Géographique des Textes Cunéiformes
RGTC 8	*Geographical Names According to New- and Late-Babylonian Texts*. R. Zadok. RGTC 8. Wiesbaden, 1985
RIMA	The Royal Inscriptions of Mesopotamia, Assyrian Periods
RIMB	The Royal Inscriptions of Mesopotamia, Babylonian Periods
RlA	*Reallexikon der Assyriologie*. Edited by Erich Ebeling et al. Berlin, 1928–
ROMCT	Royal Ontario Museum, Cuneiform Texts
SAA	State Archives of Assyria
SAAB	*State Archives of Assyria Bulletin*
SAAS	State Archives of Assyria Studies
SANER	Studies in Ancient Near Eastern Records
SAOC	Studies in Ancient Oriental Civilization
SBAW	Sitzungsberichte der Bayerischen Akademie der Wissenschaften
SBLDS	Society of Biblical Literature Dissertation Series
SBLMS	Society of Biblical Literature Monograph Series
SBLRBS	Society of Biblical Literature Resources for Biblical Study
SBLSymS	Society of Biblical Literature Symposium Series
SBLWAW	Society of Biblical Literature Writings from the Ancient World
SEÅ	*Svensk exegetisk årsbok*
SJOT	*Scandinavian Journal of the Old Testament*
SHANE	Studies in the History of the Ancient Near East
SJSJ	Supplements to the Journal for the Study of Judaism
SÖAW	Sitzungen der österreichischen Akademie der Wissenschaften in Wien

STDJ	Studies on the Texts of the Desert of Judah
SU	*Seal Use in Fifth Century B.C. Nippur, Iraq: A Study of Seal Selection and Sealing Practices in the Murašû Archive.* L. B. Bregstein. PhD Thesis, University of Pennsylvania, 1993. Ann Arbor: University Microfilms, 1997
TAD	*Textbook of Aramaic Documents from Ancient Egypt.* B. Porten and A. Yardeni. 3 vols. Jerusalem, 1986–1993
TAPS	*Transactions of the American Philosophical Society*
TCL	Textes cunéiformes. Musée du Louvre, Département des Antiquités Orientales
TCS	Texts from Cuneiform Sources
TEBR	*Textes économiques de la Babylonie récente.* F. Joannès. Paris, 1982
ThWAT	*Theologisches Wörterbuch zum Alten Testament.* Edited by G. J. Botterweck, H. Ringgren and H.-J. Fabry. 10 vols. Stuttgart, 1970–2000
TJ	*Trinity Journal*
TSAJ	Texte und Studien zum antiken Judentum
TuM	Texte und Materialien der Frau Professor Hilprecht Collection of Babylonian Antiquities im Eigentum der Universität Jena
TynB	*Tyndale Bulletin*
UCP	*University of California Publications in Semitic Philology*
UET	Ur Excavations: Texts
UF	*Ugarit-Forschungen*
VAB	Vorderasiatische Bibliothek
VS	Vorderasiatische Schriftdenkmäler der Königlichen Museen zu Berlin
VT	*Vetus Testamentum*
VTSup	Supplements to Vetus Testamentum
WBC	Word Biblical Commentary
WMANT	Wissenschaftliche Monographien zum Alten und Neuen Testament
WO	*Die Welt des Orients*
WVDOG	Wissenschaftliche Veröffentlichungen der deutschen Orientgesellschaft
WZKM	*Wiener Zeitschrift für die Kunde des Morgenlandes*
YNER	Yale Near Eastern Researches
YOS	Yale Oriental Series, Babylonian Texts
ZA	*Zeitschrift für Assyriologie*
ZABR	*Zeitschrift für altorientalische und biblische Rechtsgeschichte*
ZAW	*Zeitschrift für die alttestamentliche Wissenschaft*
ZDMG	*Zeitschrift der deutschen morgenländische Gesellschaft*
ZDMGSup	Zeitschrift der deutschen morgenländische Gesellschaft: Supplementbände
ZDPV	*Zeitschrift des deutschen Palästina-Vereins*

Non-bibliographical abbreviations

AC	In the contribution by Ran Zadok, the formula +x AC stands for 'with anonymous coparceners whose number is not indicated'
Art	Artaxerxes
AYMC	Āl-Yāhūdu marriage contract
BM	siglum of antiquities in the collection of the British Museum
Camb	reign of Cambyses (530–522 B.C.E.)
CBS	siglum of cuneiform tablets in the collection of the Babylonian Section, University Museum, Philadelphia
CH	Code of Hammurabi
Cyr	reign of Cyrus II in Babylonia (539–530 B.C.E.)
d.	daughter
Dar	reign of Darius I (522–486 B.C.E.)
DB	Darius, Behistun inscription
DP(e, h)	Darius, inscriptions from Persepolis
ET	English Translation
^{f}PN	female personal name
GN	geographical name
HSM	siglum of cuneiform tablets in the Harvard Semitic Museum
M	siglum of cuneiform tablets in the Aleppo Museum
NA	Neo-Assyrian
NBC	siglum of cuneiform tablets in the Nies Babylonian Collection, Yale University, New Haven
Nbn	reign of Nabonidus (556–539 B.C.E.)
Nbk	reign of Nebuchadnezzar II (605–562 B.C.E.)
Nbk IV	reign of Nebuchadnezzar IV (521 B.C.E.)
Ner	reign of Neriglissar (560–556 B.C.E.)
N-G	Nusku-gabbe, protagonist of the Neirab archive
Ni	siglum of cuneiform tablets from the Nippur expeditions in the Istanbul Museum
Npl	reign of Nabopolassar (626–605 B.C.E.)
NCBT	siglum of tablets in the Newell Collection of Babylonian Tablets, Yale University, New Haven
PN	personal name
SBV	Standard Babylonian Version (Gilgamesh Epic)
SÉ	siglum of cuneiform tablets in the Monastère Saint-Étienne, Jerusalem
VAT	siglum of cuneiform tablets in the Vorderasiatisches Museum, Berlin
WBA	Wadi Brisa inscription of Nebuchadnezzar II
Xer	reign of Xerxes (486–465 B.C.E.)
YBC	siglum of cuneiform tablets in the Yale Babylonian Collection, Yale University, New Haven

Index

1. Hebrew Bible

Genesis
17:20 285 n77
23:6 285 n77
25:16 285 n77
29:20 237 n43
34:2 285 n77, 310 n9
47:29–31 332

Exodus
16:22 285 n77
22:28 285 n77
23:15 271 n10
23:16 271 n10
25:1–9 338, 339
30:11–16 338, 339
32:1 311 n15
34:31 285 n77
35:4–29 338, 339
35:27 285 n77

Leviticus
4:22 285 n77
13:2 236 n39
13:6–8 236 n39
14:56 236 n39
16 271 n10
23:40 266
25 338, 339
25:10 247
27 338, 339, 340

Numbers
1:16 285 n77
1:44 285 n77
2:3 285 n77
2:5 285 n77
2:7 285 n77
2:10 285 n77
2:12 285 n77
2:14 285 n77
2:18 285 n77
2:20 285 n77
2:22 285 n77
2:25 285 n77
2:27 285 n77
2:29 285 n77
3:24 285 n77
3:30 285 n77
3:32 285 n77
3:35 285 n77
4:34 285 n77
4:46 285 n77
7:2–3 285 n77
7:10–11 285 n77
7:18 285 n77
7:24 285 n77
7:30 285 n77
7:36 285 n77
7:42 285 n77
7:48 285 n77
7:54 285 n77
7:60 285 n77
7:66 285 n77
7:72 285 n77
7:78 285 n77
7:84 285 n77
10:4 285 n77
13:2 285 n77
16:2 285 n77
17:2 285 n77
17:6 285 n77
25:14 285 n77
25:18 285 n77, 310 n9
27:2 285 n77
31:13 285 n77
32:2 285 n77
34:18 285 n77
34:22–28 285 n77
36:1 285 n77

Deuteronomy
12:6 336
14:22–29 336
16:1–8 271 n10
16:13–15 271 n10
17 287 n82
18:4 336
20:1 311 n15
26:1–15 336

Joshua
9:15 285–286 n77
9:18–19 285–286 n77
9:21 285–286 n77
13:21 100 n23, 285–286 n77, 310 n9
17:4 285–286 n77
22:14 285–286 n77
22:30 285–286 n77
22:32 285–286 n77

1 Samuel
18:3 237 n43
20:17 237 n43

2 Samuel
1:26 237 n43
8:17 336

1 Kings
2:10 332
2:26–27 336
4:2–4 336
5–7 336
8:1 285–286 n77
9:25 274, 285 n75
11:34 285–286 n77
11:43 332
12 275 n30
12:26–33 336
12:29 274
12:31–32 336
14:20 332
14:31 332
15:8 332
15:24 332

16:6 332
16:28 332

2 Kings
5:27 311 n15
9:15 311 n15
9:21 311 n15
12 344
12:1–8 336
12:4–16 336
15:19–20 295
16:10–16 274, 285 n75
22 312 n19
22:4 336
23:4 336
24 311 n17
24:8–17 64 n27
24:14 293
24:14–16 293
24:15–16 8 n5
25 312
25:7 9 n6
25:8–12 64 n27
25:12 293
25:23 294
25:25 294

Isaiah
1–39 261
15:7 266
29:3 260 n22
40–48 256–257, 267
40–55 253–267
40–66 254
40:1–11 257
40:12 260
40:18 263
40:(18)19–20 261
40:19–20 262, 263
40:20 261–266
41:2–3 273
41:6–7 261
41:15 260
42:11 260
42:15 260
44:4 265–266
44:9–20 261, 265
44:23 260
44:24–45-7 259
44:27–28 337
45:1–2 259
45:1–4 273
45:2 259–261
46:1–2 267
46:5–7 261
49–55 256–257
49:11 260
49:13 260
52:7 260
54:10 260
55:12 260
56–66 254, 263
60 338
61:1 247
63:9 237 n43

Jeremiah
10:1–16 261
22:14 243
23:5–6 273
30:21 274
33:16 273
34:8 247
34:15 247
34:17 247
36 312 n19
37 311 n17
38–43 312
39:1–10 64 n27
40 312 n19
40:6–41:3 294
52:1–16 64 n27
52:11 9 n6
52:27–30 293
52:28–30 64 n27

Ezekiel
1 247
1:1 227 n13
1:3 12 n22
3:15 12 n22
4:4–6 250
5 246
5:1 245
8 233
8:11 312 n19
10 247
12:19 237 n43
13 249
13:18 235
16:30 237
16:33 238–239, 241
17:13 234
18:7 242
18:12 242
18:16 242
19:9 242
21:26 233
22:24 248
23:14 243
23:44 244
26:16 310 n9
27:9 244
27:15 245
27:24 246
27:27 244
27:29 244
30:13 310 n9
31:11 234
32:21 234
32:29 310 n9
32:30 100 n23
33:15 242
34 273–274 n22
34:23–24 273
37 273–274 n22
37:24–25 273
40–42 287
40–48 268–291
40:1–43:10 286 n81
40:45 286 n78
40:46 286 n78
42:20 289 n89
43:2–4 273
43:7 275 n31
43:13–17 287
44 246, 287 n82
44:2 273
44:3 272–273, 288–289
44:9–16 287
44:15–31 286

44:24a 286
44:28–30 287
45:7 271 n13
45:7–8a 271
45:10–12 287
45:12 246
45:13–17 338, 339
45:16 271
45:17 271
45:18–25 287
45:18–46:15 271 n12
45:19 271 n10
45:21 271 n10
45:21–46:12 273 n19
45:22 271
45:25 271 n10
46* 274
46:1–12 287
46:1–15 272
46:2 272
46:4–7 271
46:9–10 288
46:10 272
46:11 271
46:12 271, 272
46:13–14 271
46:13–15 287
46:17 247
47 233
48:21 271 n13

Obadiah
10 237 n43

Jonah
1:5 244

Micah
5:4 100 n23

Zephaniah
3:17 237 n43

Haggai 292, 294, 298–300, 304, 341
1:1 276 n35, 338
1:8 304–305, 337, 339
1:9–11 299
1:12 338
1:14 276 n35, 339
2:2 276 n35, 338
2:2–9 304
2:4 338
2:7–9 337
2:15–19 299
2:21 276 n35
2:23 337

Zechariah 294, 298–300, 304
1–8 292
1:12 299, 300
1:16 299
1:16–17 299
2:8 299
3 299
4:9 299
4:9–10 299
6:10–11 338, 339
6:12–13 299
6:15 338
7:5 312 n20
8:4–5 299
8:9 299
8:10–13 299

Malachi 341
1:8 276 n35
1:14 338, 339, 345
3:6–12 338, 339
3:10–11 345

Psalms
72:10 245
83:12 100 n23
109:4–5 237 n43
110:4 274, 285 n75
137:1–6 328
137:2 266

Job
40:22 266

Proverbs
5:19 237 n43

Ruth 326–327
1:4 327
1:7 327
1:10 327
1:19–20 327
1:22 327
2:2 327
2:6 327
2:21 327
4:5 327
4:10 327

Ecclesiastes
9:6 237 n43

Esther
3:12 276 n35, 298
8:9 276 n35, 298
9:3 276 n35, 298

Daniel
1:3–4 228
3:1 260 n23
3:2 276 n35, 298
3:3 276 n35, 298
3:27 276 n35
5:2 24 n73
6:2 298
6:5 298
6:7 298
6:8 276 n35, 298

Ezra 294
1 292, 311, 315
1–6 292, 300, 303, 304, 307, 310, 321
1:1–11 337, 340
1:2–4 297
1:6 337, 339
1:8 276, 277 n37, 285–286 n77, 308
1:8–11 303, 310
1:11 308, 310–311
2 292, 302, 304, 306

2:59–63 331
2:68–69 337, 339
3 292, 350
3:3 303
3:7 304, 337, 339
3:12–13 304
4–6 292–293
4:4 303
4:13 344
5 310
5:3 18, 276 n35
5:6 18, 276 n35
5:6–17 305
5:13–16 303
5:14 276, 276 n35, 308, 311
5:16 308
6:2–5 337, 340
6:2–12 89
6:6 18, 276 n35
6:7 276 n35
6:8–10 337, 340
6:13 18, 276 n35
7–10 293, 303
7:15 337, 340
7:16 337, 339
7:21–24 337, 340
8:25 337, 339, 340
8:36 276 n35, 298
9–10 306, 307, 334, 349 n31, 350
9:1–2 303
9:2 332
9:11 303, 332
9:14 303
10:2 303
10:11 303
10:18–43 306

Nehemiah 293, 294
1–7 344
2:1–11 337
2:7 276 n35
2:9 276 n35
2:11–3:32 348 n29
2:16 345
3 345
3:7 276 n35
5:1–13 344
5:14 276 n35
5:14–15 344
5:15 276 n35
5:18 276 n35
5:19 344
6:6 346
6:17–19 305
7 302, 304, 306
7:61–65 331
9–10 306
10 338, 341, 342, 350, 351
10:1–40 (ET 9:38–10:39) 337
10:1 (ET 9:38) 341
10:33–40 (ET 10:32–39) 339
10:40 (ET 10:39) 350
12:26 276 n35
12:27–43 344
13 342, 345, 349 n31, 351
13:4–5 350
13:4–14 338
13:4–31 344
13:5 344
13:10–12 339
13:10–14 344, 347
13:14 344
13:21 344
13:23 350
13:23–27 306
13:28 306, 350
13:30 344
13:30–31 346
13:31 338, 339, 347

1 Chronicles
2:10 285–286 n77
4:38 285–286 n77
5:6 285–286 n77
7:40 285–286 n77
25 312

2 Chronicles
1:2 285–286 n77
5:2 285–286 n77
9:14 276 n35
19:8–11 287 n82
29–31 344
31 339
34 312 n19

2. Ancient Near Eastern Texts

8e *Cong.*
20 162–163

A Babylon 11
(Al-Rawi, *Iraq* 47) 281 n54

Aa = nâqu 238 n48

ABC
1 214 n133, 220 n161
2 10 n13
3 10 n13
4 10 n13, 64 n25, 65 n29
5 10 n9, 10 n10–n13, 64, 64 n25, 65 n31, 226 n7, 311 n17
6 10 n13
7 201, 212, 218, 221

ABL
238 101 n24
350 14 n27
811 14 n27

Adad-Guppi Stele 313 n26

AfO
52 86 no. 8 161, 163, 173, 175–176, 178–179
52 88 no. 9 161
52 88 no. 9 173, 175
52 90 no. 11 174

AION Suppl. 77
no. 1 173

ana ittišu 241

AnOr 8
76 317 n50

Antagal 238

ARAB
II § 765 281 n55

Ash.
§ 27 281 n55

Astronomical
Diaries 219–220

AuOr 10
219 177

AYMC (Āl-Yāhūdu marriage
contract) 36, 37–39,
44, 47–56

BaAr 2
no. 1 38 n18, 38 n21, 38
n22, 51
no. 2 38 n18, 52 n59
no. 3 37 n17, 38 n18, 39 n24,
52–53, 53 n62
no. 4 38 n18
no. 5 38 n18, 38 n21, 41, 44,
45–47, 51 n56, 53
no. 6 38 n18
no. 7 38 n18

BaAr 6
1 13
10 21, 21 n63, 22 n64
13 22 n64
43–57 12 n22
59–65 12 n22
67–76 12 n22
78–84 12 n22
86 12 n22
87 12 n22
90–95 12 n22

Babylonian King List A 212

Babylonian King List B 212

BE 8
25 65
26 14
40 63 n17
50 14
56 13 n27
62 105
65 14 n27, 319
69 104
94 105
126 133
132 102

BE 9
1 121, 173
4 12 n22, 136
5 122
7 131, 148
8 131, 136
10 137, 149
12 132
14 115
15 115, 123, 136
16 144
20 119
21 106, 115, 137
23 122, 138
24 119
26 8 n4, 148 n122
27 8 n3, 119, 148 n122
28 137, 173
29 148 n122
30 148 n122
31 136, 137, 143
32 142, 144, 148
33 149
34 141
36 140
37 140
38 140
40 143
44 115, 131
45 135
48 148 n122
49 138
50 173
55 116
56 133
58 133
60 109
63 128
64 133
65 63 n18, 104 n40,
144
66 136
67 123 n89, 137, 138, 144
68 133
69 21 n60, 105, 138
70 118, 164, 178
72 117, 143
73 131
75 114, 127, 135
77 108
79 108 n55, 119
80 143
81 164, 172 n36, 176
82 131, 137
84 12 n22
85 133, 136, 137
86 14 n27, 133, 135, 136, 147
87 105, 135
90 136
92 143
93 143
94 131
95 124
97 118
98 118
101 116
102 113, 173
107 128
108 142
109 146
BE 10
1 137, 164, 175
2 135
3 135

4 105 n44
5 138
7 21 n60, 125, 138, 143
8 142
9 13–14 n27, 105, 108, 174
10 133
12 114, 134
13 114 n76
15 169, 174, 178
18 126
19 123
20 122
21 114
23 164, 176
24 142, 143
25 123
28 114, 142
30 114, 149
31 124
32 117, 135
33 108, 136
34 136, 140
36 122
38 114, 121
39 132, 141
40 141
41 127
43 117
44 142, 146
46 119
47 138
51 129, 130
52 150
53 111
54 97, 143
55 136, 139
58 108, 113
59 105
61 132
62 137
64 129
66 164, 176
67 137
68 150
70 135, 143
71 125
72 117, 135, 143
77 137
79 135
80 119, 173
81 109, 169, 171, 179
82 109
84 109, 117
85 21 n61, 117
88 169, 177
89 137, 174
90 130
91 127, 174
92 124
93 118
94 135
95 106, 124
96 126, 145 n121
98 126
99 118, 120, 146
101 113, 114, 124
102 125, 174
103 114, 174
106 120
107 111, 145
108 141
109 134
112 116
113 114
114 112, 174
115 111
116 134, 149
118 14 n27, 125
119 144
120 144
122 130
123 146, 147, 170, 175–176
125 122, 125, 135
126 145
127 114, 135
128 122
129 161, 170, 174, 177–178
130 120
131 120
132 120, 121

Behistun inscription 315 (n33)

Berossos
Babyloniaca 205, 208, 212, 219–221, 314 n32

BIN 2
114 318 n55
118 11 n17

BM
81-4-28, 88 65
25660 168
30235 201 n93
45642 219 n158
46687 176, 179
46691 177, 178
54205 173
63003 88 n89
63926 88 n89
63984 172 n40
64155 162
64195+ 38 n21, 51, 51 n54, 52
64697 162, 163
68921 41 n29
82566 161, 176, 178
87228 177
87250 177
87264 179
103473 162, 163
120024 169, 177

BMA
no. 2 52 n59
no. 4 37 n17, 38 n21, 48, 50, 53 n60
no. 5 37 n17, 39 n24, 53, 53 n62
no. 6 52 n59
no. 7 37 n17
no. 8 52 n59
no. 11 40, 44
no. 14 37 n17
no. 15 53 n60
no. 17 40, 44, 46, 47–48, 52 n59, 53
no. 19 52 n59
no. 20 52 n59

no. 21–22 37 n17
no. 23 40, 43 n37, 47
no. 25 53 n60
no. 26 41, 44–45, 47–48, 48 n48, 52 n59, 57
no. 34 42, 43, 43 n38, 44, 46 n47, 47–48, 50–51, 51 n54, 52 n59, 53
no. 34–35 38 n21
no. 35 42, 43, 47, 51, 51 n54, 53

BRM 1
86 133

Camb.
85 166
121 167
313 159
334 160, 161

CBS
5516 106 n49
10059 175
12895 14 n27

CDCPP
no. 45 317 n51

Chronicle P 215–216

Code of Hammurabi 279 n47

Court Calendar (Nebuchadnezzar Prism EŞ 7834) 98, 185, 313, 318 n59

CT
4 34d 163, 177–179
11 28 238 n48
44 81 179
55 346 88 n89
56 755 88 n89
57 133 167
57 342 162

CTMMA 2
44 214

CUSAS 28
1 13, 13 n24, 27
2 24 n72, 25, 25 n76
3 24 n72, 25 n77, 27
4 24 n72, 25 n77, 27
5 25 n77
6 13 n25, 25 n77
9 25 n77
10 27
19 16 n40, 17
20 16 n40, 17
21 16 n40, 17
27 22 n64
29 22 n64
30 22 n64
37 21, 21 n63
39 22 n64
42 21 n63
45 21, 22 n64–65, 29 n85
84 23, 23 n68
101 14 n27

Cyrus Cylinder 184, 191, 191 n41, 195, 197, 217, 270 n6, 296 (n12)–297, 315

Dar.
274 112, 112 n70
301 162–163, 165
533 96
DB 315 (n33)

DEA
91 235 n35

Declaration of War 214

DPe 185 n18

DPh 185 n17

Dynastic Prophecy 183 n7, 205–206, 208, 212, 217–221

Ea = *nâqu* 238

EE
3 136
8 150
10 114
11 149
12 135
13 109
14 141–142
15 141–142
16 141–142
17 148 n122
19 147
20–21 115 n77
23 147
27 161, 175
30 148 n122
34 135
35 164, 179
38 111
40 105, 107, 120 n83, 126, 138, 168, 176
42 122
43 113
46 122
48 116, 149
52 129, 173
53 134
54 124 n93
55 137
55–59 123 n90
56 135–137
57 134
58–59 123 n92
59 137
59–62 124 n93
61 137
63 148
64 121
66 106 n49
69 142
72 140
72–73 119 n81
72–79 104 n39
73 127 n104, 127 n106
73–74 124 n95

74 117 n79, 126 n100, 140
75 109 n57, 113 n73, 126 n103, 145
76 125 n96, 129 n110
77 121 n86, 129 n109, 129 n111, 130 n113, 130 n114, 131 n115, 131 n116, 132 n118, 148
78 122 n88, 130 n112
79 109 n57, 141
80 133
85 125 n97
85–86 110 n62
86 111 n67
88–89 118 n80
89 141
89–90 116 n78
89–92 127 n105
94 137
95 105 n45, 126 n101
95–96 128 n107
96 116
98 106, 132
99 105
102 133, 142
106 105, 121 n85
108 120, 145
109 104 n40, 105, 106 n48, 164, 173, 177
114 130
117 120 n83, 134
118 143

Elamite Attack on Nippur 214

Enūma Eliš 188–189, 191 n41

Epic of Adad-šuma-uṣur 216

Epic of Amēl-Marduk 216, 219 n157

Erimḫuš 238, 241

Erra and Išum 248–249

Etemenanki Cylinder of Nabopolassar 282

Etemenanki Cylinder of Nebuchadnezzar 313

FuB 14
15 no. 4 170, 176
28–29 no. 21 170, 175

Gilgamesh Epic 285 n74

Hofkalender (Nebuchadnezzar Prism EŞ 7834) 98, 185, 313, 318 n59

IMT
2 128 n107
3 104 n38, 142, 164, 173, 175, 178
4 127, 135, 137, 142
8 116
9 7 143
11 149
14 109
16 104 n40, 142, 148
17 108
18 123 n89, 145
20 149
22 137
25 135
32 124, 136–137
33 109
34 119
35 139
37 139
40 105, 138
43 164, 172
48 115, 170, 175, 176
49 149
52 131
53 109, 137
54 131, 137
55 131, 138
71 108
73 145
74 118
75 118
76 118
82 110, 110 n61, 126 n99
87 130
88 134
89 149
90 109 n59
91 141
92 130
93 133
94 139
100 144
101 134
103 134
104 120 n83, 134
105 104 n40, 105, 106, 106 n48, 113, 173
107 119, 134
108 103
110 106
133 118
153 106 n48
199 114
201 122
202 116

Iraq 54
137 164, 177

JEOL
34 45–46 177
40 93–94 162

Joannès, 'Textes babyloniens' (*Mélanges Perrot*)
no. 1 41, 43, 43 n34–35, 43 n37, 44

Joannès and Lemaire, 'Contrats babyloniens' (*RA* 90)
no. 6 (48) 167 n24

Joannès and Lemaire, 'Trois tablettes cunéiformes' (*Transeu* 17)

no. 1 (18, 33) 11 n18
no. 2 (27–30, 34) 12 n22

Kudur-nahhunte and the Babylonians 215

Lament of Nabû-šuma-ukīn 216, 219 n157

Letter of Nebuchadnezzar to the Babylonians 215

lú=*ša* 246
3495 59 n7

Marduk and the Elamites 215

Nabonidus Chronicle, see ABC 7

Nabonidus Epic 217

Nabopolassar Epic 214

Naram-Sin and the Lord of Apišal 212

NBC
4757 162, 163
6156 160–161, 161 n10

NBDM

89 11 n17

Nbn.
214 172 n40
464 318 n58, 319
976 88 n89

NCBT

632 172 n40

Neirab texts 58–93

Ni
709 63 n17
2673 63 n17
3149 65

OECT
10 192 179
PBS 2/1 8 n2
1 141
2 123
3 125
4 142
5 108
6 121
7 145
8 145
9 129
10 141
12 13 n26, 21 n61, 142
13 169, 170, 176
14 63 n18
15 115, 150
17 134
18 135, 142
20 146
21 145 n121
25 123
27 108, 125
28 116, 149, 155
29 125
30 128 n107, 132, 174
31 123
32 135
33 121
34 125
36 119
38 174
41 136, 140
42 139
43 174
45 136
46 136, 137
47 110
48 110, 140, 174
51 169, 176
53 146, 147
54 164, 179
55 137
56 116
57 129
59 113 n72
63 131, 132, 173
65 109, 111, 161, 164, 173, 176–179
66 125
70 174
72 113 n72, 125
76 129, 174
79 147
81 150
83 116
84 172, 176
85 134
87 131
88 128, 135
89 108
91 124, 169, 178
94 135
95 119
96 114, 133, 174
101 132
102 136, 174
104 63 n18, 169, 172, 174, 176–177
106 116
107 146
108 116, 147
111 146
112 146
113 111, 164, 176–177, 179
115 147, 155
117 116
118 120
120 115
121 141
123 116, 120, 131, 146–147
125 130
126 109, 111, 137, 174
128 174
129 117
130 170, 175–176
133 122, 124
134 140
135 105 n45, 121, 133, 174

136 118
142 125
143 115
143+ 170, 175–176
144 120
145 120
146 120
147 120, 137
148 120
150 116, 133
151 145
153 135, 142
158 143
160 118
161 114
164 134
165 114 n76
173 105, 125
174 142
176 123
177 114, 147
178 128
179 139
180 111, 135
181 122
184 142
185 21 n60, 126, 143
187 114, 135
188 113, 115
190 114
191 109, 133, 145 n121
192 164, 172 n36, 174, 176
193 114, 131, 138
194 132
197 107
198 128, 164, 171–172, 176
200 129
203 117
206 145
207 115, 129
208 120, 146
209 115, 132, 136–137
210 144, 145
211 145 n121
212 140
213 140
214 122
215 137, 142
217 122
218 21 n60
219 134
221 144
222 116, 144–145
223 136, 140
224 174
226 120, 135, 147
227 120

RAcc. 129–146 189

RIMA
1 A.0.86.1 281 n55
3 A.0.103.1 281 n55
3 A.0.104.1 281 n55

RIMB
B.2.4.1 280 n49
B.2.4.8 280 n49
B.2.4.11 280 n49
B.3.1.1 280 n49
B.6.13 280 n49
B.6.32.1 199–200

ROMCT
2 2 14 n27, 65
2 5 198 n73
2 37 167

Royal Chronicle 217–218

SAA
7 216a 113 n73
18 143 14 n27
18 145 14 n27

Shulgi Chronicle 211 n126, 216, 221 n162

Sippar Cylinder of Nabonidus 313 n27

Stolper, *Fs. Biggs*
no. 20 165, 177

SU
5 118
27 125
35 133
38 125
49 124
51 125
55 116
65 122
84 135
99 143
111 114
114–161 112 n69
123 113
125 118
127 149
131 148
134 145
145 125
146 117
152 131
153 113
156 147
157 115
161 137
161–169 113 n71
164 114
175–179 112 n69
176 113 n72
177–178 105 n44
179–185 115 n77
184 111
189 113
191 117
192 143
211 145 n121
214 116
269 146
287 107
289 131
297 129
299 113
304 124
320 111
323 135
334 135
336 142

359 117
366 113
370 106 n46
372 120
374 124
381 147
382 125
384 115
396 145, 145 n121
398 137
400 146
404 113
426 115
444 115
458 120
466 146
473 146
480 145
489 127
497 148 n122
510 112
526 146
532 116
537 123
542 144
544 139
549 117
552 115
560 120
563 135
564 143
569 111
581 125
586 146
593 110
597 144
600 118
614 119
623 137
625 114
628 145
631 120

Sumerian King List 212

Šurpu 236

TCL
6 38 197 n69
9 103 167

TEBR

no. 47 317

TuM 2/3
29 137
91 11 n16
124 128
144 148 n122
145 104 n40
146 149
147 14, 145
179 173
180 117
181 125, 138, 143
183 127–128, 133
184 105, 126
187 121
188 126
189 103 n37, 110 n66, 145
203 134

UCP
9/1 29 159
9/3 271 125
9/3 276 125

UET
1 187 200
4 130 39 n26

ur$_5$.ra = *ḫubullu* 231, 241, 242 n67, 243

Uruk King List 203–205, 220

VAB 4
Nbk 1 278 n44
Nbk 20 290 n94
Nbn 1 281 n55
Ngl 2 283 n64
Npl 1 281 n56, 282 n59, 284 n65

VAT
9763 228 n15
15608 174
15617 17 n44

Verse Account 217–218, 275 n31

VS
3 189 161, 179
4 152 17 n46
4 194 168, 175
5 141 179
6 81 319
6 128 49 n52
6 184 179
6 188 164, 178
24 87 215 n141, 215 n142, 221 n163
24 91 215 n139, 215 n142

WBA (Wadi Brisa) 283 n62

Weidner, 'Jojachin' ration lists 9, 9 n6, 14, 225
924 14 n29
928 14 n28
929 167 n22
930 167 n21
931 167 n20

WZKM
97 252–253, 278 174
97 257–259, 279–281 169–170, 172, 177

YBC
4187 162

YNER 1
4 317

YOS
3 20 172 n40
3 77 317–318 n53
3 82 317–318 n53

3 111 12 n22
3 119 88 n89
3 126 317–318 n53
6 2 160
6 148 159
6 168 172 n40
7 8 197 n69
7 65 318
7 106 317–318

3. Elephantine and other Aramaic Texts

CAP
22 350 n33
30 346 n22
32 346 n23
37 238 n45

DEA
91 235 n35

KAI
27 244 n74
233 237 n42

Letter of Adon 313

TAD
A2.3 237 n42
A3.3 237 n42
A3.5 237 n42
A4.2 237 n42, 238 n45
A4.6–10 305–306
A4.7 346 n22
A4.9 346 n23
B2.4 328 n18
B2.5 54 n66
B2.6 54 n66, 54 n67, 55, 328 n18
B3.3 54 n66, 54 n67, 328 n18
B3.6 328 n18
B3.7 328 n18
B3.8 54–55, 54 n66, 54 n67, 55, 55 n69, 328 n18
B6.1 55, 328 n18
B6.1–4 54 n66
B6.2 328 n18
B6.3 328 n18
B6.4 328 n18
C3.15 350 n33

4. Dead Sea Scrolls

1Q20
II 10 239 n50
1QIsa[a] 260, 265
1QIsa[b] 260 n20
4Q242 216

5. Ancient Jewish Writers

Josephus
Ant. 12.4.1 §§ 158–59 295 n8

6. Rabbinic Works

Tosefta Soṭah
6:10 312 n20

7. Targums

Targum Jonathan
Isaiah 40:18 263

8. Early Christian Writings

Eusebius
F10b 207

Jerome
Comm. Isa. 11.489 263

9. Greco-Roman Literature

Berossos
Babyloniaca 205, 208, 212, 219–221, 314 n32

Herodotus
Hist. 1.123–24 301
Hist. 1.201 314 n32
Hist. 1.205–6 314 n32
Hist. 1.208 314 n32
Hist. 3.91 295 n9
Hist. 5.35 301
Hist. 7.239 301

Plutarch
Them. 30.1–2 301

Xenophon
Anab. 1.9.11–12 301
Cyr. 8.6.1–8 314 n32
Cyr. 8.6.19–21 314 n32
Cyr. 8.7 314 n32

www.ingramcontent.com/pod-product-compliance
Lightning Source LLC
Chambersburg PA
CBHW070748230426
43665CB00017B/2294